THE OXFORD HANDBOOK
OF INFORMATION
AND COMMUNICATION
TECHNOLOGIES

THE OXFORD HANDBOOK OF

INFORMATION AND COMMUNICATION TECHNOLOGIES

Edited by

ROBIN MANSELL
CHRISANTHI AVGEROU
DANNY QUAH
ROGER SILVERSTONE

OXFORD
UNIVERSITY PRESS

OXFORD

UNIVERSITY PRESS

Great Clarendon Street, Oxford OX2 6DP

Oxford University Press is a department of the University of Oxford.
It furthers the University's objective of excellence in research, scholarship,
and education by publishing worldwide in

Oxford New York

Auckland Cape Town Dar es Salaam Hong Kong Karachi
Kuala Lumpur Madrid Melbourne Mexico City Nairobi
New Delhi Shanghai Taipei Toronto

With offices in

Argentina Austria Brazil Chile Czech Republic France Greece
Guatemala Hungary Italy Japan Poland Portugal Singapore
South Korea Switzerland Thailand Turkey Ukraine Vietnam

Oxford is a registered trade mark of Oxford University Press
in the UK and in certain other countries

Published in the United States
by Oxford University Press Inc., New York

British Library Cataloguing in Publication Data

Data available

Library of Congress Cataloging in Publication Data

Data available

Typeset by SPI Publisher Services, Pondicherry, India
Printed in Great Britain
on acid-free paper by
Ashford Colour Press Ltd, Gosport, Hampshire

ISBN 978-0-19-926623-4
ISBN 978-0-19-954879-8 (pbk)

1 3 5 7 9 10 8 6 4 2

In memory of Claudio Ciborra (1951–2005)
and Roger Silverstone (1945–2006)

ACKNOWLEDGEMENTS

When we began work on this Oxford University Press Handbook, Claudio Ciborra, Professor of Information Systems at the LSE, was an enthusiastic member of our editorial team. Until his death in February 2005 he had responsibility for the second theme on Organizational Dynamics, Strategy, Design, and ICTs. Roger Silverstone, Professor of Media and Communications at the LSE, completed his work for the fourth theme on Culture, Community and New Media Literacies before his death in July 2006. We dedicate this book to Claudio and to Roger. We greatly miss their contributions now.

David Musson, commissioning editor for this handbook, was hugely encouraging throughout its lengthy gestation and we thank him for his confidence in our ability to put together a volume of this kind.

We are very grateful to each of the contributors. We understand that a handbook chapter is not necessarily at the top of the list of papers waiting for completion. Books and refereed articles claim a substantial share of the time of academics, as do teaching, administration, and other activities. We thank all the authors for their responsiveness to our comments and to those of the referees. We also thank them for their willingness to contribute to a strongly interdisciplinary handbook.

The editors of this handbook work variously in the fields of study of information systems, media and communications, and science and technology policy, as well as in economics, sociology, and cognate disciplines. We commissioned the chapters based on our knowledge of leading research in these areas. The juxtapositions of the theory and methodology from these areas of inquiry may be uncomfortable for some of our contributors as well as for some of our readers. Our conviction is that productive interdisciplinarity is not a matter of smoothing away difference. Rather, it is a matter of acknowledging the great variety of questions that need to be asked, and of developing theories and methodologies that are most appropriate. We are pleased that the contributors have shown a willingness to join us in this endeavour.

All those who refereed a chapter for this book, often at short notice, and always with great care and attention, also are to be thanked. The referees have agreed to be named and they are all actively involved in research in the areas we have included: Johannes Bauer, Nancy Baym, Sandra Braman, David Buckingham, Bart Cammaerts, Edward Comor, Philip Cooke, Wendy Currie, Peter Dahlgren, William H. Dutton, Jonathan Haskel, Richard W. Hawkins, Caroline Haythornthwaite,

Richard Hull, Frank Land, Sonia Liff, Priscilla Regan, Sundeep Sahay, Luc Soete, Harry Trebing, Frank Webster, Chris Westrup and Sally Wyatt.

Cynthia Little is to be congratulated, given the substantial size of this volume, for taking much of the detailed editing burden off our shoulders. As always, she performed well. We thank many others for their contributions including Kathy Moir in the early stages of commissioning the chapters and those who supported this work in their personal or professional capacities.

CONTENTS

PART I   THE KNOWLEDGE ECONOMY AND ICTs
Theme Editor: DANNY QUAH

PART IV   CULTURE, COMMUNITY, AND NEW MEDIA LITERACIES

Theme Editor: ROGER SILVERSTONE

LIST OF FIGURES

List of Tables

LIST OF CONTRIBUTORS

Chrisanthi Avgerou is Professor of Information Systems at the Information Systems Group, Department of Management, London School of Economics and Political Science, UK.

Sandra J. Ball-Rokeach is Professor of Communication at the Annenberg School for Communication, University of Southern California, USA.

Lisa Brooten is Assistant Professor at the Global Media Research Center, College of Mass Communication and Media Arts, Southern Illinois University Carbondale, USA.

Stephen Coleman is Professor of Political Communication at the Institute of Communications Studies, University of Leeds, UK.

Nick Couldry is Professor of Media and Communications at Goldsmiths College, University of London, UK.

Sara Cullen is a Ph.D. student at the Department of Information Systems, University of Melbourne, Australia.

Paul A. David is Professor of Economics (and History), Stanford University, USA; and Senior Fellow, Oxford Internet Institute, University of Oxford, UK.

John D. H. Downing is Professor of International Communication and Director, Global Media Research Center, College of Mass Communication and Media Arts, Southern Illinois University Carbondale, USA.

Mirko Draca is Research Economist at the Centre for Economic Performance (CEP), London School of Economics and Political Science, UK.

Patrick Dunleavy is Professor of Political Science and Public Policy at the Department of Government, London School of Economics and Political Science, UK.

Chris Freeman is Professor Emeritus at SPRU-Science and Technology Policy Research, University of Sussex, UK.

Robert D. Galliers is Provost and Vice President for Academic Affairs at the Bentley College, USA; and Visiting Professor at the Information Systems Group, Department of Management, London School of Economics and Political Science, UK.

Phil Graham is Canada Research Chair in Communication and Technology at the University of Waterloo; and Reader in Communication at the University of Queensland, Australia.

Abby Ann Goodrum is the Velma Rogers Graham Research Chair in News, Media and New Technology at the School of Journalism, Ryerson University, Canada.

Shane Greenstein is the Elinor and Wendell Hobbs Professor at the Department of Management and Strategy, Kellogg School of Management, Northwestern University, USA.

Lucas D. Introna is Professor of Organization, Technology and Ethics at the Management School, Lancaster University, UK.

Matthew R. Jones is Lecturer in Information Systems and Fellow at Darwin College, University of Cambridge, UK.

Joo-Young Jung is Visiting Research Professor at the Graduate School of Interdisciplinary Information Studies, University of Tokyo, Japan.

Jannis Kallinikos is Reader in Information Systems at the Information Systems Group, Department of Management, London School of Economics and Political Science, UK.

Yong-Chan Kim is Assistant Professor at the Department of Telecommunication and Film, College of Communication and Information Sciences, University of Alabama, USA.

Mary Lacity is Professor of Information Systems at the College of Business Administration, University of Missouri-St. Louis, USA.

William Lazonick is University Professor at the University of Massachusetts Lowell, USA and Distinguished Research Professor at INSEAD, France.

Sonia Livingstone is Professor of Social Psychology at the Department of Media and Communications, London School of Economics and Political Science, UK.

David Lyon is Queen's Research Chair at the Department of Sociology, Queen's University, Canada.

Robin Mansell is Professor of New Media and the Internet at the Department of Media and Communications, London School of Economics and Political Science, UK.

Sorin Adam Matei is Assistant Professor at the Department of Communication, Purdue University, USA.

William H. Melody is Guest Professor at the Center for Information and Communication Technologies, Technical University of Denmark and Managing Director, LIRNE.NET.

Shani Orgad is Lecturer at the Department of Media and Communications, London School of Economics and Political Science, UK.

Wanda J. Orlikowski is the Eaton-Peabody Professor of Information Technologies and Organization Studies at the Sloan School of Management, Massachusetts Institute of Technology, USA.

Jeff Prince is Assistant Professor at the Department of Applied Economics and Management, Cornell University, USA.

Danny Quah is Professor of Economics at the Department of Economics, London School of Economics and Political Science, UK.

Raffaella Sadun is Research Economist at the Centre for Economic Performance (CEP), London School of Economics and Political Science, UK.

Saskia Sassen is Ralph Lewis Professor of Sociology at the University of Chicago, USA and Centennial Visiting Professor at the London School of Economics and Political Science, UK.

Roger Silverstone was Professor of Media and Communications at the Department of Media and Communications, London School of Economics and Political Science, UK, until his death on 16 July 2006.

W. Edward Steinmueller is Professor of Information and Communication Technology Policy, Science and Technology Policy Research (SPRU) at the University of Sussex, UK.

Charles D. Raab is Professor of Government at the School of Social and Political Studies, University of Edinburgh, UK.

John Van Reenen is Professor of Economics and Director of Centre for Economic Performance (CEP) at the London School of Economics and Political Science, UK.

Judy Wajcman is Professor of Sociology at the Research School of Social Sciences, The Australian National University; formerly the Centennial Professor at the London School of Economics and Political Science, UK.

Leslie Willcocks is Professor of Technology, Work and Globalization at the Information Systems Group, Department of Management, London School of Economics and Political Science, UK.

LIST OF ABBREVIATIONS

....

ACEnet   Appalachian Center for Economic Networks
ACES   Annual Capital Expenditure Survey
ALA   American Library Association
ALP   Average Labour Productivity
AMARC   Association Mondiale des Radiodiffuseurs Communautaires
            (World Association of Community Organization Broadcasters)
AMD   Advanced Micro Device
ANT   Actor Network Theory
AOL   America Online
APC   Association for Progressive Communications
APTN   Associated Press Television News
ARPA   Advanced Research Projects Agency
ARPANET   Advanced Research Projects Administration Network
ASICs   Application Specific Integrated Circuits
ASM   Annual Survey of Manufactures
AST   Adaptive Structuration Theory
ATM   Automatic Teller Machine
BaE   British Aerospace
BBC   British Broadcasting Corporation
BEA   Bureau of Economic Analysis
BLFTZ   Bayan Lepas Free Trade Zone
BLS   Bureau of Labor Statistics
BP   Business Process
BPO   Business Process Outsourcing
BPR   Business Process Reengineering
CBO   Community Based Organizations
CBS   Columbia Broadcasting System
CCTV   Closed Circuit Television
CEN/ISSS   Comité Européen de Normalization/Information Society
            Standardization System
CEO   Chief Executive Officer
CFT   Capital Flows Table
CHAH   Coalition of Haitians for the Advancement of Haiti

CII	Computer Intelligence Intercorp
CIO	Chief Information Officer
CLEC	Competitive Local Exchange Company
CMC	Computer Mediated Communication
CNUS	Computer Network Use Supplement
CRM	Customer Relations Management
CSCW	Computer Supported Cooperative Work
CSO	Central Switching Office
CTC	Communication Technology Centers
DARPA	Defense Advanced Research Projects Agency
DNA	Deoxyribonucleic Acid
DNS	Domain Name System
DoJ	Department of Justice
DOTForce	Digital Opportunity Task Force
DRAM	Dynamic Random Access Memory
DSL	Digital Subscriber Line
DSP	Digital Signal Processing
DVB	Democratic Voice of Burma
EBP	Employment Based Preferences
ECI	Employment Cost Index
EPG	Electronic Programme Guides
EQW-NES	Educational Quality of the Workforce – National Employers' Survey
ERP	Enterprise Resource Planning
ESS	Employment Structure Survey
FBC	Free Burma Coalition
FCC	Federal Communications Commission
FDI	Foreign Direct Investment
FRTW	Fixed Reproducible Tangible Wealth
FTC	Federal Trade Commission
FTZ	Free Trade Zone
GDP	Gross Domestic Product
GE	General Electric
GGDC	Groningen Growth and Development Centre
GMM	General Method of Moment
GPT	General Purpose Technology
HICN	Health Information Community Networks
HR	Human Resource
IBM	International Business Machines
ICT	Information and Communication Technology
ICTS	Information and Communication Technology and Service
IDML	International Development Markup Language

IGC	Institute for Global Communication
IICT	International Information and Communication Technologies
IIT	Indian Institute of Technology
IMC	Independent Media Center
IMF	International Monetary Fund
IP	Internet Protocol
IPES	Information Processing Equipment and Software
IPR	Intellectual Property Rights
IS	Information System
ISDN	Integrated Services Digital Network
ISO	International Organization for Standardization
ISP	Internet Service Provider
ISV	Independent Software Vendor
IT	Information Technology
ITO	Information Technology Outsourcing
ITU	International Telecommunication Union
JV	Joint Venture
KAIS	Korea Advanced Institute of Science
KAIST	Korea Advanced Institute of Science and Technology
KIAP	Kanpur Indo-American Programme
KIET	Korea Institute of Electronics Technology
KIST	Korea Institute of Science and Technology
KMS	Knowledge Management System
KPI	Key Performance Indicator
KSC	Korea Semiconductor Company
LAN	Local Area Network
LEOS	Low Earth Orbiting Satellite
LG	Lucky-Goldstar
LRD	Longitudinal Research Database
LTCM	Long Term Capital Management
M&A	Mergers and Acquisitions
MFP	Multi Factor Productivity
MINERVA	Multiple Input Network for Evaluating Reactions, Votes and Attitudes
MIP-S	Mannheim Innovation Panel in Services
MK	Motorola Korea
MNC	Multinational Corporation
MOO	Multi-user Object Oriented
MOST	Ministry of Science and Technology
MoU	Memorandum of Understanding
MUD	Multi User Dungeon
NAICS	North American Industry Classification System

NAP	Network Access Point
NBC	National Broadcasting Company
NGO	Non-Governmental Organization
NHS	National Health Service
NIC	Newly Industrializing Country
NLD	National League for Democracy
NLG	New London Group
NLLS	Non-Linear Least Squares
NPM	New Public Management
NSF	National Science Foundation
NSFNET	National Science Foundation Network
NSM	New Social Movement
NTIA	National Telecommunications and Information Administration
OCAM	Office, Computing and Accounting Machinery
OECD	Organisation for Economic Cooperation and Development
Ofcom	Office of Communications
ONS	Office of National Statistics
OP	Olley Pakes
OSS	Open Source Software
P3P	Platform for Privacy Protection
PC	Personal Computer
PDA	Personal Digital Assistant
PEN	Public Electronic Network
PETS	Privacy Enhancing Technologies
PFI	Private Finance Initiative
PIA	Privacy Impact Assessment
PIM	Perpetual Inventory Method
PIN	Personal Identification Number
PIPEDA	Personal Information Protection and Electronic Documents Act
POP	Points of Presence
PPI	Producer Price Index
PSTN	Public Switched Telephone Network
QOS	Quality of Service
R&D	Research and Development
RBD	Reverse Brain Drain
RBOC	Regional Bell Operating Company
RBV	Resource Based View
RFA	Radio Free Asia
RFID	Radio Frequency Identification
S&E	Scientists and Engineers
S&T	Science and Technology
SCN	Seattle Community Network

SCOT	Social Construction of Technology
SI	Social Informatics
SIA	Semiconductor Industry Association
SMS	Short Message Service
STS	Science and Technology Studies
SUSE	System of Unified Statistics on Enterprises
TCE	Transaction Cost Economics
TCP/IP	Transmission Control Protocol/Internet Protocol
TFP	Total Factor Productivity
TI	Texas Instruments
TSMO	Transnational Social Movement Organization
UDP	User Data Protocol
UKCGO	UK Children Go Online
UNDP	United Nations Development Programme
USDA	United States Department of Agriculture
VLSI	Very Large Scale Integration
VOA	Voice of America
VoIP	Voice over Internet Protocol
WSIS	World Summit on the Information Society
WTN	Worldwide Television News
WTO	World Trade Organization
XML	eXtensible Markup Language

CHAPTER 1

THE CHALLENGES OF ICTs

ROBIN MANSELL

CHRISANTHI AVGEROU

DANNY QUAH

ROGER SILVERSTONE

1 INTRODUCTION

MANY scholars have documented the way information and communication technologies (ICTs) have been entwined with major changes in society since the invention of electrical telegraphy in the 1830s.[1] For some, the early ICTs, as well as those stemming from the invention of the microprocessor in the late 1960s, are best characterized as being revolutionary. This is because of the cascade of opportunities they created for new forms of media and information and communication services and for new ways of organizing society.

Enthusiasm for digital ICTs peaked towards the end of the twentieth century and began to subside with the economic downturn that occurred at the end of that century. The 'irrational exuberance' concerning the economic value of businesses in the 'new' economy began to dissipate. This made way for renewed reflection on the implications of the ways that ICT production and consumption have become embedded within societies—both historically and in the twenty-first century. In this handbook our aim is to introduce readers to these theoretical and empirical reflections as they appear within research undertaken by academics across a range of social science disciplines.

Those who study the economy, organizations, or people's everyday lives, sometimes depict ICTs as calling into existence a new, inclusive, social and economic order. Others regard these technologies as dystopian determinants of social inequality. However, there are many strands of research within the social sciences that are yielding insights about the very complex ways in which ICTs are woven into the fabric of society. We invited contributions from researchers who are sensitive to the need to develop research which avoids the strongest forms of technological determinism and of its counterpart, social constructivism. ICTs are regarded by the contributors to this book as being neither transformational, nor entirely malleable by their users. Although ICTs feature prominently in this volume, the authors see these technologies as potential enablers, not as the determinants, of particular cultural, organizational, social, political, or economic outcomes.

The United Nations-sponsored World Summit on the Information Society (WSIS) and its Action Plan[2] created many forums for discussions about how to resolve the still intractable problem of enabling all people and organizations to use ICTs in ways that they are likely to find engaging and useful. As a result not only of the WSIS, but also of a surge of interest on the part of civil society and public and private organizations in the wake of growing concerns about security and safety, it is timely to reflect on the relationships between ICTs and human rights and responsibilities, the kinds of communicative relationships that ICTs are supporting, and whether these are contributing to well-being in a globalizing world. We have organized the chapters of this handbook around four themes covering topics that we believe policy makers and those in other settings where ICTs are encountered will find informative. The four themes are:

The knowledge economy: This theme focuses on the economic and policy dimensions of the convergence of telephony, television, computing, and the Internet, and on the changing roles of national and international policy and regulation. This theme emphasizes the dynamics of the 'new' economy and the chapters include critical assessments of the extent to which ICTs are associated with far-reaching paradigmatic change as well as with less radical changes in markets and institutions.

Organizational dynamics, strategy, and design: ICT system design and implementation involves processes of negotiation that often produce conflict within organizations. This theme focuses on the ways in which the introduction and use of ICT applications are negotiated by those involved and the potential of various strategies for achieving consensus about the needs of users and the design of technology.

Governance and democracy: The focus of this theme is a critical assessment of the way ICTs are related to power relationships with respect to institutions and individuals. ICTs are examined in terms of the extent to which they are being mobilized to enhance democratic participation and to support social movements. The approaches to governance that may be required to achieve justice and fairness in the face of surveillance practices and the potential for the invasion of privacy protection are also examined.

Culture, community, and new media literacies: The role of ICTs is examined within this theme in terms of their contribution to the communicative and other resources that are needed for finding and expressing cultural identity, for fostering new kinds of 'community' and for mediating experience in ways that foster new kinds of literacies. The approach is consistently to reaffirm the commitment to understanding the relationship between technology and social change as one of mutual determination and therefore one that is crucially dependent on the actions of individuals and institutions in the modern world.

2 Social science and ICTs

Many theoretical perspectives are available within the social sciences for the investigation of ICTs. Perhaps the most predominant approach in the literature concerning ICTs is diffusion theory, one of several approaches that have influenced the research agenda on ICTs.

Diffusion of innovations

The production and spread of ICTs in society are often examined through the lens of a diffusion model. In *The Diffusion of Innovations*, Rogers' (1962) aim was to explain how to inculcate awareness and enthusiasm for technical innovations such that even those most resistant to their adoption might do so. By 1995, when the fourth edition was published, he had modified his expression of the theory to account for many of the contextual factors that influence the diffusion of new technologies. Nevertheless, his central concern was to explain the rate and direction of adoption of new technologies such as ICTs.[3] The work in the diffusion theory tradition is linked to the analysis of the technical and social networks that are involved in the diffusion process.[4] In this substantial body of research, there is little critical reflection on the kinds of societal transformations or ethical issues that are raised by innovations in ICTs when they are taken up by their users. In order to encourage such reflection on these broader issues we have not used diffusion theory as a key organizing theme in this handbook. Several chapters draw upon this theory, but we have sought to include many complementary theoretical perspectives and models.

Mapping and measuring ICTs

As ICTs have become more varied and pervasive in the post-World War II period, substantial effort has been devoted to mapping and measuring the extent of the information society or the knowledge economy. This work is represented by the early contributions of Daniel Bell, Fritz Machlup, Marc Porat and Youichi Ito,[5] who sought to document the growing contribution of information (or communication) services to economic activity and the growing share of information-related occupations in the workforce. Research in this tradition continues through the development of indicators and surveys that enable comparison or benchmarking of country or regional performance in terms of investment and use of ICTs.[6] Several contributors to this handbook comment on this research area.

Information economics and political economy

Another major strand of research is concerned with the role of ICTs in the market exchange of information. Some analysts are enthusiastic about the enormous growth of markets for information. Researchers often emphasize issues of intellectual property rights (IPR) protection and its role in stimulating economic growth and scientific endeavour.[7] Others argue that concerns about the market exchange of information need to be complemented by attention to the benefits and costs of information exchange which is less encumbered by the costs of negotiating property rights.[8] Still others direct their attention to the consequences of economic power and domination that are present in media and communication markets,[9] notwithstanding the Internet and opportunities for self-publishing. These areas of research inform several of the contributions to this handbook.

Network societies

Research, represented by the work of Manuel Castells on the relationships between networks, information flows, and time/space reconfigurations, and by the work of others such as Jan van Dijk and James Slevin who focus on 'network' or 'Internet' societies, has proliferated particularly since the mid-1990s.[10] This work is undertaken from many different perspectives. Research in this area has shown the importance of accounting for the interplay between online and offline activities if we are to comprehend the implications of the Internet and the spread of an enormous range of ICT applications that offer new means of creating and interacting with digital information. Other analysts have been very interested in ICTs and their association with 'information' or 'knowledge' societies, but those such as Nicholas Garnham and Frank Webster are sceptical of claims that these societies are radically altered by ICTs.[11] In this handbook, many of the contributors offer critical assessments of some of the myths associated with network societies and their implications for political, social, economic, and organizational change.

ICTs, mediation, and power

Much of the research on ICTs is either under- or over-theorized in the sense intended by Mark Granovetter.[12] It is under-theorized in so far as it is often based on the assumed autonomy of individual actors. In other cases, it is over-theorized, for example, in attempting to account for the relationships between ICTs and the meanings embedded in communicative relationships. In these cases, there is a tendency to neglect power relationships. As Armand Mattelart suggests, in the highly situated accounts that emphasize mediations and interactions, there is a tendency to overlook those aspects of ICT production within a given system that are 'marked by the inequality of exchanges'.[13] Alternatively, research on ICTs that privileges the analysis of political and economic power tends to neglect the agency of individuals. Our aim in this handbook has been to include research that provides insights into the embeddedness of ICTs in different contexts to show how mediation processes are influenced by ICTs, but also to include research that acknowledges power as a major factor in all socially and technologically mediated relationships.

The production and appropriation of ICTs are marked by inequalities because they mirror or reflect the inequalities of the societies that produce and use them. Inequalities are visible in the ways that ICTs enable changing social practices, provide new methods of communication and of information sharing, encourage network forms of organization, and give rise to new learning dynamics and commercial practices in the economy. The chapters in this handbook highlight research programmes that would help to improve understanding of these developments and provide a basis for assessing the desirability of encouraging innovation and experimentation in the use of ICTs.

A concise review of highlights from each of the four themes that provide the organizing framework for this book follows as an introduction to the arguments and evidence in subsequent chapters.

3 THE KNOWLEDGE ECONOMY AND ICTS

By the beginning of the twenty-first century, expenditure on research and development (R&D), education, and software, which is treated as an indicator of investment
in knowledge in studies of the economy, had reached about 9 per cent of GDP in the
OECD countries.[14] The production of ICTs is a very dynamic component of physical
capital investment and had grown to about 4 per cent of GDP in some of the OECD
countries by this time. Software investment had also been increasing at a very rapid
rate. By the middle of the first decade of this century, the rate of participation on the
Internet exceeded 50 per cent of the population in more than half of these countries.
Mobile telephone use had expanded rapidly, in some countries overtaking the
penetration of fixed telephone service. Network interactivity had become a 'routine'
facet of social and economic life in the wealthy economies of the world.

Most industrial sectors of these economies had become dependent on the use of
ICTs although there were large variations in the rate of investment in ICTs by
sector. The Internet and the World Wide Web had created the possibility of
producing and consuming information and media inside and outside the confines
of formal institutions. There were still gaps or digital divides within the wealthy
countries and the production and use of ICTs in developing countries continued,
in many cases, to lag far behind the industrialized countries. There was also
increasing evidence that the way that the Internet and other ICTs are introduced
or localized in different regions of the world varies considerably.[15]

The 'knowledge economy' is a static concept that shifts each time a map of the
economy is redefined and when boundaries change through time. This concept also
suggests that an invasive and transformational process is underway that alters the
rationale for, and outcomes of, economic relationships. The rapid decline in the cost
of ICTs and their growing use in the acquisition, storage, and processing of information link them to the knowledge economy. This is because of the way these technologies influence the creation and use of knowledge in the economy and the exchange of
information. Knowledge is essential to organizations that exist to coordinate the
actions of individuals and to maintain continuity to some degree in their various
purposes. For individuals, their knowledge is a basic component of their 'human
capital' and this strongly influences their wage and employment opportunities. As a
result, we cannot ignore the significance of ICTs if we are concerned about economic
growth, even if we may choose to critique the terminology that is used.[16]

By the end of the twentieth century, these developments had become associated
with labels such as the 'knowledge economy', the 'new economy', the 'weightless
economy', and the 'information society'.[17] The growing emphasis of economic
activity on the circulation of information has led to questions about the extent
to which investment in ICTs and in human capital are major contributors to
economic growth and to gains in productivity. There is a substantial body of

research on the relationship between investment in ICTs and the relative performance of national economies as well as on the relationship between ICT investment
and the competitiveness of firms. One conclusion about which there is little
argument is that 'ICT seems to offer the greatest benefits when ICT investment is
combined with other organizational assets, such as new strategies, new business
processes, new organizational structures and better worker skills'.[18] The contributors to this theme examine the features of the knowledge economy from different
standpoints employing the tools of economic analysis, and all of them find lacunae
in our ability to fully understand the contribution of ICTs to the economy. Several
important features of their arguments stand out.

General purpose technologies and the ICT paradigm

For analytical purposes, ICTs are treated by economists as 'general purpose technologies' (GPTs).[19] Because of their enormous adaptability and their ubiquity they
are expected to play a major role in the economy. In his chapter, however, Freeman
points out that despite characteristics that make ICTs subject to increasing rates of
return in use, there are many social and institutional factors that create resistance to
their smooth take-up. There is a substantial body of research that aims to measure
the uneven economic gains from ICTs, which result from differences in the rate and
direction of processes of adjustment to ICTs, as discussed by Draca, Sadun, and Van
Reenen. One of these processes is the standardization process, which smooths
adjustment to ICTs, creating platforms upon which applications can be built, as
shown by Steinmueller. An important concept which informs the work of economists who study ICTs is the notion of paradigmatic change.[20] Freeman claims that
the remarkable features of ICTs have led some enthusiasts of the ICT paradigm to
adopt 'missionary zeal' in advancing the diffusion of these technologies and to
exaggerate the 'exemplary' aspects of the paradigm. He argues that it is necessary
to distinguish clearly between the way the knowledge economy might be expected to
develop and its real expansions and contractions, which produce uneven development, an argument that is further developed by Melody. The malleability or adaptability of ICTs also provides the starting point for Greenstein and Prince's
examination of the diffusion of the Internet. They show, as do the other contributors
to this theme, that institutions of various kinds are essential if economic value is to
be created through the application of ICTs.

Productivity and ICTs

Economic theory suggests that a shift toward the predominance of the ICT
paradigm should result in productivity gains and provide a stimulus for economic

growth. In their chapter, Draca, Sadun and Van Reenen use growth accounting and econometric methods to examine productivity gains and learning effects that may be attributable to the widespread use of ICTs. They review the literature on the 'Solow Paradox' (computers everywhere except in the productivity statistics), and consider possible explanations for the greater acceleration of productivity in the US compared to Europe in the 1990s. One explanation may be differences in the way that US and other multinational firms have introduced organizational changes alongside their investments in ICTs. The contribution of ICTs to major changes in the banking and finance sector is examined by Melody who also discusses the public sector's lagging take-up of ICTs and the difficulties of assessing efficiency gains in this area.[21]

ICTs and human capital

Investment in human capital is essential to foster ICT innovations at the technological frontier and to build demand for these technologies and related services. Freeman and Melody both highlight the fact that such investment currently reaches a relatively small proportion of the global population. They argue that the rate of investment is not fast enough to avert inequality within knowledge economies or to eliminate digital divides. There is a need for a much better understanding of 'organizational capital', as Draca, Sadun, and Van Reenen suggest, if we are to explain differences in productivity performance between firms, industries, and countries. Some developing countries have prioritized investment in human capital to promote their capacity for ICT production. This is especially the case in the East Asian countries, which have used different combinations of development, and national innovation and education strategies, alongside the investment and the employment strategies of multinationals, to reverse the 'brain drain' to higher wage countries and to become world leaders in semiconductor production, as outlined by Lazonick.

ICTs and information

The claim that ICTs are GPTs is evocative of the breadth of their application, but the economic factors underpinning their influence hinges upon the unique properties of information as an economic commodity. Expansibility, that is, the ability to instantly and costlessly reproduce information, and its implication that the use of information may be non-rival, challenge the scarcity foundations upon which economic theories of value and price are constructed. Institutional arrangements for governing scarcity, such as the assignment of property rights, should not obscure the augmentation of productive resources enabled by this property. As Steinmueller explains, ICTs not only offer new 'shovels' that may be reproduced at will and at no cost, but also may provide the means for replacing those who are currently doing the shovelling. Melody, in his chapter, considers the conflicts between the goal of maximizing profits in quasi-monopoly information markets (where markets are created by strong IPR protection) and of maximizing the societal distribution of information. Like David and Steinmueller in their contributions, he argues that these conflicts are major issues that need to be addressed through changes in governance systems and new means of regulation.

ICT infrastructure and the state

State institutions have an important role in shaping knowledge economies. Regulatory agencies, standards-setting institutions, and public sector investment in ICTs and in the workforce influence the ICT industry structure and, as Melody argues, contribute to the emergence of highly concentrated oligopolistic markets. Freeman observes that there are few signs that the network features of ICTs are leading to the demise of the state or the firm, a myth that became prevalent in the 1980s and 1990s. Regulation by the state has played a central role in the rate of expansion of telecommunication infrastructures, including the spread of the Internet and broadband capacity. In the case of the Internet, David shows that innovation is strongly influenced by interdependencies between technology and policy. He highlights the implications of the concentration of market power among a small number of Internet Service Providers for the continued development of global networks, whereas Greenstein and Prince focus on the economics of Internet developments in the US to explain the factors contributing to its uneven geographic development. Like David, they highlight the importance of examining whether changes in the design of the Internet, new services such as VoIP (Voice over Internet Protocol), and new wireless networks will slow innovation or alter the geographic distribution of digital divides.

Diffusion and ICTs

The diffusion model, as highlighted earlier in this chapter, has dominated studies of the demand side of the ICT industry for decades. Economists have few means of examining the organizational changes that affect the diffusion process and as a result they often examine labour skills, as does Lazonick, or undertake surveys at the firm level, as recommended by Draca, Sadun and Van Reenan, in order to provide an empirical basis for examining the organizational changes that occur with investment in ICTs. The need for more systematic data to understand how ICTs are used by organizations, and in the economy as a whole, gives rise to studies that endeavour to 'map and measure' the knowledge economy, as noted by

Steinmueller. Despite the inadequacies of the indicators that are used, these efforts provide data for econometric research on the dynamics of knowledge economies and help to explain differences in the diffusion of ICTs between the rich and the poor, and between urban and rural areas, an issue that is discussed by Freeman, Greenstein and Prince, and Melody in their respective chapters.

4 ORGANIZATIONAL DYNAMICS, STRATEGY, DESIGN, AND ICTs

Ever since the first uses of computers in business organizations the development of ICT-based information systems has been inseparable from the dynamics of organizational change.[22] Some 30 years of information systems research have highlighted multiple crucial aspects of this complex socio-technical process. A great deal of early research focused on the construction of technology applications. Such research has been driven not only by the principle that it is the designer's duty to achieve a good fit of new information processing artefacts in existing organizational structures and practices, but also by the expectation that the organizations implementing the new ICTs will adjust themselves to more efficient and effective technology-mediated practices and structures.[23] Other research streams, though, have sought to shift the starting point and the overall orientation of the ICT innovation process in organizations from designing innovative technologies for existing organizational settings to anchoring innovation in business strategy and organizational reform interventions. But whether the primary research emphasis has been on the construction and implementation of new technologies, the perceived imperatives of organizational change for business survival, or the interaction between them, it has become increasingly clear that ICT innovation and organizational change are not contained in good design practices—for technology or organizations. Instead, they are more accurately understood as a continuous sense-making and negotiation process among multiple parties and as Claudio Ciborra argued, involve care and cultivation of new, emerging, socio-technical, organizational conditions.[24]

The role of management

One persistent research theme in information systems research concerns the capabilities for the managerial direction of ICT innovation towards desirable business ends. There have been numerous management principles and 'best practice' prescriptions for exploiting ICTs. These provide guides for identifying the strategic and operational value to be gained from new technology information systems, objectives that should be targeted, organizational models that should be followed, and systematic activities through which all of these might be achieved. A great deal of such knowledge has been ephemeral, or of dubious empirical validity, but as Galliers shows in his critique of three major themes in information systems research—alignment, competitive advantage, and knowledge management—decades of empirical research and critical scrutiny have developed valuable knowledge of effective technical/rational action beyond the faddish prescriptions. Moreover, we have now a better understanding of the nature of the process of strategic management of ICT innovation.

Similarly, the review by Willcocks, Lacity and Cullen of more than 15 years of research on experiences of outsourcing shows the gradual development of knowledge for managing organizations' relations with the ICT services vendors that they rely heavily on. One lesson is clear from their review: 'outsourcing cannot be contracted for and then not managed'. Large organizations are pursuing continuous ICT innovation involving partnerships and contractual arrangements with multiple ICT service providers across continents. Offshore outsourcing is an increasingly visible phenomenon, with opportunities and risks that require management at both government policy and business management levels, as the chapter by Willcocks, Lacity, and Cullen shows.[25] The challenges of steering such across-the-globe, organizational, business arrangements in developing and sustaining information system resources should not be underestimated; but, as the chapters by Galliers and Willcocks, Lacity, and Cullen suggest, a core of valuable lessons for practice is being produced from longitudinal empirical research.

ICT and new organizational forms

Many predictions of changes in the structure of organizations have been associated with ICTs. Some of them, such as the flattening of the hierarchical organizational pyramid that has been prevalent in the industrial era, have been confirmed by empirical evidence. Others, such as the formation of new structures—for example, the 'matrix' or 'platform' organization—have been demonstrated in particular cases, but have not become widespread.[26] Nevertheless, with the spread of intranets and the Internet the hierarchical organization seems to have been eroded, both through internal restructuring of the organization of work, and through business processes crossing organizational boundaries in the outsourcing arrangements and industrial partnerships of producer firms with suppliers and customers.

The network form has been heralded as the emerging dominant organizational form. Yet Kallinikos in his chapter suggests the need for caution in making predictions about the transition to the network organization as the dominant feature of the information society. He points out that such a transformation is not just a matter of technology-induced design of organizational structures and practices; it involves fundamental institutional changes. The spreading of network organizational arrangements is confronted by existing institutions and will not go very far unless the institutional contexts also change. Analyses of the merits of network organizational arrangements, in terms of business gains, effective management, and market reach, need to be complemented by studies of changes occurring in the broader institutional context of modernity, such as the legal frameworks governing labour markets, property rights, and social welfare, nation-state bound societies, and cultural patterns.

Knowledge and information in organizations

ICTs are closely linked with issues of knowledge in organizations. Galliers critiques the stream of research on 'knowledge management' and proposes a way of considering knowledge issues strategically without oversimplifying them. Kallinikos puts forward a different critique, on the basis of an analysis of ICTs as means of representation and processing of information, as well as of codifying and formalizing knowledge produced in the course of an organization's activities. Thus, ICTs may empower or constrain action on the basis of tacit knowledge, facilitate or inhibit new ideas and creativity, and alter power/knowledge dynamics in an organizational context.

Moreover, Kallinikos draws attention to the phenomenon of information growth, which is to a large extent facilitated by ICTs. Against the euphoria surrounding the Internet as providing almost unlimited access to information and knowledge repositories, Kallinikos detects a self-referential generation of information, which poses a challenge to the existing cognitive capabilities of organizations. So far there is limited understanding of the way the unprecedented circulation of information, disembedded from the context that gave rise to it, affects knowledge formation in organizations.

Multiple perspectives in the study of ICT and organizational and social change

Research aiming at understanding the role of ICTs in organizational change has addressed a range of fundamental conceptual questions regarding the relationship between technology and society. At the very least, such research has enriched the language we use to present and discuss information systems phenomena, to justify and explain expectations and consequences associated with ICT innovation, and to chart courses of action to that end. For example, sensitized by theoretical critiques of deterministic perspectives of technology, information systems researchers and their practice avoid assumptions of cause and effect relationships between particular technology properties and the direction of organizational change. Instead, they have developed accounts of complex processes of change that complement technological potential with consideration of intentions, interests, cognitive and emotional dispositions of multiple agents, and power relations unfolding in the organizational context.

Moreover, as Jones and Orlikowski demonstrate in their chapter, specific theoretical perspectives shed light on particular facets of the complex relationships between ICT innovation and organizations or society at large. There is ongoing debate on the validity and explanatory merits of specific perspectives, but few scholars see progress in this research field as a matter of establishing the superiority of one particular theoretical perspective over others, thus resulting in a 'correct' general theory of ICTs, organizations, and society. This line of argument is clearly followed by Introna, who presents and discusses three distinct theoretical approaches for understanding ethical issues raised by new ICTs in organizations and society. There is much to be gained in terms of in-depth understanding of new ICT associated phenomena from pursuing research through multiple theoretical perspectives, with analytical consistency within each of them and critical awareness of alternatives.

5 GOVERNANCE, DEMOCRACY, AND ICTs

The growing use of ICTs has generated considerable discussion of how this may influence the institutions and processes of governance and democracy. In whatever form they are conceived, democratic processes and regimes of governance at all levels of society are likely to be profoundly influenced by the use of these technologies. This is because of how they offer opportunities for the production and circulation of information in new ways, and how they support new communicative relationships. At least theoretically, this provides a new foundation for citizens' participation in democratic processes and for their numerous interactions with services provided by the state.

The Internet, in particular, has provided new virtual spaces for public discussion and deliberation and the expansion in the use of the World Wide Web by governments is supporting a host of e-services. However, as the contributors to this theme emphasize, before conclusions are drawn about the implications of ICTs, analysis of the potentially disruptive implications of ICTs for democratic practices and for governance systems needs to be undertaken in relation to the specific nature of the technologies and the particular contexts in which they are used. The digital technologies that are encountered within this theme include public and private networks based on the Internet Protocol (IP) as well as networks that support conventional telephony. They include e-government services at all levels developed for citizens' use, as well as large-scale information technology systems involving databases for internal use of public sector employees. They include web-based e-voting systems and 'social software' such as blogs, wikis, email, and privacy enhancing technologies, as well as closed circuit television cameras, and embedded technologies such as radio frequency identification (RFID) tags used for monitoring the movement of goods and people. ICTs are also associated with growth in the collection, retention, and analysis of data generated by computerized commercial and non-commercial transactions.[27] In many instances, what distinguishes advanced ICTs from earlier generations of technology is their use to support global networks and the consequences of these networks for governance systems and democratic processes that are bounded by nation states.[28] The following are some of the topical insights that come to light under this theme.

Questioning determinism

In their respective chapters, all the contributors to this handbook illustrate the importance of avoiding deterministic claims about the impact of ICTs on governance and democracy. Simplistic assumptions about the 'transformative' nature of ICTs are challenged in the light of empirical observations indicating that the political and social relationships engendered by the spread of ICTs are inevitably complex. In some cases, these relationships give rise to new social movements and greater interaction between governments and citizens, but in others, the transparency of governance and the effectiveness of governance systems may be reduced, and power hierarchies reinforced.

Sassen draws attention to the complex ways in which the design of ICTs and social processes interact, a theme that is addressed in studies of ICTs informed by social science theories concerning power and its embeddedness in both technological and social systems. This demonstrates how the technical design of the Internet as an open, non-hierarchical network can be associated with more distributed power relationships, as in the case of some social movements, or with the greater coalescence of power, as in the case of the financial services industry. As Sassen puts it, the outcomes associated with global networks are 'mixed, contradictory, and lumpy'. It is crucial to examine empirically how and by whom ICTs are used, before reaching conclusions about whether they are associated with greater empowerment for citizens or better governance practices.

Technological convergence has given rise to many new ICT platforms and to greater capabilities for large-scale processing of personal and transaction-related information. The use of these ICTs has the potential to alter the relationships between those invested with the power to govern and those who are governed, with major, albeit uncertain, implications for democratic freedoms and responsibili-ties.[29] In the light of these developments, Couldry draws attention to the need to consider the communicative resources that are necessary to enable citizens to participate effectively in democratic processes, while Coleman emphasizes the need to challenge claims that e-democracy leads to greater direct communication between politicians and citizens. Similarly, Dunleavy's account of the way e-government services have been introduced questions the notion that investment in ICTs automatically leads to improved service provision or to more effective means of managing information within public sector organizations. Both Raab and Lyon show that ICTs can be used in ways that are inconsistent with particular values associated with democracy. It is clear from the research traditions included under this theme that ICTs do not transform relationships of power in society in predictable ways.

Resources for empowerment

The unequal distribution of the communicative and information resources that may be deemed essential to underpin democratic processes is a central issue in many of the chapters. Coleman argues that asymmetries in information resources can lead to the suppression of public engagement with the political processes that are essential to democracy. He questions the assumption that individuals will gain in social capital simply as a result of their interactions within online communities. The promise of e-democracy is often said to be related to the fact that new ICTs can support a two-way dialogue between citizens and their government, but since the early 1970s there have been fervent debates about whether the majority of citizens will want to access online forums and about whether politicians will have an inclination to listen.[30] Online voting and blogging during elections are just two of the many developments that continue to fuel debates about whether the use of ICTs creates new possibilities for a public sphere in which rational debate can occur.[31] Couldry emphasizes that the distribution of communicative and information resources is central to achieving social justice.

The use of ICTs also is giving rise to new and unequal distributions of risk as demonstrated by Lyon in his discussion of surveillance societies and by Raab in his observations about the problems created by the unequal incidence of privacy intrusions and distribution of privacy protection. There are many unanswered questions about the nature of the resources that are needed to enable individuals to protect themselves from such risks and about the role that the state should play in protecting citizens' interests. The issue of resources is raised in a different context by Dunleavy in connection with the unequal resources available at different levels of government for investment in e-government services and the implications of this for the way these services are designed and implemented.

Digital divides, democratic participation, and governance

There is no shortage of controversy over what has come to be known as the 'digital divide'.[32] There are those who treat the uneven spread of ICTs and the capabilities to use them as a reflection of a relatively early phase in a diffusion process within the ICT paradigm. In their view, market forces will ensure that these technologies are available and affordable for all.[33] The alternative view is that the concept of the digital divide is misleading because it calls too much attention to the technology rather than to whether the distribution of ICTs is a reflection of inequalities that have their origins in society.[34] Inasmuch as ICTs can play a role in enabling new forms of participatory democracy it is important to reflect on what 'participation' means and whether citizens should be entitled to acquire capabilities that would enable them 'to be informed and to be heard', as Couldry suggests. The decisions about what specific resources citizens should be entitled to, and the practicalities of who should provide them, are issues for continuing research and debate. Central research topics in this area include whether ICT networks give rise to new patterns of political power, to the need to develop more effective means of political communication, and to the need for a 'civic commons in cyberspace'.

The contributors to this theme challenge the idea that the availability of ICTs necessarily overcomes various forms of social exclusion. Sassen shows, for example, that the use of these technologies by civil society activists is not inclusive in any straightforward way, a finding that is in line with other research findings on how social movements have been making use of ICTs to support their activities.[35] The reproduction of pre-existing social inequalities and the potential for exclusion is emphasized also in the context of Raab's discussion of the social distribution of privacy protection where differences in the protection of individuals' personal information can influence their access to social services and health care. Similarly, as Lyon indicates, 'social sorting' can lead to discrimination or divides between social groups that have been characterized, for whatever reason, as 'desirable' or 'undesirable'. Dunleavy's research on e-government services illustrates that the design and organization of such services also produces new forms of exclusion, in this case, in the form of problems of access to relevant information by those who provide services or by those who are intended to benefit from them.

Regimes of power

Effective governance and participatory democracy are predicated on the notion that citizens' views will be taken into account by those who are deemed to be accountable. The changing regimes of power that are emerging with globalization and the spread of digital networks give rise to the need to reassess the roles of dominant actors and to consider the need for a new 'politics of information'. Sassen emphasizes the power of global flows of financial capital beyond the control of the states. Dunleavy highlights the power of the large ICT companies that design and manage information systems and e-government services for the public sector. Differences in regimes of power are also visible in the authority accorded to ICT professionals in different countries which leads to different outcomes in the way e-government and e-democracy services are developed. Coleman's analysis of e-democracy services indicates that, while their use may make elections more transparent and alter the relations of power between political parties and citizens, their use does not overcome differences in citizens' abilities to discriminate between sources of information, nor does it indicate whether the use of ICTs will lead to new regimes or 'manifestations of political power'.

Legitimacy, enforcement, and freedoms

The legitimacy accorded to legislative and regulatory measures as forms of governance has a major bearing on a variety of rights and freedoms normally associated with democracy. Questions about the legitimacy of authority and political representation are raised by Coleman in terms of the public's confidence in political actors. Couldry raises issues concerning the role that governments can legitimately play in ensuring that citizens are able to acquire communicative resources for democratic participation. Dunleavy's discussion of public sector information management practices raises questions about the legitimacy of the norms governing decisions about how information is controlled and who has the authority to decide what information should be processed and shared inside and outside government.

Both Lyon and Raab raise issues concerning the public acceptance of safety measures in the cases of surveillance and privacy protection, especially in the light of variations in the capacity to enforce legislation and regulations in a 'boundary-less' world. Couldry regards individual agency or freedom as a social commitment to ensure that goods and resources are distributed fairly, and Lyon raises ethical issues concerning citizens' expectations about freedom from surveillance as a result of data processing. Raab questions whether it is reasonable to retain existing standards of privacy protection in a globalizing world. The protection of individual privacy is far more difficult in the face of government measures aimed at enhancing the 'safety state', and the emergence of 'surveillance societies' is a response to concerns about the threat of attacks of various kinds.

The research agendas set out by the contributors to this theme provide clear evidence of the need to assess changes in political power relations in the light of ethical considerations, aspirations for human welfare, and the rights and freedoms that we wish to sustain, rather than mainly in terms of what a given technology might enable.

6 Culture, community, and new media literacies

The final theme in this handbook addresses the relationship between technological change, and the social and cultural, where the social and cultural can be considered as both context for, and consequence of, the logic of innovation. We have framed it as a whole in these terms, and in some ways it could be argued that this part of the book, rather than coming at the end, should have been placed at the beginning. This is because it is clear that there is no possibility of disentangling technology either from the structures of symbolic and material power—the power of institutions, the power of traditions—or from its embedding in the conflicts and continuities of experience—the experience of producers, users, and consumers in their everyday interactions both with each other and with the technologies and services on which they have become so dependent.

In Habermassian terms ICTs are clearly part of both system and life world, and indeed crucially can be seen in many, if not most, respects to be articulating the relationship between the two. Economy, polity, and organizational life are all products of this interaction, and the dialectic between all their elements—structure, action, organization, machine, intention, value—increasingly depends on what we do, and on how we live with these technologies and the resources they release.

From this perspective there are as many questions to ask about technological change as there are questions to be asked about the social world as a whole. And an understanding of the place of ICTs in that world requires the deployment of theoretical approaches and empirical research which is not hide-bound to a single discipline or to a mechanical, more or less positivist, methodology. The contributors to this theme reflect on this complexity.

The contributors approach this complexity from a number of different perspectives and with a number of different foci. The discussion here is framed through five key windows. The first is literacy, the second the interdependence of online and offline communication, the third the political appropriation of the affordances of ICT, the fourth the role of ICTs in the formation and functioning of community, and the fifth their equivalent role in relation to identity.

ICTs and literacy

Thinking about the social dimensions of ICT as an issue of literacy directs attention to them as being constituted through social practice and, in their turn, requiring or perhaps more accurately inviting, the development of particular skills to engage with them at all, but more importantly to engage with them in socially and culturally coherent and productive ways. Each moment in the evolution of both communication and information technologies, since the age of writing, has offered new and different possibilities for communication,[36] and challenged cultures and societies to respond in creative and ultimately non-exclusive ways. Literacy, democracy, and economy went hand in hand in the nineteenth century. The question, ultimately posed in the first two chapters within this theme, is the extent to which they might still be intimately connected in the twenty-first century. Some of these issues have been discussed under the third theme of this handbook.

Literacy, media literacy, new media literacy, or information literacy (the terms are necessarily imprecise and fluid) involves more than merely a set of practical skills. Engaging in the products of a complexly mediated world, and one indeed of information overload, is not just a matter of knowing one's way around and having a certain degree of competence in what might once have been called *reading*. It involves much more than that, as Graham and Goodrum, and Livingstone, in their different ways argue. What is involved is the opportunity and the capacity meaningfully to engage in a discourse which is public, highly mediated, technologically sophisticated, and symbolically powerful. Literacy is a matter of making sense, of constructing and communicating understandings in a world of great dissonance and great ambiguity, one which ICTs both create as well as help to resolve. But literacy is also a matter of participation and protection, as individuals confronted with the bewildering and otherwise indecipherable presence of the social, need the skills to find, absorb, and use the resources that in one way or another are a precondition for citizenship, a satisfactory level of economic and financial activity and sustainability, and the overall quality of their everyday life.

ICTs, culture, and participation

New ICTs offer quite new possibilities. The capacity for interaction, the blurring of the boundaries between production and consumption, together and convergently, enable the *a priori* possibility for greater participation in what might be seen as the blurred world of public/private communication that is the web and, increasingly, mobile telephony. There are primary concerns of inclusion and exclusion here, and a sufficient degree of media and information literacy is a precondition, at the very least, for the former.

There are two issues involved. The first is the relationship between the offline and the online world. And the second is the politics of it all.

It has been customary, indeed it was once deemed almost self-evident, to find in the Internet the basis for a self-contained specific realm—it was called cyberspace—which worked according to its own patterns, and which in its seductiveness, encompassed a world that was *sui generis*. Research then began to question this, and offered an account of the relationship between online and offline communication (and culture) as being determined not by the technology but by the actions of those in the real world (most notably, but by no means exclusively, by Daniel Miller and Don Slater).[37] One determinism replaced another, and actually neither was, nor is, sustainable.

As Shani Orgad argues in those significant realms of personal or institutional action that involve communication, negotiation, and organization online, there is nevertheless a much more complex set of interactions to be understood. These involve a degree of substantial interdependence within what takes place in both domains; that both domains, the online and the offline, exercise a materiality in relation to the other, and that this needs to be addressed both methodologically and substantively.

Individuals may meet and fall in love online, but they still have to meet in some real setting if they are to marry or procreate. Likewise, the realities of social and political action in the real world increasingly, and in certain increasingly vivid settings, can be enhanced and even directed by the communications that take place exclusively online or on-mobile. The two domains nevertheless are neither substitutable nor separable.

Politics, community, and identity

The political realities of online interaction and communication both reflect and engage with the politics of the world. Political movements, political mobilizations, alternative accounts of political realities, are believed to be significantly the stuff of online interaction, for all the obvious reasons: the weakness or lack of state regulation, the low cost of entry, and the ease of global communication. However, as Downing and Brooten also suggest, what seems uniquely possible online is also available, and continues to be significant, across many media, both old and new. Media are essential to the conduct of politics of all kinds in the modern world. And of course the new digital environment has spawned a range of technologies that can be, and often are being, used to sustain a range of alternative activities from the support of local communities to the coordination of information and political action across continents.

Indeed the nature of online community and its relationship to place-based communities have been the focus of continuous and contentious concern in the literature on ICTs. Online interaction has been seen as facilitative, and it has also been seen as destructive, of the kinds of otherwise unmediated interactions that in their continuity and intensity have the capacity to create a sense of meaningful, place-based belonging. Research has tended to show that effective networking online emerges from, and to a degree depends on, pre-existent live communities, but it has also indicated the profound a-social potential in online interaction,[38] both from the point of view of the seduction of its users into an electronic realm, and in terms of the ephemerality and invasive dangers of such communication.

It is clear, however, as Jung, Ball-Rokeach, Kim, and Matei argue in their chapter, that such communicative spaces are as complex and problematic as those in real space, where communities are just as fractured and difficult. They also suggest that where and when such 'real' communities do work, they have the capacity to mobilize the potential of online communication and information access in creative and supportive ways. This goes both for the local and the more or less sedentary, as much as it does for the migrant and the displaced, though in the case of the latter, the capacity of ICTs meaningfully to provide a framework for social interaction is dependent very much on the prior circumstances, both the resources and the literacies, of the group concerned.

The argument from the study of community, and indeed the argument we are at pains to articulate throughout this volume, that the relationship between technology and the society is one of mutual shaping, is sustainable too at the level of the individual. Again the literature is replete with both determinist and essentialist figures, most evidently in arguments about gender and especially the status of ICTs as, in one way or another, necessarily gendered. Such positions are not sustainable. And while it is the case that in many societies women are denied the possibility of equivalent access to the full range of literacies, which in turn enable participation in the ICT-based culture and where indeed such exclusions are both the product of established patterns of disadvantage, and more or less motivated strategies in design. There is, as Wajcman points out, no immutable fixing of position or identity, and no singularity either, in the effects or consequences of engaging with ICTs.

7 CONCLUSION

This handbook cannot encompass all the research on the development and application of ICTs within the social sciences and it has been necessary to set some boundaries. We do not include lines of research that view these technologies as being linked to a smooth evolution of society towards a network arrangement that propagates itself throughout the world in a *singular* way. We also have not included detailed discussions of the technical characteristics of ICTs,[39] research on ICTs and cognition, or on the legal frameworks for the management and control of the way ICTs are used.

The research included here is limited by the fact that it highlights work by those who publish in the English language and who are based in universities in Australia, Canada, France, Japan the UK and the US. Although some of the contributors draw upon empirical research undertaken within or about developing countries, this handbook does not include research that is responsive to the ICT or communication 'for development' debates; although it does take account of research on the principles and practices that might guide discussions about digital divides.[40]

Research in the physical sciences, computer science, and engineering is devoted to promoting innovations in ICTs.[41] For example, research on ubiquitous or ambient computing, applications of RFID technology, software automation, multimedia content, the Semantic Web, and Knowledge Management is receiving substantial financial support. Frequently, this work gives rise to calls for cross-, inter- or multidisciplinary research which embraces the social sciences as a means of addressing the uncertainties—ethical, social, economic or political—that research in the natural sciences and engineering field brings to light, but often fails to address.

This handbook provides a resource for those working in other traditions embracing research that is informed principally by the disciplines of anthropology, economics, philosophy, politics, and sociology.[42] The contributors set out an intellectual agenda that encourages reflection on the implications of ICTs for individuals, organizations, democracy, and the economy. Many of the media accounts of ICTs present them as 'new' and appear to suggest that a wholly new way of thinking is required in order to understand their implications. The discussions in this handbook confirm our view that it is the continuous interpenetration of the old and new ICTs, older and new practices and meanings, and innovations in institutions and governance systems that need to be investigated to achieve a deeper understanding of the place and consequences of these technologies for society.

REFERENCES

ADAM, L. and contributors (2005). *Towards an African e-Index: ICT Access and Usage*, Research ICT Africa Report, http://www.researchictafrica.net/modules.php?op=modload&name=News&file=article&sid=504&CAMSSID=e6501939a722422e76cfe7915ff21cdc, accessed 24 Mar. 2006.

AGRE, P. E. and ROTENBERG, M. (eds) (1997). *Technology and Privacy: The New Landscape*. Cambridge, MA: MIT Press.

ARTERTON, F. C. (1987). *Teledemocracy: Can Technology Protect Democracy?* London: Sage.

ATTEWELL, P. (1992). 'Technology Diffusion and Organizational Learning: The Case for Business Computing'. *Organization Studies*, 3(1): 1–19.

AVISON, D. E. and FITZERALD, G. (1996). *Information Systems Development Methodologies, Techniques and Tools.* Oxford: Blackwell.

AXFORD, B. and HUGGINS, R. (eds) (2001). *New Media and Politics.* London: Sage.

BELL, D. (1973). *The Coming of Post-Industrial Society: A Venture in Social Forecasting.* New York: Basic Books.

BENNETT, W. L. and ENTMAN, R. M. (eds) (2000). *Mediated Politics: Communication in the Future of Democracy.* Cambridge: Cambridge University Press.

BRAMAN, S. (1995). 'Alternative Conceptualizations of the Information Economy'. *Advances in Librarianship,* 19: 99–116.

BRANCHEAU, J. C. and WETHERBE, J. C. (1990). 'The Adoption of Spreadsheet Software: Testing Innovation Diffusion Theory in the Context of End-User Computing'. *Information Systems Research,* 1(2): 115–43.

BRAUDEL, F. (1981). *Civilization And Capitalism, 15–18th Century, 3 Volumes* (trans. S. Reynolds). London: Fontana Press.

BRESNAHAN, T. F. and TRAJTENBERG, M. (1995). 'General Purpose Technologies "Engines of Growth"?' *Journal of Econometrics,* 65(1): 83–108.

CALHOUN, C. (ed.) (1992). *Habermas and the Public Sphere.* Cambridge, MA: MIT Press.

CAMINER, D., LAD, F., ARIS, J. and HERMON, P. (1997). *LEO: The Incredible Story of the World's First Business Computer.* New York: McGraw Hill.

CAMMAERTS, B. (2005). 'Through the Looking Glass: Civil Society Participation in the WSIS and the Dynamics between Online/Offline Interaction'. *Communications & Strategies* (SI), Nov.: 151–74.

—— and VAN AUDENHOVE, L. (2005). 'Online Political Debate, Unbounded Citizenship and the Problematic Nature of a Transnational Public Sphere'. *Political Communication* 22(2): 179–96.

CARPENTIER, N. (2003). 'Access and Participation in the Discourse of the Digital Divide: The European Perspective at/on the WSIS', in J. Servaes (ed.), *The European Information Society: A Reality Check.* Bristol: Intellect, 99–120.

CARTER, F. J. T., JAMBULINGAM, V., GUPTA, K. and MELONE, N. (2001). 'Technological Innovations: A Framework for Communicating Diffusion Effects'. *Information & Management,* 38(5): 277–87.

CASTELLS, M. (1996). *The Information Age: Economy, Society and Culture Volume I: The Rise of the Network Society.* Oxford: Blackwell.

—— (1997). *The Information Age: Economy, Society and Culture Volume II: The Power of Identity.* Oxford: Blackwell.

—— (1998). *The Information Age: Economy, Society and Culture Volume III: End of Millennium.* Oxford: Blackwell.

—— (2001). *The Internet Galaxy: Reflections on the Internet, Business and Society.* Oxford: Oxford University Press.

CHIN, W. W. and MARCOLIN, B. L. (2001). 'The Future of Diffusion Research'. *Data Base Advances in Information Systems,* 32(3): 8–12.

CIBORRA, C. U. (2002). *The Labyrinths of Information: Challenging the Wisdom of Systems.* Oxford: Oxford University Press.

COYLE, D. and QUAH, D. (2002). *Getting the Measure of the New Economy.* London: Work Foundation.

COMPAINE, B. M. (ed.) (2001). *The Digital Divide: Facing a Crisis or Creating a Myth?* Cambridge, MA: MIT Press.

DAHLGREN, P. (2001). 'The Transformation of Democracy', in B. Axford and R. Huggins (eds), *New Media and Politics*. London: Sage, 64–88.

DAMSGAARD, J. (1996). 'The Diffusion of Electronic Data Interchange: An Institutional and Organizational Analysis of Diffusion Patterns'. Institute of Electronic Systems, Department of Computer Science, Aalborg University, Unpub. Ph.D. Thesis, R-96-2041.

DAVID, P. A. (1993). 'Intellectual Property Institutions and the Panda's Thumb: Patents, Copyrights, Trade Secrets in Economic Theory and History', in M. B. Wallerstein, M. E. Mogee and R. A. Schoen (eds), *Global Dimensions of Intellectual Property Rights in Science and Technology*. Washington DC: National Academy Press, 19–61.

—— (2005a). 'Can "Open Science" be Protected from the Evolving Regime of IPR Protections?' Economics Working Paper, EconWPS, http://econwpa.wustl.edu:80/eps/io/papers/0502/0502010.pdf, accessed 21 Mar. 2006.

—— (2005b) 'A Tragedy of the Public Knowledge "Commons"? Global Science, Intellectual Property and the Digital Technology Boomerang'. Economics Working Paper, EconWPS, http://econwpa.wustl.edu:80/eps/dev/papers/0502/0502010.pdf, accessed 21 Mar. 2006.

DEROIAN, F. (2002). 'Formation of Social Networks and Diffusion of Innovations'. *Research Policy*, 31(5): 835–46.

DeSANCTIS, G. and FULK, J. (eds) (1999). *Shaping Organizational Form: Communication, Connection, and Community*. Thousand Oaks, CA: Sage.

ETZIONI, A. (1992). 'Teledemocracy: the Electronic Town Meeting'. *The Atlantic*, 270(4): 34–9.

FICHMAN, R. G. and KEMERER, C. F. (1999). 'The Illusory Diffusion of Innovation: An Examination of Assimilation Gaps'. *Information Systems Research*, 10(3): 255–75.

FREEMAN, C. and SOETE, L. (1997). *The Economics of Industrial Innovation*, 3rd edn. London: Pinter–Cassel Imprint.

—— and LOUÇÃ, F. (2001). *As Time Goes By: From the Industrial Revolutions to the Information Revolution*. Oxford: Oxford University Press.

GARNHAM, N. (2000). *Emancipation, the Media and Modernity: Arguments about the Media and Social Theory*. Oxford: Oxford University Press.

GRANOVETTER, M. (1985). 'Economic Action and Social Structures: The Problem of Embeddedness'. *American Journal of Sociology*, 91(3): 481–510.

GUTHRIE, K. K. and DUTTON, W. H. (1992). 'The Politics of Citizen Access Technology: The Development of Public Information Utilities in Four Cities'. *Policy Studies Journal*, 20(4): 574–97.

HABERMAS, J. (1989/1962). *The Structural Transformation of the Public Sphere: An Inquiry into a Category of Bourgeois Society*. Cambridge: Polity Press.

—— (1989). 'The Public Sphere: An Encyclopedia Article', in S. E. Bonner and D. M. Kellner (eds), *Critical Theory and Society: A Reader*. London: Routledge, 136–42.

INNIS, H. A. (1950). *Empire and Communication*. Toronto: University of Toronto Press.

—— (1951). *The Bias of Communication*. Toronto: University of Toronto Press.

ITeM (Instituto del Tercer Mundo) (ed.) (2005). *Information Society for the South: Vision or Hallucination?* Montevideo: ITeM with support of IDRC.

ITO, Y. (1991). 'Johoka as a Driving Force of Social Change'. *KEIO Communication Review*, 12: 33–58.

KEANE, J. (1995). 'Structural Transformations of the Public Sphere'. *The Communications Review*, 1(1): 1–22.

KELLNER, D. (1990). *Television and the Crisis of Democracy*. Boulder, CO: Westview Press.

KIM, B.-K. (2005). *Internationalizing the Internet: The Co-evolution of Influence and Technology.* Cheltenham: Edward Elgar.

KRAUT, R., STEINFIELD, C., CHAN, A., et al. (1998). 'Coordination and Virtualization: The Role of Electronic Networks and Personal Relationships'. *Journal of Computer Mediated Communication,* 3(4): np.

LAMBERTON, D. (ed.) (1971). *The Economics of Information and Knowledge: Selected Readings.* Harmondsworth: Penguin.

—— (2006). 'New Media and the Economics of Information', in L. Lievrouw and S. Livingstone (eds), *The Handbook of New Media, Updated Student Edition.* London: Sage, 364–85.

LATHAM, R. and SASSEN, S. (eds) (2005). *Digital Formations: IT and New Architectures in the Global Realm.* Princeton, NJ: Princeton University Press.

LESSIG, L. (2001). *The Future of Ideas: The Fate of the Commons in a Connected World.* New York: Random House.

LIEVROUW, L. A. and LIVINGSTONE, S. (2002). *The Handbook of New Media.* London: Sage.

—— and —— (2006). *The Handbook of New Media, Updated Student Edition.* London: Sage.

LONDON, S. (1995). 'Teledemocracy vs Deliberative Democracy: A Comparative Look at Two Models of Public Talk'. *Journal of Interpersonal Computing and Technology,* 3(2): 33–55.

LYYTINEN, K. and DAMSGAARD, J. (2001). 'What's Wrong with the Diffusion of Innovation Theory? The Case of a Complex and Networked Technology', IFIP 8.6 Working Conference, Banff, 173–90.

MACHLUP, F. B. (1962). *The Production and Distribution of Knowledge in the US Economy.* Princeton, NJ: Princeton University Press.

MANSELL, R. and COLLINS, B. S. (eds) (2005). *Trust and Crime in Information Societies.* Cheltenham: Edward Elgar.

—— and STEINMUELLER, W. E. (2000). *Mobilizing the Information Society: Strategies for Growth and Opportunity.* Oxford: Oxford University Press.

—— and WEHN, U. (eds) (1998). *Knowledge Societies: Information Technology for Sustainable Development.* Published for the UN Commission on Science and Technology for Development by Oxford University Press.

MARVIN, C. (1988). *When Old Technologies were New: Thinking about Communications in the Late Nineteenth Century.* Oxford: Oxford University Press.

MATTELART, A. (1996/2000). *Networking the World: 1794–2000* (trans. J. A. Cohen). Minneapolis, MN: University of Minnesota Press.

MAY, C. (2002). *The Information Society: A Sceptical View.* Cambridge: Polity Press.

McCHESNEY, R. and SCHILLER, D. (2003). 'The Political Economy of International Communications: Foundations for the Emerging Global Debate about Media Ownership and Regulation', Geneva, UNRISD Working Paper.

MILLER, D. and SLATER, D. (2000). *The Internet: An Ethnographic Approach.* Oxford: Berg.

MILWARD-OLIVER, G. (ed.) (2005). *Maitland+20: Fixing the Missing Link.* Bradford-on-Avon: The Anima Centre Ltd.

MONGE, P. R. and CONTRACTOR, N. S. (2003). *Theories of Communication Networks.* Oxford: Oxford University Press.

MOSCO, V. (1996). *The Political Economy of Communication.* London: Sage Publications.

NOAM, E. (2001). 'Two Cheers for the Commodification of Information', New York, Columbia University, http://www.citi.columbia.edu/elinoam/articles/Commodification.htm accessed 25 Mar. 2006.

NORRIS, P. (2000). *A Virtuous Circle: Political Communications in Post-industrial Societies.* Cambridge: Cambridge University Press.

—— (2001). *Digital Divide: Civic Engagement, Information Poverty, and the Internet Worldwide.* Cambridge: Cambridge University Press.

OECD (2001). *New Economy? The Changing Role of Innovation and Information Technology in Growth.* Paris: OECD.

—— (2005). 'Guide to Measuring the Information Society', Working Party on Indicators for the Information Society', DSTI/ICCP/IIS/2005/6/final, Paris.

ONG, W. (1982). *Orality and Literacy: The Technologizing of the Word.* London: Methuen.

PEREZ, C. (1983). 'Structural Change and the Assimilation of New Technologies in the Economic and Social System'. *Futures*, 15(4): 357–75.

—— (2002). *Technological Revolutions and Financial Capital: The Dynamics of Bubbles and Golden Ages.* Cheltenham: Edward Elgar.

PORAT, M. U. and RUBIN, M. R. (1977). 'The Information Economy' (9 vols). Washington DC: Department of Commerce Government Printing Office.

QUAH, D. (1996). 'The Invisible Hand and the Weightless Economy', London, LSE Centre for Economic Performance, Occasional Paper No. 12, Programme on National Economic Performance, April.

—— (2003). 'Digital Goods and the New Economy', in D. C. Jones (ed.) *New Economy Handbook.* London: Academic Press Elsevier Science, 289–321.

RABOY, M. (ed.) (2003). *Global Media Policy in the New Millennium.* Luton: University of Luton Press.

ROGERS, E. M. (1962). *The Diffusion of Innovations.* New York: Holt, Rinehart and Winston.

ROOM, G. (2005). *The European Challenge: Innovation, Policy Learning and Social Cohesion in the New Knowledge Economy.* Bristol: The Policy Press.

SAMARAJIVA, R. (1996). 'Surveillance by Design: Public Networks and the Control of Consumption', in R. Mansell and R. Silverstone (eds), *Communication by Design: The Politics of Information and Communication Technologies.* Oxford: Oxford University Press, 129–56.

SCHILLER, D. (1999). *Digital Capitalism: Networking the Global Market System.* Cambridge, MA: MIT Press.

SCHUDSON, M. (1992). 'The Limits of Teledemocracy'. *The American Prospect*, 3(11), 41–5.

SLEVIN, J. (2000). *The Internet and Society.* Cambridge: Polity.

STAUFFACHER, D. and KLEINWÄCHTER, W. (eds) (2005). *The World Summit on the Information Society: Moving from the Past into the Future.* New York: United Nations ICT Task Force.

STONEMAN, P. (2002). *The Economics of Technological Diffusion.* Oxford: Blackwell.

UNESCO (2005). *Towards Knowledge Societies: UNESCO World Report.* Paris: UNESCO Publishing.

VAN DIJK, J. A. G. M. (2005). *The Deepening Divide.* London: Sage.

—— (2006). *The Network Society* (2nd edn). London: Sage.

WARSCHAUER, M. (2004). *Technology and Social Inclusion: Rethinking the Digital Divide.* Cambridge, MA: MIT Press.

Webster, F. (2002). *Theories of the Information Society (2nd edn)*. London: Routledge.

World Bank (1998). *World Development Report 1998/99: Knowledge for Development*. Washington DC: The World Bank.

Notes

1. Or even before as optical telegraphy had been in use since the 1790s. ICTs also may be taken to include mechanical devices in which case, movable type that was first used in China for printing in the eleventh century, could be included. For historical studies, see Braudel (1981), Castells (1996), Innis (1950, 1951), Freeman and Soete (1997), Marvin (1988), and Mattelart (1996/2000).
2. The WSIS was held in 2003 and 2005, see http://www.itu.int/wsis/ accessed 24 Mar. 2006.
3. For research in this tradition see, for example, Attewell (1992), Brancheau and Wetherbe (1990), Carter et al. (2001), Chin and Marcolin (2001), Damsgaard (1996), Deroian (2002), Fichman and Kemerer (1999), Lyytinen and Damsgaard (2001), and Stoneman (2002).
4. See, for example, Monge and Contractor (2003).
5. See Bell (1973), Machlup (1962), Porat and Rubin (1977), and Ito (1991).
6. For example, OECD (2005), and Room (2005).
7. For example, Lamberton (1971, 2006) on the variety of roles that information plays in the economy, Noam (2001) on the institutional rules governing the development of new markets, and Quah (2003) on the potential of ICTs for creating digital goods such as digital music and novel software algorithms.
8. For example, David (1993, 2005a, b), Lessig (2001), and Mansell and Steinmueller (2000).
9. For example, McChesney and Schiller (2003), Mosco (1996), and Schiller (1999).
10. See Castells (1996, 1997, 1998, 2001), van Dijk (2006), and Slevin (2002).
11. See Garnham (2000), Webster (2002), and Braman (1995) for a review of some of these works.
12. See Granovetter (1985).
13. See Mattelart (2000: 107).
14. See Science, Technology, and Industry Scoreboard 2005: Towards a Knowledge-based Economy, OECD, http://titania.sourceoecd.org/vl=2609992/cl=23/nw=1/rpsv/ij/oecdthemes/99980134/v2005n15/s1/p1l, accessed 18 Mar. 2006.
15. For example, see Kim (2005) and Adam (2005).
16. See May (2002) and Webster (2002) for critical appraisals of these labels.
17. See Coyle and Quah (2002), Mansell and Wehn (1998), Quah (1996), OECD (2001), UNESCO (2005), World Bank (1998), for examples.
18. See OECD (2001: 12).
19. See Bresnahan and Trajtenberg (1995).
20. See Perez (1983, 2002), and Freeman and Louçã (2001).
21. Sassen examines the financial sector and Dunleavy discusses the public sector and ICTs in Pt III of this Handbook.
22. See Caminer et al. (1997).

23. For example, research on systems development methodologies in the 1980s presented in Avison and Fitzerald (1996).

24. See Ciborra (2002).

25. Lazonick also addresses outsourcing in Pt I of this Handbook.

26. For example, DeSanctis and Fulk (1999).

27. See Agre and Rotenberg (1997), and Samarajiva (1996).

28. This volume does not contain a chapter on the governance of the Internet from a technical or regulatory perspective, although some aspects of Internet governance are discussed by David in Chapter 6 in terms of the need for social regulation of the Internet. See Stauffacher and Kleinwächter (2005), ITeM (2005), Milward-Oliver (2005), and Raboy (2003) for discussions of Internet governance.

29. For access to literature on the role of the media in this context see, for instance, Axford and Huggins (2001), Bennett and Entman (2000), Dahlgren (2001), Kellner (1990), and Norris (2000).

30. See Arterton (1987), Etzioni (1992), Guthrie and Dutton (1992), London (1995) and Schudson (1992).

31. For discussion of the nature of the public sphere, see Calhoun (1992), Habermas (1989/ 1962, 1989), and Keane (1995).

32. The digital divide generally refers to differences—socio-economic or geographical—in access to ICTs and the Internet and to differences in people's capabilities to use ICTs. Inequality is said to have implications for the economy, and political and social processes.

33. This argument is made by some of the contributors to Compaine (2001).

34. See Norris (2001), van Dijk (2005), and Warschauer (2004).

35. See, e.g. Cammaerts (2005), Cammaerts and Van Audenhove (2005) and Carpentier (2003).

36. See, e.g. Ong (1982).

37. See Miller and Slater (2000).

38. See Kraut et al. (1998).

39. The technical features are explained at: http://en.wikibooks.org/wiki/Wikibooks: Information_technology_bookshelf; http://en.wikibooks.org/wiki/Wikibooks: Computer_ software_bookshelf; http://en.wikibooks.org/wiki/Wikibooks:Computer_science_bookshelf; and esp., Wiley publishers at http://eu.wiley.com/WileyCDA/Section/id-2925.html, accessed 22 Mar. 2006.

40. ICTs are mentioned in the United Nations Millennium Goals http://www.un.org/ millenniumgoals/ and work in this area has been growing rapidly, often supported by development agencies and government departments. The web resources are too numerous to cite here, but readers might start with http://www.dfid.gov.uk/aboutdfid/ organisation/icd.asp or http://www.idrc.ca/en/ev-43441-201-1-DO_TOPIC.html. See also Latham and Sassen (2005).

41. See, e.g. Mansell and Collins (2005).

42. A complementary *Handbook of New Media* (Lievrouw and Livingstone 2002, 2006) focuses more directly on 'new media'.

PART I

THE KNOWLEDGE ECONOMY AND ICTs

THEME EDITOR:
DANNY QUAH

Introduction

THIS part of the handbook focuses on the economic and policy dimensions of the convergence of telephony, television, computing, and the Internet. By mapping out the dynamics of the new economy, it assesses the changing roles of national and international regulation, and evaluates how deeply the new economy entails far-reaching paradigmatic change.

The phrase 'change of paradigm' has been used to describe the changes associated with information and communication technologies (ICTs). In Chapter 2, Freeman explains the technological and economic factors that have contributed to those changes. He examines the origins and definition of the paradigm concept, the formation and collapse of the Internet Bubble, and the reality of, and myths about, the consequences of rapid ICT innovation. Freeman pays particular attention to the conjectured decline of institutions such as large firms and nation states.

In Chapter 3, Melody examines characteristics of new knowledge economies with a view towards understanding their implications for market development and for government policy and regulation. In his view what is new about new knowledge economies is not the central role assumed by information in generating economic value, but instead the institutional structures for creating and using information in the modern economy. Melody looks at network access, intellectual property rights, and the growing importance of human capital. He highlights the contributions of ICT-based services to productivity improvements, and studies trends on the emergence of network oligopolies. Against this background Melody suggests how the new knowledge economy might achieve yet greater efficiency and inclusiveness.

Lazonick, in Chapter 4, looks at 'offshoring'—the large-scale movement of jobs overseas in general and in ICT in particular. He shows how the initial search for low-wage labour to perform low-skill work changed into a search for low-wage labour to perform *high*-skill work. Those pressures were incipient from as early as the 1970s, as ever greater price competition emerged globally and indigenous high-skilled engineers assumed increasingly significant roles in offshored locations. Lazonick focuses on the history of East Asian inward and outward migration—on South Korea, Malaysia, and India in particular—and on policy measures in education and employment undertaken in those countries to retain highly skilled workers.

In Chapter 5, Draca, Sadun, and Van Reenen summarize the literature on the productivity impact of ICTs. They point out that this work shows that the 'Solow Paradox'—the apparent absence of an impact of ICT on productivity—has disappeared. The resolution of the paradox is not particularly subtle: Solow's statement in the late 1980s on seeing computers everywhere except in the productivity statistics simply had its hypothesis incorrectly stated. No one could have seen computers everywhere since, until about the same time that the productivity numbers picked up, computers constituted only a small part of any nation's capital stock. Both growth accounting and econometric evidence now suggest an important role for ICTs in productivity. The authors discuss empirical estimates showing a much larger impact of ICT on productivity than expected and suggest that 'organizational capital' might account for this impact.

Chapters 6 and 7 focus on economic aspects of the Internet. In Chapter 6, David discusses how some of the main approaches to the 'economics of the Internet' have drawn on features common to broader categories of economic activity and public policy. He argues that much of this is not especially helpful; what is crucial, instead, is how this new Internet infrastructure differs from earlier systems of connection-oriented communications. David describes how many current recommendations for regulating the Internet might jeopardize its social value and vitiate its role as a platform for innovation. Such recommendations have emerged from two distinct sources: first, research attempting inappropriately to impose policy lessons gleaned elsewhere onto what might be a truly new communication system; and second, private interests seeking to re-engineer the infrastructure of the Internet to improve its commercial exploitation, but then disrupting its unique and valuable public-good operations. David argues that public policy needs to take into account such dangers if the Internet is to serve its proper socially beneficial task. At the same time, David points to what economists need to understand better about these emerging technologies, for their likely massive significance in determining the shape of future economic performance.

In Chapter 7, Greenstein and Prince analyse Internet diffusion across the US, with an eye to understanding the persistent 'digital divide'—unequal availability and use of the Internet. They compare Internet adoption with repeat and first-time purchases of personal computers, highlighting how these have different determinants. They examine the historical and geographical evolution of Internet usage within an economic theory of diffusion, that is, by clarifying the costs and benefits on both the demand and supply sides. In doing this they provide insight into the Internet's physical presence based on economics-based measurement techniques. They also raise questions about how the finer details on evolving, emerging technologies might affect the future relation between physical geography and the Internet: these are important questions on which, necessarily, we have as yet very little empirical evidence.

In Chapter 8, Steinmueller concludes this theme in the handbook with an explanation of how the exploitation of technological and market opportunities in the ICT industries has produced changes in market supply and demand that regulate or channel the rate and direction of industrial growth. He focuses on the way ICT innovations integrate with existing and other newly emerging technologies through standardization. Finally, he examines the underlying economic processes that influence the new economy's emerging industrial structure and the resulting consequences for policy. This chapter shares with David's Chapter 6 two important messages. First, observers will probably miss the critical features and key implications of ICTs when they seek to shoehorn the economic analysis of ICTs into previously understood, but likely inappropriate, categories. Secondly, for future economic development and policy formulation, the stake involved in getting our understanding of ICTs right is enormous.

CHAPTER 2

THE ICT PARADIGM

CHRIS FREEMAN

1 INTRODUCTION

DURING the 1990s, the use of the expression 'change of paradigm' to describe the advance of information and communication technology (ICT) became commonplace. This fashionable change in language can be explained by three main events. First, in the intellectual world, a debate was initiated by the publication of a provocative new book, which made the concept of paradigm change familiar to both natural and social scientists (Kuhn 1970). Secondly, in the real economy, the production and extremely widespread sale by Intel of a cheap microprocessor encouraged a focus on ICTs. Finally, the use of the expression by Greenspan, the then Chairman of the US Federal Reserve, drew the financial world's attention to the potential and hazards of ICTs.

By the end of the twentieth century it was already clearly evident that the new leading ICT industries (computers, software, electronic components, and telecommunications equipment) were firmly established as the leading sectors of the economy in the US. Indeed, although they still accounted for a relatively small proportion of aggregate production and employment, their rate of growth was so high that they accounted for over half of total growth in the US economy in the 1990s, and gave rise to a huge financial bubble early in the next century.

The second section of this chapter deals with the origins and definition of the paradigm concept; the third with the formation and collapse of the Bubble; and the final section with a critique of some myths that have attended diffusion of the ICT paradigm which were (and to some extent still are) the intellectual counterpart of the financial bubble. Among them were the supposed decline and even possible disappearance of some familiar institutions, such as the large firm and the nation state. How wrong they were.

2 ORIGINS OF THE EXPRESSION 'CHANGE OF PARADIGM'

Dictionaries (for example, the *Oxford English Dictionary* 1965) trace the word paradigm to both Greek and Latin derivations and distinguish the emergence of two distinct meanings of the word. In the first place, a paradigm was an *observed pattern* and later came to mean an *exemplary pattern* of human behaviour. Not surprisingly, the latter sense was characteristic of religious literature in the Middle Ages. This chapter will discuss both uses of the word, but only in relation to recent literature in the social and the natural sciences.

In terms of economics, a new pattern may be construed as a new basic *structure* of the economy, and a new exemplary pattern as a set of principles designed to guide the behaviour of managers, firms, government organizations, and others, which are striving to understand, to develop, and to modify or adapt to such a newly emerging structure of the economy.

Although historians have consistently emphasized the revolutionary changes in technology in the leading economies ever since the British industrial revolution in the late eighteenth century, there are many still who argue that the ICT revolution surpasses the industrial revolution itself in terms of the breadth of its applications and the depth of its social consequences. ICT not only affects every industry and every service, but also every function within these industries and services. Not only production, but also design, distribution, and marketing are all profoundly affected by ICT. Multinational entities enjoy a new freedom in the location of these functions and in the networks that provide them. Moreover, eBay's new trading market brings together the greatest collection of small buyers and sellers in history. These and other remarkable features of the new ICTs have led some enthusiasts for the expression 'paradigm' to adopt missionary zeal with respect to its characteristics and diffusion, and to exaggerate its exemplary aspects.

The expression 'change of paradigm' was not widely used in the social sciences before the 1970s and not at all in economics. The main stimulus for its more widespread use was undoubtedly the debate among historians of science, which followed the publication of Thomas Kuhn's (1970) book on *The Structure of Scientific Revolutions*. Although certainly controversial, this work made familiar the concept of a paradigm as a commonly agreed theoretical approach, based on a set of principles and methods, which might however periodically be challenged by new ideas, derived from discoveries and evidence not consistent with this received theory. In Kuhn's view the accumulation of such anomalies led discontented (and usually younger) scientists within a discipline to rebel against the established norms, and ultimately to develop and propagate a revolutionary new paradigm, which would become in its turn a new orthodoxy of normal science.

Some historians and philosophers of science never accepted Kuhn's theory and strongly criticized his use of the paradigm concept as inaccurate and misleading (see, for example, Lakatos and Musgrave 1970; Fuller 2004). Nevertheless, partly because of this controversy, Kuhn's book did serve to popularize the idea of a paradigm and paradigm change among both scientists and historians. It was not long before economists and technologists took the fairly obvious step of applying some of these ideas about the history of science to the history of technology. The notion of a dominant design was one advanced in various branches of technology and was in some ways analogous to Kuhn's theory of normal science. The stretching of robust and dominant designs may be compared with normal scientific work within an established paradigm (Gardiner and Rothwell 1985).

In his pioneering comparison of scientific and technological paradigms, Norman Clark (1985) pointed to some significant differences, as well as similarities. In his view, technological paradigms show greater structural heterogeneity because of the variety of inter-industry linkages and the complexity of socio-economic relationships. He cited Constant's (1973, 1980) study of the origins of the turbojet revolution to illustrate this point. The transition from propeller-driven engines to jet engines required not only a major change among designers and producers of aero-engines and manufacturers of aircraft, but also changes in the attitudes and behaviour of airlines, airports, and regulatory authorities.

It was a paper by Giovanni Dosi (1982) that brought the concept of technological paradigms explicitly to the attention of a wider circle of economists and other social scientists. He systematically related such paradigm changes to changes in the structure of specific industries and in particular the electronics industry. Defining a technological paradigm as 'an outlook, a set of procedures, a definition of the relevant problems and of the specific knowledge related to their solution' (Dosi 1982: 148), he argued that new paradigms could not emerge simply from changes in market demand or in consumer tastes.

A new paradigm could emerge only as a result of an interplay between economic pressures and new developments in technology and in science. In this early phase, new, small 'Schumpeterian' firms often played an important role together with public agencies and a variety of technological and scientific institutions. As the new paradigm became dominant, normal incremental technological change would often correspond to a phase of oligopolistic maturity in the relevant industry.

Dosi was primarily concerned with paradigm change in specific industries and did not attempt to identify or analyse paradigm changes which might affect a large number of industries and services, or even the entire economy. However, he did hint at the possibility that 'broad new technological trajectories' could influence economic cycles in the wider economy (Dosi 1982: 160) in rather the same way as Nelson and Winter (1977) had spoken of 'generalized natural trajectories' of technology, such as electrification.

Quite independently of the discussion on paradigm change, economists and sociologists had become familiar with the notion of a general structural change in the economy arising simply from the large increase in the proportion of the total labour force engaged in information or knowledge production and distribution. Although they did not use the expression paradigm change, several studies (for example, Bernal 1939) analysed this trend even before World War II. In the post-war period, among the most influential works published were those of Machlup (1962) on *The Production and Distribution of Knowledge* and Daniel Bell (1973) on *The Coming of Post-industrial Society*, and, in the management literature, Peter Drucker's (1945) concept of the corporation.

In contemporary discussion, the ICT paradigm is generally taken to refer to electronic technologies, but neither Machlup nor Bell spoke of paradigms, nor did they assign a central role to electronics in their analysis of the knowledge economy and structural change. A survey of research and development (R&D) in the electronic capital goods industry (Freeman et al. 1965) did however already show that by the early 1960s, the general view among those active in research was that the telephone communications network would increasingly depend on new electronic exchanges and that this network would be used for massive data transmission as well as voice telephony. The extraordinarily rapid growth of data processing in the computer industry would be complemented by a corresponding growth of the links between computers. Thus, the basic elements of a new pattern, or ICT paradigm, were present and observed long before the expression was coined and came into general use. The key industries in this newly emerging pattern were the computer industry, storing, processing, and transmitting vast quantities of information, the telecommunications network enabling worldwide and very rapid communication between these computers, and the micro-electronics industry supplying large numbers of cheap reliable components. This was, however, not yet regarded as an exemplary pattern, except by a few visionaries at, or near, the leading edge among researchers in science and technology policy, such as Diebold (1952, 1990).

It was especially the work of Carlota Perez (1983, 1985, 2002) that brought into general use both of the original meanings of paradigm. While the new pattern of very rapid growth of the core electronics industries could be fairly easily observed in the US, it was by no means so clear how far the new technologies could be developed in other industries and services beyond the early applications, and in other countries beyond the shores of the US. Working at this time in California, but with a background in the oil industry of her native Venezuela, Carlota Perez was particularly well qualified to recognize and study the problems of change of paradigm in industries hitherto dominated by an older technological style—the paradigm of oil-intensive mass production. She became convinced that there were potential profitable applications of ICT in every industry and service. Intel's development, production and sale of an extremely cheap but efficient 'computer on a chip' made computing universally accessible. Similarly to Dosi, she recognized the importance of the intense interaction between technology and economic pressures, which is why she used the expression 'techno-economic paradigm'. But like Kuhn, she recognized the strength of the resistance to change from those who were accustomed to a different way of thinking. Hence her insistence on the exemplary aspect of paradigm change and on the process of institutional change as an essential condition for successful diffusion. The specific characteristics of the new technologies meant that organizational changes had to accompany and facilitate technical change.

In later work Perez (2002) distinguished two phases in the diffusion of a new technological paradigm. In the first phase, which she designated as installation, investment in a new infrastructure and in new core industries are the dominant features. In the later phase, designated as deployment, it is the applications of the technological revolution in all the other industries and service activities and in many other countries that characterize the period. Clearly, in this conceptualization of the second phase the exemplary features of the new paradigm, and the institutional changes needed to establish its hegemony everywhere, are the predominant characteristics of social, economic, and technical change. While experimental and early applications of new technology would of course already be made during the installation phase, it is only after major institutional changes that the incremental process innovations in every part of the economy and in many countries can be fully deployed.

In her model, exceptional importance attaches to the role of infrastructural change, especially the communications infrastructure, in propagating the exemplary paradigm, since this can reach almost all potential actors. Only when the economic and technical advantages of the new technologies have been clearly demonstrated far beyond the industries of early applications can the paradigm become a meta-paradigm and generate widespread increases in productivity. Recognition of the potential profitability and universal applicability of the new paradigm would be driven by many events, experiments, and experiences but frequently in the past history of paradigm change one particular event had been especially significant, designated by her as a 'big bang'. For the ICT paradigm this big bang was the Intel microprocessor; in earlier times for another paradigm, the

Liverpool to Manchester railway trials played the role of a big bang for the age of railways and steam power (see Table 2.1).

It was the extent of opposition and scepticism that in the early days retarded the growth of infrastructural investment and other related investments. But once the dam was breached the opposite situation began to prevail. Local flash floods occurred because of the rush to invest in new projects. Finance capital became hyperactive in the desire to stimulate this investment. Some kind of investor mania was characteristic of canals and railways as it was of the Internet in the 1990s. The flood of new investment became so great that it often exceeded for some time the real possibilities of profitable application, both in the case of the ICT paradigm and of earlier changes of paradigm (see Table 2.1). A salutary reminder of the excesses comes when bubbles burst, but not before a vitally important new infrastructure and other facilities had been established by the wave of investment that has been labelled as a spell of 'irrational exuberance'.

Alan Greenspan was not the first to use this expression to describe the surge of expansion in the ICT industries in the 1990s and the later associated Internet Bubble (Shiller 2000). Nor of course was he the first to speak of the new paradigm in connection with the new economy, and with the surge of

Table 2.1 Five successive technological revolutions, 1770s to 2000s

Technological revolution	Popular name for the period	Core country or countries	Big-bang initiating the revolution	Year
First	The Industrial Revolution	Britain	Arkwright's mill opens in Cromford	1771
Second	Age of steam and railways	Britain (spreading to Continent and US)	Test of the 'Rocket' steam engine for the Liverpool–Manchester railway	1829
Third	Age of steel, electricity and heavy engineering	US and Germany forging ahead and overtaking Britain	The Carnegie Bessemer steel plant opens in Pittsburgh, PA	1875
Fourth	Age of oil, automobile and mass production	US (with Germany at first vying for world leadership), later spreading to Europe	First Model-T Ford plant in Detroit, MI	1908
Fifth	Age of information and telecommunication	US (spreading to Europe and Asia)	The Intel microprocessor is announced in Santa Clara, CA	1971

Source: Adapted from Perez (2002: 11).

growth in the ICT industries in mind. But his status and reputation as Chairman of the US Federal Reserve were such that, from 1996 onwards, the expression *paradigm change* entered common parlance far beyond the investor community, the economics profession or scientific research. The ICT paradigm had become both an established pattern and an exemplary pattern.

Among professional economists and historians, the notion of periodic revolutionary changes in technology, and periods of dominance of specific technologies, gained currency not only through the concept of paradigm change, but also through Bresnahan and Trajtenberg's (1995) work on General Purpose Technologies (GPT), which influenced many industries and services over long periods.

3 THE ICT PARADIGM
AND THE REAL ECONOMY

As a new pattern or structure of the economy, the ICT paradigm was clearly established by the end of the twentieth century in the US. The leading producing industries of the ICT paradigm were also growing very rapidly in Europe, in Japan, and in East and South-East Asia, influencing other industries. The rise of the Internet spawned new forms of transacting business in many of these other industries and services, including retail and wholesale distribution, travel and tourism, financial services, auctioneering and gambling, as well as publishing and information services. Of course, the penetration of e-commerce, as these new methods became known, was not instantaneous and was very uneven, but it was sufficient to fuel Internet mania in all of the numerous service activities, listed by Machlup (1962) as being those affected by the growth of the knowledge economy. These could all be transacted now, at least partly and sometimes preponderantly, by electronic means.

Obviously, changes of this magnitude could not possibly pass unnoticed by almost the entire population and expressions such as the Information Revolution, the Computer Revolution, or the Internet Revolution had become commonplace by the end of the century. Many exaggerated estimates were made about both the scale and the speed of the transformation that was occurring although, as *The Economist* (2004) observed in its *Survey of E-Commerce*, the changes that were actually occurring in the real economy were sometimes not those predicted by exuberant speculation during the heady years of the expansion of the Internet Bubble.

Among the services most deeply affected was retail distribution, and according to the US Department of Commerce, online retail sales rose to $56 billion in 2003, but this was still only 1.7 per cent of total retail sales.[1] Although the annual rate of increase at this time was 26 per cent, the biggest change was not so much in total sales as in the behaviour of consumers, and whether they bought online or not. For example, buyers of cars, armchairs, electrical appliances, or other large items, frequently did research online even if they made the final purchase offline. They came in to buy, armed with information from the Internet. The interplay between shops, showrooms online, and offline information was transformed so that a potential buyer might often go to a shop or a showroom, ask for a demonstration, but then make some excuse and get more information from the Internet, and finally make the purchase in a different shop. *The Economist Survey of E-Commerce* (2004) described this as the 'unbundling' of product information from the transaction, an expression first used by Professor Sawhney of the Kellogg School of Management in Chicago (Sawhney and Parkh 2001).

Most shops will probably not disappear as a result of the e-commerce revolution, even though the American statistics actually under-estimated the extent of the change. Travel, tourism, and auctioneering were some of the areas excluded from the Department of Commerce estimates, although they were very fast-growing e-businesses. Moreover, many shops and showrooms are changing their product range and the ways in which they operate. For example, bookshops may turn themselves also into cafes or snackbars, where potential customers may peruse books or journals in comfort before they buy them. What will eventually emerge is probably a new form of co-existence of shops, showrooms, and Internet. University of Michigan Surveys of consumer satisfaction showed a slightly higher rating for e-tail than traditional retail, but the difference was not great and traditional shopping offers advantages of personal interaction, physical exercise, and neighbourly contact so often underestimated by conventional cost-benefit techniques.[2]

Wholesale and retail distribution are of course by no means the only service industries to be deeply affected by the ICT change of paradigm, but they are among the most important and provide a good illustration of the type of structural change facilitated by the ICT paradigm. Two good examples of the ways in which firms could grow and prosper, taking advantage of new possibilities afforded by new infrastructures, were given by Fields (2004). PC's Limited, later to become Dell Computer Corporation, only began operations in 1984 in a hall of residence at the University of Texas at Austin, but by 2001 it had gained the largest share of any company in the world market for personal computers (PCs). The elimination of the retailer by direct sales over the Internet was one, but by no means the only one, of the business innovations introduced by Dell Computer to fuel its meteoric rise. The organization of production in several sites in different parts of the world was also very important. Fields makes an extremely interesting comparison with the rise of G. F. Swift in the US meat-packing industry in the late nineteenth century. In this case too, the new communication and transport infrastructure (the railways) made possible the radical transformation of both distribution and production in a major industry.

During the period around the end of the twentieth century, when e-business was taking off and the Internet Bubble was being inflated, the new information infrastructure was often referred to as The Information Highway or, using the distinctively American phraseology, as The Super-Highway. Even before the arrival of broadband technology it was capable of conveying and processing vast quantities of information at very high speeds. Broadband technology accelerated this speed by at least an order of magnitude. Not surprisingly the future of the Internet became the subject of heated political debate as well as e-business investment. The candidate for the Democratic Party in the US election for the Vice-Presidency in 1996 emphasized the crucial role of government in ICT research in his contribution to a 1991 special issue of the *Scientific American*: 'Federal policies can make a difference in several key areas of the computer revolution... most important we need a commitment to build the high-speed data highways. Their absence constitutes the largest single barrier to realizing the potential of the information age' (Gore 1991: 150).

Although some of his Republican opponents also advocated more active policies to build the super-highways, not everyone was in favour of such proactive government policies, either then or later. A good example of a more sceptical standpoint was *The Economist* magazine which, in a characteristically sharp article in 1995, entitled 'Let the Digital Age Bloom' argued that: 'Apart from imposing a few familiar safeguards, the cleverest thing that governments can do about all these changes is to stand back and let them happen' (*The Economist* 1995: 16). However, later in the same article under the sub-heading 'The case for watering and a little weeding', *The Economist* conceded that 'governments cannot ignore cyber-space altogether. There are some regulating functions which governments have to perform, at least for the foreseeable future, even if they wish to disengage as much as possible'.

Controversy over the role of government in the ICT paradigm has continued to this day and is likely to continue indefinitely since ICT cannot and does not resolve of itself the most fundamental problems of political life, which have persisted for several thousand years (Aristotle 330BC [English translation 1905]). One of the most difficult issues involving the role of government is the whole question of access to the Internet (Alexander 1999; Kruger and Gilroy 2001; see also Cabinet Office 2005) and another is control over the content. These issues are dealt with at length in Parts III and IV of this handbook. Here it will suffice to note that the policy of non-intervention prescribed by *The Economist* was never consistently followed even in the US; in some Asian countries, notably the so-called Tigers, a more radical attitude prevailed and ten years later they were ahead of the US in numbers of broadband connections as a proportion of the population and of Internet users. How far this rapid catch-up could be ascribed to a little judicious watering and weeding by governments was a matter of intense debate (Wade 1990;

Hobday 1995), but the changes in the real economy were now a matter of established fact.

Yang (2004) lamented that the US had fallen behind in the world league of broadband connections from third place in 2000 to tenth place in 2004. In her article entitled 'Behind in Broadband: New policies are needed to help the US catch up', she explained the relative decline of the US in terms of insufficient market competition. Whereas the leaders, especially South Korea, forced the incumbent companies to let start-ups use their networks at reasonable, government-set prices, and these start-ups drove speeds up and prices down, in the US the regional Bell companies prevailed in their long battle to stop this happening there. According to Yang, the US was 'in dire need of stronger leadership in broadband. The country is alone among developed nations in not having a comprehensive broadband plan' (Yang 2004: 70; see also Fransman 2006). Controversy on government policy in the US was further stimulated by the 'Brand X' decision of the Supreme Court affecting both access and content (Mossberg 2005; Supreme Court of the US 2005a, b). It was not only in broadband diffusion that catch-up of the US lead was taking place. In mobile telephony too, the erstwhile leader of the technological revolution had fallen behind.

Mobile telephones, as they evolved, also began to perform many of the functions performed by computers, television sets, and cameras. Some commentators even spoke of another change of paradigm. A big change *within* the ICT paradigm is probably a more accurate description. In this case, the competition came not only from Asia, but from Northern Europe too. However, the fact that firms in these and other countries have overtaken and often surpassed American firms in particular sectors, does not mean the end of US domination in general. The leadership of the US was based on some more enduring factors including military power, strong fundamental research, and higher education (Rosenberg and Nelson 1994).

It had at one time seemed probable that Japan would take the lead in the introduction of the ICT paradigm. In the 1970s and 1980s Japanese firms out-competed their American rivals in consumer electronics and established a world-wide lead in such areas as robotics, leading to some pessimism among American economists about the capacity to shake off the habits of the old mass production paradigm and move on to a new paradigm in the US (Dertouzos, Lester and Solow 1989). However, the Internet, the American advances in micro-electronics, computers, and software—the most basic elements of the new paradigm—combined with the enduring strengths in basic research to re-establish American hegemony. Hicks, Breitzman and Olivastro (2000) used patent statistics to demonstrate the depth of industrial leadership by American ICT firms. In this period too, the Japanese economy suffered from the explosion of a different type of bubble, based not on over-investment in the new paradigm, but on a huge rise in the price of land and financial assets. Whereas in the previous (mass production) bubble of the 1920s, bubbles in land prices were intimately associated with the growth of new transport infrastructure, this was no longer the case with ICT.

It took a fairly long time to make the necessary reforms in the Japanese financial system (and in the political system) before many Japanese firms were in a strong enough position to strike back again, but according to some observers (for example, Kunii and Tashiro 2004) they were doing so by the early years of the twenty-first century after substantial restructuring. Their renewed expansion was mainly in the 'high end' of the world markets for digital cameras, digital video disc players, plasma television, and camera phones. Here they were soon faced with intense competition from other Asian countries.

The broadband connections of the millions of computers in the information highways were of course very different from the highways of earlier technological paradigms, such as railways and motor highways. Nevertheless, the expression 'highway' is itself revealing of the ways in which the economy receives and digests new technological systems. The information highway and the earlier highways all have certain features in common despite their completely different technological characteristics. All of them facilitated the performance of a vast range of other industrial and service activities and changed the ways in which their business affairs were conducted. The railways changed the pattern of livestock breeding in Scotland, and meat marketing in London, just as fundamentally as they allowed for the transformation of the meat-packing industry in the US, described by Fields (2004), or the activities of the publishing industry that were transformed by the Internet. In poor countries, diffusion was accelerated by the use of Internet cafés. Following Korea's experience of rapid growth in the number of Internet cafés, China had an estimated 2 million cafés by 2005.

No less important, although more familiar, have been the changes in the computer and software industries themselves that have made PCs available in almost every firm, laboratory, school, office, hospital, and home. Technical change and competition constantly lead to the introduction of new models of computers while organizations are themselves constantly changing too. Finally, networks of organizations and links with the Internet are also continuously forming, re-forming, and dissolving. All of this leads to continual new requirements for software. Crime too strives to keep up with technology so that one of the main demands on the software industry is for new encryption and security methods (Giarratana 2004; Grow 2005). Military organizations engender the same or even greater pressures.

The future of the ICT paradigm depends, on the one hand, on the continuation of this enormous process of 'normal' technical change within the now well-established paradigm and, on the other hand, on the continuing extension and deployment of the new industries, services, and activities to all parts of the world (Mansell 2002; Perez 2002). Heated controversy has surrounded the worldwide deployment of the ICT paradigm. The technology undoubtedly facilitates and accelerates communication between all parts of the world as well as interception of those communications, but there are many different possible outcomes of this global deployment and big problems of institutional change.

In a capitalist economy it is mainly market competition that drives the world deployment process; but, as is evident from the foregoing, there is scope for considerable variation in the ways in which the exemplary paradigm is interpreted, modified, and applied. Moreover, it is not only the dominant firms whose inter-action is determining the outcome. As was clearly recognized in the European Commission's (1997) High Level Expert Group report *Building the European Information Society for Us All*, government policies and the general culture of society are also extremely influential. Nor is it only those countries that dominated the world economy in the twentieth century that will continue to dominate it through the twenty-first century. In their book *New Technologies and Global Restructuring*, Brundenius and Göransson (1993), and more recently, Baskaran and Muchie (2006) in *Bridging the Digital Divide*, illustrate how rapidly catch-up countries such as Brazil, China, India, and South Africa are closing the gap, and how varied are the circumstances and strategies of these and other catch-up countries. Uneven development is the rule both within and between countries, despite some counter-tendencies towards convergence and the more extreme view that the spread of the ICT paradigm involves the disappearance of the nation state.

4 MYTHS AND REALITY IN THE DEPLOYMENT OF THE ICT PARADIGM

Corresponding to the irrational exuberance that fuelled the Internet Bubble, the early period of installation of the ICT paradigm was accompanied by various myths about the economic and social consequences of its diffusion. Among these were some that related to such basic institutions of contemporary society as the state and the large firm.

There were indeed big changes in the real economy and in social institutions in the last quarter of the twentieth century and it was not surprising that some of these were so impressive that they were exaggerated and extrapolated into the future. One extreme example was Ohmae (1990: xii) who argued in his book *The Borderless World* that the 'interlinked economy' was now becoming so powerful that 'it has swallowed most consumers and corporations, made traditional national borders almost disappear and pushed bureaucrats, politicians and the military towards the status of declining industries'. More recent accounts would use the expression globalized economy rather than interlinked economy, but many others have emphasized the decline of the nation state and have postulated a close connection between the ICT paradigm and globalization.

Among the reasons for such beliefs were obviously the sheer speed and facility of global communications using ICT. These in their turn may plausibly be held to have facilitated both intra-firm and inter-firm connections on a worldwide basis, as well as inter-governmental communications, and all kinds of inter-personal communications. The rise of the multinational corporation (MNC) cannot in itself be directly attributed to the spread of the ICT paradigm, since it began much earlier. Nevertheless, most ardent opponents and enthusiasts for globalization do tend to associate them (Friedman 1999).

Critics of a strong globalization thesis often point out that there was an earlier period of globalization in the late nineteenth century which was brought to an end by the First World War and the Great Depression (Hirst and Thompson 1999; Held et al. 1999). It is even claimed that in that earlier period, globalization went further than it has today. However, Krugman (1995) is one of several well-known economists who forcefully argued that globalization has recently gone much further than in any earlier period. While not accepting all of Krugman's arguments on the nature and extent of the increase in international trade, Eichengreen (1996) in a balanced and careful survey did accept some of his main points. The change in the composition of trade in manufactures and the huge increase of trade in services occurred mainly in the 1980s and 1990s (Bordo, Eichengreen and Irwin 1999), that is, when the ICT paradigm had clearly taken off and when the speed advantages of that paradigm were already obvious. The relative decline in the purely physical volume of production and trade had given rise to the expression 'weightless economy' to describe the impact of ICT. Thus, there were reasonable grounds for associating ICT with some prominent aspects of globalization.

Eichengreen placed even greater emphasis on the recent reduction in trade barriers and obstacles to the flow of capital, and contrasted this with what Williamson (1998) called the 'globalization backlash' of the late nineteenth and early twentieth centuries, when tariffs were often increased and pressures to restrict migration of both labour and capital were increasing in the US and other countries. While there were certainly some indications of a similar backlash early in the twenty-first century, the formal commitments in the international community to the Washington Consensus and their embodiment in the World Trade Organization and the International Monetary Fund may constitute a stronger movement towards globalization. This was the clear-cut conclusion of Bordo, Eichengreen and Irwin (1999: 56) that 'the globalization of commodity and financial markets is historically unprecedented. Facile comparisons with the late nineteenth century notwithstanding the international integration of capital and commodity markets goes further and runs deeper than ever before.'

The weightless ICT paradigm made some significant contribution to this unprecedented degree of globalization, but this is a long way from the Ohmae thesis on the decline and disappearance of the nation state. On the contrary, there are still many good reasons for maintaining that in spite of and even because of financial and trade globalization, the nation state has actually become more important. This somewhat paradoxical argument was forcefully presented by Michael Porter (1990: 19) when he said that:

Competitive advantage is created and sustained through a highly localised process. Differences in national economic structures, values, cultures, institutions and histories contribute profoundly to competitive success. The role of the home nation seems to be as strong or stronger than ever... the home nation takes on growing significance because it is the source of the skills and technology that underpin competitive advantage.

At first sight, the ICT paradigm might appear to undermine these national advantages since ICT can facilitate international flows of scientific and technical information as well as financial information. Indeed, Rothwell's (1992) study of the 'electronification' of design and development in MNCs appears to lend support to this proposition. He pointed out that MNCs were already locating specialized aspects, or stages of product and process design, in their subsidiary operations or related organizations abroad. In fact, even before electronification of design, it was quite a normal feature of the activity of large multinational chemical engineering firms, to take advantage of the huge cost differences, to locate various parts of their design activities in different international locations. Electronification (that is, application of the ICT paradigm) offered the possibility of greatly accelerating this process as well as lowering the cost, but it did not initiate the globalization of design, or the demise of the large firm.

One of the major advantages of ICT is indeed that it facilitates and accelerates all kinds of networking arrangements, both inter-firm and intra-firm (see, e.g. Callon 1992; Coombs, Saviotti and Walsh 1992; Coombs et al. 1996; Dertouzos 1991; Chesnais 1996; Green et al. 1999; Mansell and Steinmueller 2000, Weiser 1991). This is surely one of the main exemplary features of the new paradigm. But the subcontracting of some parts of design activities, or their transfer, under exchange agreements with other independent firms, did not necessarily weaken the role of the large multinational firm itself.

Just as some economists construed ICT and globalization to signify the malaise and impending death of the nation state, others have construed the rapid growth of networking activities in the late twentieth century to foreshadow the displacement of the firm by the network. One of the best and most comprehensive studies of the information society (Castells 1996: 198; 1997, 1998) argues that 'the basic unit of economic organization' is no longer the entrepreneur, the family, the corporation, or the state, but a network composed of a variety of organizations. This network is held together by the 'spirit of information', which is a cultural code 'informing and enforcing powerful economic decisions at every moment in the life of the network'. Castells makes an analogy with Weber's spirit of accumulation and enterprise in the rise of capitalism, suggesting that the 'spirit of informationalism' is 'the culture of creative destruction accelerated to the speed of the opto-electronic circuits that process its signals, Schumpeter meets Weber in the cyberspace of the network enterprise' (Castells 1996: 199).

This analogy with Weber is reminiscent of the notion of a paradigm in its secondary meaning as an exemplary pattern, but neither Weber nor Castells saw either the spirit of accumulation or the spirit of information in quite this prescriptive way. Speaking of the last stage of the cultural development of capitalism, Weber referred to the possibility of 'mechanical petrification, embellished with a sort of convulsive self-importance' represented by 'specialists without spirit' and 'sensualists without heart', who imagine that they have attained a level of civilization never before achieved (Castells 1996: 200, quoting from Weber's *Protestant Ethic and the Spirit of Capitalism*). Although never so contemptuous as Weber, Castells nevertheless recognizes that the networking information society can develop in a variety of different directions, not all of them easily recognizable as a 'culture of creative destruction'.

This too is very much the attitude of Perez (2002) who envisages a wide range of possibilities for the future of the techno-economic paradigm of ICT, depending on the selective strength of contending political and cultural forces and the process of institutional change within each country and in the international arena. The fact that some social scientists were very optimistic about the future of democratic ideals within the ICT paradigm reflected to some degree the relatively early stage of development of the information society, when Utopian ideals had more currency.

It is reasonable to express some scepticism about the notion that the 'network' is displacing, or soon will displace, the large firm as the basic unit of economic organization in the capitalist economy. Whereas in the early days many economists and sociologists stressed the role of small- and medium-sized firms in the new economy, and the huge new opportunities offered to them by the Internet, after the collapse of the Internet Bubble the emphasis has been swinging back to demonstrating the advantages of the very large global firm, itself becoming a giant network. Nor have the numerous networks in which these large firms undoubtedly participate (Hagedoorn and Schakenraad 1992) shown the durability and purposeful strategic direction characteristic of some of these large firms.

It is of course true that the ICT revolution did actually weaken, or even destroy, the monopolistic power of the old telecommunication utilities, which were often state-owned or at least closely regulated. This did facilitate the rapid development of many new services and new technologies as well as many new firms. Moreover, the former mass production paradigm was frequently accompanied by a marked trend towards centralization of economic decision making and often by extensions of public ownership. This has certainly not been the case so far during the diffusion of the ICT paradigm. On the contrary, there was a wave of privatization and a repudiation, not only of socialism, but even of Keynesian or dirigiste state economic policies. Thus it is hardly surprising that many commentators should see this latter trend as characteristic of the paradigm itself.

However, neither privatization nor deregulation are necessarily permanent features of ICT, and neither does this paradigm necessarily lead to the disappearance of either large oligopolistic firms or the nation state. In their analysis of the changing population of the 200 largest US-manufacturing firms, Louçã and Mendonça (1999) show that the picture has been rather one of a new set of oligopolies establishing themselves side by side with the old oligopolies of the twentieth century. Right at the heart of the Internet, the new service providers have been described by Javary and Mansell (2002) as an 'emerging Internet oligopoly'.

Neither the electronification of design, nor the undoubted rapid growth of technology exchange and partnership agreements are unimportant developments. Both do reflect aspects of the diffusion of the ICT paradigm, but it is difficult not to reject the conclusion that their significance has been exaggerated. Qualitative analysis of the transnational activities of large MNCs shows that most of it is either local design modification to meet local regulations, or monitoring of local scientific and technological activities (Brundenius and Göransson 1993). However, both in the drug and in the electronics industry, there are important exceptions (Reddy and Sigurdson 1994) and these are sufficient to merit continuous re-examination of the distribution of MNC R&D activities in relation to national systems of innovation. This is especially important in view of the determined efforts of some erstwhile 'under-developed' third world countries to use science and technology, and especially the ICT paradigm, to aid their struggle to overcome poverty, ill health, and economic backwardness. It is at this point that the myth of the disappearance of the nation state connects with the myth of the displacement of the firm in the ICT paradigm.

Far from mythical is the rise of the two most populous countries in the world—China and India—in their share of world production and world trade, based to a considerable extent on their capability in the ICT paradigm. Regrettably, their extraordinary economic growth has led to a polarization of income distribution and ownership of wealth, which, however, has been a general trend in the world economy, including both North and South America, East and West Europe, and Africa. Kuznets (1930) suggested that such long-term swings in inequality may well be associated with the absorption of technological and demographic changes in the world economy, and there are many reasons to think that those who are the quickest and most proficient in the adoption of this ICT paradigm will gain at the expense of the laggards. Such a widening of inequality has been characteristic of the emerging ICT paradigm, both at the international level between countries, and within each country. The European Commission's Expert Group on *Building the European Information Society for Us All* (European Commission 1997) analysed the influence of the gap between the 'information rich' and the 'information poor' households and individuals, and advocated various policies to reduce this new dimension of poverty, including both fiscal proposals and much wider social and educational policies (see also Graham 2002; ILO 2004; Burrows, Ellison, and Woods 2005).

Perez (2002) has argued that the inequality effects of the early stages of installation of ICT are not so much inherent characteristics of the paradigm, as features of its cyclical development and deployment. It is not unreasonable, therefore, to hope that in the later stages they may be at least partly reversed, as occurred in the case of the deployment of the mass production paradigm. Whether or not such a reversal does occur is a matter of political and social policies and conflicts, but Reinert (2004) and his colleagues are probably right in their contention that there would have to be a massive change in social justice on a global scale if such a golden age is to emerge from the deployment of the ICT paradigm. In the period of installation of the new industries and infrastructure, the pressures towards polarization of income and wealth are very strong because of the exceptionally high monopoly profits won by the innovators due to the bubble phenomena, and acute skill shortages for developing and using the new processes and products. These things persist for quite a long time and can easily be reinforced by government policies or inertia. The need for strong countervailing policies, especially for expansion in the less developed countries, was first articulated by Tylecote (1985) and has been strongly re-emphasized by Mansell (2002) and Perez (2003). It is to be hoped that such policies prevail to aid the expansion of the world economy, as well as to promote social justice worldwide.

REFERENCES

ALEXANDER, D. L. (1999). *Internet Access: Government Intervention or Private Innovation?* Mackinac Center for Public Policy. http://www.mackinac.org/archives/1999/s1999-08.pdf, accessed 5 May 2006.

ARISTOTLE (330BC, English translation 1905). *The Politics* (trans. B. Jowett). Oxford: Clarendon Press.

BASKARAN, A. and MUCHIE, M. (2006). *Bridging the Digital Divide: Innovation Systems for ICT in Brazil, China, India, Thailand and Southern Africa.* London: Adonis & Abby.

BELL, D. (1973). *The Coming of Post-Industrial Society: A Venture in Social Forecasting.* New York: Basic Books.

BERNAL, J. D. (1939). *The Social Function of Science.* London: Routledge.

BRESNAHAN, T. E. and TRAJTENBERG, M. (1995). 'General Purpose Technologies: "Engines of Growth"?' *Journal of Econometrics*, 65(1): 83–108.

BRUNDENIUS, C. and GÖRANSSON, B. (1993). *New Technologies and Global Restructuring.* London: Taylor Graham.

BORDO, M. D., EICHENGREEN, B. and IRWIN, D. A. (1999). 'Is Globalization Really Different Than Globalization a Hundred Years Ago?' *Brookings Trade Policy Forum*, Washington DC, April 15–16.

BURROWS, R., ELLISON, N. and WOODS, B. (2005). 'Neighbourhoods on the Net: The Nature and Impact of Internet-based Neighbourhood Information Systems'. Report for the Joseph Rowntree Foundation, Bristol: The Policy Press, http://www.jrf.org.uk/bookshop/eBooks/1861347723.pdf, accessed 5 May 2006.

CABINET OFFICE (2005). 'Connecting the UK: The Digital Strategy', Prime Minister's Strategy Unit, March, http://www.strategy.gov.uk/downloads/work_areas/digital_strategy/digital_strategy.pdf, accessed 5 May 2006.

CALLON, M. (1992). 'The Dynamics of Techno-Economic Networks', in R. Coombs, P. Saviotti, and V. Walsh (eds), *Technological Change and Company Strategies: Economic and Sociological Perspectives.* London: Academic Press, 72–102.

CASTELLS, M. (1996). *The Information Age: Economy, Society and Culture Volume I: The Rise of the Network Society.* Oxford: Blackwell.

—— (1997). *The Information Age: Economy, Society and Culture Volume II: The Power of Identity.* Oxford: Blackwell.

—— (1998). *The Information Age: Economy, Society and Culture Volume III: End of Millennium.* Oxford: Blackwell.

CHESNAIS, F. (1996). 'Technological Agreements, Networks and Selected Issues in Economic Theory', in R. Coombs, A. Richards, P. Saviotti and V. Walsh (eds), *Technological Collaboration: The Dynamics of Cooperation in Industrial Innovation.* Cheltenham: Edward Elgar, 18–33.

CLARK, N. (1985). *The Political Economy of Science and Technology.* Oxford: Basil Blackwell.

CONSTANT, E. W. (1973). 'A Model for Radical Technological Change Applied to the Turbojet Revolution'. *Technology and Culture,* 14(4): 553–72.

—— (1980). *The Origins of the Turbojet Revolution.* Baltimore, MD: Johns Hopkins University Press.

COOMBS R., RICHARDS, A., SAVIOTTI, P. and WALSH, V. (eds) (1996). *Technological Collaboration: The Dynamics of Cooperation in Industrial Innovation.* Cheltenham: Edward Elgar.

——, SAVIOTTI, P. and WALSH, V. (eds) (1992). *Technological Change and Company Strategies: Economic and Sociological Perspectives.* London: Academic Press.

DERTOUZOS, M. (1991). 'Communications, Computers and Networks'. *Scientific American,* 265(3): 62–71.

——, LESTER, R. and SOLOW, R. (eds) (1989). *Made in America: Report of the MIT Commission on Industrial Productivity.* Cambridge, MA: MIT Press.

DIEBOLD, J. (1952). *Automation: The Advent of the Automatic Factory.* New York: Van Nostrand.

—— (1990). *The Innovators: The Discoveries, Inventions and Breakthroughs of our Time.* New York: Dutton.

DOSI, G. (1982). 'Technological Paradigms and Technological Trajectories – A Suggested Interpretation of the Determinants and Directions of Technological Change'. *Research Policy,* 11(3): 147–208.

DRUCKER, P. (1945). *The Concept of the Corporation.* New York: Mentor.

EICHENGREEN, B. (1996). *Globalizing Capital: A History of the International Monetary System.* Princeton, NJ: Princeton University Press.

Economist, The (1995). 'Let the Digital Age Bloom'. *The Economist,* 25 Feb.: 16–17.

—— (2004). 'A Perfect Market: A Survey of E-Commerce'. *The Economist,* 15 May.

EUROPEAN COMMISSION (1997). *Building the European Information Society for Us All.* Final Policy Report of High-Level Expert Group, Directorate-General Employment, Industrial Relations and Social Affairs, Luxembourg: OOPEC.

FIELDS, G. (2004). *Territories of Profit: Communications, Capitalist Development and the Innovative Enterprises of G. F. Swift and Dell Computer.* Stanford, CA: Stanford University Press.

FRANSMAN, M. (ed.) (2006). *Global Broadband Battles: Why the US and Europe lag while Asia leads.* Stanford, CA: Stanford Business Books.

FREEMAN, C., FULLER, J. K., HARLOW, C. J. et al. (1965). 'Research and Development in Electronic Capital Goods'. *National Institute Economic Review*, No. 34, November, 40–91.

FRIEDMAN, T. L. (1999). *The Lexus and the Olive Tree: Understanding Globalization.* New York: Farrar, Straus Giroux.

FULLER, S. (2004). *Kuhn Versus Popper.* London: ICOM.

GARDINER, P. and ROTHWELL, R. (1985). 'Tough Customers: Good Designers'. *Design Studies*, 6(1): 7–18.

GIARRATANA, M. S. (2004). 'The Birth of a New Industry: Entry by Start-ups and the Drivers of Firm Growth: The Case of Encryption Software'. *Research Policy*, 33(5): 787–806.

GORE, A. (1991). 'Infrastructure for the Global Village: Does the Information Highway Need Government Investment? *Scientific American*, 265(3): 150 ff.

GRAHAM, S. (2002). 'Bridging Digital Divides? Urban Polarisations and ICT'. *Urban Studies*, 39(1): 33–56.

GREEN, K., HULL, R., McMEEKIN, A. and WALSH, V. (1999). 'The Construction of Techno-Economic Networks vs. Paradigms'. *Research Policy*, 28(7): 777–92.

GROW, B. (2005). 'The Hacker Hunters'. *Business Week*, 6 June, 46–54.

HAGEDOORN, J. and SCHAKENRAAD, J. (1992). 'Leading Companies and Networks of Strategic Alliances in Information Technologies'. *Research Policy*, 21(2): 163–91.

HELD, D., McGREW, A., GOLDBLATT, D. and PERRATON, J. (1999). *Global Transformations.* Stanford, CA: Stanford University Press.

HICKS, D., BREITZMAN, T. and OLIVASTRO, D. (2000). *Innovations in IT in the United States – A Portrait Based on Patent Analysis.* Haddon Heights, NJ: CHI Research Inc.

HIRST, P. and THOMPSON, G. (1999). *Globalization in Question* (2nd edn). Cambridge: Polity Press.

HOBDAY, M. (1995). *Innovation in East Asia: The Challenge to Japan.* Cheltenham: Edward Elgar.

INTERNATIONAL LABOUR OFFICE (ILO) (2004). *A Fair Globalization: Creating Opportunities For All.* Report of the World Commission on the Social Dimension of Globalization. Geneva: ILO, 108.

JAVARY, M. and MANSELL, R. (2002). 'Emerging Internet Oligopolies: A Political Economy Analysis', in E. S. Miller and W. J. Samuels (eds), *An Institutionalist Approach to Public Utilities Regulation.* East Lansing, MI: Michigan State University Press, 162–201.

KRUGER, L. G. and GILROY, A. A. (2001). 'IB10045: Broadband Internet Access: Background and Issues', CRS Issue Brief for Congress, 18 May, http://www.ncseonline.org/NLE/CRSreports/Science/st-49.cfm?&CFID=4942178&CFTOKEN=85462795#_1_1, accessed 5 May 2006.

KRUGMAN, P. (1995). 'Growing World Trade, Causes and Consequences'. *Brookings Papers on Economic Activity*, 1: 327–62.

KUHN, T. S. (1970). *The Structure of Scientific Revolutions*. Chicago, IL: Chicago University Press.

KUNII, I. M. and TASHIRO, H. (2004). 'Japan's Tech Comeback'. *Business Week*, 9 Feb.: 38–9.

KUZNETS, S. (1930). *Secular Movements in Production and Prices*. Boston, MA: Houghton Miflin.

LAKATOS, I. and MUSGRAVE, A. (1970). *Criticism and the Growth of Knowledge*. Cambridge: Cambridge University Press.

LOUÇÃ, F. and MENDONÇA, S. (1999). 'Steady Change: The 200 Largest US Manufacturing Firms in the Twentieth Century'. Working Paper No. 14, CISEP/ISEG, UTI, Lisbon.

MACHLUP, F. (1962). *The Production and Distribution of Knowledge in the United States*. Princeton, NJ: Princeton University Press.

MANSELL, R. and STEINMUELLER, W. E. (2000). *Mobilizing the Information Society: Strategies for Growth and Opportunity*. Oxford: Oxford University Press.

MANSELL, R. (ed.) (2002). *Inside the Communication Revolution: Evolving Patterns of Social Interaction*. Oxford: Oxford University Press.

MOSSBERG, W. S. (2005). '"Wireless Carriers" Veto over how Phones Work Hampers Innovation', Personal Technology – Walt Mossberg, 2 June, at http://ptech.wsj.com/archive/ptech-20050602.html, accessed 5 May 2006.

NELSON, R. R. and WINTER, S. G. (1977). 'In Search of a Useful Theory of Innovation'. *Research Policy*, 6(1): 36–76.

OHMAE, K. (1990). *The Borderless World*. New York: Harper.

Oxford English Dictionary (1965). Shorter Third Edition. Oxford: Oxford University Press.

PEREZ, C. (1983). 'Structural Change and the Assimilation of New Technologies in the Economic and Social System'. *Futures*, 15(4): 357–75.

—— (1985). 'Microelectronics, Long Waves and World Structural Change: New Perspectives for Developing Countries'. *World Development*, 13(3): 441–63.

—— (2002). *Technological Revolutions and Financial Capital: The Dynamics of Bubbles and Golden Ages*. Cheltenham: Edward Elgar.

PORTER, M. (1990). *The Competitive Advantage of Nations*. New York: Free Press.

REDDY, A. S. P. and SIGURDSON, J. (1994). 'Emerging Patterns of Globalisation of Corporate R&D and Scope for Innovation Capability Building in Developing Countries'. *Science and Public Policy*, 21: 283–99.

REINERT, E. S. (ed.) (2004). *Globalization, Economic Development and Inequality*. Cheltenham: Edward Elgar.

ROSENBERG, N. and NELSON, R. R. (1994). 'American Universities and Technical Advance in Industry'. *Research Policy*, 23(3): 323–48.

ROTHWELL, R. (1992). 'Successful Industrial Innovation: Critical Factors for the 1990s'. *R&D Management*, 22(3): 221–39.

SAWHNEY, M. and PARKH, D. (2001). 'Where Value Lives in a Networked World'. *Harvard Business Review*, Jan.: 79–86.

Scientific American (1991). 'Computers, Networks and Public Policy [Introduction to articles on US Government ICT Policy]'. *Scientific American*, 265(3): 150.

SHILLER, R. (2000). *Irrational Exuberance*. Princeton, NJ: Princeton University Press.

SUPREME COURT OF THE UNITED STATES (2005a). 'National Cable and Telecommunications Association, et al., Petitioners v. Brand X Internet Services et al. (04–277); Federal Communications Commission and United States, Petitioners v. Brand X Internet Services et al. (04–281) on Writs of Certiorari to the United States Court of Appeals for the Ninth Circuit', 27 June, http://wid.ap.org/scotus/pdf/04–277P.ZO.pdf, accessed 5 May 2006.

SUPREME COURT OF THE UNITED STATES (2005b). 'J. Scalia dissenting, National Cable & Telecommunications Association, et al., Petitioners v. Brand X Internet Services et al.; (04–277); Federal Communications Commission and United States, Petitioners v. Brand X Internet Services et al. (04–281) on Writs of Certiorari to the United States Court of Appeals for the Ninth Circuit, 27 June', http://wid.ap.org/scotus/pdf/04–277P.ZD.pdf, accessed 5 May 2006.

TYLECOTE, A. (1985). 'Inequality in the Long Wave: Trend and Cycle in the Core and Periphery'. *European Association of Development Institutes Bulletin*, 1: 1–23.

—— (1992). *The Long Wave in the World Economy: The Current Crisis in Historical Perspective*. London: Routledge.

UNITED STATES DEPARTMENT OF COMMERCE (2003). 'E-Stats' http://www.census.gov/eos/www/papers/2003/2003finaltext.pdf, accessed 5 May 2006.

WADE, R. (1990). *Governing the Market: Economic Theory and the Role of Government in East Asian Industrialisation*. Princeton, NJ: Princeton University Press.

WEBER, M. (1930). *The Protestant Ethic and The Spirit of Capitalism*. London: George Allen and Unwin.

WEISER, M. (1991). 'The Computer in the 21st Century'. *Scientific American*, 265(3): 94 ff.

WILLIAMSON, J. G. (1998). 'Globalisation, Labour Markets and Policy Backlash in the Past'. *Journal of Economic Perspectives*, 12(1): 51–72.

YANG, C. (2004). 'Behind in Broadband: New Policies are Needed to Help the US Catch Up'. *Business Week*, 6 Sept.: 70–1.

NOTES

1. See http://www.census.gov/eos/www/papers/2003/2003finaltext.pdf, accessed 5 May 2006.
2. See 'E-Commerce Customer Satisfaction Outpaces Most Other Industries, New Report Shows', University of Michigan, http://www.foreseeresults.com/Press_ACSIFeb2004.html, accessed 5 May 2006.

CHAPTER 3

MARKETS AND POLICIES IN NEW KNOWLEDGE ECONOMIES

WILLIAM H. MELODY

1 INTRODUCTION

ALL economies are shaped significantly by the opportunities provided for generating and communicating information. These activities are essential for the development and sharing of knowledge, and for markets to function at all. They have powerful influences over how and what knowledge is developed, as well as the scope, efficiency, and limits of markets, and the nature of economic development. Continuing dramatic improvements in information and communication technologies and services (ICTS)—for example, the Internet, mobile phones, electronic banking, and so on—are changing quite significantly the ways in which knowledge is generated and communicated, and thereby the ways that firms operate, markets function, and economies develop. They are providing a new electronic communication foundation or infrastructure for the economy, capable of transmitting all forms of information (voice, data, pictures, music, film, and video) instantly over global networks at dramatically reduced costs, providing a quantum leap in the number and variety of opportunities for generating and communicating informa-tion in advanced twenty-first century economies.

As these new ICTS are being applied ever more widely and intensively there is increasing evidence that the economies of technologically advanced countries are in the process of moving beyond the industrial capitalism of the twentieth century to information and communication based 'knowledge economies' for the twenty-first, that is, economies where the major driving force for economic growth and development is activities relating to the generation, distribution, and application of knowledge. This transformation is exhibited not only by the rapid growth and development of new ICTS, but more importantly by their pervasive application throughout virtually all sectors of the economy (Freeman and Louçã 2001).

The electronics, computing, telecommunication, media and information content (film, television (TV), publishing, libraries, etc.) industries constitute a trillion-pound-plus global industry sector. It is the fastest growing sector of the global economy and is expected to remain so for the foreseeable future. Most national governments are counting on these industries to provide the primary stimulus to their future economic growth by stimulating productivity improve-ments in all sectors of the economy. Moreover, this transformation is expected to bring profound changes in the form and structure not only of economic systems, but also of social, cultural, and political systems. Thus, there is considerable research, public discussion, and government policy rhetoric relating to 'informa-tion' and 'knowledge' societies, as well as economies (Castells 1996, 1997, 1998).

The twentieth century industrial economy has been influenced greatly by ICTS (for example, telephone, radio and TV, computing) and the development of new knowledge for economic applications, particularly from new industrial technolo-gies in many fields (Mokyr 2002). The telephone, and even the earlier telegraph, facilitated the geographical expansion of business activity, and radio and TV provided an efficient mechanism for the mass marketing necessary to justify mass production. Therefore, the twenty-first century economy under examination here is labelled the 'new knowledge economy'. The focus is placed on the more recent ICTS and knowledge resource developments—that is, in the post-Internet period beginning in the mid-1980s—that are expected to play a much greater role in the future economy than ICTS and knowledge have played in the past industrial economy, and make possible structural and institutional changes of even greater significance.

This chapter examines some of the generic developments and key characteristics of evolving twenty-first century new knowledge economies that are becoming evident, their implications for market development, and the important issues they are raising for government policy and regulation relating to market govern-ance in the new economy. It does not take up the very important issues arising from the great differences among national economies, most particularly the enor-mous gulf between developed and developing country economies.

2 THE INFORMATION/COMMUNICATION
FOUNDATION OF INSTITUTIONS

The term 'information' is a static 'stock' concept. It suggests inventories of different kinds of knowledge as valuable assets. The term 'communication' is a dynamic 'flow' concept, reflecting the process of transmission and exchange of information, knowledge, and values. The exchanges often create new information influencing knowledge and values. The concepts of 'information' and 'communication' provide different analytical perspectives on two essential dimensions of knowledge.

An examination of the information characteristics of any economy must focus on its communication characteristics, for they will determine the terms of access to information, and the possibilities for sharing it and thereby developing new information. New communication networks are often the driving force behind the distribution of vast quantities of new information that have been generated precisely because of the new opportunities for communication. This interdependence between information and communication as essential elements of knowledge generation, distribution, and application has led to the adoption of a variety of labels for the new twenty-first century economies, including 'information', 'network', 'weightless', and 'knowledge', the label adopted here. They are all examining aspects of the same trends, although often from very different perspectives (Webster 1995).

In the broadest sense, the social, cultural, political, and economic institutions in any society can be defined in terms of the characteristics of the shared information within and among those institutions. In the narrower economic sense, it has been recognized generally that the most important resource affecting the economic efficiency of any economy, industry, production process, or household is information and its effective communication. Now that entire industries and major sectors of technologically advanced economies are devoted to information—the search for it, the creation of it, the manufacture, storage, classification, summarization, selection, editing, interpretation, hoarding, purchase, sale, and broadcast of it— the economic characteristics of information and communication are being recognized as key factors shaping the new knowledge economy.

Perhaps the most significant change between technologically advanced economies today and the oral tradition of the Greek city-state—still practised by some indigenous cultures today—is not in the role of information in the economy, but in the way that information processes and communication networks are institutionalized. The dominant form of information creation and exchange has shifted from oral discourse flowing outside the bounds of formal market arrangements to the establishment of formal information generating, storage, and transmission institutions, the commoditization of information and its exchange through markets. Perhaps the most significant change is not the overwhelming volume of information now available, but the institutional structure for its generation and distribution, and the increasing centrality of markets and government policies in shaping that structure (Melody 1987).

The importance of information flows and communication networks to the establishment and maintenance of particular institutions and power structures has been understood since earliest times. Trade routes and communication links were deliberately designed to maintain centres of power and to overcome international comparative disadvantages. Britain and other former colonial powers still benefit substantially from their historically established communication links with their former colonies, long after the formal demise of the empires. Universal telephone service was adopted as an important government policy objective in the US and other countries to encourage economic and social interaction within the country as a way of promoting national markets and political unity. The EU is specifically promoting increased communication and information exchange among EU member countries as a foundation for stimulating trade, creating a single European market, fostering a new European identity, and making Europe a stronger competitor in international markets and a more influential player in world affairs (Melody 2003).

3 THE TRANSFORMATION TO NEW KNOWLEDGE ECONOMIES

The primary forces driving the transformation of national, regional, and global economies have arisen from major changes in technologies, markets, and governance policies. It is the synergistic combination of the development and increasingly pervasive applications of ICT, and the worldwide movement to market liberalization and deregulation, that is stimulating quite fundamental changes in many markets and industries. A change in national telecommunication governance policies around the world during the latter part of the twentieth century, from public service monopolies to more open competitive markets, prepared the ground for the convergence of information technologies (IT) from the computing and electronics industries with communication technologies from telecommunication and broadcasting. This fundamental change in telecom sector policy and regulatory governance marks the beginning of the ICT revolution (Melody 1996).

In an agricultural economy, land is the most valuable resource attracting investment capital. In an industrial economy, manufacturing plants, machinery, and other forms of physical capital are the focal points of investment activity. In the evolving knowledge economy, the expectation is that skilled and well-trained people, and the information and communication tools they use, will be the central resource attracting investment because knowledge is produced, stored, and applied primarily by humans. New knowledge of course is central to technological and economic development in both agricultural and industrial economies. However, whereas the agricultural and industrial economies have been eras of physical capital where labour has been employed primarily to facilitate the requirements of machines, the new knowledge economy is optimistically expected to be one where investment in the skills, competences, and capabilities of people, that is, human capital, will be the central investment activity involving a far greater portion of the labour force (Freeman and Soete 1994).

One important distinction between the industrial economy and the evolving new knowledge economy is the shift in emphasis from a primary focus on the transformation of material resources, that is, the physical production of goods, to a focus on improving and facilitating transaction capabilities, that is, generating and communicating information to facilitate exchange transactions. The ICTS sector is driving productivity reforms primarily by improving the information and communication activities related to transactions. Although transaction activities as a measurable sector of the macro economy have not been subject to systematic ongoing research, the available evidence indicates that despite significant improvements in information processing and communication opportunities during the twentieth century, the proportion of resources allocated to transactions increased significantly. One major study of the US economy concluded that between 1870 and 1970 transactional activities, as compared to transformational activities, had risen from one quarter to almost one half of US gross domestic product (GDP) (Wallis and North 1986).

This trend is explained primarily by the geographic expansion of markets in many industries to international and global dimensions, which increased transaction costs, but often made possible significant economies of scale and scope in mass production, thereby justifying the allocation of increased resources to transactions in expanded geographical markets. In new knowledge economy markets, advances in IT are making it possible to push back the intensive limits on information by reducing the cost of generating more and more kinds of data and information services. Advances in telecom technologies are making it possible to push back the extensive geographical limit of efficient communication to extend markets (Melody 1985).

4 Distinguishing features of new knowledge economies

The most important features of the new knowledge economy that require detailed examination of their essential characteristics, and their implications for market governance policies, are:

- the development and use of advanced high speed (broadband) telecom networks—the *information infrastructure*—for electronic commerce and related next generation Internet and knowledge economy activities;
- the conditions governing the increased generation and use of *information content* both as economic resources and as products exchanged in markets;
- a much greater emphasis on the role of *human capital* as the principal producer, repository, disseminator and applier of information and knowledge;
- *applications* of ICT services and content to increase productivity throughout all sectors of the economy, initially by improving transactional capabilities and reducing transaction costs, and then by stimulating changes in the structure of organizations, industries, and markets;
- the likely *structure* and *efficiency* of new knowledge economy markets, and the significance of major market failures (for example, monopoly) and market externalities (benefits or costs to society that cannot be captured in market relations);
- the implications for *international trade* in a global knowledge economy.

Based on an understanding of the evolving market characteristics in the new knowledge economy, updated government policies and regulations will need to be developed. They will need to clear away the barriers of inherited policies and regulations that have become obsolete in the new economy, facilitate the desired and constrain the undesired market developments in the new knowledge economy at both national and international levels, and ensure that non-market policy objectives are implemented, for example, universal access to the communication network (Melody 2003; Sheehan 1997).

Access to the new information infrastructure network

The foundation for the advanced information and communication services that will drive the knowledge economy will be a transformed and upgraded telecom network that will provide the information infrastructure over which the new electronic services and information content will be supplied. Broadband telecom network connections will be needed in the workplace, home, schools, and other centres of activity, just as the telephone is needed now. This new information infrastructure will be the most important public utility of the twenty-first century economy.

The conversion of telecom networks and all forms of communication and information content to the digital standards of computing has created an electronic network infrastructure that facilitates the convergence of formerly discrete telecom services on a single telecom network. More recently, extended applications of Internet Protocol (IP) have permitted the convergence of services on the Internet to include, not only data, pictures, music and video, but also voice communication, including public voice services. Voice over IP (VoIP) is a major step in the ongoing convergence process. It means that now IP permits all types of communication services to be provided in an integrated manner over the Internet by many different service providers. These Internet services in turn are provided over the digital network facilities of telecom operators.

The convergence of telecom services using IP also completes a technical unbundling process that allows for a clear separation of facility network capacity from the services supplied over those facilities. In the historic model of telephone service supply, services and facilities were integrated by technical design as both were supplied by a single telephone monopoly in any geographical area. IP has permitted a clear separation between network facilities and services, first for data, then pictures, audio, video, and private voice networks, and now public voice networks as well. This is illustrated in Figure 3.1.

In Figure 3.1, Layer 1 is the Network Infrastructure Facilities (cables, wires, microwave towers, mobile cells, satellites, etc.) that provide the raw capacity that enables telecom connections. Layer 2 is Network Management, the standards and protocols that permit the routing and determine the technical quality of network

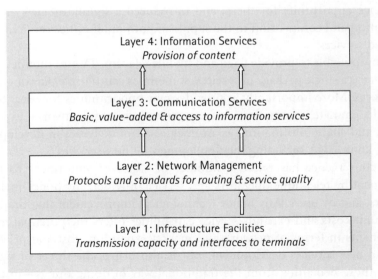

Fig. 3.1 From vertical to horizontal markets

services. IP has permitted the gradual unbundling of network services from infrastructure facilities. Layer 3 is the provision of Communication Services using IP (for example, voice, data, Internet access). Layer 4 is Information Content Services (for example, websites) that are accessible on a network using IP (Melody 1996).

With IP applied to all services, the structure of the overall market for communication services is radically changed from the former vertically integrated structure where most services and facilities were licensed and provided together by a vertically integrated monopoly telephone company, to a horizontally structured market consisting of separate markets for network infrastructure capacity, network management, communication services, and information services. This significantly reduces the barriers to entry to this market and its new submarkets and provides new opportunities for increased participation by new players, entering markets at any level, and providing a wide variety of different service packages. It allows new services and network intelligence to be developed by users at the fringes of the telecom network, rather than only by telecom operators at the centre. This is the open network model extending the unbundled network access opportunities of the Internet to a new level in next generation networks.

Although IP was developed for, and initially applied on, the Internet, the largest users of IP are the incumbent telephone operators around the world. They are in the process of converting their entire telecom systems to IP because of the enormous cost reductions to be achieved and the potential for providing new converged services in the future information economy, including e-commerce, e-government and other e-application services. At the same time, the extended application of IP by Internet service providers to include public voice services has opened a major new service opportunity for them, and introduced a significant new element of participation and competition in the supply of both public voice services and new converged services.

It is now possible to provide fixed and mobile telecom, TV and Internet access to consumers as a single package of services, sometimes called triple play or quadruple play services. More importantly, it provides new opportunities for users to search for and disseminate information, develop common interest networks, experiment, innovate and share information, as an integral set of activities in developing and applying knowledge, including the development of new services.

ICTS convergence has raised a number of issues of adjustment to the new environment by telephone operators and service providers, by policy makers and regulators, and by users. Any major technological improvement that dramatically reduces unit costs and expands service capabilities offers the potential for enormous benefits in terms of network and market expansion, cost and price reductions, and new services development. But it also brings the threat of significant losses to those benefiting from the traditional way of doing things—in this case incumbent telecom operators—in a process of 'creative destruction' (Schumpeter 1950). This also requires that the inherited structure of policies and regulations be reassessed and modified to meet the new challenges and opportunities unfolding.

Although the telecom sector has been liberalized and competition permitted or encouraged in some or all communication services markets, telecom regulatory authorities are being given new policy remits by governments for the new environment. In the UK, for example, five communication regulatory authorities were merged into one (Ofcom) early in the twenty-first century. Competition has proven to be an effective instrument for stimulating new information services development on the physical infrastructure, but infrastructure competition, especially for local distribution and in rural areas, generally has not developed significantly. Most incumbent former monopoly telecom operators have not willingly unbundled their physical networks to provide access to ISPs and other competitive services suppliers, and in many countries they are attempting to reassert their monopoly control over next generation network development. In addition, the upgrading of existing telecom networks to broadband standards is far from universally available in most countries (Trebing 1997).

Thus, most countries are in the process of developing and/or implementing policies and regulations relating to the development of new national broadband information infrastructures and the terms of access to them by information service providers and users. It is now being recognized that in the future economy those without access to basic information infrastructure services will be denied access to information and the ability to act on the content conveyed, whether it relates to economic, social, cultural, or political activity. The universal access requirements established during the telephone era will need to expand in the new knowledge economy as people will need not only the opportunity to communicate electronically, but also access to a variety of public information. For example, increasingly job opportunities are only advertised on Internet websites.

At both national and international levels there is already concern about a 'digital divide' in access to a modern information infrastructure both within countries, including the UK, the US, and other wealthy countries, and between the rich and poor countries. In the industrial economy, the majority of the world's population never had access to a telephone. Although the mobile phone explosion of recent years has expanded global coverage significantly, it is apparent that based on current trends the problem of information infrastructure access will deny the majority of the world's population access to the new knowledge economy (Melody 2003).

It is now clear that the conditions for access to the information infrastructure of the knowledge economy, at both national and international levels, will be heavily influenced by the governance policies that are established and the effectiveness of their implementation. If the matter is left to the market alone, access to the knowledge economy could be even more narrow and exclusive than it has been to the industrial economy. Although the need for governance policies to extend access beyond that which the market is likely to provide is widely recognized, the extent of government policy commitments to maintain and extend access opportunities has yet to be determined.

Information content and intellectual property rights

The stock of knowledge in society at any time, that is, the skills and education of the populace, the detailed factual information relating to such things as the working of production processes, the interrelationships and interdependencies of different sectors of the economy, and so forth, collectively represent a primary resource of the economy. The value of this stock of knowledge to society depends upon how pervasively it is spread throughout society, and upon the institutions for maintaining, replenishing, and expanding the stock of knowledge: that is, its education and training system, research generating new knowledge, and experience.

Once information has been generated, the cost of replicating it is very much lower than the cost of generating it in the initial instance. The use or consumption of information by one user does not destroy it, as occurs with almost all other economic resources and products. The information remains to be consumed by others, the only additional costs being those associated with bringing the same information and additional consumers of it together under conditions where it can be consumed, that is, learned. And once a given level of penetration is reached, with many types of information a multiplier effect comes into play as the information is spread throughout society by informal communication processes outside the formal processes of learning and training.

In addition, many information and knowledge markets are characterized by large positive externalities. They provide significant benefits to many people other than those engaged in the market transaction exchanging information. Thus the cost and benefit economics of replicating, consuming, and sharing knowledge are extremely favourable for its widespread distribution (Varian and Shapiro 1999).

Information and knowledge markets have been heavily influenced by governance policies throughout the history of the industrial economy. Governance policies have been directed toward balancing society's interest in promoting innovation by protecting the innovator's new knowledge, and in permitting access to that knowledge for useful application and the development of additional knowledge. For the industrial economy, patent laws have provided protection for knowledge relating to new inventions and their applications for a specified period of time—in most developed countries about 17 years. Alexander Graham Bell obtained his telephone patent in 1878, after which he licensed the development of monopoly telephone systems in many countries. The patent expired in 1895, after which there was a flurry of new entrants to the telephone industry in the US and some other countries who introduced a number of innovations building on Bell's original work.

For cultural products produced by authors, artists, musicians, and others, copyright laws have served a similar purpose, to protect the intellectual property of the producer so as to encourage production, but to limit this protection to a specified time period so as to encourage distribution and further development. For example, the US Copyright Act of 1790 granted American copyright holders a monopoly right to publish their work for 14 years, and to renew for another 14 years. Most other countries have copyright laws applying the same principles. At the end of the specified periods this knowledge enters the public domain. Although patent laws have been a cornerstone of the industrial economy, it is already apparent that copyright laws may be even more important in the knowledge economy.

Over the recent period of implementation of liberalization policies in telecom, changes in patent and copyright laws have moved in the opposite direction. Patent and copyright protection in the ICTs and other sectors of the economy have been expanded significantly. Developments in the US have set the standard that has tended to be followed in other countries. Until the 1980s, computer software was routinely excluded from patent protection. Beginning in the late 1980s, a series of US court decisions has permitted and strengthened patent protection for software programs. This has both enhanced the monopoly power of Microsoft and other firms, and helped spawn LINUX and the open-source software movement in response to Microsoft's monopoly power (Lessig 2001).

Since its inception, the breadth and time period of the US Copyright Act has been extended several times. In 1976, the third major revision extended the term of protection to life of the author plus fifty years, but introduced the doctrines of fair use (for example, for education) and first sale (allowing a resale market). In 1998, with the Internet threatening uncontrolled electronic distribution of copyrighted material, especially music and potentially film, the Sonny Bono Copyright Term Extension Act extended the protection period to the life of the author plus 70 years, and the Digital Millennium Copyright Act prohibits gaining unauthorized access to a work by circumventing a technological protection measure put in place by the copyright owner. During the late twentieth century period of transformation towards a new knowledge economy, as the basic characteristics of information and communication-based knowledge markets in the new knowledge economy have come into play, monopoly rights over both old and new information content and its transmission have been strengthened significantly by governance policies.

This in turn has influenced the development of new information services. Specialized information services for the private consumption of a restricted clientele are growing rapidly. They range from special research studies of the details of international markets for transnational corporations to confidential assessments of the negotiating strength of a specific customer, competitor, trade union, or government. They include remote sensing satellite data identifying the detailed swimming patterns of schools of fish, and pinpointing the location of mineral resources and the progress of crop growth in distant countries. They include the DNA of specialized crops and even people in distant lands. At the same time many governments have taken steps to attempt to restrain the march of information markets into the details of people's personal lives and to regulate the conditions of access to certain kinds of data banks, for example, credit, medical, and tax files, under new privacy laws.

It is already apparent that the economic characteristics of (1) the relatively high costs of establishing most databases, and information and knowledge services, and (2) the relatively low costs of extending the market for services already created, provide a powerful tendency toward centralization and monopoly on an international basis. Thus, competitive forces in most information and knowledge markets will be rather weak or non-existent. This raises fundamental issues of national and international government policy relating to IPR and competition policy (Melody 2003).

The inherent conflict between maximizing profit in quasi-monopoly information and knowledge markets and the social efficiency of societal distribution at marginal costs approaching zero has become a central issue in policy debates about knowledge economy governance policies. The current application of intellectual property rights in software, publishing, music, film, as well as in pharmaceuticals, medicine, and other areas is directed to increasing protection for monopoly owners of content, thereby limiting distribution severely. Thus, information and knowledge markets will continue to function inefficiently and lead to increases in the gap between rich and poor, both within countries and between countries. The efficiency, productivity, and innovation in these knowledge economy markets will be determined by the governance policies established as the new knowledge economy develops.

Human capital

The industrial economy has been characterized by waves of investment in capital-intensive physical assets such as the railway, electricity, natural gas, vehicles and roads, airlines, and the mass production of machines and durable goods. These past innovations required massive employment of relatively unskilled and semi-skilled labour. In contrast, the knowledge economy revolution is being driven primarily by skilled labour, but so far representing a much smaller portion of the total labour force. For the first time in the history of capitalism, the primary driving economic force may not be physical capital, but human capital—the investment in skilled labour. At this stage of development, the open questions are, how much investment, and what proportion of the labour force (Freeman and Soete 1994)?

Increased investment in skilled labour is evident in the research and development (R&D) that is yielding continuous innovations in the ICTS and many other industries, which are increasingly dominated by software, services, and content development. Just as computer software grew from almost nothing in the mid-1960s to become over ten times larger than the computer hardware industry by the turn of the century, so a similar process has now begun in the telecom sector, most dramatically illustrated by the explosion of Internet services. The driving force is the information content and the communication capabilities, not the physical facility systems.

This is also true in the applications of ICTS throughout the economy, and even in the delivery of new services to the home. Experimental trials around the world have demonstrated that investments in state of the art technologies and services are not enough. There must be far more investment both in understanding consumer needs and in enhancing the consumer skill base before there will be widespread acceptance of these services. Thus there is increasing evidence that the pace at which the new technologies and services are driving the process of transformation to a knowledge economy depends primarily on the pace of productive investment in human capital, that is, the skill base of labour, management, consumers, and policy makers (Sheehan and Tegart 1998).

In some respects this could be a very positive state of affairs for it implies some very promising tendencies. First, it could significantly reduce the oscillations in the business cycle, which in the past have been aggravated by the rise and fall of enormous investments in location-specific fixed physical capital. Investment in human capital can avoid these aggravated fluctuations. Further, in times of deficient aggregate demand in a knowledge economy, it will be investment in human capital that should be the priority need to stimulate renewed economic growth.

A second important characteristic of investment in human capital is that it narrows the gaps between the traditional distinct economic activities of investment, employment, service provision and benefit to the population. In the industrial economy, investment frequently does not provide satisfactory employment, and a significant portion of the economy cannot take advantage of the goods and services on offer. If the priority infrastructure investment is in human capital, then the needs of people as workers, as consumers and as citizens, can be met with the same investment. It is both a resource input and a service output at the same time.

Yet despite the rhetoric about the knowledge economy and human capital, the commitment to investment in education and training by governments in the leading industrialized countries has been declining in the early years of the twenty-first century. Corporate training remains limited and specialized because of a recognition that firms may not realize the benefits of their investments in human capital as enhanced skill may open opportunities for employees with competitors. Privately funded education and training is increasing among the wealthy. Moreover, many jobs and people are being disadvantaged in the new economy as a result of losses of job security, benefits, and real wages. Some evidence suggests that it is only a relatively small minority that is benefiting from employment in new knowledge economy jobs (Huws 2002a, b).

These trends suggest that current governance policies with respect to human capital development are directed toward enhancing the human capital of a smaller rather than a larger portion of the population. This is likely to promote an effective labour participation rate in the knowledge economy that is far lower than it need be and conceivably even lower than in the industrial economy. Once again, the shape and direction of a key resource for the knowledge economy will be influenced significantly by governance policies.

ICTS applications for productivity improvement

Although the information and communication sector of the economy is extremely important in providing a foundation for a modern economy, the major transformations that will bring about a new knowledge economy lie elsewhere. For the most part, the new ICTS are intermediate goods. Their primary benefit lies not in their intrinsic value, but in their applications for other purposes. The productivity potential for a new knowledge economy lies in the potential for applying these technologies and services to change the way business is done, for example, electronic commerce, the way organizations and industries are structured, and the way people choose to conduct their lives (Castells 1996, 1997, 1998).

Banking and finance have been the leading applications sector. The industry has been restructured on a global basis. Banks have reorganized the way they function. One can readily recognize that we do our banking and finance very differently today than ten or even five years ago. The international liberalization of finance has created highly liquid and flexible global currency and securities markets. But the deregulation of financial markets, in combination with new global information and communication financial networks, has permitted such rapid movements of money capital around the world that it has become a major cause of economic instability. The value of international financial exchanges is now more than 300 times greater than the value of trade in goods and services, which has prompted some analysts to interpret the information economy as 'casino capitalism' (Kay 2003: 362). This is associated with increased volatility in stock markets, currency markets, and economic activity in regions and small nations that are vulnerable to the resource allocation decisions of financial speculators. Effective financial governance for the new economy has not yet been established.

Other industry sectors, including transport and tourism, manufacturing, education, and other services are at earlier stages in their applications of ICTS for sector transformation. Public sector applications lag noticeably behind private sector applications. This is particularly ironic because it is in the sectors of education, health, and government administration that the potential benefits of ICTS are arguably the greatest. The extent of productivity improvements for the economy will depend significantly upon innovative service applications in the public sector. The governance policies for the applications sectors will determine the scope and extent of applications and the productivity improvements achieved.

The prevalent market structure: Network oligopoly

It is apparent that the knowledge economy increasingly will become a network economy as electronic communication networks provide the platform for the supply of ever more services and content. Communication networks are characterized by significant economies of scale and scope, and many also enable extensive positive network externalities. The primary industries of the ICT sector—telecom, network software and services, and the content sectors of music, film, television, etc., are already increasingly concentrated oligopolies, many on a global basis. Many of these firms are linking directly into services applications, most of which will also be supplied on a network basis. The available evidence suggests that the dominant industry characteristic in the knowledge economy will be highly concentrated network oligopoly markets. This raises a dilemma for governments with respect to the application of existing competition laws and/or direct industry regulation.

The economic theory of oligopoly markets (only a few large suppliers) explains how they tend to be characterized by inefficiency, instability, and indeterminacy. Too little output is produced and too much capacity is established for that output so that excess capacity will serve as an artificial barrier to entry. The rivalry among the few suppliers tends to focus on non-price factors, often heavy marketing which provides an additional artificial barrier to entry. Prices are generally set well above costs, and significant price discrimination to exploit monopoly market segments and erect barriers to entry is typical, except when external factors or an increase in uncertainty stimulate a price war. Concentrated oligopolies often engage in explicit or implicit self-regulation to preserve market share and oligopoly profits. With significant market power, they are capable of negotiating terms for minimal payments to resource suppliers, including labour, and distributors, capturing the productivity gains from the new economy for themselves (Dew-Becker and Gordon 2005).

Some oligopolies engage in significant R&D and technological development, which can lead to crashing the barriers to entry of another industry, inter-industry rivalry, and 'waves of creative destruction'. But under these circumstances the transition to the new knowledge economy is likely to be highly inefficient and unstable, leading to new industry arrangements that are most often simply restructured oligopoly (Lynn 2005).

The implications for international trade

At the international level, ongoing negotiations with respect to knowledge economy issues are focused on the establishment of patent and copyright laws in developing countries paralleling those in the developed countries, for the purpose of protecting information products, services, and content that they wish to sell into developing country markets. This trend is strengthening concentrated oligopoly in global markets both in ICTS and other sectors, pointing to a global knowledge economy that will be even more unbalanced with respect to the disparities between rich and poor countries than has been experienced in the industrial economy.

Markets with the characteristics of concentrated oligopoly need rules if operator initiative is to be directed towards efficiency and the expansion, rather than the restriction, of supply. Regulation can influence where the oligopoly market rivalry is focused in the information infrastructure sector. Strengthened competition laws focused particularly on concentrated oligopoly, rather than simply on monopoly power, will be necessary to help make information and knowledge network services markets workable. For consumers there will be countervailing benefits in some markets in terms of the availability of more complete information that will facilitate increased and more informed consumer choice, for example, purchases over the Internet. However, on balance the imperfections in the most prevalent knowledge economy markets will be greater than in industrial economy markets, requiring more active and sophisticated industry structure governance policies than in the past. Thus, the efficiency, productivity and innovation of new knowledge economy markets will depend heavily upon the effectiveness of the market governance policies (Melody 2003).

5 DEFINING THE PUBLIC INTEREST IN PUBLIC INFORMATION

Liberalization reforms of the telecom and other infrastructure segments of the economy have provided much-needed new opportunities for private initiative for the development of the infrastructure, services, content, and applications that will drive new knowledge economy development. But governments have yet to mark out the domain of the public interest in the new economy. In addition to universal access to Internet services, there will be the universal information needs of the general public in the new knowledge economy. If economies and societies are going through a transformation to a condition where information and knowledge take on increasing importance, and are provided over next generation networks, then presumably there will be a definable set of public information needs essential to the maintenance of participatory democracy. This information will be necessary for individuals to function effectively as workers (job information, tele-working), consumers (tele-shopping, banking, entertainment information), citizens (e-voting, government information), and community participants (social and cultural networks). A rich public information commons in the new electronic space will be essential if new knowledge economies are to be inclusive rather than exclusive and fragmented. How it is defined and developed will be determined by government policies (Melody 1990; Ruggles 2005).

6 CONCEPTUALIZING AND MEASURING THE NEW KNOWLEDGE ECONOMY

The new economy is based increasingly on new ICTS, new applications throughout the economy, new production processes, and new resource requirements. These do not fit well into the established ways of conceptualizing and measuring economic activity that were developed for the industrial economy, especially as knowledge, information, and communication activities have not even been recognized as significant factors in the underlying economic theory and measurement methodologies. There is no conceptual foundation for determining economic values for knowledge or the human 'assets' in which it is embodied (Miles and contributors 1990).

New theory and measurement tools need to be developed to fully understand and measure economic activity in new knowledge economies. Increasing attention is being addressed to such issues as human capital and knowledge capital as important new resources in addition to physical production and financial capital. Education, training, and R&D expenditures are beginning to be recognized as important investments. The OECD and other international agencies are examining various aspects of these issues, and academic research is increasing. However, there is a long way to go before the transformation in economic theory and measurement will provide a satisfactory understanding of the new knowledge economy and its implications.

7 CONCLUSION

This chapter has demonstrated that the most distinctive features of the new knowledge economy are the predominance of advanced telecom networks and information content produced and distributed over those networks. It is an electronic, or e-economy. But both communication networks and information content are characterized by major market imperfections, accentuated by high initial investment costs, major economies of scale and scope, extensive positive externalities, and low marginal costs. In addition, there are important extra market public interest objectives to be satisfied, including universal access to a minimal set of communication opportunities and public information. More than the industrial economy, the new knowledge economy will require the guidance of effective governance policies if the potential benefits are to be achieved. As a result government policy and regulation at national, regional, and international levels will play a very large role in shaping the growth and development of the new knowledge economy (Sheehan 1997).

This chapter has identified some distinctive characteristics and priority policy implications of the new knowledge economy, and signalled the directions in which governance policies must change if the new knowledge economy is to function more efficiently and inclusively than the old industrial economy. The analysis has demonstrated that it cannot be assumed the new economy will generate superior results to the old, or be more inclusive than the old. Although it offers great potential, it also offers possibilities for systemic market failure if it is not governed effectively.

Sustained growth in future knowledge economies will require investments in human capital as a high priority policy issue for governments—for macroeconomic management of the economy, for enhancing the microeconomic performance of specific economic sectors, for building competitive advantage in regional and global markets, and for enhancing individual income and well-being. This suggests that the new knowledge economy could provide for a considerably higher level of human development than the industrial economy, for the conversion of the majority of the labour force into information or knowledge workers, and for a significant expansion in investment in education, training, research, and development—the major formal knowledge generating and distribution activities.

It also suggests the possibility for a more widespread distribution of the wealth generated in the knowledge economy because the human resources attracting this increased investment are also workers and consumers. If successful, the so-called 'economic man' of industrial capitalism, the servant of accumulating physical capital, may be transformed into a multi-dimensional human being whose human development is served by investment in the accumulation of human capital. But as of this writing, governments have not yet begun to implement the governance structure necessary to realize the potential benefits of the new knowledge economy. That remains as a major challenge of our time.

REFERENCES

CASTELLS, M. (1996). *The Information Age: Economy, Society and Culture Volume I: The Rise of the Network Society.* Oxford: Blackwell.

—— (1997). *The Information Age: Economy, Society and Culture Volume II: The Power of Identity.* Oxford: Blackwell.

—— (1998). *The Information Age: Economy, Society and Culture Volume III: End of Millennium.* Oxford: Blackwell.

DEW-BECKER, I. and GORDON, R. J. (2005). *Where did the Productivity Growth Go?* Washington DC: Center for Economic Policy Research.

FREEMAN, C. and LOUÇÃ, F. (2001). *As Time Goes By: From the Industrial Revolutions to the Information Revolution.* Oxford: Oxford University Press.

—— and SOETE, L. (1994). *Work for All or Mass Unemployment.* London: Pinter Publishers.

HUWS, U. (2002a). 'The Restructuring of Employment in the Information Society and its Implications for Social Protection', in G. Bechmann, B.-J. Krings, and M. Rader (eds), *Work Organization and Social Exclusion in the European Information Society.* Frankfurt: Campus Frankfurt/M, 139–52.

—— (2002b) 'E-work in a Global Economy', in B. Stanford-Smith, E. Chiozza, and M. Edin (eds), *Challenges and Achievements in E-business and E-work.* Amsterdam: IOS Press, 43–69.

KAY, J. (2003). *The Truth About Markets: Why Some Nations are Rich but Most Remain Poor.* London: Penguin Books.

LESSIG, L. (2001). *The Future of Ideas: The Fate of the Commons in a Connected World.* New York: Vintage.

LYNN, B. C. (2005). *End of the Line, The Rise and Coming Fall of the Global Corporation.* New York: Doubleday.

MELODY, W. H. (1985). 'The Information Society: Implications for Economic Institutions and Market Theory'. *Journal of Economic Issues*, 19(2): 523–39.

—— (1987). 'Information: An Emerging Dimension of Institutional Analysis'. *Journal of Economic Issues*, 21(3): 1313–50.

—— (1990). 'Communication Policy in the Global Information Economy: Whither the Public Interest?', in M. Ferguson (ed.), *Public Communication: The New Imperatives. Future Directions for Media Research.* London: Sage, 16–39.

—— (1996). 'Toward a Framework for Designing Information Society Policies'. *Telecommunications Policy*, 20(4): 243–59.

—— (2003). 'Policy Implications of the New Information Economy', in M. Tool and P. Bush (eds), *Institutional Analysis and Economic Policy.* Dordrecht, NL: Kluwer, 411–32.

MILES, I. and contributors (1990). *Mapping and Measuring the Information Economy.* Boston Spa: British Library (LIR Report 77).

MOKYR, J. (2002). *The Gifts of Athena.* Princeton, NJ: Princeton University Press.

RUGGLES, M. (2005). *Automating Interaction: Formal and Informal Knowledge in the Digital Network Economy.* Cresskill, NJ: Hampton Press.

SCHUMPETER, J. A. (1950). *Capitalism, Socialism and Democracy* (3rd edn). New York: Harper.

SHEEHAN, P. (1997). 'Learning to Govern in the Knowledge Economy: Policy Coordination or Institutional Competition?', in OECD (ed.), *Industrial Competitiveness in the Knowledge-Based Economy: The New Role of Governments.* Paris: OECD, 239–47.

SHEEHAN, P. and TEGART, G. (eds) (1998). *Working for the Future: Technology and Employment in the Global Knowledge Economy.* Melbourne: Victoria University Press.

TREBING, H. M. (1997). 'Emerging Market Structures and Options for Regulatory Reform in Public Utility Industries', in W. H. Melody (ed.), *Telecom Reform: Principles, Policies and Regulatory Practices.* Lyngby: Technical University of Denmark, 29–40.

VARIAN, H. R. and SHAPIRO, C. (1999). *Information Rules: A Strategic Guide to the Network Economy.* Boston, MA: Harvard Business School Press.

WALLIS, J. J. and NORTH, D. C. (1986). *Measuring the Transaction Sector in the American Economy, 1870–1970.* Chicago, IL: University of Chicago Press.

WEBSTER, F. (1995). *Theories of the Information Society.* London: Routledge.

CHAPTER 4

GLOBALIZATION OF THE ICT LABOUR FORCE

WILLIAM LAZONICK

1 INTRODUCTION[*]

IN THE first half of the 2000s Americans became aware of the globalization of the high-tech labour force. 'Offshoring' entered the lexicon as US-based companies engaged in a large-scale movement of jobs overseas, with India and China as prime locations. Offshoring, however, is by no means a new phenomenon. For decades US information and communication technology (ICT) companies have been routinely offshoring production activities, usually through foreign direct investment (FDI). Previously offshoring had been driven largely by the search for low-wage labour to perform relatively low-skill work. New in the 2000s was the extent to which offshoring represented a search for low-wage labour to perform relatively high-skill work. In the 2000s US ICT companies have been able to access an abundance of such labour in developing countries, first and foremost in India and China.

Many of the engineering and programming jobs offshored in the 2000s are ones that observers of US high-tech industry thought could not be done abroad. The

* I gratefully acknowledge research funding provided by the Upjohn Institute for Employment Research and the European Commission, and research assistance provided by Bob Bell, Isa Cann, Ben Hopkins, Sarah Johnson, and Yue Zhang. Susan Houseman and Robin Mansell provided helpful comments on an earlier draft.

development of sophisticated products and processes generally requires interactive learning that is both collective and cumulative. Workers engaged in interactive learning have to be in close communication with one another. With the US at the centre of the ICT revolution, the assumption has been that these jobs could not be relocated to a low-wage developing economy. Indeed, precisely because the US dominates ICT, it is the place to which people come from around the world for ICT-related higher education and work experience. Why would many of the best ICT jobs be migrating to India and China if Indians and Chinese are migrating to the US for ICT education and experience?

This chapter seeks to answer this question by showing how, over the past four decades or so, the development strategies of the East-Asian nations interacted with the investment strategies of US-based ICT companies to generate a global supply of ICT labour.[1] This process of developing a global ICT labour supply has entailed flows of US capital to East-Asian labour as well as flows of East-Asian labour to US capital. As a result new possibilities to pursue high-tech careers, and thereby develop their productive capabilities, have opened up to vast numbers of individuals in East-Asian nations. Many found the relevant educational programmes and work experience in their home countries. But many gained access to education and experience by following global career paths that included study and work in the US. For the East-Asian nations, the existence of these global career paths has posed a danger of 'brain drain': the global career path could come to an end in the US (or another advanced economy) rather than in the country where the individual had been born and bred. At the same time, education and experience in the US created valuable 'human capital' that could potentially be lured back home. A major challenge for the East-Asian nations has been the creation of domestic employment opportunities, through either FDI or investment by national governments and indigenous businesses, to enable career paths to be followed back home, thus transforming a potential brain drain into an actual 'brain gain'.

In Section 2, I trace the origins and evolution of the offshoring movement as it occurred in the semiconductor industry from the 1960s to the 1980s. In Section 3, I show that national investments in educating the future labour force provided the foundations for the development of indigenous ICT capabilities. Section 4 examines the extent of the potential brain drain faced by nations such as South Korea and Taiwan by the 1960s by documenting the flow of East-Asians to the US for higher education and work experience over the last four decades. In Section 5, I analyse how the East-Asian nations sought to reverse the brain drain. In the conclusion to this chapter I consider some of the implications of this analysis of the globalization of the ICT labour supply for national development trajectories, and I raise the question of the impact of offshoring on ICT employment opportunities in the US.

2 ORIGINS AND EVOLUTION
OF ICT OFFSHORING

Subsequent to the invention of the transistor at Bell Labs in 1947, with the support of Cold War military spending, an array of US companies including Western Electric, Raytheon, GE, RCA, Westinghouse, IBM, Texas Instruments, Motorola, and, from 1957 a new firm, Fairchild Semiconductor, made the US the centre of the global semiconductor industry (Tilton 1971). From the late 1950s, however, US companies began to feel competitive pressure in the production of transistors from the Japanese, who had successfully transferred the technology from the US (Flamm 1985: 70). By the early 1960s US semiconductor manufacturers began to consider the option of doing labour-intensive assembly work in low-wage offshore locations.

In 1971 a UN research report stated: 'Every established United States semiconductor firm appears to be engaged in some offshore assembly without exception' (Chang 1971: 17). The report listed 33 offshore facilities established during 1963–1971 by 22 different US semiconductor companies, of which eight, with 16 offshore plants among them, were based in Silicon Valley (Chang 1971: 19–20). From 1972 Malaysia became a favoured location for semiconductor assembly, with Hewlett-Packard and Intel being among the first to open plants in the new Free Trade Zone (FTZ) in Penang. In 1974, Malaysia hosted 11 US-owned semiconductor facilities, Korea nine, Hong Kong eight, Taiwan three, and the rest of Asia six, while there were 15 US facilities in the Latin-American countries, primarily Mexico (Davis and Hatano 1985: 129).

By 1970 almost all of the assembly work that still remained in the US was automated. But rapid changes in technology that rendered automated processes obsolete, combined with the availability of hard working, low-wage labour in a number of developing countries, favoured the use of labour-intensive methods. By the first half of the 1980s US-based merchant producers did 80 per cent of their semiconductor assembly offshore. Much of the assembly operations that remained in the US were for military purposes (Davis and Hatano 1985: 129).

Sections 806.30 and 807 of the US Tariff Schedule permitted goods that had been exported from the US for foreign assembly to be imported with duty charged only on the value-added abroad (Flamm 1985). As late as 1974 Mexico was the most important single national location for '806/807' semiconductor exports, but from 1975 its share eroded sharply (Flamm 1985: 76). In 1970, the average hourly wage in semiconductor assembly in Singapore, Hong Kong, and Korea was less than one-tenth that in the US, and about half that in Mexico (Chang 1971: 27; Sharpston 1975: 105). The relatively high value and low weight of semiconductor products meant that the proximity of Mexico to the US did not offer an appreciable transportation advantage over an Asian location (Davis and Hatano 1985: 129). Within Asia during the 1970s and early 1980s there was a marked shift of '806/807' activity from Hong Kong to Malaysia and the Philippines, while Korea and Singapore sustained substantial market shares.

In 1985 there were 63 US semiconductor plants in East Asia, employing just under 100,000 people (Scott 1987: 145–7). Although the impetus to offshore was the search for low-wage labour, the lowest-wage Asian locations such as Indonesia and Thailand did not dominate. Other considerations, most notably political stability and the productivity of labour, entered into plant location. In the 1960s and 1970s Korea and other prominent East-Asian nations had much to offer multinational companies (MNCs) in addition to low-wage, hard-working female labour for assembly operations. Of great significance for the persistence of these offshored investments even as wage levels rose was the fact that when in the 1960s and 1970s foreign semiconductor companies employed relatively low-wage (female) labour to perform low-skill production jobs, they could find relatively low-wage (male) labour to perform *high-skill* engineering and managerial jobs. The availability of an indigenous supply of high-skill labour was critical for upgrading productive capabilities so that the ICT industries of these nations, and the offshored facilities, could remain competitive as these East-Asian economies transformed themselves from relatively low-wage to relatively high-wage.

The fact that qualified indigenous engineers were available to the US semiconductor companies when they offshored their assembly operations in the 1960s and 1970s is of great importance for understanding what in the early 1990s the World Bank (1993) would call the 'East Asian miracle'. The type of economic transformations that occurred in East Asia depended on the availability of both a highly educated high-tech labour force and employment opportunities that would enable the members of this labour force to contribute to the growth process. The transformations in productive capabilities that occurred in Korea, Taiwan, Hong Kong, Singapore, and Malaysia from the 1970s and in the world's two most populous nations, India and China, since the 1980s were the results of the interaction of the investment strategies of developmental states, innovative enterprises, and educated individuals in the pursuit of high-tech careers.

3 EDUCATION AND GROWTH
IN THE ASIAN NICs

Between 1970 and 2000, real GDP per capita increased by 7.5 times in Korea, 5.4 times in Taiwan, 4.7 in Singapore, and 3.7 in Hong Kong (Maddison 2004). The increases in wages that these higher levels of GDP per capita both permitted and reflected did not undermine the competitive advantage of the 'Tiger economies' (as they became known) in ICT. On the contrary, by further mobilizing the skills and efforts of the indigenous labour force as well as increasing the extent of domestic product markets that enjoyed a degree of protection, rising wages were integral to the dynamics of the growth process of these East-Asian nations.

These cases of rapid growth entailed active and purposeful government initiatives to build communications and educational infrastructures, develop domestic high-tech knowledge bases, and provide subsidies to business enterprises, both foreign and domestically owned, to make use of these infrastructures and knowledge bases to generate products that could ultimately be competitive at home and abroad.[2] These government and business investments in high-tech capabilities created large numbers of indigenous high-tech employment opportunities. In so far as these investments generated higher productivity than previously (which was by no means inevitably the case), they could contribute to the economic growth of the nation. In general, a portion of these productivity gains accrue as higher returns to labour, thus eliminating to some extent the low-wage advantage that the nation may have had. Given the presence of other lower wage nations that are in the process of developing their productive capabilities, economic growth that results in higher wages creates an imperative to upgrade employment opportunities by moving into higher value-added activities. Under these circumstances, the emergence of ever more remunerative high-tech employment opportunities may be both the cause and effect of sustained economic growth.

The most fundamental, and costly, expenditure for a developmental state is on a primary, secondary, and tertiary education system. In the case of Japan, investments in education that began in the late nineteenth century laid the foundations for the nation's economic transformation from the 1950s (Koike and Inoki 1990: 227–8). Investments in education meant that in 1960 only 2.4 per cent of Japan's population, aged 15 and over, had no schooling while on average this population had 7.78 years of schooling (the US figures were 2.0 per cent and 8.49 years). By contrast, in 1960 the no-schooling proportions were Korea, 42.8 per cent; Taiwan, 37.3 per cent; Singapore, 46.2 per cent; and Hong Kong 29.7 per cent; while the average years of schooling of these populations were Korea, 4.25; Taiwan, 3.87; Singapore, 4.30, and Hong Kong, 5.17 (Barro and Lee 2000). A major challenge that faced the would-be Tigers, and other East-Asian nations such as Malaysia, Indonesia, the Philippines, and Thailand, was to transform their national educational systems into foundations for industrial development.

Korea dramatically transformed its education system after 1960. The average years of schooling of Korea's 15-plus population rose from 7.91 years in 1980 to 10.84 in 2000, surpassing Japan's 2000 figure of 9.47 and not far behind the US figure of 12.05 (Barro and Lee 2000). By the last half of the 1990s Korea had the highest number of Ph.D. graduates per capita of any country in the world (Kim and Leslie 1998: 154).

India, a nation of 680 million people aged 15 or over in 2000 compared with Korea's 37 million, has not experienced such a dramatic transformation of its mass education system. In 1960, the Indian 15-plus population included 72.2 per cent with no schooling, and had on average 1.68 years of schooling. By 2000 India's no-schooling figure remained high at 43.9 per cent, while the average years figure was only 5.06. India, with one-sixth of the world's population, has one-third of the world's illiterates.

Yet, at the same time, India has become a leading source of supply of engineers and programmers to the global ICT labour force. The stage was set by government investments made in the 1950s and 1960s, of which the decision to create a number of Institutes of Technology (originally four), modelled on the Massachusetts Institute of Technology, stand out (Sebaly 1972; Bassett 2005). The first Indian Institute of Technology (IIT) was founded at Kharagpur, West Bengal in 1952 (Shenkman 1954: 28; Bassett 2005). A 1959 Act of Parliament established IIT Kanpur, which became the leading technological institute in India. From 1962 to 1972 IIT Kanpur received assistance from the Kanpur Indo-American Programme (KIAP), through which a consortium of nine US universities assisted in setting up research laboratories and academic curricula.

IIT Kanpur was the first IIT to have a computer, receiving an IBM 1620 from the US in 1963 (Bassett 2005). Subsequently, according to Ross Bassett (2005), 'Kanpur's masters and doctoral programs in electrical engineering were widely acknowledged to be the best graduate programmes in computing in India and became the place to go for Indians who wanted to stay in India for their graduate education' (Bassett 2005: 13). At the same time, he argues:

The development of IIT Kanpur and the computer centre marked the beginning of a regular flow of computer talent from India into the American academic and industrial systems. Indian engineering students had come to the US long before the establishment of IIT Kanpur, but Kanpur routinized and regularized that process. (Bassett 2005: 16)

It was estimated that in the late 1960s India was second only to the US in the number of students in universities, even though on a per capita basis the number of university students in India was extremely low (Ilchman 1969: 783). Indeed, for 1975–1990, India's 1,907,944 bachelor's degrees in natural sciences represented over 97 per cent of the US total, and, by the late 1980s, India was granting more such degrees than the US. India's output of undergraduate engineers was less prodigious, but significant nonetheless, rising from 35 per cent to 45 per cent of the US engineering graduates from 1975 to 1990. China, by contrast, focused much more on producing engineers than natural scientists. The total Chinese output of undergraduate engineers for 1982–1990 (the period for which Chinese data are available) exceeded the totals for 1975–90 of Japan by 29 per cent, of the US by

35 per cent, and of the combination of Taiwan-Korea-India by 72 per cent. From 1975 to 1990, Korea's output of engineers with bachelor's degrees quadrupled while Taiwan and India both doubled their annual outputs (NSF 1993, Appendix, Table A-3). Between 1990 and 2000 India increased its total enrolments in engineering from 258,284 to 576,649,[3] while China increased its undergraduate engineering degrees awarded from 114,620 to 207,459, and Korea from 28,071 to 56,508 (NSB 2004, Appendix Table 2–34).

For the latest years available, natural science doctorates and engineering (plus maths/computer science) doctorates awarded per 100,000 population were, respectively, 0.65 and 2.82 in Taiwan (2001); 1.30 and 4.02 in Korea (2000); 0.24 and 0.02 in India (1998); 0.21 and 0.34 in China (2001); 1.25 and 3.12 in Japan (2001); and 3.44 and 2.20 in the US (2001) (NSB 2004, Appendix Tables 2–38 and 2–39). The US figures, however, include large proportions of people, especially from Asia, who were not US citizens or permanent residents. While the US was not the only destination for the pursuit of a graduate degree, it was by far the most favoured nation (see NSB 2004 Appendix Tables 2–14, 2–40, 2–41, 2–42, and 2–43). In 1998–2001, of all non-US citizens who received US engineering doctorates, 55 per cent had 'firm plans to stay' in the US after graduation, while the proportions for Chinese and Indians specifically were 67 per cent and 77 per cent respectively (NSB 2004, Appendix Table 2–31). The greater ease with which graduates on temporary visas were able to secure 'green cards' from the late 1990s may also have been a factor in keeping these numbers high (see Vaughan 2003).

4 Brain drain?

For an investment in high-tech education to contribute to the growth of a developing nation requires employment opportunities in the domestic economy that can make productive use of the labour that has been educated. Employment experience in turn augments the productive capabilities of the labour force, especially in industries that make use of sophisticated technologies. The problem of high-tech brain drain occurs when a developing nation invests in the education of scientists and engineers (S&E) but the most attractive employment opportunities for these university graduates are abroad rather than at home. The S&E brain drain was a major problem in the 1960s and 1970s for the developing Asian economies (see, for example, Adams 1968). In the late 1960s, Asia surpassed Europe as the main source of S&E coming to the US from abroad (Schmeck 1973). The US stood accused of taking the best that the newly industrializing countries (NICs) had to offer, thus building US high-tech capabilities at the expense of economies that could ill afford it.

Encouraging the brain drain was the US Immigration and Naturalization Law of 1965, which abolished the national quota system in favour of preference to people whose skills could be 'especially advantageous' to the US (Fortney 1970, 217). Of 7,913 scientists, engineers, and physicians who immigrated to the US from developing countries in 1967, 48 per cent were students who were already in the US. For Taiwan this proportion was 89 per cent, for Korea 80 per cent, and for India 78 per cent (Fortney 1970: 220).

By one account over 30,000 college graduates went abroad from Taiwan between 1956 and 1972, with only 2,586 returning (Ho 1975: 40). Nearly 60 per cent of those who left had a science or engineering education, and they tended to be the best students, exacerbating the loss to Taiwan. In the 1950s and 1960s Korea also had a serious brain drain; 10,412 students, of whom 5,376 were in science and engineering, requested permission from the Korean Ministry of Education to study in the US in 1953–72, with over 90 per cent not returning after graduation (Yoon 1992: 6). One study estimated that, given the cost of educating S&E and their lost value-added, India transferred $51 billion to the US between 1967 and 1985. Between 1974 and 1988 the number of immigrant S&E as a proportion of all S&E increased from 5.8 per cent to 10.5 per cent, with the five leading sources being India, UK, Taiwan, Poland, and China (see Arnst 1991).

The Immigration Act of 1990 increased the annual maximum number of employment-based visas from 54,000 to 140,000. From 1996 through 2004, 454,000 Indians received green cards, with 190,000 of these admissions being 'employment-based preferences' (EBP). Indians received 11 per cent of the EBP visas in 1996–2000, but 24 per cent in 2001–04. China was next with 13 per cent in 1996–2000, and 11 per cent in 2001–04 (US INS 1997–2001; US DHS 2002–04b).

Also of great importance in enabling educated Asians to engage in high-tech employment in the US have been H-1B and L-1 non-immigrant visas. Created in 1970, the L-1 visa category enables an MNC to bring foreign employees from abroad to work in the US for as many as seven years. There is no limit to the number of L-1 visas that can be issued. Such was also the case with H-1B visas prior to the Immigration Act of 1990, when an annual cap was set at 65,000 initial visas. The cap was raised to 115,000 in FY1999–2000, and 195,000 in FY2001–03. As of 1 October 2003 the 65,000 cap was restored, but with an extra 20,000 visas available to employees of institutions of higher education and nonprofit or government research organizations.

Annually, Indians have been the top H-1B visa recipients since 1993, and the top L-1 visa recipients since 2000. In 2000–03, Indians received 57 per cent of the 547,000 initial H-1B visas and 48 per cent of the 457,000 continuing visas issued (US DHS 2002–04a). Chinese were a distant second with shares of 10 per cent and 8 per cent respectively. The proportion of L-1 visas that went to Indians climbed dramatically from 5 per cent in 1997 to 38 per cent in 2004 (US Department of State 1997–2005). Indians, therefore, have become the leading source of both immigrant and non-immigrant entrants to the US in search of work and education.

H-1B visas are predominantly high-tech visas. In FY 2003, 50 per cent of visa recipients had bachelor's degrees, 31 per cent master's degrees, 12 per cent doctorates, and 6 per cent professional degrees. At 39 per cent of the total, the largest occupational category among visa holders was 'computer-related' (US DHS 2004a). Under the Immigration Act of 1990 an H-1B visa is issued for an initial period of three years, with the possibility of an extension for another three years, and eligibility for yet another six years after a one-year absence from the US. H-1B visa holders can apply for permanent resident status, and often have employer sponsorship, with one-year extensions while waiting for their green card to be issued. In 2001 more than 228,000 NIV holders became permanent residents (Vaughan 2003).

5 REVERSING THE BRAIN DRAIN

Korea

Over the last four decades of the twentieth century, therefore, the career paths of vast numbers of well-educated people from around the world took them to the US for specialized education and specialty occupations. The challenge that faced the developing nations experiencing this potential brain drain was to create employment opportunities that could bring these people, with their enhanced capabilities, back home. In its 1993 report on the development of Asia's human resources in science and technology (S&T), the National Science Foundation (NSF) (1993: 1) stated: 'Asian countries with high technology economies will compete with the US for the Asian-born graduates of US universities. Though Asian scientists and engineers will continue to contribute to the US labor force, more will probably return to Asia.' Korea in particular was very aggressive from the late 1960s in the implementation of various policies designed to reverse the brain drain. In his study of the process, undertaken in the early 1990s, Yoon (1992: 5) argued that '[t]he Korean model of RBD is without precedent in the world and has been highly successful... Brain drain is no longer considered a social problem by [Korean] policy-makers'.

How was such a reversal achieved? By the 1990s the successful development of Korea and Taiwan in the ICT industries had created employment opportunities that entailed sufficiently high salaries and sufficiently challenging jobs to lure back large numbers of nationals—in the well-documented case of Taiwan an annual average of over 6,000 from 1993 to 1996 (Saxenian and Hsu 2001: 905–6)—who had acquired high-tech education and experience abroad. As a dynamic historical process, the reversal of the brain drain was an effect as well as a cause of successful industrial development. It could not have occurred but for the investment strategies of developmental states and innovative enterprises, which from the 1960s and 1970s had upgraded the quality of higher education and employment opportunity available to indigenous high-tech labour.

From the outset, as we have seen, MNCs that had come to Korea and Taiwan in search of low-wage labour for labour-intensive assembly operations in the 1960s and 1970s created a demand for university-educated labour, and over time, as these companies invested in higher value-added activities the high-end employment opportunities increased. Encouraged by this internal transfer of technology to build an indigenous knowledge base, national governments made investments in research institutes and graduate programmes that generated attractive high-tech employment opportunities. This indigenized knowledge in turn supported the emergence of indigenous Korean and Taiwanese companies as world-class competitors. Indeed, in many cases highly educated and very experienced Koreans or Taiwanese who had been pursuing successful careers in the US played key roles in building indigenous research institutes and companies.

Let us look at how indigenization reversed the brain drain in the case of Korea.[4] Among the pioneering US MNCs in Korea, Motorola made the most significant contribution to reversing the brain drain. Motorola trained a group of 50 Korean engineers to start-up Motorola Korea (MK), which at the outset employed 300 people in total. By 1972 MK was Korea's largest electronics company, both in terms of sales and exports (Bloom 1992: 38). Two years later MK had 5,000 employees, including two-thirds of the original 50 Korean engineers (Behrman and Wallender 1976: 267, 299). Automation in the 1980s reduced MK's headcount to 3,800 in 1988, with about 2,100 employees in its semiconductor operations. In December 1988, in the midst of labour demands for better pay and work conditions that marked Korea's transition from its 'newly industrializing' stage, MK closed its plant after a group of workers, carrying cans of gasoline, had occupied a computer room, and threatened to set themselves on fire.[5] A non-union company around the world, Motorola had agreed to recognize the union, but had balked at some of the union demands. The plant was reopened within a week.[6]

In May 1989, a *Business Week* article asked, 'Is the era of cheap Asian labour over?', and answered that 'rising wages and union strife are sending some companies packing' (Yang and Nakarmi 1989: 45). Among the US chip companies, National Semiconductor, in the midst of rationalizing its global capacity, closed down its Korean facility, laying off 250 employees.[7] Motorola, however, never considered leaving Korea, in part because it was building a major presence there in wireless communications. At the end of 1993, MK employed 2,500 people, and had shipped $3.2 billion in electronics products since it had opened in 1967.[8]

In 2004, Motorola spun off its entire semiconductor product division as Free-scale Semiconductor. As an independent company, Freescale had plants in Hong Kong and Malaysia, but no Korean operation. In May 2005, however, Freescale announced that, attracted by Korea's expertise in mobile technology, it would open a research and development (R&D) centre in Seoul, with six engineers. Freescale was not the only US semiconductor company navigating back to Korea in search of high-skill labour for high-end work. National Semiconductor, absent from Korea since 1989 when it closed its assembly facility in the midst of labour unrest, came back to Korea in 2005 to launch both a design centre and an R&D centre (Wohn 2005).

In the 2000s, there is no question that Korea has the research capability to serve the high end of the high-tech market. The brain drain has not only been reversed; with MNCs now locating in Korea to access highly skilled ICT labour, it can no longer be taken for granted that the centre of the world of high-end work is the US or even Japan. Beginning in the mid-1960s, as we have seen, MNCs in search of low-wage labour played a critical role in beginning the reversal process by offering Korean engineers and managers opportunities to accumulate ICT experience while staying at home. In the process, they transferred considerable technology to, and developed considerable capability in, Korea. The investments that permitted the economic transformation of Korea did not come, however, from MNCs alone. Building on the capabilities that FDI brought to Korea, as well as on the capabilities of Koreans who had been studying and working abroad, the Korean government and indigenous businesses made the investments in ICT that made Korea a leading 'career path' location.

Of particular importance, more in terms of quality than quantity, was the repatriation of Korean scientists and engineers who had worked abroad. In 1968 some 2,000 Korean scientists and engineers lived outside the US (Kim and Leslie 1998: 168). Their very existence presented an opportunity for Korea to build indigenous high-tech capabilities if only the brain drain could be reversed. From the last half of the 1960s, the Korean government saw the creation of an industrial research complex as a way to bring back some of those expatriate Koreans to contribute to the development of Korea's knowledge base (Bloom 1992: 54; Yoon 1992). Specifically, the desire of Korea's policy makers to transform the nation's brain drain into its brain gain served as both opportunity and impetus in the establishment of two seminal knowledge-creating institutions, the Korea Institute of Science and Technology (KIST) and the Korea Advanced Institute of Science and Technology (KAIST).

KIST came into being in 1966 after USAID funded a team of US scientists to visit Korea in May 1965 to offer advice on the formation of a national institute for scientific research. The US government provided substantial initial funding, including a $3.1 million contract to Battelle Memorial Institute to provide technical advice. In 1967, the government ensured KIST's autonomy in research and management and its financial stability through special legislation, The Assistance Act of the Korea Institute of Science and Technology (Yoon 1992: 16–17). The same year saw the creation of the Ministry of Science and Technology (MOST) (Bloom 1992: 54).

In conducting a search for its first scientists and engineers, KIST's ideal profile was an undergraduate degree from Seoul National University, plus a graduate degree and five years of work experience abroad. In its first year, 1969, KIST had 494 employees, of whom 18 were repatriated scientists and engineers (14 with doctorates) (Yoon 1992: 13–14). To attract key personnel from abroad, KIST paid high salaries and offered such perquisites as relocation expenses, free housing, and education expenses for children. Such compensation packages subsequently became the norm in government repatriation initiatives (Yoon 1992: 14–16). By 1975, out of a total of 984 employees, KIST had 137 repatriates, 69 of whom were permanent and 69 temporary (Yoon 1992: 13).

During the 1970s there was a proliferation of government research institutes in Korea, some of them spin-offs of specialist departments of KIST (Lee, Bae and Lee 1991). The Korea Institute of Electronics Technology (KIET) emerged in 1976 to conduct research into semiconductor design, processes, and systems. At the head of each of KIET's three research divisions was a Korean with research experience in the US semiconductor industry (Bloom 1992: 56; Mathews and Cho 2000: 118). In a joint venture with the Silicon Valley chipmaker, VLSI (very large-scale integration) Technology, KIET put in place Korea's first VLSI pilot wafer-fabrication plant in 1978, and by 1979 had launched a fully operational 16K DRAM fab (Mathews and Cho 2000: 118).

Overall from 1968 through 1980 MOST-sponsored repatriation programmes yielded public R&D institutes 130 overseas Koreans on a permanent basis and 182 on a temporary basis (Yoon 1992: 10). The repatriates brought knowledge, experience, connections, and leadership to Korea. Given the rapid growth in demand for scientists, engineers, and technicians in Korea from the late 1970s however, the vast majority of those employed by the public research institutes had to be homegrown. The number of researchers in Korea grew from 14,749 in 1978 (0.40 researchers per 1,000 population), to 18,434 in 1980 (0.48) and 28,448 in 1982 (0.72), with the government share in R&D expenditures constituting 49 per cent of the total in 1978, rising to 52 per cent in 1980, and then falling to 41 per cent in 1982 as business enterprises began to invest heavily in their own R&D (Arnold 1988: 439).

Government investments in indigenous R&D capability demanded complementary investments in indigenous academic institutions to generate a homegrown supply of high-tech labour. Analogous to KIST, the keystone educational investment was the founding in February 1971 of the Korea Advanced Institute of Science (KAIS), the nation's first specialized graduate school of sciences and engineering. KAIS admitted its first master's students in 1973, its first doctoral students in 1975, and its first undergraduate students in 1986. Along the way, KAIS became KAIST when, at the end of 1980, KIST and KAIS were merged. The name of the academic institution remained KAIST when the two organizations demerged in 1989 and KAIST moved its campus 100 miles south of Seoul to become the centrepiece of Taedok Science Town (Kim and Leslie 1998: 178–80). As with KIST, USAID provided financial assistance and advice, and the first faculty hires were Koreans repatriated from the US.

The government provided all KAIST students with tuition, room and board, a stipend, and a conversion of the normal compulsory three years of military service into three years of work in a government research facility subsequent to receiving their master's degrees (Kim and Leslie 1998: 169). From its inception through 1996, KAIST awarded a total of 3,108 bachelor's degrees, 9,566 master's degrees, and 2,647 doctoral degrees. Of the master's recipients 43 per cent went to industry, 17 per cent to government research institutes, and as many as 34 per cent to advanced training. Of the doctoral recipients, 45 per cent went to industry, 27 per cent to government research institutes, and 26 per cent to academic positions (Kim and Leslie 1998: 174).

By the 1990s there were plenty of good employment opportunities for these graduates in Korean industry with not only MNCs such as Motorola Korea or government research institutes such as KIST, but also, and indeed, primarily, Korean chaebol such as Samsung, Hyundai, and LG (Lucky-Goldstar), which through indigenous innovation had transformed knowledge transferred from abroad into world-leading products in a number of high-technology sectors. In no Korean industry was this transformation so dramatic as in semiconductors. In 1980 semiconductors represented 2.5 per cent of Korea's production and 2.5 per cent of exports; in 1990 7.3 per cent of production and 7.0 per cent of exports (Byun 1994: 709).

In semiconductors, no Korean company was as successful as Samsung. With $16.1 billion in revenues, in 2004 Samsung was the world's number 2 supplier of semiconductors, behind Intel with revenues of $30.4 billion, and one rank ahead of Texas Instruments with revenues of $10.9 billion. In the DRAM business, which in the face of Japanese competition Intel had abandoned in the mid-1980s, Samsung was the leader, its $8.3 billion in revenues almost double that of Micron Technology in second position. Samsung was also the leader in the flash memory business, with revenues of $4.5 billion compared with $2.3 billion each for AMD and Intel (Samsung 2005).

Samsung entered the semiconductor industry in 1975 when it bought Korea Semiconductor Company (KSC), a just-launched semiconductor firm that had run into financial trouble. The founder of KSC, Ki-Dong Kang, a Korean-American Ph.D. who had worked in semiconductor design at Motorola, now provided Samsung with his knowledge. Samsung also took over the assets of an abortive transistor joint venture between Goldstar and National Semiconductor (Mathews and Cho 2000: 116). Thus, in 1975 it acquired the capability to fabricate wafers and produce LSI chips for consumer electronics products just as the Korean government promulgated a six-year plan to promote the semiconductor industry (Kim 1997a: 88).

In 1982, Samsung started its Semiconductor R&D Laboratory to reverse engineer semiconductors from Japan and the US. At the same time Samsung organized a task force to formulate a strategy for entering into the production of VLSI chips. After six months of information gathering and analysis, the team spent a month on a fact-finding trip to the US where it especially sought advice from Korean-Americans with semiconductor expertise. The major semiconductor companies in the US had already rebuffed Samsung's requests to license 64K DRAM technology, so the task force identified smaller companies, strapped for cash, that would make the technology available. One such company was Micron Technology, founded by former Texas Instruments engineers in 1978, which in 1982 had just generated its first revenues from its new fabrication facility in Idaho (Spaeth 1984). As part of the deal, Samsung sent its engineers to Micron for training. Subsequently, in 1985 Samsung was also able to buy an advanced high-speed MOS process for $2.1 million from Zytrex, a 1983 Silicon Valley start-up that had just gone bankrupt (Chira 1985; Pollack 1985).

In 1983, Samsung announced a massive investment to design and produce 64K VLSI chips. As the biggest chaebol in Korea, Samsung was able to fund the investments in semiconductors from earnings from other divisions. It was also able to avail itself of government subsidies. When Samsung released its 64K DRAM in 1984, it lagged behind the US chipmakers by 40 months and the Japanese by 18 months. Samsung repeated this product development process for its 256K chip released in 1985, and further reduced the technology gap with the US and Japan—as indeed it continued to do with the 1M DRAM in 1987, the 4M in 1989, and the 16M in 1992, at which point it had caught up (Byun 1994: 713).

Linsu Kim (1997a: 95) has charted the transformation in R&D at Samsung Electronics that was integral to this process of indigenous innovation. Between 1980 and 1994 the company's sales soared from 2.5 billion Won to 115.2 billion Won. In the process Samsung Electronics increased its R&D as a proportion of sales from 2.1 per cent in 1980, to 3.0 per cent in 1985, 4.2 per cent in 1990, and 6.2 per cent in 1994. In 1980 the company employed 690 R&D staff, who in that year produced only 18 local patent applications and 4 local patent awards, and no foreign patent applications or awards. In 1994 8,919 R&D staff could claim credit for 2,082 local applications and 1,413 local awards, along with 1,478 foreign applications and 752 foreign awards. The generation of one local patent award for Samsung Electronics required 116.8 R&D staff in 1985, 10.4 in 1990, and 6.3 in 1994, while the generation of one foreign patent award required 992.5 R&D staff in 1985, 52.2 in 1990, and 11.9 in 1994.

As a result of the employment opportunities that Samsung as well as other leading chaebol such as Hyundai and Lucky-Goldstar had created, by the early 1990s the brain drain had been reversed. Of 13,878 foreign S&E doctorate recipients with temporary visas from US universities in 1990–91, almost 56 per cent were from China (2,779), Korea (1,912), Taiwan (1,824), or India (1,235). In 1995, 47 per cent of the 1990–91 recipients were working in the US, including 88 per cent of the Chinese, 79 per cent of the Indians, 42 per cent of the Taiwanese, but only 11 per cent of the Koreans—a proportion that was even lower than the 13 per cent of the 227 Japanese doctoral recipients (Johnson and Regets 1998).

Malaysia

The case of Korea strongly suggests that, in ICT, the transition from FDI to investment by indigenous companies can result in step increases in the development of innovative capability and its translation into rapid economic growth. Not all of the East-Asian nations that have built up significant ICT capabilities since the 1960s, however, have been able to make this transition to 'indigenous innovation'. Malaysia in particular has, since the 1970s, become a world centre for electronics manufacturing based on FDI by MNCs from the more economically advanced nations. During 2003–2005, the Malaysian economy grew at about 6 per cent per annum, with electronics still dominating its manufacturing base and exports.[9] The fact that Malaysia has grown on the basis of FDI over these decades raises the question of the types of investments in productive capabilities that MNCs have been making there.

In offshoring, the rule among US MNCs was to employ nationals rather than expatriates in the host countries. As an important example, in 1984 Intel employed about 26,000 people worldwide. In reporting its international locations in 1984, Intel stated that: '[a] hallmark of Intel's international expansion has been its sparing use of US expatriates, reflecting a practical view that the innate understanding of language and custom possessed by each country's nationals provides the best opportunity for Intel's success. As of this writing, fewer than 60 US citizens are employed in Intel's non-domestic workforce of more than 8,500 employees' (Intel 1984: 40–1).

The overwhelming reliance of MNCs on indigenous labour at all levels of the local organization, even in NICs, is confirmed by data from the early 1980s on employment in the Bayan Lepas Free Trade Zone (BLFTZ) in Penang, the location of Intel's Malaysian assembly plant. In 1982, 27 electronics/electrical factories employed a total of 24,446 people, of whom 5,389 (22 per cent) were male and 6,625 (27 per cent) were non-factory workers. Only 34 of these employees 0.14 per cent of the total, 0.63 per cent of males, and 0.51 per cent of non-factory workers were expatriates. For BLFTZ as a whole there were 226 expatriates out of 52,073 employees, representing 0.43 per cent of the total, 1.16 per cent of males, and 1.55 per cent of non-factory workers (Salih and Young 1987: 184). Given the small absolute number of expatriates—just 1.26 per electronics/electrical factory in 1982, the indigenization of the labour force at the MNCs obviously extended high up the organizational hierarchy. From a survey done in the mid-1990s, Ismail

(1999: 27–8) found that National Semiconductor's only expatriate in Penang was the managing director. Texas Instruments, with 2,800 employees in Malaysia, and Motorola, with 4,000 employees, each had only three expatriate managers (Ismail 1999: 28).

Intel's history in Malaysia from the early 1970s to the present illustrates the upgrading of indigenous capabilities by a US MNC in the semiconductor industry. Intel was one of the first semiconductor manufacturers to offshore to BLFTZ when it was launched in 1972, and as a company itself only founded in 1968, the Penang facility was Intel's first offshore plant. In 1974, Intel employed about 1,000 people in Penang,[10] and about 2,000 a decade later. Over the next ten years Intel's Penang production tripled, but its labour force remained around 2,000 because of automation of labour-intensive assembly processes. In 1994, engineers represented one in six of Intel employees in Penang, whereas in 1980 this ratio had been one in forty (Zachary 1994; Ismail 1999: 27). Over time Malaysia became Intel's main source of expertise on assembly operations. It was reported, for example, that in the mid-1980s, when Intel was setting up its assembly line in its automated chip factory in Chandler, Arizona, it had to bring in its Malaysian experts from Penang (Dreyfack and Port 1986). In 1990, when Intel established a design optimization lab at the Penang facility, it sent ten engineers to Silicon Valley for training. At that time, Intel announced that it would continue to invest in automation in Penang with the goal of attaining zero-defect production. It also declared its intention of making Penang its offshore manufacturing headquarters over the next ten years (Dennis 1990).

In July 1992, Intel decided to shift its entire microcontroller design, manufacturing, and marketing operations out of the Chandler facility to its Penang plant, a move that Lai Pin Yong, Intel Malaysia's managing director, called a milestone for the local electronics industry. 'This is the first time in Malaysia', Yong said, 'that a multinational is giving its offshore plant total responsibility of an important product.' As a result, Intel Malaysia expected to add another 50 engineers to the 300 that it already employed.[11] Plans for the Design Centre had been laid a few years earlier; in preparation a team of 30 Malaysians had received training in the US and Japan for two to three years. When the Intel Penang Design Centre opened in November 1992, it was said to be the first of its kind in South-East Asia (Leow 1992; see also Ismail 1999: 32–3).

In 2003, Intel claimed to have invested US$2.3 billion in Malaysia since 1972. At that time, Intel Malaysia employed about 1,000 Malaysians in R&D, and had secured 21 US patents. The latest addition to Intel Malaysia's R&D capabilities was a design and development centre with a focus on manufacturing processes and packaging technology for Intel's various products. In December 2005, with almost 10,000 employees, about 10 per cent of its global labour force, at five sites in Malaysia, including the original Penang location, Intel announced plans to invest $230 million in a 2,000-person assembly and test site, along with a design and development centre, in Kulim. On the occasion of this investment, Craig Barrett, Intel's chairman, stated: 'Intel is working with the Education Ministry to help grow Malaysia's globally competitive ICT workforce' (Ismail 2005: 4).

India

As in Malaysia, but beginning in the mid-1980s, US MNCs have also played an important role in creating employment opportunities for indigenous high-tech labour in India and China. In this section I focus on the case of Texas Instruments (TI), the first MNC to set up a software centre in Bangalore, India. In the wake of a Memorandum of Agreement (MoU) on high-technology transfers from the US to India, signed after years of negotiation by the two countries in May 1985 (Weisman 1985), the Indian Department of Electronics announced its intention to build 'technology parks' that would permit foreign companies to be wholly owned for the purpose of developing and exporting large-scale software systems (Tenorio 1985). In June 1985, TI began exploratory talks with the Indian government about establishing a software development centre in Bangalore. For TI, two key conditions were that it would have 100 per cent ownership of the facility and permission to connect the centre to an internal global communications network (Mitchell 1986). The Indian government acceded to both conditions. In July 1985, TI contracted with British Telecom and AT&T to install a private single-hop satellite link between TI's corporate headquarters in Dallas and its plant in Bedford, UK.[12] Subsequently, in launching its Bangalore design centre, TI invested in a satellite link between the Indian software development centre and Bedford.

In the mid-1980s TI was a global company with an Asian presence in Japan, Taiwan, Singapore, and Malaysia. It was, however, facing a major competitive challenge from the Japanese in commodity memory chips, TI's stock-in-trade. In 1985, TI saw its revenues fall by $817 million, or 14 per cent, from the previous year, losing $118 million. Whereas TI's rival, Intel, was able to move into the microprocessor segment with the IBM PC franchise, TI's future lay in custom memory chips, particularly application-specific integrated circuits (ASICs) and VLSI (Mitchell 1986). These types of semiconductors called for a major amount of software programing, using computer-aided design.

Robert Rozeboom, vice-president of TI's semiconductor group design automation department, told a reporter in August 1985 that TI had started to look at India seriously in 1984 as a potential site for software development for our computer-aided design. Software development is critical to our semiconductor operations. India has such a strong educational system in the sciences and it has such a large number of graduates who are underemployed, it became an obvious choice for us.[13]

The technology transfer MoU created an opening for TI to locate a software development centre in India. It was a small investment for TI: $5 million out of total 1986 capital expenditures of $446 million (TI, *1986 10-K*). TI recognized that the investment held the added long-term advantage of positioning the company to compete for the growing Indian electronics market.

TI India employed 17 engineers and programmers when it began operations in 1986, 85 in 1990, 275 in 1995, 500 in 2000, and 1,300 in 2005, by which time TI India employment represented almost 4 per cent of TI's worldwide labour force. A report in 2002 stated that among the 750 engineers and programmers who TI employed in Bangalore, there were no expatriates.[14] In 1997, an article in the *Electronic Engineering Times* called TI India 'a dream company for local engineers' (Bindra 1997). In 2003, TI India topped 'India's first ever list of Top 25 Great Places to Work'.[15]

In 2002, TI India expected to expand to 1,400 employees by 2005, with 75 per cent of them working on digital signal processing (DSP) chips, used in cell phones, modems, MP3 players, digital still cameras and Voice over Internet Protocol (VoIP) phones.[16] In DSP, TI India had become, according to a company press release, 'the research base for its parent company'. By the end of 2003, TI India had garnered 225 US patents (Rai 2003). In April 2004, Biswadip Mitra, managing director of TI India, told a Bangalore conference on IT innovation that a large number of his company's employees were working on systems and software for a single-chip cell phone. The challenge for TI's engineers was to integrate digital, analog, radio frequency, and modem in the single chip.[17]

By this time, almost two decades after it had been the first MNC to locate in Bangalore, TI was not alone. Also in April 2004, for example, Advanced Micro Devices (AMD) announced that it would invest $5 million over the next three years to put in place a microprocessor design centre that would employ 120 chip designers and development engineers by the end of 2005. AMD was joining the increasing number of American companies setting up engineering design plants in India's technology hub, Bangalore (Sharma 2004).

With the increased demand for designers, engineers, and programmers in Bangalore, and India generally, TI does not simply wait for qualified labour to apply for jobs. Rather, according to its website, through an initiative that the company calls UniTI, the company has become deeply involved in the Indian system of higher education.[18] With more than 275 operational DSP labs at Indian engineering institutions, UniTI is TI's second largest such programme worldwide. The company asserts that UniTI is 'a mutually beneficial relationship between academia and industry in the field of digital signal processing, and is the forum in which TI India interacts with universities and interested technical institutions in the role of a facilitator'. In the case that UniTI does not yield the quality and quantity of new recruits that TI India requires, the TI website also has a series of pages, aimed especially at Indians working in the US, dedicated to the proposition that 'the time has never been better to come back to India'.[19]

6 CONCLUSION

I began by asking why, if so many educated people are coming from East Asia to the US for further study and work experience, are so many jobs going from the US to the places from which most of these people are coming to employ people just like them. The answer is that the flows of people from East to West and jobs from West to East are both central to a process of the globalization of the high-tech labour force that has been unfolding since the 1960s. AnnaLee Saxenian (2006), focusing mainly on East-Asian entrepreneurs who have spent time starting or managing companies in Silicon Valley, has characterized these flows as 'brain circulation', an apt characterization for the global career paths that increasing numbers of East-Asians are pursuing. What I have outlined in this chapter are the historical forces, beyond the desire of talented individuals to pursue creative and rewarding careers, that created the global ICT labour force and that have enabled nations such as Korea, Taiwan, India, and China to reap the returns on national investments in education by bringing large numbers of the educated and experienced people back home and, more important quantitatively, by creating attractive employment opportunities so that it is not necessary for them to go abroad in the first place.[20]

These historical forces cannot be understood as 'market forces'. Rather their essence resides, as I have illustrated, in a triad of investment strategies of multi-national companies engaged in FDI, national governments that construct indigenous science and technology infrastructures, and indigenous companies that build on the investment strategies of foreign companies and domestic governments to become world-class competitors in their own right. The investment triad takes as its historical starting point the existence of a national education system that creates a highly educated labour supply in advance of indigenous employment demand. In the absence of jobs at home, market forces (aided by changes in US immigration policy) directed this labour abroad, with a brain drain as the result. Through their participation in the investment triad, nations such as Korea and Taiwan in effect confronted these market forces, and helped to generate a dynamic of indigenous job creation that reversed the brain drain, and transformed expatriate scientists and engineers from a wasted investment into a precious resource.

While, among developing economies, East-Asian nations have been the most prominent participants in, and beneficiaries of, this globalization process, the three cases that I have highlighted in this chapter reveal distinctive development paths. In each case—Motorola in Korea, Intel in Malaysia, and Texas Instruments in India—US-based MNCs invested early, and then upgraded and expanded their investments over substantial periods of time. In addition, in each case great emphasis was placed on the almost exclusive employment of indigenous engineers and managers, and in the early years created some of the first attractive opportunities for nationals to pursue high-tech careers at home.

In the case of Korea, domestic investment by government and business rather than FDI is now driving the development of indigenous high-tech capabilities. Indeed, these indigenous investments are creating new opportunities for high-end investment by MNCs in Korea, including new investments by Motorola which has been doing business there for almost 40 years.

In contrast, in the absence of leading indigenous ICT companies, Malaysia's growth still remains highly dependent on the upgrading strategies of MNCs such as Intel. Like Motorola in Korea, Intel originally went to Malaysia in search of low-wage assembly labour in a politically stable country that had made a commitment to mass education. And like MK, Intel Malaysia upgraded its capabilities over time, employing a higher proportion of high-skill labour in higher value-added activities at rising wages.

Like Motorola in Korea and Intel in Malaysia, TI originally went to India in the mid-1980s in search of low-wage labour. TI, however, was not searching for low-skill labour. What attracted TI to India in the mid-1980s was the ready availability of highly educated engineers and programmers at low wages. Over time TI expanded and upgraded its Indian operations, employing larger numbers of educated labour to design increasingly complex products. Two decades after TI came to Bangalore, India is experiencing a growth dynamic in which, with both skill levels and wages rising, indigenous companies such as Tata Consultancy Services, Infosys, and Wipro are taking the lead, and in which MNCs are being attracted to India more for the high quality of its ICT labour supply than for its low cost. A similar process of indigenous innovation has been taking place in China; for example in 2005 China's leading computer manufacturer Legend, with its name changed to Lenovo, acquired IBM's PC business, and even moved its global headquarters to New York.

Given the growth dynamic that has taken hold in these nations, sheer size ensures that Indians and Chinese will dominate the expansion of the global ICT labour supply. In 2001 the combined population of India and China was 33 times that of Korea and Taiwan. As part of the growth process, India and China have rapidly growing domestic markets that both provide a home demand for the products of indigenous companies and give their governments leverage with MNCs in gaining access to advanced technology as a condition for FDI. While India and China offer indigenous scientists and engineers rapidly expanding employment opportunities at home, vast numbers of their educated populations are studying and working abroad. Aided by the ongoing liberalization of US immigration policy (impeded just temporarily by the reaction to 9/11), the global career path is much more of a 'mass' phenomenon for Indian and Chinese scientists and engineers than it has been for the Koreans and Taiwanese.

Finally, what are the implications for employment opportunities in a high-wage country such as the US?[21] 'Offshoring' has been a major political issue in the US in the 2000s (see Hira and Hira 2005), precisely because of the globalization of the ICT labour force, whose evolution I have just analysed. One need not take literally a recent statement by Intel chairman Craig Barrett that 'companies like Intel can do perfectly well in the global marketplace without hiring a single US employee' to fathom the employment insecurity that now faces the US high-tech labour force (see Lazonick 2006: np).

As for Intel, its vision of the labour market may be global, but its perspective on the role of the US government in providing it with new technology remains distinctly national. On 16 March 2005 the Semiconductor Industry Association (SIA) organized a Washington DC press conference in which it exhorted the US government to step up support for research in the physical sciences, including nanotechnology, to assure the continued technological leadership of the US. Intel CEO Craig Barrett was there to warn: 'U.S. leadership in the nanoelectronics era is not guaranteed. It will take a massive, coordinated U.S. research effort involving academia, industry, and state and federal governments to ensure that America continues to be the world leader in information technology'.[22]

The globalization of the ICT labour force is an ongoing process in which the transnational flows of labour and capital can only be understood in terms of the economic development strategies and outcomes of the nations involved. Future research needs to continue to document the origins, directions and extent of these flows, and in particular the characteristics of the most prevalent global career paths in ICT and the offshoring activities of MNCs. In addition, as in Section 5 on reversing the brain drain, future research needs to understand what I have called the 'investment triad': the dynamic interactions among the upgrading strategies of MNCs, the development strategies of national and local governments, and the innovative strategies of indigenous enterprises that result in the creation of ICT employment opportunities in certain places and times. Going forward, the cases of India and China demand special attention.

References

ADAMS, W. (ed.) (1968). *The Brain Drain*. London: Macmillan.

AMSDEN, A. (1989). *Asia's Next Giant: South Korea and Late Industrialization*. Oxford: Oxford University Press.

AMSDEN, A. and CHU, W. (2003). *Beyond Late Development: Taiwan's Upgrading Policies.* Harvard, MA: MIT Press.

ARNOLD, W. (1988). 'Science and Technology Development in Taiwan and South Korea'. *Asian Survey*, 28(4): 437–50.

ARNST, C. (1991). 'Poor Nations Seen Aiding Rich by Brainpower Export in Billions'. *Reuters News*, 7 April: 7.

BARRO, R. and LEE, J.-W. (2000). 'International Data on Educational Attainment: Updates and Implications,' Harvard Center for International Development Working Paper No. 42, April, Appendix Data Files, available at http://www.cid.harvard.edu/ciddata/ciddata. html, accessed 25 Mar. 2006.

BASSETT, R. (2005). 'Facing Two Ways: The Indian Institute of Technology Kanpur, American Technical Assistance, and the Indian Computing Community, 1961–1980'. Paper presented at the Society of the History of Technology meetings, Minneapolis, 5 Nov.

BEHRMAN, J. N. and WALLENDER, H. W. (1976). *Transfers of Manufacturing Technology Within Multinational Enterprises.* New York: Ballinger.

BINDRA, A. (1997). 'Silicon Influx puts India on World Electronics Map', *Electronic Engineering Times*, 7 April: 27.

BLOOM, M. (1992). *Technological Change in the Korean Electronics Industry.* Paris: OECD Development Centre.

BRANSCOMB, L. and CHOI, Y.-H. (eds) (1996). *Korea at the Turning Point: Innovation-Based Strategies for Development.* New York: Praeger.

BYUN, B. M. (1994). 'Growth and Recent Development of the Korean Semiconductor Industry'. *Asian Survey*, 34(8): 706–20.

CHANG, S. (1992). 'Causes of Brain Drain and Solutions: The Taiwan Experience'. *Studies in Comparative International Development*, 27(1): 27–43.

CHANG, Y. S. (1971). *The Transfer of Technology: Economics of Offshore Assembly, The Case of the Semiconductor Industry.* UNITAR Research Report no. 11, United Nations Institute for Training and Research.

CHIRA, S. (1985). 'Korea's Chipmakers Race to Catch Up'. *New York Times*, 15 July: D4.

DAVIS, W. and HATANO, D. (1985). 'The American Semiconductor Industry and the Ascendancy of East Asia'. *California Management Review*, 27(1): 128–43.

DENNIS, W. (1990). 'Intel to Start MPU Production in Malaysia'. *Electronic World News*, 9 April.

DREYFACK, K. and PORT, O. (1986). 'Even American Knowhow is Headed Abroad'. *Business Week*, 3 March.

FORTNEY, J. (1970). 'International Migration of Professionals'. *Population Studies*, 24(2): 217–32.

FLAMM, K. (1985). 'Internationalization in the Semiconductor Industry', in J. Grunwald and K. Flamm (eds), *The Global Factory: Foreign Assembly in International Trade.* Washington DC: Brookings Institution, 38–136.

HIRA, R. and HIRA, A. (2005). *Outsourcing America: What's Behind our National Crisis and How We Can Reclaim American Jobs.* New York: American Management Association.

HO, S. P. S. (1975). 'Industrialization in Taiwan: Recent Trends and Problems'. *Pacifica*, 48(1): 27–41.

HOBDAY, M. (1995). *Innovation in East Asia: The Challenge to Japan.* Cheltenham: Edward Elgar.

ILCHMAN, W. F. (1969). '"People in Plenty": Educated Unemployment in India'. *Asian Survey*, 9(10): 781–95.

INTEL (1984). *A Revolution in Process: A History of Intel to Date*, Intel Corporation, http://www.intel.com/museum/archives/brochures/brochures.htm, accessed 25 Mar. 2006.

ISMAIL, I. (2005). 'Intel Steps up Local Investment'. *New Straits Times*, 12 Dec.

ISMAIL, M. N. (1999). 'Foreign Firms and National Technological Upgrading: The Electronics Industry in Malaysia', in K. S. Jomo, G. Fulker, and R. Rasiah (eds), *Industrial Technology Development in Malaysia: Industry and Firm Studies*. London: Routledge, 21–37.

JOHNSON, J. and REGETS, M. (1998). 'International Mobility of Scientists and Engineers to the United States—Brain Drain or Brain Circulation?', Division of Sciences Resources Studies Issue Brief, MSF 98-316, Revised, 10 Nov.

JOMO K. S., FULKER, G. and RASIAH, R. (eds) (1999). *Industrial Technology Development in Malaysia: Industry and Firm Studies*. London: Routledge.

KIM, D.-W. and LESLIE, S. (1998). 'Winning Markets or Winning Nobel Prizes? KAIST and the Challenges of Late Industrialization'. *Osiris*, 2nd ser. (13): 154–85.

KIM, L. (1997a). 'The Dynamics of Samsung's Technological Learning in Semiconductors'. *California Management Review*, 39(3): 86–100.

KIM, L. (1997b). *Imitation to Innovation: The Dynamics of Korea's Technological Learning*. Cambridge, MA: Harvard Business School Press.

KOIKE, K. and INOKI, T. (eds) (1990). *Skill Formation in Japan and Southeast Asia*. Tokyo: University of Tokyo Press.

LAZONICK, W. (2004). 'Indigenous Innovation and Economic Development: Lessons from China's Leap into the Information Age'. *Industry & Innovation*, 11(4): 273–98.

—— (2007). 'Evolution of the New Economy Business Model', in E. Brousseau and N. Curien (eds), *Internet and Digital Economics*. Cambridge: Cambridge University Press 55–119.

LEE, D. H., BAE, Z.-T. and LEE, J. (1991). 'Performance and Adaptive Roles of the Government-Supported Research Institute in South Korea', *World Development*, 19(10): 1421–40.

LEOW, C. (1992). 'Intel Corp Plans US$80m Investment in Penang Plant'. *Business Times Singapore*, 13 Nov.

LU, Q. (2000). *China's Leap into the Information Age: Innovation and Organization in the Computer Industry*. Oxford: Oxford University Press.

MADDISON, A. (2004). 'Historical Statistics, World Population, GDP, and per capita GDP, 1-2001 AD', http://www.eco.rug.nl/~Maddison/.

MATHEWS, J. A. (1997). 'A Silicon Valley of the East: Creating Taiwan's Semiconductor Industry'. *California Management Review*, 39(4): 26–54.

—— and CHO, D.-S. (2000). *Tiger Technology: the Creation of the Semiconductor Industry in East Asia*. Cambridge: Cambridge University Press.

MITCHELL, J. (1986). 'TI Grasping the Future with Both Hands'. *Dallas Morning News*, 26 Sept.: 1d.

NSB (National Science Board) (2004). *Science and Engineering Indicators 2004* (2 vols). Arlington, VA: National Science Foundation.

NSF (National Science Foundation) (1993). *Human Resources for Science and Technology: The Asian Region*. Surveys of Science Resources Series, Special Report, NSF 93-303. Arlington, VA: National Science Foundation.

POLLACK, A. (1985). 'US-Korea Chip Ties Grow'. *New York Times*, 15 July, D1.

RAI, S. (2003). 'In India, a HighTech Outpost for US Patents'. *New York Times*, 15 Dec.: 4.

SALIH, K. and YOUNG, M.-L. (1987). 'Social Forces, the State and the International Division of Labour: the Case of Malaysia', in J. Henderson and M. Castells (eds), *Global Restructuring and Territorial Development*. London: Sage, 168–202.

SAMSUNG (2005). 'Corporate Backgrounder: Samsung Components', Samsung Semiconductor.

SAXENIAN, A. (2006). *The New Argonauts: Regional Advantage in a Global Economy*. Cambridge, MA: Harvard University Press.

—— and HSU, J. Y. (2001). 'The Silicon Valley-Hsinchu Connection: Technical Communities and Industrial Upgrading'. *Industrial and Corporate Change*, 10(4): 893–920.

SCHMECK, Jr., H. (1973). 'Asia Biggest Source of Brain Drain to US'. *New York Times*, 13 Jan.

SCOTT, A. J. (1987). 'The Semiconductor Industry in South-East Asia: Organization, Location, and the International Division of Labour'. *Regional Studies*, 21(2): 143–60.

SEBALY, K. P. (1972). 'The Assistance of Four Nations in the Establishment of the Indian Institutes of Technology, 1945–1970', unpub. Ph.D. dissertation, University of Michigan.

SHARMA, D. (2004). 'AMD to Open Engineering Center in India'. *CNETNews.com*, 22 Apr.

SHARPSTON, M. (1975). 'International Sub-Contracting'. *Oxford Economic Papers*, 27(1): 94–135.

SHENKMAN, A. (1954). 'Higher Education in India'. *Far Eastern Survey*, 23(2): 24–8.

SPAETH, A. (1984). 'Korean Companies Set Expensive Plans to Make Microchip Plants Competitive'. *Wall Street Journal*, 8 Feb.: 30.

TENORIO, V. (1985). 'The Big Computer Catch-up Begins'. *Australian Financial Review*, 31 July: 13.

TILTON, J. E. (1971). *International Diffusion of Technology: The Case of Semiconductors*. Washington DC: Brookings Institution.

US DHS (Department of Homeland Security) (2002–2004a). 'Characteristics of Specialty Occupation Workers (H-1B)'. US Government Printing Office, April 2002, September 2003, July 2004.

—— (2002–2004b). *Yearbooks of Immigration Statistics*. Washington DC: US Government Printing Office.

US DS (Department of State) (1997–2005). 'Tables on Non-Immigration Visas Issued, Fiscal Years', http://travel.state.gov/visa/about/report/report_1476.html, accessed 24 Mar. 2006.

US INS (Immigration and Naturalization Service) (1997–2001). *Statistical Yearbooks of the Immigration and Naturalization Service*. Washington DC: US Government Printing Office.

WADE, R. (1990). *Governing the Market: Economic Theory and the Role of Government in East Asian Industrialization*. Princeton, NJ: Princeton University Press.

WEISMAN, S. (1985). 'US-India Technology Accord Gains'. *New York Times*, 4 May.

WOHN, D.-H. (2005). 'Chip Developers See Korea as Ideal for R&D Centers', *Joins.com*, 20 May.

World Bank (1993). *The East Asian Miracle: Economic Growth and Public Policy*. Oxford: Oxford University Press.

VAUGHAN, J. (2003). 'Shortcuts to Immigration: The "Temporary" Visa Program is Broken', Center for Immigration Studies, Washington DC, January.

YANG, D. J. and NAKARMI, L. (1989). 'Is the Era of Cheap Asian Labour Over?' *Business Week*, 15 May: 45.

YOON, B.-S. L. (1992). 'Reverse Brain-Drain in South Korea: State-Led Model'. *Studies in Comparative International Development*, 27(1): 4–26.

ZACHARY, G. P. (1994). 'Trading Places: Malaysians Become Stars at US Electronic Firms'. *Asian Wall Street Journal*, 3 Oct.: 1.

NOTES

1. A longer version of this chapter, with more detailed documentation of its various parts, can be found at http://faculty.insead.edu/Lazonick.
2. See for example Amsden (1989); Wade (1990); Branscomb and Choi (1996); Hobday (1995); Kim (1997b); Jomo et al. (1999); Lu (2000); Mathews and Cho (2000); Amsden and Chu (2003); Lazonick (2004).
3. *Statistical Abstract India*, 2002 and 2003, http://mospi.nic.in/mospi_cso_rept_pubn.htm, accessed 25 Mar. 2006.
4. For the case of Taiwan, see Chang (1992); Mathews (1997); Saxenian and Hsu (2001); Amsden and Chu (2003: 41–7); Saxenian (2006).
5. 'Workers occupy computer room of Motorola factory,' *Reuters News*, 1988, 29 Dec.
6. 'Union flare-up cools at Korean Motorola site'. *Electronic Buyers' News*, 1989, 9 Jan.: 2.
7. 'National Semiconductor closes plant in S. Korea'. *Electronic World News*, 1989, 15 May.
8. 'Key contributor to Korea's semiconductor industry exported $3.2 billion of semiconductors, communications equipment'. *Business Korea*, 1994, 1 Feb.: 53.
9. See http://www.tdctrade.com/mktprof/asia/mpmal.htm, accessed 25 Mar. 2006.
10. 'Intel closes two plants in California for week due to slowing business'. *Wall Street Journal*, 1974, 4 Sept.
11. 'Intel to move microcontroller operations to Penang plant'. *Electronic Times*, 1992, 30 Jul.
12. 'Dallas, Texas, is to be connected to Bedford, England, by a 4,500 mile, single-hop, satellite communications link under a contract signed in New York'. *Textline Multiple Source Collection* (1980–1994), 1985, 26 Jul.
13. 'Texas Inst. looks to grab fast-growing Asia market'. *United Press International*, 1985, 19 Aug.: 50.
14. 'Business as usual for US firms in India'. *Reuters News*, 2002, 3 June.
15. 'Geek haven: Texas Instruments'. *Business World*, 2003, 1 Sept.: 28.
16. 'India to increase staff strength'. *Business Line*, 2002, 11 Mar.
17. 'Texas Instruments building single chip mobile phone in India'. *The Press Trust of India Limited*, 2004, 3 Nov.
18. http://www.ti.com/asia/docs/india/dsp-universities.html, accessed 25 Mar. 2006.
19. http://www.ti.com/recruit/docs/india/info.shtml, accessed 25 Mar. 2006.
20. Space limitations make it impossible to cover the full gamut of national experiences and no attempt is made to deal with China (but see Lu 2000; Lazonick 2004).
21. This question is addressed in my forthcoming book on the subject, funded by the Upjohn Institute for Employment Research.
22. 'US could lose race for nanotech leadership, SIA panel says'. *Electronic News*, 2005, 16 Mar.

CHAPTER 5

PRODUCTIVITY AND ICTs: A REVIEW OF THE EVIDENCE

MIRKO DRACA

RAFFAELLA SADUN

JOHN VAN REENEN

1 INTRODUCTION[*]

PAUL KRUGMAN has remarked that productivity is not everything, but in the long run it is almost everything. This is because the key indicator of material well-being, national income per person, is fundamentally determined by the growth of labour productivity. Because of greater productivity, society has the option to enjoy more leisure, pay lower taxes, increase public spending, or redistribute wealth without making a large proportion of people worse off.

Given the importance of productivity it is somewhat disturbing that for many years 'we could see computers everywhere but in the productivity statistics'. Nobel

* We would like to thank the Economic and Social Research Council for financial support through the Centre for Economic Performance. This review draws on joint work with Nick Bloom. All mistakes remain our own.

Laureate Robert Solow (1987) made this remark in response to the simultaneous apparent widespread adoption of computers and slowdown in US productivity growth from the mid-1970s. Much research effort has been devoted since that time to addressing this 'Solow Paradox' and analysing the impact of information and communication technologies (ICTs) on productivity. Because of this research, the outlook in the early twenty-first century appears more optimistic than it did from the perspective of the 1980s.

This explosion of research has involved academics, statistical agencies and international bodies. There has been greater collaboration between these sectors, which has enabled progress in the generation and analysis of data. The work of private sector organizations and consultancies has also contributed significantly to the debate. In addition to the intrinsic interest of researchers in this question, the availability of very large longitudinal datasets following the same firms and industries over many years has enabled significant progress in research. These large electronic datasets would have been virtually impossible to compile and analyse if the ICT revolution had not occurred.

In this chapter, we offer a guided tour to some of the main aspects of ICTs and productivity. Section 2 discusses a neoclassical theoretical framework that has been extensively used (either explicitly or implicitly) by most of the studies we survey. We also consider extensions to these theoretical approaches. In Section 3 we detail some of the econometric issues involved in estimating the productivity of ICT. This requires some consideration of the estimation of production functions, an area where there has been considerable econometric advance in recent years. In Section 4 we discuss issues relating to the data, both ideal and actual. The final two sections discuss the results of the empirical studies covering both growth accounting (Section 5) and econometric approaches (Section 6) at the industry and firm level. The studies are presented in summary in Tables 5.2, 5.3 and 5.4.

Given the size of the task, there are several caveats. Our focus is mainly economic, and thus we largely ignore the contributions of many other social scientists. Our justification is that we want to focus on the quantitative work where economists have tended to dominate. For this reason, we have not attempted to survey the large case study literature, which has thrown up some interesting insights on the role of organizational factors (for example, the McKinsey Global Institute studies). Furthermore, for reasons of space we present only the basics of the many empirical studies in this area.

Within the class of econometric studies, we focus on the estimation of cross industry production functions. There are several econometric studies of particular types of ICT in particular sectors, such as trucking (Baker and Hubbard 2004); emergency medical care (Athey and Stern 2002) and schools (Angrist and Lavy 2002; Machin, McNally and Silva 2006). These studies represent some of the future directions of the discipline and their scant mention should not be interpreted to be a sign of their small importance.

Somewhat preempting the conclusions of our study we want to highlight the following findings. The key finding in the macro-economic literature is the remarkable productivity acceleration in the US since the 1990s, which would appear to be related (at least in part) to ICT. Europe has not achieved similar productivity acceleration, which is probably due to the greater 'organizational capital' in US firms. There is some suggestive recent evidence from micro panel studies supporting this, but more work needs to be done to (a) specify more concretely the type of organizational features that promote successful ICT usage, and (b) deal with the inherent endogeneity of ICT choices.

2 THEORY

Basic approach

We begin by outlining the basic neoclassical approach, which in addition to being the most common approach in the literature, provides a very useful framework for organizing our thinking.

The basic neo-classical approach begins with a production function ($F(.)$), which relates output, Y, to inputs. One of these inputs is capital; the components of capital are ICT capital (denoted C), and non-ICT capital K (which includes, for example, buildings). There are also factors of production such as hours of labour L, and materials M.[1] We also allow different levels of efficiency, A (Hicks neutral technology). Consequently,

$$Y = AF(X) = AF(L,K,C,M) \qquad (2.1)$$

To illustrate the issues we will assume that the production function can be written in Cobb-Douglas form (although the results we discuss are suitable for much more general forms of the production function). In natural logarithms the production function can be written as:

$$y = a + \alpha_l l + \alpha_k k + \alpha_c c + \alpha_m m \qquad (2.2)$$

where lower case letters indicate that a variable has been transformed into a natural logarithm (e.g. $y = lnY$). In discrete time, the growth rate of output can be written as:

$$\Delta y = \Delta a + \alpha_l \Delta l + \alpha_k \Delta k + \alpha_c \Delta c + \alpha_m \Delta m \qquad (2.3)$$

where Δa is Total Factor Productivity (TFP) growth and the other terms are the growth rates of the inputs. Usually, we can think of Δ as the first difference transformation (e.g. $\Delta y_t = y_t - y_{t-1}$) but we can also consider longer differences (e.g. the average annual growth rate between 1995 and 2000: $\Delta_5 y = (y_t - y_{t-5})/5$).

Several approaches are now possible. The first approach we consider is called growth accounting, which is popular in the macro literature. The second approach is to estimate some form of the production function directly, an approach popular in the micro literature. However, it should be noted that growth accounting is also possible at the micro level and production function estimation is also possible at the macro level.

Growth accounting

Under the assumption that factor markets and product markets are perfectly competitive their shares in revenue can replace the coefficients on factor inputs. These are strong assumptions, but there are many ways to relax them and allow for degrees of imperfect competition. Denoting a revenue share by s, we can write:

$$\alpha_x = s_x = \frac{\rho_x X}{pY} \tag{2.4}$$

where ρ_x is the unit cost of factor X and p is the output price (so pY is revenue). For example, ρ_c will be the Hall-Jorgenson user cost of ICT capital. For labour, ρ_l is simply the wage rate. Given this, we can re-write the production relation as:

$$\Delta y = \Delta a + s_l \Delta l + s_k \Delta k + s_c \Delta c + s_m \Delta m \tag{2.5}$$

Note that, with the exception of TFP growth, Δa, all the objects on the right-hand side of this equation are observed. Growth accounting (over a period) divides output growth into the contribution of the (weighted) growth of inputs and the contribution of the residual. Since Solow (1957), the contribution of the residual has generally been found to be a large component of total labour productivity growth. This is sometimes labelled technical change, but obviously it includes everything in the economy that improves (or reduces) the efficiency with which factors are used (as well as some amount of measurement error).[2]

Under constant returns to scale (i.e. $\alpha_l + \alpha_k + \alpha_c + \alpha_m = 1$), we can re-write the growth equation in terms of labour productivity growth:

$$\Delta(y - l) = \Delta a + s_k \Delta(k - l) + s_c \Delta(c - l) + s_m \Delta(m - l) \tag{2.6}$$

Therefore, output growth per hour is a function of inputs per hour and TFP growth. Clearly the contribution of ICT capital will be $s_c \Delta(c - l)$. If the production function is Leontief in materials, we can write the relationship in value added (v) terms as:

$$\Delta(v - l) = \Delta a + s_k \Delta(k - l) + s_c \Delta(c - l) \tag{2.7}$$

This provides a basic picture of growth accounting. In the ICT literature growth accounting has focused, naturally enough, on the importance of the ICT contribution by decomposing the equations by industry because ICT contributes to aggregate productivity growth in two distinct ways. First, through ICT-capital deepening, $s_c \Delta(c - l)$ as sectors increase the intensity of their ICT use. Second, through TFP growth in ICT producing sectors.

There are several well-known problems with growth accounting. First, it describes, but does not explain. There is no attempt to claim that there is any causal connection between changes in inputs, such as ICT, and productivity. Secondly, the assumptions underlying growth accounting are strong and generally not tested (for example, perfect competition). It is simply assumed in growth accounting that the share of ICT capital measures its contribution, and no attempt is actually made to estimate the strength of the relationship in the data. Thirdly, if there are externalities related to factors they will be included in the residual, and the contribution of these factors will be underestimated. Modern endogenous growth theorists emphasize that there may be important knowledge spillovers from human capital, especially the highly skilled workers employed in the research and development (R&D) sector (see, e.g. Aghion and Howitt 1998). Consequently, traditional growth accounting will systematically underestimate the importance of these factors in accounting for economic growth (see Sianesi and Van Reenen (2003) for a survey of the role of human capital in growth). Finally, the model is one of static long-run equilibrium and takes no account of adjustment costs.

Some extensions to the basic model

Complementary organizational capital and ICT

There has been considerable discussion in the literature that the measured ICT may be only the tip of the iceberg. Successful implementation of an ICT project requires reorganization of the firm around the new technology.[3] Reorganization incurs costs, whether in the shape of fees paid to consultants, management time, or expenditure on the retraining of workers. There is much anecdotal evidence supporting this view, and it has been claimed that the total cost of an ICT project can be four or more times the amount paid for the equipment and software. Yang and Brynjolffson (2001) cite evidence that the total start-up cost (that is, the costs incurred within the first year) of an Enterprise Resource Planning (ERP) suite is five times the cost of the hardware and software licences. Based on econometric evidence of the effect on stock prices of ICT investment, Brynjolffson, Hitt and Yang (2002) suggest that as much as $9 of total investment is associated with $1 of ICT investment. This additional expenditure could be interpreted simply as adjustment costs, which are perhaps particularly high in the case of ICT. These adjustment costs can be estimated econometrically.

More generally, a production function can be estimated where there are inter-actions between organizational capital, O, and ICT capital (the previous discussion was in terms of perfect complementarity—a firm has to spend \$9 extra on organization when it buys ICT). One form of the production function could be (cf. Bresnahan, Brynjolfsson and Hitt 2002)

$$y = a + \alpha_l l + \alpha_k k + \alpha_c c + \alpha_m m + \alpha_o o + \alpha_{oc}(c \times o) \qquad (2.8)$$

where the hypothesis is $\alpha_{oc} > 0$.[4] Note that this is different from the situation where the firm may simply have more organizational capital in general, and this is positively correlated with ICT capital ($\alpha_{oc} = 0$, but $\text{cov}(C,O) > 0$). In this case, the importance of ICT capital will be overestimated if organizational capital is not properly measured.

In another scenario, O is essentially fixed and exogenous to the firm. For example, entrepreneurs establish firms that have a distinctive managerial culture, which it is extremely difficult to change unless the firm (or plant) closes down or is taken over (for models of this type see Syverson 2004). A differenced version of this equation would be

$$\Delta y = \Delta a + \alpha_l \Delta l + \alpha_k \Delta k + \alpha_c \Delta c + \alpha_m \Delta m + \alpha_{oc}(o^* \Delta c) \qquad (2.9)$$

There will be systematic variation in the ICT coefficient depending on whether firms have a high or low value of O. For example, if US multinationals have systematically greater organizational capital than non-US multinationals this implies a positive estimate of the interaction between ICT capital and a dummy for whether the firm was a US multinational (see Bloom, Sadun and Van Reenen 2005 for evidence in favour of this hypothesis).

Skills

There is much evidence to show that technology and skills are complementary (e.g. Chennells and Van Reenen 2002; Machin and Van Reenen 1998). Failure to account for skills in equation (2.2) could also bias upwards the estimated effects of ICT, just as would the omission of organizational capital. Caroli and Van Reenen (2001) examine an extended version of the production function allowing for interactions between ICT, organizational capital, and skills. They find that the complementarity between ICT and organization is not significant when organization, skills, and the interaction between them are controlled for.

General purpose technologies and spillovers

It is frequently argued that ICT is a 'general-purpose' technology (GPT). This has some implications. Firstly, adoption of a GPT entails experimentation that may lead to innovation by the adopting firms, which in turn shows up as TFP growth. Secondly, as well as innovating themselves, firms can learn from the (successful or unsuccessful) innovation efforts of others, so there are spillover effects (Bresnahan and Trajtenberg 1995). Thirdly, there may be network effects specific to the wide-spread use of ICT: ICT may be more effective when many firms in a region or industry are using similar levels or types of ICT.

These considerations cause researchers to look for spillovers from ICT in the same way that researchers looked for R&D spillovers.[5] The method generally employed is to augment the production function with a spillover term (denote this SPILL), which is the ICT of some of the other firms in the economy.

$$y = a + \alpha_l l + \alpha_k k + \alpha_c c + \mu SPILL + \alpha_m m \qquad (2.10)$$

We are interested in whether $\mu > 0$.

The main problem here is how to construct the SPILL measure. In general, this requires the specification of weights or 'distances' (d_{ij}) between firms i and j. So in general $SPILL_i = \sum_{j,i \neq j} d_{ij} C_j$. The distances could be based on industry—for example, all the other firms in firm i's industry are given a weight of unity ($d_{ij} = 1$), while firms outside firm i's industry are weighted zero ($d_{ij} = 0$). If spillovers come from forward or backward linkages, input-output matrices or trade matrices could be used. Alternatively, weighting can be based on geography or technology class.

It should be emphasized, however, that ICT, unlike R&D, is embodied, therefore knowledge spillovers will be less likely. Network effects may be more important, but these might apply to specific forms of ICT (like operating systems or communication networks) rather than ICT in general.

3 ECONOMETRIC MODELS

There are many problems involved in estimating the production function for ICT. Some of these are generic issues related to the estimation of production functions. For instance, unobserved heterogeneity: there are many factors correlated with productivity that we do not measure. If unobserved heterogeneity is constant over time then panel data can help. The unobserved factor can be treated as a fixed effect and then the estimation can proceed with either dummy variables for each firm being included, (that is, the within groups estimator) or by differencing the data (e.g. first differences). Another problem is endogeneity. The factor inputs (such as ICT) are chosen by firms and are not, therefore, exogenous when included on the right-hand side of the production function. One solution to this is to find external instrumental variables that affect the decision to invest in ICT, but do not affect the productivity of the firm directly.[6]

The literature has not followed up the instrumental variable solution, however, and most studies ignore these issues and simply estimate a production function using ordinary least square (OLS) methods. However, some studies examine various approaches for dealing with these problems and a minority[7] actually compare the results derived from alternative advanced econometric techniques. We now discuss three approaches: TFP-based, General Method of Moment (GMM), and Olley Pakes (OP).

TFP-based approaches

A common approach in the ICT literature dealing with this issue is to consider a transformation that constructs a measured TFP growth term. For example, Brynjolfson and Hitt (2003) estimate the following forms of equations:

$$\Delta \tilde{a} = \beta_1 \Delta c \qquad (3.1)$$

where the dependent variable is measured TFP (or 'four factor' TFP)

$$\Delta \tilde{a} = \Delta y - s_l \Delta l - s_k \Delta k - s_c \Delta c - s_m \Delta m \qquad (3.2)$$

If ICT earned 'normal returns' then the estimated coefficient in equation (3.1) would equal zero ($\beta_1 = 0$). Unfortunately, although this resolves the endogeneity problem for the non-ICT factor inputs by moving them from the right-hand side to the left-hand side of the equation, the endogeneity of ICT remains a problem. In fact, it is likely to be exacerbated as the construction of measured TFP involves the variable of interest on the right-hand side of the equation. Any measurement error in ICT will be transmitted into a biased coefficient on β_1.[8]

An additional problem is that classical measurement errors in ICT will generate an attenuation bias towards zero for β_1. This is one reason for turning to longer differenced models, the approach adopted by Brynjolffson and Hitt (2003) (although they interpret their increasing coefficients as being due to unmeasured organizational capital rather than measurement error). In general, the attenuation bias should be less for longer differences than for shorter differences as the transitory shocks will be averaged out increasing the signal to noise ratio for the ICT measure (Griliches and Hausman 1986). Unfortunately, in econometrics as in life there is no free lunch. Although long-differencing the data reduces the random measurement error, endogeneity problems are exacerbated because the transformed error term now includes more time periods.

General method of moment (GMM) approaches

For notational simplicity, re-consider the basic production function as,

$$y_{it} = \theta x_{it} + u_{it} \qquad (3.3)$$

where θ is the parameter of interest on a single factor input, x. Assume that the error term, u_{it}, takes the form

$$u_{it} = \eta_i + \tau_t + \omega_{it}$$
$$\omega_{it} = \rho\omega_{it-1} + v_{it}$$

(3.4)

τ_t represents macro-economic shocks captured by a series of time dummies, η_i is a correlated individual effect, and v_{it} is a serially uncorrelated mean zero error term. The other element of the error term, ω_{it} is allowed to have an AR(1) component (with coefficient ρ), which could be the result of measurement error or slowly evolving technological change. Substituting (3.4) into (3.3) gives the dynamic equation:

$$y_{it} = \pi_1 y_{it-1} + \pi_2 x_{it} + \pi_3 x_{it-1} + \eta_i^* + \tau_t^* + v_{it}$$

(3.5)

The common factor restriction (COMFAC) is $\pi_1\pi_2 = -\pi_3$. Note that $\tau_t^* = \tau_t - \rho\tau_{t-1}$ and $\eta_i^* = (1 - \rho)\eta_i$.

Blundell and Bond (2000) recommend a system GMM approach to estimate the production function and impose the COMFAC restrictions by minimum distance. If we allow inputs to be endogenous, we will require instrumental variables. We consider moment conditions that will enable us to construct a GMM estimator for equation (3.5). A common method is to take first differences of (3.5) to sweep out the fixed effects:

$$\Delta y_{it} = \pi_1 \Delta y_{it-1} + \pi_2 \Delta x_{it} + \pi_3 \Delta x_{it-1} + \Delta\tau_t^* + \Delta v_{it}$$

(3.6)

Since v_{it} is serially uncorrelated the moment condition:

$$E(x_{it-2}\Delta v_{it}) = 0$$

(3.7)

ensures that instruments dated t-2 and earlier[9] are valid and can be used to construct a GMM estimator for equation (3.6) in first differences (Arellano and Bond 1991). A problem with this estimator is that variables with a high degree of persistence over time (such as capital) will have very low correlations between their first difference (Δx_{it}) and the lagged levels being used as an instrument (e.g. x_{it-2}). This problem of weak instruments can lead to substantial bias in finite samples. Blundell and Bond (1998) point out that under a restriction on the initial conditions another set of moment conditions is available:[10]

$$E(\Delta x_{it-1}(\eta_i + v_{it})) = 0$$

(3.8)

This implies that lags of first differences of the endogenous variables can be used to control for the levels in equation (3.5) directly. The econometric strategy is to combine the instruments implied by the moment conditions (3.7) and (3.8). We can obtain consistent estimates of the coefficients and use these to recover the underlying structural parameters.

The Olley-Pakes method

Reconsider the basic production function[11] as:

$$y_{it} = \alpha_l l_{it} + \alpha_m m_{it} + \alpha_k k_{it} + \alpha_c c_{it} + \omega_{it} + \eta_{it} \tag{3.9}$$

The efficiency term, ω_{it} is the unobserved productivity state that will be correlated with both output and the variable input decision, and η_{it} is an independent and identically distributed error term. Assume that both capital stocks are predetermined and current investment (which will react to productivity shocks) takes one period before it becomes productive, that is, $K_{it} = I_{t-1}^K + (1 - \delta^K)K_{it-1}$ and $C_{it} = I_{t-1}^C + (1 - \delta^C)C_{it-1}$.

It can be shown that under certain regulatory conditions the investment policy functions for ICT and non-ICT are monotonic in non-ICT capital, ICT capital, and the unobserved productivity state.

$$i_{it}^K = i_t^K(k_{it}, c_{it}, \omega_{it}) \tag{3.10}$$

$$i_{it}^C = i_t^C(k_{it}, c_{it}, \omega_{it}) \tag{3.11}$$

The investment policy rule, therefore, can be inverted to express ω_{it} as a function of investment and capital. Focusing on the non-ICT investment policy function it can be inverted to obtain the proxy: $\omega_t^K(i_{it}^K, k_{it}, c_{it})$. The first stage of the OP algorithm uses this invertibility result to re-express the production function as:

$$\begin{aligned} y_{it} &= \alpha_l l_{it} + \alpha_m m_{it} + \alpha_k k_{it} + \alpha_c c_{it} + \omega_t^K(i_{it}^K, k_{it}, c_{it}) + \eta_{it} \\ &= \alpha_l l_{it} + \alpha_m m_{it} + \phi(i_{it}^K, k_{it}, c_{it}) + \eta_{it} \end{aligned} \tag{3.12}$$

where $\phi(i_{it}^K, k_{it}, c_{it}) = \phi_t = \omega_t^K(i_{it}^K, k_{it}, c_{it}) + \alpha_k k_{it} + \alpha_c c_{it}$.

We can approximate this function with a series estimator or non-parametric approximation and use this first stage result to get estimates of the coefficients on the variable inputs. The second stage of the OP algorithm is:

$$y_{it}^* = y_{it} - \alpha_l l_{it} - \alpha_m m_{it} = \alpha_k k_{it} + \alpha_c c_{it} + \omega_{it} + \eta_{it} \tag{3.13}$$

Note that the expectation of productivity, conditional on the previous period's information set (denoted Ω_{t-1}) is:

$$\omega_{it}\big|_{\chi_{it}=1} = E[\omega_{it}|\omega_{it-1}, \chi_{it} = 1] + \xi_{it} \tag{3.14}$$

where $\chi_{it} = 1$ indicates that the firm has chosen not to shut down (a selection stage over the decision to exit can be incorporated in a straightforward manner). This expression for productivity state is based on the assumption that unobserved productivity evolves as a first order Markov process. Again, we assume that we can approximate this relationship with a high order series approximation $g(\omega_{it-1})$.

Substituting this into the second stage, and making expectations conditional on the previous period's information set gives:

$$E(y_{it}^* | \Omega_{t-1}) = \alpha_k k_{it} + \alpha_c c_{it} + g[\phi(i_{it-1}^K, k_{it-1}, \alpha_c c_{it-1}) - \alpha_k k_{it} - \alpha_c c_{it}] \quad (3.15)$$

Since we already have estimates of the ϕ_{t-1} function this amounts to estimating by Non-Linear Least Squares (NLLS). We now have all the relevant parameters of the production function.[12]

4 Data issues: Measuring ICT

Ideal measures of capital in a production function context

The ideal measure capturing the economic contribution of capital inputs in a production theory context is *flow of capital services*. Building this variable from raw data entails non-trivial assumptions regarding: the measurement of the investment flows in the different assets, and the aggregation over vintages of a given type of asset.[13] Assuming for the moment that we can measure investments in the specific asset without error, we investigate the latter point.

For the sake of simplicity, we assume a framework in which only one type of capital is used for production. Output will depend on the aggregation of the different vintages of investments made over the years, after allowing for the fact that the capacity of earlier investments decays after installation. Defining the decay factor for an investment of s years old d_s, and I_{t-s} as the real gross investment of vintage s, the aggregate *capital* stock can be written as:

$$K_t = \sum_{s=0}^{t} (1 - d_s) +_{-s} \quad (4.1)$$

If we assume that the rate of decay is constant over time (geometric rate of decay), then Equation 4.1 takes the very simple form:

$$K_t = I_t + (1 - d)K_{t-1} \quad (4.2)$$

In the case of geometric decay, the rate of decay is equal to the *depreciation rate* (δ) (Oulton and Srinivasan 2003). Depreciation measures the difference between the price of a new and a one-year old asset at time t. Defining the price of a specific asset of age j at time s as $p_{s,j}$, then the depreciation rate is:

$$\delta_t = \frac{(p_{t,j} - p_{t,j+1})}{p_{t,j}} \quad (4.3)$$

Assuming that the depreciation rate of the asset does not vary over time we can omit the time subscript. A concept related to depreciation rate is the capital gain/loss (f) associated with the investment in the specific asset. The capital gain/loss is defined as the change in the price of a new asset between periods $t-1$ and t, that is:

$$f_{t,j} = (p_{t,j} - p_{t-1,j}). \tag{4.4}$$

Both depreciation and capital gain/loss affect the definition of the rental price $(\rho_{t,j})$ for the capital services of a capital input of age j at time t. This is defined as:

$$\rho_{t,j} = r_t \cdot p_{t-1,j} + \delta \cdot p_{t,j} - f_{t,j} \tag{4.5}$$

where r_t is the actual nominal rate of return during period t. The rental price is what the company would pay if instead of buying the capital good, it rents it from another firm. A profit-maximizing firm will hire the capital good up to the point when the rental price equals the marginal revenue of the product of the capital good. Under perfect competition, the rental price will be equal to the value of the marginal product of the asset. In this case, the asset is said to deliver normal returns. When the marginal product is higher than the rental price, then the asset is said to deliver excessive returns.[14]

Basic capital theory applies equally to both ICT and non-ICT assets. As this brief description suggests, empirical implementation of the theory of capital measurement is far from simple. This seems to be particularly true for ICT assets, as they entail several problematic issues related to the measurement of investment flows, and of depreciation rates and price deflators. In the next two sections we explore how the research has dealt with these issues, focusing first on industry level data, and then looking at firm level studies.

Measurement of ICT capital at the industry level

This section describes the main sources and methodologies used to measure ICT assets in an industry level framework, with a specific focus on the methodologies developed within the main US statistical offices—the Bureau of Economic Analysis (BEA) and the Bureau of Labor Statistics (BLS). The BEA and BLS are the major data sources for studies that apply industry data to examine the productivity impact of ICT in the US economy. Moreover, US methodologies represent the frontier for ICT capital measurement and have been widely applied in non-US contexts[15] to derive industry level measures of ICT capital.

US data

Both the BEA and the BLS develop data on capital stocks, by asset and industry, applying the Perpetual Inventory Method (PIM) to real investment figures. The BEA publishes basic industry level data on ICT spending for the US economy.[16]

These estimates are derived using a top down approach. First, gross investments in ICT for the total US economy are computed starting from micro data—produced monthly by the Census Bureau—on computer shipments. Exports, intermediate, households, and government purchases[17] are deducted from this total, and imports are added. Secondly, industry totals on overall investments are built from micro data on establishments from the Economic Census and the Annual Capital Expenditures Survey (ACES) (since 1992) or the Plant and Equipment Survey (before 1992). To obtain series of ICT (and non-ICT investments) by industry, the industry and asset totals are combined and distributed across the different industries using an occupational-employment-by-industry matrix developed by the BLS, as documented in Bond and Aylor (2000), (implicitly) assuming a labour-capital fixed coefficient technology. BEA publishes the estimated asset-by-industry flows of all assets in the Capital Flows Table (CFT) and the Fixed Reproducible Tangible Wealth (FRTW) Investment Matrix.[18]

Measuring nominal ICT flows is the first of a series of adjustments needed to obtain proper ICT capital. A basic step is the creation of appropriate deflators—to convert nominal flows into real flows. This issue is of particular relevance for ICT assets, which have experienced dramatic price and quality changes over the years. The BEA and the BLS, in concert with academic and computer industry econo-mists, have made significant improvements in developing quality-adjusted prices for computer equipment.[19] Since the early 1990s, the deflators used by BEA for computers and peripheral equipment have been derived from the producer price index (PPI) and the import price index, quality adjusted by BLS using hedonic techniques (briefly described in Holdway 2001).[20]

Another component is the creation of appropriate depreciation schemes—to take account of the rate of decay of the different vintages of investments. BEA's depreciation schemes differ from those used by the BLS. Since 1997, the BEA has used age-price depreciation for its weights, the assumption being that the depre-ciation pattern of most assets declines geometrically over time.[21] In contrast, the BLS uses a hyperbolic age-efficiency function.[22]

European Data

European statistics offices' published industry data on ICT assets lag behind the US. They have produced various country specific industry level data sets on ICT investment flows.[23] The dataset developed by van Ark et al. (2002) is an example of combining official statistics on ICT flows at industry level for EU economies with US methodologies (especially on depreciation patterns and hedonic prices), to produce broadly comparable estimates of ICT stocks from the late 1970s to 2003.[24] In order to build series for real ICT investments, they applied country specific data deflators obtained through the price index harmonization method developed by Schreyer (2002), using US deflators adjusted for each country's general inflation. Once the flows are obtained, capital stocks are derived applying PIM to US depreciation rates taken from Jorgenson and Stiroh (2000a).

Discussion

Despite the major effort made by US statistical offices in the context of ICT measurement, and especially the development of robust ICT deflators based on hedonic techniques, the construction of the asset-by-industry investment matrix from which capital stocks are derived seems to suffer from potentially problematic measurement issues[25] (Becker et al. 2005). Similarly, available European data rely on interpolation techniques, as, for most European countries, the investment series are available only for specific years.[26]

Crepon and Heckel (2002) give examples of some of the problems that can arise when using industry level estimates of ICT stocks developed in a national accounting framework. In their work, measures of ICT capital at the two-digit level are built using firm level data on ICT assets declared by firms in their tax returns. The industry data are built for an average of 300,000 firms per year over the period 1984–1998, and compared to the figures reported by Cette, Mairesse, and Kocoglu (2000) based on National Accounts. The share of ICT capital in value added, obtained through the aggregation of firm level data, is 1.7 per cent, while the share derived from National Account sources is 0.5 per cent. This stark difference may be due to the more detailed data entries obtained from micro sources, but also could be due to the different assumptions related to the PIM employed in the National Accounts' estimations.[27]

Measures of ICT capital at firm level

Using micro data rather than industry data allows the well-documented firm level heterogeneity in productivity and investment patterns to be taken into account, which is particularly relevant in the context of ICT assets. ICT frequently is found to have a differential impact on firm level productivity according to characteristics such as organizational structures and skills that are likely to differ even across firms within the same industry.

Micro context, private surveys

The first attempts to estimate the role of ICT assets on firm level productivity data were made by Brynjolfsson and Hitt (1995, 2003). The data they used typically refer to volume measures of firms' hardware stocks on site, collected through telephone surveys organized and managed by private organizations such as the Computer Intelligence Intercorp (CII). These volume measures are translated into value measures of hardware stocks using price and computing capacity information provided by CII.[28]

There are two advantages of such data. First, the detailed information collected (hardware stocks by type of equipment) provides a very precise snapshot of the type of ICT stocks existing at a specific site, and does not require PIM. Secondly, as many of the firms in these surveys were sampled in different years, the data are suitable for longitudinal productivity analysis.

However, there are also some problematic aspects to their use. First, for the purposes of productivity analysis the ICT data—collected at site level—needs to be matched with data from other financial information sources (such as Compustat for the US or Amadeus for several European countries), which refer to firms rather than sites within a firm. This implies that the ICT data need to be adjusted by aggregation if multiple sites belonging to a single firm are sampled, or by applying weighting schemes to project the site level information to firm level. Secondly, as these types of ICT surveys target very large firms (for the US the sample is Fortune 1000 firms), there might be a selection issue biasing the productivity results.

Micro context, census based data

In the last decade, statistical offices have played a major role in collecting ICT information at firm level. These data now represent a valid alternative to the micro level ICT measures collected by private organizations, and are typically matched to other census-based information on output and inputs, or to publicly available databases (such as Compustat), which contain firm level financial information.

In most cases, statistical offices collect information related to the *use* of ICT equipment, rather than precise measures of ICT expenditure or ICT stocks. The surveys are at the employee level (that is, an employee of a specific firm is surveyed about his/her own particular use of ICT), as in Greenan and Mairesse (1996),[29] or at firm level (that is a representative of the firm is asked about the number of employees using ICT in general, about a specific type of ICT equipment or procedure, such as broadband or e-commerce), as in Maliranta and Rouvinen (2004).[30] Using a similar approach, Atrostic and Nguyen (2005) for the US, and Atrostic et al. (2004) for Japan, employ firm level information on ICT infrastructures (a dummy variable taking value one if the firm uses computer networks) to explore how firms use ICT,[31] rather than how much they spend on it.

More recently, statistical offices have begun to collect micro level information on investment expenditures in ICT. This type of information has the clear benefit of providing a direct measure of investment that can be quite easily used in a production function context. However, the ICT investment data typically have been collected on a cross sectional basis, requiring the use of different approximations to recover measures of productive stocks of ICT equipment for use in a production function context from flows.[32]

The existence of detailed information on ICT flows over consecutive time periods allows researchers to build measures of ICT stocks more closely following the procedure established in the PIM (see Bloom, Sadun and Van Reenen 2005; Hempell 2005).[33] However, estimating capital stocks using PIM implies specific assumptions regarding the starting point of the PIM recursion.[34] This introduces a degree of measurement error in the estimates of stocks, especially when the time series is short. This problem is partially offset for ICT assets, as they typically have a very high depreciation rate ($\approx$ 30 per cent).

Discussion

Compared to ICT data collected by private organizations, the census-based data yield larger and more representative samples. Moreover, although the ICT measures and the data collection criteria were generally determined independently by each country, recently there has been some multinational collaboration (such as the OECD International Micro Data Initiative), which it is to be hoped will facilitate cross-country comparisons of ICT studies. The main issues in the use of these data are the scant availability of time series information (for both categorical variables and expenditure information) and the problems related to software measurement.

Conclusions on data

Despite recent improvements, the gap between the theoretical conception of ICT capital services and empirical measures of ICT assets is still wide. This applies to industry level data where the estimation of the ICT stocks may be undermined by problems related to the imprecise allocation of flows across different industries (US) and to the use of heavy interpolation techniques (Europe). The problem also applies to firm level data where information about investments is often not available, and if it is, it often covers a very short (or no) time series. In fact, many of the studies discussed rely on even cruder indicator variables whose connection with the theory is likely to be even looser. Software continues to be a major problem as, below the macro level, it is rarely measured directly.

5 RESULTS FROM GROWTH ACCOUNTING EXERCISES

In our view, four stylized facts, which we discuss here, emerge from the macro growth accounting literature:

1. The Solow Paradox arose because ICT was a small part of the capital stock;
2. Productivity growth has accelerated in the US since 1995;

3. This acceleration appears to be linked to ICT;

4. There has been no general acceleration of productivity growth in the EU, mainly due to the poorer performance of the ICT using sectors.

The macro studies are described in Table 5.2. All our summary tables take the same form. Column 1 lists the authors; column 2 the countries and levels of aggregation; column 3 presents the data; and column 4 the measure of ICT used. Columns 5 and 6 respectively present the methods and results.

Some of the earliest studies aimed at understanding the Solow Paradox: that computers were visible everywhere except in the productivity statistics (Solow 1987). Oliner and Sichel (1994) used a growth accounting framework and careful analysis of BEA and BLS data to show that this paradox was more apparent than real. Computers could not make a large contribution to aggregate productivity growth in the 1970s and 1980s because they constituted a very small proportion of aggregate US capital stock (about 2 per cent in 1993). Since then the importance of ICT has grown considerably. Basu et al. (2004) estimate that the share of ICT in US value added in 2000 in the private non-farm economy was 5.5 per cent (1.6 per cent computer, 2.31 per cent software and 1.59 per cent communication). Although it remains a relatively small share of total value added, ICT makes a substantial contribution to productivity growth because of its fast growth rate and high rate of depreciation.

One of the most remarkable facts has been the rapid growth of labour productivity in the US economy since 1995 (see Fig. 5.1). This has continued despite the high-tech crash and the 9/11 terrorist attacks, and reversed a period of slow US productivity growth that set in after the oil shocks of the mid-1970s. Many authors point to ICT as having an important role in this acceleration.

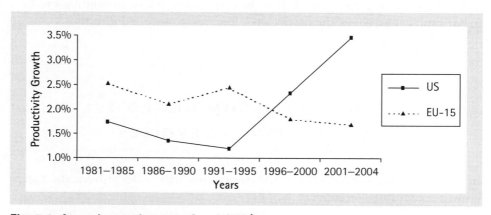

Fig. 5.1 Annual growth rates of real GDP/hour

Source: Groningen Growth and Development Centre

Notice that the acceleration of productivity growth is a double difference (where the Δ is annual averages over many years):

$$\Delta\Delta(y - l) = \Delta\Delta a + s_k\Delta\Delta(k - l) + s_c\Delta\Delta(c - l) + s_m\Delta\Delta(m - l) \qquad (5.1)$$

An example of a growth accounting exercise is given in Table 5.1 (Jorgensen and Stiroh 2000a, b). The authors examine the sources of output growth in the 1974–90 period and the 1995–99 periods (the 1990–95 period covered a deep recession and therefore was not included; however, its inclusion does not have much effect). Looking first at column (1) output growth in the early period was 3.13 percentage points per annum. The contribution of ICT was relatively small—about 0.37 percentage points per year or about 10 per cent ($= .37/3.13$) of the total. In the later period, the contribution made by ICT is more prominent. Output growth rose to 4.76 percentage points per year, 20 per cent, of which 1.01 percentage points were due to ICT. Furthermore, there was a significant increase in TFP growth from a third of a percentage point per year to just less than 1 per cent per year. Some of this TFP growth was concentrated in the ICT producing sectors (semi-conductors, computers, etc.).

Oliner and Sichel (2000, 2002) corroborate Jorgensen's results that ICT made an important contribution to US productivity acceleration. By splitting the economy

Table 5.1 Example of growth accounting: Contributions to US output growth: (US Non–Farm non–Government business sector annual rates of change—% points)

Category	(1) 1974–90	(2) 1995–99	Acceleration (2)–(1)
Output growth	3.13	4.76	1.63
Capital services:[b]	1.62	2.34	0.72
of which: ICT[a]	0.37	1.01	0.64
other capital	1.25	1.33	0.08
Labour services	1.17	1.44	0.27
of which: hours	0.97	1.19	0.22
labour quality	0.20	0.25	0.05
Multi-factor productivity (MFP)	0.33	0.99	0.66
Average labour productivity (ALP)	1.44	2.56	1.12

Source: Derived from Jorgenson and Stiroh (2000a, b), Table 2.
[a] Includes services of consumer computers and software, but not consumer communications equipment.
[b] Includes services of consumer durables.

into ICT producing and using sectors they found that there were important contributions made by ICT in both sectors.

What drives these ICT-led increases in productivity? In the growth accounting framework the model is relatively simple: there has been rapid technological progress in the ICT producing sectors. In particular, the technology cycle for semi-conductors appears to have speeded up after 1994 and this led to a very rapid fall in quality-adjusted prices for ICT goods (Jorgenson 2001). This was reflected in TFP growth in the ICT producing sectors and ICT capital deepening in other sectors (that is, since the user cost of ICT capital had fallen there was substitution into ICT capital and away from other factors of production). Both elements contributed to productivity growth, but the underlying factor is rapidly falling ICT prices.

In a provocative series of articles, Gordon (2000, 2003) takes issue with the view that ICT use played an important role in US productivity growth post-1995. He is sceptical about the ability of ICT to affect productivity growth and in Gordon (2000), he claims that outside the ICT producing sector, productivity growth in the US economy was entirely cyclical. Despite the inherent problems of knowing exactly how to correct for the cycle, this view had some plausibility in the late 1990s. It seems very implausible at the end of 2005. The US economy has suffered some cyclical downturns with the 2000 stock market crash, 9/11, the Iraq War, high oil prices, etc. but productivity growth has continued to power ahead. Furthermore, Stiroh (2002a) produced econometric evidence based on industry data that there was significant productivity growth in the intensive ICT using sectors, even after controlling for macro-economic shocks.

Figure 5.1 also shows productivity growth in Europe. European productivity growth over the whole period since World War II has outstripped US productivity growth, generating a convergence in productivity levels. Since 1995, however, European productivity growth has shown no acceleration.

This is also illustrated in Figure 5.2, which depicts a more straightforward comparison of productivity growth between sectors when we divide the economy into ICT producing sectors, ICT using sectors (those that use ICT extensively, for example, retail, wholesale, and finance), and the rest of the economy (excluding public administration, health, and education). The bars show the acceleration of productivity. In the US economy, illustrated on the left hand-side of the diagram we can see the acceleration in productivity growth, and that this acceleration was strongest in the ICT using sectors (up from 1.2 per cent per annum in the early 1990s to 4.7 per cent per annum after 1995). There is also a smaller acceleration in the ICT producing sectors (up by 1.9 percentage points). Outside these sectors, there was a deceleration in productivity of about half a percentage point. The right hand side of the diagram shows the picture

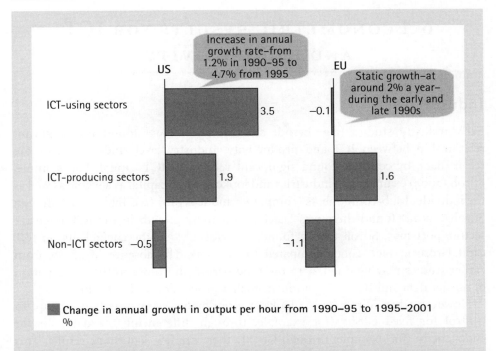

Fig. 5.2 US and European acceleration in productivity growth (market sector)
Source: Derived from O'Mahoney and van Ark 2003.

for the European Union (the 15 members pre-2004). Again, there is productivity acceleration in the European ICT producing sectors, and a deceleration in the non-ICT sectors, but unlike the US, no acceleration of productivity in the ICT using sectors. This is somewhat surprising when the price of ICT is similar throughout the world.

There has been much discussion over this productivity difference between the US and Europe, but no consensus has emerged. Some authors claim it is simply a matter of time before Europe resumes the catching-up process (Blanchard 2004) while others point to more long-term structural problems in Europe such as over-regulated labour and product markets (Gust and Marquez 2004). Basu et al. (2003) examine the differences between the US and the UK—unlike the US but like other European countries, the UK did *not* experience a productivity acceleration 1995–2000 relative to 1990–1995.[35] They found the US–UK difference difficult to account for, but argued that the UK is likely to catch up because of its later investment in complementary organizational capital.

6 Econometric results for ICT and productivity

Industry level

Early industry studies (e.g. Berndt and Morrison 1995) found no significant relationship between ICT and productivity. Industry level studies using more recent data, by contrast, found significant returns to ICT capital. For example, Stiroh (2004) examined 58 industries and looked at ICT capital as a whole as well as the individual sub-components (computers and telecom) (see Table 5.3). Although Stiroh (2002a) found there was faster productivity growth in the ICT intensive sectors post-1995, Stiroh (2004) found no evidence that the coefficients on ICT capital rose in 1996–2000 (compared to 1987–95). The absence of effects from earlier studies may be due less to the time period and more to the combination of noisier data and ICT being a much smaller proportion of total capital.

However, when Stiroh (2004) looks at econometric estimators that attempt to control for fixed effects (for example, through differencing the data) and/or endogeneity (for example, through GMM) there are few significant results. This may be due to genuine misspecification and the absence of an ICT effect or, more plausibly, because the industry data are too coarse for some of the more sophisticated econometric approaches.

Most of the other studies in the industry level literature focus on TFP growth equations of the type discussed above. Overall, the results mirror Stiroh's findings. The ICT coefficients tend to be generally insignificant, and unstable across time and across countries (e.g. Basu et al. 2003, Table 8). The TFP regressions have the problems of the aggregate industry data and the problems discussed in the section on TFP approaches, that ICT is included on the left hand-side and the right hand-side of the estimating equations.

Given concerns about aggregation and other biases attention has shifted to the more micro-level.

Firm level

What do we know?

The results at firm level (or below) are summarized in Table 5.4. There are some prominent features. Firstly, most studies do reveal a positive and significant association of ICT with productivity. This is reassuring as many were undertaken in response to the Solow paradox, which suggested there was no productivity impact from ICT. Secondly, the magnitude of the ICT coefficients is larger than might be expected from the standard neoclassical assumptions underlying the growth accounting framework. A well-known example here is Brynjolfssen and Hitt (2003). Thirdly, the explanation that the high magnitudes are due to organizational capital gets some support from Bresnahan, Brynjolfsson and Hitt (2002) who conducted a survey containing explicit questions on decentralization within firms. Black and Lynch (2001, 2004) and Caroli and Van Reenen (2001) do not find support for interactions between ICT and organization, but they have less sophisticated measures of ICT capital than Brynjolfsson and his colleagues. Bloom, Sadun and Van Reenen (2005) find some support for the organizational capital hypothesis as they find much higher returns for the ICT in US multinationals compared to non-multinationals than between statistically similar establishments in the UK. Fourthly, there is a very wide range of estimates of the elasticity of output with respect to ICT capital. The Stiroh (2004) meta-study is very useful for comparing the sub-set of studies considered here. He finds that the mean of the estimates across studies is about 0.05, which is well above the share of the ICT stock in revenue as noted above. However, the estimates range from an upper end of over 25 per cent to minus 6 per cent. This wide variation is in part driven by methodological choice, but also is strongly suggestive of heterogeneity in the ICT coefficient by country, industry, and type of firm. Bloom, Sadun and Van Reenen's (2005) findings of systematically different returns by ownership type and industry corroborate this. In particular they find that US firms receive a higher return from ICT and this higher return is driven by the sectors that intensively use ICT (the same sectors underlying the US productivity acceleration highlighted in Figure 5.2).

Finally, the evidence for spillovers is very weak. Most studies struggle to find convincing impacts from spillover effects. This suggests that the GPT effects stressed by the theorists may be somewhat exaggerated. While the spillover mechanism is pretty clear for innovation, or R&D, it is much less clear for ICT.[36]

What we do not know

None of the literature has produced convincing evidence of a causal impact on ICT on productivity, for example by analysing a natural experiment. Even the more sophisticated studies rely on standard panel data techniques for dealing with endogeneity. In the economics of education there are some studies examining the impact of computers on school productivity, which use policy variation to try to address the endogeneity issue. Angrist and Lavy (2002), in a study of learning in Israeli schools, find that treating computers as endogenous shows that there may actually be a negative effect from ICT. Machin, McNally and Silva (2006), however, did find some positive effects of ICT in their study of English schools. Despite the absence of a consensus, the attempt to find alternative credible instrumental variables should be a priority for future research.

Another area where more work is needed is specification of the types of com-plementary organizational practices in more detail. What are they? What deter-mines their distribution? Why do some firms appear to be better than others at introducing these organizational practices? Is this the explanation for differences between the US and other OECD countries?

On a more mundane level, the micro studies have focused more on hardware than software because of the lack of good data. Using software as well as hardware, and building in communications, has been done much more systematically at the macro than at the micro level.

Another lacuna exists in establishing a solid link between micro and macro. For example, micro studies may tend to overestimate the benefits of productivity growth if the impact of ICT mainly comes from redistributing the quasi-rents between oligopolistic firms (e.g. in finance). This would not occur if we had 'true' productivity measures, but the dependent variable is usually deflated sales divided by labour which mixes productivity and the mark-up. Some element of the profit mark-up is legitimate product quality, but others may simply be market power from other sources.

Finally, the most prominent studies are still US based. There is a need for more cross-country comparisons at the micro level to examine why there may be differential returns for similar firms in different countries.[37]

6 CONCLUSION

There has been significant progress made since the mid-1990s in the analysis of ICT and productivity. The fall in the quality-adjusted price of computers has enabled researchers to build and analyse very large-scale databases that have revolutionized our understanding of the role of ICT and productivity. The proliferation of databases covering thousands of firms and decades of data has enabled significant intellectual advance.

In this chapter we have presented a very basic neoclassical framework (with a few extensions), which we think is helpful in considering the problem. There does seem to be some reasonable evidence of a strong firm level association between ICT and firm performance (although causality has still to be convincingly demonstrated). We need a much greater understanding of the interactions between the techno-logical and organizational dimensions of firm performance.

Table 5.2 Macroeconomic studies

Authors	Country & level of aggregation	Data	Measure of ICT	Method	Key results
Gordon (2000)	US, 1972–99	Uses data developed by Oliner & Sichel (2000)	Distinguishes between computer hardware, software & communication equipment. Productive stocks are calculated for hardware using detailed BLS equipment data. From Oliner & Sichel (2000).	Builds on previous growth accounting exercises, decomposing output/hour according to (i) cyclical effects; (ii) contribution of ICT producing sector.	Finds no evidence of structural acceleration in productivity during 1995–9 after accounting for cyclical and ICT producing sector effects.
Gordon (2003)	US, 1972–2002	Business cycle analysis uses quarterly BLS data on 4 sectors: non-farm private business, manufacturing, durables, non-durables.	Focus on Oliner & Sichel (2000) results.	Performs further business cycle decomposition Main argument is that role of ICT investment is exaggerated. Stresses that productivity gains have occurred but source lies outside ICT alone.	Main arguments: (1) Results such as Oliner & Sichel (2000) assume an unrealistic instant pay-off to ICT investment. (2) Micro evidence in retail suggests productivity revival is uneven – concentrated in new establishments only. (3) Cross-state comparisons do not exhibit the expected relationship between ICT intensity and state productivity.

(Continued)

Table 5.2 (*Continued*)

Authors	Country & level of aggregation	Data	Measure of ICT	Method	Key results
Gust & Marquez (2004)	13 OECD countries, 1993–2000	OECD national data and regulations database.	2 measures: • Share of ICT producing sectors in GDP (OECD); • ICT expenditure: GDP ratio (World ICT and Service Alliance).	Models labour productivity growth as a function of ICT and other controls (e.g. employment population ratio, country fixed effects). Also look at ICT investment equations.	ICT production and (to a lesser extent) ICT expenditure are associated with higher productivity growth. Labour and start-up regulation significantly retards ICT (although no controls for country fixed effects).
Jorgenson (2005)	G7 economies (Canada, France, Germany, Italy, Japan, UK, US)	van Ark et al. (2002) for Europe. BEA & BLS (US). Statistics Canada. Jorgenson and Motohashi (2005) (Japan).	Investment in ICT hardware and software. Uses internationally consistent prices following Schreyer (2000) and Wyckoff (1995).	Detailed growth accounting analysis of input per capita, output per capita and TFP 'Capital quality' represented by capital input: capital stock ratio.	Late 1990s surge in ICT capital investment is found across the G7. Declining contributions of non-ICT capital offset effect of ICT surge in Japan, France and Germany.

Table 5.3 Industry level studies of ICT and productivity

Authors	Country & level of aggregation	Data	Measure of ICT	Method	Key results
Basu et al. (2003)	US	Manufacturing and Services, 1977–2000 (some only since 1987), BLS, BEA 44 sectors in final regressions.	US data from the BLS capital input data disaggregated by industry. Among equipment, BLS provides additional detail for • information • processing • equipment, and • software (IPES). IPES is composed of 4 broad classes of assets: • computers and related equipment • software • communications equipment • other IPES equipment.	Objective to test the GPT hypothesis by focus on potential presence of unmeasured complementary investments and presence of TFP gains amongst ICT-using and non-using sectors. Run OLS TFP growth regressions in long differences in 3 periods, 1980-90, 1990-95, and 1995-2000.	Lagged ICT capital services growth positively and significantly related to post-1995 growth in TFP. Current ICT capital services growth negatively related to TFP growth (interpet this as suggesting current ICT growth reflects building up organizational capital, their table 8).
Basu et al. (2003)	UK	28 industries, 1979–2000 (BE, Bank of England dataset) in final regressions.	ICT capital services derived using US methodology (Jorgenson & Stiroh 2000a, b) hence geometric, depreciation rate with US prices converted to sterling. Note software levels multiplied by three.	(See above)	Results not clear. ICT generally insignificant, their table 8.

(Continued)

Table 5.3 (*Continued*)

Authors	Country & level of aggregation	Data	Measure of ICT	Method	Key results
Berndt & Morrison (1995)	US industries	2-digit manufacturing, 1968–86.	Define high tech capital as aggregate of office and ICT capital. Covers 4 asset codes OCAM including: • office and computing machinery; • communications equipment; • scientific and engineering instruments; and • photocopy equipment.	Aim is to examine diffusion and impact of high-tech capital. Labour productivity and profitability equations.	Limited evidence of positive relationship between profitability and share of high-tech capital. High-tech capital share negatively correlated with MFP. Greater levels of high-tech capital associated with superior economic performance. However, increasing rates of such capital within industries not necessarily associated with improved performance.
Chun & Nadiri (2002)	US 4-digit industry	NBER-CES Manufacturing industry database.	Decomposes TFP growth in 4 computer industries.	Uses hedonic price information to separate out TFP growth due to product innovation (i.e. quality improvements); process innovation (i.e. technological efficiency improvements) and economies of scale.	Computer industry TFP growth explained by product innovation (30%); process innovation (50%) and economies of scale (20%). Increasing role for product innovation during late 1990s.

					Computer industry contribution to aggregate productivity growth estimated to be 1/3 of total TFP growth.
Crepon & Heckel (2002)	France	Firm data aggregated up to 2-digit sectoral and macro level, 1987–98.	OCAM—office, computing and accounting machinery. Comes from tax declarations of 300,000 French firms (outside financial sector).	Growth accounting exercise.	ICT contributes 0.7%/annum on average (0.4% from production of ICT, 0.3% from capital deepening). Av. value added growth 1987–98 is 2.6% per annum. Share of ICT capital much higher than suggested by French National Accounts (Cette, Mairesse, & Kocoglu 2000).
O'Mahony & Vecchi (2003)	UK & US industries	UK (24), US (31) 1976–2000.	ICT capital stock built from supply and use tables.	TFP regressions including heterogeneous panel estimates.	LR effect of ICT above its factor share.
Oulton & Srinivasan (2003)	UK industries	34 industries 1970–2000 (BE Dataset).	ICT capital stock built from supply and use tables.	Growth accounting, TFP and labour productivity regressions.	ICT capital deepening has positive and significant effect post 1990 (accounts for large proportion of 1990s productivity growth).
Stiroh (2004)	US 2-digit (61 industries)	BEA Industry data on output, investment and capital stocks	(1) ICT capital stock comprising computer hardware and software.	(1) Meta-analyses of 20 existing studies based on methods, type of data and resulting ICT elasticity.	(1) ICT elasticity predictable based on approach and estimation method. Mean estimates include 0.042

(Continued)

Table 5.3 (*Continued*)

Authors	Country & level of aggregation	Data	Measure of ICT	Method	Key results
			(2) Telecoms equipment as separate category of capital.	(2) 'Full disclosure' regression analysis of BEA data using many alternative approaches and reporting all findings.	(value-added) and 0.066 (gross output). (2) BEA data regressions indicate ICT elasticities fall as estimation moves from levels to methods accounting for unobservables. System GMM provides the most sensible estimates (0.05 ICT elasticity).
Stiroh (2002a)	61 US 2-digit industries (1987–2000) 49 US 2-digit industries (1977–2000)	BEA data on industry gross output, labour input and intermediate input. BEA Tangible Wealth Survey used to build capital stocks.	ICT capital built up from wealth stocks on computer hardware (8 types); software (3 types); and communication equipment. Capital Service Flow measure constructed by aggregating individual capital stocks using asset-specific prices.	Uses pre-1995 ICT intensity (both discrete and continuous measures) to assess whether acceleration argument for ICT-using industries is valid. Decomposes labour productivity growth according to 3 sectors: ICT producing industries, ICT using industries, those sectors 'isolated' from ICT	Pre-1995 ICT intensity related to patterns of acceleration for discrete and continuous measures. Acceleration for ICT intensive industries approximately 2% more than other industries. Decomposition finds that ICT using industries contribute 0.83% of total acceleration with ICT producing industries accounting for 0.17%. Isolated industries made a −0.21% contribution.

Stiroh (2002b)	US 2-digit Manufacturing (18 industries *15 years)	BLS multifactor productivity database for manufacturing (18 industries from 1984–1999).	ICT capital including total value of hardware, software and telecommunications equipment Computer capital defined as hardware and software assets only.	Tests a key spillover hypothesis: that ICT impacts on TFP if network effects or externalities are present. Uses traditional difference-in-difference, and traditional labour productivity, and TFP regressions to test above hypothesis.	Finds some positive effects of ICT on average labour productivity but not TFP. Tele-communications capital has a negative association with productivity. In general, no strong evidence of spillover-type effects of ICT on productivity.
van Ark et al. (2002)	12 EU countries and US (EU countries include Austria, Denmark, Finland, France, Germany, Ireland, Italy, Netherlands, Portugal, Spain, Sweden, UK)	Manufacturing and Services, 1980–2000 (Using input-output tables).	(1) Broad definition of ICT as comprising the whole category of office and computer equipment—including peripherals; (2) Separate investment series on ICT investments used where available (applies to most assets for Denmark, France, Netherlands, Italy, UK, only to specific assets for Germany and Spain). (3) Used a Commodity Flow Method to fill gaps.	Concentrates on building comparable ICT investment and ICT capital data across EU and US then employs standard growth accounting and labour productivity equations.	Similar growth rates ICT real capital formation and capital services for US and EU. Investment patterns similar—office equipment grew strongly in the 1980s and from the late 1990s. Growth of communication equipment and software accelerated after 1995 (more so in the US). ICT investment share levels lower in the EU—2/3 of US level throughout the period.

(Continued)

Table 5.3 (*Continued*)

Authors	Country & level of aggregation	Data	Measure of ICT	Method	Key results
			This supply side method first computes total amount of ICT commodities available in a specific year as value of total ICT production less ICT exports plus ICT imports.		Relative contribution of ICT to EU labour productivity growth close to US but slowdown in EU growth reduces the absolute contribution. Stronger TFP effects for ICT producing sectors in the US during the 1990s.
van Ark & Inklaar (2005)	US and European industries (France, Germany, Netherlands, UK)	60 industries, 1987–2004 Specially constructed GGDC dataset.	Investment series for different types of ICT-related capital expenditure.	Growth accounting equations for macro-level data. Labour productivity equations for industry data ('shift-share' approach following Stiroh (2002b). TFP equation to test for spillovers.	Lower ICT contribution to EU growth has continued through early 2000s. US–EU differential increased following strong labour productivity gains in US market services (i.e. non-government sector). No evidence of ICT spillovers to TFP. Hypothesis of U-shaped ICT returns pattern: initial 'hard savings' followed by experimentation period then 'soft savings' as capital complementarities develop.

Table 5.4 Firm–level studies of ICT and productivity

Authors	Country and level of aggregation	Data	Measure of ICT	Method	Key results
Atrostic and Nguyen (2005)	US establishments	Computer Network Use Supplement (CNUS) of the 1999 Annual Survey of Manufactures (ASM). Approximately 30,000 plants.	Discrete indicator of whether establishment uses a computer network.	3 factor production function (incorporating materials). Endogeneity of networks addressed by explaining network presence as function of past performance (2SLS).	OLS indicates that labour productivity is 3.7% higher for network-using establishments. 2SLS indicates a 7.2% effect. Lower productivity in earlier periods associated with networks. Interpreted as evidence that establishments may use networks to catch up.
Black and Lynch (2001)	US establishments	Educational Quality of the Workforce– National Employer's Survey (EQW-NES) matched with Longitudinal Research Database (LRD) 638 establishments in manufacturing, 1987–1993.	Proportion of non-managers within establishment using computers. Many controls for workplace practices and characteristics (education, union presence) to account for complementarities.	Cross-sectional Cobb-Douglas production function. 2-step fixed effects approach (i.e. second stage involves regressing firm effects on a set of explanatory variables).	ICT variable significant and positive in cross-sectional production function. ICT significant in 2-step within estimator, but not GMM version.
Black and Lynch (2004)	US establishments	1993 and 1997 waves of the EQW-NES. Panel of 766 establishments (again matched with LRD).	Proportion of non-managers within establishment using computers. Again, controls for other (complementary) workplace practices and characteristics.	Cross-sectional Cobb-Douglas production functions for 1997 wave. Includes interaction effects in production functions.	ICT variable significant and positive in cross-sectional production function Interaction terms of ICT variable with workplace practices and characteristics not significant.

Table 5.4 (*Continued*)

Authors	Country and level of aggregation	Data	Measure of ICT	Method	Key results
		284 establishments in the balanced panel.		Production functions with fixed effects (for balanced panel).	ICT variable significant in fixed effect model for balanced panel.
				Uses estimates in a decomposition of MFP growth (benchmarked against BLS estimates).	Workplace innovation makes 1.4% contribution to MFP growth (approximately 89% of total MFP growth).
Bloom, Sadun & Van Reenen (2005)	British establishments 1995–2004 (un-balanced panel).	7,000 establishments.	ICT capital constructed from 3 ONS surveys (FAR, Quarterly Capital expenditure Survey, BSCI) PIM.	Estimation of panel production functions and TFP regressions. Compare OLS, within–groups, GMM and OP.	ICT significant impact on productivity. Effect greater for US than non-US multinationals or domestic firms. US effect also stronger in ICT intensive industries.
Bloom, Draca, Kretschmer and Van Reenen (2005)	Britain (1994–2004).	About 3,000 firms in 1994–2004.	Constructed using Harte-Hanks hardware and software data (recorded at business site level). Measures include: (i) Value of ICT hardware (ii) PCs/employee.	Production functions estimated by OLS, within-groups and GMM. Tests for heterogeneity of ICT impact across different firm characteristics (e.g. size, sector, time period). Tests for spillovers at the regional and industry level.	Significant and positive effect of ICT on productivity (elasticity with respect to output 0.035 on within–groups specification). No evidence of ICT spillovers at industry or region level.

				Reduced form investment models.	
Bresna-han, Brynjo-lfsson & Hitt (2002)	US firms across all types of industries.	331 firms (NB survey asked managers about characteristics at level of the 'typical establishment').	ICT capital calculated using CII data on firm computer hardware inventories only. Author's (cross-sectional) survey of organizational practices and skills circa 1995–6. Compustat accounts information.	Correlation analysis of relationship between potential complemen-tary inputs. Input choice functions. Production functions with interaction terms.	Complements (ICT, organization and skills) significantly and positively co-vary. Skills and organization significant as determinants of ICT demand. ICT-Skill and ICT-Organization interaction variables significant in production function.
Brynjo-lfsson, Hitt & Yang (2002)	US firms	1987–97 Compustat firms matched with CII data and author's (cross-sectional) organizational practices survey. Final sample features 272 firms with matched data and 2,097 observations in total.	CII measure of the market value of computer equipment at a firm (calculated based on replacement cost).	Estimates market value equation focusing on how IT and organizational practices represent intangible assets. OLS, Least absolute deviations, Fixed and Random Effects estimation of market value equation. Also, use long difference specification. Nonpara-metric plot of relationship between organization, ICT and market value.	Key organizational characteristics correlated with ICT capital but not physical capital. ICT capital associated with higher market value. Interaction term between organization and ICT significant – firms with combinations of ICT and good organizational practices have the highest market value.

(Continued)

Table 5.4 (*Continued*)

Authors	Country and level of aggregation	Data	Measure of ICT	Method	Key results
Brynjo-lfsson & Hitt (2003)	US firms	527 large Compustat firms 1987–94.	Computer capital stock CII (Harte Hanks) value of total ICT stock; IDG (firms stated value of mainframes plus no. PCs).	OLS, short and long differences. Production function and TFP equation.	In long differences ICT coefficient above ICT capital share in revenue.
Dewan & Min (1997)	US firms	Computerworld data matched to Compustat 1,131 observations (unbalanced) with maximum of 304 different firms observed in a single year (1988–92).	Market value of computer hardware and labour expenses for ICT staff.	CES-Translog production functions.	Some evidence of excess returns to ICT capital.
Forth & Mason (2003)	UK firms	1997–9 International Benchmarking Survey; 308 firms, c. 900 observations.	Categorical indicators of different types of ICT.	OLS and IV estimation.	Generally positive impact; interactions with skill shortages.
Gilchrist, Gurbaxani & Town (2003)	US firms, 1986–93	CII matched to Compustat. Unbalanced panel of 580 firms.	ICT hardware value PCs/employee.	GMM estimation of production function. Regressions of Solow residual on inputs.	ICT coefficient approximately equal to cost share; PCs have additional impact in durable goods sectors. Growth of PCs significant in Solow residual regression, also with additional impact in the durable goods sector.

Greenan, Mairesse & Topiol-Bensaid (2001)	French firms, 1986–94	SUSE (System of Unified Statistics on Enterprises) and ESE (Employment Structure Survey). Approximately 3,000 manufacturing firms and 2,500 in services.	Value of office and computing equipment. No. of specialized workers (computer, electronics, research and analysis staff).	Mainly examines correlations between ICT, R&D and skills. Some production function estimation.	ICT effect is not significant when firm fixed effects are included. Share of blue-collar workers falls with increase in ICT (for all indicators).
Greenan & Mairesse (1996)	French firms, 1987–93	TOTTO (specialized survey of techniques and organization of work) matched to INSEE firm database for 1987, 1991, 1993. Approximately 3,000 observations/year.	No. of employees using computers at work (calculated from sample).	OLS Cobb-Douglas production function, no fixed effects.	ICT coefficient stable across models for all 3 years. Coefficient of approximately 0.20.
Gretton, Gali & Parham (2004)	Australian firms	Australian Business Longitudinal Study Panel of three years 1988-9; 1993-4; 1998-9. Sample sizes not clearly stated.	Binary indicator and duration dummies.	OLS productivity growth equation. Controls include lagged level of productivity, capital growth separately for 8 sectors.	ICT positive in most specifications, significant in only 2 specifications.
Halti-wanger, Jarmin & Schank (2003)	US and Germany	Matched ASM and CNUS for the US, 1999–2000. 22,000 observations IAB manufacturing sector panel for Germany, 2000-1.	Total investment in computers and peripheral equipment (US) Total investment in information and communication technology in previous business year (Germany).	Compares the productivity outcomes for similar ICT intensive firms in both countries High ICT intensity defined by whether firms are in the top 25% viz ICT	ICT intensive US firms exhibit greater productivity dispersion, particularly among younger businesses.

(Continued)

Table 5.4 (*Continued*)

Authors	Country and level of aggregation	Data	Measure of ICT	Method	Key results
		3,500 observations used in regression analysis.	Proportion of employees with internet access (US and Germany).	investment and internet access. Assumes that the most ICT intense firms have a propensity to 'change technologies'.	
Hempell (2005)	German and Dutch firms	1998 CIS (but with lags as IVs); distribution and business services; Netherlands 972; Germany 995.	ICT expenditure converted into a stock.	GMM SYS (but instruments appear invalid as Sargan-Hansen test rejects).	Significant ICT effect; many complementarities.
Hendel (1999)	US establishments	Comtec survey of 7,895 establishments (conducted 1994 and 1998). Note studies only 240 banking and insurance establishments from 1988 survey. PC price and characteristics data (used by Berndt & Griliches 1993).	Detailed information PC hardware, including brand, type, quality.	Explicit model of establishment-level demand for differentiated types of PCs. Based on buyers making multiple discrete choices. Task-based model of why establishments choose different types of computer equipment.	Estimated return on PC investment calculated as 92%. 10% increase in performance-to-price ratio for microprocessors estimated to raise user surplus by 2.2%.
Lehr & Lichtenberg (1998)	US govt agencies (1987–92)	BLS Productivity Measurement Program (Data on agency output and productivity).	Replacement value of computer capital (via CII).	Production functions based on BLS estimates of the output of government	Excess returns to computer capital (with 0.061 co-efficient on computer

		CII 44 agencies in matched data.			services (44 agencies).	capital compared to 0.014 share of IT capital in total cost).
Lehr & Lichtenberg (1999)	US 1977–93	Enterprise Survey (Census Bureau). Auxiliary Establishment Survey. Compustat CII Matched sample includes 5,000 firms.	Replacement value of computer capital (via CII). Investment in computer equipment (Census Bureau).	Production function regressions, including terms for specific types of equipment. Inventory regressions (i.e. test whether computers facilitate just-in-time style production strategies).		Excess returns to computer capital still found after including firm fixed effects. These returns peak in 1986–7. Negative association between computer capital and inventories.
Lichtenberg (1995)	US	190 to 450 firms.	Computer and non-computer capital stock, ICT and non-ICT labour.	OLS, no IV or fixed effects.		In long differences ICT coefficient above cost share.
Matteucci et al. (2005)	Germany, Italy and UK	Germany IAB 3,168 observations 1997–2000. Italy 'Capitalia' manufacturing firms 1995–2000, 3,918 observations (unbalanced) and 1,119 (balanced) ABI linked with 2001 ONS E-commerce survey (2,422 observations).	Lagged ICT investments plus instruments based on firm training patterns (Germany). Single year of ICT investment information. Duration of internet access at firm and proportion of workers using a PC.	Regressing firm fixed effects on various characteristics to explain determinants of productivity TFP Equation. Cross-sectional Cobb-Douglas production function.		Significant effect of ICT in manufacturing but not services. Weakly significant effect of ICT (10% level). Significant impact for PCs/worker in service sector.
Wilson (2004)	US 1998	1998 ACES matched with Compustat firms. 3,000 firms in matched sample.	Total Computer and Peripheral Equipment Investment as measured in ACES.	Looks at the effects of different capital types on variously defined measures of TFP.		Positive effects of computer capital on TFP 'High-tech' capital complementary with 'low-tech' capital.

(Continued)

Table 5.4 (*Continued*)

Authors	Country and level of aggregation	Data	Measure of ICT	Method	Key results
				Uses interaction effects to examine complementarities and substitutability between capital types Calculates marginal products for different capital types.	Different types of capital are substitutable within their technology class (i.e. high-tech vs low-tech). Marginal products for computers, communication equipment and software are higher than those suggested by BLS rental prices.

REFERENCES

AGHION, P. and HOWITT, P. (1998). *Endogenous Growth Theory*. Cambridge, MA: MIT Press.

ANGRIST, J. and LAVY, V. (2002). 'New Evidence on Classroom Computers and Pupil Learning'. *Economic Journal*, 112(482): 735–65.

ARELLANO, M. and BOND, S. (1991). 'Some Tests of Specification for Panel Data: Monte Carlo Evidence and an Application to Employment Functions'. *Review of Economic Studies*, 58: 277–97.

ATHEY, S. and STERN, S. (2002). 'The Impact of Information Technology on Emergency Health Care Outcomes'. *RAND Journal of Economics*, 33(3): 399–432.

ATROSTIC, B. K. and NGUYEN, S. V. (2005). 'IT and Productivity in US Manufacturing: Do Computer Networks Matter?' *Economic Enquiry*, 43(3): 493–506.

——, BOEGH-NIELSEN, P., MOTOHASHI, K. et al. (2004). 'Information Technology, Productivity, and Growth in Enterprises: Evidence from New International Micro Data', in OECD (ed.), *The Economic Impact of ICT: Measurement, Evidence and Implications*. Paris: OECD, 279–98.

BAKER, G. and HUBBARD, T. (2004). 'Contractability and Asset Ownership: On Board Computers and Governance in US Trucking'. *Quarterly Journal of Economics*, 119(4): 1443–80.

BASU, S., FERNALD, J. G., OULTON, N. and SRINIVASAN, S. (2004). 'The Case of the Missing Productivity Growth: Or, Does Information Technology Explain Why Productivity Accelerated in the United States but not the United Kingdom?' in M. Gertler and K. Rogoff (eds), *NBER Macroeconomics Annual 2003*. Cambridge, MA: MIT Press, 9–63.

BECKER, R., HALTIWANGER, J., JARMIN, R., et al. (2005). 'Micro and Macro Data Integration: The Case of Capital', CBS (Census Bureau Staff) Working Paper, http://www.nber.org/books/CRIW-naccts/becker-et-al4-17-05.pdf.

BERNDT, E. R. and GRILICHES, Z. (1993). 'Price Indexes for Microcomputers: An Exploratory Study', in M. F. Foss, M. Manser and A. H. Young (eds), *Price Measurements and their Uses. National Bureau of Economic Research Studies in Income and Wealth, Vol. 57*. Chicago: University of Chicago Press, 63–93.

—— and MORRISON, C. J. (1995). 'High-tech Capital Formation and Economic Performance in U.S. Manufacturing Industries: An Exploratory Analysis', *The Journal of Econometrics*, 65: 9–43.

BLACK, S. and LYNCH, L. (2001). 'How to Compete: The Impact of Workplace Practices and Information Technology on Productivity'. *The Review of Economics and Statistics*, 83(3): 434–45.

—— (2004). 'What's Driving the New Economy? The Benefits of Workplace Innovation'. *The Economic Journal*, 114: F97–F116.

BLANCHARD, O. (2004). 'The Economic Future of Europe'. *Journal of Economic Perspectives*, 18(4): 3–26.

BLOOM, N., GRIFFITH, R. and VAN REENEN, J. (2002). 'Do R&D Tax Credits Work?' *Journal of Public Economics*, 85: 1–31.

——, SADUN, R. and VAN REENEN, J. (2005). 'It Ain't What You Do It's the Way You Do IT: Testing Explanations of Productivity Growth Using US Affiliates'. Mimeo. Centre for Economic Performance, London School of Economics.

——, SCHANKERMAN, M., and VAN REENEN, J. (2005). 'Technology Spillovers and Product Market Rivalry', CEP Discussion Paper No. 675. Centre for Economic Performance, LSE.

—— DRACA, M., KRETSCHMER, T. and VAN REENEN, J. (2005) 'IT Productivity, Spillovers and Investment: Evidence from a Panel of UK Firms'. Mimeo. Centre for Economic Performance, LSE.

BLUNDELL, R. and BOND, S. (1998). 'Initial Conditions and Moment Restrictions in Dynamic Panel Data Models', *Journal of Econometrics*, 88: 115–43.

—— (2000). 'GMM Estimation with Persistent Panel Data: An Application to Production Functions'. *Econometric Reviews*, 19(3): 321–40.

BOND, B. and AYLOR, T. (2000). 'Investment in New Structures and Equipment in 1992 by Using Industries'. Survey of Current Business, December.

BOND, S. and SODERBOM, M. (2005). 'Adjustment Costs and Identification of Cobb Douglas Production Functions'. Mimeo. University of Oxford.

BOSWORTH, B. and TRIPLETT, J. (2001). 'Productivity in the Services Sector', in R. M. Stern (ed.), *Services in the International Economy*. Ann Arbor, MI: Michigan State University Press, 240.

BRESNAHAN, T. F. and TRAJTENBERG, M. (1995). 'General Purpose Technologies: "Engines of Growth"?', *Journal of Econometrics*, 65(1): 83–108.

BRESNAHAN, T. F., BRYNJOLFSSON, E. and HITT, L. M. (2002). 'Information Technology, Workplace Organization and the Demand for Skilled Labour: Firm-level Evidence', *Quarterly Journal of Economics*, 117(1): 339–76.

BRYNJOLFSSON, E., HITT, L. M. and YANG, S. (2002), 'Intangible Assets: Computers and Organizational Capital'. *Brookings Papers on Economic Activity: Macroeconomics*, 1, 137–99.

BRYNJOLFSSON, E. and HITT, L. (1995). 'Information Technology as a Factor of Production: The Role of Differences Among Firms'. *Economics of Innovation and New Technology* (SI on Information Technology and Productivity Paradox) 3(4): 183–200.

—— (2003). 'Computing Productivity: Firm-level Evidence'. *Review of Economics and Statistics*, 85(4): 793–808.

CAROLI, E. and VAN REENEN, J. (2001). 'Skill-Biased Organizational Change? Evidence from a Panel of British and French Establishments'. *Quarterly Journal of Economics*, 116: 1449–92.

CHENNELLS, L. and VAN REENEN, J. (2002). 'The Effects of Technical Change on Skills, Wages and Employment: A Survey of the Micro-econometric Evidence', in Y. L'Horty, N. Greenan and J. Mairesse, *Productivity, Inequality and the Digital Economy*. Cambridge, MA: MIT Press, 175–225.

CETTE, G., MAIRESSE, J. and KOCOGLU, Y. (2000). 'La mésure de l'investissement en technologies de l'information et de la communication: quelques considérations métho-dologiques'. *Economies et Statistique*, 339(40): 73–91.

CHUN, H. and NADIRI, M. I. (2002). 'Decomposing Productivity Growth in the US Computer Industry'. *NBER Working Paper 9267*.

CREPON, B. and HECKEL, T. (2002). 'Computerization in France: An Evaluation based on Individual Company Data'. *Review of Income and Wealth*, 1: 1–22.

CRISCUOLO, C. and WALDRON, K. (2003). 'Computer Network Use and Productivity in the United Kingdom'. Mimeo. Centre for Research into Business Activity and Office of National Statistics.

DEWAN, S. and MIN, C. (1997). 'The Substitution of Information Technology for Other Factors of Production: A Firm-Level Analysis'. *Management Science*, 43(12): 1660–75.

DEDRICK, J., GURBAXANI, V. and KRAEMER, K. (2003). 'Information Technology and Economic Performance: A Critical Review of the Empirical Evidence'. *ACM Computing Surveys*, 35(1): 1–28.

DOMAR, E. D. (1961), 'On the Measurement of Technological Change'. *Economic Journal*, LXXI: 709–29.

DOMS, M., DUNN, W., OLINER, S. and SICHEL, D. (2004). 'How Fast Do Personal Computers Depreciate? Concepts and New Estimates', *NBER Working Paper No. 10521*.

FORTH, J. and MASON, G. (2003). 'Persistence of Skill Deficiencies across Sectors, 1999–2001', in G. Mason and R. Wilson (eds), *Employers Skill Survey: New Analyses and Lessons Learned*. Nottingham: Department for Education and Skills, 71–89.

FRAUMENI, B. M. (1997). 'The Measurement of Depreciation in the U.S. National Income and Product Accounts'. *Survey of Current Business*, July: 7–23.

GESKE, M. J., RAMEY, V. A. and SHAPIRO, M. D. (2004) 'Why do Computers Depreciate?' *NBER Working Paper 10831*, http://www.nber.org/papers/w10831.pdf.

GILCHRIST, S., GURBAXANI, V. and TOWN, R. (2001). 'Productivity and the PC Revolution', CRITO Research Papers.

GORDON, R. (2000). 'Does the New Economy Measure up to the Great Inventions of the Past?' *The Journal of Economic Perspectives*, 14(4): 49–74.

—— (2003). 'High-Tech Innovation and Productivity Growth: Does Supply Create its Own Demand?' NBER Working Paper No 9437.

GREENAN, N. and MAIRESSE, J. (1996). 'Computers and Productivity in France: Some Evidence'. NBER Working Paper 5836.

GRILICHES, Z. (1992). 'The Search for R&D Spillovers'. *Scandinavian Journal of Economics*, 94(SI): S29–47.

—— and HAUSMAN, J. (1986). 'Errors in Variables in Panel Data'. *Journal of Econometrics*, 31: 93–188.

GRIMM, B., MOULTON, B. and WASSHAUSEN, D. B. (2002). 'Information Processing Equipment and Software in the National Accounts'. BEA Working Paper 02, April.

GUST, C. and MARQUEZ, J. (2004). 'International Comparisons of Productivity Growth: The Role of Information Technology and Regulatory Practices'. *Labour Economics*, 11: 33–58.

—— and TOPIOL-BENSAID, A. (2001) 'Information Technology and Research and Development Impact on Productivity and Skills: Looking for Correlations on French Firm Level Data', in M. Pohjola (ed.), *Information Technology Productivity and Economic Growth*. Oxford: Oxford Univerisity Press, 119–48.

HALTIWANGER, J., JARMIN, R. and SCHANK, T. (2003). 'Productivity, Investment in ICT and Market Experimentation: Micro Evidence from Germany and the U.S.' *Center for Economic Studies Working Paper CES-03-06*. Washington DC: Bureau of the Census.

HEMPELL, T. (2005). 'What's Spurious? What's Real? Measuring the Productivity Impacts of ICT at the Firm Level'. *Empirical Economics*, 30(2): 427–64.

HELPMAN, E. and TRAJTENBERG, M. (1998). 'A Time to Sow and a Time to Reap: Growth Based on General Purpose Technologies', in E. Helpman (ed.), *General Purpose Technologies and Economic Growth*. Cambridge, MA: The MIT Press, 85–119.

HENDEL, I. (1999). 'Estimating Multiple Discrete Choice Models: An Application to Computerization Returns'. *The Review of Economic Studies*, 66(1): 423–46.

HOLDWAY, M. (2001). 'Quality-Adjusting Computer Prices in the Producer Price Index: An Overview', http://www.bls.gov/ppi/ppicomqa.htm, accessed 3 Nov. 2006.

JORGENSON, D. W. (2001). 'Information Technology and the U.S. Economy'. *American Economic Review*, 91: 1–32.

—— (2005). 'Information Technology and the G7 Economies'. Mimeo.

—— and STIROH, K. J. (2000b). 'Raising the Speed Limit: US Economic Growth in the Information Age'. *Brookings Papers on Economic Activity*, 1: 125–211.

——, Ho, M. and STIROH, K. J. (2003). 'Growth of U.S. Industries and Investments in Information Technology and Higher Education'. *Economic Systems Research*, 15(3): 279–325.

—— and MOTOHASHI, K. (2005). 'Information Technology and the Japanese Economy', NBER Working Papers 11801, National Bureau of Economic Research, Inc., http://www.nber.org/papers/w11801.pdf

—— and STIROCH, K. J. (2000a). 'US Economic Growth at the Industry Level'. *American Economic Review*, 90: 161–8.

LANDEFELD, S. and GRIMM, B. (2000). 'A Note on the Impact of Hedonics and Computers on Real GDP'. *Survey of Current Business*, Dec. 17–22, http://www.bea.gov/bea/articles/NATIONAL/NIPAREL/2000/1200hm.pdf

LANE, R. N. (1999). Appraisal Report, 'Large Aerospace Firm', personal property, Los Angeles County, March 1, 1995 (revised February 2, 1999), Lane, Westly Inc.: Burlinghame, CA.

LEHR, B. and LICHTENBERG, F. (1998). 'Computer Use and Productivity Growth in US Federal Government Agencies, 1977–1992'. *The Journal of Industrial Economics*, 46(2): 257–79.

—— and —— (1999). 'Information Technology and its Impact on Firm-level Productivity: Evidence from Government and Private Data Sources, 1977–1993'. *Canadian Journal of Economics*, 32(2): 335–62.

LEVINSOHN, J. and PETRIN, A. (2003). 'Estimating Production Functions using Inputs to Control for Unobservables'. *Review of Economic Studies*, 70: 317–42.

LICHTENBERG, F. (1995). 'The Output Contributions of Computer Equipment and Personnel: A Firm Level Analysis'. *Economics of Innovation and New Technology*, 3: 201–17.

MACHIN S., McNALLY, S. and SILVA, O. (2006). 'New Technology in Schools: Is There a Payoff?' Mimeo. CEP-LSE, http://personal.lse.ac.uk/silvao/ICTinSchools.pdf

—— and VAN REENEN, J. (1998). 'Technology and Changes in Skill Structure: Evidence from Seven OECD Countries'. *The Quarterly Journal of Economics*, 113(4): 1215–44.

MALIRANTA, M. and ROUVINEN, P. (2004). 'ICT and Business Productivity: Finnish Micro-level Evidence', in OECD (ed.), *The Economic Impact of ICT – Measurement, Evidence and Implications*. Paris: OECD. 213–39.

MATTEUCCI, N., O'MAHONEY, M., ROBINSON, C. et al. (2005). 'Productivity, Workplace Performance and ICT: Evidence for Europe and the US'. *The Scottish Journal of Political Economy*, 52(3): 359–86.

NADIRI, I. and MUN, S. (2002). 'Information Technology Externalities: Empirical Evidence from 42 U.S. Industries'. NBER Working Paper 9272.

OLINER, S. D. and SICHEL, D. (1994). 'Computers and Output Growth: How Big is the Puzzle?' *Brookings Papers in Economic Activity*, 2: 273–334.

—— and —— (2000). 'The Resurgence of Growth in the Late 1990s: Is Information Technology the Story?' *Journal of Economic Perspectives*, 14: 3–22.

—— and —— (2002). 'Information Technology and Productivity: Where Are We Now and Where Are We Going?' *Federal Reserve Bank of Atlanta Review*, 87(3): 15–44.

OLLEY, S. and PAKES, A. (1996). 'The Dynamics of Productivity in the Telecommunications Industry'. *Econometrica*, 64: 1263–97.

O'MAHONY, M. and DE BOER, W. (2002). 'Britain's Relative Productivity Performance: Has Anything Changed?' *National Institute Economic Review*, 179 (Jan.): 38–43.

—— and VECCHI, M. W. (2003). 'Is There an ICT Impact on TFP? A Heterogeneous Dynamic Panel Approach'. National Institute of Economic and Social Research.

—— and B. VAN ARK (eds) (2003). 'EU Productivity and Competitiveness: An Industry Perspective. Can Europe Resume the Catching-up Process?' Luxembourg: Office for Official Publications of the European Communities.

OULTON, N. (2002). 'ICT and Productivity Growth in the UK'. *Oxford Review of Economic Policy*, 18(3): 363–79.

—— and SRINIVASAN, S. (2003). 'Capital Stocks, Capital Services, and Depreciation: An Integrated Framework'. Bank of England Working Paper no. 192, www.bankofengland.co.uk.

SCHREYER, P. (2000). *The Contribution of Information and Communication Technology to Output Growth: A Study of the G7 Countries*. Paris: OECD.

—— (2002). 'Computer Price Indices and International Growth and Productivity Comparisons'. *Review of Income and Wealth*, 48(1): 33–57.

SIANESI, B. and VAN REENEN, J. (2003). 'Education and Economic Growth: A Review of the Literature'. *Journal of Economic Surveys*, 17(2): 157–200.

SOLOW, R. (1957). 'Technical Change and the Aggregate Production Function'. *Review of Economics and Statistics*, 39: 312–20.

—— (1987). 'We'd Better Watch Out'. *New York Times Book Review* (July 12): 36.

STIROH, K. J. (2002a). 'Information Technology and the US Productivity Revival: What Do The Industry Data Say?' *American Economic Review*, 92(5): 1559–76.

—— (2002b). 'Are ICT Spillovers Driving the New Economy?' *Review of Income and Wealth*, 48(1): 33–57.

—— (2004). 'Reassessing the Impact of IT in the Production Function: A Meta-analysis and Sensitivity Tests'. Mimeo, New York Federal Reserve.

SYVERSON, C. (2004). 'Market Structure and Productivity: A Concrete Example'. *Journal of Political Economy*, 112(6): 1181–222.

VAN ARK, B. and INKLAAR, R. (2005). 'Catching Up or Getting Stuck? Europe's Troubles to Exploit ICT's Productivity Potential'. *GGDC Research Memorandum GD-79*, http://www.ggdc.net/pub/online/gd79(online).pdf

——, MELKA, J., MULDER, N., TIMMER, M. et al. (2002). 'ICT Investment and Growth Accounts for the European Union, 1980–2000'. Final Report on 'ICT and growth accounting' prepared for the DG Economics and Finance of the European Commission, Brussels, http://www.eco.rug.nl/GGDC/dseries/Data/ICT/euictgrowth.pdf.

WILSON, D. (2004). 'IT and Beyond: The Contribution of Heterogeneous Capital to Productivity'. Working Papers in Applied Economic Theory, 2004-13. Federal Reserve Bank of San Francisco.

WOLFF, E. (2002). 'Productivity, Computerization and Skill Change'. NBER Working Papers 8743.

WYCKOFF, A. W. (1995). 'The Impact of Computer Prices on International Comparisons of Productivity'. *Economics of Innovation and New Technology*, 3–4(3): 277–93.

YANG, S. and BRYNJOLFSSON, E. (2001). 'Intangible Assets and Growth Accounting: Evidence from Computer Investments', www.ebusiness.mit.edu/erik.

NOTES

1. Of course, we could consider multiple sub-divisions of the capital stock and other factors of production.
2. The inputs should be expressed in terms of the flows of services that the input stocks create, which feeds into the flow of output. See the discussion of the data.
3. Helpman and Trajtenberg (1998); Yang and Brynjolffson (2001).
4. Note that finding a positive coefficient on the interaction is not sufficient to establish that the two factors are complementary in the Hicks-Allen sense. A positive coefficient makes Allen elasticity more likely, however.
5. See Griliches (1992); Bloom, Schankerman and Van Reenen (2005).

6. Such as changes in the tax price, see Bloom, Griffith, and Van Reenen (2002) for examples from R&D.

7. Stiroh (2004); Bloom, Sadun and Van Reenen (2005) and Hempell (2005).

8. Although note that the bias will be towards zero and researchers in the micro literature generally find IT coefficients that are higher than we would expect.

9. Additional instruments dated t-3, t-4, etc. become available as the panel progresses through time.

10. The conditions are that the initial change in productivity is uncorrelated with the fixed effect $E(\Delta y_{i2} \eta_i) = 0$ and that initial changes in the endogenous variables are also uncorrelated with the fixed effect $E(\Delta x_{i2} \eta_i) = 0$.

11. For notational simplicity we abstract from plant age.

12. Numerous extensions to the basic OP methodology have been suggested. First, we consider the additional selection correction originally suggested by the authors. Second, Levinsohn and Petrin (2003) suggest using intermediate inputs as an alternative proxy for the unobserved productivity term. This has attractions for plant level data where investment is zero in a non-trivial number of cases. Ackerberg, Caves, and Frazer (2005) and Bond and Soderbom (2005) emphasize the identification problems underlying the original OP set-up, which implicitly requires variation in firm-specific input prices. Bond and Soderbom argue for the GMM approach discussed in the previous sub-section, which is identified in the presence of differential adjustment costs.

13. If one is willing to work with an aggregate measure of capital, extra care must be taken in aggregating the different asset types. For a detailed treatment of the issue see Oulton and Srinivasan (2003).

14. Rental prices are also very important in constructing Tornqvist aggregate service flows of assets of different types. Rental prices rather than asset prices are used as weights to account for differences in the rate of return to capital, the rate of economic depreciation, the rate of nominal appreciation of assets and their tax treatment.

15. Oulton and Srinivasan (2003), O'Mahony and de Boer (2002), van Ark et al. (2002).

16. In this framework ICT is defined as the aggregation of the different ICT investment series produced by the BEA, i.e. mainframe computers, personal computers (PCs), direct access storage devices, printers, terminals, tape drivers, storage devices.

17. The BEA also makes adjustments to reflect trade costs and transportation margins (to convert into purchaser value).

18. These two tables represent the main sources for the construction of the ICT capital stocks used in Jorgenson and Stiroh (2000a, 2000b), Jorgenson, Ho and Stiroh (1999), Stiroh (2002a, 2002b, 2004), Oliner and Sichel (2000), Bosworth and Triplett (2002), Basu et al. (2003), Nadiri and Mun (2002), Chun and Nadiri (2002), Berndt and Morrison (1995).

19. The ICT deflators are described in Grimm, Moulton and Wasshausen (2002).

20. The basic principle of the hedonic deflators is as follows. The estimated prices of specified characteristics (e.g. speed for PCs) are used to quality adjust the price of a newly introduced model so that it is consistent with the discontinued model. For software the deflators are derived from PPI's, a BEA cost index, and a BLS employment cost index (ECI) and are applied to three subcategories (pre-packaged, own account,

and custom software). A detailed description of the methodologies can be found in Landefeld and Grimm (2000).

21. This is fully described in Fraumeni (1997). Until the 1999 revision, the estimated depreciation rates for computers were cohort and asset specific, taken from studies by Oliner. With the 1999 revision of the National Income and Product Accounts (NIPA) a new depreciation rate was introduced for PCs only. The value is 0.3119, based on Lane (1999), assuming that the value of a PC declines to 10 per cent of its initial value after 5 years. As noted by Doms et al. (2004), this schedule incorporates the full loss in PC value as it ages, capturing both depreciation and devaluation. Starting from the 2003 revision of the NIPA, and based on new evidence in Doms et al. (2004), the depreciation rate for PCs has been changed to 0.34.

22. Other differences between the BEA and the BLS estimates relate to the construction of the aggregate capital stock measures. The BLS uses the Jorgenson methodology to build a service measure of capital stocks (also defined as an estimation of 'productive capital stocks') instead of the BLS wealth measure (the methodology is summarized in http://www.bls.gov/web/mprcaptl.htm).

23. Note for the UK O'Mahony and de Boer (2002) and the Bank of England dataset introduced in Oulton and Srinivasan (2003).

24. In this context ICT is defined very broadly as comprising the whole category of office and computer equipment—including peripherals such as printers, photocopiers, etc.—radio, television and communication equipment, and software.

25. Since the information on occupational activities by industry is used to produce an asset by industry matrix, this embedded relationship between industry ICT flows and employment may introduce dangerous spurious correlations. For example, this issue may put at risk studies that use the data to investigate correlations between capital mix and employment mix choices (Chennells and Van Reenen, 2002). Moreover, the specific occupational categories used to break down the ICT flows by industry are not published. Bosworth and Triplett (2002) note that the latest year for which the BEA flow table was used to allocate ICT capital by industry is 1992. Another problematic issue is the measurement of software investments, especially custom-made software Dedrick, Gurbaxani and Kraemer (2003).

26. The country specific matrices of ICT investments by industries are interpolated for intermediate years. For longer gaps in the data the Commodity Flow Method is employed. (This supply-side method first computes the total amount of ICT commodities available in a specific year by taking the value of total ICT production plus the net value of ICT imports less ICT exports.) Then the shares of investments across the different industries are allocated using as weights the shares of total investments over production minus exports plus imports computed from the input output tables.

27. Interestingly, the higher shares reported by Crepon and Heckel do not seem to be related to selection issues.

28. Several adjustments are made to apply the data in a production function framework. In Brynjolfsson, Bresnahan, and Hitt (2002) the nominal values are deflated using price information. Brynjolfsson, Bresnahan, and Hitt (2002) use prices developed by Robert Gordon (19.3% yearly changes). In Brynjolfsson and Hitt (2003) the data are transformed from wealth stocks (market value of the assets) into productive stock (the value of assets based on output capability) by multiplying the wealth stocks by the annual aggregate ratio of the productive stock to the wealth stock of computer assets

computed by the BLS. The CII data have been extensively used in other research on productivity. Some recent examples include Lehr and Lichtenberg (1999)—where CII data are combined with additional census based data on firm level IT investments—and Gilchrist, Gurbaxani and Town (2001)—where CII data are used in the context of TFP growth regressions. More recently, Bloom, Draca, and Van Reenen (2005) used a similar type of data (detailed information on the volume of IT equipment existing in a specific site of a firm, collected via a telephone survey) to analyse the impact of IT on productivity in the UK economy.

29. Greenan and Mairesse (1996) use the questions on IT use by workers collected in the framework of the French survey TOTTO (Enquête sur les Techniques et l'Organisation du Travail) to build firm level measures on computer use, which they match with the INSEE firm database. Clearly, the worker-level information requires specific assumptions regarding the degree of representativeness of the employees surveyed.

30. Maliranta and Rouvinen (2004) use as IT measures the percentage of employees in Finnish firms using computers and/or LAN and Internet systems. These data were collected in the framework of Statistics Finland's Internet use and e-commerce in enterprises surveys. A similar measure was collected in the UK in the e-commerce survey (Criscuolo and Waldron 2003).

31. These studies combine basic information on the existence of computer networks within a firm with more detailed data on specific types of IT resources such as fully integrated ERP software.

32. These data require very specific assumptions on the depreciation or the growth patterns of the capital stocks. If we assume full depreciation ($\delta = 1$) then the investment flows represent a valid proxy for capital stocks. This is the choice implicitly made by Doms et al. (2002) in a study focusing on the role of IT in US retail sector productivity, where the ratio of IT investments over total investments (drawn from the 1992 Asset and Expenditures Survey) is used to proxy for IT capital intensity for some 2000 retail firms. The same type of measure (IT investment share in total investments) is employed by Haltiwanger, Jarmin, and Schank (2003) in a comparison of IT effects in the US and Germany. Wilson (2004) uses a slightly more sophisticated framework to exploit the 1998 ACES on detailed firm level investments in IT (and in 54 other types of assets) in a production function context. He rewrites the PIM formula as:

$$K_{t-1} = (g_t + \delta)^* I_t$$
$$g_t = \frac{\Delta K_t}{K_{t-1}}$$

He then assumes that in the steady state g should be approximately equal to zero, and states a direct proportionality between stocks and flows, running through the depreciation rate.

33. Bloom et al. (2005) use four different surveys on micro level IT investments in the UK economy collected by the Office of National Statistics for the years 1995–2003. Hempell (2005) employs IT investment data from the Mannheim Innovation Panel in Services (MIP-S), collected by the ZEW on behalf of the German Federal Ministry of Education and Research since 1994.

34. Bloom et al. (2005) build the initial conditions of the PIM assuming a direct proportionality between industry and firm level capital stocks.

35. Oulton (2002) shows that the contribution of ICT to UK productivity growth increased from 13.5% in total growth in 1979–89 to 21% in 1989–98. This is less than the US experience, but greater than the European average.

36. Griliches' (1992) survey and some recent contributions (e.g. Bloom, Schankerman and Van Reneen 2005) provide compelling evidence about the importance of spillovers from R&D.

37. Bloom et al. (2005) have developed a UK dataset on ICT and firm performance; they plan to produce comparable data for France, Germany, and the US.

CHAPTER 6

ECONOMIC POLICY ANALYSIS AND THE INTERNET: COMING TO TERMS WITH A TELECOMMUNICATIONS ANOMALY

PAUL A. DAVID

1 INTRODUCTION: THE EVOLVING NATURE AND SCOPE OF 'INTERNET ECONOMICS'*

EVERYDAY life in the world's economically advanced societies has been touched and in some parts substantially altered by the advent of the Internet. Some among the developing economies also have felt the impacts of the explosive growth in

* In this contribution I have drawn upon previously published writings of mine that benefited from the informative comments of Marjory Blumenthal, Andrew Glyn, Andrew Graham, Robert Spinrad, Gregory Rosston, and Raymund Werle. I am particularly grateful to Robin Mansell and W. Edward Steinmueller for their substantive and editorial improvements upon an earlier draft of this chapter, but responsibility for errors, omissions, and the sometime captious views expressed remains mine alone.

global connectivity and the astounding proliferation of diverse innovations in applications software. These marvels distinguish the performance of the Internet as a communication infrastructure from that of its historical predecessors—such as the telegraph and telephone networks. It would have been truly remarkable had economists not been drawn to study the implications of this novel technology for commercial activities and the organization of material life more generally.

Those economists who focus on industrial organization and regulation of industry (including antitrust and merger law) have found new scope for application of their expertise to issues arising from the Internet's consequences for the entire telecommunications sector. Another, more macroeconomically-oriented segment of the profession was absorbed, first, by the puzzling disjuncture between signs of rapid innovation in digital information technologies and the sluggish growth of productivity in the US economy—the so-called 'computer productivity paradox'. Then, in the late 1990s they found themselves absorbed in trying to understand what role (if any) had been played by the Internet in the sudden, and for many rather surprising productivity upsurge which has now outlived the bursting of the dotcom bubble and the post-2000 recession. In recent years, various debates concerned with the nature and implications of the digital divide—in both its domestic and its international aspects—have engaged attention in still other quarters of the discipline, especially among researchers concerned with distributive inequalities and policies intended to address these.

As scholars responding in their professional capacities to the developments that followed from the privatization and commercialization of the Internet in the mid-1990s, economists manifested an understandable inclination to 'lead from strength'—that is, to discuss matters that they had already worked out thoroughly in other contexts of application. In academic economics circles during the 1990s emphasis was placed on counteracting the hype of media and industry presentations of the Internet as a revolutionary and transformative technological advance, primarily by showing how the familiar concepts and tools of microeconomic analysis could be used to illuminate the commercial developments that were emerging in cyberspace.

This approach to the economics of the Internet drew on prior research that dealt with the special properties of information goods on the one hand, and on the extensive literature in the field of industrial organization that was concerned with competition and the regulation of telecommunications industries on the other. Key topics featured in the early 'positive' economics of the Internet literature included:

- the pricing of information goods and services sold online, and business strategy in markets characterized by network externalities;
- digital payment systems and electronic banking;
- the effects of particular instantiations of e-commerce such as financial brokerage and auctions;

- the pricing of access to the network backbone;
- regulation of Internet interconnection agreements and their implications for competitive entry and market structure.

The latter topics occupied pride of place among the Internet policy issues on which economists initially focused, in good part because the regulation of network access had emerged as a prominent subject of analysis in the era following the break-up of the Bell System and the movement to liberalization of telecommunications markets. McKnight and Bailey (1997) provide an influential collection of papers reflecting the leading edge of research on 'Internet economics' in the mid-1990s. The programmes of the annual Telecommunications Policy Research Conference during 1995–99 reveal the same pattern of concentration on the part of the participants drawn from university faculties of economics in the US.[1] Although the canvas of research has broadened subsequently, the foregoing remain core topics of university courses on 'the economics of the Internet'.[2]

The general thrust of this approach to the economics of the Internet, therefore, has been that of 'naturalizing' the subject matter by focusing on those generic features that were common to broader categories of economic activity and public policy, particularly those affecting the telecommunications sector. There were, however, several respects in which it was recognized that the new communications infrastructure differed significantly from its precursors, and moreover, that these differences impeded an immediate application of the pre-existing corpus of telecommunications economics that had been formulated in the context of connection-oriented public switched telephone systems. The differentiating features manifested themselves in a variety of awkward, or anomalous performance dimensions that became apparent when the 'network of networks' was thrown open to the general public and commercial traffic in the mid-1990s.

Most salient among them, at least for economists, were the difficulties of pricing the usage of bandwidth in order to reduce delays in transmission arising from congestion, and of establishing commercial ventures based on the same 'fee-for-service' business model that telephone operators were able to support. Related, but of less immediate economic interest, were the difficulties of providing users with services that permitted blocking delivery of nuisance messages (spam), offensive content, or politically disturbing material (whether of the neo-Nazi or Falun Gong variety); and protecting users from damage resulting from the malicious actions of others (for example, release of destructive software viruses, and denial of service attacks on web servers). Economic analysts could readily construe all of these as posing challenges for the design of resource allocation mechanisms that would render the Internet more efficient as a system of communication.

What was not equally appreciated, however, was that each of those problematic aspects of the Internet was rooted in the technical specifications that were responsible for the performance capabilities of the Internet, which its users perceived to be its uniquely beneficial properties. The openness and transparency of the softly integrated 'network of networks' were attributes that derived from the distinctive 'end-to-end' design of the architecture and transmission control mechanisms of the new, connection-less communications system. These features enable the Internet to tolerate extreme diversity in the technical specifications of its constituent networks and platforms. That, in turn, made joining the system cheap, and highly attractive to new network operators, Internet service providers (ISPs) and users. In addition to facilitating the rapid extension of the system, the transparency of the end-to-end architecture—which placed the intelligent components at the ends rather in the core of the network—afforded a particularly accommodating platform for developers of applications innovations (David 2001a). Software could be designed to run on the computers situated at the network's edges, taking data input and generating data output that traversed the intervening channels without having to pay attention to the specifics of the computer hardware and software that executed the message routing functions of the system.

The existence of a significant set of public policy issues for economics to address, arising from the tension between the 'anomalous drawbacks' and the 'special benefits' of the Internet, is the focus of this chapter. Yet, for a considerable number of years it was not recognized explicitly in the emerging literature on Internet economics. One hesitates to fault a discipline that disposes its expert practitioners to talk about things they really do understand—and what the first economists to enter the field understood well was the pre-Internet world of telecommunications. The question is how far it is possible to go on the basis of understandings gained in contexts that have some similarities, but within which the subject of interest appears quite anomalous. I suggest that economists working in this area have tended—for rather too long—either to avoid focusing on the points of divergence between connection-oriented and connection-less communications systems, or to propose 'solutions' to perceived inefficiencies that would have the effect of bringing the economics of the Internet more closely into line with that of the class of telecommunications systems with which they were already familiar.

The understandable inclination of analysts to focus on features of a new phenomenon that allow them to speak authoritatively, may fail adequately to address core policy issues that are posed by radical innovations in technology—or in institutional design, for that matter. Therefore, I shall not review here the many important questions on which economists examining the Internet have been able to proceed quite usefully by recapitulating their prior concerns, and deploying familiar and well-honed tools to illuminate new developments. These have been ably surveyed elsewhere (Graham 2001). Instead, this chapter is directed to some policy issues that were avoided by initial forays into the economics of the Internet, and whose importance only lately has begun to come into clearer view.

The discussion will proceed through the following steps. In the second section it will be shown, first, that the problem of congestion which was widely perceived to be a critical economic resource allocation challenge turned out to be largely chimerical; and, second, that economists were quite blasé in proposing solutions for that and other, related problems by introducing pricing mechanisms whose implementation required radical engineering modifications to the Internet. The latter, however, would jeopardize, and possibly vitiate, the unique, socially valuable performance capabilities of the system. The third section takes note of the fact that the recommendations for usage-sensitive pricing that were advanced by economists on static and rather narrow 'efficiency' grounds probably posed less of an actual threat to the continuation of the end-to-end design principle than the pressures that presently emanate from the private sector. The source of the latter are business ventures seeking the engineering modifications needed to enable them to offer users more profitable services, such as voice telephony over the Internet. The fourth section therefore addresses the questions of whether, and on what grounds, public policy might be mobilized to protect the architecture of the Internet—and thus preserve its beneficial properties of flexibility, extensibility, and hospitality as a platform for innovation. The final section concludes with some observations and suggestions regarding future policy-relevant directions for Internet economics.

2 Remedies for 'an unpriced resource'

Among the early contributions to the economics of the Internet perhaps the best known were those concerned with the sources of congestion, and how to deal with them (Mackie-Mason and Varian 1996; 1995a; 1995b). What economists typically brought to this discussion, perhaps all too predictably, was an abstract understanding of the phenomenon of congestion as a negative externality suffered by all users as a consequence of the lack of some effective mechanism restraining individuals' claims on the limited available capacity. Casual analogies were drawn with the phenomena of overfishing and overgrazing of common resources, and the spectre was thus raised of the Internet becoming another case of a resource whose utility was seriously degraded by congestion arising from the absence of (bandwidth) usage-sensitive pricing. The mantra that subsequently has been imparted to novitiates in the field of Internet economics carries the same message, formulated in a less normative way (McKnight and Bailey 1997: 12): 'Flat rate pricing does not provide an economic congestion control mechanism for bandwidth resource allocation'.

Most of the proposals put forward by economists to correct this deficiency have favoured usage-pricing and a useful review is provided by Gupte (2001), although their schemes have varied considerably both in the degree of their economic sophistication and their complexity. At the upper end of that scale, the 'smart market' mechanism advocated in the pioneering work of Mackie-Mason and Varian (1995a) applies the principles of a Vickery auction: users would enter bids for network access that indicated a maximum willingness to pay, and routers would recognize the bids attached to each of the data-packets; all packets with bids exceeding some cut-off value would be admitted for forwarding. Given a fixed supply of bandwidth, the cut-off value would therefore be the lowest bid that corresponded to the transmission capacity of the system, and that price would be charged to all users whose bids were accepted. Consistent with marginal cost pricing principles, when there were only bids for network access that fell below the router's cut-off value, the price would fall to zero.

As the authors of this proposal soon acknowledged (Mackie-Mason and Varian 1995b): 'usage-based pricing is itself expensive—it requires an infrastructure to track usage, prepare bills, and collect revenues.' A subsequent publication (MacKie-Mason and Varian 1997) took the matter further by recognizing that designing a congestion accounting and billing mechanism for a packet network is not so straightforward a proposition: Who should be charged, the sender of packets, or the receiver? Consider the situation in which a user downloads a file from a public archive: both the applications that are parties to the communication-transaction originate their own packets, but there is no way for the routers to identify the many packets forwarded from the archive as being responses to the session initiated by the small number of packets carrying the user's request for the file. If such requests resulted in congestion, how could the behaviour of the users be modified by charging the costs to the passive party in the transaction (the archive)? To allocate the congestion costs between the parties, the public archive in this case would have to have installed a billing mechanism, permitting the subsequent re-assignment of the charges to the user that had instigated the file transfer.

Just what changes would be required in the architecture and transmission control algorithms to enable the routers to do all this was not considered. But, the design of the Internet's transmission control protocols (TCP) does not allow monitoring the state of congestion everywhere in the network, and so the implementation of the suggested pricing mechanism, like that of quality of service (QOS) schemes, would require monitoring and information collection functions that are not supported and—with the continuing growth of the network—would become increasingly taxing for the simple routers to accomplish in real time. Moreover, the cost allocation and billing requirements for congestion control via QOS systems would call for the collection, transmission, and processing of *internal* traffic information as well as user bids, and the provision of discretionary network routing capabilities. To imagine all that being implemented without substantial engineering departures from the principles of an end-to-end architecture is difficult indeed (Odlyzko 1998: 26–7; CSTB 2001: 99–100), and so it seems rather remarkable that the larger implications of such changes have not been more prominent matters of concern for the proponents of such schemes.

More remarkable still is the continuing robustness of the economics literature's fixation on congestion-pricing, the pertinent facts notwithstanding. Congestion was not a major problem on the Internet during the early 1990s, when its opening to commercial traffic first directed attention to the problem posed by the impending need to introduce usage-pricing; nor has the forecast condition of chronic congestion materialized subsequently. Delays experienced on the Internet will indeed be caused by queues, which are an intrinsic part of congestion control and the sharing of capacity (CSTB 2001: 98ff). But there can be other sources of delay. Indeed, because ISPs are not required either to collect or release data on transmission delays, dropped packet rates, or other network performance variables, there continues to be much disagreement over the exact extent to which many of the service problems experienced by Internet users are properly attributable to congestion, rather than other causes. The frequently observed delays in the delivery of e-mail, for example, are thought to be almost always the result of mail server faults that result in a large proportion of the load being generated by the retransmission of packets; and the painful slowness that web surfers encounter during peak hours is ascribed to nonresponding web servers (Odlyzko 1998; Huitema 1997, as cited by Cave and Mason 2001).

True congestion delay occurs on the Internet whenever the combined traffic needing to be forwarded on to a particular outgoing link exceeds the capacity of that link. The design of the TCP assigns to the sending nodes the responsibility for regulating the flow of packets on the basis of cumulative acknowledgments from (adjacent) receiving nodes of the arrival of packets sent to them. This adaptive control mechanism operates in response to 'packet losses' that reach a rate signalling the presence of congestion to the routers that share the link. Thus, when congestion occurs, a packet may be delayed, sitting in an adjacent router's queue awaiting dispatch, and so will arrive later than some other packet from the same message that has not been subject to queuing. The result is delay in the reassembly of all the packets that contain the message, a condition described as 'latency' in the language of telecommunications engineers. (When queue lengths vary, and some queues fill up, packets will be dropped by the router and therefore need to be resent, causing variations of the duration of delays and the condition known as 'jitter'.) Congestion typically is a transient phenomenon, however, lasting only for the interval during which the TCP mechanism adapts to the available capacity by slowing the outgoing packet rate. It can reach drastic levels, however, if the capacities of the nodes available to each router fall below the minimum transmission rate provided by the control protocol.

The mechanism of congestion control provided by TCP, therefore, is simply to push back on the traffic source dynamically, in response to the detection of congestion inside the network, until it no longer is able to accept the offered load. This simple algorithm is incapable of discriminating among the initiators of the offered load, or among various types of applications that are generating traffic. Hence it cannot serve to shape the behaviour of individual users on the Internet, or even that of classes of users. Moreover, this congestion control algorithm is neither enforced on the Internet, nor is it even part of the protocol architecture of some applications that do not implement TCP—such as streaming video and UDP (User Data Protocol) (CSTB 1994: 189, 201 n. 40). Those applications consequently can be viewed as taking unfair advantage of other applications, such as email programs that do implement TCP.

Today, congestion generally is understood to be rare within the backbone networks of North American ISPs. The obvious explanation for the failure of chronic, paralysing congestion to materialize under the conditions of unpriced usage lies in the rapid expansion of capacity to accommodate the growth of Internet hosts and traffic; and because most of the widely used applications tolerated the congestion control mechanisms provided by TCP. Whether bandwidth increases can continue to keep pace with the growth of demand, of course, depends on whether QOS-enabling enhancements are made in the network that will greatly increase the offering of bandwidth-hungry services, and the degree to which competition will either check the ability of ISPs to differentially price such services in a manner that curtails their needs for heavy investment in capacity, or result in rivalries among the larger ISPs to stake out more real estate on the Net in order to attract an expanded customer base.

Instead of appearing ubiquitously throughout the rest of the network, however, congestion does appear to be concentrated at particular bottlenecks created by disparities in the provision of capacity. As has been noted above, the links (exchange points) between ISPs—and especially the public network access points (NAPs)—are as a rule much more heavily congested than the links *within* the service providers' respective networks (Odlyzko 1998; CSTB 2001: 99, 117). Although the links between customers' local area networks (LANs) or residences and their ISPs are also frequently congested, the difficulty arises from the organizational delays or the expense entailed in increasing the capacity of the connection. Persistent congestion has been documented at several international links, where long and variable queuing delays, as well as high packet loss rates, have been measured (Paxson 1999; CSTB 2001: 99–100). Here again, however, the proximate source of the problem appears to be rooted in institutional circumstances affecting the provision and allocation of capacity at strategic connection points, rather than the endemic condition of unrestrained bandwidth usage envisaged by economic theorizing.

A cynical commentator might conclude that the stream of ingenious proposals from economists to fix the problem of congestion on the Internet, in typically ignoring the possible strategic explanations for congestion at the public NAPs, and proposing the introduction into the network's core of the intelligence needed to operate a sophisticated pricing mechanism, come down to the expedient of making the network less and less like the Internet, and more closely akin to a connection-oriented conventional public switched telephone network (PSTN). Quite obviously, however, had such a design been embraced to begin with, many other difficulties posed by the peculiar open-architecture would have been obviated as well. Along with removal of the obstacles to a mass transfer fee-for-service business model, this would reduce the myriad *practical* difficulties that local communities linked to the Internet now encounter in seeking to control the content of messages bearing objectionable content. In a connection-oriented system it is much more feasible to rapidly and accurately identify the locations, if not the identities of agents engaging in the electronic transmission of content that recipients deem to be pernicious—and to set about mobilizing political, social, and legal countermeasures. There would, therefore, be less need than presently exists to devote resources to the development of the still rather coarse-grained 'geo-locator technologies' that are being used to create targets for direct mail advertising and sales techniques based on the characteristics of the recipients' neighbourhoods. Less attention would also have to be given to figuring out whether such technologies can be made sufficiently reliable to be employed to control the distribution of objectionable content on the Internet, in the ways that would parallel the familiar content-regulating actions of political authorities who can identify the originating parties and have legal jurisdiction over the geographical territories in which they are situated.

Whether or not the removal of anonymity, and the reimposition of greater controls on individuals' access to content are desirable in some circumstances, is quite another matter (Engel and Keller 2000). The point is simply that the congestion-pricing solution envisaged for the Internet is not the narrow matter of economic efficiency that economists have appeared to be presenting; its implementation would require an architectural revolution in which the Internet as we know it would have disappeared. Correspondingly, in that brave new world, debates about the conflicting desiderata of privacy, anonymity, and security would continue, but they would cease to be policy matters that had a peculiar 'Internet' aspect and would simply reprise the issues that society has found ways of resolving for other communications media—physical newspapers and books, plain old telephones, radio, films, and television (de Sola Pool 1990).

3 A PATH TO THE END OF 'END TO END'?

Will the pressures to insert new capabilities into the core of the network really have the deleterious effects envisaged, and if undesirable consequences materialize, would it not be possible to restore the *status quo ante*? The likelihood is that even the unintended ending of an integral end-to-end Internet would not be readily reversible, and that the benefits thereby lost might prove difficult if not virtually impossible to recover on a later, improved successor to the global information infrastructure. This last point deserves further elaboration, which can conveniently be provided by returning to consideration of the concrete issue of permitting cable companies in the ISP market to create proprietary sub-networks on which QOS technologies are used to offer differentiated service choices to subscribers. Users of a particular service, however, would have access only to the music and the video that their ISP had designated, possibly also to a designated IP voice telephony service, and might be similarly locked in to a particular suite of other web-based services and applications software.

A concrete scenario in which this possibility might be realized is suggested by the emergence of the Skype VoIP (Voice over Internet Protocol) service in 2003.[3] This service is based upon the distinctive end-to-end features of the 'old' Internet and, as a consequence, free-rides on the bandwidth made available for services like the World Wide Web or email. Skype's business model, which offers free voice calls between users who are connected to the Internet, is based upon charges for receiving and placing calls to users who are using other networks as well as charging for additional, premium, services such as voice mail. According to the market research company Evalueserve,[4] Skype had recruited 13 million users worldwide within two years of its founding. Sustained rapid growth of Skype will not only have a significant impact on the revenues and profitability of telecommunications network operators, but also is likely to generate significant congestion in the Internet. In addition, since Skype is a peer-to-peer technology, its use involves employing resources from individual user machines and their networks to 'relay' calls or store voice messages. This has raised corporate concerns about security and local network congestion and has led to responses such as the products offered by Bitek International that block Skype services.[5]

This situation is very similar to the past use of peer-to-peer networks to transfer music files (Skype was created by the same individuals that created Kazaa, a leading peer-to-peer file exchange application). However, Skype involves a more complex set of issues. In some countries, for example, Israel, the use of Skype to bypass the local telecommunications operator is illegal and it is likely that congestion effects will prompt ISPs and network operators to employ blocking technologies such as those available from Bitek International. In other countries, the employment of blocking or filtering technologies is likely to be more decentralized and thus, to involve corporate networks or specific ISPs. These developments are likely to lead to a growth in 'restricted web' services, that is, those that utilize some applications and block others. It is a short step from these developments to legitimizing Skype by incorporating it as a specific service offered by leading ISPs. Skype users would thus be assured (in countries permitting such services) that they would be able to retain connectivity with other Skype users as well as telephone services to connect to others.

There are reasons to expect that having put in place a restricted-web ISP service offering, such as Skype, the ISP in question might well be receptive to allowing compatibility between this sub-network and other similar sub-networks. The economic logic of this situation differs from that which governs in the general analysis of compatibility standardization for network interoperability—where it is generally found that small networks seek connectivity with larger ones, and the latter have stronger incentives to remain aloof from rivals of comparable size (Farrell and Saloner 1986; David and Greenstein 1990, for a review of the early literature; Shapiro and Varian 1998, especially chapters 7 and 9 on strategies in standards wars; and Varian, Farrell and Shapiro 2004). By linking with similarly sized networks, an ISP with a large network base could offer subscribers other enhanced services that are latency-sensitive, such as voice telephony, and a larger choice among the set of preselected applications. The value of integrating to achieve compatibility with smaller ISPs would remain comparatively small, and so, in this market setting, the dynamics lead toward a high degree of market power concentrated in the hands of a small number of ISPs, and a large fringe of ISPs whose clientele remains cut-off from these enhanced services.

Thus entrenched, the dominant ISPs would be in a position to extract some, if not most, of the rent that might otherwise flow to the developers of applications innovations, in exchange for making these available for use by their clientele. Lacking that access, the developers would be confined to exploiting niche markets at the fringes of the network, where their products would remain beyond the reach of the subscribers to the large ISPs. Nothing in this picture suggests that the emergent structure of a partitioned network would be likely to be voluntarily dismantled by the incumbent, or vertically integrated ISPs, nor successfully attacked by an entrant possessing a novel and superior application technology. An entrant with the capital resources required to establish a new, competitive, vertically integrated ISP, moreover, would have every incentive to seek compatibility with an existing large service provider; indeed, an aggressive newcomer and, were the newcomer aggressive, it might expand by stealing the original incumbent's clientele. But, in addition to requiring the financial backing to create the additional network capacity required for the implementation of that strategy, the successful entrant would replicate the initial situation, and pose an even greater entry barrier to the next innovator.

A mitigating consideration to be noted in the foregoing scenario is that although the technological enhancements to the Internet would create new opportunities for ISPs to extract greater rents (consumer surplus) from their customers by means of discriminatory pricing schemes (Mandjes 2004; Odlyzko 2004), the strategy of vertical bundling of networking services and Internet-based applications nevertheless would provide additional benefits for a large segment of the Internet population. The technologists who created an end-to-end architecture, and who value it particularly for the support it provided to applications innovators, are less burdened than the typical Internet user by having to install, configure, upgrade, and maintain the software of each and every one of the rapidly growing number of applications that must be attached at the networks' end points. This state of affairs can be expected only to become more burdensome. As Blumenthal and Clark perceptively observe:

The importance of ease of use will only grow with the changing nature of consumer computing. The computing world today includes more than PCs. It has embedded processors, portable user interface devices such as computing appliances or personal digital assistants (PDAs, such as Palm devices), Web-enabled televisions and advanced set-top boxes, new kinds of cell-phones, and so on. If the consumer is required to set up and configure separately each networked device he [*sic!*] owns, what is the chance that at least one of them will be configured incorrectly? That risk would be lower with delegation of configuration, protection, and control to a common point, which can act as an agent for a pool of devices. This common point would become a part of the application execution context. With this approach, there would no longer be a single indivisible end-point where the application runs. (Blumenthal and Clark 2001: 72)

While pointing to the threat to the preservation of the open-network architecture, this acknowledges that the creation by ISPs of enclaves containing advanced services would be one way in which the multitude of less technically sophisticated users could obtain specialized (and correspondingly standardized) network applications-integrating services. Thus, in regard to this issue—as so frequently is the case, network policy makers face the classic trade-off of securing the immediate benefits of closed standardization by sacrificing the technological flexibility that is conducive to future radical innovations (David 1995).

4 POLICY PRIORITIES AND PROTECTION OF THE INTERNET'S ARCHITECTURE

It has been seen that among the many technological fixes proposed for enhancing the Internet's performance some are not so innocuous, because they would entail inserting intelligence into the core of the network. The likely impact of these induced innovations therefore would be the alteration of the distinctive end-to-end architecture, pushing the future path of the network's evolution more towards emulating the performance features (both good and bad) associated with a connection-oriented telecommunications system—the familiar paradigm of which exists in the PSTN (David and Steinmueller 1996). Will the changing balance among the interests of the communities using the information infrastructure, inevitably force a sacrifice of the global infrastructure's transparency and openness, thereby raising new barriers to the invention and diffusion of valuable applications?

Inasmuch as a technological drift away from the original Internet's end-to-end architectural design should not be regarded as an inexorable process beyond the reach of social control, there is scope for policy interventions to check such a course of evolution. It must be hoped then, that promoting wider understanding of the issues at stake can increase the political feasibility of arriving at rational policy priorities. At least, that is the spirit in which the following commentary on the identification and balancing among conflicting goods will proceed.

A first appropriate step is to ask whether the net impact of any proposed movement in that direction would be socially beneficial. In view of the prospective emergence of a broadband Internet on which QOS will be more widely implemented by ISPs competing for customers while seeking the means to charge what the (multimedia) traffic will bear, the question might be asked whether the time has come for end-to-end to terminate. It could be argued that inasmuch as the days of Internet1 as a unified global infrastructure providing a receptive platform for rapid innovation and experimentation with networks are numbered, the best course of action would be to make whatever changes are required in the core of the network to quickly reap the benefits of the available new services on a 'users' Internet,' that is to say, we should come to terms with the immanent tendency of the evolutionary dynamics driven by the needs of the maturing market for a differentiated Internet service, and think about other ways to provide a network environment that would stimulate the continuation of amazing innovations.

Such a view would counsel turning attention to the construction of a separate, very high speed internetwork as the test bed and experimental commercial market for advanced services, which would be designed to provide the features of openness and flexibility that have proved so encouraging to the development of more powerful digital technologies. This might be called Internet2+ to distinguish it from the actual federally funded backbone created in the US to continue the National Science Foundation's Network (NSFNET) research role. There is something to be said for this vision of a cyclical regeneration of a new inter-networking environment that would revive some characteristics of the original. It acknowledges the important symbiotic relationship between the mature PSTN infrastructure on which packet switching and the novel technologies of the ARPANET (Advanced Research Projects Administration Network) and NSFNET could be erected; and it recognizes the fertility of experimental research communities as sources of user-designed technological innovations. But, unfortunately, it ignores the crucial fact that an important aspect of the historical experience cannot be replicated or revived by these means.

The nub of the problem is that to develop innovations that are readily available for deployment on the Internet as it exists, one needs a test bed with its technical features. Yet, for the communities that would have access to Internet2+, and especially for those groups that are engaged in advancing the frontiers of network engineering, the high value use would be to develop applications that utilized the enhanced properties of that infrastructure rather than the more limited capabilities of Internet1—or the still less accommodating infrastructure into which the latter would be tending to evolve.

Next, one should consider the net balance of gains against losses: would the contemplated enhancements in the quality of differentiated services, and in the ability of service providers to engage in price discrimination among the users of the Internet, compensate for the economic welfare costs entailed—in terms of curtailed future scaleability and a slowed pace of innovation in applications? Several grounds for scepticism regarding the value of the gains seem worth keeping in mind.

To begin with, the incremental social benefit of upgrading the Internet to carry real-time audio traffic is not obviously overwhelming, given the existence of other technological means of providing a large part of the world's population with access to voice telephony (via cellular radio and satellite transmission) at lower fixed costs than those entailed in laying copper wire or fibre-optic cabling. Certainly, Internet telephony could be integrated into new, multimedia services. Yet, there is a disjunction here between a strategy directed toward opening profit opportunities in the developed economies—to elicit continued private sector investment in augmenting the broadband infrastructure available to users in those countries—and a policy that also takes account of the situation in the world at large.

While cellphone technology has opened the benefits of rapid, global communications to large cohorts in the developing economies, it remains unsuitable for sparsely populated regions and geographically remote sites, just as it is not capable of supporting the very high bandwidth communications that are likely eventually to be in demand there. But systems of low earth orbit satellites (LEOS), which are designed to provide two-way, low-latency, point-to-point transmissions, will be available to fill these significant service gaps. According to expert engineering opinion, the seamless linking of LEO satellite constellations into the worldwide communications infrastructure is a development that can be expected to take place in the relatively near future.[6]

For the developing economies, however, it is accepted that even to provide substantial narrowband coverage, considerable amounts of public funding for upgrading existing telecommunications infrastructures would be necessary; and some of that is likely to be provided by subsidized loans and transfers through multinational cooperative agencies. It must therefore be recognized that the social rate of return on public (and private) investments in this infrastructure would be reduced substantially if the present core of the Internet were to be modified by engineering changes that deviated from the principles of end-to-end. To permit alterations to the architecture of the backbone networks in the high income countries, in order to provide users there with Internet voice telephony (along with business or entertainment services integrating real-time video), would effectively mean curtailing the access afforded newly connected users in the world's poorer societies to existing information tools and global data resources.

The foregoing remarks address possible discrepancies between the private incentives driving the Internet's technological evolution, and the social value of the enhancements that would thus be achieved. They have not touched on the need to explore engineering improvements that can be implemented (at the edges of the network) in ways that would not compromise the performance attributes that derived from the Internet's end-to-end architecture. Content labelling conventions, are one example of the kind of 'improvements' that could be made (voluntarily or enforced upon content providers) to enhance the efficiency of filtering at the endpoints of the network.

But another important set of alternatives to introducing control mechanisms in the network's core that remains to be considered is the large class of *non*-technological options. In view of the fact that the origins of many of the vexing dysfunctionalities of the Internet derive from the historical displacement of this technology system from the peculiar, highly regulated behavioural and organizational contexts within which it was created and initially used, an obvious option to be considered is the restoration of some of the former modes of regulating users' behaviours. The Internet may have been a technology that quite by accident was well-attuned to the *laissez-faire* spirit of the era in which it was publicly introduced. Yet, an ideologically driven commitment to go on thinking exclusively in the same vein about ways to overcome the problems posed by the 'network of networks', rejecting social engineering in favour of solutions found through Internet re-engineering, is most likely to sacrifice the Internet's unique and valuable pro-innovation features. There is no *a priori* reason to conclude that the most efficient solution path is one that relies solely on fixes that can be technologically implemented.

Yet, proposed regulation and interventions by public authorities continue to be opposed on the argument that such actions are inimical to the Internet's survival as a global interaction space free from governmentally imposed structures of social regulation. Current rhetorical support for relying on engineers to fix whatever might really need mending, rather than letting legislators and lawyers loose in cyberspace, presents a curious mixture of attitudes. These are compounded from the libertarian philosophy that is pervasive among survivors of the Internet's pioneering user groups, strains of anarchosyndicalism that have emerged in the ethos of the latter-day hacker culture, and the generic *laissez-faire* disposition of the Internet's more recently arrived community of business entrepreneurs. The holders of pro-commercial and anti-commercial sentiments alike appear quite comfortable making common cause against the intrusion of government regulations that are socially engineered. This, it should be recognized, presents an essential political and philosophical position, quite distinct from the utilitarian rationale that would give priority to preserving the distinctive end-to-end architecture of the Internet—especially inasmuch as serving the latter priority might call for the development of new, institutional mechanisms of governance.

Lawyers looking at the evolving Internet are naturally disposed to pose this issue in terms of a political choice between the regulation of human actions by laws or governance by 'Code'—the encompassing term used by Lessig (1999) in referring to the architectural configuration of networks and the location of access points, the design of hardware, operating systems, languages, data formats, and applications software. Economists, it would seem, would have something helpful to contribute to debates on these questions, by directing attention to the relative costs of alternative modes of regulation in network environments, especially in view of the significant externalities and irreversibilities that are likely to be entailed by introducing either technological or institutional modifications in the existing regime (see Mueller 2002).

Furthermore, approaching some questions that involve the governance of human behaviour in cyberspace from the perspective of the economics of crime and punishment also may be a useful way to mediate in debates between the engineers and the lawyers: the quest for perfect technological mechanisms of detection and suppression of malefactors is only relevant in a perfect world, and it is possible to compensate for reduced probabilities of being caught by raising the penalties visited on those who are. This approach may not be good enough in some areas of concern, and other technological safeguards will be needed to protect humans and vital technological systems alike from grave damage. But much of the 'protective' control of behaviour afforded under the law has been found to work tolerably well with this mixed approach.

For those reasons and still others, the relevant policy questions ought not to be construed in terms of making either–or choices. It is important to resist the rhetoric of much contemporary discussion of economic policy, which tends to offer only extreme alternatives. Participants are too often driven into opposing camps, one side calling for the introduction of government controls, and the other placing its faith in the further development of decentralized, automatic, supposedly neutral, and (market-like) regulatory mechanisms that can better resist political manipulation and so preserve greater scope for human volition. The following statement exemplifies the polarizing impact of applying the technologists' Internet philosophy to decide on the best means of protecting privacy on the Net:

[T]he cyperpunk credo can be roughly paraphrased as 'privacy through technology, not through legislation'. If we can guarantee privacy protection through the laws of mathematics rather than the laws of men and whims of bureaucrats, then we will have made an important contribution to society. It is this vision which guides and motivates our approach to Internet privacy. (Goldberg, Wagner and Brewer 1997, quoted in Blumenthal and Clark 2001: 84 n. 52)

A full-blown systems design approach, by contrast, would hold that if the benefits of the Internet's end-to-end architecture are to be retained, some technological solutions simply cannot be substituted for other, socio-legal modes of governing the behaviour of agents on the Internet. Rather than being viewed as antithetical substitutes, the potential complementarity of technological and institutional mechanisms governing the digital communications infrastructure should be explored in a coordinated manner.

There is thus a case to be made for devoting greater attention to matching the technological innovations of the Internet by mobilizing other, non-technologically implemented modes of regulation. Greater consideration surely is worth directing to the design of legal, political, and social rule structures and administrative procedures, of the kind that proved to be efficacious in supporting successful economic exploitation of previous technical advances in communications networks. In this connection, it is worth recalling that the oldest international treaty organization in existence today is the International Telecommunication Union (ITU). This institution, which began its life in 1865 as the International Telegraph Union, provided the model in whose image virtually all subsequent international treaty-based organizations were created (David and Shurmer 1996; Schmidt and Werle 1998). While that may suffice to suggest the possibility that fruitful innovations in international rule-making fora can be driven by the opportunities, or problems, that new technologies create, there is no doubt that today very formidable challenges are posed for the adaptive coevolution of international laws governing cyberspace (Gamble 1999).

5 CONCLUSION

Even as the Internet comes of age, the technology of the global information infrastructure and the organization of the communications service industries based on it continue to undergo significant changes. The main message carried by the foregoing discussion is that many microeconomic policy recommendations and engineering proposals that have been presented as incremental modifications to enhance the performance capabilities of the Internet actually may have radical implications for the future course of its technological evolution. These have been seen to involve rather esoteric matters that might appear best left to be decided by engineering specialists, and experts in the intricacies of telecommunications regulations. But decisions taken in those realms will powerfully shape the future performance characteristics of the Internet. In that way, they will have important consequences for the nature, size, and distribution of the economic and social benefits that it yields.

It is understandable that the initial reaction of many economists who had developed familiarity and expertise in the context of studying mature telecommunications networks (i.e. the PSTN) found it natural to transfer to the sphere of

Internet economics the modes of analyses and policy prescriptions that were, so to speak, most ready to hand. Thus, a great deal of prominence has been given to the discussion of principles that should govern optimal pricing of access to the transport/bearer layer of the Internet, a matter of undoubted importance for existing and would-be service providers. In a technologically dynamic network setting such as that of the Internet, however, the feasibility and terms of entry also depend on non-price policies, including those affecting technical compatibility standards, and regulations governing the interconnection strategies of incumbent service providers (Cave and Mason 2001). Over the long run, the technical rules of the game affecting physical interconnection are likely to be more consequential than pricing formulae in their effects on the growth and distribution of available bandwidth, competition in the ISP market, and the rate of innovation in applications on the Internet.

Bertrand Russell once remarked that we must 'tolerate specialists because they do good work'. Perhaps it would be more generous to speak of appreciation rather than toleration, but the point remains that in matters whose potential implications for human welfare are as important as those at hand, more than narrow expertise is wanted. The story of the Internet's development justly can be presented as a remarkable case of 'success by design' (CSTB 2001: 34) invokes this phase in discussing architectural principles). Equally, it may be read as a path-dependent tale of fortuitous engineering design decisions that were made with little consideration for aspects that have turned out to be problematic for many of the purposes and social contexts in which the resultant, wonderfully open and flexible technology would be used. (On concepts of irreversibility, path-dependence, and 'path-constrained melioration', see David 2001b.)

As societies around the world continue to wrestle with difficult technical challenges and policy quandaries that have their origins in historically remote decisions that proved to be essentially irreversible, an obvious question to be asked is whether it has become possible now to proceed differently. The historical economics approach (David 2001b) that informs much of the foregoing discussion carries some additional, and potentially more provocative suggestions for rethinking the economics of the telecommunications regulation in the age of the Internet. Because economic analysis of industrial organization and public regulation of telecommunications utilities was developed with reference to industries based on a mature network technology, practitioners in this area remain too inclined to start from the assumption that the technology is given. This is seldom the case, and it is palpably misleading when applied to the situation of the Internet. Therefore, perhaps the most important general lesson to be drawn for the future of Internet policy analysis is for economists to start thinking about the ways in which the structure of the existing markets, and the uneven and uncoordinated regime of regulation and nonregulation, can induce research and technological innovation to take some directions, while discouraging it from proceeding in others.

REFERENCES

BLUMENTHAL, M. S. and CLARK, D. D. (2001). 'Rethinking and Design of the Internet: The End to End Argument vs. the Brave New World'. *ACM Transactions on Internet Technology*, 1(1): 70–109.

CANNON, R. (2005) 'State Regulatory Approaches to VoIP: Policy, Implementation, and Outcome'. *Federal Communications Law Journal*, 57(3): 479–510.

CAVE, M. and MASON, R. (2001). 'The Economics and Regulation of the Internet'. *Oxford Review of Economic Policy*, 17(2): 188–201.

CSTB (Computer Science and Telecommunications Board) (1994). *Realizing the Information Future: The Internet and Beyond*. Washington DC: CSTB.

—— (2001). 'Computer Science and Telecommunications Board, National Research Council'. *The Internet's Coming of Age*, Washington DC: National Academy Press.

DAVID, P. A. (1995). 'Standardization Policies for Network Technologies: The Flux Between Freedom and Order Revisited', in R. Hawkins, R. Mansell and J. Skea (eds), *Standards, Innovation and Competitiveness: The Political Economy of Standards in Natural and Technological Environments*. Cheltenham: Edward Elgar, 15–35.

—— (2001a). 'The Evolving Accidental Information Super-highway'. *Oxford Review of Economic Policy*, 17(2): 159–87.

—— (2001b). 'Path Dependence, Its Critics and the Quest for "Historical Economics"', in P. Garrouste and S. Ionnides (eds), *Evolution and Path Dependence in Economic Ideas: Past and Present*. Cheltenham: Edward Elgar Publishing, 15–40.

—— and GREENSTEIN, S. (1990). 'The Economics of Compatibility Standards: A Review of Recent Research'. *Economics of Innovation and New Technology*, 1(1&2): 3–41.

—— and SHURMER, M. (1996). 'Formal Standards-Setting for Global Telecommunication and Information Services'. *Telecommunications Policy*, 20(10): 789–815.

—— and STEINMUELLER, W. E. (1996). 'Standards, Trade and Competition in the Emerging Global Information Infrastructure Environment'. *Telecommunications Policy*, 20(10): 817–30.

DE SOLA POOL, I. (1990). *Technologies Without Boundaries: On Telecommunications in a Global Age*. Cambridge, MA and London: Harvard University Press.

ENGEL, C. and KELLER, K. H. (eds) (2000). *Understanding the Impact of Global Networks on Local Social, Political and Cultural Values*. Baden-Baden: Nomos Verlagsgesellschaft.

FARRELL, J. and SALONER, G. (1986). 'Installed Base and Compatibility: Innovation, Product Preannouncements and Predation'. *American Economic Review*, 76(4): 940–55.

GAMBLE, J. K. (1999). 'New Information Technologies and the Sources of International Law: Convergence, Divergence, Obsolescence and/or Transformation'. *German Yearbook of International Law*, Berlin: Duncker and Humbolt, 170–205.

GOLDBERG, I., WAGNER, D. and BREWER, E. (1997). 'Privacy-enhancing Technologies for the Internet', University of California, Berkeley, 42nd IEEE COMPCOM'97 Conference, Spring, http://www.cs.berkeley.edu/~daw/papers/privacy-compcon97-www/privacy-html.html, accessed 16 Mar. 2006.

GRAHAM, A. (2001). 'The Assessment', Introduction to Special Issue on the Economics of the Internet. *Oxford Review of Economic Policy*, 17(2): 145–58.

GUPTE, R. P. (2001). 'Pricing to Control Congestion: An Economist's Bias', Trinity Term Research Paper in Economics 168X, Stanford University Centre in Oxford, June.

HUITEMA, C. (1997). 'The Required Steps Towards High Quality Internet Services', unpubl. Bellcore Report.

LESSIG, L. (1999). *Code and Other Laws of Cyberspace.* New York: Basic Books.

MACKIE-MASON, J. K. and VARIAN, H. R. (1995a). 'Pricing the Internet', in B. Kahin and J. Keller (eds), *Public Access to the Internet.* Cambridge, MA: MIT Press, 269–314.

—— and —— (1995b). 'Pricing Congestible Network Resources'. *IEEE Journal of Selected Areas in Communications,* 13(7): 1141–9.

—— and —— (1996). 'Some Economics of the Internet,' in W. Sichel (ed.), *Networks, Infrastructure and the New Task for Regulation.* Ann Arbor, MI: University of Michigan Press, 107–36.

—— (1997). 'Economic FAQs About the Internet', in L. W. McKnight and J. P. Bailey (eds), *Internet Economics.* Cambridge, MA: MIT Press, 27–62.

McKNIGHT, L. W. and BAILEY, J. P. (1997). 'An Introduction to Internet Economics', in L. W. McKnight and J. P. Bailey (eds), *Internet Economics.* Cambridge, MA: MIT Press, 3–26.

MANDJES, M. (2004). 'Pricing Strategies and Service Differentiation'. *Netnomics,* 6(1): 59–81.

MUELLER, M. (2002). *Ruling the Root: Internet Governance and the Taming of Cyberspace.* Cambridge, MA: MIT Press.

ODLYZKO, A. (1998). 'The Economics of the Internet: Utility, Utilization, Pricing and Quality of Service', AT&T Labs-Research, http://www.dtc.umn.edu/~odlyzko/doc/internet.economics.pdf, accessed 17 Mar. 2006.

—— (2004). 'Privacy, Economics, and Price Discrimination on the Internet', in L. J. Camp and S. Lewis (eds), *Economics of Information Security – Advances in Information Security,* Vol. 12. Boston, MA, Dordrecht and London: Kluwer Academic, 187–211.

OECD (2006). 'Policy Considerations of VoIP', Working Party on Telecommunication and Information Services Policies', DSTI/ICCP/TISP(2005)13/Final, Paris, 20 March.

PAXSON, V. (1999). 'End-to-End Internet Packet Dynamics'. IEEE/ACM Transactions on Networking, 7(3): 277–92.

SCHMIDT, S. K. and WERLE, R. (1998). *Coordinating Technology. Studies in the International Standardization of Telecommunications.* Cambridge, MA: The MIT Press.

SHAPIRO, C. and VARIAN, H. R. (1998). *Information Rules: A Strategic Guide to the Network Economy.* Boston, MA: Harvard Business School Press.

VARIAN, H. R., FARRELL, J. and SHAPIRO, C. (2004). *The Economics of Information Technology: An Introduction.* Cambridge: Cambridge University Press.

NOTES

1. See http://www.tprc.org/ARCHIVES.HTM, accessed 17 Mar. 2006.
2. For a representative example, drawn more or less at random from online listings, see Prof. P. K. Dutta's course lectures: www.columbia.edu/~pkd1/lecture20002.html, accessed 3 Nov. 2006.
3. For a discussion of policy and regulatory approaches to VoIP in the US, see Cannon (2005) and, more generally, OECD (2006).
4. See http://www.evalueserve.com/, accessed 17 Mar. 2006.
5. See http://www.bitek.com/, accessed 17 Mar. 2006.
6. Private communication from Robert Spinrad, 9 May 2000.

CHAPTER 7

INTERNET DIFFUSION AND THE GEOGRAPHY OF THE DIGITAL DIVIDE IN THE UNITED STATES

SHANE GREENSTEIN

JEFF PRINCE

1 INTRODUCTION*

THIS chapter analyses the rapid diffusion of the Internet across the US over the past decade for both households and firms. We put the Internet's diffusion into the context of economic diffusion theory where we consider costs and benefits on the demand and supply side. We also discuss several pictures of the Internet's current physical presence using some of the current main techniques for Internet measurement. We highlight different economic perspectives and explanations for the digital divide, that is, unequal availability and use of the Internet.

* We thank the Kellogg School of Management for financial support. We thank an anonymous reviewer and the editors for extensive comments. All errors contained here are our responsibility.

The Internet is unlike any communications network that came before it. It is a complex technology embedded in a multi-layered network, and many different participants operate its pieces. The National Science Foundation (NSF) began to commercialize the Internet in 1992. Within a few years there was an explosion of commercial investment in Internet infrastructure in the US. By October of 2003, 61.5 million (54.6 per cent) homes in the US had Internet connections (NTIA 2004).

As with any new technology, the diffusion of the Internet follows predictable regularities. For example, it always takes time to move a frontier technology from a small cadre of enthusiastic first users to a larger majority of potential users. In this sense the economic patterns found throughout the early diffusion of the Internet are general. The diffusion of the Internet also possesses some unique features. It has thus far proceeded in two waves. There is a clear difference between low-speed/dial-up connection and high-speed/hard-wire connection. In the early 1990s, those with dial-up connections were considered at the frontier, but by the turn of the millennium, dial-up connection had clearly become a non-frontier technology, with the new frontier consisting of high-speed connections, mainly through xDSL and cable.

This experience raises pressing policy issues. A pessimistic view emerged in the mid-1990s, one that became affiliated with the notion labelled 'the digital divide'. It forecast that the Internet was diffusing disproportionately to urban areas with their complementary technical and knowledge resources for supporting personal computers (PCs) and other computing, leaving rural areas behind. A related recent concern highlights the uneven use of frontier technologies in the second wave: in this case, broadband access and related complementary applications.

This chapter provides an overview of the economic processes underlying the geographic digital divide. This involves two goals—to analyse a specific phenomenon, and to communicate general lessons. We provide a survey of the growing and detailed literature concerning the diffusion of the Internet in the US during its first two waves. This is a specific story told about a specific technology in a particular time period, and, at the same time, throughout this chapter we use this story to understand broader questions about the economic workings of diffusion processes. In addition, we will conceive the Internet as a general purpose technology (GPT), using it to build a framework about the economic determinants of its diffusion.

2 Brief history of the Internet

The digital divide did not arise overnight, nor did the Internet. What became the Internet began in the late 1960s as a research project of the Advanced Research Projects Administration of the US Department of Defense, the ARPANET.

From these origins sprang the building blocks of a new communications network. By the mid-1980s, the entire Internet used Transmission Control Protocol/Internet Protocol (TCP/IP) packet-switching technology to connect universities and defence contractors.

Management for large parts of the Internet was transferred to the National Science Foundation, or NSF, in the mid-1980s. Through NSFNET, the NSF was able to provide connection to its supercomputer centres and a high-speed backbone, from which to develop the Internet. Since use of NSFNET was limited to academic and research locations, Alternet, PSInet, and SprintLink developed their own private backbones for corporations looking to connect their systems with TCP/IP (Kahn 1995).

By the early 1990s the NSF had developed a plan to transfer ownership of the Internet out of government hands and into the private sector. When NSFNET was shut down in 1995, for-profit organizations were left running the commercial backbone. Thus, with the Internet virtually completely privatized, its diffusion path within the US was dependent on market forces and economic incentives (Greenstein 2005).

Unlike many other technologies embedded in a single type of durable good, the Internet is a malleable technology the form of which is not fixed across time and location. As with malleable GPTs, to create value, the Internet must be embedded in investments at firms that employ a suite of communications technologies, TCP/IP protocols, and standards for networking between computers. Often organizational processes also must change to take advantage of the new capabilities.

3 THE DIFFUSION PROCESS

Because of the unusual origins of the Internet, it is not immediately obvious that economic theories of diffusion provide an effective guide for analysing the geographical diffusion of the Internet. According to such economic diffusion theory, the rate of adoption of a new technology is jointly determined by consumers' willingness to pay for the new product, and suppliers' profitability from entering the new market. Both typical users and typical suppliers change over time. We consider each of these factors in turn.

Standard diffusion analysis

We begin our analysis with simple definitions. Any entity (household, individual, or firm) is considered to be connected to the Internet if it has the capability of communicating with other entities (information in and/or information out) via the physical structure of the Internet. We will defer discussion about connections coming at different speeds (56K dial up versus broadband) and from different types of suppliers (AOL versus a telephone company).

With regard to consumers, it is the heterogeneity of adopters that generally explains differences in the timing of adoption (Rogers 1995). When a technology first reaches the frontier, a group of risk-taking innovators adopts first and, over time, the technology moves down the hierarchy to mainstream users seeking pragmatic gains. If these groups are not evenly dispersed geographically, there will be an uneven rate of adoption across regions of the country.

In addition, a good deal of heterogeneity in user response in this case is the direct result of another technology's diffusion—that of PCs. The Internet is a 'nested innovation' in that heterogeneity among its potential adopters depends heavily on the diffusion process of PCs (Jimeniz and Greenstein 1998). In addition to this nesting, within the class of PC users there are also differences in their willingness to experiment and the intensity of their use.[1] There are differences in types of adopters across regions in terms of the following five attributes of a new technology widely considered as the most influential for adoption speed across different types of users: relative advantage, compatibility, complexity, trialability, and observability. Any increase in the relative advantage over the previous technology, the compatibility of the new technology with the needs of potential adopters, the ability of adopters to experiment with the new technology, or the ability of users to observe the new technology, will speed up the diffusion process. Similarly, any decrease in technological complexity will also speed up the diffusion process (Rogers 1995).

The Internet has relative advantages along many dimensions. It provides written communication faster than postal mail, allows for purchases online without driving to the store, and dramatically increases the speed of information gathering. The Internet is also easy to try out (perhaps on a friend's PC, or at work), easy to observe, and compatible with many consumer needs (information gathering, fast communication); and its complexity has been decreasing consistently.

The above attributes hold across the US, but the degree to which they hold is not geographically uniform. Specifically, we see differences between rural and urban areas. For example, people living in rural areas might find greater relative advantage since their next-best communication is not as effective as that of their urban counterparts. Also, they might find the Internet more difficult to try or observe, and possibly more complex if they have less exposure to, or experience with, PCs.

GPT framework

Within general diffusion theory there can be much dispute as to why the adoption of a new technology is actualized in a specific way. Here, we apply a GPT framework to our study of the diffusion of the Internet. Bresnahan and Trajtenberg (1995) define a GPT as a capability whose adaptation to a variety of circumstances raises the marginal returns to inventive activity in each of these circumstances. GPTs are often associated with high fixed costs and low marginal costs to use. The invention of the Internet follows this pattern, in the sense that the technology was largely invented and refined by the early 1990s (Bresnahan and Greenstein 2001).

The GPT framework further predicts that additional benefit from the technology comes from co-invention of additional applications. Co-invention costs are the costs affiliated with customizing a technology to particular needs in specific locations at a point in time. These costs can be quite low or high, depending on the idiosyncrasy and complexity of the applications, as well as the economies of scale within locations. They may also depend on regulatory rules over access to network. For example, in the case of dial-up access, Internet service providers (ISPs) faced comparatively low incremental costs because they were complementary to the telephone system. In contrast, particularly in the case of broadband, provision of the Internet in a region involves high fixed costs of operating switches, lines, and servers.

We expect to see firms wishing to minimize fixed costs or exploit economies of scale by serving large markets. Also, the cost of 'last mile' connections (e.g. xDSL or cable) in rural areas is far greater due to their longer distance from the backbone. This basic prediction frames much of the research on the diffusion of the Internet. There will necessarily be a margin between those who adopt and those who do not. What factors are correlated with the observed margin? We can divide these factors into those associated with raising or lowering the costs of supply or the intensity of demand.

The marginal PC adopter

According to the NTIA (2004) study, as of 2003, approximately 61.8 per cent of American homes owned a PC, with Internet participation rates at 54.6 per cent. These adoption rates suggest that the diffusion of each technology is moving into the late majority category of adopters, though there is considerable disagreement about how to portray the rate of adoption for the remaining households. As mentioned above, the Internet is a nested innovation whose adoption at home strongly depends on adoption of a PC.[2] Since the vast majority (87.6 per cent) of PC owners have home Internet access, the marginal Internet adopter looks very similar to the marginal PC adopter and, related, it is natural to hypothesize that the determinants of adoption among non-adopters will differ from its determinants in the late 1990s.

Prince (2005) conducts a structural analysis of the demand for (desktop) PCs in 2001 in the US. A main objective of the paper is to model two very different-looking demand curves—PC demand for households already owning a PC (repeat purchasers), and PC demand for households that have never owned a PC (first time purchasers). His data indicate a large difference between these two groups: the likelihood of buying a new PC in 2001 was more than two times greater for a repeat purchaser than for a first time purchaser. The demand for first time purchasers is especially relevant since it represents the marginal adopters for PCs, and therefore, strongly resembles the marginal adopters of the Internet.

In his paper, Prince describes three main determinants of the 'divide' in PC ownership: heterogeneity (in the marginal utility of PC quality and PC holdings), start-up costs,[3] and dynamics. His results indicate that the marginal utility of PC quality is strongly increasing in income and education, and strongly decreasing in age. Further, forward-looking behaviour also affects the demand for PCs. As prices fall and quality rises over time, the decision about whether to buy a new PC is complicated by the decision of when to buy a new PC. The results show that households' expectations about what PCs will be available in the future affect current demand. Finally, regarding the two demand curves, the paper finds that first time purchasers are more price sensitive than repeat purchasers, and face large start-up costs.

These results show that, as the diffusion of the PC moves deeper into mainstream use, the marginal PC adopter is a household with low marginal value for PC quality, high start-up costs, significant price sensitivity, and potential difficulty in determining when (not necessarily if) to buy. These findings show why the early experience in the adoption of the Internet provides little help for understanding user adoption in later periods. Quite a different set of factors shapes later adoption than shaped early adoption.

Demand by households

Data from 2001 (NTIA 2002) show Internet usage to be positively correlated with household income, employment status, and educational attainment. With regard to age, the highest participation rates were among teenagers, while Americans in their prime working ages (20–50 years of age) were also well connected (about 70 per cent) (NTIA 2002). Although there did not appear to be a gender gap in Internet usage, there did appear to be a significant gap in usage between two widely defined racial groups: (1) whites, Asian Americans, Pacific Islanders (approximately 70 per cent); and (2) Blacks and Hispanics (less than 40 per cent) (NTIA 2002). Much of this disparity in Internet usage can be attributed to observable differences in education and income. For example, at the highest levels of income and education there are no significant differences in adoption and use across ethnicities.

In general, Internet and PC demanders have much in common, and differences in adoption rates across the above variables are similar for both technologies. However, specific to the Internet, a great deal of literature points to a digital divide between rural and urban areas, contending that rural residents are less connected to the Internet than urban ones. Some argue that rural citizens are less prone to use computers and digital networks because of exacerbating propensities arising from lower income, less education, and less technological skills (on average) than those living in the city. The evidence for this hypothesis is mixed, however, with many rural farm households using the Internet at high rates (USDA 2000). In addition, over the two-year span from 1998 to 2000, Internet access went from 27.5 per cent to 42.3 per cent in urban areas, 24.5 per cent to 37.7 per cent in central cities, and 22.2 per cent to 38.9 per cent in rural areas. Thus, there was at least a narrowing of the gap in participation rates between rural and urban areas; and there certainly was no evidence of the gap widening on any front.[4]

Furthermore, when we divide American geography into three sections—rural, inner city urban, and urban (not inner city)—we see lower participation in the first two categories; inner city participation also is low potentially due to a greater percentage of citizens with lower income and education levels. With the higher concentration of Blacks and Hispanics in the inner city, there then arises the correlation between education and income and socioeconomics. As we previously stated, ethnicity is not the cause of lower adoption rates; instead, lower education and income levels, which in turn are caused by socioeconomic factors, create lower adoption rates in the inner cities (Strover 2001). There is also increasing evidence that there is considerable variance in the abilities and skills to take advantage of what the technology has to offer. While this variance correlates somewhat with socioeconomic factors, it also raises a distinct set of issues.[5]

It has been argued that the benefits of adoption are greater for rural areas, because rural residents can use the Internet to compensate for their distance from other activities. Adopting the Internet improves retail choices, information sources, education options, and job availability more than for urban residents (Hindman 2000; Sinai and Waldfogel 2004). However, these benefits may or may not be translated into actual demand, depending on many factors, such as income, education, local support services, or a host of social factors.

Demand for business purposes

Businesses adopt different aspects of Internet technology for a variety of reasons. In the standard framework for analysing diffusion, the decision to adopt or reject the Internet falls within three categories: (1) optional, where the decision is made by the individual; (2) collective, where it is made by consensus among members; or (3) authoritative, where it is made by a few people with authority (Rogers 1995). For businesses, the decision process generally falls under one of the latter two categories.

Business adoption of the Internet came in a variety of forms. Implementation for minimal applications, such as email, was rather straightforward by the late 1990s. It involved a PC, a modem, a contract with an ISP and some appropriate software. In contrast, investment in the use of the Internet for an application module in a suite of Enterprise Resource Planning (ERP) software, for example, was anything but routine during the latter half of the 1990s. Such an implementation included technical challenges beyond the Internet's core technologies, such as security, privacy, and dynamic communication between browsers and servers. Usually organizational procedures also changed.

A further motivating factor will shape business adoption: competitive pressure. As Porter (2001) argues, there are two types of competitive motives behind Internet adoption. First, the level of 'table stakes' may vary by region or industry. That is, there may be a minimal level of investment necessary just to be in business. Secondly, there may be investments in the Internet that confer competitive advantage vis-à-vis rivals. Once again, these will vary by location, industry, and even the strategic positioning of a firm (e.g. price leader, high service provider) within those competitive communities. The key insight is that such comparative factors shape competitive pressure.

Several recent studies look empirically at determining factors for Internet adoption by firms and the possible existence of a digital divide among them. Premkumar and Roberts (1999) test the former by measuring the relevance of ten information technology attributes for the adoption rate of small rural businesses. The ten attributes are: relative advantage, compatibility, complexity, cost-effectiveness, top management support, information technology expertise, size, competitive pressure, vertical linkages, and external support. They found that relative advantage, cost-effectiveness, top management support, competitive pressure, and vertical linkages were significant determinants of Internet adoption decisions.

Forman (2005) examines the early adoption of Internet technologies at 20,000 commercial establishments from a few select industries. He concentrates on a few industries with a history of adoption of frontier Internet technology and studies the microeconomic processes shaping adoption. He finds that rural establishments were as likely as their urban counterparts to participate in the Internet and to employ advanced Internet technologies in their computing facilities to enhance their computing facilities. He attributes this to the higher benefits received by remote establishments, which otherwise had no access to private fixed lines for transferring data.

Forman, Goldfarb, and Greenstein (2002, 2003a, b) measured national Internet adoption rates for medium and large establishments from all industries.[6] They distinguish between two purposes for adopting, one simple and the other complex. The first purpose, labelled 'participation', relates to activities such as email and web browsing. This represents minimal use of the Internet for basic communications. The second purpose, labelled 'enhancement', relates to investment in frontier Internet technologies linked to computing facilities. These latter applications are often known as e-commerce, and involve complementary changes to internal business computing processes. The economic costs and benefits of these activities are also quite distinct; yet, casual analysis in the trade press tends to blur the lines between the two.

Forman, Goldfarb, and Greenstein examined business establishments with 100 or more employees in the last quarter of 2000. They show that adoption of the Internet for purposes of participation is near saturation in most industries. With only a few exceptional, laggard industries, the Internet is everywhere in medium to large business establishments. Their findings for enhancement contrast sharply. There is a strong urban bias towards the adoption of advanced Internet applications. The study concludes, however, that location, *per se*, does not handicap adoption decisions. Rather, the industries that 'lead' in advanced use of the Internet tend to be disproportionately located in urban areas.

They conclude that a large determinant of the location of the Internet in e-commerce was the pre-existing distribution of industrial establishments across cities and regions. This conclusion highlights that some industries are more information intensive than others and, accordingly, make more intensive use of new developments in information technologies, such as the Internet, in the production of final goods and services. Heavy Internet technology user industries have historically been banking and finance, utilities, electronic equipment, insurance, motor vehicles, petroleum refining, petroleum pipeline transport, printing and publishing, pulp and paper, railroads, steel, telephone communications and tyres (Cortada 1996).

Forman, Goldfarb and Greenstein (2005) find evidence consistent with the 'urban leadership' hypothesis. In this view the infrastructure necessary for the geographic diffusion of the Internet, such as the equipment to enable high-speed Internet access, initially appeared to be difficult to deploy and use. Technically difficult technologies favour urban areas, where there are thicker labour markets for specialized engineering talent. Similarly, close proximity to thick technical labour markets facilitates the development of complementary service markets for maintenance and engineering services. Labour markets for technical talent were relevant to the diffusion of new technologies in the Internet. As with many high-tech services, areas with complementary technical and knowledge resources are favoured during the early use of technology.

These findings raise an open question. Early use of advanced technology favours growth in a few locations, such as Silicon Valley, the Boston area, or Manhattan—for a time at least, particularly when technologies are young. But will it persist? This depends on how fast the technology matures into something standardized that can be operated at low cost in areas with thin supply of technical talent.

Furthermore, complex Internet applications are linked to computing facilities, which are often known as e-commerce or e-business. Most often, these technologies involve inter-establishment communication and/or substantial changes to business processes. Cross-establishment Internet technologies, in contrast, represent Internet investments that involve communication among establishments within the value chain (e.g. an extranet) or between an establishment and its end consumers.

Forman, Goldfarb and Greenstein (2005) hypothesize that geographically isolated establishments will have higher gross benefits from communicating with external suppliers and customers. Changes in location size and density will primarily influence costs (and not benefits) for communication within an establishment, but, on the other hand, such changes will influence both costs and benefits of communicating with external parties. They found evidence consistent with these views. That is, controlling for other factors, advanced Internet applications for communication outside the establishment had a higher propensity in rural establishments than Internet applications for communication within an establishment.

Supply by private firms

Since the Internet privatization in 1995, private incentives have driven the supply side of Internet access. ISPs are divided into four classes: (1) transit backbone ISPs; (2) downstream ISPs; (3) online service providers (e.g. AOL); and (4) firms that specialize in Web-site hosting. Provision incentives are profit based, and for a technology with significant economies of scale, profits are likely to be higher in markets with high sales quantity. Thus, we see high numbers of ISPs in regions with high population concentrations (Downes and Greenstein 1998, 2002).

The ISPs also decide on the services they provide (e.g. value-added services) and the price at which they provide them. Greenstein (2000a, b) highlights two types of activities other than basic access in which ISPs partake—high-bandwidth applications, and services that are complementary to basic access. He notes that differences in firm choices are due to 'different demand conditions, different quality of local infrastructure, different labor markets for talent,' or differing qualities of inherited firm assets.

Geography plays a role in these differences and can explain much of the variation in quality of access. We expect the local infrastructure quality to be higher in urban areas. The quality of ISP service will be higher there as well. In addition, rural ISPs often have less incentive to improve due to lack of competition, that is, they are the only provider in their area and thus there is little incentive to enhance their service.

Supply by regulated telephone firms

Every city in the US has at least one incumbent local telephone provider. The deregulation of local telephony has been proceeding in fits and starts in many parts of the US, since the AT&T divestiture in the early 1980s. By the mid-1990s there had been significant attempts at, and success in, allowing competitive access providers to enter local markets to provide alternative local access paths, predominantly for data communications and large volume voice users in business. This movement is an attempt to increase the number of potential providers of local voice services beyond the monopoly incumbent and, in so doing, increase the competitiveness of markets for a variety of voice and data services. This form of deregulation became indirectly linked to the growth of broadband because the rules affecting telephony shaped the entry of potential broadband suppliers. Deregulation also had an indirect impact on the Internet's deployment because it altered the organization of the supply of local data services, primarily in urban areas.[7]

For our purposes here, the key question is, did the change in regulation shape the geographic diffusion of Internet access across the US? The answer is almost certainly, yes—at least in the short run. However, the answer is more ambiguous in the long run. By the end of the millennium the largest cities in the US had dozens of potential and actual competitive suppliers of local telephone service that interconnected with the local incumbent. By the end of 2000, over 500 cities in the US had experience with at least a few competitive suppliers of local telephony, many of them focused on providing related Internet and networking services to local businesses, in addition to telephone service (New Paradigm Research Group 2000).

Prior to the commercialization of the Internet, decades of debate in telephony had already clarified some regulatory rules for interconnection with the public switched network for what the Federal Communications Commission (FCC) defined as an enhanced information service (Cannon 2001). This set of rules applied to dial-up ISPs, but there would be considerable debate about applying them to broadband suppliers. In the dial-up era this set of rules eliminated some potential local delays in implementing this technology on a small scale. In treating ISPs as enhanced service providers and not as competitive telephone companies, the FCC did not pass on access charges to them, which effectively made it cheaper and administratively easier to be an ISP (Oxman 1999).[8]

The new competitor for the deregulated network is known as a Competitive Local Exchange Company, or CLEC for short. No matter how it is deployed, every CLEC has something in common: each offers phone service and related data carrier services that interconnect with the network resources offered by the incumbent provider (e.g. lines, central switches, local switches). In spite of such commonalities, there are many claims in the contemporary press and in CLEC marketing literature that these differences produce value for end users. In particular, CLECs and incumbent phone companies offer competing versions of (sometimes comparable) DSL services and networking services.

Something akin to CLECs existed prior to the 1996 Telecommunications Act, which was the watershed federal bill for furthering deregulation across the country. These firms focused on providing high-bandwidth data services to business in high volume situations, as noted. After the passage of this bill, however, CLECs grew even more and quickly became substantial players in local networks, accounting for over twenty billion dollars a year in revenue in 2000.[9] More to the point, CLECs became the centre of focus of the deregulatory movement. Many CLECs grew very rapidly and often took the lead in providing solutions to issues about providing the last mile of broadband, particularly to businesses and targeted households. In addition, many CLECs already were providing direct line (for example, T-1) services to businesses (as was the incumbent local phone company). After the 'telecom meltdown' in 2001, however, the biggest hopes for CLECs did not become reality. The market capitalization of the entire sector declined even as the number of customers served increased. Instead of developing new initiatives, many firms simply repackaged the Incumbent Local Exchange Providers' services.[10]

The incumbent delivered services over the switch, and so did CLECs. In recognition of the mixed incentives of incumbents, regulators tried to set rules for governing the conduct of the transactions and these were challenged in court. As directed by the 1996 Telecommunications Act, this included setting the prices for renting elements of the incumbent's network, such as the loops that carried the DSL line.[11] However, interpreting and implementing this area of regulation became one of the most contentious chapters in the US telecommunications policy. Legal challenges continued for some time, altering both the rules for unbundling and, eventually, the definition of the boundary between an information service and a telecommunications service. By 2005 Incumbent Local Exchange Providers were no longer obligated to make most DSL service available on a wholesale basis.[12]

Though short lived and constantly changing, this opportunity extended to virtually all cities with a population of more than 250,000, and even to many cities with a population under 100,000. Very few rural cities, however, were afforded this opportunity except for those in the few states that promoted it. So, at the outset, if there were any effects at all, the entry of CLECs only moderately increased broadband supply (and in only urban locations, and in these, primarily to business), if at all.

Due to the uneven availability of the Internet in some locations, local government authorities also intervened to speed deployment, during both the first (dial-up) and second (broadband and wireless) waves of diffusion. Local governments acted as agents for underserved demanders by motivating broadband deployment in some neighbourhoods through select subsidies or the granting of rights of way (Strover and Berquist 2001). Public libraries often received help; the presence of a federal subsidy enables even the poorest rural libraries to have Internet access at subsidized rates (Bertot and McClure 2000). There is considerable variance in these practices over time and across locations, depending on local political circumstances and ever-shifting interpretations of national policy (see, e.g., Gillett, Lehr and Osorio 2004).

Because CLECs did not play a large role in household markets, the second wave of diffusion, involving broadband, ultimately looked somewhat different from the first wave.[13] Provision to business continued to involve a wide mix of providers, as described above. In contrast, both existing cable firms and incumbent local telephone companies became the dominant providers of high speed broadband services to homes in the US. The only exceptions occurred in dense urban environments, such as Manhattan, where private carriers could provide connections to businesses as well as apartment buildings or condominiums (see Crandall and Alleman 2002).

Altogether, CLECs had two effects, on availability of Internet services and on costs/prices for services related to the Internet, such as broadband. During the diffusion of dial-up, the costs of operating an ISP were brought down by the presence of CLECs in urban areas, a factor that surely speeded up adoption. Due to the ambiguities of, and frequent changes to, regulatory rules, however, the effect of CLECs on prices in the second wave of diffusion is much more indirect and, therefore, more ambiguous.

4 Mapping the Internet's dispersion

A number of alternative methods have been devised for measuring the Internet's presence, or its adoption in a location. None is clearly superior, as they are all valid ways of measuring the diffusion of the technology across geographic regions.

Backbone

The commercial Internet consists of hubs, routers, high-speed switches, points of presence (POPs), and high-speed high-capacity pipes that transmit data. These pipes and supporting equipment are sometimes collectively referred to as the backbone. The backbone consists mostly of fibre-optic lines of various speeds and capacity. However, no vendor can point to a specific piece of fibre and call it 'backbone'. This label is a fiction, but a convenient one. Every major vendor has a network with lines that go from one point to another, but it is too much trouble to refer to it as 'transmission capacity devoted primarily to carrying traffic from many sources to many sources'.

Comparing the backbones in different regions is not straightforward. Their presence depends on many things such as population size, type of local industry, and other facets of local demand. Their maximum flow rate is only exploited at peak times, not most of the day, so statistics about capacity must be interpreted with care. Moreover, nobody would expect connection and bandwidth to be equally distributed across geographic space, so the appropriate benchmark for assessing the geographic dispersion of backbone is subject to debate.[14]

Despite this inherent interpretive ambiguity, there is intense policy interest in understanding the geography of commercially supplied backbone. There are concerns that some areas (e.g. small towns) are underserved while others (e.g. major cities) are served too well. There are also concerns that the industry is too concentrated, as well as nearly the opposite, that the competitive situation motivated firms to make impertinent and redundant investments.

One common theme in almost every article addressing the Internet's backbone is the following: a handful of cities in the US dominate in backbone capacity, and, by extension, dominate first use of new Internet technology. Specifically,

San Francisco/Silicon Valley, Washington DC, Chicago, New York, Dallas, Los Angeles, and Atlanta account for the vast majority of backbone capacity (Moss and Townsend 2002, 2000). As of 1997, these seven cities accounted for 64.6 per cent of total capacity, and the gap between this group and the rest remained even during the intense deployment of new networks and capacity between 1997 and 1999. By 1999, even though network capacity had quintupled over the previous two years, the top seven still accounted for 58.8 per cent of total capacity.

In addition, the distribution of backbone capacity does not perfectly mimic population distribution, since metropolitan regions such as Seattle, Austin, and Boston have a disproportionately large number of connections (relative to their populations), whereas larger cities such as Philadelphia and Detroit have dispro-portionately fewer connections (Townsend 2001a, b). Overall, the largest metropol-itan areas are well served by the backbone, while areas such as the rural south have few connections (Warf 2001).

Domain name registrations

Domain names are used to help map intuitive names (such as www.northwestern.edu) to the numeric addresses computers use to find each other on the network. This address system was established in the mid-1990s and diffused rapidly along with the commercial Internet.

The leaders in total domain names are New York and Los Angeles; however, Chicago—normally considered along with New York and Los Angeles as a global city—only ranks a distant fifth, far behind the two leaders. Furthermore, when ranking metropolitan areas according to domain names per 1,000 persons, of these three cities, only Los Angeles ranks among the top 20 (17th). The full ranking of domain name density indicates that medium-sized metropolitan areas dominate, while global cities remain competitive, and small metropolitan areas show very low levels of Internet activity (Townsend 2001a).

Moss and Townsend (2002) looked at the growth rate for domain name regis-trations between 1994 and 1997. They distinguish between global information centres and global cities, and find that global information centres, such as Man-hattan and San Francisco, grew at a pace six times the national average. In contrast, global cities such as New York, Los Angeles, and Chicago grew only at approxi-mately one to two times the national average.

Kolko (2000) examines domain names in the context of questioning whether the Internet enhances the economic centrality of major cities in comparison to geo-graphically isolated cities.[15] He argues, provocatively, that reducing the 'tyranny of distance' between cities does not necessarily lead to proportional economic activity between them. That is, a reduction of communications costs between locations yields ambiguous predictions about the location of economic activity in the periphery or the centre. Lower costs can reduce the costs of economic activity in isolated locations, but it can also enhance the benefits of locating coordinative activity in the central location. As with other researchers, Kolko presumes that coordinative activity is easier in a central city where face-to-face communication takes place.

Kolko (2000) documents a heavy concentration of domain name registrations in a few major cities. He also documents extraordinary per capita registrations in isolated medium-sized cities. He argues that the evidence supports the hypothesis that the Internet is a complement to, not a substitute for face-to-face communication in central cities. He also argues that the evidence supports the hypothesis that lowering communication costs helps business in remote cities of sufficient size (that is, medium-sized, but not too small).

Hosts, ISPs, and POPs

Measurements of host sites, ISPs, and POPs also have been used to measure the Internet's diffusion. Indeed, the growth of the Internet can be directly followed in the successive years of *Boardwatch Magazine*. The earliest advertisements for ISPs in *Boardwatch Magazine* appear in late 1993, growing slowly until mid-1995, at which point *Boardwatch* began to organize their presentation of pricing and basic offerings. There was an explosion of entries in 1995, with thousands being present for the subsequent few years. Growth only diminished after 2001.

Internet hosts are defined as computers connected to the Internet on a full-time basis. Host-site counting may be a suspect measurement technique due to its inability to differentiate between various types of equipment, and to the common practice of firms not to physically house Internet-accessible information at their physical location. Nevertheless, we do see results similar to those found with other measurement techniques, since, as of 1999, five states (California, Texas, Virginia, New York, and Massachusetts) contain half of all Internet hosts in the US (Warf 2001).

Downes and Greenstein (2002) analyse the presence of ISPs throughout the United States. Their results show that, while low entry into a county is largely a rural phenomenon, more than 92 per cent of the US population had access by a short local phone call to seven or more ISPs as of 1997. Strover, Oden, and Inagaki (2002) look directly at ISP presence in areas that have traditionally been under-served by communications technologies (for example, the Appalachian region). They examine areas in the states of Iowa, Texas, Louisiana, and West Virginia. They determine the availability and nature of Internet services from ISPs for each county and find that rural areas suffer significant disadvantages in relation to Internet service (see also, Strover 2001).

Measurements of POPs help to identify 'urban and economic factors spurring telecommunication infrastructure growth and investment' (Grubesic and O'Kelly 2002: 260). The POPs are locations where ISPs maintain communications equipment for network access. This is often a switch or router that allows Internet traffic to enter or proceed on commercial Internet backbones. Through POP measurement,

Grubesic and O'Kelly derived similar results to those concerning the backbone, namely the top seven cities, Chicago, New York, Washington DC, Los Angeles, Dallas, Atlanta, and San Francisco provide the most POPs. Furthermore, Boston and Seattle are emerging Internet leaders.

Grubesic and O'Kelly (2002) use POPs to measure which metropolitan areas are growing the fastest. Their data indicate that such areas as Milwaukee, Tucson, Nashville, and Portland saw major surges in POPs at the end of the 1990s. They provide several explanations for these surges: (1) proximity to major telecommunications centres (e.g. Tucson and Milwaukee); (2) intermediation between larger cities with high Internet activity (e.g. Portland); and (3) centralized location (e.g. Nashville). Greenstein (2005) offers an additional interpretation of these findings, arguing that hub-and-spoke economics for networks in geographic space explains the general patterns for many advantageously-located large and medium sized cities.

Content, e-commerce

Zook (2000, 2001) proposes two additional methods for measuring the presence of the Internet. The first measures the Internet by content production across the US. Zook (2000: 412; 2001) defines the content business as enterprises involved in the creation, organization, and dissemination of informational products to a global marketplace where a significant portion of the business is conducted via the Internet. He plotted the location of each firm with a dotcom Internet address and found that San Francisco, New York, and Los Angeles are the leading centres for Internet content in the US with regard to absolute size and degree of specialization.[16]

The second method looks at the locations of the dominant firms in e-commerce. Again, Zook (2000, 2001) finds the top Internet companies based on electronically generated sales and other means, and their location. His analysis shows San Francisco, New York, and Los Angeles as dominant in e-commerce, with Boston and Seattle ranking 4th and 5th. When measured on a scale relative to the number of Fortune 1000 companies located in the region, his results indicate greater activity on the coasts (especially the West coast) with many midwestern cities such as Detroit, Omaha, Cincinnati, and Pittsburgh lagging.

5 DIFFUSION OF ADVANCED INTERNET ACCESS

Internet connection generally comes in two forms: (1) dial-up (technology now behind the frontier); and (2) broadband (the new frontier technology).

Provision and adoption

While dial-up connection has moved past the frontier stage in the US, broadband access is still at the frontier. For a few years it was far from ubiquitous, though that is changing at the time of writing.[17] However, as the volume and complexity of traffic on the Internet increases dramatically each year, the value of high-capacity and universal 'always on' broadband service is constantly increasing. Furthermore, broadband access will enable providers to offer a wider range of bundled communications services (e.g. telephone, email, Internet video, etc.) as well as promote more competition between physical infrastructure providers already in place.

In the earliest years of diffusion to households—that is, prior to 2003—the diffusion of broadband Internet access was very much supply-driven in the sense that supply-side issues were the main determinants of Internet availability and, hence, adoption. Cable firms and telephone firms needed to retrofit existing plant, and this constrained availability in many places. In these years the spread of broadband service was much slower and less evenly distributed than that of dial-up service. Highly populated areas were more profitable due to economies of scale and lower last mile expenses. As building has removed these constraints, demand-related factors—such as price, speed, and reliability—should play a more significant role in determining the margins between who adopts and who does not.

As from October 2003, 37.2 per cent of Internet users possessed a high-speed connection; the dominant types of broadband access were cable modems and xDSL. In addition, broadband penetration has been uneven, as 41.2 per cent of urban and 41.6 per cent of central city households with Internet access used broadband compared to a rate of only 25.3 per cent for rural households. Consistent with the supply-side issues, the FCC estimates that high-speed subscribers were present in 97 per cent of the most densely populated zip codes at the end of 2000, whereas they were present in only 45 per cent of the zip codes with the lowest population density (NTIA 2002). Research by Prieger (2003) shows that high speed access and rural location are negatively correlated even after controlling for demographic variables, lending further support to the argument that the supply side is driving lower rural broadband adoption.

Most of the additional empirical evidence comes from these earliest years. For example, Augereau and Greenstein (2001) analyse the evolution of broadband provision and adoption by looking at the determinants of ISPs' upgrade decisions. Although their analysis only looks at upgrades from dial-up service to 56K modem or ISDN service occurring by 1997, it addresses issues related to the provision of high-speed service and warrants mention as an empirical paper with the earliest evidence on ISP upgrade behaviour. In their model, they look for firm-specific factors and location-specific factors that affect firms' choices to offer more advanced Internet services. Their main finding is that 'the ISPs with the highest propensity to upgrade are the firms with more capital equipment and the firms with propitious locations' (Augereau and Greenstein 2001: 1099). The most expansive ISPs locate in urban areas. They further argue that this could lead to inequity in the quality of supply between ISPs in high-density and low-density areas.

Grubesic and Murray (2002) look at differences in xDSL access for different regions in Columbus, Ohio. They point out that xDSL access can be inhibited for some consumers due to the infrastructure and distance requirements. The maximum coverage radius for xDSL is approximately 18,000 feet from a central switching office (CSO), which is a large, expensive building.[18] Furthermore, the radius is closer to 12,000 feet for high-quality, low-interruption service. Therefore, those living beyond this radius from the CSOs already built before xDSL was available are more likely to suffer from lack of service. As a counter-intuitive result, affluent areas such as Franklin County in Ohio might lack high-speed access, which is contrary to the usual notion of there being a socioeconomic digital divide (Grubesic and Murray 2002). However, this does give more insight into why many rural residents (those living in places with more dispersed populations) might also lack high-speed access.

Gillett and Lehr (1999) compiled a database of communities in the US where cable modem service is offered, and linked it to county-level demographic data. They found that broadband access is not universal. Only 43 per cent of the population live in counties with available cable modem service.[19] Broadband access is typically available in counties with large populations, high per capita income, and high population density; and there is a notable difference in the strategies of cable operators, with some being more aggressive than others.

In a very data-intensive study, Gabel and Kwan (2001) examine deployment of DSL services at central switches throughout the US and provide a thorough census of upgrade activity at switches. They examine the choice of providers to deploy advanced technology—to make broadband services available to different segments of the population. The crucial factors in the decision to offer service are listed as: (1) cost of supplying the service; (2) potential size of the market; (3) cost of reaching the Internet backbone; and (4) regulations imposed on Regional Bell Operating Companies (RBOCs).[20] They find that advanced telecommunications service is not being deployed in low-income and rural areas.

In summary, even before considering the impact of geographic dispersion on demand, the issues involved in the cost of supply guaranteed that the diffusion process of broadband would differ from dial-up. The earliest broadband ISPs, primarily cable companies and telephone companies, found highly dense areas more profitable due to economies of scale in distribution and lower expenses in build-out. Moreover, the build-out and retrofit activities for broadband are much more involved and expensive than was required for the build-out of dial-up networks. So within urban areas, there was uneven availability during the earliest years of the build-out.

The underlying economic situation has shaped this outcome. As long as prices for broadband are much higher than for dial-up, users face a price/quality trade-off, and different preferences over that trade-off shape the margin between adopter and non-adopter. If prices decline and become much closer to dial-up prices, then broadband's superior qualities should diminish the importance of that trade-off. In addition, providers of broadband may put together bundles of services (e.g. voice, video, and Internet service) that have marketing appeal. Finally, and more speculatively, if a low-cost wireless solution for providing high-bandwidth applications emerges, then it may have features that might induce adoption where none has yet occurred. For a number of years one should expect next generations of Internet access to grow primarily by taking market share from dial-up, and secondarily by inducing first time adoption. There is little evidence to suggest that broadband will induce anything other than slow adoption by households who had not experienced the Internet by 2003.

Rural versus urban divides

We can make several key observations concerning a geographical divide. First, a divide for basic dial-up Internet services is generally nonexistent, or, at worst, it is relegated to a very small part of the population. Due to the pre-existing telephone service infrastructure, the cost of provision is relatively low; thus, we see over 92 per cent of households just a local call away from Internet connection. Furthermore, as of 2001, 52.9 per cent of rural residents were using the Internet, higher than the central city average of 49.1 per cent, and not much lower than 57.4 per cent for urban residents who are not in a central city (NTIA 2002).

Businesses participate at high rates, over 90 per cent for medium and large establishments (over 100 employees). While we do see lower basic participation rates in rural areas, this essentially is due to the type of industries we find there (i.e. industries deriving less relative benefit from Internet connection). Thus, in this particular case, we see that it is not necessarily availability of Internet access, but largely the private incentives of the adopters (commercial businesses) that is determining the adoption rate.

Augereau and Greenstein (2001) warn of the possibility of the divide in availability worsening as large firms in large cities continue to upgrade their services rapidly while smaller firms in smaller cities move forward more slowly. Now that basic service is available almost everywhere in the country, the real issue of concern is the evolution of *quality* of service geographically, as well as value per dollar. Several authors warn that we may be headed down a road of bifurcation where large urban areas get better service at a faster pace, while smaller cities and urban conurbations fall behind. Greenstein (2000a: 408) suggests that these areas get more new services due to two factors: '(1) increased exposure to national ISPs, who expand their services more often; and (2) the local firms in urban areas possess features that lead them to offer services with propensities similar to the national firms.'

Along a different line of argument, Strover (2001) arrives at a similarly pessimistic assessment, one shared by many observers.[21] She points out that the cost structure for ISPs is unfavourable because of their dependence on commercial telecommunications infrastructure providers, which are reluctant to invest in rural areas due to the high costs necessary to reach what often are relatively few customers. A lack of competition in rural areas among telephone service providers serves to exacerbate the low incentives. Furthermore, the fact that the economics of small cities are shaped more by the private sector than government initiatives, makes small cities less prone to initiating plans to develop telecommunications (Alles, Esparza and Lucas 1994).

Many studies place a much greater emphasis on other variables along which they find the divide is much more pronounced. Hindman (2000) suggests that there is no strong evidence of a widening gap between urban and rural residents' use of information technologies, but that such predictors as income, education, and age have become even more powerful in predicting usage over the years (specifically from 1995 to 1998).

Forman, Goldfarb, and Greenstein (2002, 2003a, b) find that, as from December 2000, 12.6 per cent of establishments engage in some form of Internet enhancement activities. Furthermore, they find much higher enhancement adoption rates in large cities (consolidated metropolitan statistical areas) as the top ten ranges from Denver at 18.3 per cent to Portland at 15.1 per cent. In addition, enhancement adoption rates in large urban counties (metropolitan statistical areas) is 14.7 per cent, while that of small counties is only 9.9 per cent on average. However, they also find that the industries of 'management of companies and enterprises' (NAICS 55) and 'media, telecommunications, and data processing' (NAICS 51) had enhancement adoption rates of 27.9 per cent and 26.8 per cent, respectively—rates far exceeding all other industries.[22] This strongly points to the idea that geographical differences may largely be explained by the pre-existing geographical distribution of industries.

6 OVERVIEW

What happened during the first wave of diffusion?

It was unclear at the outset which of several potential maturation processes would occur after commercialization. If advancing Internet infrastructure stayed exotic and difficult to use, then its geographic distribution would depend on the location of the users most willing to pay for infrastructure. If advancing Internet infrastructure became less exotic for a greater number of users and vendors, then commercial maturation would produce geographic dispersion over time, away from the areas of early experimentation. Similarly, as advanced technology becomes more standardized, it is also more easily serviced in outlying areas, again contributing to its geographic dispersion.

As it turned out, the first wave of the diffusion of the Internet (from 1995 to 2000) did not follow the most pessimistic predictions. The Internet did diffuse to urban areas with their complementary technical and knowledge resources, but the location of experiments was necessarily temporary, an artefact of the lack of maturity of the applications. As this service matured—as it became more reliable and declined in price so that wider distribution became economically feasible—the geographic areas that were early leaders in technology lost their comparative lead or ceased to be leaders. As such, basic ISP technology diffused widely and comparatively rapidly after commercialization. On-the-margin users in urban areas had a better experience than users in rural areas, but many of these differences arose from straightforward economic reasons, such as the cost of provision and the lack of economies of scale brought about by thin demand.

Open questions remain as the next wave proceeds. There is little experience with uncoordinated commercial forces developing a high-speed communication network with end-to-end architecture. This applies to the many facets that make up advanced telecommunications services for packet switching, such as switching using frame relay or Asynchronous Transfer Mode, as well as Synchronous Optical Network equipment or Optical Carrier services of various numerical levels (Noam 2001).

The spread of broadband service has been seemingly slower and almost certainly much less evenly distributed than that of dial-up. This is not surprising once their basic economics is analysed; moreover it is possibly an artefact of early limitations on availability. The broadband ISPs find highly dense areas more profitable due to economies of scale in distribution and lower expenses in build-out. Moreover, the build-out and retrofit activities for broadband are much more involved and expensive than was required for the build-out of the dial-up networks.

7 OPEN QUESTIONS ABOUT THE
SECOND WAVE

How will the Internet's geographic characteristics shape economic growth during the second wave of diffusion? The answer is not clear for a variety of reasons. First, it is not clear whether new technologies for delivering the Internet will alter the bilateral relationship between geography and the Internet. For example, will Internet connection via satellite emerge as the connection of choice, and if so, how much would this dampen the argument that location matters? Will another fixed wireless solution emerge for delivery of high-speed data services, and will it exhibit low enough economies of scale to spread to suburban areas? Secondly, and perhaps more speculatively, the Internet will affect the diffusion of other new products. As the majority of American homes becomes hard-wired, how drastic will the effect be on local media, such as local newspapers (see, e.g. Chyi and Sylvie 2001)? If individuals can access any radio station in the country at any time, how can all incumbent stations possibly stay in existence? These were mostly rhetorical questions about hypothetical scenarios during the earliest years of the Internet's diffusion, but have become less so with increasing numbers of Internet users. The Internet has diffused to a sufficiently large population that researchers have begun to accumulate evidence based on actual firm behaviour (see, e.g. Ting and Wildman 2002).

Thirdly, it is not clear whether the digital divide will accelerate or decelerate, as new technologies diffuse on the existing network. Consider the following: use of some peer-to-peer technologies, such as ICQ and Napster and Skype, spread very fast worldwide because these were nested within the broader use of the Internet at the time. Was their speed of adoption exceptional, a by product of the early state of the commercial Internet, or something we should expect to see frequently? There are related questions about the spread of new technologies supporting improvements in the delivery of Internet services. Will the diffusion of IPv6 occur quickly because its use is nested within the structure of existing facilities? Will various versions of XML spread quickly or slowly due to the interrelatedness of all points on the Internet? What about standards supporting IP telephony? Will 802.11b (aka WiFi) diffuse to multiple locations because it is such a small scale technology, or will its small scale interfere with a coordinated diffusion?

As we speculate about future technologies, two overriding lessons from the past shape our thinking. First, once the technology was commercialized, private firms tailored it in multiple locations in ways that nobody had foreseen. Indeed, the eventual shape, speed, growth, and use of the commercial Internet were not foreseen within government circles (at NSF), despite (comparatively) good intentions and benign motives on the part of government overseers, and despite advice from the best technical experts in the world. Second, Internet infrastructure grew because it is malleable, not because it was technically perfect. It is better thought of as a cheap retrofit on top of the existing communications infrastructure. No single solution was right for every situation, but a TCP/IP solution could be found in most places. The US telephone system provided fertile ground because backbone used existing infrastructure when possible. What existing infrastructure will the next generation of Internet use?

REFERENCES

ALLES, P., ESPARZA, A. and LUCAS, S. (1994). 'Telecommunications and the Large City–Small City Divide: Evidence from Indiana cities'. *Professional Geographer*, 46: 307–16.

ATROSTIC, B. K. and NGUYEN, S. V. (2002). 'Computer Networks and US Manufacturing Plant Productivity: New Evidence from the CNUS Data'. Working Paper #02-01, Center for Economic Studies, US Census Bureau, Washington DC.

AUGEREAU, A. and GREENSTEIN, S. (2001). 'The Need for Speed in Emerging Communications Markets: Upgrades to Advanced Technology at Internet Service Providers'. *International Journal of Industrial Organization*, 19: 1085–1102.

BAUER, J. M. (2005). 'Unbundling Policy in the United States: Players, Outcomes and Effects'. *Communications & Strategies*, 57: 59–82.

BERTOT, J. and MCCLURE, C. (2000). *Public Libraries and the Internet, 2000*. Report prepared for National Commission on Libraries and Information Science, Washington DC, http://www.nclis.gov/statsurv/2000plo.pdf.

Boardwatch Magazine (various years). Directory of Internet Service Providers, Littleton, CO.

BRESNAHAN, T. and GREENSTEIN, S. (2001). 'The Economic Contribution of Information Technology: Towards Comparative and User Studies'. *Journal of Evolutionary Economics*, 11: 95–118.

—— and TRAJTENBERG, M. (1995). 'General Purpose Technologies: "Engines of Growth"?' *Journal of Econometrics*, 65(1): 83–108.

CANNON, R. (2001). 'Where Internet Service Providers and Telephone Companies Compete: A Guide to the Computer Inquiries, Enhanced Service Providers, and Information Service Providers', in B. Compaine and S. Greenstein (eds), *Communications Policy in Transition: The Internet and Beyond*. Cambridge, MA: MIT Press, 3–34.

CASTELLS, M. (2001). *The Internet Galaxy: Reflections on the Internet, Business and Society*. Oxford: Oxford University Press.

CHYI, H. I. and SYLVIE, G. (2001). 'The Medium Is Global, the Content Is Not: The Role of Geography in Online Newspaper Markets'. *Journal of Media Economics*, 14(4): 231–48.

CORTADA, J. W. (1996). *Information Technology as Business History: Issues in the History and Management of Computers*. Westport, CT: Greenwood Press.

CRANDALL, R. W. and ALLEMAN, J. H. (2002). *Broadband: Should We Regulate High-Speed Internet Access?* Washington DC: AEI-Brookings Joint Center for Regulatory Studies.

DODGE, M. and KITCHIN, R. (2001a). *Atlas of CyberSpace*. London: Addison Wesley.

—— and —— (2001b). *Mapping CyberSpace*. London: Routledge.

DOWNES, T. and GREENSTEIN, S. (1998). 'Do Commercial ISPs Provide Universal Access?' in S. Gillett and I. Vogelsang (eds), *Competition, Regulation and Convergence: Current Trends in Telecommunications Policy Research*. Mahwah, NJ: Lawrence Erlbaum Associates, 195–212.

—— and —— (2002) 'Universal Access and Local Internet Markets in the U.S'. *Research Policy*, 31: 1035–52.

FORMAN, C. (2005). 'The Corporate Digital Divide: Determinants of Internet Adoption'. *Management Science*, 51(4): 641–54.

——— GOLDFARB, A. and GREENSTEIN, S. (2002). 'Digital Dispersion: An Industrial and Geographic Census of Commercial Internet Use'. Working Paper, NBER, Cambridge, MA.

——— and ——— and ——— (2003a). 'The Geographic Dispersion of Commercial Internet Use', in S. Wildman and L. Cranor (eds), *Rethinking Rights and Regulations: Institutional Responses to New Communication Technologies*. Cambridge, MA: MIT Press, 113–45.

——— and ——— and ——— (2003b). 'Which Industries use the Internet?', in M. Baye (ed.), *Organizing the New Industrial Economy*. Amsterdam: Elsevier, 47–72.

——— and ——— and ——— (2005). 'How did Location Affect Adoption of the Internet by Commercial Establishments? Urban Density versus Global Village'. *Journal of Urban Economics*, 58(3): 389–420.

GABEL, D. and KWAN, F. (2001). 'Accessibility of Broadband Communication Services by Various Segments of the American Population', in B. Compaine and S. Greenstein (eds), *Communications Policy in Transition: The Internet and Beyond*. Cambridge, MA: MIT Press, 295–320.

GARCIA, D. L. (1996). 'Who? What? Where? A Look at Internet Deployment in Rural America'. *Rural Telecommunications*, Nov./Dec.: 25–9.

GILLETT, S. E. and LEHR, W. (1999). 'Availability of Broadband Internet Access: Empirical Evidence', http://itel.mit.edu/itel/docs/MISC/LehrGillettTPRC99_0523.doc, accessed 17 Mar. 2006.

———, LEHR, W. H. and OSORIO, C. (2004). 'Local Government Broadband Initiatives'. *Telecommunications Policy*, 28: 537–58.

GOOLSBEE, A. and KLENOW, P. (1999). 'Evidence on Learning and Network Externalities in the Diffusion of Home Computers'. NBER Working Papers 7329, NBER, Cambridge, MA.

GORMAN, S. P. and MALECKI, E. J. (2000). 'The Networks of the Internet: An Analysis of Provider Networks in the USA'. *Telecommunications Policy*, 24(2): 113–34.

GREENSTEIN, S. (2000a). 'Building and Delivering the Virtual World: Commercializing Services for Internet Access'. *The Journal of Industrial Economics*, 48(4): 391–411.

——— (2000b). 'Empirical Evidence on Commercial Internet Access Providers' Propensity to Offer new Services', in B. Compaign and I. Vogelsang (eds), *The Internet Upheaval, Raising Questions and Seeking Answers in Communications Policy*. Cambridge, MA: MIT Press, 253–76.

——— (2005). 'The Economic Geography of Internet Infrastructure in the United States', in M. Cave, S. Majumdar and I. Vogelsang (eds), *Handbook of Telecommunications Economics, Vol. II*. Amsterdam: Elsevier Publishing, 289–374.

——— and MAZZEO, M. (2006). 'The Role of Differentiation Strategy in Local Telecommunication Entry and Market Evolution: 1999–2002', *Journal of Industrial Economics*, 54(3): 323–50.

GRUBESIC, T. H. and MURRAY, A. T. (2002). 'Constructing the Divide: Spatial Disparities in Broadband Access'. *Papers in Regional Science*, 81(2): 197–221.

——— and O'KELLY, M. E. (2002). 'Using Points of Presence to Measure Accessibility to the Commercial Internet'. *Professional Geographer*, 54(2): 259–78.

HARGETTAI, E. (2003). 'The Digital Divide and What To Do About It', in D. C. Jones (ed.), *The New Economy*. San Diego, CA: Academic Press, 822–38.

HINDMAN, D. B. (2000). 'The Rural–Urban Digital Divide'. *Journalism and Mass Communication Quarterly*, 77(3): 549–60.

JIMENIZ, E. and GREENSTEIN, S. (1998). 'The Emerging Internet Retailing Market as a Nested Diffusion Process'. *International Journal of Innovation Management*, 2(3): 281–308.

KAHN, R. (1995). 'The Role of Government in the Evolution of the Internet,' in National Academy of Engineering (ed.), *Revolution in the U.S. Information Infrastructure*. Washington DC: National Academy Press, 13–24.

KENDE, M. (2000). 'The Digital Handshake: Connecting Internet Backbones'. Working Paper No. 32., Federal Communications Commission, Office of Planning and Policy, Washington DC.

KITCHIN, R. M. (1998). 'Towards Geographies of Cyberspace'. *Progress in Human Geography*, 22(3): 385–406.

KOLKO, J. (2000). 'The Death of Cities? The Death of Distance? Evidence from the Geography of Commercial Internet Usage', in I. Vogelsang and B. Compaine (eds), *The Internet Upheaval: Raising Questions, Seeking Answers in Communications Policy*. Cambridge, MA: MIT Press, 73–98.

—— (2002). 'Silicon Mountains, Silicon Molehills, Geographic Concentration and Convergence of Internet Industries in the U.S.' *Economics of Information and Policy*, 14(2): 211–32.

MALECKI, E. J. (2002). 'The Economic Geography of the Internet's Infrastructure'. *Economic Geography*, 78(4): 399–424.

—— and GORMAN, S. (2001). 'Maybe the Death of Distance, But not the End of Geography: The Internet as a Network', in T. Leinbach and S. Brunn (eds), *Worlds of E-Commerce: Economic, Geographical and Social Dimensions*. New York: John Wiley and Sons, 87–105.

MOSS, M. L. and TOWNSEND, A. M. (1999). 'How Telecommunications Systems are Transforming Urban Spaces', in J. O. Wheeler and Y. Aoyama (eds), *Cities in the Telecommunications Age*. New York: Routledge, 31–41.

—— and —— (2000). 'The Internet Backbone and the American Metropolis'. *Information Society*, 16(1): 35–47.

—— and —— (2002). 'The Role of the Real City in Cyberspace: Measuring and Representing Regional Variations in Internet Accessibility', in D. Janelle and D. Hodge (eds), *Information, Place, and Cyberspace*. Berlin: Springer Verlag, 171–86.

MOWERY, D. C. and SIMCOE, T. S. (2002). 'The Origins and Evolution of the Internet', in R. Nelson, B. Steil and D. Victor (eds), *Technological Innovation and Economic Performance*. Princeton, NJ: Princeton University Press, 229–64.

NTIA (National Telecommuncations and Information Administration) (1995). 'Falling Through the Net: A Survey of the "Have Nots" in Rural and Urban America', http://www.ntia.doc.gov/reports.html, accessed 17 Mar. 2006.

—— (1997). 'Falling Through the Net: Defining the Digital Divide', http://www.ntia.doc.gov/reports.html, accessed 17 Mar. 2006.

—— (1998). 'Falling Through the Net II: New Data on the Digital Divide', http://www.ntia.doc.gov/reports.html, accessed 17 Mar. 2006.

—— (2002). 'A Nation Online: How Americans Are Expanding Their Use of the Internet', http://www.ntia.doc.gov/reports.html, accessed 17 Mar. 2006.

—— (2004). 'A Nation Online: Entering the Broadband Age', http://www.ntia.doc.gov/reports.html, accessed 25 Mar. 2006.

New Paradigm Resources Group (2000). *CLEC Report*, Chicago, IL.

NOAM, E. (2001). *Interconnecting the Network of Networks*. Cambridge, MA: MIT Press.

NUECHTERLEIN, J. E. and WEISER, P. J. (2005). *Digital Crossroads: American Telecommunications Policy in the Internet Age*. Cambridge, MA: MIT Press.

OXMAN, J. (1999). 'The FCC and the Unregulation of the Internet'. Working Paper 31, Federal Communications Commission, Office of Planning and Policy, Washington DC.

PARKER, E. B. (2000). 'Closing the Digital Divide in Rural America'. *Telecommunications Policy*, 24(4): 281–90.

PORTER, M. (2001). 'Strategy and the Internet'. *Harvard Business Review*, 79(3): 62–78.

PREMKUMAR, G. and ROBERTS, M. (1999). 'Adoption of New Information Technologies in Rural Small Businesses'. *Omega-International Journal of Management Science*, 27(4): 467–84.

PRIEGER, J. E. (2003). 'The Supply Side of the Digital Divide: Is There Equal Availability in the Broadband Internet Access Market?' *Economic Inquiry*, 41(2): 346–63.

PRINCE, J. (2005). 'Measuring the Digital Divide: Structural Estimation of the Demand for Personal Computers'. Mimeo, Cornell University.

ROGERS, E. M. (1995). *Diffusion of Innovations*. New York: Free Press.

ROSSTON, G. and WIMMER, B. (2001). ' "From C to Shining C" Competition and Cross-Subsidy in Communications', in B. Compaine and S. Greenstein (eds), *Communications Policy in Transition: The Internet and Beyond*. Cambridge, MA: MIT Press, 241–64.

SINAI, T. and WALDFOGEL, J. (2004). 'Geography and the Internet: Is the Internet a Substitute or a Complement for Cities?' *Journal of Urban Economics*, 56(1): 1–24.

STAFFORD, T. F. (2003). 'Differentiating between Adopter Categories in the Uses and Gratifications for Internet Services', *IEEE Transactions on Engineering Management*, 50(4): 427–35.

STROVER, S. (2001). 'Rural Internet Connectivity'. *Telecommunications Policy*, 25(5): 331–47.

—— and BERQUIST, L. (2001). 'Developing Telecommunications Infrastructure: State and Local Policy Collisions', in B. Compaine and S. Greenstein (eds), *Communications Policy in Transition: The Internet and Beyond*. Cambridge, MA: MIT Press, 221–40.

STROVER, S., ODEN, M. and INAGAKI, N. (2002). 'Telecommunications and Rural Economies: Findings from the Appalachian Region', in L. F. Cranor and S. Greenstein (eds), *Communication Policy and Information Technology: Promises, Problems, Prospects*. Cambridge, MA: MIT Press, 317–46.

TING, C. and WILDMAN, S. (2002) 'The Economics of Internet Radio'. Paper presented at the 30th Telecommunications Policy Research Conference, Alexandria, VA, 29 Sept.

TOWNSEND, A. M. (2001a). 'Network Cities and the Global Structure of the Internet'. *American Behavioral Scientist*, 44(10): 1697–716.

—— (2001b). 'The Internet and the Rise of the New Network Cities, 1969–1999'. *Environment and Planning B-Planning & Design*, 28(1): 39–58.

USDA (US Department of Agriculture) (2000). *Advanced Telecommunications in Rural America, The Challenge of Bringing Broadband Communications to All of America*. April, Washington DC http://www.ntia.doc.gov/reports/ruralbb42600.pdf accessed 1 Aug. 2006.

VAN DIJK, J. A. G. M. (2005). *The Deepening Divide: Inequality in the Information Society*. Thousand Oaks, CA: Sage Publications.

WARF, B. (2001). 'Segue Ways into Cyberspace: Multiple Geographies of the Digital Divide'. *Environment and Planning B-Planning and Design*, 28(1): 3–19.

WEINBERG, J. (1999). 'The Internet and Telecommunications Services, Access Charges, Universal Service Mechanisms, and Other Flotsam of the Regulatory System', in S. Gillett and I. Vogelsang (eds), *Competition, Regulation and Convergence: Current Trends in Telecommunications Policy Research*. Mahwah, NJ: Lawrence Erlbaum Associates, 297–316.

WERBACH, K. (1997). *A Digital Tornado: The Internet and Telecommunications Policy*. Working Paper 29, Federal Communication Commission, Office of Planning and Policy, Washington DC.

WOROCH, G. (2001). 'Local Network Competition', in M. Cave, S. Majumdar and I. Vogelsang (eds), *Handbook of Telecommunications Economics*. Amsterdam: Elsevier Publishing, 642–716.

ZOOK, M. A. (2000). 'The Web of Production: the Economic Geography of Commercial Internet Content Production in the United States'. *Environment and Planning A*, 32(3): 411–26.

——— (2001). 'Old Hierarchies or New Networks of Centrality? The Global Geography of the Internet Content Market'. *American Behavioral Scientist*, 44(10): 1679–96.

NOTES

1. For more on the diffusion of PCs, see Goolsbee and Klenow (1999), US Department of Agriculture (2000), or NTIA (1995, 1997, 1998, 2002).
2. As of 2003, approximately 1% of households accessed the Internet using a mobile telephone or some other home Internet access device. More than this, only 14.2% of Internet users did not have home access, further highlighting the strong relationship between Internet use and home adoption (NTIA 2004).
3. These are the one-time costs of learning how to use a PC and all its peripherals.
4. For the full historical trend, see also NTIA (1995, 1997, 1998).
5. This is a large topic and outside the scope of this review. See, e.g. Hargettai (2003) or van Dijk (2005).
6. See, also, Atrostic and Nguyen (2002), who look at establishments in manufacturing. To the extent that they examine adoption, their study emphasizes how the size of establishments shapes the motives to adopt networking for productivity purposes.
7. For a comprehensive review of the literature, see Woroch (2001).
8. The FCC's decision was made many years earlier for many reasons, and extended to ISPs in the mid-1990s with little notice at the time, since most insiders did not anticipate the extent of the growth that would arise. As ISPs grew in geographic coverage and revenues and threatened to become competitive voice carriers, these interconnection regulations came under more scrutiny (Werbach 1997, Kende 2000, Weinberg 1999).
9. See Crandall and Alleman (2002).
10. Some ISPs operated as CLECs and vice versa, but many did not. This is a complex topic, still changing as of this writing. See www.alts.org, New Paradigm Resources Group (2000), or Greenstein and Mazzeo (2006).
11. For a review of the determinants of pricing within states, see Rosston and Wimmer (2001).
12. This is a complex topic that necessarily strays into matters outside the scope of this review. For extensive description and analysis of these disputes and their resolution, see e.g. Bauer (2005) or Nuechterlein and Weiser (2005).
13. For example, Greenstein and Mazzeo (2006) find that most CLECs explicitly targeted their services at businesses and few CLECs offered *only* household service. In low density areas the CLECs were largely existing phone companies who tried to cream skim business customers in neighbouring small towns. With only a few exceptions, in

the major urban areas those CLECs that targeted households did so in conjunction with their business services and only when the costs of doing so were not cost-prohibitive, such as in a high density location like Manhattan, or in downtown Chicago, or Boston, or San Francisco.

14. For a variety of perspectives, see Kitchin (1998), Moss and Townsend (1999), Dodge and Kitchin (2001a, b), Castells (2001), Malecki and Gorman (2001), Gorman and Malecki (2000) and reviews in Malecki (2002) and Greenstein (2005).

15. See, also, Kolko (2002).

16. Degree of specialization is measured by relating the number of .com domains in a region relative to the total number of firms in a region to the number of .com domains in the US relative to the total number of firms in the US (Zook 2000).

17. Broadband is defined by the FCC as the capability of supporting at least 200 Kbps in at least one direction (supplier and/or consumer), http://www.fcc.gov.

18. This is the non-amplified radius; with amplifiers the signal could reach further. However, the 18,000 feet only applies to service of up to 1.5 Mbps; for higher speeds, the radius is even more limited. For example, for speeds of 8 Mbps, the limit is 9,000 feet and for VDSL, which could supply up to 55 Mbps, the limit is a mere 1,000 feet.

19. They point out that this population is actually closer to 27% (as was stated by Kinetic Strategies), but explain that their data are not fine enough to show this measurement.

20. Data were obtained concerning wire centres; also data on DSL and cable modem service availability were collected via web sites and calling service providers. They supplemented these with Census data.

21. See also Garcia (1996), Parker (2000), Hindman (2000).

22. NAICS stands for the North American Industry Classification System.

CHAPTER 8

THE ECONOMICS OF ICTs: BUILDING BLOCKS AND IMPLICATIONS

W. EDWARD STEINMUELLER

1 INTRODUCTION

As IN much of economics, the most direct or 'simplest' analytical approach to analysing a specific industry is to consider how supply and demand are articulated in response to market opportunities. Information and communication technologies (ICTs) are not an exception. Both popular and academic accounts have highlighted how a very rapid rate of technological progress in components such as integrated circuits, opto-electronics, and magnetic storage have produced a myriad of new application (or supply) opportunities—making it possible to create the personal computer, Internet, and software industries.

The proliferation of new ICTs is often portrayed in the popular and business literatures as an instance of 'supply push'—a cascade of initiatives from technology producers. For economists, supply and demand are inextricably linked—'supply push' suggests a short term aberration or disequilibrium, which must either be absorbed by corresponding changes in demand or which will create unprofitable surplus production that will result (in fairly short order) in a scaling back of supply.

As this chapter will illustrate, the exploitation of technological and market opportunities in the ICT industries has produced a series of changes in both supply and demand that serve to regulate or channel the rate and direction of industrial growth. On the supply side, these changes are manifested in two ways. The first, which will only be indirectly considered in this chapter (particularly in Section 3 which considers demand and diffusion of technology), is that the industry has experienced and is likely to continue to experience marked fluctuations in rates of output and employment. These fluctuations are the consequence of the rapid and sometimes uneven pace of technical advance requiring major accommodations and adjustments by both suppliers and their customers. The second way in which these changes are apparent is the evolution of new institutions (rules, norms, and standards) governing the production of variety or diversity in the industry. Because ICT innovations seldom 'stand alone' and, most often, must be integrated with existing and other newly emerging technologies, compatibility standardization plays a central role in *how* technological opportunities are exploited. A central theme of this chapter (developed in Section 2) is that technological compatibility standards represent a strategic 'building block' that shapes the structure of the ICT industries as well as the rate and direction of the exploitation of new technological and market opportunities.

The micro-economic foundation approach of this chapter is distinct from but also parallels previous economic analyses of the industry, which have emphasized the 'meso' or industry unit of analysis. These earlier studies have reflected three complementary perspectives. The first originated from treating these industries as exemplars of the research intensive or science-based industries (Tilton 1971; Freeman 1974; Braun and Macdonald 1982); the second concerned questions of industrial structure, and specifically the extent to which these industries are subject to producer concentration and incipient monopolization (Brock 1981; Fisher, McGowan and Greenwood 1985), and the third addressed the strategies chosen by specific actors which may be related to government policies and linked to market success or failure (Malerba 1985; Fransman 1990; Flamm 1987, 1988; Langlois and Steinmueller 2000). In effect, these three perspectives reflect different views about industrial performance in high technology industries—the first emphasizing the exploitation of technological opportunity, the second, the factors (including the presence or absence of government regulation) influencing the structure and competitive performance of the ICT industries and the third, the role of government policy in promoting these industries.

The focus of this chapter is on the micro or building block level, where the programme of economic research has been directed by the goal of explaining the origins and consequences of rapid technological change and cost reduction—in other words, the foundations of the first of the perspectives identified above.

By focusing on this level, it is possible to illuminate some of the underlying processes influencing industrial structure (the focus of the second perspective in the literature and the subject of Sections 2 and 3) and to suggest consequences for policy aimed at promotion of industrial growth and success (Section 4). The central theme of this chapter is that the micro foundations or building blocks of supply and demand shape industrial structure and performance as well as influencing the opportunities and limits for government policy (including policies aimed both at promoting industrial growth and regulating economic concentration).

Introducing the supply side

On the supply side, the most basic building blocks supporting the economics of firms and industries are to be found in influences on the cost of production. The ICT industries are distinguished by peculiarities in how key determinants of cost, and economies of scale, scope, and industrial coordination[1] operate, which is due to the unusual features of information as an economic input—specifically that, unlike other inputs such as labour or capital, information is inexpensively reproduced (it is expansible) and its use is non-rivalrous (use of information for one purpose does not interfere with its use for other purposes).[2]

The expansibility and non-rivalrous properties of information, operating through the re-use of design information, are the primary bases for economies of scale in the production of ICTs.[3] These qualities of information are by no means unique features of ICTs—they are also the basis for economic savings in many other activities where designs are replicated, and especially in other information industries such as print or software publishing where the costs of the first copy may be amortized over subsequent identical copies. As in other industries where first copy costs are important, a market leader can achieve a pricing or quality advantage over rivals that are producing smaller quantities of output, a feature that is closely linked to economists' concerns with the relation between market structure and market power.[4] A rapid rate of take-up or diffusion of a particular ICT product model—computer, mobile telephone, software—can provide a market leader with a cost advantage that can be reinvested in quality improvements in subsequent models and a persistent market advantage. However, this 'first mover' advantage need not be stable since continuing technological progress offers designers, not only at the 'first mover' firm, but also rival firms, opportunities to make new and improved designs.

The basis for economies of scope in the production of ICTs stems from the ability to address different application needs with similar designs. This possibility also draws upon the peculiarities of information as an economic input—information can be transferred from an old to a new application (through expansibility) without detracting from its previous use (non-rivalry). Within a firm, it is possible to produce different models of a commodity employing ICTs for different applications and therefore for different market demands. This creates important opportunities for product differentiation, attracting users with different application needs, while allowing producers to re-use much of what has been learned about the design of earlier models. Economies of scope in the ICT industries are often extended over time—earlier generations of products and services provide a basis for new generations. An important technological basis for economies of scope is the use of 'programmable components' (specifically microprocessor-based design), which permits the creation of different systems based upon similar 'embedded' software instructions.

Most modern electronic systems employ digital integrated circuit components, which came into widespread use around 1971, the year of the invention of the microprocessor. A new approach to system design emerged with these components. Systems were based on assembly of standardized components (Blakeslee 1975) and, later, the design of components from standardized libraries of functional building blocks (Mead and Conway 1980). Interconnection standards, which are discussed later in this chapter emerged for assembling these and other components into electronic systems, permitting the economies of scope identified in the previous paragraph to be extended across different firms.

Economies of industrial coordination are a hybrid of economies of scale (because interoperable components, components that can be connected to one another in many different designs, have a higher level of demand than one-off or customized products, their costs will generally be lower) and economies of scope (because the same component may be used in the production of different systems, designs with these components will be less expensive than designs using purpose-built components). Unlike the traditional meaning of economies of scope, however, the economies of industrial coordination mean that the lower costs of jointly producing many different designs are not necessarily confined to a single firm, but apply to all of the products incorporating these components. In economics terminology, economies of industry coordination are the consequence of positive externalities from producing inter-operable or inter-connectable components. These externalities encourage suppliers to define more 'general purpose' modular components, the result being the creation of a very large, complex, and global 'technological infrastructure' supporting ICT system production.

Industrial coordination economies appear to lead to two different types of industrial structure. One involves wide dispersion of component production and supports frequent entry of new firms, and can be called open standards modularity (Baldwin and Clark 2000). The other common ICT industrial structure reflecting economies of industrial coordination is based upon proprietary 'product platforms', assembled by a system integrator who takes a major responsibility for coordinating suppliers and directing the technological design of the family of products identified with the platform (Hobday 1995). Examination of the implications of these two different industrial structures is the subject of the latter half of Section 2.

These three supply-side economic features of ICTs are complementary—each amplifies the effect of the other two. The expansibility of information (which enables the reuse of design information in ICT hardware designs) also amplifies the dissemination of new applications—a device can, in principle and often in fact, be reconfigured to meet a different application need as easily as 'downloading' a new set of computer instructions. The standardization created by digital electronics enables the creation of ever-larger networks of inter-operable 'systems' (outputs from one part of the system can be processed as inputs by other parts of the system). In such systems, the ability to devise new software means that the use of the system can be improved and modified as perceptions of new opportunities arise—the same data can be reused for purposes distinct from those that led to its initial capture. For example, the personal computer can be used to gather, distribute, or display a vast array of types of information (multimedia programming, scientific data, emails, instrumentation and automation of laboratory or home instrumentation, etc.)

Although some of these examples in the use of personal computers allude to the origins of the computer as a 'general purpose scientific instrument', it can be said that personal computers and ICTs, more generally, constitute a general purpose technology (GPT) (Bresnahan and Trajtenberg 1995)—wherever a useful application can be reduced to the acquisition, storage, processing, and distribution of information, a personal computer or other ICT device can be readily configured to address the application. GPTs are subject to very extended and increasing rates of return in their use by society and therefore may be expected to influence the long-term macroeconomic prospects of modern economies. The theme and consequences of GPTs are developed in the first half of Section 2 below.

Introducing the demand side

Economic examination of ICT demand originated in a somewhat different set of concerns about performance, a questioning of the potential of 'automation'—the replacement of labour with capital animated by software rather than by human operators (e.g. Diebold 1953; Michael 1963). While concerns about the consequences of automation have persisted for more than three decades—(Braverman 1974; Rifkin 1995)—the transformation of wealthier societies in the second half of the century into 'service economies' raised an entirely different issue—would ICTs provide tools for improving productivity in the service sector that would be comparable to the tools of mechanization in agriculture and manufacturing (Baumol et al. 1989). Draca et al. in Chapter 5 of this handbook examine the progress that has been made in resolving this question.

One reason that demand-side issues have been dominated by questions about the productivity of ICTs is the difficulty of other approaches. Some progress is made by recognizing that the purchase of ICT commodities and services involves the construction of networks of information exchange and, therefore, that individual customer demands are interdependent (Rohlfs 1974). Because these networks span and connect social actors, collective action in their regulation and design seems warranted and such action can be informed by political economy and sociological studies (Mansell 1996). The interaction of supply and demand has therefore not been a simple matter of establishing market-clearing prices, but a complex process of adaptation and accommodation. To make the difficult problem of understanding demand more tractable, studies of the ICT industries have most often relied upon models of technology diffusion or take up of new technologies (Tilton 1971; Stoneman 1976, 1995).

The diffusion perspective provides a way of marrying the mysteries of individual choices in which new technologies are adopted with the seemingly autonomous advance in the capabilities of the technology. There are, however, several alternatives for explaining the S-shaped path followed over time in cumulative adoption, including the uneven spread of information and the heterogeneity of customer preferences (Geroski 2000).

In the preceding account of the features of the ICT industries, technology is predominant. The humans that employ these technologies play a relatively peripheral role as opportunistic agents taking advantage of the cornucopia of benefits that they produce, apparently autonomously. This perspective, sometimes pejoratively labelled 'technological determinism' neglects the processes of adaptation and accommodation that humans make to technological change in ICTs and, indeed, ignores the roles that humans have in their design—the purposes, the ideals and dreams that motivate those who create these technologies. As purposes, ideals and dreams are not the stock in trade of economists, the economic literature on ICTs has a 'technological determinist' flavour (Freeman 1987). The particular deus ex machina used to resolve questions about the origin of demand for ICTs, whose applications often lag behind the adoption decision, is the 'diffusion perspective', which is considered in more detail in Section 3.

Economics offers very little critical theory for understanding the forces shaping adoption processes. This has left the field open for speculative examinations. For example, the opinions of non-economist writers who have considered the influence of ICTs on economic and societal advance are diverse. At one extreme they accept the principle of the inevitability of technological diffusion and argue that ICTs are transformational technologies—harbingers of a new economic order (see, e.g. Gilder 1990; Leadbeater 1999). At the other extreme, it is argued that the promise of the new technologies is inflated and that their advance extends the control of elites and creates patterns of exclusion whose costs substantially erode the benefits that might be expected from them (Webster 2002). The claim of inexorable advance and crisis may also be combined—recalling fears of the consequences of automation raised by many writers including economists, for example, Freeman and Perez (1988). A more systematic examination of these claims is likely to be based on research drawn from institutional economics (the study of how the evolution of rules, norms, and standards influences economic behaviour and outcomes rather than industrial economics) that is to say, the economics of firms and industries operating within a fixed institutional framework (see, e.g. Noam (1987) and Mansell (1993)).

Accounts of the assembly of the building blocks of ICTs are thus stories with alternative plots and endings—ones that often challenge existing understandings. This chapter can only identify a limited number of the opportunities for economic and industrial analysis that follow from the basic building blocks introduced here. In particular, this chapter does not attempt to provide a balanced coverage of the vast array of ICT industries, but uses illustrative examples that will be familiar to most readers.

The next two sections are structured around two themes that have been central to the literature aimed at understanding the economic influences of ICTs. Section 2 examines the nomination of ICTs as an exemplar of GPTs—technologies that are so adaptable and ubiquitous that they have a major influence on the evolution of economies. Central to this theme are the processes responsible for creating the general purpose nature of this technology—technical compatibility standards and processes of technological convergence among the ICT industries. Section 3 examines the diffusion perspective, its limitations, and some tentative alternatives that economists have proposed for addressing the determinants of demand for ICT products and services. The concluding section suggests some paths forward in the analysis of the industrial economics of ICTs and their social and economic influences.

2 ICTs AS GENERAL PURPOSE TECHNOLOGIES

As indicated in the introduction, the advance of technology provides an ever-expanding array of possible applications for ICTs and these applications involve accommodations and adjustments that may be time-consuming and expensive to make. This observation has led to the claim that ICTs constitute a GPT—a technology whose scope of application is so widespread throughout an economy that it influences the economy as a whole (David 1991; Bresnahan and Trajtenberg 1995; Helpman 1998). The idea of a GPT is based upon two elements: first, the observation that the take-up and uses of new technology have disruptive effects—it provides powerful new opportunities for re-configuring existing productive activities; secondly, these disruptive effects must be widespread. While many technologies are disruptive in a specific industry or application, the distinguishing feature of GPTs is the extensiveness of their application and disruptive effects.

To borrow from the historical example offered by David (1991), the electrical motor can be considered as an early twentieth century example of a GPT. The disruptive qualities of the electrical motor arose from the possibilities it created for distributing motive power in ways that were simply not possible using steam and internal combustion engines. With the electrical motor, as is also the case with ICTs, new application possibilities were not localized to the application of the technology itself—but disrupted existing practice in factory design and operations management.[5] Moreover, the opportunities generated by electrical motors were *extensive*—they not only fostered change across the vast array of human activities in which motive power was already used (ranging from street cars to washing machines), they also fostered innovations, new goods and services, that were only possible or economic with the use of the electrical motor such as refrigerators and escalators.

ICTs have exercised a disruptive and extensive influence for over a century, a disruption that has gained momentum over time. During the first decades of the twentieth century, these disruptive elements were concentrated in telecommunications—telegraphic and telephonic communication linked markets and suppliers, reconfiguring the boundaries of firms and markets (Beniger 1986). More recently, the 'distribution' of information processing has evolved through successive generations of manual, wired, and wireless data communication—for example, moving data collection from arrangements requiring pencil and paper tabulation of data and data entry, to handheld barcode scanners—and data processing from 'centres' to desktops. At each of these stages in development, new possibilities for revisions in the structures of control and feedback have encouraged new patterns of organization. For example, the information systems of modern express parcel services in which details about shipments are logged at pickup, used to route their carriage and to allocate transport capacities, and logged at delivery, make it possible to schedule transport better and to offer new services such as parcel tracking. In such a system virtually every job performed by human beings is transformed—delivery van operators become data entry clerks, workers responsible for scheduling and routing transportation become data analysts, and managers have to develop greater skills at being system analysts.

Employing ICTs for purposes of accountability and control creates a 'virtual' information environment in which physical objects and processes can be represented as data, providing new insights into the bottlenecks and constraints governing the operation of productive activities. This creates a basis for analyses and simulations in which different organizational arrangements can be tested and which stimulate thought about new ways to profit from the division and specialization of labour and capital (Pavitt and Steinmueller 2002).

In addition to their use in control and accountability, ICTs support other human communication needs, some of which are also the basis for major new markets. ICTs enable:

- social expression through the mediation of interpersonal communication over space and time and the opening of new channels of communication for establishing social networks;
- cultural expression through mass communication of written and audiovisual content to audiences, both large and small;
- market exchange through the exchange of myriad information from the design to the delivery of products and services; and
- general education and training through the provision of teaching and learning resources as well as the interpersonal communication needed to exploit these resources for learning.

In sum, ICTs are different in kind as well as degree, from all previous human technologies involving tangible artefacts. They are best compared to certain intangible 'technologies' such as human language, or specific domains of human knowledge such as science, where processes of evolution and re-configuration of the methods by which inputs are converted to outputs are both extraordinarily complex and flexible and, at the same time, create manifold opportunities to re-use and re-apply basic capabilities and knowledge.

While these manifold opportunities support the claim that ICTs have widespread economic influence, the costs of adjustment and transformation are substantial (Freeman and Perez 1988; David and Abramovitz 2000). This is because, despite their general purpose nature, ICTs require the construction of an immense infrastructure of new types of information that can be productively exchanged using ICTs and because the competitive processes stimulated by the transformational use of ICTs creates waste as well as progress. A central issue in the construction of the ICT infrastructure is the creation of technical compatibility standards (David and Greenstein 1990).

For information to be exchanged and re-used, it must be codified (Cowan, David, and Foray 2000) in formats that allow it to be digitally represented. Digital representations of information are necessarily arbitrary—there is no 'natural' digital representation of a letter in the Roman alphabet or the information contained in a high-resolution colour photograph. For letters and, therefore, texts or pictures to be digitally represented a code has to be devised and it is more efficient if this code is standardized. Such standards can be achieved through market processes—the producers of ICTs have an incentive to establish such codes as a means of extending the range of information that can be utilized (thereby making their products more desirable). However, it is not only commonplace to disagree about such standards, but such disagreements provide a basis for product differentiation and the maintenance or extension of market power by dominant producers.

The same principle applies to the information embedded in ICT designs—it may reflect standards that are in widespread use or this information may be protected by laws governing intellectual property such as patents, copyright, and trademarks (David and Steinmueller 1996). As is the case with other information, producers have a choice between open standards—standards that are freely published and that are either non-exclusively licensed or made freely available—or proprietary standards whose use is governed by a sponsor. Open standards may encourage others to create complementary information and artefacts, but also enable others to produce *substitutes*—products that employ the same standards and compete directly with a producer's offerings. Proprietary standards may impede the production of complements and serve as a barrier to the production of substitutes.

Standards and markets

Regardless of whether standards are open or proprietary, market competition will select among standards. Market competition does not, however, lead to rapid or reliable convergence to standards that create the highest social welfare. This is because there are consumption externalities in the use of standards (Rohlfs 1974; Swann, Cowan and Cowan 1997, 2004; Shapiro and Varian 1998)—standards create benefits that are not priced in the market and hence are external to it. For example, the addition of one more user employing a specific standard increases that individual's ability to exchange information or 'connect' with other users employing the same standard—while the adopter is motivated by this benefit, the existing users reap a windfall gain from this additional user.

Correspondingly, if a specific user elects for a different and 'incompatible' standard because it offers specific advantages other than connection with existing users, the potential for collective gain is lost. This disconnection in the market exists because users already employing the technology cannot directly offer an incentive to new users to join in the common use of an existing standard. The value of connecting to the new user, *for other users*, is not priced (it is not something that can easily be traded in markets) and is therefore not taken into account in market choices.

Since there are always incentives to improve upon existing standards and to offer specific benefits to some sub-community of users, the potential social welfare loss from the fragmentation of standards may be substantial (Barrett and Yang 2001). Of course, it must be recognized that long-term improvements in the quality of standards can only occur at the cost of short-term losses to users of what will become obsolete standards, as and when superior and incompatible standards emerge. These conditions provide the basis for the emergence of some form of governance structure attempting to raise collective welfare while still providing sufficient flexibility for technological progress (Tassey 2000). Three basic forms of governance structure have emerged so far in the ICT industries.[6] The first is the governance of compatibility standards by voluntary standards organizations, the second is the explicit setting of standards for the international interoperability of telecommunication networks by intergovernmental organizations, and the third involves the emergence of coalitions of firms that 'sponsor' standards. In the third case, these coalitions may represent the shared aims of virtually all producers to improve the market acceptance of new technologies or they may serve the interest of a group of firms aimed at strategic promotion of one standard over one or more alternatives (Augereau, Greenstein and Rysman 2004). Instances of this third case appear to be increasing in recent years, a development that may be explained by the flexibility it offers for extending or restricting access to standards and the greater speed that it offers for establishing new standards.

Leaderless and sponsored modular platforms

As a means of concentrating market control, compatibility standards can be employed strategically to create 'platforms' that are most often sponsored by one or more dominant competitors and serve to enhance their competitive position (Greenstein 1990). Alternatively, compatibility standards may support the emergence of 'modular' platforms, platforms based upon compatibility standards that are either not proprietary or where proprietary elements are not used for purposes of excluding competitive entry. The economic incentive to produce modular systems stems from the advantages that may flow from a more rapid rate of market growth and a higher degree of competitive discipline and entry opportunity for innovative firms.

The alternatives to modular platforms based upon public and open (or non-proprietary) standards are platforms based on 'sponsored' or proprietary standards. These two uses of the standards needed to assemble multi-component systems are alternatives for exploiting the rapidly advancing frontier of technological opportunity to produce new products and services. The principal advantage of the proprietary platform is the concentration of revenues in a smaller group of firms that can thereby mount larger research efforts and undertake more extensive activities in coordinating upstream suppliers and downstream marketing channels. The principal, and offsetting, advantage of platforms based on open standards (compatibility standards that are not subject to proprietary controls such as exclusive licensing or high licence fees) is the impetus that they provide for competitive entry and competition, which may hasten the pace of technological advance and create a greater diversity for market selection. Baldwin and Clark (1997) suggest that the advantages stemming from relatively or totally open modular platforms will provide a competitive advantage to producers following this strategy for market development. Their argument depends upon emergent coherence in modular design stemming from the effect of modularity in directing individual actors towards the greatest opportunities for market growth.

The abstraction of purely proprietary and purely modular platforms is a useful analytical device. As Baldwin and Clark (2000) recognize, however, hybrid strategies are possible in which interfaces in a proprietary platform are 'opened' to a modular approach, allowing the sponsor of the proprietary system to benefit from competitive entry and pricing for components that are complementary in demand for their proprietary platform. Correspondingly, producers of modular components will seek to produce 'super sets' or 'higher order' features of devices that both conform to compatibility standards and permit the construction of higher performance (and value) systems, thus benefiting from both the demand for widely standardized components and creating a proprietary application niche for their products.

In summary, the rapid rate of technological progress in ICTs, their vast range of applicability to problems of measurement and control, and the potentials they offer for supporting processes of human communication in social, cultural, market, and educational contexts indicate that their influence is sufficiently widespread to suggest that they meet the 'pervasiveness' requirements of a GPT. The range of adjustments and accommodations required to take advantage of ICTs suggest that they also have the disruptive features of GPTs. This section has focused on technical compatibility standards as one of the principal methods for extending the applicability, and mitigating the disruptive influence of ICTs. Institutions for the governance of technical compatibility standards reduce the risks of excessive variety and welfare-reducing incompatibilities and support earlier and more confident adoption of new ICTs. Several different methods for compatibility standardization have emerged, in part because market competition has not yet provided a general answer as to whether sponsored or open compatibility standards provide the best means of taking advantage of technological and market opportunities.

3 DEMAND AND DIFFUSION

The preceding section stressed the supply-side dynamics of ICT markets—demand was largely taken to be exogenous and pre-determined by the preferences of users. In other words, potential adopters of ICT products and services were assumed to be able to make rational choices between alternative offerings based upon their perceived applicability and value. There were, however, two important ways in which demand-side issues played an important role in the discussion. The first was the idea of 'interdependent' demand—the demand of one user depends upon the choices made by other users, and provides an incentive to create governance systems for achieving compatibility standards. The second, related, way in which demand-side issues played a role in the previous section was the implicit assumption that users were able to make rational choices in favour of systems that are compatible with existing systems or that offer, or might offer, a range of complementary goods and services. Without this second demand-side assumption, the evolution of ICT markets would be entirely subject to 'bandwagon' effects in which early 'small events' providing a small lead for an innovative ICT product or service would, because of inter-dependent demand, favour its universal adoption (see Arthur 1994 for the relevant theory governing such processes).

Obviously, there are significant differences in capabilities between users—a larger corporation with an information systems department is likely to have greater capabilities for choosing and constructing integrated systems than an individual consumer. It can therefore be expected that the 'influence of small events' might be greater in markets dominated by consumers, and that more forward-looking and less haphazard patterns of innovation might be present in markets dominated by larger organizations which, in turn, might be more capable of acting in concert. However, the capabilities of both organizations and individuals are likely to be evolving over time as greater experience in the use of ICTs accumulates. In particular, the capabilities for individual users to provide increasingly coherent and forceful critical views on new product offerings appear to have increased over the past several decades (Warschauer 2003).

Economists have generally responded to the complexities of the demand for ICT products by assuming that the processes of choice involved in users' adoptions of a particular technology or product are too complex to analyse in a direct way (some exceptions are considered later in this section). Instead, to the extent that demand is considered, it is considered within the framework provided by economic models of technology diffusion (Griliches 1958; Mansfield 1963).

The diffusion perspective has dominated studies of the demand side of the ICT industry for several decades, for example, Stoneman (1976); Antonelli (1986); OECD (2004). Despite its *ad hoc* and determinist character it remains the most straightforward way to stitch together into a common framework the complexities of heterogeneous products that have rapidly changing characteristics, and the diversity of user needs and capabilities that are also evolving rapidly over time.

Three basic approaches have been used to augment the 'stylized fact'-based approach to diffusion mentioned in the introduction. One approach relies upon measuring changes in product attributes over time as a way of explaining how, by adjusting for quality, the quantity demanded of an ICT (such as units of computers) might increase faster than could be reasonably explained only by a reduction in the purchase price (Chow 1967; Stoneman 1976). The second approach takes up the issue of the user characteristics directly attempting to identify the main factors responsible for the adoption decision (OECD 2004). A third approach, based on the role of signalling, and of information in influencing adoption decisions, is relatively new and worth explaining in more detail.

In the face of uncertainty about the potential value of a new ICT product or service, users may not be able to make a rational assessment of whether the benefits that it offers justify incurring the costs of its adoption. An alternative is to rely upon information gleaned from other users or some 'signal' (Spence 1974) of potential benefits. Both approaches suggest the existence of an information exchange process within a network of users. As yet, economists have not used this approach to specifically address ICT but the foundations have been established in two different analytical approaches. One analytical approach is to examine what structure of social networks might be optimal for the spread of information (Bala and Goyal 1998). The other analytical approach is to make assumptions about the network structure in order to analyse or simulate adoption outcomes (Midgley, Morrison and Roberts 1992; Cowan and Jonard 2004).

The alternatives to diffusion theory for explaining user demand for ICTs are relatively fragmented and partial. A more sociological approach is to examine how users adapt to, resist, and seek accommodations with product offerings, which may provide richer information about future paths that the ICT industries may follow (Haddon 2002). In many cases, it may still be true, however, that supply offerings dominate this 'co-evolving' process—what users want to do with ICTs may be largely determined by what they *can* do with existing product offerings. From the economics perspective, a few studies have sought to identify explanatory variables influencing demand for software (Doucouliagos and Torre 2004), Internet services (Beckert 2005), or additional phone lines for dial-up modem services (Eisner and Waldon 2001) as well as the influence of specific features in ICT product offerings (Andersson, Fjell and Foros 2004).

Several of these studies as well as others, for example, Brown and Greenstein (1995), have employed the hedonic price approach. Griliches (1971) is an indispensable guide to the origins and early applications of this technique. Hedonic prices are a method for taking account of the fact that the characteristics of relatively complex goods such as automobiles, washing machines, and computers are changing over time. Since any such product has a number of different characteristics and these characteristics are changing at different rates over time, it is useful to have a reference point for assessing how changes in these characteristics influence consumer behaviour. By assuming that customers respond to changes in characteristics, as well as price in their purchasing behaviour, it is possible to make statistical inferences about the value they attribute to individual characteristics. This makes it possible to draw conclusions about the sensitivity of consumer behaviour to technological changes in the qualities of goods that they consume and also provides a means to adjust the price indexes to these changes. Triplett (1989) provides a survey of the use of these indexes in the case of computers and

Wyckoff (1995) provides a useful commentary on how the application influences international comparisons of productivity between the US and Europe.

Studies of individual markets do provide some indication of the demand elasticity for specific features. They are, however, 'snapshots' of particular eras in the evolution of demand and do not provide much insight into the ways in which the use of ICTs is evolving.

One reason for the scarcity of ICT demand studies is the variety of the applications, forcing investigators into highly situated (in time and place) research that makes it difficult to reach broader generalizations or to utilize aggregate data. It can be observed, for example, that computer users have, over time, become far more involved in the exchange of emails, raising questions about the extent to which such involvement is productivity enhancing. However, only two economic studies (studies indexed by the *Journal of Economic Literature*'s EconLit electronic repository) so far have taken up the issue of email use in the workplace outside the legal liabilities involved—both propose taxes on emails as a way of reducing the negative externality (costs imposed on others) of unsolicited messages (Shiman 1996; Willmore 1999). While the apparent disinterest in this topic may reflect economists' presumption that people necessarily make rational use of their time, it is also possible that the problem is one of measurement—associating email use with individual or group productivity may simply be a difficult problem to address unless it is pursued in highly situated contexts, that is, a particular organization, at a particular time.

There are, however, three areas where the evolution of user capabilities and behaviours in the use of ICTs do leave traces that provide a basis for studies that, while situated, provide a basis for replication or that involve larger-scale investigation. There are studies of the effects of ICT use on organizational change, the interaction between ICT use and the accumulation of labour skills, and user activities in co-invention and adaptation of software and information systems.

Studies of ICT use and organizational change are more often the subject of management, industrial relations, and sociology where a principal concern is with ways in which to characterize change processes, assess their impacts on particular groups of workers and reach conclusions about how to better manage these processes (see, e.g. Frenkel et al. 1998). Much of this literature appears to be influenced by the earlier generation of literature (e.g. Braverman 1974) on the perils of automation, where a main concern was with how the new technologies might displace worker skills—creating a workforce controlled by, rather than controlling, the pace and content of work. Economists have struggled with the same problems and the, often necessarily, situated nature of such studies—for example, Autor, Levy, and Murnane (2000) consider a single case study of work reorganization stemming from the adoption of automated image processing in a bank in which routine work is automated, eliminating lower skilled jobs and requiring additional skills from those remaining.

Perhaps because economics provides few avenues for examining organizational change, economists combine studies of organizational change with examinations of changes in skills. The great advantage of examining labour skills is that national statistical offices regularly and extensively gather such data. Studies conducted on the changing content of skills clearly indicate that ICT-related skills are becoming more prevalent in the industrialized countries. In countries with detailed surveys, such as France, this evidence can be very specifically linked with ICT use (Greenan and Mairesse 2000) while in other countries with less detailed surveys, evidence is more circumstantial (Autor, Levy and Murnane 2003; Bresnahan, Brynjolfsson and Hitt 2002). As users become more sophisticated in their use of ICTs, it is reasonable to believe that they may become more active in attempting to influence the nature of product offerings. How this influence will be manifested over time, however, remains quite uncertain.

Evidence is also accumulating that organizations other than the producers of ICTs are actively involved in a process of 'co-invention' to make better use of these technologies (Bresnahan and Greenstein 1996, 2001). While it is again difficult to find appropriate indicators of the scale or extent of these activities, one measure is the extent to which non-ICT industry companies are taking out ICT-related patents, and several authors have noted a strong trend in this direction (Rao, Vemuri and Galvin 2004; Cantwell and Santangelo 2000, 2002). Again, this is a fragmentary indicator that does not provide much insight into how changes in the producer–user relationship may be changing over time. However, it is an indicator of 'signs of life' consistent with the GPT hypothesis—that such companies are accommodating the disruptive effects of the new technologies by developing capabilities for modifying and extending them in use.

In short, empirical economic studies of demand evolution in ICTs are fragmentary. The diffusion approach provides important information about the rate and location of the spread of new technologies, but diffusion-based explanations are generally constructed after the processes that they seek to explain have occurred. More economic studies of the adoption process indicate that ICTs are supporting organizational change, but fall short of confirming hypotheses such as that the number of vertical layers in organizations is shrinking as the consequence of information system use. They indicate that worker skills related to the use of ICTs are increasing, but do not tell us how these skills are shaping the demand for new generations of ICT products and services. Existing studies indicate that organizations other than ICT producers are engaged in co-inventing in the area of ICT application without telling us whether these co-inventions have a broader influence or impact on ICT producing industries. Even more significantly, there is very little evidence concerning the role of ICTs in supporting the internationalization of productive activities in services or manufacturing—one facet of the complex process referred to as globalization. These shortcomings suggest that the economic analysis of ICTs is still young and offers numerous opportunities for future research, some of which are discussed in Section 4.

4 CONCLUDING REMARKS

The evolution of the supply-side of the ICT industries has major implications not only for the future structure of the ICT industries, but also for economic policy more generally. If it is true that a 'leaderless' modularity emerges from the processes of competition between alternative platform suppliers seeking lower cost components, the recent history of global trade liberalization can only further support the process—entry opportunities are likely to be widespread at different technological levels and abundant. If, on the other hand, the cost-reducing features of ICT component supply are combined with a small number of dominant platform producers, many countries may find that they are unable to generate or attract the sponsors of platforms. In this case, the global liberal trade order will look less attractive and issues of technological and economic dependency and competitiveness will play a more prominent role in international discussions.

Improving the foundations for better understanding the supply side is a challenging problem due to the variety of skills needed to properly analyse competing claims concerning the economic implications of ICTs. For example, over the past decade, very rapid growth has occurred in a class of contract manufacturers—companies that serve as intermediaries between platform sponsors in the industrialized world and lower wage economies. Contract manufacturers have played a major role in the export success of China, where nearly one-third of total exports are electronics or ICT-based.[7] This is only one of several examples where economic studies have lagged behind developments in industrial structure that are likely to be influential in the future course of economic affairs.

To illustrate this, let us consider what might improve the discussion of demand-side issues in the ICT industry. For progress to be made in this area, at least two important developments need to occur. First, a way must be found to conceptualize the use of ICTs in modern organizations that allows researchers to understand the composition of activities in which ICTs are employed—studies of task productivity and task composition are likely to be needed. It is likely that the composition of activities has changed over the past decade as the result of the 'network revolution' in which computers are connected not only locally, but on a global basis through the Internet, and used in supply chain management, online procurement, and complex patterns of inter-organizational cooperation in research, marketing, and distribution. At the same time as ICTs have been used more *extensively* as a means of information exchange, however, organizations also have developed more *intensive* applications of information systems—data warehousing, group collaboration in design and implementation, internal accounting, and inventory control. All of these activities feature prominently in the technical literature on information systems applications, but have not been translated into concepts or measures to which economic analysis could be applied. Although there have been several attempts to provide over-arching frameworks for understanding the processes by which information is generated and used in organizations (see, e.g. Boisot 1995; Nonaka and Takeuchi 1995), this area of research is still organized around conceptual development and validation and, as yet, provides little basis for systematic data gathering or analysis.

Secondly, further progress is needed in understanding how the increasing experience of individuals and organizations in the use of ICTs can influence the processes of innovation and design. Several interesting historical studies (Caminer et al. 1996; van den Ende and Kemp 1999) have been produced that provide insights into this process. At present, the most dynamic area of research contributing to this area is on Open Source Software (OSS) (Weber 2004). Several theories have been developed to explain why individuals volunteer their efforts in producing OSS[8] including a bid for status or 'career concerns' (Lerner and Tirole 2002), cooperation to serve users' own needs (von Hippel 2005), and personal fulfilment (Raymond 1999). The various explanations of the phenomenon of OSS (as well as some of the arguments concerning its effectiveness) are worth applying to the more general problem of how users employ ICTs within organizations—the processes of structuring workgroups, defining the efforts that need to be undertaken to create value from their efforts, and the actual processes by which information system development work is actually carried out. A major reason for the amount of attention devoted to studies of OSS is that this is one of the few activities of the ICT industries where researchers have a sustained ability to observe the design and implementation process.

A central conclusion of this chapter is that the ICT industries are distinguished from other industries by their micro-foundations, which shape the exploitation of technological opportunity. While some of these micro foundations, particularly on the structure and strategy of suppliers are becoming clearer, large gaps remain in the understanding of influences governing demand and diffusion. The current state of knowledge is of serious concern given the interest of many governments in promoting policies supporting the information society (Mansell and Steinmueller 2000; Melody 1996; Mansell and Wehn 1998; Webster 2002) and in regulating ICT industries where dominant competitors have emerged (Fisher, McGowan, and Greenwood 1985, Economides 2001). Even if retrospective studies indicate substantial government roles in the origins and early development of particular ICT industries (e.g. Flamm 1987, 1988), major questions remain about how government policies might promote the growth of such industries in the future. Addressing these issues will require a deeper understanding than is currently available.

REFERENCES

ANDERSSON, K., FJELL, K. and FOROS, O. (2004). 'Are Interactive TV-Pioneers and Surfers Different Breeds? Broadband Demand and Asymmetric Cross-Price Effects'. *Review of Industrial Organization*, 25(3): 295–316.

ANTONELLI, C. (1986). 'The International Diffusion of New Information Technologies'. *Research Policy*, 15(3): 139–47.

ARTHUR, W. B. (ed.) (1994). *Increasing Returns and Path Dependence in the Economy*. Ann Arbor, MI: University of Michigan Press.

AUGEREAU, A., GREENSTEIN, S. and RYSMAN, M. (2004). 'Coordination vs Differentiation in a Standards War: 56K Modems', National Bureau of Economic Research, Inc. NBER Working Papers, No. 10334, Mar.

AUTOR, D. H., LEVY, F. and MURNANE, R. (2000). 'Upstairs, Downstairs: Computer-Skill Complementarity and Computer-Labor Substitution on Two Floors of a Large Bank', National Bureau of Economic Research, Inc. NBER Working Papers., No. 7890, Sept.

——, —— and —— (2003). 'The Skill Content of Recent Technological Change: An Empirical Exploration'. *Quarterly Journal of Economics*, 118(4): 1279–333.

BALA, V. and GOYAL, S. (1998). 'Learning from Neighbours'. *Review of Economic Studies*, 65(3): 595–621.

BALDWIN, C. Y. and CLARK, K. B. (1997). 'Managing in an Age of Modularity'. *Harvard Business Review*, 75(5): 84–93.

—— and —— (2000). *Design Rules: Volume 1 The Power of Modularity*. Cambridge, MA: MIT Press.

BARRETT, C. B. and YANG, Y.-N. (2001). 'Rational Incompatibility with International Product Standards'. *Journal of International Economics*, 54(1): 171–91.

BAUMOL, W. J., BATEY BLACKMAN, S. A. and WOLFF, E. N. (1989). *Productivity and American Leadership: The Long View*. Cambridge, MA: MIT Press.

BECKERT, W. (2005). 'Estimation of Heterogeneous Preferences, with an Application to Demand for Internet Services'. *Review of Economics and Statistics*, 87(3): 495–502.

BENIGER, J. A. (1986). *The Control Revolution: Technological and Economic Origins of the Information Society*. Cambridge, MA: Harvard University Press.

BLAKESLEE, T. R. (1975). *Digital Design with Standard MSI and LSI*. New York: John Wiley and Sons.

BOISOT, M. H. (1995). *Information Space – A Framework for Learning in Organizations, Institutions and Culture*. London: Routledge.

BRAUN, E. and MACDONALD, S. (1982). *Revolution in Miniature: The History and Impact of Semiconductor Electronics* (2nd edn). Cambridge: Cambridge University Press.

BRAVERMAN, H. (1974). *Labor and Monopoly Capital*. New York: Monthly Review Press.

BRESNAHAN, T. F. and GREENSTEIN, S. (1996). 'Technical Progress and Co-invention in Computing and the Uses of Computers'. *Brookings Papers: Microeconomics 1996*, 1–77.

—— and —— (2001). 'The Economic Contribution of Information Technology: Towards Comparative and User Studies'. *Journal of Evolutionary Economics*, 11(1): 95–118.

—— and TRAJTENBERG, M. (1995). 'General Purpose Technologies "Engines of Growth"?' *Journal of Econometrics*, 65(1): 83–108.

——, M., BRYNJOLFSSON, E. and HITT, L. M. (2002). 'Information Technology, Workplace Organization and the Demand for Skilled Labor: Firm-level Evidence'. *Quarterly Journal of Economics*, 117(1): 339–76.

BROCK, G. W. (1981). *The Telecommunications Industry: The Dynamics of Market Structure*. Cambridge, MA: Harvard University Press.

BROWN, K. H. and GREENSTEIN, S. M. (1995). 'How Much Better is Bigger, Faster & Cheaper? Buyer Benefits from Innovation in Mainframe Computers in the 1980s', National Bureau of Economic Research, Inc. NBER Working Papers, No. 5138, May.

BRUNSSON, N., JACOBSSON, B. and Associates (2002). *A World of Standards*. Oxford and New York: Oxford University Press.

CAMINER, D., ARIS, J., HERMON, P. and LAND, F. (1996). *User-Driven Innovation: The World's First Business Computer*. London: McGraw-Hill Book Company.

CANTWELL, J. and SANTANGELO, G. D. (2000). 'Capitalism, Profits and Innovation in the New Techno-Economic Paradigm'. *Journal of Evolutionary Economics*, 10(1–2): 131–57.

—— and —— (2002). 'The New Geography of Corporate Research in Information and Communications Technology (ICT)'. *Journal of Evolutionary Economics*, 12(1–2): 163–97.

CARGILL, C. F. (1996). *Open Systems Standardization: A Business Approach* (2nd edn). Upper Saddle River, NJ: Prentice Hall.

CHOW, G. C. (1967). 'Technological Change and the Demand for Computers'. *American Economic Review*, 57(5): 1117–30.

COWAN, R., DAVID, P. A. and FORAY, D. (2000). 'The Explicit Economics of Knowledge Codification and Tacitness'. *Industrial and Corporate Change*, 9(2): 211–54.

—— and JONARD, N. (2004). 'Network Structure and the Diffusion of Knowledge'. *Journal of Economic Dynamics and Control*, 28(8): 1557–75.

DAVID, P. A. (1991). 'Computer and Dynamo: The Modern Productivity Paradox in a Not-Too-Distant Mirror', in OECD (ed.) *Technology and Productivity: The Challenge for Economic Policy*, Paris: OECD, 315–48.

—— and ABRAMOVITZ, M. (2000). 'American Macroeconomic Growth in the Era of Knowledge-Based Progress: The Long Run Perspective', in S. Engerman and R. Gallman (eds), *The Cambridge Economic History of the United States*. Cambridge: Cambridge University Press, 1–92.

—— and GREENSTEIN, S. (1990). 'The Economics of Compatibility Standards: An Introduction to Recent Research'. *Economics of Innovation and New Technology*, 1(1): 3–41.

—— and STEINMUELLER, W. E. (1996). 'Standards, Trade and Competition in the Emerging Global Information Infrastructure Environment'. *Telecommunications Policy*, 20(10): 817–30.

DIEBOLD, J. (1953). 'Automation–The New Technology'. *Harvard Business Review*, 31(6): 63–71.

DOUCOULIAGOS, H. and TORRE, A. (2004). 'The Market for Software in the US'. *Empirical Economics Letters*, 3(1): 11–20.

DUBOFF, R. B. (1979). *Electric Power in American Manufacturing, 1889–1958*. New York: Arno Press.

ECONOMIDES, N. (2001). 'The Microsoft Antitrust Case'. *Journal of Industry, Competition and Trade: From Theory to Policy*, 1(1): 7–39.

EISNER, J. and WALDON, T. (2001). 'The Demand for Bandwidth: Second Telephone Lines and On-Line Services'. *Information Economics and Policy*, 13(3): 301–9.

FISHER, F. M., McGOWAN, J. J. and GREENWOOD, J. E. (1985). *Folded, Spindled and Mutilated: Economic Analysis and US vs. IBM*. Cambridge, MA: MIT Press.

FLAMM, K. (1987). *Targeting the Computer: Government Support and International Competition*. Washington DC: The Brookings Institution.

—— (1988). *Creating the Computer: Government, Industry, and High Technology*. Washington DC: The Brookings Institution.

FRANSMAN, M. (1990). *The Market and Beyond*. Cambridge: Cambridge University Press.

FREEMAN, C. (1987). 'The Case for Technological Determinism', in R. Finnegan, G. Salaman and K. Thompson (eds), *Information Technology: Social Issues. A Reader*, London: Hodder and Stoughton, 5–18.

—— and PEREZ C. (1974). *The Economics of Industrial Innovation*. Harmondsworth: Penguin.

—— and —— (1988). 'Structural Crises of Adjustment, Business Cycles and Investment Behaviour', in G. Dosi, C. Freeman, R. Nelson, et al. (eds), *Technical Change and Economic Theory*. London: Pinter, 38–66.

FRENKEL, S. J., TAM, M. KORCZYNSKI, M. and SHIRE, K. (1998). 'Beyond Bureaucracy? Work Organization in Call Centres'. *International Journal of Human Resource Management*, 9(6): 957–79.

GEROSKI, P. (2000). 'Models of Technology Diffusion'. *Research Policy*, 29: 603–25.

GILDER, G. (1990). *Microcosm: The Quantum Revolution in Economics and Technology*. New York: Touchstone Books.

GREENAN, N. and MAIRESSE, J. (2000). 'Computers and Productivity in France: Some Evidence'. *Economics of Innovation and New Technology*, 9(3): 275–315.

GREENSTEIN, S. (1990). 'Creating Economic Advantage by Setting Compatibility Standards: Can "Physical Tie-ins" Extend Monopoly Power?' *Economics of Innovation and New Technology*, 1(1–2): 63–83.

GRILICHES, Z. (1958). 'Research Costs and Social Returns: Hybrid Corn and Related Innovations'. *Journal of Political Economy* (Oct.): 419–31.

—— (ed.) (1971). *Price Indexes and Quality Change*. Cambridge, MA: Harvard University Press.

HADDON, L. (2002). 'Information and Communication Technologies and the Role of Consumers in Innovation', in A. McMeekin, K. Gren, M. Tomlinson and V. Walsh (eds), *Innovation by Demand: An Interdisciplinary Approach to the Study of Demand and its Role in Innovation*. Manchester and New York: Manchester University Press distributed by Palgrave, New York, 151–67.

HELPMAN, E. (ed.) (1998). *General Purpose Technologies and Economic Growth*. Cambridge, MA: MIT Press.

HOBDAY, M. (1995). *Innovation in East Asia: The Challenge to Japan*. Cheltenham: Edward Elgar.

LANGLOIS, R. and STEINMUELLER, W. E. (2000). 'Strategy and Circumstance: The Response of American Firms to Japanese Competition'. *Strategic Management Journal*, 21(10/11): 1163–73.

LEADBEATER, C. (1999). *Living on Thin Air: The New Economy*. London: Viking.

LERNER, J. and TIROLE, J. 2002. 'Some Simple Economics of Open Source'. *Journal of Industrial Economics*, 52 (June): 197–234.

MALERBA, F. (1985). *The Semiconductor Business: The Economics of Rapid Growth and Decline*. Madison, WI and London: University of Wisconsin Press and Frances Pinter.

MANSELL, R. (1993). *The New Telecommunications: A Political Economy of Network Evolution*. London: Sage Publications.

—— (1996). 'Communication by Design?' in R. Mansell and R. Silverstone (eds), *Communication by Design: The Politics of Information and Communication Technologies*. Oxford: Oxford University Press, 15–43.

—— and STEINMUELLER, W. E. (2000). *Mobilizing the Information Society: Strategies for Growth and Opportunity*. London: Oxford University Press.

—— and WEHN, U. (eds) (1998). *Knowledge Societies: Information Technology for Sustainable Development*. Oxford: Published for the UN Commission on Science and Technology for Development by Oxford University Press.

MANSFIELD, E. (1963). 'Intrafirm Rates of Diffusion of an Innovation'. *Review of Economics and Statistics*, 45 (Nov.): 348–59.

MEAD, C. and CONWAY, L. (1980). *Introduction to the VLSI Systems*. Reading, MA: Addison-Wesley.

MELODY, W. H. (1996). 'Toward a Framework for Designing Information Society Policies'. *Telecommunications Policy*, 20(4): 243–59.

MICHAEL, D. N. (1963). *Cybernation: The Silent Conquest, A Report to the Center for the Study of Democratic Institutions*. Santa Barbara, CA: Center for the Study of Democratic Institutions.

MIDGLEY, D. F., MORRISON, P. D. and ROBERTS, J. H. (1992). 'The Effect of Network Structure in Industrial Diffusion Processes'. *Research Policy*, 21(6): 533–52.

NOAM, E. (1987). 'The Public Telecommunications Network: A Concept in Transition'. *Journal of Communications*, 37(1): 30–48.

NONAKA, I. and TAKEUCHI, H. (1995). *The Knowledge-Creating Company: How Japanese Companies Create the Dynamics of Innovation*. New York: Oxford University Press.

OECD (2004). *The Economic Impact of ICT: Measurement, Evidence and Implications*. Paris: OECD.

PAVITT, K. and STEINMUELLER, W. E. (2002). 'Technology and Corporate Strategy: Change, Continuity and the Information Revolution', in A. Pettigrew, H. Thomas and R. Whittington (eds), *Handbook of Strategy and Management*, London: Sage Publications, 344–72.

RAO, P. M., VEMURI, V. K. and GALVIN, P. (2004). 'The Changing Technological Profile of the Leading ICT Firms: Evidence from US Patent Data, 1981–2000'. *Industry and Innovation*, 11(4): 353–72.

RAYMOND, E. S. (1999). *The Cathedral and the Bazaar: Musings on Linux and Open Source by an Accidental Revolutionary*. Sebastopol, CA: O'Reilly and Associates, Inc.

RIFKIN, J. (1995). *The End of Work: The Decline of the Global Labor Force and the Dawn of the Post-Market Era*. New York: Tarcher/Putnam.

ROHLFS, J. (1974). 'A Theory of Interdependent Demand for a Communications Service'. *Bell Journal of Economics*, 5(1): 16–37.

SHAPIRO, C. and VARIAN, H. R. (1998). *Information Rules: A Strategic Guide to the Network Economy*. Boston, MA: Harvard Business School Press.

SHIMAN, D. R. (1996). 'When E-Mail Becomes Junk Mail: The Welfare Implications of the Advancement of Communications Technology'. *Review of Industrial Organization*, 11(1): 35–48.

SPENCE, A. M. (1974). *Market Signaling: Informational Transfer in Hiring and Related Processes*. Cambridge, MA: Harvard University Press.

STONEMAN, P. (1976). *Technological Diffusion and the Computer Revolution: The UK Experience*. Cambridge: Cambridge University Press.

STONEMAN, P. (ed.) (1995). *Handbook of the Economics of Innovation and Technological Change*. Oxford: Blackwell.

SWANN, P., COWAN, R. and COWAN, W. (1997). 'A Model of Demand with Interaction Between Consumers'. *International Journal of Industrial Organization*, 15: 711–732.

——, —— and —— (2004). 'Waves in Consumption with Interdependence Between Consumers'. *Canadian Journal of Economics*, 37(1): 149–77.

TASSEY, G. (2000). 'Standardization in Technology-Based Markets'. *Research Policy*, 29(4–5): 587–602.

TILTON, J. E. (1971). *International Diffusion of Technology: The Case of Semiconductors*. Washington DC: Brookings Institution.

TRIPLETT, J. E. (1989). 'Price and Technological Change in a Capital Good: A Survey of Research on Computers', in D. W. Jorgenson and R. Landau (eds), *Technology and Capital Formation*. Cambridge, MA: MIT Press, 127–213.

VAN DEN ENDE, J. and KEMP, R. (1999). 'Technological Transformations in History: How the Computer Regime Grew Out of Existing Computing Regimes'. *Research Policy*, 28(8): 833–51.

VARIAN, H. R. and SHAPIRO, C. (1999). *Information Rules: A Strategic Guide to the Network Economy*. Boston, MA: Harvard Business School Press.

VON HIPPEL, E. (2005). *Democratizing Innovation*. Cambridge, MA: MIT Press.

WARSCHAUER, M. (2003). *Technology and Social Inclusion: Rethinking the Digital Divide*. Cambridge, MA: MIT Press.

WEBER, S. (2004). *The Success of Open Source Software*. Cambridge, MA: Harvard University Press.

WEBSTER, F. (2002). *Theories of the Information Society* (2nd edn). London: Routledge.

WILLMORE, C. (1999). 'A Penny for your Thoughts: E-Mail and the Under-Valuation of Expert Time', Department of Economics, University of Warwick.

WYCKOFF, A. W. (1995). 'The Impact of Computer Prices on International Comparisons of Labour Productivity'. *Economics of Innovation and New Technology*, 3(3–4): 277–93.

ZUBOFF, S. (1988). *In the Age of the Smart Machine: The Future of Work and Power*. New York: Basic Books.

NOTES

1. Formally speaking, the last two of these concepts are nearly identical—they both provide cost advantages to firms based upon joint output of several different types or models of ICT commodities. The distinction is that economies of scope are generally taken to apply to joint production *within* firms while the term economies of industrial coordination (and specific variants such as 'platforms' and 'modular systems' discussed below) can be taken more generally to apply to combinations of inputs produced by many different firms.

2. The principle of non-rivalry can be confusing. Obviously, the spread of information can influence behaviour in ways that are adverse to its original possessor, e.g. the disclosure of the immanent bankruptcy of a company. From the viewpoint of resource inputs, however, a piece of information can be used in two different production processes

without diminishing the amount available for use—something that cannot be said of many physical inputs such as shovels or labourers.

3. In addition, over the past 20 years, the minimum efficient scale for integrated circuit fabrication facilities and for the R&D efforts required to produce large telecommunication switches has become very large—creating more traditional plant or firm level economies of scale for these sectors.

4. These features are particularly well explained in Varian and Shapiro (1999).

5. See DuBoff (1979) and David (1991).

6. See Cargill (1996) and Brunsson (2002) for comprehensive reviews of standards-making processes.

7. See http://www.chinadaily.com.cn/en/doc/2003–12/05/content_287725.htm, accessed 26 Feb. 2006.

8. Software created that uses copyright to preserve the availability of the source code in which humans write software.

PART II

ORGANIZATIONAL DYNAMICS, STRATEGY, DESIGN, AND ICTs

THEME EDITOR:
CHRISANTHI AVGEROU

INTRODUCTION

THE often conflictual processes of ICT system design and implementation in a wide variety of organizational contexts are the focus of the contributions to this part. The contributors in this section focus on various aspects of the way the outcomes of ICT applications are negotiated by the actors involved in these processes and they consider developments both inside organizations and between them.

The general principles of information systems planning—alignment, competitive advantage and knowledge management—that are often taken as being axiomatic are examined by Galliers in Chapter 9. He develops a perspective on information system (IS) strategy that emphasizes 'strategizing' rather than the outcome of processes, and advocates inclusive and exploratory approaches to planning so as to discern the problems that might be addressed through the application of ICTs and the unintended consequences of such applications.

Willcocks, Lacity and Cullen review the diverse definitions, approaches, focus, and results of ICT outsourcing studies in Chapter 10. They identify the findings from a stream of studies of outsourcing practices that they have been engaged in since the early 1990s, concentrating particularly on lessons of success and failure. They examine the degree of learning that has occurred over time through empirical evidence of changes in outsourcing portfolios, methods of evaluating market options, ways of crafting outsourcing arrangements, and in the way such relationships are managed.

Kallinikos critically assesses claims that ICTs are associated with new patterns of interaction, work, and communication that give rise to the structure of networks. In Chapter 11, he elaborates on two sets of conditions related to the emerging significance of networks: institutional changes of deregulation and globalization, and the contemporary growth of information and ICTs. He argues that the dynamic of networks is manifested in the decomposability and mobility of a growing number of operations and resources in ways that challenge important principles underlying formal organizations.

Research in the past decades has provided important insights on the role and influence of ICTs in organizational change. Jones and Orlikowski in Chapter 12 examine the new challenges posed by ICT innovations when they support more permeable and less hierarchical organizations with multiple horizontal and networked relationships. They review key perspectives that have emerged in the IS literature and they discuss empirical data on the emergence of online news reporting to illustrate the nature and dynamics of technology-based organizational change.

In Chapter 13, Introna shows how understandings of the ethical implications of ICTs are conditioned by assumptions about the relationship between humans and

ICTs. He presents three such theoretical assumptions, namely, that new media and ICTs are tools that have an impact on human society, that new media and ICTs are socially constructed and therefore serve particular interests better, and exclude others, and that the new media and ICTs are the way modern human beings express their existence, conducting themselves in an ongoing challenging and ordering of the world. He discusses the different questions each of these three approaches raises and clarifies their implications for ICT regulators, designers, users, and researchers.

CHAPTER 9

ON CONFRONTING SOME COMMON MYTHS OF IS STRATEGY DISCOURSE

ROBERT D. GALLIERS

I wonder if we could contrive...some magnificent myth that would in itself carry conviction to our whole community...

Plato: *Republic*, Bk 3: 414

1 INTRODUCTION[*]

IN the above quotation from Plato's *Republic*, the word 'myth' is sometimes translated as 'the noble lie'. Whether or not the myths—or lies—common in the mainstream treatment of Information Systems (IS) strategy are noble, or deliberate, I am uncertain. Irrespective of the answer, these myths—let us call them misconceptions—certainly need to be confronted. This is the purpose of my contribution to this collection.

Over the relatively short history of IS planning and strategy,[1] a number of general principles have arisen that are often taken as being axiomatic. Three such principles that have appeared in the mainstream literature include:

- *alignment*: information and communication technology (ICT) systems should align with the business strategy;
- *competitive advantage*: ICT systems can provide a firm with an advantage over its competitors, and
- *knowledge management*: ICT systems can and should be a repository of an organization's knowledge resources.

As with other management fields,[2] IS has been subject to a faddishness that fails to answer Keen's (1981) challenge for a more cumulative tradition. The 'holy grail' of IS has taken a number of different forms over the years. One can reasonably argue that the database was the IS 'solution' of the 1970s, soon to be followed, later in the decade and into the 1980s, by decision support systems. The competitive advantage to be gained from information technology (IT) took root as a key topic in the mid-1980s. The advent of the business process reengineering (BPR) movement in the early 1990s presaged a feeding frenzy in the mainstream academic and popular literature. Later in the decade, perhaps as a result of the loss of organizational knowledge that occurred as a result of the more extreme applications of BPR, the concept of knowledge management and knowledge management systems appeared on the scene. Since then, we have been subjected to enterprise systems and, latterly, the off shoring phenomenon.

Given the strategic focus of this contribution, I shall focus in this chapter on two key considerations—one more prevalent in the 1980s, the other a focus of attention in the 1990s and into the twenty-first century—namely, competitive advantage and knowledge management. The third consideration—alignment—has been a major focus, and a source of some contention, and I shall therefore incorporate this into my treatment of the subject matter.

---

* This chapter builds on, and extends, arguments first presented in Galliers and Newell (2003a, b) and Galliers (2004).

A further admission before we begin: I am a self-confessed adherent to the trans-disciplinary school of thought in the field of IS. There are some who argue for disciplinary purity, preferring our sole focus of attention to be on the IT artefact (see, e.g. Benbasat and Zmud 2003) and the design of IT-based IS. In fact, I do not perceive IS as a discipline at all. I see it—like all organizational subjects—as a transdisciplinary field of interest, possibly even a meta-discipline (see, e.g. Galliers 2003), and our focus of attention, I argue, should not simply be the artefact 'IT', but the complex and mutually constituted nature of IT use by human beings in and between organizations—and in society.

I shall take each in turn—alignment, competitive advantage and knowledge management and question these 'self evident truths' with a view to developing an alternative perspective on IS strategy. This perspective focuses more on the process of *strategizing* than on the outcome of the process, that is, the strategy itself. I argue that benefit is to be gained from a more inclusive, exploratory approach to the strategy process. This perspective is set against the common view, which is concerned more with exploiting the potential of ICT systems for business gain. Implicit in my arguments is the view that it is to be intellectually bankrupt to accept these myths as 'self evident truths'; that it would actually be a dangerous game we would play were we to do so. Too often, our IT solutions are ped-dled without attention being paid to the questions they are meant to 'solve', and certainly without an appreciation of their unintended consequences (Robey and Boudreau 1999).

After providing a critique of each of the myths, I attempt to synthesize the arguments, utilizing concepts of, *inter alia*, architecture and infrastructure (e.g. Star and Ruhleder 1996) and of 'ambidextrousness' (Tushman and O'Reilly 1996), with a view to refining a revised framework of IS strategizing, introduced in Galliers (2004). The aim is to provide a more balanced perspective, a sense-making device (Weick 1995), that will have an impact in both theory and practice.

2 ALIGNMENT

A central plank on which much of IS strategy theory and practice has been built is the concept of alignment. For example, almost 30 years ago, McLean and Soden (1977) compared the theoretical need for a 'strong link' between the business plan and the IS plan with the then current practice. They found that in less than 50 per cent of cases in their US study was there this strong link. A similar figure was reported by Earl (1983) in the UK. In a later work, Earl (1989) makes the important distinction between an information *systems* strategy and an information *technology* strategy. He notes that the IS strategy should be concerned with identifying what information is needed to support the business, and what information services need to be provided. In other words, the IS strategy is demand-oriented. Conversely, he sees the IT strategy as being supply-oriented. It demarcates what is and will be available in terms of IT infrastructure, applications, and services. His argument is that these two aspects of IS/IT strategy should be aligned. Other proponents of alignment include, for example, Parker, Benson, and Trainor (1988), MacDonald (1991), Baets (1992), Henderson and Venkatraman (1992; 1999), and Peppard and Ward (2004). These different perspectives on alignment make a telling point: what is being aligned with what? The examples given here refer to alignment between the business and IT strategies; between IS and IT strategies, between business performance and IT acquisitions; between the internal and external environments, and between IS capability and organizational performance.

While the alignment concept may be intuitively appealing, an issue that has remained relatively unchallenged and unquestioned is how to align ICT that is relatively fixed, once implemented in an organization, with a business strategy and associated information requirements that are constantly in need of adjustment, in line with the dynamic nature of the organization's business imperatives.[3] Despite the useful distinction made between IS and IT strategies, Earl's (1989) model, for example, is relatively static and does not account adequately for the changing information requirements of organizations, in line with a changing business strategy. While a subset of those requirements will doubtless remain relatively constant over time, the dynamic nature of the competitive, collaborative, and regulatory environments in which organizations conduct their business, dictates that constant and careful attention should be paid to the ever-changing nature of information need. In addition, and as I have pointed out elsewhere (Galliers 1991, 1993, 1999), information is needed to question whether an existing strategy continues to remain appropriate, given the changing environmental context—*external* considerations in other words—and lessons learned from the unintended consequences of actions taken and IT systems implemented (Robey and Boudreau 1999)—the *internal* considerations.

This issue leads us to the conclusion that information itself is a medium through which alignment might take place, and that this might usefully be perceived to be, at the very least, a two-way process: 'top-down' and 'bottom-up'. Indeed, this is implied by Earl's (1989) model. I say at the very least a two-way process because, as indicated above, alignment between the internal and external environments is an additional dimension to be incorporated into the alignment debate. Note, however, that from the perspective that information is the alignment medium, the focus is on such artefacts as technology, the strategic plan, and bottom-line business benefit. There are, however, those whose approach is more focused on exploration rather than exploitation (cf. March 1991). The former approach is otherwise known as coming from the processual school (see, e.g. Whittington 1993), being more concerned with the process of strategizing than with the strategy itself.

This brings us to the issue of emergence—a topic of debate in the business strategy literature for the past 20 years or so (see, e.g. Mintzberg and Waters 1985). In practice, IS strategy approaches tend to be based on a rational analysis of need— either in response to an extant business strategy, and/or an analysis of current ICT capability—or in a proactive manner, based on a 'clean slate' approach, such as with business process engineering. With respect to the latter, the argument was essentially that revolutionary change would lead to 'order of magnitude' business benefits (Hammer 1990; Davenport and Short 1990; Venkatraman 1991; Davenport 1993). The approach was based on identifying and streamlining key business processes and key customer requirements, and then on identifying how ICT might support (and often automate) these processes and requirements, with a view to improving efficiency and effectiveness, and cutting costs. The approach involved quite some risk (Galliers 1997) and often led to what was euphemistically called 'downsizing', with many middle managers being required to leave the company. This had a consequent, unintended (cf. Robey and Boudreau 1999) deleterious effect on organizational memory and available expertise (Davenport 1996; Galliers and Swan 1999).

But what of innovation and serendipity? As indicated above, there is a school of thought that argues for the emergent nature of strategic processes. In the field of IS, Ciborra used terms such as bricolage (after Lévi-Strauss 1966), drift, and tinkering (Ciborra 1992, 2000, 2002) to propose a more incremental, ad hoc approach to strategizing. He argued that even in situations where strategic advantage had been gained from the astute application of ICT, the resultant gain was by no means always expected and in no way pre-ordained. Rather, the organizations concerned had benefited from creating an environment—or infrastructure—in which innovation might emerge. The approach he advocated smacks of playfulness. Others see benefit in combining incremental and radical change. Tushman and O'Reilly (1996), for example, speak of 'ambidextrous' organizations, while He and Wong (2004) confirm this hypothesis in a study of more than 200 manufacturing firms (see also Gibson and Birkinshaw 2004).

All in all, then, the question of alignment is a vexed one. I posed the question 'alignment with what?' earlier. There is the question of 'alignment with whom?' in addition. Given the advent of inter-organizational systems, and more so, of the Internet, alignment is also presumably required along the virtual value chain, with relationships with suppliers and customers, for example, needing to be taken into account. It is in such circumstances that we note the need for human interaction, rather than an almost total reliance on rational analysis of organizational need or on ICT per se. As will be argued in the context of knowledge management, there is a need for 'boundary-spanning' (Tushman and Scanlan 1981) activity, for under-standing, and trust (Newell and Swan 2000), and the natural development of 'communities of practice' (Brown and Duguid 1991; Lave and Wenger 1991)—both within organizations and externally—in order for new knowledge to emerge.

But let me use the conclusion to this discussion regarding the contentious issue of alignment, as a means of providing something of a link between it and the discussion that follows on ICT and competitive advantage. We have seen that alignment has been considered from different perspectives—alignment between 'what' and 'whom' are key questions. There is a more basic point to consider here though, and that is the conceptual link that appears to be missing between what is after all a conceptual business strategy and a physical, technological artefact. I earlier pondered whether the missing ingredient might be information, and there is certainly a reasonable argument here. In addition, however, it should be remembered that organizations often comprise many technologies and many, often dispersed, individuals.[4] Increasingly, these individuals are 'organized' on a project-by-project basis, thereby adding increased dynamism to the mix, and compounding the issue of alignment still further. Hansen (1999) talks of the need for weak ties across organizational sub-units. Gheradi and Nicolini (2000) call for the establishment of safety for individuals to form communities of practice for sharing understanding and knowledge. The processes of developing weak ties and safe communities are learned—and these learning processes are as important as the content knowledge itself (Newell et al. 2003).

3 COMPETITIVE ADVANTAGE

Considerable attention was paid in the 1980s and 1990s to what became something of a holy grail of IS: the gaining and retention of competitive advantage from the astute and proactive use of ICT in and by organizations. ICT 'changes the way you compete' noted one venerable proponent of the cause (McFarlan 1984). Later, during the 1990s, and as already indicated, radical business transformation on the back of business process change—and enabled by ICT—was all the rage (Hammer 1990; Davenport and Short 1990; Venkatraman 1991; Davenport 1993). But rage of a different kind soon ensued and the bubble burst as the millennium dawned. Why was that? There are many answers to this question of course, but let me highlight two of them. One relates to the purchase of so-called 'best practice' solutions, such as enterprise systems, off-the-shelf. The other relates to the question of sustainability.

It was always the case that ICT in and of itself would not provide a firm with competitive advantage, despite the more popular press claiming this to be the case. And this is certainly even more the case these days with the commoditization of ICT.

The advent of the Internet and enterprise systems has seen to that. What is perhaps surprising is that we are still treated to claims of 'best practice' solutions [*sic*] as if there were no contradiction between an advantage to be gained over others by the purchase of a 'solution' that could be obtained just as easily by those same competitors, from the same vendors. Thus, vendors of off-the shelf 'best practice' enterprise systems make the implausible claim that advantage will ensue with the purchase of a technology and services that are equally available to one's competitors.[5] But there is more: this so-called 'best practice' technology—this readily implementable solution—also turns out to require on-going support and consultancy.[6]

Even in the 1980s, it became clear that there was an issue of sustainability that had to be addressed. While there may have been first mover advantage from the purchase of new technology, the lead gained needed to be sustained over time (see, e.g. Porter 1985; Ghemawat 1986; Hall 1993; Suarez and Lanzolla 2005). It was Porter who provided something of an answer to those who proclaimed advantage from the technology alone (Porter and Millar 1985). The important point he raised at that time was that it was the use made of the technology that mattered—it was information that could provide the advantage, not the technology. Later, others joined the fray. Senn (1992), for example, echoed the later thoughts of Ciborra and others in criticizing the very concept of strategic IS, and later still, Land (1996) questioned the basic premises on which the BPR movement was built.

What is perhaps both surprising and disappointing about the faddishness of much of the literature on IS strategy is that many key lessons were soon forgotten as a new technology or movements emerged. Thus, for example, Leavitt's (1965) argument that organizations could usefully be viewed as complex socio-technical systems comprising four elements: objectives, structure, technology and people, seems to have become lost in the excitement, the *zeitgeist*, if you will. The focus in the age of BPR was primarily on ICT and processes, and in the age of enterprise systems, it appears to be primarily on a technological architecture that actually dictates how processes should be undertaken. Even one of the founding fathers of the BPR movement proclaimed that it had become 'the fad that forgot people' (Davenport 1996)—of which more in Section 4 on knowledge management.

With the emergence of the Internet and e-business, again we are confronted with considerable hyperbole, notwithstanding the bursting of the dot.com bubble. Again, we have been treated to many arguments that another new technology would fundamentally change the basis of competition. In his compelling *Harvard Business Review* article, Porter (2001) refutes any such suggestion. Porter sees the Internet as something that complements rather than cannibalizes organizations and organizational ICT as we have come to know them. As I have noted previously (Galliers 2004: 254), 'while some have argued that "the Internet renders strategy obsolete . . . the opposite is true . . . it is more important than ever for companies to distinguish themselves through strategy"' (Porter 2001: 63). While Porter sees the Internet as just another means of doing business, opening up a new channel, he makes the point that it is likely to increase competition and make it more difficult for companies to sustain their competitive advantage. Thus, in his view, ICT in and of itself, rather than being a force *for* competitive advantage, becomes a force *against* competitive advantage. He goes on to argue that 'only by integrating the Internet into overall strategy will this powerful new technology become an equally powerful force for competitive advantage' (Porter 2001: 78).

To develop this argument further, competitive advantage may be gained by those companies that can integrate uses of the Internet with their core competences (Prahalad and Hamel 1990). Porter's contention is that it may well be easier for 'traditional' companies to do this than for dot coms to adopt, develop, and integrate such competencies themselves. He argues that these core competencies and traditional strengths are likely to remain the same, with or without the Internet, and it is these that will provide competitive advantage, not the technology.

Thus, we might argue that the impact of ICTs on competitiveness may well be negative rather than the more positive, view most often expounded in the mainstream literature. In addition, we have seen companies attempting to utilize ICT in an attempt to increase efficiency and reduce costs. Having said that, and as noted in the discussion on BPR and enterprise systems, in adopting this approach, companies run the risk of reducing their effectiveness, dexterity and innovative capacity. Unless they can develop the ambidextrousness of which Tushman and O'Reilly (1996) speak, they face the common dilemma of gaining efficiency at the expense of innovation (Clark and Staunton 1989; March 1991; McElroy 2000). They also run the risk of losing their capacity for organizational learning and knowing. This is now discussed in the following section.

4 KNOWLEDGE MANAGEMENT

Knowledge is considered by many to be a key organizational resource, and the knowledge management movement that followed the BPR era has encouraged organizations to attempt to exploit more strategically their knowledge assets (e.g. Grant 1996; Kogut and Zander 1992).[7] Companies are thus lured by the suggestion that they can 'gain competitive advantage' (that ubiquitous expression) by managing their knowledge assets more astutely, and in particular, by transferring knowledge across individuals, groups, and organizational units, using ICT to achieve this end. There is a knowledge management aspect to the enterprise systems phenomenon, and I shall introduce this section by attacking these myths before progressing to a consideration of knowledge management systems (KMS) themselves. Incorporating knowledge management considerations into a discourse on IS strategizing will be left to the final section of this chapter, but it is perhaps worth noting the current relative lack of such considerations in mainstream IS strategy discourse. This is somewhat surprising given the common view that knowledge is a strategic organizational resource, and that ICT systems are means by which such knowledge can be transferred across time and space.

As already discussed, enterprise systems are often promoted as a means of transferring 'best practice' knowledge. An enterprise system's built-in processes require the adopting organization to adapt its existing processes to the exigencies of the software. The argument is that, since these inbuilt processes are based on 'best practice' industry standards, the organization concerned will automatically benefit as a result. But, as we have seen, vendors of enterprise systems make much of the consultancy services they offer during and after implementation. Presumably, these services are provided in order for the 'best practice' solution to become 'better', and the off-the-shelf 'solution' to be customized. Research undertaken by Wagner (Scott and Wagner 2003; Wagner and Newell 2006) demonstrates how these so-called best practices have to be moulded and adapted to the realpolitik of organizations, to some extent at least, *despite* the services of the vendor. In addition, and in relation to the earlier discussion on alignment, enterprise systems are often implemented to replace legacy systems, which presumably have drifted out of alignment—presumably, too, to become legacy systems in their own right over time.

Moreover, by advocating copying best practices to improve efficiency, organizations are, potentially at least, running the risk of actually reducing their ability to create the new knowledge needed to innovate and respond creatively to changing imperatives. Given that this is a key concern of business strategy, and that KMS are meant to support and inform the process of strategizing, it appears we may have another problem here. ICTs such as enterprise systems and the Internet can be thus seen to be a force for standardization, thereby speeding competitive convergence, given that the technology is more or less common—and increasingly commoditized—irrespective of the organization implementing it. But there is more to this enigma, as presaged by the earlier comments on knowing as opposed to knowledge.

The myth of KMS emerged in the 1990s. That is, ICT-based KMS can store and transfer knowledge. Thus, existing knowledge can be collected and re-used, utilizing ICT. From this perspective, knowledge is 'out there', ready to be mined, harvested. We thus return to the mythology of 'best practice' that underpins much of this kind of thinking. Presumably, for such knowledge to be worth re-using, knowledge of what is best practice is required.[8] But, let us consider some basic principles here. Checkland (1981) reminds us that, while ICT can be exceptionally powerful and proficient in processing data, it is human beings who apply meaning (their knowledge) to selected data in order to make sense (Weick 1990) of these data, for a specific purpose. Data may therefore be context-free, while information can only be informative within a particular context. ICT systems are therefore data processing systems—nothing more, nothing less. IS require the presence of human beings who apply their knowledge to turn data into information. Knowledge is therefore tacit (cf. Polanyi 1966) and embedded. 'It resides within our brains, and enables us to make sense of the data we [choose to] capture' (Galliers 2004: 253). It is also 'sticky' (Szulanski 1996; Szulanski and Jensen 2004) in that its contextual nature means that it is less easily transferred than the KMS perspective might otherwise suggest.

Responsibility for the myth of codified knowledge that can be captured in ICT systems can, partially at least, be laid at the doorstep of Nonaka (e.g. Nonaka and Takeushi 1995). Their model depicts the transformation of tacit knowledge into codified knowledge and is widely known and frequently cited in this context. An alternative perspective has also appeared on the scene, however, one that is much more in line with the perspective adopted in this essay. Blackler (1995), Boland and Tenkasi (1995), Tsoukas (1996), and Cook and Brown (1999), among others, raise issues of knowledge transfer and *knowing* rather than knowledge capture and codification. Individuals working with colleagues in organizations learn (see, e.g. Bogenreider and Nooteboom 2004) from their interactions with each other and their interactions with formal (and informal) data processing systems (see Land 1982). Similarly, Wenger (1998) talks of situated learning in the context of communities of practice, while Sole and Edmondson (2002) develop the concept further in relation to geographically dispersed teams. The contrast between these perspectives on knowledge and knowing, on capture and creation, and on explicit and tacit knowledge is similar to the personalization–codification distinction of Hansen, Nohria, and Tierney (1999), and the community–codification distinction made by Scarbrough, Swan, and Preston (1999). In taking the more processual perspective, I would argue that there is potentially considerably more to be gained from the process of knowing, of knowledge creation, of learning and human interaction—in the context of this essay, the process of strategizing[9]—than the mere transfer of 'knowledge' [*sic*] per se.

5 SYNTHESIS: TOWARDS A REVISED FRAMEWORK FOR IS STRATEGIZING

An attempt is made in this final section to bring together aspects of the foregoing arguments as a basis for the development of a revised framework for IS strategizing. Thus far, we have considered the issues of alignment, competitive advantage, and knowledge management, as they each relate to the development and use of ICT systems in and between organizations. An attempt has been made to raise serious doubts about some of the mythology that has surrounded these concepts in the more popular, mainstream literature. With regard to the topic of alignment, we have noted, *inter alia*, that there are vexed issues associated with aligning dynamic information needs with a relatively static technology. Alignment with what and with whom were issues that were also raised. Competitive advantage on the back of an increasingly commoditized technology also presents us with something of a conundrum, with the importance of ICT use and capability, core competence, and the key role of information each being highlighted. In relation to knowledge management and KMS, questions were raised as to whether ICT systems could in fact capture and transfer knowledge and, just as importantly, the process of knowing and knowledge creation was privileged over knowledge capture and transfer.

In attempting to synthesize these arguments, with a view to developing a revised, integrated framework for IS strategizing, the socio-technical concept of an infor- mation architecture or infrastructure is a useful building block (e.g. Ciborra 2000; Hanseth 2004; Monteiro 1998; Star and Ruhleder 1996), as argued in Galliers (2004). In introducing this framework, it was argued that organizations could be ambidextrous (cf. the arguments introduced earlier, based on the work of Tushman and O'Reilly 1996) in combining an ability both to exploit current capability and to explore new possibilities. Modes of exploitation and exploration, I argue, may be facilitated by an environment—an information infrastructure or architecture— that provides a supportive context for learning and interaction. I shall take each of these components of the proposed framework in turn, as a means of refining the framework and describing how it might be used as a sense-making (cf. Weick 1995) device in organizations.

The process of exploitation adopted in the revised framework bears many of the hallmarks of mainstream thinking on IS strategy. This is the deliberate—as compared to the emergent—strategy of which Mintzberg speaks (Mintzberg and Waters 1985). A deliberate attempt is made to identify and develop ICT applications that both support and question the organization's strategic vision, and current need for information and expertise. Here, we find both the IS and IT strategies that Earl (1989) proposes. It is likely that enterprise systems and so-called KMS, and standardized procedures for adopting ICT products, hiring ICT personnel, and developing customized applications will each contribute to this exploitation strat- egy. Moreover, in line with the models introduced in Galliers (1991, 1999), an aspect of this strategy will relate to the organizational arrangements for IS/IT services, including sourcing considerations (cf. Lacity and Willcocks 2001). Policies on such issues as risk, security, and confidentiality will also need to be considered in this context (e.g. Backhouse et al. 2005).

With respect to the exploration aspects of strategizing, here the emphasis is much more on issues associated with situated learning, communities of practice, and cross-project learning. Ciborra and colleagues (Ciborra 2000) talk of drift in this context—as against control—but there is nonetheless a sense of direction and purpose associated with this activity. I therefore prefer the term emergence in this regard, but there is certainly a sense of bricolage (cf. Lévi-Strauss 1966) and tinkering at play here, to return to terms favoured by Ciborra (1992). As already noted, organizations are increasingly reliant on project teams whose membership may well be in flux and distributed. Considerations of trust (Sambamurphy and Jarvenpaa 2002) and learning from one project to another (e.g. Scarbrough, Swan and Preston 1998) are key features at play here. The role of communities of practice (e.g. Wenger 1998) is crucial in knowledge creation as we have seen, as is the role of boundary spanning individuals (Tushman and Scanlan 1981), or what we might term knowledge brokers (see also, Lave and Wenger, 1991; Hansen 1999).

While the concept of the ambidextrous organization has been postulated (Tushman and O'Reilly 1996), and some empirical research has been conducted to test the thesis (e.g. He and Wong 2004), there remains little in the literature that might be of assistance to organizations in providing an enabling, supportive environment that might foster this sought-after 'ambidexterity'. Relating concepts of infrastructure introduced earlier to the concept of ambidexterity would appear to hold some promise in this regard.

In the 1980s and 1990s, the term 'information infrastructure' usually connoted the standardization of corporate ICT, systems, and data, with a view to reconciling centralized processing and distributed applications. Increasingly, however... the concept has come to relate not just to data and ICT systems, but also the human infrastructure. (Galliers 2004: 256)

Thus, the kind of socio-technical environment proposed by Star and Ruhleder (1996), Ciborra (2000), and Hanseth (2004), for example, would combine information and knowledge sharing services—both electronic and human—that would facilitate both exploration and exploitation of knowledge, and the kind of flexibility necessary to enable appropriate responses to changing business imperatives. In some ways, this kind of infrastructure would help circumvent the alignment issue that was introduced at the beginning of this chapter.

I have also stressed the importance of on-going learning and review, given the processual view adopted here, the unintended consequences arising not only from ICT implementations (Robey and Boudreau 1999) and the dynamic nature of alignment (Sabherwal, Hirschheim and Goles 2001), but also the emergent nature of strategizing (Mintzberg and Waters 1985). The whole process of strategizing is one of visioning, planning, taking action, and assessing outcomes, all with an eye to changing circumstance and imperatives, and the actions of individuals and groups outside, and notwithstanding, any formal strategy process. There are countless books on breakthrough change management focusing on the role of ICT (e.g. Lientz and Rea 2004) and on so-called transformational leaders (e.g. Anderson and Anderson 2001). The major features of this genre include prescriptive, deliberate approaches that suggest guaranteed, order-of-magnitude gains. Organizational realities suggest an alternative, incremental approach more akin to 'muddling through' (Lindblom 1959), however. The incremental exploration of possibilities—the tinkering (Ciborra 1992) and bricolage (Lévi-Strauss 1966)—along with the more deliberate, analytical approaches that incorporate oversight of implementations and review of outcomes (e.g. Willcocks 1999) is what is envisaged here.

Bearing all this in mind, the following concept is an attempt to refine further the IS strategizing concept introduced in Galliers (2004: 256). The framework is not meant to be a prescriptive tool, nor a solution. It is a sense-making (cf. Weick 1995) device, meant more as an aide-mémoire, to be used to raise questions and facilitate discussion concerning the strategizing elements and connections that may or may not be in place in any particular organization.

One final point in closing: the fact that I continue to refer to the strategizing framework as one concerned with IS (as opposed to either ICT at one pole or knowledge sharing and creation at the other) is deliberate. There are two primary reasons for this. The first relates to the preceding discussion of the nature of data, information, and knowledge. The socio-technical infrastructure depicted in Figure 9.1 comprises human beings who can make sense of data provided by both formal and informal systems via the application of their (situated) knowledge. In doing so, they turn data into purposeful information. The second reason is to provide an otherwise missing link between the literatures on IS/IT strategy, on knowledge management, and on organizational strategies for change—the transdisciplinary

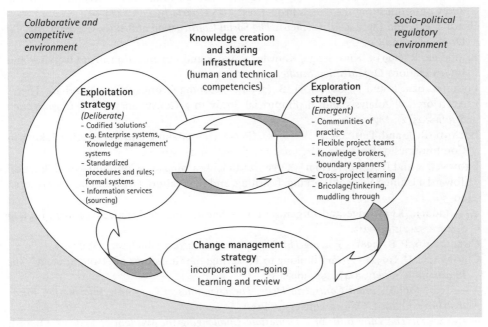

Fig. 9.1 A revised IS strategizing framework

perspective mentioned in the introduction. Too often viewed as discrete, an underlying argument in this chapter is that the concepts emerging from these literatures should be viewed as complementary and synergistic. If I may be permitted to misquote Porter (2001: 78), the next stage of strategy evolution will involve a shift in thinking from business strategy and knowledge strategy, to IS strategizing. By integrating IS considerations into the discourse on business and knowledge strategy, the resultant thinking and practice will become mutually constituted and significantly more robust. In saying this, I realize that I may have unintentionally constructed a new myth. Please accept though that my intentions—my 'lies' if you will—are 'noble'.

References

Anderson, D. and Anderson, L. A. (2001). *Beyond Change Management: Advanced Strategies for Today's Transformational Leaders*. San Francisco, CA: Jossey-Bass/Pfeffer.

Backhouse, J., Bener, A., Chauvidul, N. et al. (2005). 'Risk Management in Cyberspace', in R. Mansell and B. Collins (eds), *Trust and Crime in Information Societies*. Cheltenham: Edward Elgar, 349–79.

Baets, W. (1992). 'Aligning Information Systems with Business Strategy'. *Journal of Strategic Information Systems*, 1(4): 205–13.

Benbasat, I. and Zmud, R. (2003). 'The Identity Crisis within the IS Discipline: Defining and Communicating the Core's Properties'. *MIS Quarterly*, 27(2): 183–94.

Berger, P. L. and Luckman, T. (1966). *The Social Construction of Reality*. Garden City, NY: Doubleday and Co.

Blackler, R. (1995). 'Knowledge, Knowledge Work and Organizations: An Overview and Interpretation'. *Organization Studies*, 16(6): 1021–46.

Bogenreider, I. and Nooteboom, B. (2004). 'Learning Groups: What Types are There? A Theoretical Analysis and an Empirical Study in a Consultancy Firm'. *Organization Studies*, 25(2): 287–313.

Boland, R. J. and Tenkasi, R. V. (1995). 'Perspective Making and Perspective Taking in Communities of Knowing'. *Organization Science*, 6(4): 350–72.

Brown, J. S. and Duguid, P. (1991). 'Organizational Learning and Communities of Practice: Toward a Unified View of Working, Learning, and Innovation'. *Organization Science*, 2(1): 40–56.

—— (2001). 'Knowledge and Organization: A Social-Practice Perspective'. *Organization Science*, 12(2): 198–213.

Checkland, P. B. (1981). *Systems Thinking. Systems Practice*. Chichester: Wiley.

Ciborra, C. U. (1992). 'From Thinking to Tinkering: the Grassroots of IT and Strategy'. *The Information Society*, 8(4): 297–309.

—— (ed.) (2000). *From Control to Drift: The Dynamics of Corporate Information Infrastructures*. Oxford: Oxford University Press.

—— (2002). *The Labyrinths of Information: Challenging the Wisdom of Systems*. Oxford: Oxford University Press.

CLARK, P. A. and STAUNTON, N. (1989). *Innovation in Technology and Organization*. London: Routledge.

COOK S. D. and BROWN J. S. (1999). 'Bridging Epistemologies: The Generative Dance between Organizational Knowledge and Organizational Knowing'. *Organization Science*, 10(4): 381–400.

CUMMINGS, S. and ANGWIN, D. (2004). 'The Future Shape of Strategy: Lemmings or Chimeras?' *The Academy of Management Executive*, 18(2): 21–36.

DAVENPORT, T. H. (1993). *Process Innovation: Re-engineering Work through Information Technology*. Boston, MA: Harvard Business School Press.

—— (1996). 'Why Re-engineering Failed. The Fad that Forgot People'. *Fast Company*, Premier Issue, 70–4.

—— and SHORT, J. E. (1990). 'The New Industrial Engineering: Information Technology and Business Process Redesign'. *Sloan Management Review*, 3(4): 11–27.

EARL, M. J. (1983). 'Emerging Trends in Managing New Information Technologies', in N. Piercey (ed.) (1986), *The Management Implications of New Information Technology*, London: Croom Helm, 189–215.

—— (1989). *Management Strategies for Information Technology*. London: Prentice Hall.

GALLIERS, R. D. (1991). 'Strategic Information Systems Planning: Myths, Reality and Guidelines for Successful Implementation'. *European Journal of Information Systems*, 1(1): 55–64.

—— (1993). 'Towards a Flexible Information Architecture: Integrating Business Strategies, Information Systems Strategies and Business Process Redesign'. *Journal of Information Systems*, 3(3): 199–213.

—— (1995). 'Reorienting Information Systems Strategy: Integrating Information Systems into the Business', in F. A. Stowell (ed.), *Information Systems Provision: The Contribution of Soft Systems Methodology*. London: McGraw-Hill, 51–74.

—— (1997). 'Against Obliteration: Reducing Risk in Business Process Change', in C. Sauer, P. W. Yetton and Associates (eds), *Steps to the Future: Fresh Thinking on the Management of IT-Based Organizational Transformation*. San Francisco: Jossey-Bass, 169–86.

—— (1999). 'Towards the Integration of e-Business, Knowledge Management and Policy Considerations within an Information Systems Strategy Framework', *Journal of Strategic Information Systems*, 8(3): 229–34.

—— (2003). 'Change as Crisis or Growth? Toward a Trans-disciplinary View of Information Systems as a Field of Study - A Response to Benbasat and Zmud's Call for Returning to the IT Artifact. *Journal of the Association for Information Systems*, 4(6): 337–51.

—— (2004). 'Reflections on Information Systems Strategizing', in C. Avgerou, C. Ciborra, and F. Land (eds), *The Social Study of Information and Communication Technology: Innovation, Actors, and Contexts*. Oxford: Oxford University Press, 231–62.

—— and NEWELL, S. (2003a). 'Strategy as Data + Sense Making', in S. Cummings and D. C. Wilson (eds), *Images of Strategy*. Oxford: Blackwell, 164–96.

—— and NEWELL, S. (2003b). 'Back to the Future: From Knowledge Management to the Management of Information and Data'. *Information Systems and e-Business Management*, 1(1): 5–13.

—— and SWAN, J. A. (1999). 'Information Systems and Strategic Change: A Critical Review of Business Process Re-engineering', in W. L. Currie and R. D. Galliers (eds), *Rethinking Management Information Systems: An Interdisciplinary Perspective*. Oxford: Oxford University Press, 361–87.

GHEMAWAT, P. (1986). 'Sustainable Advantage'. *Harvard Business Review*, 64(5): 53–8.

GHERARDI, S. and NICOLINI, D. (2000). 'The Organizational Learning of Safety in Communities of Practice'. *Journal of Management Inquiry*, 9(1): 7–18.

GIBSON, C. B. and BIRKINSHAW, J. (2004). 'The Antecedents, Consequences, and Mediating Role of Organizational Ambidexterity'. *The Academy of Management Journal*, 47(2): 209–26.

GRANT, R. M. (1996). 'Prospering in Dynamically-competitive Environments: Organizational Capability as Knowledge Integration'. *Organization Science*, 7(4): 375–87.

HALL, R. (1993). 'A Framework Linking Intangible Resources and Capabilities to Sustainable Competitive Advantage'. *Strategic Management Journal*, 14(8): 607–18.

HAMMER, M. (1990). 'Don't Automate, Obliterate'. *Harvard Business Review*, 68(4): 104–12.

HANSEN, M. T. (1999). 'The Search Transfer Problem: The Role of Weak Ties in Sharing Knowledge across Organizational Sub-units'. *Administrative Science Quarterly*, 44(1): 82–111.

HANSEN, M., NOHRIA, N. and TIERNEY, T. (1999). 'What's your Strategy for Managing Knowledge?' *Harvard Business Review*, 77(2): 106–16.

HANSETH, O. (2004). 'Knowledge as Architecture', in C. Avgerou, C. Ciborra, and F. Land, (eds), *The Social Study of Information and Communication Technology: Innovation, Actors, and Contexts*. Oxford: Oxford University Press, 103–18.

HE, Z.-L. and WONG, P.-K. (2004). 'Exploration vs. Exploitation: An Empirical Test of the Ambidexterity Hypothesis'. *Organization Science*, 15(4): 481–94.

HENDERSON, J. and VENKATRAMAN, N. (1992). 'Strategic Alignment: A Model for Organizational Transformation through Information Technology', in T. A. Kochan and M. Useem (eds), *Transforming Organizations*. New York: Oxford University Press, 97–117.

—— and —— (1999). 'Strategic Alignment: Leveraging Information Technology for Transforming Organizations'. *IBM Systems Journal*, 38(2–3): 472–84.

KEEN, P. G. W. (1981). 'MIS Research: Reference Disciplines and a Cumulative Tradition'. *Proceedings of the 1st International Conference on Information Systems*, Philadelphia, PA, 8–10 Dec, 9–18.

KOGUT, B. and ZANDER, U. (1992). 'Knowledge of the firm, combinative capabilities, and the replication of technology'. *Organization Science*, 3(3): 383–97.

KRIEBEL, C. H. (1968). 'The Strategic Dimension of Computer Systems Planning'. *Long Range Planning*, 1(1): 7–12.

LACITY, M. C. and WILLCOCKS, L. (2001). *Global Information Technology Outsourcing: In Search of Business Advantage*. Chichester: John Wiley & Sons.

LAND, F. (1982). 'Adapting to Changing User Requirements'. *Information and Management*, 5(2): 59–75.

—— (1996). 'The New Alchemist: Or How to Transmute Base Organisations into Corporations of Gleaming Gold'. *Journal of Strategic Information Systems*, 5(1): 5–17.

LAVE, J. and WENGER, E. (1991). *Situated Learning: Legitimate Peripheral Participation*. Cambridge: Cambridge University Press.

LEAVITT, H. J. (1965). 'Applying Organizational Change in Industry: Structural, Technological and Humanistic Approaches', in J. G. March (ed.), *Handbook of Organizations*, Chicago, IL: Rand McNally.

LEIDNER, D. E. (ed.) (2000). *Journal of Strategic Information Systems*. SI on Knowledge Management and Knowledge Management Systems, 9(2–3): 101–261.

LÉVI-STRAUSS, C. (1966). *The Savage Mind*. London: Weidenfeld & Nicolson.

LIENTZ, B. P. and REA, K. P. (2004). *Breakthrough IT Change Management: How to Get Enduring Change Results*. Oxford: Elsevier Butterworth Heinemann.

LINCOLN, T. J. (1975). 'A Strategy for Information Systems Development'. *Management Datamatics*, 4(4): 121–28.

LINDBLOM, C. (1959). 'The Science of Muddling Through'. *Public Administration Review*, 19(2): 79–88.

MACDONALD, H. (1991). 'Business Strategy Development, Alignment and Redesign', in M. Scott Morton (ed.), *The Corporation of the 1990s*. New York: Oxford University Press, 159–86.

MARCH, J. (1991). 'Exploration and Exploitation in Organizational Learning'. *Organization Science*, 2(1): 71–86.

MCELROY, M. (2000). 'Integrating Complexity Theory, Knowledge Management and Organizational Learning'. *Journal of Knowledge Management*, 4(3): 195–203.

MCFARLAN, F. W. (1971). 'Problems in Planning the Information System'. *Harvard Business Review*, 49(2): 75–89.

—— (1984). 'Information Technology Changes the Way You Compete'. *Harvard Business Review*, 62(3): 98–102.

MCLEAN, E. R. and SODEN, J. V. (1977). *Strategic Planning for MIS*. New York: Wiley.

MINTZBERG, H. and WATERS, J. A. (1985). 'Of Strategies, Deliberate and Emergent'. *Strategic Management Journal*, 6(3): 257–72.

MONTEIRO, E. (1998). 'Scaling Information Infrastructure: The Case of the Next Generation IP in Internet'. *The Information Society*, 14(3): 229–45.

NEWELL, S. and SWAN, J. (2000). 'Trust and Inter-organizational Networking'. *Human Relations*, 53(10): 1287–328.

——, EDELMAN, L., SCARBROUGH, H. et al. (2003)., '"Best Practice" Develoopment and Transfer in the NHS: The Importance of Process as well as Product Knowledge'. *Journal of Health Services Management*, 16: 1–12.

NONAKA, I. and TAKEUCHI, H. (1995). *The Knowledge-Creating Company: How Japanese Companies Create the Dynamics of Innovation*. New York: Oxford University Press.

PARKER, M., BENSON, R. and TRAINOR, E. (1988). *Information Economics: Linking Business Performance to Information Technology*. Englewood Cliffs, NJ: Prentice Hall.

PEPPARD, J. and WARD, J. (2004). 'Beyond Strategic Information Systems: Towards an IS Capability'. *Journal of Strategic Information Systems*, 13(2): 167–94.

POLANYI, M. (1966). *The Tacit Dimension*. Garden City, NY: Doubleday and Co.

PORTER, M. E. (1985). *Competitive Advantage: Creating and Sustaining Superior Performance*. New York: The Free Press.

—— (2001). 'Strategy and the Internet'. *Harvard Business Review*, 79(3): 63–78.

—— and MILLAR, V. E. (1985). 'How Information Gives You Competitive Advantage'. *Harvard Business Review*, 63(4): 149–60.

PRAHALAD, C. K. and HAMEL, G. (1990). 'The Core Competence of the Corporation'. *Harvard Business Review*, 68(3): 79–91.

ROBEY, D. and BOUDREAU, M. C. (1999). 'Accounting for the Contradictory Organizational Consequences of Information Technology: Theoretical Directions and Methodological Implications'. *Information Systems Research*, 10(2): 167–85.

SABHERWAL, R., HIRSCHHEIM, R. and GOLES, T. (2001). 'The Dynamics of Alignment: Insights from a Punctuated Equilibrium Model'. *Organization Science*, 12(2): 179–97.

SAMBAMURTHY, V. and JARVENPAA, S. (eds) (2002). *Journal of Strategic Information Systems*. SI on Trust in the Digital Economy, 11(3–4): 183–346.

SCARBROUGH, H., BRESNEN, M., EDELMAN, L. F. et al. (2004). 'The Processes of Project-based Learning: An Exploratory Study'. *Management Learning*, 35(4): 491–506.

SCARBROUGH, H., SWAN, J. and PRESTON, J. (1998). *Knowledge Management and the Learning Organization*. London: IPD.

SCOTT, S. V. and WAGNER, E. L. (2003). 'Networks, Negotiations and New Times: The Implementation of Enterprise Resource Planning into an Academic Administration'. *Information and Organization*, 13(4): 285–313.

SENN, J. A. (1992). 'The Myths of Strategic Systems: What Defines True Competitive Advantage?' *Journal of Information Systems Management*, 9(3): 7–12.

SOLE, D. and EDMONDSON, A. (2002). 'Situated Knowledge and Learning in Dispersed Teams'. *British Journal of Management*, 13: S17–S34.

STAR, S. L. and RUHLEDER, K. (1996). 'Steps Towards an Ecology of Infrastructure: Design and Access to Large Information Spaces'. *Information Systems Research*, 7(1): 111–34.

SUAREZ, F. F. and LANZOLLA, G. (2005). 'The Half-Truth of First-Mover Advantage'. *Harvard Business Review*, 83(4): 121–7.

SZULANSKI, G. (1996). 'Exploring Internal Stickiness: Impediments to the Transfer of Best Practice within the Firm'. *Strategic Management Journal*, 17(1): 27–44.

—— and JENSEN, R. J. (2004). 'Overcoming Stickiness: An Empirical Investigation of the Role of the Template in the Replication of Organizational Routines'. *Managerial and Decision Economics*, 25(6–7): 347–63.

TSOUKAS, H. (1996). 'The Firm as a Distributed Knowledge System: A Constructionist Approach'. *Strategic Management Journal*, 17 (Winter SI): 11–25.

TUSHMAN, M. L. and SCANLAN, T. (1981). 'Boundary Spanning Individuals: Their Role in Information Transfer and their Antecedents'. *Academy of Management Journal*, 24(2): 289–305.

—— and O'REILLY, C. (1996). 'Ambidextrous Organizations: Managing Evolutionary and Revolutionary Change'. *California Management Review*, 38(1): 8–30.

VENKATRAMAN, N. (1991). 'IT-induced Business Reconfiguration', in M. Scott Morton (ed.), *The Corporation of the 1990s: IT and Organizational Transformation*. New York: Oxford University Press, 122–58.

WAGNER, E. and NEWELL, S. (2006). 'Repairing ERP: Producing Social Order to Create a Working Information System'. *Journal of Applied Behavioral Research*, 42(1): 40–57.

WEICK, K. E. (1990). 'Technology as an Equivoque: Sensemaking in New Technologies', in P. S. Goodman and L. Sproull (eds), *Technology and Organizations*. San Francisco, CA: Jossey-Bass, 1–44.

—— (1995). *Sensemaking in Organizations*. Thousand Oaks, CA: Sage.

WENGER, E (1998). *Communities of Practice: Learning, Meaning, and Identity*. Cambridge: Cambridge University Press.

WHITTINGTON, R. (1993). *What is Strategy? And Does it Matter?* London: Routledge.

WILLCOCKS, L. (1999). 'Managing Information Technology Evaluation: Techniques and Processes', in R. D. Galliers, D. E. Leidner and B. S. H. Baker (eds), *Strategic Information Management: Challenges and Strategies in Managing Information Systems* (2nd edn). Oxford: Butterworth-Heinemann, 271–90.

YOUNG, R. C. (1967). 'Systems and Data Processing Departments Need Long-Range Planning', *Computers and Automation*, May, 30–3, 45.

NOTES

1. Early academic literature on these topics dates back to the work, e.g. of Young (1967); Kriebel (1968); McFarlan (1971), and Lincoln (1975).
2. I take an organizational/managerial perspective in this chapter in providing a critique of the mainstream literature, rather than a social science perspective.
3. Sabherwal, Hirschheim, and Goles (2001) being an exception—these authors refer to the concept of punctuated equilibrium in noting the natural tendency of organizations' IS strategies and business strategies to fall in and out of alignment over time.
4. Indeed, it is instructive in this context to recall that the Department of Organisation, Work and Technology in the Lancaster University Management School was known formerly as the Department of Behaviour *in* Organisations [my emphasis], rather than by the more usual term, Organisational Behaviour.
5. For example: (i) 'Oracle ROI Series studies document the quantifiable values and strategic benefits of Oracle-enabled business transformations', http://www.oracle.com/customers/index.html; (ii) 'You've stretched every budget and trimmed every expense. Or have you? SAP solutions give you real-time visibility across your entire enterprise, so you can streamline your supply chain, bring products to market faster, get more out of procurement, and eliminate duplication of effort. SAP is a world leader in business solutions, offering comprehensive software and services that can address your unique needs', http://www.sap.com/solutions/index.epx.
6. For example: (i) 'Oracle Consulting builds creative solutions for modern businesses. Drawing on industry best practices and specialized software expertise, Oracle consultants help you assess your current infrastructure, create your enterprise computing strategy, and deploy new technology. With Oracle's flexible and innovative global blended delivery approach, we assemble the optimal team for your organization by matching the right expertise, at the right time for the right cost in every phase of your project. Whether you have a new Oracle implementation or a system upgrade, Oracle Consulting helps you face today's most complex technology challenges and increase the financial return on your Oracle investment', http://www.oracle.com/consulting/index.html; (ii) 'Ensuring the value of your SAP investment takes more than software. It takes SAP Consulting—and the expertise and skill we've gained from 69,000 implementations over 30 years. With more than 9,000 consultants, plus a global network of 180,000 certified partners, SAP Consulting can provide the depth and breadth of coverage your business demands' (http://www.sap.com/services/consulting/index.epx).
7. A special issue of the *Journal of Strategic Information Systems* is devoted to the issue of knowledge management and KMS (Leidner 2000).
8. Nonaka and Takeuchi (1995) define knowledge as 'justified true belief', following Plato. Given adherence to the social construction of reality (cf. Berger and Luckman 1966), knowledge here might better be interpreted as 'justified belief'.
9. Building on the concept of alternative interpretations of the same data, and thus alternative futures, or scenarios (cf. Galliers 1993, 1995), Cummings and Angwin (2004) use the metaphor of the chimera to discuss potential future developments in strategic thinking.

INFORMATION TECHNOLOGY SOURCING: FIFTEEN YEARS OF LEARNING

LESLIE WILLCOCKS

MARY LACITY

SARA CULLEN

1 INTRODUCTION

THE information technology outsourcing (ITO) and business process outsourcing (BPO) services markets, together with more recent offshore variants, have been dynamically expanding revenues, capabilities, and associated rhetoric, in equal measure, for over a decade. Outsourcing makes up a substantial and rapidly rising part of expenditure across corporations and government agencies alike. On our estimates, ITO global revenues exceeded $US200 bn per year at the end of 2005. After, and indeed partly because of, the slow-down between 2001 and 2004 this figure will rise by at least 7 per cent per annum in the subsequent five years. Of this, offshoring ($US7 bn in 2004) will probably rise to $US17 bn by 2008. Additionally, mainstream BPO expenditure in areas such as the human resource function, procurement, back office administration, call centres, finance and accounting, is set to rise from $US110 bn in 2003 to $US175 bn in 2008 (Willcocks and Lacity 2006). Use of external IT/BP services combined is likely to move from a 2005 average of 12 per cent to 20 per cent of the corporation's total costs by 2008/9. For many organizations, then, outsourcing is well above the parapet in sheer expenditure terms. However, much of this increase has been happening incrementally, as a response to immediate market conditions and specific opportunities to cut costs, rather than through long-term strategic thinking. Moreover, despite the accumulated experience, learning has been painfully slow; there has been mixed success, and much conflicting advice.

2 EVOLUTION AND CRITIQUE OF THE LITERATURE

ITO has a long history stretching back to the 1960s. Computing power was expensive and many organizations bought data processing services from computer bureaux, often run by large IT manufacturers. Subsequently, as IT became relatively affordable, many organizations built their own IT capabilities. By 1989, some major corporations were wondering whether this process had gone too far. The ITO literature as a genre got its official start in 1991 with studies of Eastman Kodak's landmark, large-scale outsourcing initiative (Applegate and Montealegre 1991; Loh and Venkatraman 1992a), along with the first works around that time focused on software outsourcing (Whang 1992; Ang and Beath 1993). The early ITO studies (1991–4) concerned themselves predominantly with the identification of characteristics regarding firms that outsource, and this concern continues (Oh 2005). In addition, the tradition of empirical work that still dominates ITO research began in 1993 with Huber's (1993) classic case study on Continental Bank, and Lacity and Hirschheim's (1993) case studies, along with the first ITO survey-based research (Heinzl 1993). Work on success in ITO began in 1994 (see Heckman and King 1994) with work focusing on satisfaction. Also, the first of many studies on the impact of outsourcing on various variables was published during this period, for instance, Loh and Venkatraman's (1992b) finding that stock prices in the US were positively affected by ITO announcements—still highly cited today.

There has been a steady stream of ITO research since that time, peaking first in 1995 and again in 1998. Figure 10.1 depicts the major academic studies in the 1991–2004 period, which appeared as books, or articles published in top ranking journals. The most comprehensive review of the ITO literature, by Dibbern et al. (2004), lists 212 references, but many of these are not specifically IT outsourcing

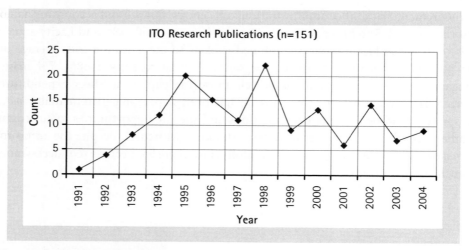

Fig. 10.1 ITO research chronology

studies. We also leave out non-academic studies—of which there have been many, and the recently burgeoning parallel literature on BPO.

The years 1995 to 1998 were a defining period in ITO research growth, averaging 17 published studies a year from the sample—a period of research growth not experienced since, though ITO/BPO and offshore studies, which started in the 2004–5 period experienced a real acceleration. Much of the work performed during 1995–8 remains the cornerstone of current ITO research. For example, Grover, Cheon, and Teng's (1996) success instrument, based in part on Parsuraman, Zeithaml and Berry's (1988) SERVQUAL instrument, is still used today unchanged from its original form (see, e.g. Lee, Miranda and Kim 2004).

This period began the flow of a wide variant of theories, assumptions, mixed findings, and contradictions that continues to the time of writing (2006). Solutions to the many inconsistencies were a major plea to researchers from the two most comprehensive reviews of the ITO literature (Hui and Beath 2002; Dibbern et al. 2004). Those wanting a more comprehensive analysis of the ITO literature are referred to these studies. Here we focus on the more limited aim of identifying four areas of inconsistency in the academic literature, before reporting on our own detailed findings from 15 years of research in the area.

Defining outsourcing

ITO definitions abound, with little consistency or agreement in sight. Why do we need to understand how each study defines outsourcing? Simply because minor variants in terminology can result in the study of different phenomena, or of various subsets of the possible outsourcing population. For instance, Loh and Venkatraman (1992a,b) kicked off an early definition of ITO as, 'a significant contribution by external vendors in the physical and/or human resources associated with the entire or specific components of the *IT infrastructure* in the user organization', which is still employed today (Oh 2005). This definition emphasizes IT infrastructure, and could be interpreted to exclude applications development to which much ITO research has been devoted. However, the studies that employ the infrastructure definition either do not explicitly state any exclusions to this definition, or where they do (e.g. Grover, Cheon and Teng 1996) appear to unintentionally exclude other phenomena in the outsourcing population.

Some ITO definitions see it as involving a transfer or turning over of something to a vendor, such as functions, assets, responsibilities, and/or people (Apte et al. 1997; Cheon, Grover and Teng 1995). Consequently, if a researcher uses this definition, arguably outsourcing that did not involve a transfer would be excluded, although no researcher adopting this definition makes this explicit. Here, many non-transfer types of outsourcing would not be considered as outsourcing. For example, in a survey of 235 organizations in Australia, only 27 per cent involved staff transfers (Cullen and Willcocks 2003). Therefore, a transfer-based definition restricts the study to a small subsection of the possible outsourcing population—in effect under 30 per cent.

Other studies limit the definition of outsourcing to only those services or functions previously conducted in house (Lacity and Hirschheim 1993), thereby excluding work performed by third parties that had not been conducted previously by the client organization. Still others describe ITO as commissioning, or contracting a vendor to run the organization's resources (Willcocks and Fitzgerald 1994), inferring that the organization still owns the resources. But many possible variants of resource ownership occur and the client organization may not retain all or part of the resource base (assets, facilities, and staff). Lastly, some merely state that outsourcing is, 'the provision of services by a vendor firm to a client' (Klepper and Jones 1998), or 'third-party provision of IT products and services' (Hancox and Hackney 1999), hence, anything a third party can do for a firm, echoing Williamson (1985).

Defining types of outsourcing

ITO researchers have not standardized on definitions of types of ITO. Thus, different perspectives on the phenomenon under study fall under a common label, despite there being no common terminology in which to take and test ideas, constructs, or theories. For example, Millar (1994) describes value-added outsourcing as where the supplier is able to add value to the activity that could not be cost-effectively provided in house. Klepper and Jones (1998) describe it as an 'intermediate' relationship characterized by complex work and substantial benefits. Lacity and Willcocks (2001) define it as when the parties combine to market new products and services. As another example, Currie (1998) identified 'facility sharing' as sharing all the key tangible resources including facility, assets, and labour, which Lee, Miranda, and Kim (2004) identified as a partnership. Lacity and Hirschheim (1993), however, define partnerships as descriptors of negotiation techniques, power balancing, and a collection of intangible characteristics such as compatible cultures, finding the term at odds with the actual contractual relationship, but without referring to the expression in terms of resource ownership as do Currie, and Lee and colleagues. Grover, Cheon, and Teng (1996) selected 'partnership' as a mediating variable in their study. Partnership was defined in terms of descriptive elements ranging from long-term commitment, sense of mutual cooperation, shared risk and benefits, and equal responsibility. Again, no single definition has been adopted. It is not surprising, then, that Lacity and Willcocks (2001) found partnerships to be more unsuccessful, for which Lee, Miranda, and Kim (2004) found no support. If nothing else, ITO research needs a common dictionary.

As a result, studies offer conflicting advice regarding how firms should go about making outsourcing successful. For example, conflicting advice over long- versus short-term contracts abounds. Earl (1996) believes the uncertainty involving IT and the requirement to experiment in its application precludes long-term contracts. Klepper and Jones (1998) argue that long-term contracts enable the supplier to learn about the organization, and for the parties to establish mutual trust. Lee, Miranda, and Kim (2004) note that in certain cultures, for example, South Korea, longer-term contracts are a reflection of the value that the culture places on long-term relationships. Lacity and Willcocks (1998) found that short-term contracts yielded greater cost savings. Lee, Miranda, and Kim (2004) found the reverse. However, all these studies assume a single term, which has not been the norm for some time.

Another example of conflicting advice regarding successful outsourcing structures is the degree of outsourcing performed. Lacity and Willcocks (2001) and Sambamurthy, Straub, and Watson (2001) suggest that selective outsourcing is more successful than total outsourcing. The latter occur where at least 80 per cent of the IT budget is outsourced to a single supplier—the assumption being success is a function of exposed risk to a single supplier. Yet Lee, Miranda, and Kim (2004) found selective sourcing to be no more successful than other degrees of outsourcing.

How is one to interpret such contradictory findings? One possibility is that success has been measured differently (therefore incomparably) in different studies. Another possibility is that it is a mistake to treat all ITO arrangements as instances of the same phenomenon: outsourcing involves a variety of choices that result in widely differing types and forms of arrangements.

There has been no definitive work on the different forms ITO takes. Many studies identify limited options, for example, Lacity and Willcocks (2001) in differentiating total outsourcing from selective outsourcing. Different functional or service scope has been well recognized, with many studies on specific IT functions such as software outsourcing (Ang and Beath 1993), application service provider (ASP) (Kern, Lacity and Willcocks 2002) as well as more comprehensive studies (Ang and Straub 1998; Oh 2005). But all the possible alternatives have not been brought together in such in a manner that every study has a common base from which to refer to the type of outsourcing under study.

Defining success

We have long known that outsourcing success is hardly guaranteed (Lacity and Hirschheim 1993). But each study regarding success, and advice on how to achieve it, is dependent on how the researcher defines success, outcomes, and benefits, terms used interchangeably in the research, but varying considerably in meaning. For example, Grover, Cheon, and Teng (1996) identified three categories: economic, technological, and strategic, which were further broken down into eight attributes. Domberger, Fernandez, and Fieberg (2002) performed a simple analysis of what drove a single attribute, 'desired performance'. Lacity and Willcocks (2001), in their summary of the experiences of 116 organizations, used three factors: objectives against results, cost reductions, and satisfaction. Lee, Miranda, and Kim (2004) used three dimensions: strategic competence, cost efficiency, and technology catalyst from the Chief Information Officer's (CIO) perspective. Not surprisingly, different perceptions of what constitutes successful outsourcing have yielded conflicting advice about the degree to which outsourcing practices have been successful.

Defining ITO processes

A decade of in depth studies demonstrates that outsourcing cannot be contracted for, and then not managed (Cullen and Willcocks 2003; Dibbern et al. 2004). Many researchers attempt to identify 'best practices', or processes that positively affect performance. However, all the studies we reviewed look at 'process' merely as a means to provide background information, or descriptive information—process is not the primary purpose of the study. There is a great deal of practitioner literature advising clients as to the process to adopt when outsourcing (Klepper and Jones 1998; Aalders 2001). But these do not use any rigorous research methods and typically are based on a few case studies. Up to 2006, the only academic study that purposely set out to study the process and form a theory as to what process works best is Cullen (2005), which provides a comprehensive and granular

Table 10.1 The 151 ITO research sample

Year	Studies	n
1991	Applegate & Montealegre	1
1992	Whang	4
1993	Loh & Venkatraman (a, b, c); Ang & Beath; Heinzl; Huber; Reponen; Willcocks & Fitzgerald; Lacity & Hirschheim (a, b, c)	8
1994	Arnett & Jones; Cullen; Fitzgerald & Willcocks; Heckman; Juri-Looff; Klepper & King; Lacity, Willcocks & Fitzgerald; Grover, et al. (a, b); Quinn & Hilmer; Wibbelsman & Maiero; Willcocks & Fitzgerald; Millar	12
1995	Chaudhury, et al.; Grover, et al.; Clark, et al.; Cronk and Sharp; De Cross; Jurison; Klepper; Lacity (a, b); Lacity & Hirschheim; Loh & Venkatraman; McFarlan; McLellan & Fitzgerald; Nolan; Palvia; Sobol & Apte; Teng, et al.; Willcocks & Choi; Willcocks, et al.	20
1996	Aubert, et al.; Currie; Early; Goodstein; Grover, et al.; Gurbaxani; Heiskanen, et al.; Lacity & Willcocks (a, b); Lacity, et al. (a, b); Nam, et al.; Slaughter & Ang; Willcocks, et al.	15
1997	Ang & Cummings; Apte & Sobol; Elitzur & Wensley; Hu, et al.; Lacity & Willcocks; Michell & Fitzgerald; Saunders, et al.; Venkatraman; Wang, et al.; Willcocks & Currie; Slaughter & Currie	11
1998	Ang & Slaughter; Ang & Straub; Aubert, et al.; Beath & Walker; Chalos & Sung; Currie; Currie & Willcocks (a, b); DiRomualdo & Gurbaxani; Domberger; Duncan; Fowler & Jeffs; Hirschheim & Lacity; Klepper & Jones; Lacity & Willcocks (a, b); Marcolin & McLellan; Poppo & Zenger; Smith, et al.; Willcocks & Lacity; Willcocks & Kern	22
1999	Aubert, et al.; Gallivan & Oh; Hancox & Hackney; Lacity & Hirschheim; Lee & Kim; Quinn; Sabherwal; Willcocks & Lacity; Willcocks, et al.	9
2000	Bennett & Timbrell; Dewire; Goo, et al.; Hirschheim & Lacity; Kern & Willcocks (a, b, c); King & Malhotra; Lacity & Willcocks (a, b, c); Lee, et al.; Schultze & Boland; Useem & Harder	13
2001	Barthélemy & Geyer; Goles; Kern & Willcocks; Kern et al.; Lacity & Willcocks; Rouse, et al.	6
2002	Carmel & Agarwal; Dibbern & Heinzl; Domberger, et al.; Goles & Chin; Hui & Beath; Kern & Willcocks (a, b); Kern, et al.; Kern, et al.; Kern, et al.; Klein; Knolmayer; Seddon, et al.	14
2003	Hindle, et al.; Lacity & Willcocks (a, b); Lacity, et al.; Levina & Ross; Susarla, et al.; Willcocks & Plant	7
2004	Dibbern, et al.; Koh, et al.; Lee, at al.; Linder; Plant & Willcocks; Willcocks & Willcocks; Willcocks & Plant; Willcocks, et al. (a, b)	9

framework describing the key management choices regarding the outsourcing process. See Table 10.1 for a summary of the 151 ITO research sample.

3 INFORMATION TECHNOLOGY SOURCING: FIFTEEN YEARS OF LEARNING

Having identified the difficult work still needed to synthesize the diverse definitions, approaches, foci of interest, and findings across ITO studies so far, this chapter moves to a more constructive process of identifying the findings from a more limited, but coherent and internally consistent stream of studies we have been conducting since the early 1990s. One key feature of this body of research is that we measure actual outcomes compared to expected outcomes in our 600 plus longitudinal case studies and six surveys. This enables us to draw conclusions as to the practices associated with success and failure and to analyse results over time. The rest of the chapter summarizes the findings from this extensive research. First, we comment on the degree of learning experienced in those 15 years. Next we organize the research findings under four headings: assessing the portfolio, evaluating market options, crafting deals, managing relationships. The key summary sources are Cullen (2005), Cullen and Willcocks (2003), Lacity and Willcocks (2001), Lacity, Willcocks, and Cullen (forthcoming), Kern and Willcocks (2001), and Willcocks and Lacity (1998; 2006).

The outsourcing learning curve

Most of our participants were from large North American, European, and Australian companies, and few at the outset approached outsourcing from a strategic perspective. Most organizations initially engaged in outsourcing for tactical reasons, such as seeking lower labour rates for staff augmentation on specific projects. Only after pilot tests were completed, supplier relationships established, and viability proven, did senior executives seek more radical and strategic uses of global resources. This incremental approach, we found, allowed organizations to gain experience with outsourcing options at an operational level before seeking more strategic objectives.

Figure 10.2 illustrates the typical customer learning curve for ITO and BPO approaches and more recent offshore variants. The learning curve is demonstrated through the typical learning of one particular outsourcing model, namely offshore outsourcing. The general mass of organizations using ITO are weighted towards phases 3 and 4 (see Figure 10.2), with some organizations on their third or fourth generation ITO, while most BPO and offshore clients, as at 2006, were much further down the learning curve.

During phase I, senior executives we interviewed became aware of offshore outsourcing through marketing hype ('you'll save 60 per cent off your costs') or irrational propaganda about whether software outsourcing would hurt US competitiveness (see Hof and Kerttetter 2004; McGee 2003). Senior executives quickly learned about potential benefits, costs, and risks by talking to peers and consultants, and by reading research. Most senior executives initially engaged in offshore outsourcing (phase 2) to seek lower costs, primarily through favourable labour arbitrage. During pilot testing, senior executives learned about the immense amount of in-house management required to effectively work with global suppliers and to achieve real cost savings. As learning accumulated, some senior executives moved to phase 3 when they exploited global sourcing for quality as well as cost reasons. One phrase we heard over and over again from participants was, 'we went for the price, we stayed for the quality'.

More mature adopters in phase 4 used offshore outsourcing to strategically enable corporate strategies, such as increasing business agility, bringing products to market faster and cheaper, financing new product development, accessing new markets, or creating new business. These strategic initiatives often evolved over time. For example, in 2005 a large financial services firm in the US, used global sourcing of IT and back office functions primarily to enable strategic agility. It had captive centres in Manila and Mumbai, and various joint ventures (JV) and fee-for-service relationships with 14 Indian suppliers. During the refinancing boom, the

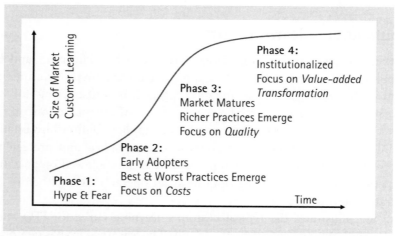

Fig. 10.2 Outsourcing learning curve

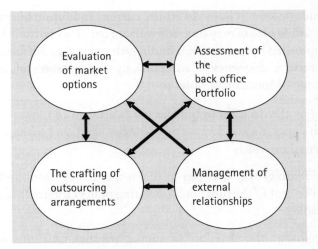

Fig. 10.3 Learning and feedback in IT sourcing

company was able to beat competitors by quickly meeting the immense surge in demand for IT and BP services. As the refinancing boom burst, the company was able to immediately scale back resources. But it took them 15 years to develop this well-oiled global network.

While at an aggregate level the learning curve suggests a sequential progression, at the micro level learning has been iterative and concurrent. Customers continually learned how to assess better their own service portfolio, evaluate suppliers' capabilities, craft contracts, and manage supplier relationships. Even within the same customer–supplier relationship, customers frequently revisited the scope of the deal and re-crafted contracts several times. This iterative learning process is depicted in Figure 10.3. In the next sections we look at each of these four areas in detail.

4 ASSESSMENT OF THE BACK-OFFICE PORTFOLIO

IT as a portfolio of capabilities

We increasingly found sourcing strategies beginning with the assumption that back offices should be treated as a portfolio of activities and capabilities. Some

IT activities must be kept in house to ensure current and future business advantage and flexibility, while others may be safely outsourced. This portfolio perspective is empirically supported by our research findings that selective outsourcing decisions had a higher relative frequency of success than total outsourcing decisions.[1] We defined the scope of sourcing options as:

Total outsourcing: the decision to transfer the equivalent of more than 80 per cent of the function's operating budget for assets, leases, staff, and management responsibility to external providers.

Total in-house sourcing: the decision to retain the management and provision of more than 80 per cent of the function's operating budget internally after evaluating the services market.

Selective outsourcing: the decision to source selected functions from external provider(s) while still providing between 20 per cent and 80 per cent of the function's operating budget internally.

Selective outsourcing decisions have been generally successful during the past 10 years, with 85 per cent successes reported by 1995, and 77 per cent reported by 2001 (Lacity and Willcocks 2001). This relates to the finding that selective outsourcing is also the most common sourcing practice.[2] The most commonly outsourced functions in IT were mainframe data centres, software development and support services, telecommunications/networks, and support of existing systems. The most commonly outsourced applications in human resources were payroll, benefits administration, and employee training and education (Lawler et al. 2004). In most cases, suppliers were judged to have an ability to deliver these products and services less expensively than internal managers. The ability to focus in-house resources on higher-value work also justified selective outsourcing.

Participants frequently encountered one or more of the following problems with total outsourcing:

- excess fees for services beyond the contract due to increase in user demand
- excess fees for services participants assumed were in the contract
- hidden costs, such as software licence transfer fees
- fixed-prices that exceeded market prices two to three years into the contract
- inability to adapt the contract to even minor changes in business or technology without triggering additional costs
- lack of innovation from the supplier
- deteriorating service in the face of patchy supplier staffing of the contract.

In-house sourcing has remained generally successful (67 per cent up to 1995, 76 per cent up to 2001) (Lacity and Willcocks 2001). We found, however, that success stemmed from the potential threat of outsourcing. Once empowered through the threat of competition, internal managers often had cost advantages over suppliers (such as no marketing expense, no need to generate a profit). In addition, they often had service advantages, such as knowledge of idiosyncratic business applications. These findings are consistent with our more recent (2001–5) research (Willcocks and Lacity 2006).

Core in-house IT capabilities

There are many frameworks and theories to help managers assess which core capabilities to keep in-house. The most popular portfolio assessment models are based on theories such as resource dependency theory, agency theory, auction theory, game theory, institutional theory, and, by far the two most dominant theories, transaction cost economics (TCE), and the resource-based view (RBV). In many ways, TCE is the ideal theoretical foundation because it specifically addresses make-or-buy decisions based on generic attributes of assets, and describes appropriate ways to govern customer–supplier relationships. For example, TCE posits that transactions with high asset specificity (essentially customization), high uncertainty, and/or that occur frequently are best managed internally, while the rest would be more efficiently outsourced.[3] Indeed, a number of empirical outsourcing studies have found that asset specificity, the degree to which assets can be redeployed elsewhere without losing value, has been a significant factor.[4] RBV has been the second most widely-applied theory in the outsourcing context.[5] RBV suggests that managers keep valuable, rare, non-imitable, and non-substitutable strategic assets in-house,[6] while potentially outsourcing the rest. TCE and RBV are both valuable perspectives. They also guide managers to treat the entire business function as a portfolio of transactions/capabilities—some of which must be kept in-house, some which may be outsourced.

The most direct assessment of IT as a portfolio has been the model developed by Feeny and Willcocks (1998). By synthesizing research findings this suggests four broad categories that customers must keep in-house, even if they intend to outsource nearly all of the IT (or another—for example, human resources, legal, procurement, accounting) function:

- Governance
- Eliciting and delivering business requirements
- Ensuring technical ability and architecture
- Managing external suppliers.

Table 10.2 Different portfolio assessment perspectives: What core activities should be kept in-house?

Transaction cost economics	Resource-based view	Core capabilities model
High asset specificity: The physical or human assets are non-redeployable for alternative uses or users. The activities are so idiosyncratic & customized that keeping them in-house is less costly than outsourcing.	*Valuable:* Activities can be used to exploit strategic opportunities or ward off threats	*Governance:* Strategy, mission, and coordination
High uncertainty: Activities cannot be clearly defined for effective third-party contracting. Threat of supplier opportunism is high unless customer incurs excessive transaction costs.	*Rare:* Few competitors offer the activities	*Business requirements:* Understanding business needs as they relate to the service function (IT, HR, etc), and relationship building among management, users, and the service function
High Frequency: Transactions that occur frequently and are highly asset-specific are less costly if kept in house.	*Non-imitable:* It is difficult or costly for competitors to imitate the activity	*Ensure technical ability:* The architecture operation may be outsourced, but the customer maintains control over architecture design.
	Non-substitutable: The activity has no immediate equivalents	*External supplier management:* Customers must make informed buying decisions, monitor and facilitate contacts, and seek added-value opportunities from suppliers.

Feeny and Willcocks suggest that these four essential tasks can be delivered by nine core capabilities. On the technical side, technical architecture and making technology work are vital. Business facing capabilities include relationship building and business systems thinking. External supply is managed through vendor development, contract facilitation, informed buying and contract monitoring capabilities, while leadership is required along with informed buying to support governance and coordination. Table 10.2 summarizes the activities to be kept in-house from three different perspectives.

'Best-sourcing' of non-core capabilities

Once organizations identify core IT capabilities, it does not automatically follow that the remaining, non-core, capabilities will be outsourced. We found that those customers that considered additional business, economic, and technical factors relating to non-core capabilities were most frequently happy with their sourcing decisions (Lacity, Willcocks and Feeny 1996).

A much more complex picture of best-sourcing practice emerged. From a business perspective, some capabilities that currently are non-core could become core in the future. Outsourcing such non-core functions could well impede strategic exploitation in the future. For example, one of our case studies outsourced its web site design and hosting in 1995, which initially served as a marketing tool. As the web became increasingly important to their strategy, including online sales and customer service, the customer found its outsourcing relationship was impeding strategic exploitation of the web. It subsequently terminated the supplier at a significant switching cost and brought the function back in-house.

From an economic perspective, some non-core activities may well be more efficiently kept in-house. For example, several of our case study participants were willing to outsource their large data centres, but could not find suppliers who could do it more cheaply. From a technical perspective, some non-core capabilities are highly integrated with other core activities. This makes outsourcing extremely difficult, and we have many examples of organizations that ran into difficulties as a result. Assuming non-core capabilities pass these tests, we found clients still needing to evaluate the market options, in order to further validate an outsourcing model and to identify viable suppliers, as discussed in the next section.

5 EVALUATION OF MARKET OPTIONS

An important and ongoing sourcing process we identified was to keep abreast of market options, even where an organization was currently, almost exclusively, in house. Recent work (Feeny, Lacity and Willcocks 2005) has identified 12, potentially core supplier capabilities along with practices in four general outsourcing models. These models are fee-for-service (time and materials or exchange-based), netsourcing, JVs, and enterprise partnerships (see Table 10.3). These models are often blended, for instance, having a JV component to structure a shared risk and reward and a traditional outsourcing component for operational delivery. In general, we found each model was suited to particular types of activities, as discussed under the following headings.

Time and materials model

Here, supplier capabilities are bought in to supplement in-house capabilities under in-house management. A typical example is hiring consultants to help in-house

Table 10.3 Suitability of various outsourcing models

Model	Resource ownership (Infra-structure & People)	Resource management	Customer/supplier relationship	Typical location of supplier staff	Typical customer/supplier contract	Activities most suited for this model
Fee for Service Outsourcing: Time & Materials	Supplier	Customer	One-to-one	Supplier staff on customer site	Time & Materials	Core or non-core capabilities; Customized products & services; Uncertain business or technical requirements
Fee for Service Outsourcing: Exchange-based	Supplier	Supplier	One-to-one or One-to-some	Mixed (some supplier staff on customer site, some staff centralized at supplier site)	Highly customized contract defining costs and service levels for that particular customer	Non-core capabilities; Customized products or services; Stable business & technical requirements
Netsourcing	Supplier	Varies	One-to-many	Supplier staff not on customer site	Generic contract specifying rental costs and very minimal service guarantees	Non-core capabilities; Standard products or services; Stable business & technical requirements
Joint ventures	Venture	Supplier–investor	One-to-one: Customer is both investor and first major customer	Mixed (some supplier staff on customer site, some staff centralized at venture)	Highly customized for operations delivery; broadly defined for revenue-sharing	Customer non-core, supplier core capabilities; Significant market for venture's product & services; Frequently used to access offshore resources
Enterprise partnerships	Partnership	Customer & supplier	One-to-one	Mixed (some supplier staff on customer site, some staff centralized at venture)	Broadly defined for revenue-sharing; customized after partnership is formed	Customer non-core, supplier core capabilities; Significant market for venture's product & services; Used for large scale transform of large back offices

teams implement customer relationship management (CRM) systems. Because requirements are uncertain, the customer cannot negotiate a detailed contract, and thus the variable price based on time and materials emerged as more appropriate. We found this time and materials model to be the most common, and posed the least risk to customers.

Exchange-based or traditional outsourcing contracts

In this situation, the customer pays a fee to the supplier in exchange for a customized product or service. In this model, the customer typically transfers its assets, leases, licences, and personnel to the external supplier. The supplier manages the resources and provides to the customer a set of products and services governed by a one-to-one contract.

In our early studies of IT outsourcing, we found that customers often had naive expectations about this model. For example, many customers expected to save 25 per cent on IT costs by signing 10-year, fixed-price contracts for a set of baseline services they assumed would remain stable for the duration of the contract. Many customers subsequently re-negotiated, terminated, or switched suppliers midstream. For example, one 2000 survey found that 32 per cent of respondents had terminated at least one IT outsourcing contract. Of those, 51 per cent switched suppliers, 34 per cent brought the function back in-house, and the remainder eventually reinstated their initial suppliers due to prohibitively high switching costs (Cullen and Willcocks 2003).

Survey respondents generally provided a healthy report card for exchange-based outsourcing. For instance, in one 2001 survey, respondents rated overall supplier performance as 'good'; respondents realized some, or most of the benefits they expected from outsourcing; and respondents characterized the majority of problems/issues as only 'minor' in nature. This is explained by the scope and type of IT outsourcing practised by responding organizations. The vast majority of respondents pursued selective outsourcing; most respondents also used multiple suppliers (82 per cent) rather than a single supplier, which allows for best-of-breed supplier selection. These results may also be explained by the types of activities selected for outsourcing. For IT, respondents generally targeted stable, non-core IT activities such as disaster recovery, mainframe operations, network management, midrange operations, personal computer (PC) support, and help desk operations rather than IT development or IT strategy (Lacity and Willcocks 2001).

Netsourcing

With netsourcing, the customer pays a fee to the supplier in exchange for a standard product or service delivered over the Internet or other networks. Netsourcing promises to deliver best-of-breed, scaleable, and flexible business applications to customer desktops, for a low monthly fee based on number of users or number of transactions at the customer site. Customers can rent nearly all popular independent software vendor (ISV) products from netsourcing providers, including enterprise resource planning (ERP), CRM, personal productivity and communications, e-commerce, and e-business packages. Our early research (Kern, Lacity and Willcocks 2002) shows that this model is suited to customers wanting lower back-office costs at the expense of accepting standardized solutions.

The revenues generated in this space are still modest, less than $US3 bn annually in 2005. Our preliminary research on this space found that early adopters were mainly small- to mid-sized enterprises (Kern et al. 2001). These companies primarily netsourced standard applications such as email, communications, and personal productivity tools.

Customer–supplier JVs

In the JV model, the supplier and customer create a new company.[7] Deals are typically structured so that the customer investor provides personnel, becomes the venture's first major customer, and shares in future profits if the venture attracts external customers.

In the past, we found JVs between customers and suppliers often failed to attract external customers, and the relationships were often redefined as exchange based. Examples include Delta Airlines and AT&T, Xerox and EDS (technology services), and UBS (finance) and Perot Systems (IT services). But in the offshore outsourcing space, JVs have been the preferred vehicle for large organizations to create a large offshore facility without the risks involved in a fully-owned captive centre. Customers such as MasterCard, CSC, Perot Systems, and TRW (aerospace and automotive) chose this model over a fully owned model, trading-off some control in exchange for less risk. For example, MasterCard created a JV called MPACT with the Chennai-based Mpower Software Services. MPACT had 250 employees performing IT work for MasterCard in 2005.

Enterprise partnerships

The goal here is often to transform the back-offices of large organizations that have grown through mergers and acquisitions (M&A). We have tracked how old ITO and new start-up BPO suppliers have entered the new market space since 1999, offering to transform their larger customer's back offices through leadership, streamlined processes, and new technology (see Willcocks and Lacity 2006).

For example, the UK-based company, Xchanging, created three JVs with customers, beginning in 2001. The first, called Xchanging HR Services, was with British Aerospace (BAe) for BPO of human resource management. BAe signed a 10-year contract worth £250 million and transferred 430 human resources (HR) employees to the venture. The second JV, named Xchanging Procurement Services, also with BAe, provided BPO for procurement. Again, the venture's first customer was BAe, which signed an £800 million, 10-year contract. The third JV, with Lloyd's of London and the London insurance market generally, originally called Ins-sure, as at 2006 was continuing to provide policy and claims processing BPO. Lloyd's signed a 10-year contract worth £400 million with Ins-sure. In these three ventures, BAe and Lloyd's were guaranteed an undisclosed amount of cost savings on the business process and a share in the ventures' future profits. In these deals, success will depend partly on Xchanging's ability to deliver on the contracts while simultaneously attracting external customers beyond BAe and the London insurance market.

Comparing requests-for-proposal to internal bids

During the last 15 years, organizations that invited both internal and external bids had a higher relative frequency of success than organizations that merely compared a few external bids to current performance (89 per cent successful by 1995, 83 per cent successful by 2001) (Lacity and Willcocks 2001). We believe that this was because formal external supplier bids were often based on efficient managerial practices that could be replicated by internal managers.[8]

In some cases, internal managers could not implement cost reduction tactics because the internal politics often resisted such tactics as consolidating departments, reducing headcount, and standardizing processes and technology. Based on 85 case studies, we found that when customers allowed internal bid teams to compete with external suppliers, 83 per cent of those decisions were successful. When no in-house bid was invited and existing costs were compared with one or two supplier bids, only 42 per cent of those decisions were successful. The use of an internal bid team served to provide a baseline for what could be attained internally if the in-house staff were empowered to behave like a supplier, for example, proposing unfavourable consolidation and standardization of technology (Lacity and Willcocks 2001).

Senior management and sourcing decisions

Our case study and survey data both suggest that multiple stakeholder involvement and strong outsourcing performance are correlated. In our 2001 survey data,

68 per cent of respondents had at least two stakeholders driving the decision, most frequently the back-office manager and lawyers, or the back-office manager and senior executives. Our case study data show that joint senior executive/back-office manager decisions or back-office managers acting alone had higher relative frequencies of success than senior executives acting alone (Lacity and Willcocks 2001).

We defined the decision sponsor as the person that initiated or championed the sourcing decision and made or authorized the final decision. In our study, joint sourcing decisions made with both senior executive and back-office manager input had the highest success rate (76 per cent of joint decisions). It appears that successful sourcing decisions require a mix of political power and technical skills.[9] Political power helped to enforce the larger business perspective—such as the need for organization-wide cost cuts—as well as the 'muscle' to implement such business initiatives. Domain expertise on back-office services, service levels, measures of performance, rates of service growth, and price/performance improvements were needed to develop requests-for-proposals, evaluate supplier bids, and negotiate and manage sound contracts.

6 THE CRAFTING OF OUTSOURCING ARRANGEMENTS

This section looks at how organizations craft outsourcing contracts, and with what results.

Exchange-based contracts revisited

Of the outsourcing models presented in Table 10.3, the exchange-based model is still the most common model. But our data reveal that there are several types of exchange-based contracts:

Standard contracts: the customer signed the supplier's standard, off-the-shelf contract. This is primarily restricted to the netsourcing space.

Detailed contracts: the contract included special contractual clauses for service scope, service levels, measures of performance, and penalties for non-performance.

Loose contracts: the contract did not provide comprehensive performance measures or contingencies, but specified that the suppliers perform 'whatever the customer was doing in the baseline year' for the duration of the contract at 10–30 per cent less than the customer's baseline budget.

Mixed contracts: For the first few years of the contract, requirements were fully specified, connoting a detailed contract. However, participants could not define requirements in the long run, and subsequent requirements were only loosely defined, connoting a loose contract.

Detailed contracts achieved expectations with greater relative frequency than other types of contracts (75 per cent of detailed contracts were successful). These organizations understood their own functions very well, and could therefore define their precise requirements in a contract. They also spent up to 18 months negotiating the details of contracts, often with the help of outside experts.

In our 2001 survey, we found that customers included the following clauses in their detailed contracts:

- costs (100 per cent)
- confidentiality (95 per cent)
- service level agreements (88 per cent)
- early termination (84 per cent)
- liability and indemnity (82 per cent)
- change contingency (65 per cent)
- supplier non-performance penalty (62 per cent).

Increasingly, contracts have also included responsibility matrices, which outline the responsibilities for both customers and suppliers. This innovation recognizes that suppliers sometimes missed service levels because of their customers' inaction.

No matter how detailed contracts become, changes in requirements occur. At the time of writing (2006), many detailed contracts now have mechanisms of change, including:

- planned contract realignment points to adapt the contract every few years
- contingency prices for fluctuation in volume of demand
- negotiated price and service level improvements over time, or even
- external benchmarking of best-of-breed suppliers to reset prices and service levels.

In contrast to the success of the detailed contract, all seven of the loose contracts we studied were disasters in terms of costs and services. Two of these companies actually terminated their outsourcing contracts early and rebuilt their internal departments. Another company threatened to sue the supplier. Senior executives in these companies had signed flimsy contracts having been swayed by the rhetoric of 'strategic alliance'. However, the essential elements of a strategic alliance were absent from these deals. There were no shared risks, no shared rewards, and no synergies from complementary competencies, nor any other of the critical success factors identified by researchers. Instead, these loose contracts created conflicting goals. Specifically, customers were motivated to demand as many services as possible for the fixed-fee price arguing that 'You are our partners'. Suppliers' account managers countered that their fixed-fee price only included the services outlined in the contract. The additional services triggered supplier costs, which were passed on to the customer as excess fees.

Six of the 11 mixed contracts we studied achieved expectations. The contracts contained either shared risks and rewards, or significant performance incentives. A Dutch electronics company spin-off of the IT department to a wholly-owned subsidiary. Because the newly-formed company's only source of revenue was from the electronics company, the venture was highly motivated to satisfy its only client's needs (Lacity, Willcocks, and Cullen, forthcoming).

Length of contract

From the customer perspective, there is clear evidence that short-term contracts have higher frequencies of success than long-term contracts. From the 85 case studies we examined 87 per cent of outsourcing decisions with contracts of three years or less were successful, compared to a 38 per cent success rate for contracts of eight years or longer. Short-term contracts involved less uncertainty, motivated supplier performance, allowed participants to recover from mistakes quicker, and helped to ensure that participants were getting a fair market price. Participants also only outsourced for the duration in which requirements were stable. Thus, they could articulate adequately their cost and service needs. Some participants noted that short-term contracts motivated supplier performance because suppliers realized customers could opt to switch suppliers when the contract expired (Lacity, Willcocks and Cullen, forthcoming).

In contrast, long-term contracts have remained troublesome, with failure to achieve cost savings being the primary reason. As at 2006, we found that few total outsourcing mega-deals had reached maturity without a major stumbling block. Conflicts are increasingly being resolved through contract re-negotiations. Suppliers, however, have a clear preference for long-term relationships to recoup excessive transition and investment costs. In the case of the DuPont/Computer Science Corporation/Andersen Consulting deal, the transition activities lasted over 18 months as the contract was operationalized in 22 countries for a population of nearly 100,000 users. The transition also included massive investments by one supplier in IT infrastructure, which the supplier could only recoup in a long-term deal. Clearly, the customer's incentives for short-term deals must be balanced with the supplier's incentives for long-term deals. The DuPont arrangements were subsequently restructured and renewed in 2003, with different terms and a different proportion of work to the suppliers.

7 THE MANAGEMENT OF EXTERNAL RELATIONSHIPS

For all the sourcing models, there is an inherent adversarial nature in ITO and BPO contracts in that a dollar out of the customer's pocket is a dollar in the supplier's pocket. A knowledgeable, capable customer following good practices up to the point of signing the contract may well be sufficiently protected from the devastatingly negative consequences experienced in many early 1990s deals. If a supplier negotiates a favourable deal, it should be able to deliver on the contract and still earn a profit margin. But, as Kern and Willcocks (2001) detail, even under the most favourable circumstances, relationship management in outsourcing has emerged as difficult. Here we will mention from our consolidated research three areas where customers and suppliers found ways of improving the relationship dimension in their outsourcing arrangements.

Core capabilities for managing external supply

Earlier we mentioned nine core capabilities that need to be retained in-house. Of these, five are orientated towards managing external supply, including Leadership and Informed Buying. These two tend to be more strategic in orientation, but require relationship skills for dealing with senior executives and negotiators within suppliers. The remaining three involve key tasks, but also major skills in, and time on, relationship management at many different levels within the supplier.

Thus contract facilitation is the capability to provide a vital liaison role between the supplier and the customer's user and business communities to ensure supplier success. We found the role arising for a variety of reasons: for example (a) to provide one-stop shopping for the business user; (b) the supplier or user demanded it; (c) users were demanding too much and incurring excessive charges.

Contract monitoring is the capability to ensure that the supplier delivers on the contract. While the contract facilitator is working to 'make things happen' on a day-to-day basis, the contract monitor is ensuring that the business position is protected at all times.

Vendor development is the capability beyond the legal requirements of a contract to explore increasing ways that customers and suppliers can engage in win-win activities. It is in the customer's interest to maximize the contribution of existing suppliers and guard against what we call 'mid-contract sag' where minimal contractual commitments are met, but little else.

Relationship dynamics

Even with these capabilities in place, we found customer and supplier relationships sometimes troublesome, but the parties still tended to have a good relationship overall. Rather than seek to extinguish such troubles, the best relationships embraced the dynamics of these quite complex interactions. We identified four common types of customer–supplier interactions: adversarial, tentative, cooperative, and collaborative (Lacity and Willcocks 2001). These are based on the extent of goal alignment for the task at hand.

- Tentative interactions occurred when goal alignments are unknown, such as during the bidding process. At such times, each side tended to exaggerate their strengths and hide their weaknesses.
- Adversarial interactions occurred when goals were conflicting, such as interpreting ambiguous statements in the contract about which party, for instance, should pay for something.
- Cooperative interactions occurred when goals were complementary, such as the customer wanted the service, the supplier wanted the payment.
- Collaborative interactions occurred when both sides had shared goals, such as educating the user community about what they could expect from the contract.

By attending to the expectations and goals of many outsourcing stakeholders, apparent anomalies in relationships could be clarified. Why, for example, did customer contract managers and supplier account managers collaborate to mediate user expectations, then feel perfectly comfortable 'fighting' over a monthly bill? Quite simply, the dynamics of stakeholder relationships vary with the task.

Supplier capabilities

A major recent stream of our research has focused on an area much neglected in academic studies of outsourcing, namely, supplier core capabilities. Depending on what is trying to be achieved, our work suggests that an outsourcing supplier needs three competencies. Delivery competency encompasses how well a supplier can respond to the client's requirement for day-to-day operational services. Transformation competency represents how well a supplier can radically improve and even transform cost, quality, and functionality in line with the client's formal and informal expectations. Relationship competency relates to the supplier's motivation and ability to align with client needs over time.

Our on-going work points to 12 capabilities needed to underpin these competencies (Feeny, Lacity and Willcocks 2005).

- Domain expertise—sufficient professional knowledge of the target process domain to meet user requirements.
- Business management—ability to deliver both client service level agreements and supplier business and financial goals.
- Behaviour management—ability to motivate and manage people, including transferees, to deliver service with a 'front office' mind-set.
- Sourcing—expertise and access to whatever resources are necessary to deliver service cost targets.
- Technology exploitation—ability to develop and deploy technology required to meet service improvements swiftly and effectively.
- Process re-engineering—ability to design and implement changes to the service process to meet improvement targets.
- Customer development—ability to transform 'users' of a service into 'customers' who make informed choices about service level and functionality.
- Planning and contracting—ability to develop and contract for business plans that deliver 'win-win' results for client and provider over time.
- Organizational design—ability to design and implement organizational arrangements that enable access to the capabilities required within the provider firm; and delivery of them where and when needed within the client.

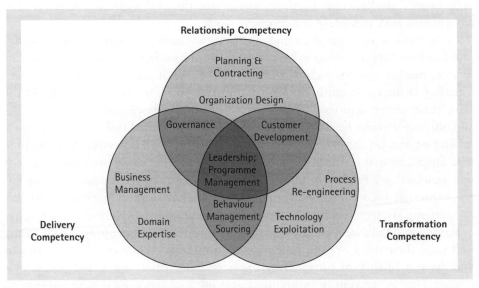

Fig. 10.4 Core capabilities in the outsourcing services provider

- Governance—establishment and operation of processes that allow service performance to be defined and agreed, tracked, and assessed over time.
- Programme management—ability to orchestrate and deploy transformational capabilities to successfully achieved required changes over time.
- Leadership—ability to identify, communicate, and ensure delivery of the mix of delivery, relationship, and transformation activities to achieve present and future success for client and provider.

Of these 12, six capabilities emerged from our research as seeming to have major direct bearing on the quality of relationships achieved (see Figure 10.4).

8. CONCLUSION

The IT sourcing literature is already rich in empirical survey and case research findings, but is still marked by inconsistencies, a plethora of concepts, research approaches, ambivalent terminology, and a lack of consistency and common focus across different research groupings. To some extent this reflects the relatively youthful state of IT sourcing research, and it could be concluded that the research has been remarkably productive, rigorous in many respects within individual studies, and also insightful in terms of the learning achieved over time. One can posit that over time researchers will come to standardize much more, learn from each other's studies, and begin to appreciate the real value of cross-research comparison and, indeed, of collaborative work.

As to the outsourcing phenomenon itself, we have consolidated our findings into a rich picture of evolution over 15 years, from its origins as a relatively small IT services market in some sectors, through to the rise of selective multiple supplier sourcing as the consistently dominant approach in IT in the present day. At the same time, under semi-recessionary conditions in the developed economies, BPO and offshore variants of ITO and BPO have greatly increased their share of an ever-expanding market for external business processing and IT services. We conclude that organizational learning on outsourcing has on the whole been quite slow. It may well be that a lower risk approach, and a safer way to accumulate learning has been through incremental outsourcing, and that customers have adopted this outsourcing strategy precisely to develop in-house knowledge about outsourcing.

Having said that, we regularly find that organizations do not apply their learning well until their third or even fourth generation deals. While client organizations may have a history of outsourcing experiences to draw upon, the problem is change. First generation outsourcing clients often changed what they outsourced and how they outsourced the second and third times around. Each time, they found themselves in a relatively new situation, having to learn anew. Furthermore, if their knowledgeable people had left and not been replaced, organizational learning was not able to occur until sometimes the fourth generation deal. At the same time, people providing the service to a client might move on, and take with them valuable knowledge that cannot easily be replaced, and that will no longer be applied to improving the specific outsourcing arrangement. One of our overall conclusions is that though customer and supplier maturity definitely looks set to evolve further in the next five years, we have seen few signs of the knowledge issues inherent in outsourcing IT, or other back-office functions being addressed in the strategies and practices that these parties have brought to bear in the outsourcing arena. By 2006, there were promising signs of some studies in this area appearing in the academic journals. But it remains to be seen whether practitioners themselves, beyond intellectual property issues, will start recognizing knowledge issues implicit in the act of outsourcing large parts of the back-office, let alone standardizing practices on ensuring key retained knowledge, and on suppliers possessing and fully deploying complementary knowledge in the service of their customers.

REFERENCES

ALDERS, R. (2001). *The IT Outsourcing Guide*. Chichester: Wiley.

ANG, S. and BEATH, C. (1993). 'Hierarchical Elements in Software Contracts'. *Journal of Organizational Computing*, 3(3): 329–61.

—— and STRAUB, D. W. (1998). 'Production and Transaction Economies and IS Outsourcing: A Study of the U.S. Banking Industry'. *MIS Quarterly*, 22(4): 535–52.

APPLEGATE, L. and MONTEALEGRE, R. (1991). 'Eastman Kodak Organization: Managing Information Systems Through Strategic Alliances'. *Harvard Business School Case 9-192-030*, Boston, MA: Harvard University.

APTE, U., SOBOL, M., HANAOKA, S., et al. (1997). 'IS Outsourcing Practices in the USA, Japan, and Finland: A Comparative Study'. *Journal of Information Technology*, 12(4): 289–304.

BARNEY, J. (1991). 'Firm Resources and Sustained Competitive Advantage'. *Journal of Management*, 17(1): 99–121.

BEATH, C. (1996). 'The Project Champion' in M. Earl (ed.), *Information Management: The Organizational Dimension*. Oxford: Oxford University Press, 347–58.

CHEON, M. J., GROVER, V. and TENG, J. T. C. (1995). 'Theoretical Perspectives on the Outsourcing of Information Services'. *Journal of Information Technology*, 10(4): 209–10.

CULLEN, S. (2005). 'Reframing Outsourcing: A Study Of Choices Regarding Processes, Structures and Success'. Unpub. Ph.D. thesis, University of Melbourne.

CULLEN, S. and WILLCOCKS, L. P. (2003). *Intelligent IT Outsourcing: Eight Building Blocks to Success*. Chichester: Elsevier.

CURRIE, W. L. (1998). 'Using Multiple Suppliers to Mitigate the Risk of IT Outsourcing at ICI and Wessex Water'. *Journal of Information Technology*, 13: 169–80.

DIBBERN, J., GOLES, T., HIRSCHHEIM, R. et al. (2004). 'Information Systems Outsourcing: A Survey and Analysis of the Literature'. *The Data Base for Advances in Information Systems*, 35(4): 6–102.

DOMBERGER, S., FERNANDEZ, P. and FIEBIG, D. (2002). 'Modelling the Price, Performance and Contract Characteristics of IT Outsourcing'. *Journal of Information Technology*, 15(2): 107–18.

EARL, M. J. (1996). 'The Risks of Outsourcing IT'. *Sloan Management Review*, 37(3): 26–32.

FEENY, D., LACITY, M. C. and WILLCOCKS, L. P. (2005). 'Taking the Measure of Outsourcing Service Providers'. *Sloan Management Review*, 46(3): 41–8.

—— and WILLCOCKS, L. P. (1998). 'Core IS Capabilities for Exploiting Information Technology'. *Sloan Management Review*, 39(3): 9–21.

GROVER, V., CHEON, M. Y. and TENG, J. (1996). 'The Effect of Service Quality and Partnership on the Outsourcing of Information Systems Functions'. *Journal of Management Information Systems*, 12(4): 89–116.

HANCOX, M. and HACKNEY, R. (1999). 'Information Technology Outsourcing: Conceptualizing Practice in the Public and Private Sector', in R. Sprague et al. (eds), *Proceedings of the 32nd Annual Hawaii International Conference on Systems Sciences*. Hawaii: HICSS, 183–91.

HECKMAN, R. and KING, W. (1994). 'Behavioral Indicators of Customer Satisfaction with Vendor-Provided Information Services', in J. DeGross, S. L. Huff and M. C. Munro (eds), *Proceedings of the 15th International Conference on Information Systems*. Vancouver: ICIS, 429–44.

HEINZL, A. (1993). 'Outsourcing the Information Systems Function Within the Company: An Empirical Survey', *Proceedings of the International Conference of Outsourcing of Information Services*. University of Twente, The Netherlands: ICOIS.

HIRSCHHEIM, R. and LACITY, M. (2000). 'Information Technology Insourcing: Myths and Realities'. *Communications of the ACM*, 43(2): 99–107.

HOF, R. and KERTTETTER, J. (2004). 'Software: Will Outsourcing Hurt America's Supremacy?' *Business Week*, 1 March, 84–95.

HUBER, R. L. (1993). 'How Continental Bank Outsourced its "Crown Jewels"'. *Harvard Business Review*, 71(1): 121–29.

HUI, P. P. and BEATH, C. M. (2002). 'The IT Sourcing Process: A Framework for Research'. Working Paper, McCombs School of Business, University of Texas at Austin.

KERN, T. and WILLCOCKS, L. P. (2001). *The Relationship Advantage: Information Technologies, Sourcing and Management*. Oxford: Oxford University Press.

—— LACITY, M. C. and WILLCOCKS, L. P. (2002). *Net Sourcing: Renting Business Applications and Services Over a Network*. Princeton, NJ: Prentice-Hall.

——, ——, —— et al. (2001). *ASP Market-Space Report 2000: Mastering the Customer's Expectations*. Amsterdam: CMG.

KANTER, R. (1994). 'Collaborative Advantage, The Art of Alliances'. *Harvard Business Review*, 25(4): 96–108.

KLEPPER, R. and JONES, W. O. (1998). *Outsourcing Information Technology Systems and Services*. Princeton, NJ: Prentice Hall.

LACITY, M. C. and HIRSCHHEIM, R. A. (1993). *Information Systems Outsourcing: Myths, Metaphors, and Realities*. Chichester: Wiley.

—— and WILLCOCKS, L. P. (1996). 'Interpreting Information Technology Sourcing Decisions From A Transaction Cost Perspective: Findings and Critique'. *Accounting, Management and Information Technology*, 5(3–4): 203–44.

—— and —— (1998). 'Practices in Information Technology Outsourcing: Lessons From Experience'. *MIS Quarterly*, 22(3): 363–408.

—— and —— (2001). *Global Information Technology Outsourcing: In Search of Business Advantage*. Chichester: John Wiley & Sons.

——, —— and CULLEN, S. (2007 forthcoming). *Global IT Outsourcing: In Search of Business Advantage* (2nd edn). Chichester: Wiley.

——, —— and FEENY, D. (1996). 'The Value of Selective IT Sourcing'. *Sloan Management Review*, 37(3): 13–25.

LAWLER, E., ULRICH, D., FITZ-ENZ, J. and MADDEN, J. (2004). *Human Resources Business Process Outsourcing*. San Francisco, CA: Jossey-Bass.

LEE, J.-N., MIRANDA, S. M. and KIM, Y.-M. (2004). 'IT Outsourcing Strategies: Universalistic, Contingency, and Configurational Explanations of Success'. *Information Systems Research*, 15(2): 110–31.

LOH, L. and VENKATRAMAN, N. (1992a). 'Diffusion of Information Technology Outsourcing Influence Sources and the Kodak Effect'. *Information Systems Research*, 3(4): 334–58.

—— and —— (1992b). 'Stock Market Reaction to IT Outsourcing: An Event Study', Sloan School of Management. *Working Paper*. MIT, Boston.

MCFARLAN, F. W. and NOLAN, R. (1995). 'How to Manage an IT Outsourcing Alliance'. *Sloan Management Review*, 35(1): 9–23.

MCGEE, M. (2003). 'Offshore Outsourcing Drags Down U.S. Bonus Pay'. *Information Week*, 25 Aug., 13.

MILLAR, V. (1994). 'Outsourcing Trends', in *Proceedings of the Outsourcing, Cosourcing and Insourcing Conference*. Berkeley, CA: University of California at Berkeley.

NAM, K., RAJAGOPALAN, S., RAO, H. et al. (1996). 'A Two-level Investigation of Information Systems Outsourcing'. *Communications of the ACM*, 39(7): 36–44.

OH, W. (2005). 'Why Do Some Firms Outsource IT More Aggressively Than Others? The Effects of Organizational Characteristics on IT Outsourcing Decisions', in R. Sprague (ed), *Proceedings of the 38th Hawaii International Conference on Systems Sciences*. Hawaii: HICSS, 1–9.

PARSURAMAN, A., ZEITHAML, V. A. and BERRY, L. L. (1988). 'SERVQUAL: A Multiple-item Scale for Measuring Consumer Perceptions of Service Quality'. *Journal of Retailing*, 64(1): 12–40.

POPPO, L. and ZENGER, T. (1998). 'Testing Alternative Theories of the Firm: Transaction Cost, Knowledge-based, and Measurement Explanations for Make-or-Buy Decisions in Information Services'. *Strategic Management Journal*, 19(9): 853–77.

SAMBAMURTHY, V., STRAUB, D. W. and WATSON, R. T. (2001). 'Information Technology Managing in the Digital Era', in G. W. Dickson and G. DeSanctis (eds), *Information Technology and the Future Enterprise, New Models for Managers*. Princeton, NJ: Prentice Hall, 151–74.

STRAUB, D., WEILL, P. and STEWART, K. (2002). 'Strategic Control of IT Resources: A Test of Resource-Based Theory in the Context of Selective IT Outsourcing'. Working Paper, Georgia State University and MIT Sloan School of Management.

TENG, J., CHEON, M. and GROVER, V. (1996). 'Decisions to Outsource IT Functions: Testing a Strategy-Theorectic Discrepancy Model'. *Decision Sciences*, 26(1): 75–103.

WHANG, S. (1992). 'Contracting for Software Development', *Management Science*, 38(3): 307–24.

WILLCOCKS, L. P. and FITZGERALD, G. (1994). *A Business Guide to IT Outsourcing*. London: Business Intelligence.

—— and LACITY, M. C. (1998). *Strategic Sourcing of Information Systems*. Chichester: Wiley.

—— and —— (eds) (2006). *Global Sourcing of Business and IT Services*. Chichester: Wiley.

WILLIAMSON, O. E. (1985). *The Economic Institutions of Capitalism: Firms, Markets, Relational Contracting*. New York: The Free Press.

—— (1991a). 'Strategizing, Economizing, and Economic Organization'. *Strategic Management Journal*, 12(8): 75–94.

—— (1991b). 'Comparative Economic Organization: The Analysis of Discrete Structural Alternatives'. *Administrative Science Quarterly*, 36(2): 269–96.

NOTES

1. A detailed description of the research methodology was published in our findings reported to 1995 and updated in Lacity and Willcocks (2001).
2. For sample surveys on selective IT outsourcing, see Apte et al. (1997), Grover, Cheon, and Teng (1996).
3. For a concise explanation of TCE, see Williamson (1991a,b).
4. For examples of empirical testing of TCE in an IT context, see Ang and Straub (1998), Lacity and Willcocks (1996), Nam, et al. (1996) and Poppo and Zenger (1998).
5. Examples of empirical testing of RBV in IT outsourcing context include Straub, Weill, and Stewart (2002), Teng, Cheon, and Grover (1996).
6. For a concise explanation of the RBV, see Barney (1991).
7. For best practices on alliance management, see McFarlan and Nolan (1995); Kanter (1994); Klepper and Jones (1978).
8. For a list of practices customers implemented themselves, see Hirschheim and Lacity (2000).
9. On the role of business executives as IT project champions, see Beath (1996).

CHAPTER 11

ICT, ORGANIZATIONS, AND NETWORKS

JANNIS KALLINIKOS

1 INTRODUCTION

NETWORKS are increasingly being seen as a key modality of social and economic coordination (e.g. Castells 1996; Nohria and Eccles 1992). The term 'networks' is undeniably vague, indeed versatile (DiMaggio 2001) while its meaning shifts substantially, depending on the kind of theoretical tradition within which it is deployed. Indeed, the literature on networks is vast and hardly surveyable. It embraces a variety of disciplines and stretches much farther back in time than the recent popularity of the term may suggest. There is an economic literature on networks stemming partly from the tradition of industrial organization (e.g. Eccles 1981; Storper 1989, 1993) and partly from institutional economics (e.g. Arrow 1974; Coase 1937, Williamson 1975, 1981), and a rather comprehensive and disparate sociological literature (e.g. Burt 1982; Cook and Whitmeyer 1992; Fukuyama 1997; Sassen 2001), itself a reflection of the conceptual diversity of sociology. Key contributions across these literatures have been brought to bear upon related issues in the narrower fields of organization theory (e.g. Aldrich, 1979; Grandori and Soda 1995; Kallinikos 1995; Powell 1990) and industrial marketing (e.g. Håkansson 1982; Hägg and Johanson 1982) and have yielded a substantial body of research on networks. Relatively recently, research on networks has acquired a novel popularity as witnessed by a burgeoning and interdisciplinary literature on the subject (see, e.g. Castells 1996, 2000, 2001; DeSanctis and Monge 1999; Wellman and Haythornthwaite 2002). There is, no doubt, considerable overlap between all these literatures, but also crucial differences as concerns the understanding of the term, the role it plays within contemporary economy and society, and the structural mechanisms and socio-economic dynamics with which it is associated (e.g. Kallinikos 2006).

There is no way to summarize these literatures within the confines of this chapter. As a matter of fact, and given the different paradigmatic roots underlying them, I doubt whether they could be fruitfully summarized at all, without indulging in great oversimplification. And yet, there are zones of convergence that partly explain the migration of the term 'network' across disciplines and the alluring explanatory valence it has acquired. One such zone is demarcated by the very (pre)understanding of networks as a coordinative arrangement alternative to those of markets and formal organizations (e.g. Fukuyama 1997; Powell 1990; Rifkin 2000). In this respect, networks are seen as governance mechanisms that challenge both the bounded and hierarchical constitution of formal organizations and the spot, price-mediated exchanges commonly associated with markets (see, e.g. Kallinikos 1995). Even though the preconception of networks as an alternative coordinative arrangement to markets and formal organizations is itself predicated on widely varying assumptions, having yielded different and often incompatible explanations, it has nonetheless helped constitute a cross-disciplinary terrain within which the term has become a sort of common currency.[1]

If, as I suggest, and the references to the literature above affirm, the term 'network' has been around for quite a while, how then is its recent popularity to be explained? There certainly are different factors to be invoked to account for the spectacular diffusion of the term over the last decade or so. Nevertheless, two sets of conditions seem to be related straightforwardly to the significance networks have recently assumed. The first relates to the institutional nexus of deregulation and globalization and the implications that the associated trends have for the formation of shifting firm alliances across institutional settings, regions, or nations, often seen as the epitome of the network form of organization. The second is closely connected to the spectacular growth of information and communication technologies (ICTs) and the transactional modalities and interaction forms they have given rise to. Often, these developments have been seen as closely interrelated, and as indicative of much broader social and economic changes that are assumed to signify the end of the prevailing social order and the decline of formal organizations as the key institution for the production of goods and services (Castells 2001; Heckscher and Donnellon 1994; Malone 2004; Mowshowitz 2002).[2]

In the following sections (2–5), I briefly review some widespread claims that associate ICTs with patterns of interaction, work, and communication that are said to be conducive to the structural arrangement of the network. In so doing, I seek to lay bare and occasionally question a few key assumptions on which these claims are predicated. I endeavour to develop an alternative explanation of networks that is closely associated with the contemporary growth dynamics of information and the technologies which sustain and give it momentum. A key element of these dynamics is manifested in the increasing decomposability and mobility of a growing number of operations and resources that can thus be lifted out of particular contexts, and transferred, reshuffled, and recombined, often on a global scale. These developments challenge important principles underlying formal organizations as bounded and hierarchical entities, and seem to be closely related to the diffusion of networks as alternative coordinative arrangements. The chapter concludes by positioning an appreciation of these claims within the nexus of institutional relationships associated with current developments, and evaluating them critically.

2 ELECTRONIC TRANSACTIVITY AND NETWORKS

The rapidly expanding involvement of ICT-based systems and the Internet in economic and institutional life has often been associated with the changing forms of interaction which contemporary technology is assumed to occasion, and the implications of such forms for the functioning of formal organizations (e.g. DeSanctis and Monge 1999; Fulk and DeSanctis 1995; Malone 2004; Mowshowitz 2002). The literature concerning the organizational implications of the diffusion of ICTs and the Internet that is relevant here entails a wide variety of arguments. In what follows I shall briefly, and rather indicatively, summarize those claims that have a direct bearing on the issues that concern us here.

To begin with, computer-based ICTs have commonly been associated with important changes in the very conditions under which the production of goods and services takes place. The gradual yet far reaching automation of materially-based processes and administrative tasks has resulted in the redefinition of a growing number of organizational operations and the emergence and diffusion of a variety of novel tasks (DiMaggio et al. 2001; Kling 1996; Sinha and Van de Ven 2005; Zuboff 1988). A major implication of these developments has been the rising significance of information in terms of its involvement in the planning, execution and monitoring of organizational operations (Zuboff 1988). Coupled with new, efficient and less costly modes of communicating across functions, hierarchical levels and sites, the significance of information and the changes it has brought in the very task infrastructure of organizations have exerted strong pressures upon the governance mechanisms and the structural morphology of organizations (i.e. role systems, hierarchical levels, span of control, standard operating procedures etc.) towards administrative simplification, flatter hierarchies and leaner processes (e.g. DiMaggio et al. 2001; Fulk and DeSanctis 1995; Malone 2004; Nohria and Buckley 1994; Sinha and Van de Ven 2005). Rather than being reflected solely in the internal restructuring of organizations, the growing involvement of ICTs and the changes it has implied have weakened the traditional crucial controlling function of organizational boundaries. Everyday duties and tasks are increasingly being carried out through extensive transactions and lateral liaisons with other actors or constituencies in the organization's environment (Sinha and Van de Ven 2005; Starkey, Barnatt and Tempest 1999).

Taken together, these developments have been associated with the emergence of alternative organizational arrangements (e.g. networks) that challenge the constitution of formal organizations as strictly circumscribed and hierarchical entities (Castells 1996, 2000; 2001; DeSanctis and Monge 1999). Despite the fact that empirical evidence suggests a much more complicated picture, in which centralization and decentralization, local autonomy and central control systems mix in various ways that resist easy generalization (Ahuja and Carley 1999; Sassen 2001; Zuboff 1988), the view that ICT is an agent of decentralization, boundary crossing, and networking has continued to enjoy widespread diffusion (see, e.g. Castells 2001; Malone 2004; Mowshowitz 2002).

In addition, ICT-based systems and the Internet have been associated with the advent and diffusion of networks clustering around distributed forms of work. As distinct from the above-mentioned implications, distributed forms of work challenge traditional work practices through a rather different route that involves the downgrading of the importance traditionally ascribed to location as a key organizing platform and instrument of control (DeSanctis and Monge 1999; Hinds and Mortensen 2005; Knorr-Cetina and Bruegger 2002; Schmidt and Bannon 1992; Sinha and Van de Ven 2005; Sproull and Kiesler 1991; Wellman et al. 1996). The primacy that site historically assumed as the very blueprint for carrying out work derives partly from the rich communicative context of face-to-face interaction and the inescapable situatedness of traditional forms of oral communication (Zuboff 1988).

Yet site organization of work has also been closely associated with the wider mechanisms of surveillance and control that spatio-temporal inclusion makes possible (Deleuze 1995; Zuboff 1988). In this respect, and via its own route, distributed work seems to challenge established work practices and the structural arrangements that have traditionally accommodated them. It undermines, or at least weakens, the importance of hierarchical mechanisms of control based on proximity, supervision, and normative compliance, the last an intrinsic attribute and accompaniment to group participation. It further accentuates the limits of hierarchy by making possible, and crucially necessary, the coordination of work participants through multiple instant feedback loops that defy or make cumbersome hierarchical mediation (Sproull and Kiesler 1991; Wellman et al. 1996). In yet another way, distributed work provides the basis for project-based temporary work arrangements that limit the efficacy of standard, location-bound, and hierarchical control structures (Castells, 1996, 2000, 2001; Malone 2004; Sproull and Kiesler 1991). Again, and despite the reasonable character of these claims, empirical evidence on the subject is contradictory (Ahuja and Carley 1999; DiMaggio et al. 2001). Distributed work is not exactly an exercise in brotherhood. It often takes place under conditions of strong individual competition and distrust that significantly moderate whatever impact ICTs may have in promoting shared and open practices. In addition, distributed work and the networks it may be associated with are framed by the prevailing stratified social topology of organizations, and the ways in which hierarchy, and the interests it embodies, seek to accommodate these technological developments (Ekbia and Kling 2005; Zuboff 1988; Sassen 2001).

Finally, ICT-based systems and the Internet make available a technological platform for the development of the practices of outsourcing and subcontracting in comprehensive and cost efficient ways. They provide novel incentives for reframing the logic upon which boundedness, location, and hierarchy as major and constitutive organizational principles, have been predicated (Castells 2001; Davidow and Malone 1992; Malone and Laubacher 1998; Rifkin 2000). Subcontracting has always involved the key question about what to produce in-house versus what to acquire from the market. This question has been addressed within the framework of the constraints imposed by the stage of technological development, and the prevailing division of labour and the institutional forms accommodating it. In this respect, ICT-mediated outsourcing substantially enlarges the scope of what is possible by reducing coordination costs and making technically feasible the polyvalent planning, communication, and control of cross-site and cross-organizational operations (Malone 2004; Rifkin 2000). To these developments should be added the far-reaching implications in terms of resource mobility that are associated with the informatization of many services and the very standardization of technologies (software and hardware) sustaining it. Less conspicuous or straightforward, the mobility of services that informatization confers is easy to overlook. Informatization that rides on software and hardware standardization increases the interoperability of the informatized functions and tasks and, provided that these are adequately modularized and packaged, also raises their transferability across contexts. As the case of finance makes clear, modularization and mobility are crucial preconditions for the tradeability or exchangeability of many services and operations, often on a global scale (Sassen 2001). Under these conditions, ICT-based outsourcing becomes a key strategy for the reshuffling and recombination of detachable and modularized operations between and among organizations. The formation of networks becomes in this respect an important means for gaining advantage of the associated economies of experience and specialization (Wigand, Picot and Reichwald 1997; Sassen 2001; Sinha and Van de Ven 2005). This is a key argument to which I will return.

Despite the reasonable character of the claims portraying ICT as a major agent of organizational change with wider implications, the empirical evidence, as already indicated, is contradictory and far from conclusive. Indeed, whatever possibilities can be associated with technologically-induced social change seem to be inescapably mediated by the nexus of power, the institutional relationships with which power is associated, and other cultural or social forms that embody the cumulative effects of experience and social learning (Douglas 1986; Fligstein 2001). This is a lesson that ought by now to be familiar (Avgerou et al. 2005; Mansell 2002).

The complex character of social and economic change is conspicuous in the case of networks and the institutional nexus of relationships (e.g. hierarchy, property rights, labour contract) that heavily condition whatever interactive patterns networks may be said to engender (Fligstein 2001). An appreciation of the possible impact such patterns may have must therefore be situated within the established legal–institutional framework of the typical modern social order. Placed within such a wider socio-historical context, formal organization emerges not simply as an administrative or production apparatus, but crucially as an institutional form accommodating the social contradictions of capitalist production as manifest in the legal-institutional arrangements of property rights and the labour contract. The appreciation of the social and institutional complexity formal organization epitomizes inevitably begs the question of the institutional status of networks and the ways in which networks challenge formal organizations—not simply as administrative/instrumental arrangements, but as key institutional forms in modernity (Kallinikos 2006). The literature on these matters has mostly been silent and, on those few occasions it has sought to deal with the issue, rather unclear (e.g. Castells 2000, 2001; DiMaggio 2001; Heckscher and Donnellon 1994; Malone 2004; Steinmueller 2002). I return to this point in the last section of this chapter after spelling out my own interpretation of networks in the next two sections.

3 ORGANIZATIONS DISSOLVED: INFORMATION PROCESSES AS A CATALYST

The straightforward causal connection between ICTs and the interaction or organizational forms they are supposed to engender, should be rejected as too simple to capture the dynamics of social and organizational change. Experience suggests that whatever effect technology may have on social forms is heavily shaped by the social, cultural, and institutional relations in which the technology is embedded. However, meaningful as it may be, such a claim is too general to be of any substantial aid to the penetrating analysis of socio-technical assemblages (Kallinikos 2004b). Socially conditioned as they are, the spread of information and the variety of technologies that sustains it, do have important implications, which need be analysed in ways that do justice to their distinctiveness (Beniger 1986; Borgmann 1999). In this respect, the current research on ICTs, work, and organizational forms I have just summarized does have the potential to contribute to a better appreciation of the relevant issues, if the empirical findings from it are adequately framed and interpreted.

A key implication that emerges from the three strands of literatures summarized is that the diffusion of technological information is involved in the remaking of the underlying conditions that have accommodated the dominant structural arrangements, and interaction in organizations (Ciborra 1996; Lilley, Lightfoot and Amaral 2004). It is quite common to associate whatever implications ICTs may have for organizations, with the changing patterns in communication and interaction that they enable. However, crucial as they may be, shifts in modes of communicating and interacting are a second-order effect that presupposes the rendition of reality at the level of information. Such a rendition, which often extends to the reconstitution of the real along technological lines, is itself predicated on the meticulous and relentless analytical parsing and decomposition of all those tasks and operations that become informatized. There is no other way to proceed to coding and informatization. The logical–mathematical foundation of software engineering is in this respect far from accidental. Two key implications follow. First, technical representation (i.e. coding and informatization) becomes increasingly crucial in conceiving and instrumenting organizational operations. Secondly, organizational reality is made pliable and its rendition/reconstitution can accordingly be explored along alternative routes (Borgman 1999). Given the grand scale that software-based codification has assumed in economic and organizational life, it comes as no surprise that an inevitable consequence of informatization has been the growing decomposability of the very texture in which organizational operations have generally been embedded (Borgman 1999; Zuboff 1988).

Coupled with the heightened control of cross-context transactions, the lowering costs of communication, and the growing interoperability of ICT-based systems, the decomposability of organizational tasks has substantially contributed to raising their transferability across settings. A far-reaching consequence of these developments, which are taking place on a grand scale, is the technical possibility of separating the inescapable context-embedded and materially-conditioned character of producing goods and services from other operations of a rather strategic or crucial nature, such as those associated with the provision of specialized, knowledge-intensive inputs (i.e. producer services) or the design, availability and monitoring of the global distribution of these goods and services (Sassen

2001). Under these conditions, the combinability of resources and activities across space and time greatly expands, and the opportunities for pursuing such combinations profitably or efficiently become substantially enlarged. Networks are the outcomes of such a separation and the inter-organizational links they provide epitomize the opportunities and coordinative challenges associated with the rising mobility and combinability of a range of operations, many of which are heavily conditioned by a variety of ICT-based systems and artefacts.

Now, such a separation could be thought of as intrinsic to the deepening division of labour characteristic of capitalist production and the economies of specialization it helps generate. Indeed, historically, the significance (producer) services have acquired in the information age could be understood that way (Bell 1973; Webster 2002). There is little doubt that economies of specialization play an important role in this process of organizational disaggregation and vertical disintegration (Sassen 2001; Storper 1989, 1993). Yet specialization in many knowledge intensive services is closely associated with information management, and the efficiency and lower costs of communication that contemporary ICTs enable. Most crucially, though, the contemporary developments that networks epitomize challenge the bounded space and hierarchical constitution of formal organizations by raising the very decomposability of what once was, or was thought to be, a functionally interwoven and hardly separable set of operations, which thus by necessity remained location dependent (Kallinikos 2004a; Mowshowitz 2002). Decomposability and specialization are no doubt related. Specialization by definition emerges from a wider context of skills and technologies against which it appears as entailing a narrower profile of skills, often performed in a more efficient way than would otherwise have been the case. Yet decomposability is a broader term that does involve differentiation, but not necessarily what we ordinarily mean by specialization and the economies underlying it.

Be that as it may, the impact of information growth is not exhausted in whatever effects it may have on specialization, but has wider implications that continue to reframe important premises upon which formal organizing has been predicated. The importance that information and information management assume in the current age is better appreciated against the background of the current dynamics underlying the spectacular growth of technological information (Hylland-Eriksen 2001; Kallinikos 2006). Rather than being accidental, such dynamics reflect the confluence of several developments, a key manifestation of which is the expanding interoperability of available information sources and the technological systems sustaining them. The interoperable character of technological information engenders a self-propelling information growth dynamics, in the sense of their being implicated in the self-referential generation of information out of information through the very juxtaposition, reshuffling, recycling, and recombination of information items within and across the interoperable information sources and systems (Ciborra 2006; Kallinikos 2006; Shiller 2003). In this way, the rendition of economic operations at the level of information is progressively removed from the referential reality of these operations. Informatization does not simply copy the contingencies in which these operations are embedded, but seeks increasingly to accommodate, or take advantage from, available information. In this sense, information growth and the ongoing interlocking of information systems and sources form the very background against which current economic, social, and organizational developments (among which specialization is just one) take place.

Thus, a major implication of the rapidly growing amount of information available is the very possibilities it offers for drawing upon it when planning or evaluating initiatives and outcomes in particular contexts of contemporary life. In this respect, information introduces the 'depth' of perspective consequent upon the possibility of relating and juxtaposing information items and sources. In so doing, however, it tends to shift the evaluation of locally-spun courses of action from the consideration of local or context-embedded factors towards criteria that derive from other context-transcending or global concerns mediated by decontextualized systems of representation (Kallinikos 2004b; Rolland and Monteiro 2002). A specific manifestation of these abstract and hardly tangible trends, which Giddens (1990) subsumes under his widely referred notion of disembeddedness, is indeed the global relocation of economic operations and the possibility of running their dispersed and heterogeneous contexts by means of information control, rather than traditional, hierarchical control or ownership (Beniger 1986; Sassen 2001). These trends, however, are more complex than these univocal accounts may imply. They are often matched by counter-trends that allow abstract or decontextualized information to be appropriated, made sense of, complemented, or further developed within the local relationship contexts into which they, sooner or later, are introduced. Both types of trends are a manifestation of the same underlying phenomenon of information growth, and tend to reinforce one another (Sassen 2001; Woolgar 2002).

4 DISAGGREGATION AND NETWORKS

The significance that pliable and decontextualized information assumes in the management of the contemporary world is to some degree indicative of the mobility of humans and resources that underlie modernity, and the consequent enlargement of the temporal and territorial scale of human operations (Borgmann 1999; Giddens 1990; Luhmann 1995, 1998). However, as the analysis above demonstrates, the significance of information, and the diffusion and interlocking of ICTs have substantially expanded the mobility of many services and raised their functional independence and pliability. An important outcome of these trends is the modularization of these services and their exchangeability across contexts. This near decomposability of what used to be completely or, at least, substantially interdependent operations, sets the stage for a significant number of developments associated with the emergence of networks as a key coordinative arrangement in the current age. The disaggregation of organizations that has been taking place over the last two or three decades, under the banner of such fads as downsizing, core business, outsourcing, and the like, could be interpreted in these terms; that is, as a means of exploring the decomposability of organizational operations and taking advantage of the possibilities for recombining them in novel ways. As indicated earlier, the perception of such opportunities is heavily contingent on the substantially broader spectrum of situations that interoperable and transferable information enables.

Disaggregation, therefore, could be seen as a managerial strategy for exploring the decomposability and recombinability of economic operations, by decoupling the pursuit of economic objectives and entrepreneurial initiatives from whatever constraints are associated with the materiality and context-embeddedness of production (e.g. DeSanctis and Monge 1999; Malone and Laubacher 1988; Rifkin 2000; Castells 2001). Perhaps the most extreme manifestation of these trends is the emergence of networks (often referred to as virtual organizations) that subcontract production (and other operations) for short periods. Contracts of this sort can be terminated when they are no longer needed. Virtual organizations exemplify the decomposability of organizations and the conditions established by the information growth dynamics and the technological infrastructure sustaining such a dynamics. By subcontracting and outsourcing the overwhelming variety of production tasks, organizations of this type concentrate on the making of higher order decisions such as the type of products to be produced, design characteristics, marketing strategies, and the like. Decisions of this sort become the premises for bringing together the contributions of a variety of spatially dispersed organizations or actors in time-bound and shifting networks that seek to accommodate the socio-cultural context of late capitalism. In this sense, virtual organizations contrasts sharply with organizations conceived as bounded, locally based, and rule-governed systems. But they also epitomize a very specific, power-mediated coordinative arrangement by means of which the decomposability of what once was a tightly interwoven set of operations is explored by those agents that are able to control the production and distribution of information (Ekbia and Kling 2005; Rifkin 2000). For, under the conditions just described, once vital operations, like the production of goods and services, become accessories to a much wider logic. This logic gives primacy to the timely and successful development of entrepreneurial initiatives that first emerge as possibilities within the growing domain of information, and within the modular and decomposable operations it helps to construct.

However, developments of this sort are not limited to the corporate world. The relevance of information, and the technological infrastructure by which information and communication processes are sustained, seem to have had consequences with respect to how the role and the organization of the state itself are conceived (Barry 2001; Castells 2001).[3] The idea that the contemporary state can exercise its political leadership through the very control of decision premises and the shaping of communication and information flows, rather than through immediate economic and administrative involvement, has, over the last two decades, won acceptance beyond the neoliberal advocates of the minimal state (see, e.g. Barry 2001; Fountain 2001; Tilly 2001).

Against such a backdrop, the disaggregation of public organizations and state agencies, accomplished either through straightforward privatization or through cross-organizational architectures known as quasi-markets (LeGrand and Bartlett 1993; Osborne and Gaebler 1992), may acquire a slightly different meaning. For, in such a model, state functions and the agencies that embody them are predominantly conceived as 'coordination centres', or the central nodes in networks whose major task is to provide the premises for other actors' actions and decisions, through the shaping of information flows, the making and transmission of higher order decisions, and the monitoring of their implementation. The power and coordinative capacity of these centres do not derive from immediate involvement with, and steering of, core and often locally embedded processes and decisions. Indeed, quite the opposite. To accomplish their task, coordination centres must remain both dissociated and detached from local engagements and seek to obtain a bird's-eye view of the actors and operations they coordinate, a task that is substantially aided by the control and management of information processes.

There are certainly important elements of normative pressure and often a strong ideological predilection behind the reformation of the public sector along these predominantly new public management lines (see, e.g. du Gay 2005). Yet the specific direction along which the entrenched interests drive these developments transcends the effects of sheer ideology and cannot exclusively be accounted for in such terms, without postulating fundamental changes in the workings of late capitalism. Some of these changes, I suggest, are ultimately associated with the significance which is attaching to information in the contemporary world, and the increasing pliability and decomposability of the economic operations it helps to bring about.[4]

5 NETWORKS AND INSTITUTIONAL CHANGE

The observations advanced so far suggest that the emergence of networks as important coordinative arrangements reflects a variety of developments that are closely associated with the possibilities information offers for reframing and reorganizing the production of goods and services in the contemporary world. However, economic and organizational change on this scale does not occur in a vacuum. As already indicated, the implications of the ongoing information growth dynamics are conditioned by the predominant cultural and institutional order that is itself the outcome of longstanding social and economic developments.

A central element of the institutional order that has dominated industrial capitalism over the last century up to our own days is the institution of formal organization, of which corporations and public agencies are typical examples (Tilly 2001). The developments associated with the significance of information and its growth dynamics undeniably exert strong pressures upon the structural arrangements (i.e., hierarchy, formal role systems, clear boundaries) with which formal organizations have been commonly identified. But do these trends really imply the historical decline and eventual extinction of the unitary, bounded, and hierarchical character of formal organizations, as the short historical memory and unrestrained functionalism of management theory seem to suggest?

The decline of the unitary, bounded, and hierarchical organization is ultimately an empirical question that remains to be resolved. For, despite the organizational implications of the developments described above, this organizational form still dominates the production of goods and services and it seems unlikely that it will be rendered extinct in the near future (du Gay 2005; Kallinikos 2004a; Kraakman 2001). I find it relevant in this respect to venture a distinction between two widely divergent approaches to social and economic reality, whose indiscriminate conflation has tended to produce a certain confusion as regards the prospects facing networks. The first approach, deriving mainly from economics and functionalist sociology, sees the development of new organizational forms as arrangements that seek to minimize the cost of social interaction. In this view, formal organizations and networks are understood as more or less effective organizational arrangements, and their prospects are consequently tied to the possibilities they offer in addressing the production of goods and services in efficient ways. Within longer time spans, less efficient arrangements gradually give way to more efficient ones (e.g. Castells 2001; Fukuyama 1997). The second approach sees the social reality of formal organizations as institutionally negotiated. The organizational arrangements associated with formal organizations (and networks) are the outcome of social compromises entailing the pursuit of benefit, and goal maximization, which are understood within the dominant cultural paradigm and the institutions it has produced. Viewed from this institutional perspective, formal organizations are not just structural configurations entailing relationships between functions, task modules, and roles. Rather, formal organizations are institutions built on other institutional arrangements (e.g. property rights and the labour contract in industrial capitalism), while their operations are underlaid by a complex and historically cumulated system of rules, laws, and regulations governing the relationships of organizational participants (e.g. du Gay 2005; Fligstein 2001).

These observations suggest that the unitary, bounded, and hierarchically constituted organization is not just an organizational arrangement or configuration that can be modified in terms of an adaptivist logic, reflecting rational calculations of what is functionally more efficient. Institutions reflect the inculcation of values by means of which function and significance are assigned to material and social arrangements (Searle 1995), and changes in values are well known not to be reducible to calculations about means. Corporations and public agencies, as already suggested, are variants of the dominant organizational form in modernity and industrialism, which, after Weber (1978), became known as the bureaucratic form of organization (du Gay 2000, 2005; Fountain 2001; Kallinikos 2004a; Perrow 1986). Bureaucracies are thick institutions. They operate under a legal–rational regime (the outcome of long-standing social developments and struggles) whose formation signified, among other things, the organization of working life away from the patronage and arbitrary exercise of rule characteristic of pre-modern communities (Weber 1978). A regime of this sort stipulates the duties and rights of organizational participants (employers and employees), and provides a variety of rules, laws, and regulations by means of which organizational operations are governed. Most crucially, organizations as institutions (as opposed to structural arrangements) embody jurisdictional responsibility on the basis of which they are rendered accountable (du Gay 2005; Fountain 2001; Perrow 1986).

It is a widespread assumption that goes beyond management and neoliberal circles that the bureaucratic organization with its strict adherence to rules, hierarchy, and boundary maintenance, may not possess the adequate flexibility for responding to the demands for shifting and scaleable forms of engagement, which the developments outlined in the preceding sections make increasingly necessary. Such a belief needs to be qualified in various ways to retain an element of truth, bureaucracy being the only organization form that has systematically separated the requirements of organizational roles from human beings conceived as an existential or anthropological unity. By this means, bureaucracy manages to sufficiently dissociate the reengineering of tasks and roles, from the time-consuming and tedious processes of personal development and reorientation, thereby providing the space for the ceaseless making and remaking of organizational arrangements.[5] The flexibility of bureaucracy, as historically witnessed by the dynamic and constantly unfolding character of the modern social order, is unmatched by all other forms of organization in which human involvement takes catholic or inclusive forms.[6] On the other hand, the heavily regulated practices of role re-engineering and the demands of accountability underlying the legal–rational regime governing the operations of the bureaucratic form may not be well attuned to the demands for the aforementioned mobile, decomposable, and scaleable arrangements that are diffusing, as the outcome of the developments outlined earlier in this text.

In this respect, the building of mobile and scaleable cooperative arrangements that networks exemplify are assumed to respond to the flexibility demands contemporary economy and society raise. Networking becomes then, as Castells (2000, 2001) suggests, the means for combining, disbanding, and recombining human and other resources to accommodate the rapidly shifting tasks and demands facing contemporary societies. But these practices do not produce an organizational form in the way that bureaucracy was able to: while profit appropriation is associated with the corporate form (Kraakman 2001), and work is predominantly carried out in institutional settings regulated by employment contracts (no matter how flexible or time limited), it is difficult to think of networks as an alternative form of organization (Kallinikos 2004a). Unless the network is constituted as a unit of jurisdictional responsibility (which would mean that it would become some sort of bureaucracy) it is destined to remain no more than a social arrangement or practice, a strategy, as it were, for the reallocation of resources in a highly versatile economy in which information and communication processes assume primary importance.

Therefore, I suggest that networks do not represent an alternative organizational form, but rather the organizational strategy rendered feasible by the developments described in the preceding pages for exploring the possibilities of recombining a variety of economic operations. These possibilities usually reside within organizations that are versions of the bureaucratic form (that is, corporations, public organizations, authorities, etc.). Indeed, the crucial effects of networks are not to be sought in the alternative form of organization they are assumed to provide if this is understood as an institutionally embedded organization with jurisdictional responsibility and a well-developed framework of laws, rules, and regulations decreeing its operations. If, on the other hand, form is conceived as a general arrangement, then the network as a temporary, project-based alliance of actors could well be understood as a form, but in this case the network would be an alternative to the market rather than to bureaucracy. Networks of this type, then, have always existed (see, e.g. Garnham 1990, 2004; Tilly 2001), even though a case can be made for the rising importance that information and communication processes assume, and the shifting or scaleable forms of management and collaboration that such processes render necessary.

6 CODA

The growth dynamics of information, and the variety of forms in which it is involved in the redefinition of the organizational and economic landscape of late capitalism are rather conspicuous phenomena, despite disagreement about their precise organizational and economic implications. It may well be that the possibilities of these developments are not exhausted in organizational dis-aggregation and the effects associated with the decomposability, exchangeability, and combinability of organizational operations. It is tempting to think that such a dissociation could be just the beginning of a long-wave change. If the self-propelling dynamics of information growth we have witnessed over recent decades continues unabated then information ordering and reduction ought to become increasingly vital and economically rewarding tasks, irrespective of their utility for the production and distribution of goods and services. Information ordering and information services will thus become valuable and constantly expanding operations, tied straightforwardly to consumption without the necessity for being redeemed by production (Baudrillard 1988).

Social and economic predictions are inherently risky however. The trends identified here develop within a multi-dimensional institutional matrix (property rights, profit accumulation, labour law, hierarchy, etc.) in which they are variously accommodated. The disaggregation of organizations goes hand in hand with corporate empire building and capital accumulation. Never before in history has such a small number of transnational corporations controlled such an immense wealth (Webster 2002). Empirical findings suggest, at least so far, that organiza-tional size has only slightly diminished since the 1970s (Kelly 1998), despite the reasonableness of predictions about disaggregation. These observations suggest that there is no cast-iron way that the developments identified here are manifest. There is little doubt that the growth and autonomous character of information and communication processes, and the technologies that sustain their development, have already altered, and radically, the conditions under which organizations operate. But the final outcome will be, as ever, a compromise between past and present, possibility and actuality. On a more general level the developments identified here might well lead to the increasing infiltration of the principle of economic performance by a significantly less consequential logic, which reflects the development of communicative, information-based transactions as an autonomous, self-propelling domain. Here the information age joins hands with postmodernity, as the boundaries of what were once different domains of economy and society become increasingly blurred (Baudrillard 1988; Baumann 1992).

References

AHUJA, M. K. and CARLEY, M. K. (1999). 'Network Structure in Virtual Organizations'. *Organization Science*, 10(6): 741–57.
ALDRICH, H. (1979). *Organizations and Environments*. Englewood Cliffs, NJ: Prentice Hall.
ARROW, K. (1974). *The Limits of Organization*. New York: Norton.

AVGEROU, C., CIBORRA, C., CORDELLA, A., et al. (2005). 'E-Government and Trust in the State: Lessons from the Electronic Tax Systems in Chile and Brazil'. Mimeo. Department of Information Systems, London School of Economics.

BARRY, A. (2001). *Political Machines: Governing a Technological Society.* London: The Athlone Press.

BENIGER, J. (1986). *The Control Revolution: Technological and Economic Origins of the Information Society.* Cambridge, MA: Harvard University Press.

BAUDRILLARD, J. (1988). *Selected Writings.* Stanford, CA: Stanford University Press.

BAUMAN, Z. (1992). *Intimations of Postmodernity.* London: Routledge.

BECK, U. (2000). *The Brave New World of Work.* Cambridge: Polity Press.

BELL, D. (1973). *The Coming of the Post-Industrial Society: A Venture in Social Forecasting.* New York: Basic Books.

BORGMAN, A. (1999). *Holding On To Reality: The Nature of Information at the Turn of the Millennium.* Chicago, IL: University of Chicago Press.

BURT, R. S. (1982). *Towards a Structural Theory of Action: Network Models of Social Structure, Perception and Action.* New York: Academic Press.

CARNOY, M (2000). *Sustaining the New Economy: Work, Family and Community in the Information Age.* Cambridge, MA: Harvard University Press.

CASTELLS, M. (1996). *The Information Age: Economy, Society and Culture, Volume 1: The Rise of the Network Society.* Oxford: Blackwell.

—— (2000). 'Materials for an Explanatory Theory of Network Society'. *British Journal of Sociology,* 51(1): 5–24.

—— (2001). *The Internet Galaxy: Reflections on the Internet, Business, and Society.* Oxford: Oxford University Press.

CIBORRA, C. U. (1996). 'The Platform Organization: Recombining Strategies, Structures and Surprises'. *Organization Science,* 7(2) 103–17.

—— (2006). 'Imbrications of Representations: Risk and Digital Technologies'. *Journal of Management Studie,* 43 (6): 1339–56.

COASE, R. (1937). 'The Nature of the Firm'. *Economica,* 4(16): 386–405.

COOK, K. S. and WHITEMEYER, J. M. (1992). 'Two Approaches to Social Structure: Exchange Theory and Network Analysis'. *Annual Review of Sociology,* 18: 109–27.

DAVIDOW, W. H. and MALONE, T. W. (1992). *The Virtual Corporation: Structuring and Revitalizing the Corporation for the 21st Century.* New York: Harper.

DELEUZE, G. (ed.) (1995). *Negotiations 1972–1990,* trans. M. Joughin. New York: Columbia University Press.

DESANCTIS, G. and MONGE, P. (1999). 'Introduction to the Special Issue: Communication Processes for Virtual Organizations'. *Organization Science,* 10(6): 693–703.

DIMAGGIO, P. J. (2001). 'Introduction: Making Sense of the Contemporary Firm and Prefiguring its Future', in P. J. DiMaggio (ed.), *The Twenty-First Century Firm: Changing Economic Organization in International Perspective.* Princeton, NJ: Princeton University Press, 3–30.

——, HARGITTAI, E., RUSSELL NEWMAN, W, et al. (2001). 'Social Implications of the Internet'. *Annual Review of Sociology,* 27: 307–36.

DOUGLAS, M. (1986). *How Institutions Think.* Syracuse: Syracuse University Press.

DU GAY, P. (2000). *In Praise of Bureaucracy: Weber, Organization, Ethics.* London: Sage.

—— (ed.) (2005). *The Values of Bureaucracy.* Oxford: Oxford University Press.

ECCLES, R. J. (1981). 'The Quasi Firm in the Construction Industry'. *Journal of Economic Behavior and Organizations,* 2(4): 335–57.

EKBIA, H. R. and KLING, R. (2005). 'Network Organizations: Symmetric Cooperation or Multivalent Negotiation?' *The Information Society*, 21(3): 155–68.

FLIGSTEIN, N. (2001). *The Architecture of Markets: An Economic Sociology of Twenty-first Century Capitalist Societies*. Princeton, NJ: Princeton University Press.

FOUNTAIN, J. (2001). *Building the Virtual State: Information Technology and Institutional Change*. Washington DC: Brooking Institution Press.

FUKUYAMA, F. (1997). *The End of Order*. London: Centre for Post-Collectivist Studies, Social Market Foundation.

FULK, J. and DeSANCTIS, G. (1995). 'Electronic Communication and Changing Organization Forms'. *Organization Science*, 6(4): 337–49.

GARNHAM, N. (1990). *Capitalism and Communication: Global Culture and the Economics of Information*. London: Sage.

—— (2004). 'Information Society as Theory and Ideology', in F. Webster (ed.), *The Information Society Reader*, London: Routledge, 165–84.

GIDDENS, A. (1990). *The Consequences of Modernity*. Stanford, CA: Stanford University Press.

GRANDORI, A. and SODA, G. (1995). 'Inter-Firm Neworks: Antecedents, Mechanisms and Forms'. *Organization Studies*, 16(2): 183–214.

HÄGG, I. and JOHANSON, J. (1982). *Foretag I Natverk*. Stockholm: Naringsliv och Samhalle.

HåKANSSON, H. (ed.) (1982). *International Marketing and Purchasing of Industrial Goods: An Interaction Approach*. Chichester: Wiley.

HECKSCHER, C. and DONNELLON, A. (eds) (1994). *The Post-Bureaucratic Organization: New Perspectives in Organizational Change*. London: Sage.

HINDS, P. and MORTENSEN, M. (2005). 'Understanding Conflict in Geographically Distributed Teams: The Moderating Effects of Shared Identity, Shared Context, and Spontaneous Communication'. *Organization Science*, 16(3): 290–307.

HYLLAND-ERIKSEN, T. (2001). *The Tyranny of the Moment: Fast and Slow Time in the Information Age*. London: Pluto Press.

KALLINIKOS, J. (1995). 'Cognitive Foundations of Economic Institutions: Markets, Organizations and Networks Revisited'. *Scandinavian Journal of Management*, 11(2): 119–37.

—— (2003). 'Work, Human Agency and Organizational Forms: An Anatomy of Fragmentation'. *Organization Studies*, 24(4): 595–618.

—— (2004a). 'The Social Foundations of the Bureaucratic Order'. *Organization*, 11(1): 13–36.

—— (2004b). 'Farewell to Constructivism: Technology and Context-Embedded Action', in C. Avgerou, C. Ciborra and F. Land (eds), *The Social Study of Information and Communication Technology: Innovation, Actors and Contexts*. Oxford: Oxford University Press, 140–61.

—— (2006). *The Consequences of Information: Institutional Implications of Technological Change*. Cheltenham: Edward Elgar.

KLING, R. (ed.) (1996). *Computerization and Controversy: Value Conflicts and Social Choices* (2nd edn). San Diego, CA: Academic Press.

KNORR-CETINA, K. and BRUEGGER, U. (2002). 'Global Microstructures: The Virtual Societies of Financial Markets'. *American Journal of Sociology*, 107(4): 905–50.

KRAAKMAN, R. (2001). 'The Durability of the Corporate Form', in P. J. DiMaggio (ed.), *The Twenty-First Century Firm: Changing Economic Organization in International Perspective*. Princeton, NJ: Princeton University Press, 147–60.

LeGrand, J. and W. Bartlett (eds) (1993). *Quasi-Markets and Social Policy*. London: Macmillan.

Lilley, S., Lightfoot, G. and Amaral, P. (2004). *Representing Organization: Knowledge, Management and the Information Age*. Oxford: Oxford University Press.

Luhmann, N. (1995). *Social Systems*, trans. J. Bednarz Jr. with D. Baecker. Stanford, CA: Stanford University Press.

—— (1998). *Observations on Modernity*, trans. W. Whobrey. Stanford, CA: Stanford University Press.

Malone, T. W. (2004). *The Future of Work: How the New Order of Business will Shape Your Organization, Your Management Style and Your Life*. Boston, MA: Harvard Business School Press.

—— and Laubacher, R. (1998). 'The Dawn of the E-Lance Economy'. *Harvard Business Review*, Sept.–Oct.: 145–52.

Mansell, R. (ed.) (2002). *Inside the Communication Revolution: Evolving Patterns of Social Interaction*. Oxford: Oxford University Press.

Mowshowitz, A. (2002). *Virtual Organization: Toward a Theory of Societal Transformation Stimulated by Information Technology*. Westport, CT: Quorum Books.

Nohria, N. and Buckley, J. D. (1994). 'The Virtual Organization: Bureaucracy, Technology and the Implosion of Control', in C. Heckscher and A. Donnellon (eds), *The Post-Bureaucratic Organization: New Perspectives in Organizational Change*. London: Sage, 108–28.

—— and Eccles, R. (eds) (1992). *Networks and Organizations: Structure, Form and Action*. Cambridge, MA: Harvard Business Press.

Osborne, D. and Gaebler, T. (1992). *Reinventing Government: How the Entrepreneurial Spirit is Transforming the Public Sector*. Reading, MA: Addison-Wesley.

Perrow, C. (1986). *Complex Organizations: A Critical Essay*. New York: Random House.

Powell, W. W. (1990). 'Neither Market nor Hierarchy: Network Forms of Organization', in B. Staw and L. Cummings (eds), *Research in Organizational Behaviour*. Greenwich, CT: JAI Press, 295–336.

—— and DiMaggio, P. J. (eds) (1991). *The New Institutionalism in Organizational Analysis*. Chicago, IL: Chicago University Press.

Rifkin, J. (2000). *The Age of Access: How the Shift from Ownership to Access is Transforming Capitalism*. London: Penguin–Tarcher.

Rolland, K. H. and Monteiro, E. (2002). 'Balancing the Local and the Global in Infrastructural Information Systems'. *The Information Society*, 18: 87–100.

Sassen, S. (2001). *The Global City: New York, London, Tokyo*. Princeton, NJ: Princeton University Press.

Schmidt, K. and Bannon, L. J. (1992). 'Taking CSCW Seriously: Supporting Articulation Work'. *CSCW*, 1(1–2): 7–40.

Searle, J. (1995). *The Construction of Social Reality*. London: Penguin.

Shiller, R. J. (2003). *The New Financial Order: Risk in the 21st Century*. Princeton, NJ: Princeton University Press.

Sinha, K. K. and Van de Ven, A. H. (2005). 'Designing Work Within and Between Organizations'. *Organization Science*, 16(4): 389–408.

Sproul, L. S. and Kiesler, S. B. (1991). *Connections: New Ways of Working in the Networked Organization*. Boston, MA: MIT Press.

STARKEY, K., BARNATT, C. and TEMPEST, S. (1999). 'Beyond Networks and Hierarchies: Latent Organizations in the UK Television Industry'. *Organization Science*, 11(3): 299–305.

STEINMUELLER, W. E. (2002). 'Virtual Communities and the New Economy', in R. Mansell (ed.), *Inside the Communication Revolution: Evolving Patterns of Social Interaction*. Oxford: Oxford University Press, 21–54.

STORPER, M. (1989). 'The Transition to Flexible Specialization in US Film Industry: External Economies, the Division of Labour, and the Crossing of Industrial Divides'. *Cambridge Journal of Economics*, 13(2): 273–305.

—— (1993). 'Flexible Specialization in Hollywood: A Response to Aksoy and Robins'. *Cambridge Journal of Economics*, 17(4): 479–84.

TILLY, C. (2001). 'Welcome to the Seventeenth Century', in P. J. DiMaggio (ed.), *The Twenty-First Century Firm: Changing Economic Organization in International Perspective*. Princeton, NJ: Princeton University Press, 200–9.

VENKATESH, M. (2003). 'The Community Network Life Cycle: A Framework for Research and Action'. *The Information Society*, 19: 339–47.

WEBER, M. (1978). *Max Weber: Economy and Society* (2 vols), ed. G. Roth and C. Wittich. Berkeley, CA: University of California Press.

WEBSTER, F. (2002). *Theories of the Information Society: Second Edition*. London: Routledge.

WELLMAN, B. and HAYTHORNHWAITE, C. (eds) (2002). *The Internet in Everyday Life*. Oxford and Malden, MA: Blackwell Publishers.

——, SALAFF, J., DIMITROVA, D., et al. (1996). 'Computer Networks as Social Networks: Collaborative Work, Telework and Virtual Community'. *Annual Review of Sociology*, 22: 213–38.

WIGAND, R., PICOT, A. and REICHWALD, R. (1997). *Information, Organization and Management: Expanding Markets and Corporate Boundaries*. New York: Wiley.

WILLIAMSON, O. E. (1975). *Markets and Hierarchies: Analysis and Anti-trust Implications*. New York: Free Press.

—— (1981). 'The Economics of Organization: The Transaction Cost Approach'. *American Journal of Sociology*, 87(3): 548–77.

WOOLGAR, S. (ed.) (2002). *Virtual Society? Technology, Cyperbole, Reality*. Oxford: Oxford University Press.

ZUBOFF, S. (1988). *In the Age of the Smart Machine: The Future of Work and Power*. New York: Basic Books.

NOTES

1. Such an account of networks excludes other contemporary social contexts which, due to the significance of the Internet and other computer-based networks, have been described as involving a variety of networking activities, i.e. electronic communities, Internet-based social networks, etc. (e.g. DiMaggio et al. 2001; Steinmueller 2002; Venkatesh 2003; Wellman and Haythornthwaite 2002).

2. For a general critique of these claims, see Garnham (2004) and for a critique of specific claims concerning the end of hierarchy and bureaucracy (see the 2004, vol. 11, no. 1, SI on Bureaucracy in the Age of Enterprise, *Organization*).

3. The rethinking of the role of the state combines with even wider processes coinciding with the sovereignty of the nation state in an increasingly globalized world. The information and communication processes analysed here are obviously associated with globalization and with the wider acceptance of neoliberal ideas and the diffusion of new public management, but this debate cannot be taken up here.

4. To account for these developments exclusively in terms of mimetic isomorphism (Powell and DiMaggio 1991) is to gloss over the underlying processes (i.e. the growth dynamics of information and the decomposability and modularization of organizational operations) that make such an isomorphism possible in the first place.

5. The reader is referred to Kallinikos (2003, 2004a).

6. That is, organizational elements which reappear in the form of an overworking culture where job concerns dominate strongly over and, in some cases rule out, personal interests or preoccupations (Beck 2000; Carnoy 2000; Kallinikos 2003).

CHAPTER 12

INFORMATION TECHNOLOGY AND THE DYNAMICS OF ORGANIZATIONAL CHANGE

MATTHEW JONES
WANDA J. ORLIKOWSKI

1 INTRODUCTION[*]

RESEARCH in past decades has provided important insights into the role and influence of information and communication technologies (ICTs) in organizational change, although the topic remains the subject of considerable debate within both the information systems (IS) and organizational literatures. Recent innovations in contemporary organizations, as well as technologies, however, are posing new challenges for such understandings. Organizations have become more permeable and less hierarchical, entailing multiple horizontal and networked relationships. Work is often conducted through temporary project teams that are cross-functional and dispersed, spanning geographic, temporal, and cultural

* This research was funded in part by the Cambridge-MIT Institute (project 074).

boundaries, and involving distributed accountability, decentralized decision making, and multiple (often competing), evaluative criteria (Child and McGrath 2001). Contemporary technologies are inter-networked and evolving (Lyytinen and Yoo 2002), ranging from complex and integrated enterprise-wide systems to distributed and ubiquitous technologies such as mobile email devices, and weblogs.

Advancing the ongoing debates and accounting for these innovations in the relationship between technology and organizational change will require rich theoretical conceptualizations and new empirical insights. In this chapter we begin by briefly reviewing some key perspectives that have emerged in the IS literature to account for the relationship between technology and organizational change. We then present a short empirical account taken from a recent field study into the emergence of online news in the traditional newspaper industry since the mid-1990s. These data provide some grounded details about the nature and dynamics of technology-based organizational change. We use the online news case to outline some of the different ways in which existing perspectives might make sense of the empirical data, and what kinds of analyses they would put forward. We conclude by suggesting opportunities for further theoretical development in the IS research repertoire.

2 Examining perspectives in studies of technology and organizations

The question of the relationship between organizational change and ICTs is a fundamental one in the literature, significantly shaping how we think about and study the role and influence of technologies in organizations. The history of this literature can be broadly characterized through a series of perspectives. Given space constraints this review is necessarily only an overview. Interested readers should consult the key papers cited for more detailed exposition of the arguments.

Deterministic perspectives

Initial research into the role and influence of technology in organizations adopted two opposing and deterministic positions (Kling 1980; Markus and Robey 1988). The technological determinist position sees organizational change as driven by the intrinsic properties of the deployed technologies. Building on early work in manufacturing technology by Woodward (1958), Harvey (1968), and Hickson, Pugh, and Pheysey (1969), researchers argue that different types of technology are consistently associated with different approaches to organizing. For example, the more complex and unpre-dictable the technology, the more likely are organizations to adopt an organic rather than a mechanistic structure. Technology is thus assumed to be an exogenous, independent, and material influence on organizations, producing predictable changes in organizational characteristics such as structure, size, decision-making, work rou-tines, information flows, and performance (Huber 1990; Leavitt and Whistler 1958; Pfeffer and Leblebici 1977).

Opposing the position of technological determinism is that of social determin-ism—viewing organizational change as driven by social forces upon which the technology has little, or no, influence. In this research, the properties and per-formance of the technology are assumed to be largely dependent on other organ-izational influences, for example, strategic choices, distributions of power, information processes, and local contexts of use (Bjørn-Andersen, Eason and Robey 1986; Child 1972; Zuboff 1988). Some researchers have gone further, arguing that technology only has influence through the interpretations made of it by humans (Fulk 1993; Prasad 1993). In this view, the properties of technology are not simply shaped by organizational influences, but are essentially socially constructed.

Emergent perspectives

Concern about the limitations of deterministic approaches led to attempts to develop intermediate positions that sought to accommodate both technological and social influences. These 'emergent perspectives' (Markus and Robey 1988), assume that organizational change emerges out of the complex and dynamic interactions of technological capacities, social histories, and contexts, as well as human choices and actions. An important stream of this research is that of the socio-technical systems literature, originating in the classic 'Tavistock' studies of the effects of technology on work organization (Trist and Bamforth 1951). Drawing on Systems Theory (Emery 1969), these studies conceptualize organiza-tions as 'open systems', in continuous, dynamic interaction with their environ-ment, whose internal arrangements reflect the mutual interplay of social and technological influences. In the IS field, Mumford has been a leading proponent of socio-technical ideas, using them in studies of system development and imple-mentation (Mumford 1981).

Another important research stream in the emergent tradition is the work of Kling and colleagues who critique the dominant 'discrete-entity model' of computing which, they argue, adopts a 'tool view', focusing on technologies in isolation and ignoring their intertwining with history, context, and the contingen-cies of development and use. In contrast, Kling proposes a 'web model of computing', that is, a view of technology, grounded in an open systems perspective, focusing on the broader ecology of people, infrastructures, resources, policies, and social relations that influence the design, adoption, use, and maintenance of ICTs (Kling and Iacono 1984; Kling and Scacchi 1982).

Another influential study within the emergent perspective is Barley's (1986) investigation of the introduction and use of CT scanning technologies in two hospitals. Drawing on negotiated order and structuration theories, Barley argues that 'technologies are better viewed as occasions that trigger social dynamics which, in turn, modify or maintain an organization's contours', leading to both intended and unintended structural changes. While technology in this view is understood as a social object whose meaning is defined by its context of use, its material properties are seen to be relatively fixed across time and contexts of use, thus leading to what Barley terms 'a soft determinism' (1986: 107).

Research from the emergent perspective has effectively displaced deterministic arguments, and shown the value of attending to material triggers, contextual influences, and socio-historical processes of development, adoption, adaptation, learning, and use. Nevertheless, such perspectives retain a certain 'technicism' (Grint and Woolgar 1997), viewing technology unproblematically as having certain material properties that are taken for granted. As such, they are not well equipped to account for the dynamic and emergent nature of technological artefacts, as they are modified, corrected, updated, and enhanced during use over time.

Perspectives from structuration theory

Another stream of research on technology-based organizational change has involved studies using structuration theory (Giddens 1984). Structurational approaches build on Giddens' notion of structures as rules and resources recurrently enacted in people's ongoing practices. As such, structures are understood to be the organizing principles behind social practices, rather than the social practices or social forms themselves. Structurational perspectives have informed many IS research studies (Jones 1999; Orlikowski and Robey 1991), and two broad structurational variants are evident.

The first variant is Adaptive Structuration Theory (AST), developed by DeSanctis and Poole (1994) to investigate the mutual influence of technology and social processes. AST emphasizes the adaptive processes through which humans produce and transform structures (understood as rules and resources) in their purposive and knowledgeable action. DeSanctis and Poole (1994) argue that because ICTs serve as only one source of structure for groups, analysing the use of a particular technology requires consideration of other sources of structure such as work tasks and the organizational environment. Thus, two types of structures are posited by the theory:

structures that are embedded in the technologies, and structures that emerge as human actors interact with those technologies.

AST is an influential research programme within IS research. Its strengths lie in its grounding within Giddens social theory, and its building of a strong research programme that has generated a large number of IS research papers, especially in the area of group decision making (Contractor and Seibold 1993; Gopal, Bostrom and Chin 1992). Its limitations lie in its inconsistencies with some aspects of Giddens' structuration theory, for example, the notion that structures are 'embedded within technology' and the positing of 'faithful and unfaithful appropriations' of structure, which produce a contingency-type logic of explanation (Jones 1999).

The second variant, developed by Orlikowski (1992), emphasizes two key aspects of technology in organizational change: that technology is both shaped by and shapes human action, and that the interaction between people and technology is ongoing and dynamic. Orlikowski argues that technology is physically and socially constructed by human action, while also becoming reified and institutionalized within processes of structuration. This focuses attention on the creative aspects of technological development and use, while also considering their physical, historical, and institutional contexts. Empirical work has applied and elaborated this approach through examining the organizational use of different kinds of technologies: computer-aided software development tools (Orlikowski 1993), e-mail (Orlikowski and Yates 1994), and groupware (Orlikowski 1996).

Weaknesses of this approach are the view that structures are embedded in technologies, and the limited attention to the materiality of artefacts. Subsequent work by Orlikowski (2000) adopts a practice lens to propose the notion of 'technologies-in-practice' that refer to the structures of technology use enacted by social actors as they interact with particular technological artefacts over time. Viewed through a practice lens, technology structures are emergent and enacted, not embodied and appropriated. This approach has been recently elaborated and extended to examine enterprise resource planning (ERP) systems (Boudreau and Robey 2005), intranets (Vaast and Walsham 2005), and nomadic computing (Cousins and Robey 2005).

Applications of structuration have highlighted the nature and influence of human agency in technological development and use, and emphasized the critical role of humans in shaping (whether deliberately or inadvertently) how technology is developed and used in organizations. While this work acknowledges the importance of technology's material properties, analysis of such properties remains underdeveloped. In addition, empirical studies have focused on micro level interactions within specific organizations, largely ignoring the broader institutional influences—industrial, economic, political, global—that significantly shape the role and influence of technology in organizational change.

Perspectives from science and technology studies

A further source of insights into the role of technology in organizational change is the literature on the history and sociology of scientific and technological systems. While identified by a common label—Science and Technology Studies (STS)—this literature comprises a number of distinct strands with significantly different theoretical orientations (Van House 2003).

One of these strands is the Social Shaping of Technology approach (Mackenzie and Wajcman 1999), which seeks to show how the design of technologies is influenced by societal forces such as gender, ethnicity, or political ideology. While providing a richer understanding of how particular technologies reflect wider social interests, it has less to say about how these technologies shape organizations. A related approach, the Social Construction of Technology (SCOT) (Pinch and Bijker 1984), is more concerned with how the 'interpretive flexibility' of technological artefacts enables them to be seen as addressing problems defined by a variety of 'relevant social groups' (rather than broader social interests). Over time, interpretive flexibility is seen to diminish as the design of an artefact stabilizes and comes to embody a particular set of interests. This notion of closure has been criticized (Wajcman 2000), however, as privileging design, thus overlooking the continuing reinterpretation of technological artefacts by different users (Oudshoorn and Pinch 2003), and the social and political consequences of technology (Winner 1993).

One interesting attempt to avoid treating technology as having universal and incontrovertible properties with particular effects is offered by Pickering (1995), who argues that the effects of technology are temporally emergent, being the outcome of a 'mangle of practice,' as humans interact with technologies in specific settings. Pickering talks of a 'dialectic of resistance and accommodation' as humans struggle to get technologies to perform in certain ways and adjust their actions in the face of difficulties they experience. Jones (1998) extends Pickering's primary focus on scientific practice to address technology in which, he proposes, there is a 'double mangling', as designers and implementers strive to get technologies to produce particular actions and users to respond to the actions of technology in undertaking certain practices.

A different, and more radical, approach to the relationship between technology and organizations is offered by Actor Network Theory (ANT) (Latour 1987, 1999). Starting from a 'ruthless application of semiotics' (Law 1999: 3), ANT proposes that entities have no inherent qualities, but acquire their form and attributes only through their relations with other entities. This principle is extended 'symmetrically' to both natural and technological artefacts and human actors. From this perspective, therefore, there are no distinct and separate social or technological forces that might shape, or be shaped by, the other. Rather, artefacts should be considered as equivalent participants in a network of human and non-human 'actants' that (temporarily) coalesce to achieve particular effects. A specific methodology—a sociology of translation—for studying the 'co-evolution of sociotechnical contexts and socio-technical content' (Law and Callon 1994: 21) is described by Callon (1986).

For critics such as Collins and Yearley (1992) and Pels (1996) this goes too far in ascribing human qualities such as intentionality, to material artefacts. ANT proponents, however, argue that technologies have become such an inextricable part of contemporary life that it is impossible to separate out the effects of humans and technologies. They should thus be seen as an ensemble, an actor-network or *hybrid collectif* (Callon and Law 1995). Mol and Law (1994) go further, conceptualizing the interrelationship between the technical and the social as a fluid, rather than a network of fixed nodes.

A further criticism of ANT is offered by Grint and Woolgar (1997) who argue that it exhibits some residual essentialism, treating technologies as having 'actual' properties that are not questioned. In contrast, they advance a position that treats technologies as texts, whose meanings are always open to alternative readings. Such thoroughgoing anti-essentialism rejects not just claims about the inherent properties of technologies, but also equivalent claims about humans. Hutchby (2001: 450), in turn, is critical of such strong constructivism, arguing that while it can show 'that humans are capable of interpreting the capacities of technologies [such as a bridge or an aeroplane] in varying ways', it does not resolve the central question: 'does the aeroplane lend itself to the same set of possible interpretations as the bridge; and if not, why not?' (Hutchby 2001: 447).

Perspectives from workplace studies, CSCW, and distributed cognition

A further significant stream of inquiry is that developed by researchers in workplace studies, computer supported cooperative work (CSCW), and distributed cognition. Over the last two decades, scholars have conducted in-depth field studies using ethnomethodology and ethnography to investigate office work, medical practice, architectural offices, traffic control rooms, and airport operations (Button 1993; Luff, Hindmarsh and Heath 2000; Suchman 1987). This stream of research has generated detailed knowledge about 'how technologies, ranging from complex systems through to mundane tools, feature in the practical accomplishment of organisational activities' (Heath and Luff 2000: 8). In addition to generating rich data about the micro practices of technology interaction, this research has informed the design and development of new technologies (Dourish and Button 1998; Heath and Luff 2000; Schmidt and Bannon 1992).

An important development within CSCW research has been scholars' uptake of the notion of 'affordances', which can be used to account for the enabling and constraining materiality of artefacts (Hutchby 2001). Initially proposed by Gibson (1979), and further elaborated by Norman (1988), affordances refer to the possibilities for action offered by the world to the actor. As such, affordances are relationships between certain objects in the world and different actors and thus differ across contexts and types of actors. This inherently relational and contingent quality, however, has not been recognized in some studies, which have treated affordances as intrinsic properties of the world (Norman 2004).

The focus on situated action within workplace studies and CSCW is echoed in recent developments in cognitive science: the recognition that cognition is emergent in practice and distributed across multiple actors and artefacts (Hutchins 1995; Lave 1988; Rogers 1993). This work has led to valuable insights about how tools are drawn on in collaborative endeavours such as ship navigation, aviation, air traffic control, and engineering work. As Rogers and Ellis (1994) elaborate, this approach focuses on how the interactions among people, as well as those between people and artefacts, dynamically coordinate the transformation of knowledge through mental, social, and technological representational states.

These research streams have many strengths: they offer detailed, up-close, and *in situ* examinations of how knowledgeable practical action is accomplished through engagement with artefacts. However, these advantages are also a limitation, as they preclude a focus on the larger institutional contexts within which the interactions are situated. Many of these studies consequently fail to consider, and thus underestimate, the broader social and political dynamics that are produced and changed through recurrent technology interactions.

Perspectives based on formative contexts, labour process, and critical realism

Another interesting stream of IS research draws on the approach of 'formative contexts'. Originally developed by Unger (1987) as an explanatory theory of society, it opposes the view that established forms of social organization reflect impersonal and irresistible forces. Unger proposes that existing social relations are the product of institutional and imaginative contexts within which routine conflicts and actions take place, and that it is always possible for social actors to disrupt these and act otherwise. Ciborra and colleagues have adopted Unger's ideas in numerous papers (e.g. Ciborra and Lanzara 1994; Ciborra, Patriotta and Erlicher 1995) exploring how organizational contexts influence the routines and frames that shape IS practices and how these practices influence routines and frames, reconstructing the context.

Another stream of work—labour process theory—builds on Braverman's (1974) critical analysis of technological deskilling. He argued that managers choose or design technologies to fragment work and separate mental from manual labour, thus de-skilling and alienating workers, while subordinating them to the dictates of technology (Noble 1977; Perrolle 1986). While carefully outlining the manner in which technology is devised and deployed to control workers and thus advances the political and economic interests of powerful organizational actors, these studies are somewhat deterministic, inadequately accounting for human agency in the workplace. Subsequent developments of this perspective have identified and moved beyond this limitation (Burawoy 1979; Knights and Willmott 1985).

An additional perspective with implications for studying ICTs and organizational change is the transformational model of social action developed by critical realists such as Bhaskar (1989) and Archer (1995). While similar to structuration theory in proposing that structure and action are mutually constitutive, critical realism differs in two respects. First, it rejects what Archer (1995) calls the 'central conflation' of structure and agency (the treatment of structure as existing only in the instant of action). Rather than individual actors creating society anew with every action, Archer proposes that social structure pre-exists individual action, but is reproduced or transformed through agency. This analytical separation of structure and agency in time, however, does not imply that either determines the other. Instead structure is seen as providing conditions, the influence of which is still subject to individual agency. The second difference concerns Giddens' insistence that agents are always able to act otherwise. Critical Realists, for whom structural power may precede and transcend individual action (Layder 1987), argue that constraints are not always negotiable through immediate interaction. This may be seen as a potentially significant issue in the context of material influences on social practice. To date, however, only a few IS studies have employed Critical Realism (e.g. Dobson 2001; Mingers 2004) and there is much scope for applying it to the empirical study of IS phenomena.

Summary of perspectives

This brief, broad, and necessarily simplified, review reveals the multiplicity of perspectives that have been used within the IS field to study the relationship between technology and organizations. These various perspectives have unquestionably enriched the theoretical repertoire of IS research, but how adequately any of them addresses the complex, multifaceted, dynamic, and emergent relationship between ICTs and organizational change remains unclear. We examine this question in the context of a contemporary empirical case which we then consider from the various perspectives, inquiring how they might address the relationship between technology and organizational change evident in the case.

3 CONSIDERING AN EMPIRICAL CASE

The data below are extracted from a recent field study that examined the emergence of online news within the newspaper industry. In particular, we consider some of the changes that have become evident in both the production and consumption of news since the mid-1990s.

The production and consumption of online news

Most print newspapers are produced once a day, presenting a survey of events of the previous 24 hours along with comment and analysis. The time required to print and distribute a hard copy morning edition means that events happening after 9 p.m. on the previous day cannot be reported until the next day. Transporting hard copy is also a factor restricting the primary distribution area of newspapers, and this is typically reflected in the nature and scope of stories covered.

While the introduction of new printing technologies and direct text entry by journalists in the 1980s has changed some aspects of newspaper production, a print journalist's or editor's work process has remained largely unchanged since the nineteenth century. Thus journalists, generally working a 10 a.m. to 6 p.m. day, write copy according to priorities decided at a late morning editorial meeting. Copy is sub-edited (and, if necessary, checked by lawyers) in order to deliver a proof of the first edition for editorial approval at 7 p.m. There is time, therefore, for journalists to do background research and check stories, but the pace and pressures of work build up towards the deadline. This shared rhythm of the regular churning out of so many words, with stress accumulating over the course of the day, and then nothing to do until the whole process starts again the next day, is seen to contribute to a distinctive culture of the hard-drinking, cynical, 'hack' journalist.

From the readers' perspective, the consumption of print news is a largely one-way process. The paper arrives with its daily quota of news and commentary, chosen and produced according to the editor's judgement of priorities and stance. Thus, while the reader can choose when, and how to read the paper, the content of a particular edition is fixed. Limited feedback may be possible via letters to the editor, but what happens to these is at the discretion of the editor.

Online news sites, in contrast, are accessible 24 hours a day from anywhere in the world, and readers have come to expect that these sites will be up-to-date with the latest stories. Readers may also be closer to the events that are being reported than the journalists, and are able to offer their own interpretations of what is happening or opinions on the paper's reporting. With email, they can provide the editor or journalist with almost instant feedback. Secondary sites, such as weblogs and news aggregators, also provide readers with story selections that are outside the control of any one source, and, in the case of weblogs, may also produce their own content. The authority and control of the news agenda previously enjoyed by newspapers has consequently been weakened.

There are related changes in terms of news content. Thus, rather than a once-a-day digest, the emphasis is now on breaking news and the continuous revising and updating of stories as they develop. Rather than addressing a specific geographical audience, site content may be more international in focus. Rather than being written to be read in hard copy, stories are typically shorter and simpler, to be readable on digital displays (including desktop computers, cellphones, and PDAs). With the emphasis on speed, moreover, traditional checks on stories tend to be superseded by an ethos of 'scrappiness and immediacy . . . [rather than] polish and presentation' as a senior editor put it, especially as errors can be fairly easily and quickly corrected.

For online journalists, therefore, much of their work may involve continuous, rapid writing of short stories. On many sites a substantial proportion of these stories will be based on content from the newspaper. Often, such reuse of content involves a lot of repetitive reformatting, a consequence of incompatibilities between print and online computer systems that reflect the initial independence enjoyed by online news sites at the time of the dotcom boom. In addition, since each story has its own (typically short) deadline, there is no common rhythm of work and pressure is continuous. Compared to newspaper staff, online news staff tend to be younger, multi-skilled, and to have limited newspaper experience. Combined with their perceived secondary role in putting up copy from the paper on the web, online news staff tend to have lower status in the organization, and certainly vis-à-vis newspaper staff. This is reflected in their pay and career prospects.

While brief, this empirical account begins to provide some details about the kinds of organizational changes associated with the shift from print newspapers to web-based online news. Notably, we see changes in the rhythm, pace, content, and control of news production, as well as shifts in the time, place, and nature of news consumption. And as we now illustrate in what follows, how we make sense of these technology-based organizational changes depends in large part on the particular theoretical stance we adopt to study this phenomenon.

Accounting for the production and consumption of online news

In examining how various theoretical perspectives might make sense of these data, we found it useful to organize our comments into five themes that characterize the research choices and practices of IS researchers: (i) nature of causality; (ii) locus of agency; (iii) conception of technology; (iv) level of analysis; and (v) scope of analysis.

Some of the theoretical perspectives take fixed and unambiguous stances towards these themes; others are either variable (researchers allow for different choices depending on the conditions of the study), or ambivalent (different researchers working within a perspective make different choices). In the discussion that follows, we focus on highlighting the dominant positions of the various theoretical perspectives (see Table 12.1 for a summary). Consequently, not all perspectives will be represented in our discussions of the five themes.

Nature of causality

This theme refers to researchers' beliefs about the primary causal influence in the relationship between ICTs and organizational change. As noted, three views are found in the literature: seeing either technology or humans as the central causal influence, and an intermediate position of mutual shaping.

In the online news context, researchers' choices would include seeing organizational changes as predictable from 'features' of the technology (e.g. the reach and speed of the Internet, digital displays, etc.), seeing the changes as dependent on how users (e.g. journalists, readers) use the technology in their practices, or seeing some combination of the two. Specific studies might include examining whether the technology imposes certain structural choices, or whether different organizations and users are able to configure online news work, for example, to reflect traditional industry practices whether or not these are most appropriate for online news. An intermediate analysis might consider which aspects of the work are harder/easier to change and why, for example, the time to print and distribute a newspaper, or supporting joint filing by journalists for both print and online.

In terms of IS theoretical perspectives, technological determinism, and some labour process theorists, have tended to emphasize technology impacts, while social determinism, SCOT, and the practice lens have privileged strategic choice and interpretive flexibility. The middle ground is offered by perspectives such as the mangle of practice, workplace studies, and critical realism—perspectives that acknowledge material constraints, but do not see these as determining social practice.

Locus of agency

This theme refers to how researchers situate agentic influence. The choices include attributing organizational change to the discrete actions of particular agents (whether human or nonhuman), and attributing changes to the complex and dynamic interrelations of humans with material objects (because the particular effects of each cannot be isolated).

In the online news context, for example, researchers focusing on discrete agentic influence might examine the characteristics of particular technologies (e.g. the amount of space visible on one screen), or the decisions and actions of certain individuals or groups (e.g. managers' decisions in organizing their online news

Table 12.1 Theoretical perspectives on ICTs and organizational change

	Description	Choices	Theoretical Perspectives
Nature of causality	Researchers' beliefs about primary causal influences in the phenomena	*Technology* as primary causal influence	Technological Determinism, Labour Process
		Human agents as primary causal influence	Social Determinism, Sociotechnical Systems, Social Construction of Technology, Labour Process
		Human and material agency as primary causal influences	Mangle of Practice, Critical Realism
Locus of agency	Researchers' choices about locating agentic influence	*Discrete* agency is the ambit of distinct actors (whether human or nonhuman)	Technological Determinism, Social Determinism, Structuration, Labour Process
		Relational agency emerges from the intertwinings of actors and the world	Actor–Network Theory, Distributed Cognition, Mangle of Practice
Conception of technology	Researchers' choices about conceptualizing technology	Technology has intrinsic *material properties* that must be understood	Technological Determinism, Adaptive Structuration Theory, Labour Process, Critical Realism, Affordances
		Technology has no essential intrinsic properties and can only be understood in terms of *people's interpretations*	Anti-Essentialism
Level of analysis	Researchers' choices about the level at which to explain phenomena	Macro: focus on *broader socio-economic context* and *institutional* forces	Social Shaping, Labour Process, Formative Contexts
		Micro: focus on *interpretations* and/or *practices of situated actors*	Workplace Studies, Actor–Network Theory
		Both: focus on *bridging the levels* by linking social contexts and practices	Web Models, Structuration, Practice Lens
Scope of analysis	Researchers' choices of domain in which to focus analytic attention	Focus is primarily on *design* of technology	Sociotechnical Systems, Social Construction of Technology, Actor–Network Theory
		Focus is primarily on *use* of technology	Workplace Studies, Practice Lens, Mangle of Practice

division). Researchers focusing on networked agentic influence might examine the emergent effects of users' interactions with Internet technology and how managers conceptualize this, perhaps reflecting their own prior experience with other technologies.

In terms of IS theoretical perspectives, technological and social determinism identify discrete agents of change, as do labour process theory and the structurational approaches in rather different ways. The relational position would be most closely associated with ANT approaches, but is also evident in such perspectives as the mangle of practice, workplace studies, and distributed cognition.

Conception of technology

This theme refers to how researchers conceptualize the nature of technology within their research, specifically—do they view technologies as having intrinsic material properties that exist independently, or do they view technologies as only relevant through the interpretive work that people engage in to make sense of them?

In the online news context, this might lead to questions such as whether multiple ways of creating and consuming online news are possible, or whether the materiality of online news technology enforces certain configurations and entails requisite consequences? Does the use of Internet technology for online news mean that all online news sites have to adopt a global focus, with breaking news and frequent updating? If all sites adopt this practice, is it because of the intrinsic nature of the Internet technology or because of how users (writers and readers) engage with it?

In terms of IS theoretical perspectives, technological determinism posits strong essential logics for technologies. Other perspectives moderate the notion of intrinsic properties to varying degrees. For example, labour process theory and AST view technologies as having some material properties designed into the artefacts by human agents. Critical realism identifies specific material constraints, as does the focus on affordances evident in some CSCW and workplace studies. Grint and Woolgar's (1997) anti-essentialism, in contrast, would adopt a strongly opposed position, acknowledging no artefactual properties outside of human interpretations.

Level of analysis

This theme refers to the level at which researchers choose to explain a phenomenon. Two primary levels of analysis have dominated researchers' accounts: a macro level of analysis that examines changes in terms of broader socio-economic contexts and institutional forces; and a micro level of analysis that examines changes in terms of the interpretations and/or practices of situated actors. Some attempts have also been made to bridge the two levels, linking a focus on social contexts with that of interpretations and practices.

In terms of online news, macro analyses might focus on how the economic and social environments have influenced news production and consumption. For example, studies might explore how the dot.com boom encouraged online news departments to be relatively independent of their parent newspapers and how this contributed to technological and organizational choices that have hampered subsequent integration; or how the low status of online departments affects the types of people employed and the design of online news production systems; or how the rise of news aggregators has weakened the authority of newspapers among consumers. Perspectives emphasizing such forms of analysis include the social shaping of technology, labour process theory, and formative contexts.

Micro level analyses in the online news context would tend to focus on the everyday work practices of producers and consumers of news. For example, studies might explore how individual journalists and editors work in specific organizations and how their micro-interactions construct the news in certain ways, or what expectations and activities are associated with the consumption of print and online news and how this affects readers' practices. Perspectives adopting such a level of analysis include ANT and workplace studies. Other perspectives such as structuration and web models may be seen to be attempting a middle ground, examining both situated activities and choices in everyday work practices, and how these constitute wider socio-economic conditions and consequences.

Scope of analysis

This theme refers to the domain on which researchers focus their analytic attention. With respect to organizational change and ICTs, the perspectives have oscillated between the influences, choices, and activities involved in *designing* a particular technology, and those involved in *using* a particular technology.

In the online news context, adopting a focus on technology design might involve looking at decisions made during the development and construction stages, such as the priority assigned to ensuring compatibility between existing print and emergent online systems, or to how frequently is updating of the website permitted, and by whom, or the extent to which reader feedback is enabled. Perspectives such as SCOT, socio-technical systems, and, according to some critics, ANT, tend to see the design stage as the key locus for interventions shaping organizational outcomes.

Adopting a focus on technology use might involve looking at the way that readers' use of weblogs influences the news agenda of online news, or how new reporting norms emerge in the work practices of online journalists, or how awareness of a more global readership shapes the technology use practices of both journalists and readers. Perspectives about which such questions are asked include workplace studies, practice lens, and mangle of practice.

Assessing the perspectives

From this brief analysis of how the emergence of online news might be understood, it is clear that the various perspectives adopt different positions on a number of themes, but also that there are similarities among different perspectives on different themes. No one perspective pays equal attention to all five themes, nor would there seem to be sufficient complementarity among them to indicate that some hybrid combination could address the complexity, dynamics, and multiplicity of the relationship between technology and organizational change. Rather than proposing and prescribing a particular perspective or combination, we suggest some topics that a considered account of the relationship would entail.

As outlined in the introduction, contemporary innovations in ICTs and organizations suggest that unprecedented technological capabilities (whether real or constructed) and forms of organizing are emerging. Within organizational studies, there is growing recognition that firms are experimenting with being continually adaptive so as to respond effectively to contemporary conditions of volatility and virtuality (Child and McGrath 2001; Ciborra 1996).

How to adequately account for the changing relationship between technology and forms of organizing in such conditions is a critical question. An emergent perspective would seem to be more helpful than deterministic ones. Accounts that attribute effects to invariant and intrinsic characteristics of technology, or entirely to the interpretations of social actors irrespective of the technology, would seem similarly limiting. More positively, there appears to be a need for approaches that develop accounts of: the broader social and economic context of technology development and implementation, as well as the particular local circumstances shaping conceptualizations of, and responses to, technological innovation; an awareness of the multiple agendas that may be affected by technological change and how technologies may be both explicitly and implicitly drawn on in discourses of organizational change; and the situated work practices through which multiple agents enact various technology-based activities, and which of these are transforming, and how and why. Rather than seeing technology as having predictable organizational effects, approaches would develop rich appreciations of the complexity and variability of organizing processes in specific socio-economic and technological contexts.

Treatments of technology would similarly explore the recursive interplay between the social and material constitution of technology. Outcomes would be understood to be emergent, not wholly dependent on material properties, yet not infinitely malleable. It would seem useful to consider technologies in terms of capabilities of specific configurations that may, or may not, be realized in specific settings rather than determinate effects of generic technology types. The way in which these capabilities are realized, moreover, would be understood to occur through the practices that social actors enact in their use of technologies. And these might be quite different from those envisaged by designers or intended by those implementing them.

4 CONCLUDING REMARKS

This chapter has explored some key perspectives that have been employed in the IS literature to account for the relationship between ICTs and the dynamics of organizational change. Initial deterministic approaches have largely been superseded by emergent accounts that see the relationship as reflecting both social and technological influences. Rather than providing a single, coherent analysis, however, such approaches have introduced further debates, reflecting differences within such fields as sociology and STS, and IS researchers' efforts to adapt these theories to what are seen to be the particular concerns of their field.

Rather than seeking to identify one best way to understand technology and organizational dynamics or to propose a definitive synthesis, this chapter has sought to highlight some of the outstanding issues that an effective understanding would need to address, especially in the current context of organizational and technological innovation. In particular, the complex, dynamic, and mutually constitutive relationship of technological influences and organizational processes in specific settings would seem to require greater attention. In terms of the themes identified this would seem to imply an emergent account that recognizes: the social construction of technological influences on organizations, but also how these are expressed in particular material capacities of technologies; the mutual intertwining of human and material agency; the influence of broader social settings as well as the specifics of local practices; and the ongoing interplay of technology and organizations throughout the design and use of specific systems. Whether involving the reworking, extending, or blending of existing perspectives, or the creation of novel concepts and perspectives, continuing theoretical and empirical development would seem necessary to enhance our understanding of the complex and dynamic relationship between ICTs and organizational change.

REFERENCES

ARCHER, M. (1995). *Realist Social Theory: The Morphogenetic Approach*. Cambridge: Cambridge University Press.

BARLEY, S. R. (1986). 'Technology as an Occasion for Structuring: Evidence from Observation of CT Scanners and the Social Order of Radiology Departments'. *Administrative Science Quarterly*, 31: 78–108.

BHASKAR, R. (1989). *The Possibility of Naturalism*. Hemel Hempstead: Harvester Wheatsheaf.

BJØRN-ANDERSEN, N., EASON, K. and ROBEY, D. (1986). *Managing Computer Impact: An International Study of Management and Organisation*. Norwood, NJ: Ablex Publishing.

BOUDREAU, M.-C. and ROBEY, D. (2005). 'Enacting Integrated Information Technology: A Human Agency Perspective'. *Organization Science*, 16(1): 3–18.

BRAVERMAN, H. (1974). *Labor and Monopoly Capital*. New York: Monthly Review Press.

BURAWOY, M. (1979). *Manufacturing Consent*. Chicago, IL: University of Chicago Press.

BUTTON, G. (ed.) (1993). *Technology in Working Order: Studies of Work, Interaction and Technology*. London: Routledge.

CALLON, M. (1986). 'Some Elements of a Sociology of Translation', in J. Law (ed.), *Sociological Review Monograph*. London: Routledge & Kegan Paul, 196–233.

—— and LAW, J. (1995). 'Agency and the Hybrid Collectif'. *South Atlantic Quarterly*, 94: 431–507.

CHILD, J. (1972). 'Organizational Structure, Environment, and Performance: The Role of Strategic Choice'. *Sociology*, 6(1): 1–22.

—— and McGRATH, R. G. (2001). 'Organisations Unfettered: Organisational Form in an Information-Intensive Economy'. *Academy of Management Journal*, 44(6): 1135–48.

CIBORRA, C. U. (1996). 'The Platform Organization: Recombining Strategies, Structures, and Surprises'. *Organization Science*, 7(2): 103–18.

—— and LANZARA, G. F. (1994). 'Formative Contexts and ICT: Understanding the Dynamics of Innovation in Organizations'. *Accounting, Management and Information Technologies* 4(2): 61–86.

——, PATRIOTTA, G. and ERLICHER, L. (1995). 'Disassembling Frames on the Assembly Line', in W. J. Orlikowski, G. Walsham, M. R. Jones et al. (eds), *Information Technologies and Changes in Organisational Work*. London: Chapman and Hall, 397–418.

COLLINS, H. M. and YEARLEY, S. (1992). 'Epistemological Chicken', in A. Pickering (ed.), *Science as Practice and Culture*. Chicago, IL: University of Chicago Press, 301–26.

CONTRACTOR, N. S. and SEIBOLD, D. R. (1993). 'Theoretical Frameworks for the Study of Structuring Processes in Group Decision Support Systems'. *Human Communication Research*, 19(4): 528–63.

COUSINS, K. C. and ROBEY, D. (2005). 'Human Agency in a Wireless World: Patterns of Technology Use in Nomadic Computing Environments'. *Information and Organization*, 15(2): 151–80.

DeSANCTIS, G. and POOLE, M. S. (1994). 'Capturing the Complexity in Advanced Technology Use: Adaptive Structuration Theory'. *Organization Science*, 5(2): 121–47.

DOBSON, P. J. (2001). 'The Philosophy of Critical Realism: An Opportunity for Information Systems Research'. *Information Systems Frontiers*, 3(2): 199–210.

DOURISH, P. and BUTTON, G. (1998). 'On "Technomethodology": Foundational Relationships Between Ethnomethodology and System Design'. *Human–Computer Interaction*, 13(4): 395–432.

EMERY, F. E. (1969). *Systems Thinking*. Harmondsworth: Penguin.

FULK, J. (1993). 'Social Construction of Communication Technology'. *Academy of Management Journal*, 36(5): 921–50.

GIBSON, J. J. (1979). *The Ecological Approach to Visual Perception*. Boston, MA: Houghton Mifflin.

GIDDENS, A. (1984). *The Constitution of Society*. Cambridge: Polity Press.

GOPAL, A., BOSTROM, R. P. and CHIN, W. W. (1992). 'Applying Adaptive Structuration Theory to Investigate the Process of Group Support Systems Use'. *Journal of Management Information Systems*, 9(3): 45–69.

GRINT, K. and WOOLGAR, S. (1992). 'Computers, Guns, and Roses: What's Social About Being Shot?' *Science, Technology & Human Values*, 17(3): 366–80.

—— and —— (1997). *The Machine at Work*. Cambridge: Polity Press.

HARVEY, E. (1968). 'Technology and the Structure of Organizations'. *American Sociological Review*, 33(2): 247–59.

HEATH, C. and LUFF, P. (2000). *Technology in Action*. Cambridge: Cambridge University Press.

HICKSON, D. J., PUGH, D. S. and PHEYSEY, D. C. (1969). 'Operations Technology and Organization Structure'. *Administrative Science Quarterly*, 14: 378–97.

HUBER, G. P. (1990). 'A Theory of the Effects of Advanced ICTs on Organisational Design, Intelligence, and Decision Making'. *Academy of Management Review*, 15(1): 47–71.

HUTCHBY, I. (2001). 'Technologies, Texts and Affordances'. *Sociology*, 35(2): 441–56.

HUTCHINS, E. (1995). *Cognition in the Wild*. Cambridge, MA: MIT Press.

JONES, M. R. (1998). 'Information Systems and the Double Mangle: Steering a Course between the Scylla of Embedded Structure and the Charybdis of Material Agency', in T. Larsen, L. Levine and J. I. DeGross (eds), *Information Systems: Current Issues and Future Challenges*. Laxenburg: IFIP, 287–302.

—— (1999). 'Structuration Theory', in W. J. Currie and R. Galliers (eds), *Rethinking Management Information Systems*. Oxford: Oxford University Press, 103–35.

KLING, R. (1980). 'Social Analyses of Computing: Theoretical Perspectives in Recent Empirical Research'. *Computing Surveys*, 12(1): 61–110.

—— and IACONO, S. (1984). 'Computing as an Occasion for Social Control'. *Journal of Social Issues*, 40(3): 77–96.

—— and SCACCHI, W. (1982). 'The Web of Computing: Computing Technology as Social Organisation', in M. V. Zelkowitz (ed.), *Advances in Computers, Volume 21*. New York: Academic Press, 1–90.

KNIGHTS, D. and WILLMOTT, H. (1985). 'Power and Identity in Theory and Practice'. *Sociological Review*, 33(1): 22–46.

LATOUR, B. (1987). *Science in Action*. Cambridge, MA: Harvard University Press.

—— (1999). 'On Recalling ANT', in J. Law and J. Hassard (eds), *Actor Network Theory and After*. Oxford: Blackwell, 15–25.

LAVE, J. (1988). *Cognition in Practice*. Cambridge: Cambridge University Press.

LAW, J. (1999). 'After ANT: Complexity, Naming and Topology', in J. Law and J. Hassard (eds), *Actor Network Theory and After*. Oxford: Blackwell, 1–14.

—— and CALLON, M. (1994). 'Life and Death of an Aircraft: A Network Analysis of Technical Change', in W. Bijker and J. Law (eds), *Shaping Technology/Shaping Society*. Cambridge, MA: MIT Press, 21–52.

LAYDER, D. (1987). 'Key Issues in Structuration Theory: Some Critical Remarks'. *Current Perspectives in Social Theory*, 8: 25–46.

LEAVITT, H. J. and WHISTLER, T. L. (1958). 'Management in the 1980s'. *Harvard Business Review*, 36(Nov.): 41–8.

LUFF, P., HINDMARSH, J. and HEATH, C. (eds) (2000). *Workplace Studies: Recovering Work Practice and Informing System Design*. Cambridge: Cambridge University Press.

LYYTINEN, K. and YOO, Y. (2002). 'Issues and Challenges in Ubiquitous Computing'. *Communications of the ACM*, 45(12): 63–5.

MACKENZIE D. and WAJCMAN, J. (eds) (1999). *The Social Shaping of Technology* (2nd edn). Milton Keynes: Open University Press.

MARKUS, M. L. and ROBEY, D. (1988). 'Information Technology and Organizational Change: Causal Structure in Theory and Research'. *Management Science*, 34(5): 583–98.

MINGERS, J. (2004). 'Realizing Information Systems: Critical Realism as an Underpinning Philosophy for Information Systems'. *Information and Organization*, 14(2): 87–103.

MOL, A. and LAW, J. (1994). 'Regions, Networks and Fluids: Anaemia and Social Topology'. *Social Studies of Science*, 24(4): 641–71.

MUMFORD, E. (1981). 'Participative Systems Design: Structure and Method'. *Systems, Objectives, Solutions*, 1(1): 5–19.

NOBLE, D. F. (1977). *America by Design: Science, Technology, and the Rise of Corporate Capitalism*. New York: Alfred A. Knopf.

NORMAN, D. A. (1988). *The Psychology of Everyday Things*. New York: Doubleday.

—— (2004). 'Affordance, Conventions and Design', first published in May 1999 in *Interactions*, 38–43, http://www.jnd.org/dn.mss/affordance_conventi.html, accessed 19 Mar. 2006.

ORLIKOWSKI, W. J. (1992). 'The Duality of Technology: Rethinking the Concept of Technology in Organizations'. *Organization Science*, 3(3): 398–427.

—— (1993). 'CASE Tools as Organizational Change: Investigating Incremental and Radical Changes in Systems Development'. *MIS Quarterly*, 17(3): 309–40.

—— (1996). 'Improvising Organizational Transformation over Time: A Situated Change Perspective'. *Information Systems Research*, 7(1): 63–92.

—— (2000). 'Using Technology and Constituting Structures: A Practice Lens for Studying Technology in Organizations'. *Organization Science*, 11(4): 404–28.

—— and ROBEY, D. (1991). 'Information Technology and the Structuring of Organizations'. *Information Systems Research*, 2(2): 143–69.

—— and YATES, J. (1994). 'Genre Repertoire: The Structuring of Communicative Practices in Organizations'. *Administrative Science Quarterly*, 39(4): 541–74.

OUDSHOORN, N. and PINCH, T. (eds) (2003). *How Users Matter: The Co-Construction of Users and Technology*. Cambridge, MA: The MIT Press.

PELS, D. (1996). 'The Politics of Symmetry'. *Social Studies of Science*, 26(2): 277–304.

PERROLLE, J. A. (1986). 'Intellectual Assembly Lines: The Rationalization of Managerial, Professional, and Technical Work'. *Computers and Social Sciences*, 2(3): 111–21.

PFEFFER, J. and LEBLEBICI, H. (1977). 'Information Technology in Organizational Structure'. *Pacific Sociological Review*, 20(2): 241–61.

PICKERING, A. (1995). *The Mangle of Practice: Time, Agency and Science*. Chicago, IL: University of Chicago Press.

PINCH, T. J. and BIJKER, W. E. (1984). 'The Social Construction of Facts and Artefacts'. *Social Studies of Science*, 14 (May): 399–441.

PRASAD, P. (1993). 'Symbolic Processes in the Implementation of Technological Change: A Symbolic Interactionist Study of Work Computerization'. *Academy of Management Journal*, 36(6): 1400–29.

ROGERS, Y. (1993). 'Coordinating Computer-Mediated Work'. *Computer Supported Cooperative Work*, (4): 295–315.

—— and ELLIS, J. (1994). 'Distributed Cognition: An Alternative Framework for Analysing and Explaining Collaborative Working'. *Journal of Information Technology*, 9(2): 119–28.

SCHMIDT, K. and BANNON L. J. (1992). 'Taking CSCW Seriously, Supporting Articulation Work'. *Computer Supported Cooperative Work*, 1(1–2): 7–40.

SUCHMAN, L. A. (1987). *Plans and Situated Actions: The Problem of Human Machine Communication.* Cambridge: University of Cambridge Press.

TRIST, E. L. and BAMFORTH, K. W. (1951). 'Some Social and Psychological Consequences of the Longwall Method of Coal-getting'. *Human Relations*, 4: 3–38.

UNGER, R. M. (1987). *False Necessity.* Cambridge: Cambridge University Press.

VAAST, E. and WALSHAM, G. (2005). 'Representations and Actions: The Transformation of Work Practices with IT Use'. *Information and Organization*, 15(1): 65–89.

VAN HOUSE, N. A. (2003). 'Science and Technology Studies and Information Studies'. *Annual Review of Information Science and Technology*, 38: 3–86.

WAJCMAN, J. (2000). 'Reflections on Gender and Technology Studies: In What State is the Art?' *Social Studies of Science*, 30(3): 447–64.

WINNER, L. (1993). 'Upon Opening the Black Box and Finding It Empty: Social Constructivism and the Philosophy of Technology'. *Science, Technology & Human Values*, 18(3): 362–78.

WOODWARD, J. (1958). *Management and Technology.* London: HMSO.

ZUBOFF, S. (1988). *In the Age of the Smart Machine: The Future of Work and Power.* New York: Basic Books.

CHAPTER 13

MAKING SENSE OF ICT, NEW MEDIA, AND ETHICS

LUCAS D. INTRONA

1 INTRODUCTION

NEW and different forms of media become possible in a world where information and communication technology (ICT) has become pervasive—media that seem very different from that which preceded them. For example, a wide variety of new media emerged around the infrastructure of the Internet such as text and video blogs, Internet radio and television, real time news sites with individualized feeds, podcasting and web portals, to name but a few. Similarly, new ways of interacting emerged such as email, online forums, virtual chat, webcams, peer-to-peer file sharing, online multiplayer games, and multi-user dungeons (MUDs). It would seem reasonable to say that the range and scope of possible connections and interactions, for those connected to the ICT infrastructure, has increased by orders of magnitude. If one adds to this the even more pervasive mobile telephone infrastructure, as well as Voice-over Internet Protocol (VoIP), then the possibilities for an ICT mediated sociality seem almost endless. The screen as an interface—a way of facing—has become almost ubiquitous. It has been claimed that there might soon be more screens in the world than people. Thus, it seems apparent that a world with ICT and new media is somehow quite different to a world without it—but in what way and for the benefit of whom?

On a mundane level we might say that ICT is making it easier, or in some cases more difficult, for us to perform certain activities; or, perhaps that it significantly increases our possibilities for doing certain things, such as communicating and interacting. On a more fundamental level one might argue that ICT and new media are changing the very nature of our society, even our understanding of what it might mean to be human. Given such a wide range of possible answers—and the importance of such questioning—it seems right to reflect on how one might approach or frame an analysis of the ethical implications of ICT and new media. Clearly there are many different ways of doing it. For example, one could develop a cultural historical account of ICT and new media similar to Mumford's (1934, 1964) accounts of other technologies. One could develop a sociological analysis of ICT and new media as seen, for example, in the work of Zuboff (1984), Turkle (1995), Hutchby (2000) and Sassen (2002); or for media more generally as available in the work of Hall (1998). One might also decide to develop a more philosophical account of ICT and new media in the manner developed, for example, by Gordon (1999); or for media more generally as was done by McLuhan (1964), Baudrillard (1983) and Virilio (1994); or for technology more generally as was done by Heidegger (1977a), Ellul (1964), Habermas (1970), Marcuse (1964, 1998) and Feenberg (1991, 1995, 1999), to name but a few.

This chapter, however, will offer a different way of approaching and ordering the analysis.[1] We will suggest that our understanding, and evaluation, of the ethical implications of ICT and new media will be conditioned—in a substantial way— by our assumptions about, or account of, the relationship between us (humans or society) and ICT/new media. Stated more generally one could say that it will be conditioned by our assumptions about, or account of, the relationship between us and technology—that is, our most basic assumptions about what society and technology are, for us, when we do our ethical analysis and accounting. For example, if we think of technology as something technical that we 'add' to society then we might evaluate it differently from when we conceive of technology as something that is social, and only social, from the start. We will also suggest that our proposals for 'solving' or regulating the ethical implications of ICT and new media will likewise be conditioned by our understanding of this assumed relationship.

The purpose of this chapter is to propose and clarify some of these different ways of seeing or approaching, as well as the implications these might have for us as regulators, designers, users, and researchers of ICT and new media, especially with regard to their ethical significance. Of course any clarification (classification, categorization, or analysis) is always problematic: incomplete, and often—in a sense—violent. It usually claims more than it can offer and forces the singular into a category in ways that deny the very idiosyncrasies that are often most important when approaching phenomena. Thus, it would be reasonable for the reader to take the analysis in the following presentation as incomplete, preliminary, and not definitive in any sense whatsoever.

Nevertheless, it does seem useful, at least as a starting point, to have some sense of the differences, even if we have to immediately admit as Jacques Derrida so often reminds us, to the perpetual deference of our concepts and categories. Furthermore, the subject matter covered by this chapter is vast—encompassing a variety of disciplines such as New Media Studies, Information Systems, Science and Technology Studies (STS), New Media Ethics, Computer Ethics, Ethical Theory, Applied Ethics, and so forth. As such, this chapter should be seen as an introductory sketch, nothing more. It will provide some distinctions and give some indication of the issues at stake. For a more detailed study it is suggested that the reader consult the references in this chapter.

The chapter will be structured around three possible approaches—and the assumptions they imply—to our ongoing relationship with ICT and new media. Others are also possible.[2] The chapter will present each of these views in turn as follows. First, we outline the particular way in which the ICT/society relationship is understood or accounted for. Secondly, we discuss how such a view of the ICT/society relation will condition the way ethical questions are approached and solutions proposed—including some examples of work that follow the particular approach to ICT and ethics.

2 New media and ICT as tools

The tool ontology

The most common view of ICT is that it is an artefact, tool, or system that is designed to be available for humans to achieve their objectives and outcomes—to email, to write, to store, to manipulate, to interact, and so forth. This view is rooted in our everyday intuitions about the world in which our tools are seen as something distinctly separate from us—thus, where the subject/object dualism is taken for granted. Tools are seen as objective and neutral 'technical things' (separate from us) that we can draw upon, or not, to achieve our particular ends. This relationship between us and our tools is often expressed as a means–ends relationship where technology is designed—based on some technical rationality—as means (or tools) to achieve particular ends. Some of these tools might be useful and others not. However, when users take up tools or artefacts (email, word processor, mobile phone, etc.) these tools will tend to have an impact on the way they do things. For example, if I send you an email, I write and communicate in a different way from sending you a paper-based letter. Thus, we need to understand the impact that ICT has on social practices, as these tools are taken up and used in these everyday practices and situations. For example, how will communication with mobile phones change or impact on our social interaction, and possibly our social relationships?

In posing these questions on the impact of this or that technology this view does not primarily concern itself with the prior process of how this or that particular technology was developed—why and how did it come about in the first instance, and why not something else? These questions are seen as 'technical' questions that are the domain of designers and engineers (working within the assumption of technical rationality). It is taken for granted that the particular technology is the outcome of a more or less technical rational attempt by designers and engineers to solve concrete practical problems by the 'technical' means available to them. From this perspective the relevant question is how society uses these technical means and how this usage impacts on, and changes, social practices. In thinking through these questions it is normally assumed that the particular technology—mobile phones in this case—operates in a more or less uniform manner in different social settings. In other words, it assumes that a particular technology has certain *determinate* effects on, or in, the context of its use. This way of conceptualizing ICT leads to questions such as: what is the impact of the Internet on education? Or what is the impact of closed circuit television (CCTV) on privacy?

This view of technology is often criticized to a lesser or greater degree for technological determinism. Technological determinism is the view that technology more or less *causes* certain ways of doing or ways of organizing social practices to come about. Determinists would suggest that one can extrapolate from certain technical features the sort of social consequences that might result. Toffler (1970, 1980) articulated a popular version of this view. Thus, a technological determinist may argue that the Internet's open and non-hierarchical architecture can more or less cause a society that uses it to become more open and less hierarchical. When they have taken this approach, various authors have come to very different evaluations of the potential impact of ICT and new media on society. For example, Rheingold (1993b: 14) argues that computer mediated communication (CMC) (in the form of the Internet) has the capacity: '[T]o challenge the existing political hierarchy's monopoly on powerful communications media, and perhaps thus revitalize citizen-based democracy. . . . a world in which every citizen can broadcast to every other citizen?'

The work of Postman (1993), in particular his book *Technopology*, is also an example of this type of critical evaluation of the impact of technology on society. For Postman the technical domain is 'colonising' the social world and leading to a 'technopolistic' society (Postman 1993: 71–2).

The impact of new media and ICT and the application of ethical theory

The fundamental (or ontological) assumption that the 'technical' and the 'social' are fundamentally different types of reality allows the tool view to retain a distinction between the 'technical' means and the 'social' ends—or between facts and values as critiqued by Latour (2002). For example, for adherents of the tool view, technology is neutral and it is humans that bring (good or bad) values to technology when they use it. This view is often expressed in the debate on guns in the following manner: 'it is people that are bad not guns'. Similarly, for them the Internet is a neutral (technical) medium that can be used for good (education, community, commerce, etc.) or for bad (pornography, gambling, terrorism, etc.). Much of the ethical and policy debate about ICT and new media has been informed by this 'tool view'. Within this tradition a number of issues have emerged as important. For example, whether ICT and new media generate new types of ethical problems that require new or different ethical theories or whether it is just more of the same (Gorniak 1996; Tavani 2002). These debates are often expressed in the language of the impact of information technology on particular values and rights (Johnson 1994; Baase 2003). Thus, we have discussions on the impact of CCTV or web cookies on the right to privacy (Bennett 2001, Marx 1998), the impact of the digital divide on the right to access information (Hacker and Mason 2003), the impact of the piracy of software on intellectual property rights (IPR) (Lipinski and Britz 2000), and so forth. In these debates Moor (1985) has argued that computers show up policy vacuums that require new thinking and the establishment of new policies. Others have argued that the resources provided by classical ethical theory such as utilitarianism, consequentialism, and deontological ethics are more than enough to deal with all the ethical issues emerging from our design and use of ICT (Gert 1999).

Irrespective of whether ICT and new media create new types of ethical problems that require new ethical theory, or whether established ethical theory is sufficient, one tends to find the debate on the ethical issues of ICT and new media centred on questions of *policy* that are intended to regulate or justify the conduct or practices that the technology now makes possible (or prevents). These policies are seen, and presented as, ways to regulate or balance competing rights or competing values as these are made possible (or not) through the new technology. For example, what sort of policies do we need to protect our children when they go on the Internet, as the Internet now allows them to go 'anywhere'? How would these policies affect the right to free speech? Or, what sort of policies do we need to secure the rights of producers of digital products? How would these policies affect the right of society to a reasonable access to these products? Furthermore, these debates are most often directed at an institutional level of discourse—that is, with the intention to justify (or not) the policies or conduct for governments, organizations, and individuals. In these debates on the impact of ICT and new media, ethics and ethicists are primarily conceived of as presenting arguments for justifying a particular policy (or set of policies) that balance certain values or rights, over and against other possible policies. In presenting these arguments ethicists normally apply ethical theories (such as consequentialism, utilitarianism, deontological ethics, etc.) to new cases or problems presented by the use, or perceived impact, of the particular technology.

3 New media and ICT as constructed artefacts and actors

The constructivist ontology

Many scholars argue that the 'impact view'—based on the tool ontology—of ICT and new media does not give an adequate account of the ongoing relationship between new media, ICT (or technology more generally) and society (Bijker, Pinch and Hughes 1987, Bijker 1995, Law 1991, Latour 1991, Pfaffenberger 1992, Berg and Lie, 1995; Bowker and Star 1999). They argue that the taken for granted ontology of the subject/object dualism (also expressed as the technology/society dualism) leads us to inappropriate conclusions about the ethical import of new media and ICT. For them means and ends cannot be separated as suggested in the impact view. They argue that this view does not take into account that the new media and ICT do not simply appear but are the outcome of a complex and socially situated development and design process. By 'socially situated' we mean subject to the aspirations, interests, power, values, assumptions, beliefs, and so on of a diverse set of potential stakeholders—such as financiers, technologists, users, markets, and others. In this development and design process, many alternative options become excluded in favour of the technology that is now available—obviously with important implications. In other words there are many cultural, political and economic forces that shape the particular options suggested as well as the way the selected options become designed and implemented (Bijker, Pinch and Hughes 1987). It is not only technology that 'impacts' on society; technology itself is already the outcome of complex, subtle, and situated social processes. Moreover, they argue that when we look at the actual uses of particular technologies we discover that users interpret and use them in many diverse and often unexpected ways, leading to many and diverse unintended consequences.

The degree to which the technology/society distinction is useful at all (ontologically or analytically) varies between the different constructivist authors. For example, Philip Brey (1997) identifies three different strands of constructivist approaches.[3]

The *strong social constructivism* position holds that technological change is *only* the outcome of diverse social practices. It tends to emphasize processes such as the interpretation or framing by the different actors and social groups, the negotiation of these interpretations, and the stabilization and enclosure of these interpretations in what is subsequently referred to as the 'technology'. According to them, technology can, and should, be explained only with reference to social practices. Technology is wholly and completely a social construction. This means that technology of itself does not have 'properties', or 'effects' in any way whatsoever. There is no distinction between the technical and the social. The technical is social 'all the way down'. There is nothing in the technology that cannot be accounted for by exclusive reference to social practices, values, beliefs, and so forth (Collins and Yearley 1992; Woolgar 1991; Grint and Woolgar 1995).

Mild social constructivism (also known as the 'social shaping' approach) tends to accept that it is meaningful to retain a distinction between the social and the technical. Its adherents suggest that it is still meaningful to attribute certain properties and effects to the technology. Nevertheless, they would argue that these properties and effects are defined relative to a particular social context (for example, MacKenzie and Wajcman 1985, MacKenzie 1990; Kling 1991). They suggest that once these properties have become stabilized and enclosed they become 'built into' these technologies, as it were, in ways that might have important consequences for some (and not for others).

Actor-network theory (also referred to as 'constructivism' more generally) is a third approach that can be identified. Actor-network theorists employ a principle of *generalized* symmetry. For them the distinctions between the natural, social, and technical are *post hoc* constructions. They are rather all seen as actors (or 'actants') that participate in a heterogeneous network of entities that become stabilized as this or that 'technology' (or society). Importantly, all the actors have a similar explanatory role in which no one can be privileged over and above any other (Callon 1987; Latour 1987; Callon and Latour 1992; Haraway 1991).

All constructivist accounts of the ICT–society relation depend on detailed empirical and historical studies to demonstrate the ongoing construction of technology. They claim that if one looks at these detailed historical studies then it is impossible to make general statements about the impact of a technology. One can, at most, speak of some general trends to which many exceptions will invariably exist. For the proponents of the constructivist view it is important to understand, through detailed descriptive accounts, the particular ways in which technologies emerge or become embedded in particular social practices. In these historical accounts the analysts remain agnostic about the knowledge claims and often implicit value judgements made by the different relevant social actors (this is often referred to as *methodological symmetry* or as *methodological relativism*).[4]

Indeed constructivist studies, based on methodological symmetry, are often criti-cized for not 'taking a stand' and getting caught up in a moral relativism (Winner 1993; Radder 1992). Wiebe Bijker, a prominent figure in the STS community, suggested that 'The STS agenda has been largely agnostic as to the normative and political issues related to the application of STS insights, (Bijker 2003: 445).

New media, ICT, and the possibilities of a disclosive ethics

The constructivists' approach to the ICT/society relationship tends to lead to a different kind of reflection on the ethical significance of ICT and new media. They do not accept the 'means–ends' distinction suggested by the tool ontology. For constructivists, technology—in its ongoing process of 'becoming' embedded in a particular context—progressively reflects the practices, aspirations, interests, values, assumptions, beliefs of those social actors that design, implement, and draw upon it for their particular purposes. Thus, constructivists tend to argue that technology emerges as political from the start; as such the ethical concern is also already there from the start. Thus, for them there is no way in which one could talk about technology as a 'mere means'—that is, for them the neutrality thesis does not make sense at all. They argue that socio-technical networks (technology/society configura-tions), through their process of design, implementation, and use, include (or rather afford) certain interests and exclude others. This does not mean that designers, implementers, and users are always aware that they are making political and ethical decisions—although they might be. Many would argue that they are mostly not. They might suggest that they are mostly trying to solve very mundane 'technical' problems. For example, the automatic teller machine (ATM) assumes a particular type of person in front of it. It assumes a person that is able to see the screen, read it, remember and enter a PIN (personal identification number) code, and so on. It is not difficult to imagine a whole section of society that does not conform to these assumptions. If you are blind, in a wheelchair, have problems remembering, or are unable to enter a PIN, because of disability (or being disabled by the machine), then your interest in getting access to your account may have become excluded by the actual design of the ATM—especially in the context of the increased closure of local branches. This does not mean that users cannot intentionally or unintentionally reinterpret the way technology suggests or 'affords' (to use Gibson's (1979) and Norman's (1988, 1990) term), possibilities to suit their own needs. Users often 'read' and use technology in ways unintended by the designers/implementers. However, as these technological affor-dances become embedded in larger infrastructures (practices, systems, spaces, organ-izations, etc.) it becomes increasingly difficult to use the technology in ways other than in the way it was set up to afford possibilities (or not).

If ICT and new media are always in the process of becoming political—including/excluding certain interests—then they are clearly also immediately ethical. Latour

(2004: 258) suggests that the moral concern for the constructivist should be: 'To maintain the reversibility of foldings'. Similarly, Bijker (2003: 446) argues that detailed STS case studies act as 'mirrors' in which detailed insights gained can connect 'the institutional level to the individual level, doing case studies is a way for individual STS researchers to conduct political interventions'. Thus, for the constructivist the ethical concern is revealing—through detailed empirical work—the particular way in which interests are being 'built into' the technology and social practices (Brey 2000; Agre and Harbs 1994; Kling 1996). Moreover, they often argue that ethical reflection should be an inherent part of the design process—referred to as value sensitive design (Friedman 1997; Blomberg, Suchman and Trigg 1996; Miller and Resnick 1996; Mumford 1996).

With regard to ICT and new media the particular concern is often the way information technology 'hides' or subsumes these values and interests in the logic of software algorithms and hardware circuits (Introna and Nissenbaum 2000; Introna and Wood 2004). This is particularly important for ICT and new media, as opposed to other everyday technologies, as these systems are mostly not evident, obvious, transparent, or open to inspection by the ordinary everyday person affected by it (Brey 1999, 2000). Rather they tend to be obscure, subsumed, and black-boxed in ways that only makes their 'surfaces' available for inspection. Embedded in the software and hardware codes of these systems are complex rules of logic and categorization that may have material consequences for those using it and for the ongoing production of social order more generally.

In this view of new media and ICT ethics the task of ethics is to influence, shape, or mediate the development, implementation, and use of new media and ICT in a democratic and inclusive way according to core human values (Feenberg 1991, 1995, 1999; Friedman 1997; Hamelink 2000) as well as continually to open up the black box of new media and ICT and reveal or disclose the values and interests they 'embody' for scrutiny and reflection (Winner 1980; Latour 2004; Brey 2000; Introna and Nissenbaum 2000). Such an approach to the ethics of ICT and new media is most often informed by situated historical studies within the STS tradition as proposed by Bijker (2003).

4 NEW MEDIA AND ICT AS AN ONGOING HORIZON OF MEANING AND ACTION

Phenomenological ontology

For the phenomenologists the 'impact view' of ICT and new media as well as the constructivist view of the ICT/society relationships is valid but not sufficient

(Heidegger 1927/1962, 1977a; Borgmann 1984, 1999; Ihde 1990, 2002; Dreyfus 1992, 1999, 2001; Heim 1987, 1993). They argue that these accounts of technology (and/or society) posit these categories as if speaking about the one (society or technology) that does not already and immediately draw upon the other for its ongoing constitution, sense or meaning. For the phenomenologist, society and ICT always and already *co-constitute* each other's possibility to be. In other words they are each other's ongoing transcendental condition or possibility for being what they are. 'Transcendental' here is understood as 'that [horizon of intelligibility] which constitutes, and thereby renders the empirical possible' (Mohanty 1997: 52). Thus for the phenomenologist the questions of which is prior (technology or society) or which should be privileged (or not) do not come up as relevant questions at all. Rather, things (humans, practices, and technology) always and already have their being in a world (or horizon of intelligibility) in which they function as such. Let us consider this argument more closely by attending to the work of Martin Heidegger (1927/1962, 1977a) as an example of the phenomenological approach.

In *Being and Time*, Heidegger argues that we humans (whom he calls *Dasein*) exist in an ongoing structural openness 'towards' the world in which the self and the world is always and already a unity, a *being-in-the-world* (Heidegger 1927/1962: 297). To say that they are 'always and already a unity' is to say that there is or was never a time when self (*Dasein*) and world (technology, practices, etc.) existed as something as such. According to Heidegger we human beings (*Dasein*) *are* always and already this unity, indeed, we are always and already *beings-in-the-world*—we have this unity as our ongoing way of being. Whenever we find ourselves, or take note of ourselves, we find ourselves already engaged in ongoing everyday activity in which things immediately show up as 'possibilities for' this or that practical intention—never as mere things or objects that are just there—strange and in need of interpretation as it were. When we encounter familiar useful things (as possibilities for this and that) in our everyday 'going about' they are already significant in some way or another. It is not our encounter that renders them significant, they are already significant and therefore we encounter them as such. One could say, to use the language of Gibson (1979) and Norman (1988), that their 'affordances' are immediately apparent to us because we have our being in that world. Their location and arrangement as well as all the implied references to a whole array of other things that constitute their possibility to be—something in particular—show them up as 'obvious' things for this or that purpose—so we simply engage with them in order to do what we want or need to do. Heidegger (1927/1962) explains:

Equipment—in accordance with its equipmentality—always is in terms of its belonging to other equipment: inkstand, pen, ink, paper, blotting pad, table lamp, furniture, windows, doors, room. These things never show themselves proximally as they are for themselves. So as to add up to a sum of *realia* and fill up the room [to be a study].... [Rather] out of this [already belonging to other equipment] the 'arrangement' [the study] emerges, and it is in this [equipmental nexus] that any 'individual' item of equipment shows itself. [But] *Before* it does so, a totality of equipment [the equipmental nexus or whole] has already been discovered. (Heidegger 1927/1962: 97–8)

When we take up these things, as this or that particular thing, we do not take them up for their own sake; we take them up with an already present reference to our projects or our concerns. As beings that are always already projected we are always already ahead of ourselves, meaning we are always already immersed in a nexus of concerns; or rather we have as our way of being already a nexus of concerns. This is why Heidegger (1927/1962: 236) claims the way of being of *Dasein* is care (care as in 'mattering'). We do not simply bang on keys, we use the laptop to type, in order to write this chapter, to do email, to surf the web, and so forth. Moreover, the writing of this chapter already refers to possible readers. Readers already refers to a possible audience, which already refers to a community of scholars or students, which already refers to institutions of learning, which already refers to teaching and research programmes, etc. Heidegger (1927/1962: 118) calls this already recursively defining and necessary nexus of projects, or for-the-sake-of relations, *the involvement whole*. The equipment whole and the involvement whole always already refer to each other and sustain each other as an ongoing horizon of meaning and intelligibility. Heidegger calls this horizon of meaning, or horizon of intelligibility, 'the world'. We humans (*Dasein*), in our human way of being, always already have a world as our being in which things show up as mostly familiar (it is simply already evidently there, 'ready-to-hand' in Heidegger's terminology). The phenomenological meaning of the world can only be understood within the always already defining referential whole, the world itself. The point of Heidegger's account is:

that things show up for us or are encountered as what they are only against a background of familiarity, competence, and concern that carves out a system of related roles [already recursively defining references] into which things fit. Equipmental things are the roles into which they are cast by skilled users of them, and skilled users are the practical roles into which they [become] cast themselves. (Hall 1993: 132)

Thus, for the phenomenologist, technology is not just this or that empirical artefact or actor. Rather, the artefact already emerges from an always *prior* 'technological' nexus, attitude, and orientation, which is our human way of being as beings always and already in-the-world.

Let us now turn briefly to Heidegger's most famous phenomenological analysis of technology: his essay *The Question Concerning Technology*.[5] In this essay Heidegger (1977a: 12) claims that: 'Technology is therefore no mere means. Technology is a way of revealing.' For Heidegger technology is—already has its meaning as—the disclosure of being, or rather our way of being. Or as Ihde (1990: 56–7) expresses it: 'Technology, in the deepest Heideggerian sense, is simultaneously material-existential and *cultural*. . . . It is a way of seeing embodied in a particular form.' In his essay *The Thing*, Heidegger (1971: 81) claims that 'the thing things the world'. Thus, for him, to see a thing is to already see, or be in the world, in a particular way. Indeed that is the only way one can make sense of his suggestion that the 'jug is not a vessel because it was made; rather, the jug had to be made because it is [already] this holding vessel' (Heidegger 1971: 168). The world (or referential whole) in which the jug, as a holding vessel, emerges as necessary is prior to this or that entity 'jug'. Therefore, in making the entity 'jug' a world (a way of being), already present, is thereby revealed. As such technology has as its being the revealing of a way of being.

It is therefore no surprise that for Heidegger the essence of modern technology is the way of being of modern humans—a way of conducting themselves towards the world—that sees the world as something to be ordered and shaped in line with our projects, intentions and desires—a 'will to power' that manifests itself as a 'will to technology'. It is in this technological mood that problems show up as requiring technical solutions. The term 'mood' here is used in a collective sense, like the 'mood of the meeting' or the 'mood of our times'. He calls this technological mood 'enframing' (*Gestell* in German). For us, in the modern technological age the world is already 'framed' as a world available 'to be made', 'to be shaped' for our ongoing possibilities to express our existence, to be whatever we are, as business men and women, engineers, consultants, academics, teenagers, and so forth. In short: the need for modern technology makes sense because we already live in the technological age or mood where the world (and we as beings that are never 'out' of the world) is already *framed* in this way—as available resources for the ongoing challenging and ordering of the world by us, which is for Heidegger the essence of the 'modern' mood.

New media, ICT, ethics, and our human way of being

From the preceding discussion, it should be clear that phenomenologists would tend not to only concern themselves with this or that artefact or technology as such. They would rather be concerned with the world (or mood as already suggested) that made these artefacts or technologies seem necessary or obvious in the first place. They would also be concerned with the ways in which particular technologies 'frame' and reveal us, or our world, as we draw on them. They would claim that it is *this ongoing co-constitution* that we should focus on if we are to understand the social and ethical implications of ICT and new media. This does not preclude the possibility that we could also consider the impact of particular technologies as well as unpack particular technologies to understand the values and interests they imply. However, the phenomenologists would argue that the impact analysis and the disclosive analysis (already outlined) could be enhanced if these were situated in a broader phenomenological analysis. Such an additional analysis might add another level of critical reflection that could be important in justifying different possible futures.

One might describe the phenomenological approach as an iterative process of *ontological disclosure* in which a world (relevant social practices or involvement whole) and technology (nexus of equipmentality) are taken as mutually constitutive, interpretive contexts in which the one renders the other intelligible—grounds it as a 'seemingly' meaningful way to be. In this iterative process there is a progressive uncovering of the constitutive conditions that are necessary for particular ways of seeing or doing in the world or in particular social practices to make sense of that which they are taken to be. For example, in Heidegger's analysis of modern technology, as already outlined, he identifies the emergence of calculative thinking as a condition to see the world as resources available for our purposes. However, this calculative orientation is itself conditioned by a particular way of approaching the world that he traces back to Greek thought.

Heim (1987), in *Electric Language*, argues that the change from handwriting to word-processing is not just a change of tools, it is also and immediately a change (or reconstitution) of a way of being a writer, and therefore our understanding of what writing is supposed to be. For example, he argues that on the screen writing loses its reflective craft-like nature. Words and ideas become constituted as fragments that can be 'cut and pasted' in a more or less thoughtless manner in pursuit of a more efficient mode of composition. According to him the electronic text, in writing on the screen, becomes constituted as never being thought. It is rather the outcome of what is possible (outlining, cutting and pasting, thesaurus replacement, etc). In a similar manner, Lyman (1984) argues that computer writing changes a craft labour into a system of production that privileges the lexical over the graphic, and in which writing becomes a medium for transmitting information rather than an artistic performance. Phenomenological analyses such as these open up the horizon of reflection to disclose some of the ontological implications of taking up seemingly innocent 'tools' (such as replacing handwriting with computer writing). At the level of the tool ontology such a shift might be analysed as a matter of taking up (or not) of a useful tool that potentially makes writing easier—a phenomenological analysis suggests that much more is happening.[6] With such a phenomenological analysis it becomes possible to reflect on the human 'cost' of technology as our world (our human way of being) becomes reconstituted. That is, such an analysis may reveal the significance of changes in our way of being, rather than simply in our ways of doing.

In reflecting on the ethics of new media a number of authors have commented on the way these technologies constitute the other as both 'close' (that is, just here on the screen) but also 'distant'. That is, they do not seem to be able to claim our responsibility in the way that face-to-face encounters do (Silverstone 2002, 2003; Introna 2002; Lyon 2001). For phenomenologists, the new media do not simply 'connect' us or bring us 'close' to each other. They also and immediately reconstitute our relation, physically, socially, and morally. For example, Silverstone (2003: 478) argues for the importance of maintaining a 'proper distance' in which proximity and responsibility are maintained. He argues that in the modern world of the Internet and increased mobility the stranger becomes 'my neighbour': 'and we are all neighbours to one another now'. In the mediated world we become inundated with the solicitations of the multitude of others that increasingly appear on our screens. How ought we to respond? We cannot allow the world, reconstituted through the new media, to turn them into mere images, pixels on the screen. We must recognize: 'that I have as much responsibility for the stranger, that other who is either, physically or metaphysically, far from me, as I do for my neighbour' (Silverstone 2003: 480). As Levinas (1974/1991: 159) (whom Silverstone draws upon) suggests, justice demands that 'there is no distinction between those close and those far off, but in which there also remains the impossibility of passing by the closest'. Thus, according to Silverstone the ambiguity of a world of 'closeness' and simultaneous 'distance' of the other that the new media constitute is an altogether different way of being with others that requires a new ethic of 'proper distance' where the possibility of facing the other, as Other, is not lost in the ethereality of our clicks. It is clear from these examples that the ethical question for phenomenology is mostly also an ontological question—that is, what sort of world or way of being are we becoming, as opposed to the sort of world we value and want? The phenomenologists would argue that these fundamental choices may only become visible if we approach new media and ICT (and the ethics they imply) from a phenomenological point of view.

One criticism levelled against the phenomenological approach, especially by the constructivists, is that it has a too 'essentialist' view of technology. They argue that if one would take a careful look at the way individuals or groups interpret and use technology one sees many idiosyncratic ways of being with technology that would suggest that one cannot really make the sort of claims discussed above, about writing, virtuality, and new media. Obviously this is an important caution to keep in mind in doing a phenomenological analysis. However, the phenomenologists would respond by suggesting that the constructivist gives far too much agency to the human actor, who is always already immersed in the world or certain horizons of intelligibility. They would suggest that the tool view as well as the constructivist position underestimates the degree to which the interpretation and use of the technology by the users are always and already conditioned within a certain horizon of intelligibility, and in which the technology already shows up in this or that way rather than as something else; or in which certain possibilities of seeing and doing would simply not even emerge as meaningful to consider in the first place. Furthermore, they would suggest that technology, once stabilized as taken for granted, becomes more or less 'essential' inasmuch as it becomes constituted as implicit choices (and founding conditions) that are no longer subjected to reinterpretation and scrutiny. The ongoing horizon of intelligibility, that technology is, becomes so obvious that it is simply taken for granted as the way the world is.

5 CONCLUSION

The purpose of this chapter was to open up a horizon within which it becomes possible to make sense of new media and ICT so as to appreciate the social and ethical implications of these 'new' technologies. It was suggested that this 'making sense' will be conditioned by a certain fundamental understanding, or assumptions about the social–technical relationship. Each of these approaches is legitimate in its own terms. However, with each approach there are also limitations, as we have tried to show. The most important limitation, however, would be to be completely unaware or naive about one's underlying assumptions in approaching the social and ethical questions raised by ICT and new media.

REFERENCES

AGRE, P. E., and HARBS, C. A. (1994). 'Social Choice about Privacy: Intelligent Vehicle-highways Systems in the United States'. *Information Technology and People*, 7(4): 63–90.

ARNOLD, M. (2003). 'On the Phenomenology of Technology: The "Janus-faces" of Mobile Phones'. *Information and Organization*, 13(4): 231–56.

BAASE, S. (2003). *A Gift of Fire: Social, Legal, and Ethical Issues for Computers and the Internet* (2nd edn). Upper Saddle River, NJ: Pearson Education.

BAUDRILLARD, J. (1983). *Simulations*. New York: Semiotext(e).

BENNETT, C. J. (2001). 'Cookies, Web Bugs, Webcams and Cue Cats: Patterns of Surveillance on the World Wide Web'. *Ethics and Information Technology*, 3(3): 197–210.

BERG, A. and LIE, M. (1995). 'Feminism and Constructivism: Do Artifacts Have Gender?' *Science, Technology & Human Values*, 20(3): 332–51.

BIJKER, W. E. (1995). *Of Bicycles, Bakelites and Bulbs. Toward a Theory of Sociotechnical Change*. Cambridge, MA: MIT Press.

—— (2003). 'The Need for Public Intellectuals: A Space for STS'. *Science Technology & Human Values*, 28(4): 443–50.

—— , PINCH, T. and HUGHES, T. (eds) (1987). *The Social Construction of Technological Systems: New Directions in the Sociology and History of Technology*. Cambridge, MA: MIT Press.

BLOMBERG, J., SUCHMAN, L. and TRIGG, R. (1996). 'Reflections on a Work-oriented Design Project'. *Human-Computer Interaction*, 11(3): 237–65.

BORGMANN, A. (1984). *Technology and the Character of Contemporary Life*. Chicago, IL: Chicago University Press.

—— (1999). *Holding On To Reality: The Nature of Information at the Turn of the Millennium*. Chicago/London: The University of Chicago Press.

BOWKER, G. C. and STAR, S. L. (1999). *Sorting Things Out: Classification and its Consequences*. Cambridge, MA: MIT Press.

BREY, P. (1997). 'Philosophy of Technology meets Social Constructivism'. *Techné: Journal of the Society for Philosophy and Technology*, 2(3/4): 56–79.

—— (1999). 'The Ethics of Representation and Action in Virtual Reality'. *Ethics and Information Technology*, 1(1): 5–14.

—— (2000). 'Disclosive Computer Ethics'. *Computers and Society*, 30(4): 10–16.

CALLON, M. (1987). 'Society in the Making: The Study of Technology as a Tool for Sociological Analysis', in W. E. Bijker, T. P. Hughes and T. J. Pinch (eds), *The Social Construction of Technological Systems*. Cambridge, MA: MIT Press, 83–103.

—— and LATOUR, B. (1992). 'Don't Throw the Baby Out with the Bath School! A Reply to Collins and Yearley', in A. Pickering (ed.), *Science as Practice and Culture*. Chicago, IL: University of Chicago Press, 342–68.

COLLINS, H. M. and YEARLEY, S. (1992). 'Epistemological Chicken', in A. Pickering (ed.), *Science as Practice and Culture*. Chicago, IL: University of Chicago Press, 301–26.

DREYFUS, H. L. (1992). *What Computers Still Can't Do: A Critique of Artificial Reason*. Cambridge, MA: The MIT Press.

—— (1999). 'Anonymity versus Commitment: The Dangers of Education on the Internet'. *Ethics and Information Technology*, 1(1): 15–20.

—— (2001). *On the Internet*. London: Routledge.

DUNLOP, C. and KLING, R. (eds) (1991). *Computerization and Controversy: Value Conflicts and Social Choices*. San Diego, CA: Academic Press.

ELLUL, J. (1964). *The Technological Society*. New York: Vintage Books.

FEENBERG, A. (1991). *Critical Theory of Technology*. Oxford: Oxford University Press.

—— (1995). *Alternative Modernity*. Los Angeles, CA: University of California Press.

—— (1999). *Questioning Technology*. London: Routledge.

FRIEDMAN, B. (ed.) (1997). *Human Values and the Design of Computer Technology*. New York: Cambridge University Press and CSLI, Stanford University.

GERT, B. (1999). 'Common Morality and Computing'. *Ethics and Information Technology*, 1(1): 57–64.

GIBSON, J. J. (1979). *The Ecological Approach to Visual Perception*. Boston, MA: Houghton Mifflin.

GORDON, G. (1999). *The Internet: A Philosophical Inquiry*. London: Routledge.

GORNIAK, K. (1996). 'The Computer Revolution and the Problem of Global Ethics'. *Science and Engineering Ethics*, 2(2): 177–90.

GRINT, K. and WOOLGAR, S. (1995). 'On Some Failures of Nerve in Constructivist and Feminist Analyses of Technology'. *Science, Technology, and Human Values*, 20(3): 286–310.

HABERMAS, J. (1970). 'Technical Progress and the Social Life-World', in J. Habermas (ed.), *Toward a Rational Society: Student Protest, Science and Politics* (trans. J. J. Shapiro). Boston, MA: Beacon Press, 50–61.

HACKER, K. L. and MASON, S. M. (2003). 'Ethical Gaps in Studies of the Digital Divide'. *Ethics and Information Technology*, 5(2): 99–115.

HALL, H. (1993). 'Intentionality and World: Division I of *Being and Time*', in C. Guignon (ed.), *The Cambridge Companion to Heidegger*. Cambridge: Cambridge University Press.

HALL, S. (1998). *Representation: Cultural Representations and Signifying Practices. Culture, Media and Identities*. London: Sage and Open University Press.

HAMELINK, C. (2000). *The Ethics of Cyberspace*. Thousand Oaks, CA: Sage.

HARAWAY, D. J. (1991). *Simians, Cyborgs, and Women: The Reinvention of Nature*. New York: Routledge.

HEIDEGGER, M. (1927/1962). *Being and Time* (trans. John Macquarrie and Edward Robinson). New York: Harper and Row.

—— (1971). *Poetry, Language, Thought* (trans. A. Hofstadter). New York: Harper and Row.

—— (1977a). *The Question Concerning Technology and Other Essays*. New York: Harper Torchbooks.

—— (1977b). 'On the Essence of Truth', in D. F. Krell (ed.), *Martin Heidegger: Basic Writings*. San Francisco, CA: HarperCollins Publishers, 113–41.

HEIM, M. (1987). *Electric Language: A Philosophical Study of Word Processing*. New Haven, CT: Yale University Press.

—— (1993). *The Metaphysics of Virtual Reality*. New York: Oxford University Press.

HUTCHBY, I. (2000). *Conversation and Technology: From the Telephone to the Internet*. Cambridge: Polity Press.

IHDE, D. (1990). *Technology and the Lifeworld: From Garden to Earth*. Bloomington and Indianapolis: Indiana University Press.

—— (2002). *Bodies in Technology*, Minneapolis, MN: University of Minnesota Press.

INTRONA, L. D. (2002). The (Im)Possibility of Ethics in the Information Age'. *Information and Organisation*, 12(2): 71–84.

—— and ILHARCO, F. M. (2004). 'The Ontological Screening of Contemporary Life: A Phenomenological Analysis of Screens'. *European Journal of Information Systems*, 13(3): 221–34.

—— and NISSENBAUM, H. (2000). 'Shaping the Web: Why the Politics of Search Engines Matters'. *The Information Society*, 16(3): 169–85.

—— and WOOD, D. (2004). 'Picturing Algorithmic Surveillance: The Politics of Facial Recognition Systems'. *Surveillance and Society*, 2(2/3): 177–98.

JOHNSON D. G. (1994). *Computer Ethics* (2nd edn). Englewood Cliffs, NJ: Prentice Hall.

—— and NISSENBAUM, H. (eds) (1995). *Computers, Ethics and Social Values* Englewood Cliffs, NJ: Prentice Hall.

KEULARTZ, J., SCHERMER, M., KORTHALS, M. et al. (2004). 'Ethics in Technological Culture: A Programmatic Proposal for a Pragmatist Approach'. *Science, Technology and Human Values*, 29(1): 3–29.

KLING, R. (1991). Computerization and Social Transformations. *Science, Technology and Human Values*, 16(3): 342–67.

—— (ed.) (1996). *Computerization and Controversy: Value Conflict and Social Values*, (2nd edn). San Diego, CA: Academic Press.

LATOUR, B. (1987). *Science in Action*. Cambridge, MA: Harvard University Press.

—— (1991). 'Technology is Society made Durable', in J. Law (ed.) *A Sociology of Monsters: Essays on Power, Technology and Domination*. London: Routledge, 103–31.

—— (2002). 'Morality and Technology: The End of the Means'. *Theory, Culture and Society*, 19(5/6): 247–60.

—— (2004). *Politics of Nature: How to Bring the Sciences into Democracy*, trans. C. Porter Cambridge, MA: Harvard University Press.

LAW, J. (1991). *The Sociology of Monsters: Essays on Power, Technology and Domination*. London: Routledge.

LEVINAS, E. (1974/1991). *Otherwise than Being or Beyond Essence*. Dordrecht: Kluwer Academic Publishers.

LIPINSKI, T. A. and BRITZ, J. J. (2000). 'Rethinking the Ownership of Information in the 21st Century: Ethical Implications'. *Ethics and Information Technology*, 2(1): 49–71.

LYMAN, P. (1984). 'Reading, Writing and Word Processing: Toward a Phenomenology of the Computer Age'. *Qualitative Sociology*, 7(1/2): 75–89.

LYON, D. (2001). 'Facing the Future: Seeking Ethics for Everyday Surveillance'. *Ethics and Information Technology*, 3(3): 171–81.

MACKENZIE, D. (1990). *Inventing Accuracy: A Historical Sociology of Nuclear Missile Guidance*. Cambridge, MA: MIT Press.

—— and WAJCMAN, J. (eds) (1985). *The Social Shaping of Technology: Second Edition*. Milton Keynes: Open University Press.

MARCUSE, H. (1964). *One-Dimensional Man*. Boston, MA: Beacon.

—— (1998). *Technology, War and Fascism*. London: Routledge.

MCLUHAN, M. (1964). *Understanding Media: The Extensions of Man*. New York: McGraw Hill.

MARX, G. T. (1998). 'An Ethics for the New Surveillance'. *The Information Society*, 14(3): 171–85.

MILLER, J. and RESNICK, P. (1996). 'PICS: Internet Access Controls without Censorship'. *Communications of the ACM*, 39(10): 87–93.

MOHANTY, J. (1997). *Phenomenology: Between Essentialism and Transcendental Philosophy*. Evanston, IL: Northwestern University Press.

MOOR, J. H. (1985). 'What is Computer Ethics?' *Metaphilosophy*, 16(4): 266–79.

MUMFORD, L. (1934/1963). *Technics and Civilization*. New York: Harcourt, Brace and Co.

—— (1964/1970). *The Myth of the Machine: The Pentagon of Power*. New York: Harcourt, Brace, Jovanovich.

—— (1996). *Systems Design: Ethical Tools for Ethical Change*. London: Macmillan.

NORMAN, D. A. (1988). *The Psychology of Everyday Things*. New York: Basic Books.

—— (1990). *The Design of Everyday Things*. New York: Doubleday.

PELS, D. (1996). 'The Politics of Symmetry'. *Social Studies of Science*, 26(2): 277–304.

PFAFFENBERGER, B. (1992). 'Technological Dramas'. *Science, Technology, and Human Values*, 17: 282–312.

POSTMAN, N. (1993). *Technopoly: The Surrender of Culture to Technology*. New York: Alfred A. Knopf.

RADDER, H. (1992). 'Normative Reflexions on Constructivist Approaches to Science and Technology'. *Social Studies of Science*, 22(1): 141–73.

RHEINGOLD, H. (1993a). 'A Slice of Life in My Virtual Community', in L. Harasim (ed.), *Global Networks. Computers and International Communication*. Cambridge, MA: The MIT Press, 57–80.

—— (1993b). *The Virtual Communities: Homesteading on the Electronic Frontier*. Reading, MA: Addison-Wesley.

RICHARDSON, W. J. (1963/2003). *Heidegger: Through Phenomenology to Thought*. New York: Fordham University Press.

SASSEN, S. (2002). 'Towards a Sociology of Information Technology'. *Current Sociology*, 50(3): 365–88.

SILVERSTONE, R. (2002). 'Complicity and Collusion in the Mediation of Everyday Life'. *New Literary History*, 33(4): 761–80.

—— (2003). 'Proper Distance: Towards an Ethics for Cyberspace', in G. Liestol, A. Morrison and T. Rasmussen (eds), *Digital Media Revisited*. Cambridge, MA, MIT Press, 469–91.

SISMONDO, S. (1993) 'Some Social Constructions'. *Social Studies of Science*, 23(3): 515–53.

SPINELLO, R. A. and TAVANI, H. T. (eds) (2001). *Readings in CyberEthics*. Boston, MA: Jones and Bartlett Publishers.

TAVANI H. T. (2002). 'The Uniqueness Debate in Computer Ethics: What Exactly is at Issue, and Why Does it Matter?' *Ethics and Information Technology*, 4(1): 37–54.

TOFFLER, A. (1970). *Future Shock*. New York: Random House.

—— (1980). *The Third Wave*. New York: William Morrow and Co.

TURKLE, S. (1995). *Life on the Screen: Identity in the Age of the Internet*. New York: Simon and Schuster.

VIRILIO, P. (1994). *The Vision Machine*. Bloomington, IN: Indiana University Press.

WINNER, L. (1980). 'Do Artefacts Have Politics'. *Daedalus*, 109: 121–36.

—— (1993). 'Upon Opening the Black Box and Finding It Empty: Social Constructivism and the Philosophy of Technology'. *Science, Technology, and Human Values*, 18(3): 362–78.

WOLF, M. (ed.) (2003). *Virtual Morality: Morals, Ethics and New Media*. London: Peter Lang Publishing.

WOOLGAR, S. (1991). 'The Turn to Technology in Social Studies of Science'. *Science, Technology and Human Values*, 16(1): 20–50.

ZUBOFF, S. (1984). *In the Age of the Smart Machine: The Future of Work and Power*. New York: Basic Books.

NOTES

1. We acknowledge this approach as one alternative among many. E.g. one of the most common approaches for discussing the ethics of ICT and new media is to bring together different perspectives and different themes in an edited collection. Examples of these would be Dunlop and Kling (1991), Kling (1996), Wolf (2003), Johnson and Nissenbaum (1995) and Spinello and Tavani (2001).

2. The approach chosen here could be located in the debates about the technology and society relationship as found in the STS literature as well as the ICT Ethics literature. Obvious omissions from our analysis are a Marxist or Critical Theory perspective as reflected in the work of culture and media theorist Stuart Hall (1998), and a poststructuralist perspective as reflected in the work of Jean Baudrillard (1983) and Paul Virilio (1994).

3. Brey suggests that his taxonomy is based on the taxonomy of Sismondo (1993). There are obviously many debates possible about the degree of constructivism (and by implication essentialism) involved in the work of various authors. The intention here is just to highlight that this might condition the way ethical issues are raised as well as how or whether interventions might be proposed—see, e.g. Keulartz et al. (2004) for a discus-

sion of this. Refer also to the debate between Kling, and Woolgar and Grint in Volumes 16 and 17 of *Science, Technology & Human Values* in 1991 and 1992.

4. The degree to which constructivists do in fact maintain such symmetry has been the subject of vigorous debate (Pels 1996).

5. Moving from the 'early' Heidegger to the 'late' Heidegger in a way that suggests continuity (rather than a break) is not uncontroversial. However, I agree with the argument in Richardson (1963/2003) that there is fundamental continuity in his work. We do not feel one has to choose in an 'either/or' fashion as Latour (2004) seems to have done.

6. See also Introna and Ilharco (2004), Arnold (2003), and Heim (1993) for similar analyses of the screen, mobile phones, and virtual reality.

PART III

GOVERNANCE, DEMOCRACY, AND ICTs

THEME EDITOR:
ROBIN MANSELL

INTRODUCTION

IN this part, the contributors focus on the power of the media and communications as institutions, the potential of new technologies to empower and disempower, and the way ICTs influence governance arrangements and democratic practices. They consider both older forms of ICTs and the new digital media, and the circumstances in which these technologies can be mobilized to enhance democratic participation, to enable new social movements, and to influence the distribution of power in public and private domains. The role of e-government is examined as well as the spread of ICTs and their implications for privacy and security.

Saskia Sassen critiques the notion that social forms are becoming inherently distributive because of the technical capacities of electronic networks such as the Internet. In Chapter 14, she distinguishes the technical capacities of digital networks from complex socio-digital formations, arguing that many factors can shape network outcomes. She examines financial and activist networks to draw out the different ways in which decentralized access, simultaneity, and interconnectivity influence their outcomes, and evaluates their implications for governance and for democratic participation.

In Chapter 15, Stephen Coleman argues for the essential need to assess the ways in which new media technologies can support the norms and practices of political communication. He suggests that if the spread of information and unrestricted communication between citizens is to be encouraged as a foundation of democratic practice, much greater attention needs to be given to assumptions about how citizens and political leaders interact with ICTs. He reviews early 'teledemocracy' experiments and evaluates the Internet as a public communication network that has the potential to influence changes in the functions of political leadership, government organization, and political parties.

Nick Couldry in Chapter 16 suggests that all citizens require a share of a society's communicative resources if they are to participate effectively in the democratic process, and considers what form such resources should take. Arguing that 'digital divide' debates have pushed this issue to the centre of policy discussions he assesses what policies might be needed to achieve improved distributive equity with respect to these resources. His review of the literature provides an insight into how the communicative preconditions of democracy might be understood in the light of the growing use of ICTs. He makes the case for government intervention to ensure that all citizens acquire communicative capabilities as a means of stemming otherwise declining prospects for political engagement.

In Chapter 17, Patrick Dunleavy exposes the polarized attitudes towards ICTs expressed in the literature on technology applications in the public sector, and in the public management and public administration literatures. These range from those who regard technology as transformational, and beneficial for all aspects of governance, to those who treat ICTs as a minor disturbance, which should be largely ignored. He offers an analysis of how ICTs are being introduced to support different approaches to e-government. He argues that a more holistic vision of the way ICTs can be used to support the organization of government information is needed, accompanied by a better understanding of the implications of all these technologies, including web-based services, for organizational change within government.

Charles Raab assesses whether privacy is conceivable in a world that is heavily dependent on the use of ICTs and the capacity to process enormous quantities of personal data. In Chapter 18 he discusses different approaches to information privacy including how governments and other organizations attempt to regulate personal data, and the practice of sharing data across organizational boundaries. He examines the implications of the safety and security political agenda and terrorism and counter-terrorism measures in the light of interests in privacy protection.

In Chapter 19, David Lyon examines the social consequences of the 'surveillance society'. He argues that ICTs are enabling the large-scale collection and processing of personal details, which, for those involved in such activities, are offering new means of achieving influence and control. He suggests that the growth of surveillance needs to be considered in the light of basic political questions about social justice, and risk and freedom, since the availability of searchable databases that can be used to categorize and profile, can influence citizens' life chances positively or negatively.

CHAPTER 14

ELECTRONIC NETWORKS, POWER, AND DEMOCRACY

SASKIA SASSEN

1 INTRODUCTION

THE rapid proliferation of global computer-based networks and the digitization of a broad array of economic and political activities which can then circulate in those global networks raise questions about the effectiveness of current framings for state authority. Thereby, network technologies also point to the possibility of democratizing a whole range of practices precisely because they can escape hierarchical state controls and give free range to the distributive potential of digital networks. The possibility of exiting state regulatory frameworks has been seen both in positive terms—for example, the democratizing of spheres once subject to hierarchical controls—and in rather more negative terms—for example, the increasingly unregulated power of global finance. The most common positions on the issue are at either end of the spectrum: some argue that digitization neutralizes the regulatory capacities of national states, while others find that states continue to have basically the same regulatory power they have had for some time.

Easily left out of these types of debates are the diversity and specificity of 'socio-digital formations' (Latham and Sassen 2005: Intro.), and hence the possibility of whole new types of articulation between state authority and territory. This takes the analysis beyond the option of exiting state regulatory frameworks. One of the organizing efforts in this chapter is to focus on distinct socio-digital formations in order to understand their variable and often novel insertions into national territories. A second organizing effort in this chapter is to examine whether electronically networked social forms are in fact inherently distributive given their technical properties, and hence push towards democratizing outcomes. The focus is on digital interactive domains and for anlaytical purposes I distinguish the technical capacities of digital networks from the more complex socio-digital formations that such interactive domains actually constitute. Intervening mechanisms that may have little to do with the technology *per se* can reshape network outcomes such as distributed outcomes (with their strong connotations of democracy and of participation). The fact of this re-shaping by the social logics of users and of digitized actors carries implications for governance and democratic participation.

In principle, the range of empirical cases we could use to examine some of these issues is vast. Further, the specifics of each case make legible particular patterns, thereby undermining generalization. Given the enormous developments in information and communication technologies (ICTs), the highly specialized character of many of the pertinent regulatory regimes, and the rapidly growing literature on the subject, details would seem preferable to generalities. Thus, I briefly review the literature that addresses some of the general questions and conclusions that arise out of the fact that the technical properties of electronic interactive domains deliver their utilities through complex ecologies partly shaped by diverse social logics. And I go into greater depth on these questions by focusing on two very different types of socio-digital formations that I have researched over the years. Here I am confined to my past research, in a trade-off between generality and in-depth analysis. This detailed examination is then a vehicle to situate the more general scholarship on computer-centred interactive domains and their multiple insertions into, and exits from, systems of authority.

The two cases used to develop the argument empirically are electronic financial networks and electronic activist networks. Both cases are part of global dynamics and both have been significantly shaped by the three properties of digital networks—decentralized access/distributed outcomes, simultaneity, and interconnectivity. But these technical properties have produced strikingly different outcomes in each case. In one case, these properties contribute to distributive outcomes: greater participation of local organizations in global networks. Thereby they help constitute transboundary public spheres or forms of globality centred in multiple localized types of struggles and agency. In the second case, these same properties have led to higher levels of control and concentration in the global capital market even though the power of these financial electronic networks rests on a kind of distributed power, that is, millions of investors distributed around the world and their millions of individual decisions.

The particularities of these two cases serve to address several larger research agendas now under way. They include specifying, among others, the actual socio-digital formations arising from these mixes of technology and social interaction (Barry and Slater 2002; Berman 2002; Bennett and Entman 2001; Schuler 1996; Mansell and Silverstone 1996; Howard and Jones 2004), the possible new forms of sociality such mixes may be engendering (e.g. Castells 1996; Dutton 1999; Whittel 2001; Elmer 2004; Himanen 2001; Latham and Sassen 2005; Olesen 2005), the possible new forms of economic development and social justice struggles enabled by these technologies (Avgerou 2002; Credé and Mansell 1998; Gurstein 2000; Leizerov 2000; Mansell and Steinmueller 2002), and the consequences for state authority of digital networks that can override many traditional jurisdictions (Indiana Journal of Global Legal Studies 1998; Rosenau and Singh 2002; Johnson and Post 1996; Klein 2005; Bauchner 2000; Sassen 2006 (chs. 7, 8 and 9); Drake and Williams III 2006; Loader forthcoming).

These two cases also illuminate an emergent problematic about the extent to which the combination of decentralized access and multiple choices will tend to produce power law distributions regardless of the social logics guiding users. Thus civil society organizations may well produce outcomes similar to finance in that a limited number of organizations concentrate a disproportionate share of influence, visibility, and resources. One way of thinking about this is in terms of political formats (e.g. Dean, Anderson and Lovink 2006; Lovink 2003). That is to say, civil society organizations have been subjected to constraints that force them into a format—akin to that of incorporated firms with conventional accountability requirements—that keeps them from using the new technologies in more radical ways. Thus I would argue that finance succeeds in escaping conventional formats when two or more financial exchanges merge and thereby constitute a networked platform, allowing them to maximize the utilities of network technologies (Sassen 2006: chs. 7 and 8). In this sense, I would argue that finance has been far ahead of civil society in the use of networked technologies. It has actually invented new formats to accommodate its use: multi-sited networked platforms, where each financial centre is a node in the network. Civil society organizations have had many obstacles put in their way towards these types of networked arrangements. In many ways they have been forced to take the form of incorporated firms rather than networked platforms. There is, in my reading, a political issue here that functions as yet another variable contributing to produce diverse socio-digital formations even when similar network technologies are used.

The first part of the chapter discusses some of the general questions raised thus far. The second part examines the role of digitization in shaping today's global capital market and the extent to which it is or is not largely electronic, supra-national, and hence able to escape all territorial jurisdictions. And the third part examines the formation of types of global politics that run through the specificities of localized concerns and struggles yet can be seen as expanding democratic participation beyond state boundaries. I regard these as non-cosmopolitan versions of global politics. These types of politics raise questions about the relation of law to place that are the opposite of those raised by global finance.

2 RESHUFFLING THE TERRITORY–AUTHORITY LINK

The condition of the Internet as a decentralized network of networks has fed strong notions about its built-in autonomy from state power and its capacity to enhance democracy from the bottom up via a strengthening of both market dynamics and access by civil society. In a context of multiple partial and specific changes linked to globalization, digitization has contributed to the ascendance and greater weight of subnational scales, such as the global city, and supranational scales, such as global markets, where previously the national scale was dominant. These rescalings do not always parallel existing formalizations of state authority. At its most general these developments raise questions about the regulatory capacities of states, and about their potential for undermining state authority as it has come to be constituted over the last century.

But there are conditionalities not even these technologies can escape. Among these we might mention the social shaping of technology (e.g. Mackenzie and Wajcman 1999; Bowker and Star 1999; Latour 1996; Coleman 2004; Seely Brown and Duguid 2002; Lievrow and Livingstone 2002), the limits of what speed can add to an outcome (e.g. Mackenzie and Elzen 1994; Sassen 2006: ch. 7), the role of politics in shaping communication (e.g. Mansell and Silverstone 1996; Howard 2006; Lovink 2002; Dean 2002; Loader forthcoming; Tennant forthcoming), the built-in stickiness of existing technical options (e.g. Shaw 2001; Woolgar 2002; Newman 2001), and the segmentations within digital space (Lessig 1996; Loader 1998; Sassen 1999; Koopmans 2004; Schiller 1995; McChesney 2000; Monberg 1998).

Thus while digitization of instruments and markets was critical to the sharp growth in the value and power of the global capital market, this outcome was shaped by interests and logics that typically had little to do with digitization per se. This brings to the fore the extent to which digitized markets are embedded in complex institutional settings (e.g. Mackenzie and Millo 2003; Pauly 2002; Knorr Cetina and Predar 2004; Sassen 1991/2001), cultural frames (Thrift 2005; Zaloom 2003; Pryke and Allen 2000; more generally see Bell 2001; Trend 2001) and even intersubjective dynamics (Knorr Cetina and Bruegger 2002; Fisher 2006). And while the raw power achieved by the capital markets through digitization also facilitated the institutionalizing of finance-dominated economic criteria in national policy, digitization *per se* could not have achieved this policy outcome—it took actual national institutional settings and actors (Helleiner 1999; Pauly 2002; Sassen 2006: ch. 5; Harvey forthcoming; for cases beyond the financial markets see, e.g. Barfield, Heiduk and Welfens 2003; Waesche 2003).

In short, the supranational electronic market, which partly operates outside any government's exclusive jurisdiction, is only one of the spaces of global finance. The other type of space is one marked by the thick environments of actual financial centres, places where national laws continue to be operative, albeit laws that have been profoundly altered with the growth of a global economy. These multiple territorial insertions of private economic electronic space entail a complex interaction with national law and state authority. The notion of 'global cities' captures this particular embeddedness of various forms of global hypermobile capital— including financial capital—in a network of well over 40 financial centres across the world.[1] This embeddedness carries significant implications for theory and politics, specifically for the conditions through which governments and citizens can act on this new electronic world (e.g. Roseneau and Singh 2002; Kamarck and Nye 2002; Bousquet and Wills 2003; Sassen 2006: chs. 5, 8, and 9), though there are clearly limits (Robinson 2004; Olesen 2005; Dean, Anderson and Lovink 2006).

Producing capital mobility takes capital fixity: state-of-the-art environments, well-housed talent, and conventional infrastructure—from highways to airports and railways. These are all partly place-bound conditions, even when the nature of their place-boundedness differs from what it may have been a hundred years ago when place-boundedness was far more likely to be a form of immobility. But digitization also brings with it an amplification of capacities that enable the liquefying of what is not liquid, thereby producing or raising the mobility of what we have customarily thought of as not mobile, or barely so. At its most extreme, this liquefying digitizes its object. Yet the hypermobility gained by an object through digitization is but one moment of a more complex condition.

In turn, much place-boundedness is today increasingly—though not completely—inflected or inscribed by the hypermobility of some of its components, products, and outcomes. More than in the past, both fixity and mobility are located in a temporal frame where speed is ascendant and consequential. This type of fixity cannot be fully captured through a description confined to its material and locational features. The real estate industry illustrates some of these issues. Financial firms have invented instruments that liquefy real estate, thereby facilitating investment in real estate and its 'circulation' in global markets. Even though the physical remains part of what constitutes real estate, it has been transformed by the fact that it is represented by highly liquid instruments that can circulate in global markets. It may look the same, it may involve the same bricks and mortar, it may be new or old, but it is a transformed entity.[2]

Perhaps the opposite kind of articulation of law and territory from that of global finance is evident in a domain that has been equally transformed by digitization, but under radically different conditions. The key digital medium is the public access Internet, and the key actors are largely resource-poor organizations and individuals (for a range of instances see, e.g. Dahlgren 2001; Bennett 2003; Dutton 1999; Friedman 2005). This produces a specific kind of activism, one centred on multiple localities yet connected digitally at scales larger than the local, often reaching a global scale. As even small, resource-poor organizations and individuals can become participants in electronic networks, it signals the possibility of a sharp growth in cross-border politics by actors other than states (Warkentin 2001; Khagram, Riker and Sikkink 2002). What is of interest here is that while these are poor and localized actors, in some ways they can partly bypass territorial state jurisdictions and, though local, they can begin to articulate with others worldwide and thereby constitute an incipient global commons.

From the perspective of state authority and territorial jurisdictions, the overall outcome might be described as a destabilizing of older formal hierarchies of scale and an emergence of not fully formalized new ones. Older hierarchies of scale, dating from the period that saw the ascendance of the nation state, continue to operate. They are typically organized in terms of institutional level and territorial scope: from the international down to the national, the regional, the urban, and the local. But today's rescaling dynamics cut across institutional size and across the institutional encasements of territory produced by the formation of national states (Swyngedouw 1997; Taylor 2003; Graham 2003; Borja and Castells 1997). The next two sections focus in detail on some of these issues.

3 ELECTRONIC FINANCIAL NETWORKS

Electronic financial markets are an interesting case because they are perhaps the most extreme example of how the digital might reveal itself to be indeed free of any spatial and, more concretely, territorial conditionalities. A growing scholarship examines the more extreme forms of this possibility, vis-à-vis both finance and other sectors (e.g. *Indiana Journal of Global Legal Studies* 1998; Geist 2003; Korbin 2001). The mix of speed, interconnectivity, and enhanced leverage evinced by electronic markets produces an image of global finance as hypermobile and placeless. Indeed, it is not easy to demonstrate that these markets are embedded in anything social, let alone concrete, as in cement.

The possibility of an almost purely technical domain autonomous from the social is further reinforced by the growing role played by academic financial economics in the invention of new derivatives, today the most widely used instrument. It has led to an increasingly influential notion that if anything, these markets are embedded in academic financial economics. The latter has emerged since the 1980s as the shaper and legitimator, or the author and authorizer, of a new generation of derivatives (Callon 1998; MacKenzie 2003; Barrett and Scott 2004). Formal financial knowledge, epitomized by academic financial economics, is a key competitive resource in today's financial markets; work in that field thus also represents the 'fundamentals' of the market value of formal financial knowledge, that is, some of these instruments or models are more popular among investors than others.[3] Derivatives, in their many different modes, embody this knowledge and its market value.

But these technical capabilities, along with the growing complexity of instruments, actually generate a need for cultures of interpretation in the operation of these markets, cultures best produced and enacted in financial centres—that is, very territorial, complex, and thick environments. Thus, and perhaps ironically, as the technical and academic features of derivatives instruments and markets become stronger, these cultures become more significant in an interesting trade-off between technical capacities and cultural capacities (Sassen 2006: ch. 7). We can then use the need for these cultures of interpretation as an indicator of the limits of the academic embeddedness of derivatives and therewith recover the social architecture of derivatives trading markets. More specifically, it brings us back to the importance of financial centres—as distinct from financial 'markets'—as key, nested communities enabling the construction and functioning of such cultures of interpretation. This role of financial centres also, then, explains why the financial system needs a network of such centres (Budd 1995; Sassen 1991/2001). This need, in turn, carries implications for territorially bounded authority, and signals the formation of a specific type of territoriality, one marked by electronic networks and territorial insertions. Global cities are a more general, less narrowly technical instance of this same dynamic, including sectors other than finance. And beyond these types of formations there are other multi-sited global geographies—such as those binding Silicon Valley to Bangalore and kindred spaces. (See generally Corbridge et al. 1994; Taylor 2003; Graham 2003; Borja and Castells 1997; Aneesh 2006.)

Yet alongside these territorial insertions that give national states some traction in regulating even the most global of financial markets (and other kinds of global firms and markets), the massive increases in values traded have given finance a good measure of power over national governments. This increase is probably one of the most significant outcomes of digitization in finance, with three of its capacities particularly critical. One is the digitizing of financial instruments. Computers have facilitated the development of these instruments and enabled their widespread use. Much of the complexity can be contained in the software, enabling users who might not fully grasp either the financial mathematics or the software algorithms involved. Further, when softwaring facilitates proprietary rights it also makes innovations more viable. Through innovations finance has raised the level of liquidity in the global capital market and increased the possibilities for liquefying forms of wealth hitherto considered non-liquid. The overall result has been a massive increase in the securitizing of previously untradeable assets, including various kinds of debt, and hence a massive increase in the overall volumes of global finance. Mediated through the specifics of contemporary finance and financial markets, digitization can then be seen as having contributed to a vast increase in the range of transactions.

Secondly, the distinctive features of digital networks can maximize the advantages of global market integration: simultaneous interconnected flows and decentralized access for investors and for exchanges in a growing number of countries. The key background factor here is that since the late 1980s countries have de- and re-regulated their economies to ensure cross-border convergence and the global integration of their financial centres. This non-digital condition has amplified the new capabilities introduced by the digitization of markets and instruments.

Thirdly, because finance is particularly about transactions rather than simply flows of money, the technical properties of digital networks assume added meaning. Interconnectivity, simultaneity, decentralized access, and software instruments, all contribute to multiply the number of transactions, the length of transaction chains (i.e. the distance between instrument and underlying assets), and thereby the number of participants. The overall outcome is a complex architecture of transactions that promote exponential growth in numbers and value.[4]

These three features of today's global market for capital are inextricably related to the new technologies. The difference they have made can be seen in two consequences. One is the multiplication of specialized global financial markets. It is not only a question of global markets for equities, bonds, futures, currencies, but also of the proliferation of enormously specialized global sub-markets for each of these. This proliferation is a function of increased complexity in the instruments, in turn made possible by digitization of both markets and instruments.

The second consequence is that the combination of these conditions has contributed to the distinctive position of the global capital market in relation to several other components of economic globalization. We can specify two major traits; one concerns orders of magnitude and the second the spatial organization of finance. In terms of the first, indicators are the actual monetary values involved and, though more difficult to measure, the growing weight of financial criteria in economic transactions, sometimes referred to as the financializing of the economy. Since 1980, the total stock of financial assets has increased three times faster than the aggregate gross domestic product (GDP) of the 23 highly developed countries that formed the Organization for Economic Cooperation and Development (OECD) for much of this period; and the volume of trading in currencies, bonds, and equities has increased about five times faster and now surpasses it by far. This aggregate GDP stood at about US$30 trillion in 2000 and US$36 trillion in 2004, while the worldwide value of internationally traded derivatives had reached over US$65 trillion in the late 1990s, a figure that rose to US$168 trillion in 2001, and US$262 trillion in 2004. In contrast, the value of cross-border trade was US$11 trillion in 2004 and that of global foreign direct investment (FDI) stock, and US$8 trillion in 2004 (IMF 2005; BIS 2004). Foreign exchange transactions were ten times as large as world trade in 1983, but (according to the triannual survey of the BIS) 70 times larger in both 1999 and 2003, even though world trade also grew sharply over this period.

Another major set of issues about the transformative capacities of digitization has to do with the limits of technologically driven change, or, in other words, with the point at which this global electronic market for capital runs into the walls of its embeddedness in non-digital conditions. There are two distinct aspects here. One is the extent to which the global market for capital even though global and digital is actually embedded in multiple environments, some indeed global in scale, but others subnational, such as the actual financial centres within which the exchanges are located (MacKenzie and Millo 2003). A second issue is the extent to which it remains concentrated in a limited number of the most powerful financial centres notwithstanding its character as a global electronic market and the growing number of 'national' financial centres that constitute it (Sassen 2006: ch. 5; GAWC 2005). The deregulation of finance could conceivably have led to wide geographic dispersal of this most electronic and global of markets.

The sharp concentration in leading financial markets can be illustrated with a few facts.[5] London, New York, Tokyo (notwithstanding a national economic recession), Paris, Frankfurt, and a few other cities regularly appear at the top and represent a large share of global transactions. This holds even after the 9/11 attacks in New York that destroyed the World Trade Center (though it was mostly not a financial complex) and damaged over 50 surrounding buildings, home to much financial activity. The level of damage was seen by many as a wake-up call to the vulnerabilities of sharp spatial centralization in a limited number of sites. London, Tokyo, New York, Paris (now consolidated with Amsterdam and Brussels as Euro-Next), Hong Kong, and Frankfurt account for a major share of worldwide stock market capitalization. London, Frankfurt, and New York account for an enormous world share in the export of financial services. London, New York, and Tokyo account for over half of the foreign exchange market, one of the few truly global markets; together with Singapore, Hong Kong, Zurich, Geneva, Frankfurt, and Paris, they account for 85 per cent in this, the most global of markets. These high levels of concentration do not preclude increased activity in a large number of other markets, even though the latter may account for a small global share.

This trend towards consolidation in a few centres, even as the network of integrated financial centres expands globally, also is evident within countries. In the US for instance, New York concentrates the leading investment banks with only one other major international financial centre in this enormous country, Chicago. Sydney and Toronto have equally gained power in continental-sized countries, and have taken over functions and market share from what were once the major commercial centres, respectively Melbourne and Montreal. So have São Paulo and Bombay, which have gained share and functions from respectively Rio de Janeiro in Brazil, and New Delhi and Calcutta in India. These are all enormous countries and one might have thought that they could sustain multiple major financial centres, especially given their multi-polar urban system. It is not that secondary centres are not thriving, but rather that the leading centres have gained more rapidly and gained disproportionately from integration with global markets. This pattern is evident in many countries, including the leading economies of the world.

In brief, the private digital space of global finance intersects in at least two specific and often contradictory ways with the world of state authority and law (for more detail, see Sassen 2006: chs. 5 and 7). One is through the incorporation into national state policy of types of norms that reflect the operational logic of the global capital market rather than the national interest. The second is through the partial embeddedness of even the most digitized financial markets in actual financial centres, which partly returns global finance to the world of national governments although it does so under the umbrella of denationalized (i.e. global-oriented) components of the state regulatory apparatus. Global digitized finance makes legible some of the complex and novel imbrications between law and territory, notably that there is not simply an overriding of national state authority even in the case of this most powerful of global actors. There is, rather, both the use of national authority for the implementation of regulations and laws that respond to the interests of global finance (with associated denational-izing of the pertinent state capacities involved), and the renewed weight of that authority through the ongoing need of the global financial system for financial centres.

These conditions raise a number of questions about the impact of this concentration of capital in global markets which allow for accelerated circulation in and out of countries. The global capital market now has the power to 'discipline' national governments, that is to say, to subject to financial criteria various monetary and fiscal policies that previously may have been subject to broader economic or social criteria. Does this trend alter the functioning of democratic governments? While the scholarly literature has not directly raised or addressed such questions, we can find more general responses, ranging from those who find that in the end the national state still exercises the ultimate authority in regulating finance (e.g. Helleiner 1999; Pauly 2002), to those who see in the larger global economy an emergent power gaining at least partial ascendance over national states (Panitch 1996; Gill 1996).

4 A POLITICS OF PLACES ON CROSS-BORDER CIRCUITS

Digital media are critical for place-centred activists focused on local issues to connect with other such groups around the world. This is cross-border political work centred on the fact that specific types of local issues recur in localities across the world.[6] These are politics which, unlike hacktivism (Denning 1999) and cyberwar (Der Derian 2001), are partly embedded in non-digital environments that shape, give meaning to, and to some extent constitute the event. Such forms of activism contribute to an incipient unbundling of the exclusive authority, including symbolic authority, over territory and people we have long associated with the national state. That unbundling may well happen even when those involved are not necessarily problematizing the question of nationality or national identity; it can be a *de facto* unbundling of formal authority, one not predicated on a knowing rejection of the national.

None of this is historically new (Lustiger-Thaler and Dubet 2004). Yet there are two specific matters that signal the need for empirical and theoretical work on their ICT enabled form. One is that much of the conceptualization of the local in the social sciences has assumed physical or geographic proximity, and thereby a sharply defined territorial boundedness, with the associated implication of closure. The other, partly a consequence of the first, is a strong tendency to conceive of the local as part of a hierarchy of nested scales amounting to an institutionalized hierarchy, especially once there are national states. Even if these conceptualizations hold for most of what is the local today, the new ICTs are destabilizing these arrangements and invite us to reconceptualize the local so that it can accommodate instances that diverge from dominant patterns. Key among these current conditions are globalization and/or globality, as constitutive not only of cross-border institutional spaces, but also of powerful imaginaries enabling aspirations *to* transboundary political practice even when the actors involved are basically localized and not mobile.

Computer-centred interactive technologies facilitate multiscalar transactions and simultaneous interconnectivity among those largely confined to a locality. They can be used to further develop old strategies (e.g. Tsaliki 2002; Lannon 2002) and to develop new ways of organizing, notably electronic activism (Denning 1999; Smith 2001; Yang 2003; Rogers 2004). Internet media are the main type of ICT used, especially email, for organizations in the global south confined by little bandwidth and slow connections. To achieve the forms of globality that concern me in this chapter, it is important that there be a recognition of these technical constraints among major transnational organizations dealing with the global south: for instance, making text-only databases, with no visuals or HTML, no spreadsheets, and none of the other facilities that demand considerable bandwidth and fast connections (Pace and Panganiban 2002: 113; Electronic Frontier Foundation 2002).[7]

As has been widely recognized, new ICTs do not simply replace existing media techniques. The evidence is far from systematic and the object of study is continuously undergoing change. But we can basically identify two patterns. One is of no genuine need for, or, at best, under-utilization of these particular technologies given the nature of the organizing.[8] The other is creative utilization of the new ICTs along with older media to address the needs of particular communities, such as using the Internet to send audio files to be broadcast over loudspeakers to groups with no Internet connectivity, or literacy. The M. S. Swaminathan Research Foundation in southern India has supported such work by setting up Village Knowledge Centres catering to populations that even when illiterate, know exactly what types of information they need or want; for example, farmers and fishermen know the specific types of information they need at various times of the year. Amnesty International's International Secretariat has set up an infrastructure to collect electronic news feeds via satellite, which it then processes and redistributes to its staff workstations (Lebert 2003).

Use of these technologies has also contributed to forming new types of organizations and activism (Donk et al. 2005). Yang (2003) found that what were originally exclusively online discussions among groups and individuals in China concerned with the environment, evolved into active non-governmental organizations (NGOs). The diverse online hacktivisms examined by Denning (1999) are made up of mostly new types of activisms. Perhaps the most widely-known case of how the Internet made a strategic difference, the Zapatista movement, became two organizational efforts—one a local rebellion in the mountains of Chiapas in Mexico, the other a transnational electronic civil society movement joined by multiple NGOs concerned with peace, trade, human rights, and other social justice struggles. The movement functioned through both the Internet and conventional media (Cleaver 1998; Arquilla and Ronfeldt 2001; Olesen 2005), putting pressure on the Mexican government. It shaped a new concept for civil organizing: multiple rhizomatically connected autonomous groups (Cleaver 1998).

Far less known is that the local Zapatistas lacked an email infrastructure (Cleaver 1998), let alone collaborative workspaces on the web. Messages had to be hand-carried, crossing military lines to bring them to others for uploading to the Internet; further, the solidarity networks themselves did not all have email, and sympathetic local communities often had problems with access (Mills 2002: 83). Yet Internet-based media did contribute enormously, in good part because of pre-existing social networks, a fact that is important in social movements initiatives (Khagram, Riker and Sikkink 2002) and in other contexts, including business (see Garcia 2002). Among the electronic networks involved, LaNeta played a crucial role in globalizing the struggle. LaNeta is a civil society network established with support from a San Francisco-based NGO, the Institute for Global Communication (IGC). In 1993, LaNeta became a member of the Association for Progressive Communications (APC) and began to function as a key connection between civil society organizations within and outside Mexico. A local movement in a remote part of the country transformed LaNeta into a transnational information hub.

All of this facilitates a new type of cross-border politics, deeply local yet intensely connected digitally. Activists can develop networks for circulating place-based information (about local environmental, housing, and political conditions) that can become part of their political work, and they can strategize around global conditions—the environment, growing poverty and unemployment worldwide, lack of accountability among multinationals, and so forth. While such political practices have long existed with other media and with other velocities, the new ICTs change the orders of magnitude, scope, and simultaneity of these efforts. This inscribes local political practice with new meanings and new potentialities. These dynamics are also at work in the constituting of global public spheres that may have little to do with specific political projects (Sack 2005; Krause and Petro 2003), though they do not always work along desired or expected lines (Cederman and Kraus 2005).

Such multi-scalar politics of the local can exit the nested scalings of national state systems (e.g. Williamson, Alperovitz and Imbroscio 2002; Drainville 2005).[9] They can directly access other such local actors in the same country and city (Lovink and Riemens 2002), or across borders (Adams 1996; Tennant forthcoming). One Internet-based technology that reflects this possibility of escaping nested hierarchies of scale is the online workspace, often used for Internet-based collaboration (Bach and Stark 2005). Such a space can constitute a community of practice (Sharp 1997) or a knowledge network (Creech and Willard 2001). An example of an online workspace is the Sustainable Development Communications Network (Kuntze, Rottmann and Symons 2002) set up by a group of civil society organizations in 1998; it is a virtual, open, and collaborative organization to inform broader audiences about sustainable development, and build members' capacities to use ICTs effectively. It has a trilingual Sustainable Development Gateway to integrate and showcase members' communication efforts. It contains links to thousands of member-contributed documents, a job bank, and mailing lists on sustainable development. It is one of several NGOs whose aim is to promote civil society collaboration through ICTs; others include the Association for Progressive Communications (APC), One World International, and Bellanet.

The types of political practice discussed here are not the cosmopolitan route to the global. They are global through the knowing multiplication of local practices. These are types of sociability and struggle deeply embedded in people's actions and activities. They also involve institution-building work with global scope that can come from localities and networks of localities with limited resources, and from informal social actors. Actors 'confined' by domestic roles can become actors in global networks without having to leave their work and roles in home communities. But from being experienced as purely domestic and local, these 'domestic' settings become micro-environments on global circuits. They need not become cosmopolitan in this process; they may well remain domestic and particularistic in their orientation and continue to be engaged with their households, and local community struggles, even as they participate in emergent global politics. One possible outcome is a community of practice can emerge that creates multiple lateral, horizontal communications, collaborations, solidarities, and supports.

5 CONCLUSION

These two cases illuminate specific aspects of the capacities of digital technologies to override existing relations of law to territory, notably the possibility even for resource-poor actors partially to exit national encasements and emerge as global political actors. But these cases also illuminate the specific conditionalities under which this takes place: the digital and the nondigital moment in the often complex processes wherein these new technologies are deployed. This signals the formation of spatio-temporal orders that need to be distinguished from those of the national and those of the global; in short, these are orders that can cut across the duality of global/national.

Using these two cases helps illuminate the very diverse ways in which this partial overriding can happen. They are extreme cases, one marked by hypermobility and the other by immobility. But they show us that both are subject to particular types of embeddedness and to particular types of novel potentials for global operation. Financial markets and electronic activism reveal two parallel developments associated with particular technical properties of the new ICTs. They also reveal a third, radically divergent outcome, one I interpret as signalling the weight of the specific social logics of users in each case.

First, perhaps the most significant feature in both cases is the possibility of expanded decentralization and simultaneous integration. That local political initiatives can become part of a global network parallels the articulation of the capital market with a network of financial centres. That the former relies on public access networks and the latter on private dedicated networks does not alter this technical outcome. Among the technical properties that produce the specific utility in each case is the possibility of being global without losing the articulation with specific local conditions and resources. In fact, this articulation with the local is not only simultaneous, but also constitutive of each of these distinct formations. As with the global capital market, there is little doubt that digital networks have had a sharp impact on resource-poor organizations and groups engaged in cross-border work.

Secondly, once established, expanded decentralization and simultaneous integration enabled by global digital networks, produce threshold effects. Today's global electronic capital market can be distinguished from earlier forms of international financial markets due to some of the technical properties of the new ICTs, notably the orders of magnitude that can be achieved through decentralized simultaneous access and interconnectivity, and through the use of software in increasingly complex instruments which enables far more traders to use these instruments. In the second case, the threshold effect is the possibility of constituting transboundary publics and imaginaries rather than being confined to communication or information searches. In so far as the new network technologies strengthen and create new types of cross-border activities among non-state actors, they enable the constitution of a distinct and only partly digital condition variously referred to as global civil society, global publics, and commons.

Thirdly, the significant difference lies in the substantive rationalities, values, objectives, and conditionings to which each type of actor is subject. Once we introduce these issues, we can see a tendency in each domain toward cumulative causation leading to a growing differentiation in outcomes. The constitutive capabilities of the new ICTs lie in a combination of digital and nondigital variables. It is not clear that the technology alone could have produced the outcome. The nondigital variables differ sharply between these two cases, even as digitization is crucial for constituting the specificity of each case. The divergence is evident in the fact that the same technical properties produced greater concentration of power in the case of the capital market, and greater distribution of power in public access civil society oriented networks.

The issues introduced in this chapter point to the enormous capabilities of these technologies, but also to their limitations. It is in good part the social logics of users and actors that contribute to the outcomes, and hence to the 'distortion' of technical properties. The logics of users may not correspond to the engineer's design. The outcome of users' interaction with the technologies is a hybrid, an ecology that mixes technical properties and social logics. The fact of this re-shaping by the social logics of users and digitized actors carries implications for governance and democratic participation. They will not necessarily allow users to escape state authority, nor will they necessarily ensure democratic outcomes. They will not inevitably globalize users and eliminate their articulation with particular localities, but they will make globality a resource for users as diverse as the two examined here. The outcomes are not unidirectional and seamless. They are mixed, contradictory, and lumpy.

REFERENCES

ADAMS, P. C. (1996). 'Protest and the Scale Politics of Telecommunications'. *Political Geography*, 15(5): 419–41.

ANEESH, A. (2006). *Virtual Migration: The Programming of Globalization*. Durham, NC: Duke University Press.

ARQUILLA, J. and RONFELDT, D. F. (2001). *Networks and Netwars: The Future of Terror, Crime, and Militancy*. Santa Monica, CA: Rand.

AVGEROU, C. (2002). *Information Systems and Global Diversity*. Oxford: Oxford University Press.

AXEL, B. K. (2002). 'The Diasporic Imaginary'. *Public Culture*, 14(2): 411–28.

BACH, J. and STARK, D. (2005). 'Recombinant Technology and New Geographies of Association', in R. Latham and S. Sassen (eds), *Digital Formations: IT and New Architectures in the Global Realm*. Princeton, NJ: Princeton University Press, 37–53.

BARFIELD, C. E., HEIDUK, G., and WELFENS, P. J. J. (eds) (2003). *Internet, Economic Growth and Globalization: Perspectives on the New Economy in Europe, Japan and the USA*. New York: Springer.

BARRETT, M. and SCOTT, S. (2004). 'Electronic Trading and the Process of Globalization in Traditional Futures Exchanges: A Temporal Perspective. *European Journal of Information Systems*, 13(1): 65–79.

BARRY, A. and SLATER, D. (2002). 'Introduction: The Technological Economy'. *Economy and Society*, 31(2): 175–93.

BARTLETT, A. (2007 forthcoming). 'The Politics of Protest: Subjectivity, Migration and the New Urban Order', in S. Sassen (ed.), *Deciphering the Global: Its Spaces, Scales and Subject*. New York and London: Routledge.

BAUCHNER, J. S. (2000). 'State Sovereignty and the Globalizing Effects of the Internet: A Case Study of the Privacy Debate'. *Brooklyn Journal of International Law*, 26(2): 689–722.

BELL, D. (2001). *An Introduction to Cybercultures*. London: Routledge.

BELLANET (2002). 'Report on Activities 2001–2002', http://home.bellanet.org, accessed 18 Mar. 2006.

BENNETT, W. L. (2003). 'Communicating Global Activism: Strengths and Vulnerabilities of Networked Politics'. *Information, Communication & Society*, 6(2): 143–68.

—— and ENTMAN, R. M. (eds) (2001). *Mediated Politics: Communication in the Future of Democracy*. Cambridge: Cambridge University Press.

BERMAN, P. S. (2002). 'The Globalization of Jurisdiction'. *University of Pennsylvania Law Review*, 151: 314–17.

BIS (Bank for International Settlements) (2004). 'BIS Quarterly Review: International Banking and Financial Market Developments'. Basle: BIS Monetary and Economic Development.

BORJA, J. and CASTELLS, M. (1997). *The Local and the Global: Management of Cities in the Information Age*. London: Earthscan.

BOUSQUET, M. and WILLS, K. (eds) (2003). *Web Authority: Online Domination and the Informatics of Resistance*. Boulder, CO: Alt-x Press.

BOWKER, G. C. and STAR, S. L. (1999). *Sorting Things Out: Classification and its Consequences*. Cambridge, MA: MIT Press.

BUDD, L. (1995). 'Globalisation, Territory, and Strategic Alliances in Different Financial Centres'. *Urban Studies*, 32(2): 345–60.

CALLON, M. (1998). *The Laws of the Markets*. Oxford: Blackwell Publishers.

CASTELLS, M. (1996). *The Information Age: Economy, Society and Culture, Volume 1: The Rise of the Network Society*. Oxford: Blackwell.

CEDERMAN, L.-E. and KRAUS, P. A. (2005). 'Transnational Communications and the European Demos', in R. Latham and S. Sassen (eds), *Digital Formations: IT and New Architectures in the Global Realm*. Princeton, NJ: Princeton University Press, 283–311.

CLEAVER, H. (1998). 'The Zapatista Effect: The Internet and the Rise of an Alternative Political Fabric'. *Journal of International Affairs*, 51(2): 621–40.

COLEMAN, G. (2004). 'The Political Agnosticism of Free and Open Source Software and the Inadvertent Politics of Contrast'. *Anthropological Quarterly*, 77(3): 507–19.

CORBRIDGE, S., THRIFT, N. and MARTIN, R. (eds) (1994). *Money, Power and Space*. Oxford: Blackwell.

CREDÉ, A. and. MANSELL, R. E. (1998). *Knowledge Societies...in a Nutshell: Information Technology for Sustainable Development*. Ottawa: International Development Research Centre (IDRC).

CREECH, H. and WILLARD, T. (2001). *Strategic Intentions: Managing Knowledge Networks for Sustainable Development*. Winnipeg: International Institute for Sustainable Development.

DAHLGREN, P. (2001). 'The Public Sphere and the Net: Structure, Space, and Communication', in W. L. Bennett and R. M. Entman (eds), *Mediated Politics: Communication in the Future of Democracy*. Cambridge: Cambridge University Press: 33–55.

DEAN, J. (2002). *Publicity's Secret: How Technoculture Capitalizes on Democracy*. Ithaca, NY: Cornell University.

——, ANDERSON, J. W. and LOVINK, G. (2006) *Reformatting Politics: Information Technology and Global Civil Society*. London: Routledge.

DENNING, D. (1999). *Information Warfare and Security*. New York: Addison-Wesley.

DER DERIAN, J. (2001). *Virtuous War: Mapping the Military–Industrial–Media–Entertainment Network*. Boulder, CO: Westview Press.

DRAINVILLE, A. (2005). *Contesting Globalization: Space and Place in the World Economy*. London: Routledge.

DRAKE, W. J. and WILLIAMS III, E. M. (2006). *Governing Global Electronic Networks: International Perspectives on Policy and Power*. Cambridge, MA: MIT Press.

DUTTON, W. H. (ed.) (1999). *Society on the Line: Information Politics in the Digital Age*. Oxford: Oxford University Press.

Electronic Frontier Foundation (2002). 'Activist Training Manual', presented at the Ruckus Society Tech Toolbox Action Camp, 24 June–2 July.

ELMER, G. (2004). *Profiling Machines: Mapping the Personal Information Economy*. Cambridge, MA: MIT Press.

FISHER, M. S. (2006). 'Navigating Wall Street Women's Gendered Networks in the New Economy', in M. Fisher and G. Downey (eds), *Frontiers of Capital: Ethnographic Reflections on the New Economy*. Durham, NC: Duke University Press, 209–36.

—— and DOWNEY, G. (eds) (2006). *Frontiers of Capital: Ethnographic Reflections on the New Economy*. Durham, NC: Duke University Press.

FRIEDMAN, E. J. (2005). 'The Reality of Virtual Reality: The Internet and Gender Equality Advocacy in Latin America'. *Latin American Politics and Society,* 47: 1–34.

GARCIA, L. (2002). 'Architecture of Global Networking Technologies', in S. Sassen (ed.), *Global Networks, Linked Cities.* London: Routledge, 39–70.

GAWC (Globalization and World Cities Study Group and Network) (2005). http://www.lboro.ac.uk/gawc/, accessed 18 Mar. 2006.

GEIST, M. (2003). 'Cyberlaw 2.0'. *Boston College Law Review,* 44: 323–58.

GILL, S. (1996). 'Globalization, Democratization, and the Politics of Indifference', in J. Mittelman (ed.), *Globalization: Critical Reflections.* Boulder, CO: Lynne Rienner Publishers, 205–28.

GLASIUS, M., KALDOR, M. and ANHEIER, J. (eds) (2002). *Global Civil Society Yearbook 2002.* Oxford: Oxford University Press.

GOLDSMITH, J. (1998). 'Against Cyberanarchy'. *University of Chicago Law Review,* 65: 1199–1250.

GRAHAM, S. (ed.) (2003). *The Cybercities Reader.* London: Routledge.

GURSTEIN, M. (ed.) (2000). *Community Informatics: Enabling Communities with Information and Communication Technologies.* Hershey, PA: Idea Group.

HARVEY, R. (2007). 'The Subnational Constitution of Global Markets', in S. Sassen (ed.), *Deciphering the Global: Its Spaces, Scales and Subjects.* New York and London: Routledge.

HELLEINER, E. (1999) 'Sovereignty, Territoriality and the Globalization of Finance', in D. A. Smith, D. J. Solinger and S. Topik and (eds), *States and Sovereignty in the Global Economy.* London: Routledge, 138–57.

HIMANEN, P. (2001). *The Hacker Ethic and the Spirit of the Information Age.* New York: Random House.

HOWARD, P. N. (2006). *New Media Campaigns and the Managed Citizen.* New York: Cambridge University Press.

—— and JONES, S. (eds) (2004). *Society Online: The Internet in Context.* London: Sage.

IMF (International Monetary Fund) (2005). 'International Financial Statistics'. Washington DC: IMF.

INDIANA JOURNAL OF GLOBAL LEGAL STUDIES (1998). 'Symposium: The Internet and the Sovereign State: The Role and Impact of Cyberspace on National and Global Governance', 5(2).

IZQUIERDO, J. A. (2001). 'Reliability at Risk: The Supervision of Financial Models as a Case Study for Reflexive Economic Sociology'. *European Societies,* 3(1): 69–90.

JOHNSON, D. and POST, D. (1996). 'Law and Borders – The Rise of Law in Cyberspace'. *Stanford Law Review,* 48: 1367–402.

JUDD, D. R. (1998). 'The Case of the Missing Scales: A Commentary on Cox'. *Political Geography,* 17(1): 29–34.

KAMARCK, E. C. and NYE, J. S. (eds) (2002). *Governance.Com: Democracy in the Information Age.* Washington DC: Brookings Institution Press.

KHAGRAM, S., RIKER, J. V. and SIKKINK, K. (eds) (2002). *Restructuring World Politics: Transnational Social Movements, Networks, and Norms.* Minneapolis, MN: University of Minnesota Press.

KLEIN, H. (2005). 'ICANN Reform: Establishing the Rule of Law', prepared for the World Summit on the Information Society (WSIS), http://www.ip3.gatech.edu/images/ICANN-Reform_Establishing-the-Rule-of-Law.pdf, accessed 18 Mar. 2006.

KNORR CETINA, K. and BRUEGGER, U. (2002). 'Global Microstructures: The Virtual Societies of Financial Markets'. *American Journal of Sociology*, 107(4): 905–50.

—— and PREDA, A. (eds) (2004). *The Sociology of Financial Markets*. Oxford: Oxford University Press.

KOOPMANS, R. 2004, 'Movements and Media: Selection Processes and Evolutionary Dynamics in the Public Sphere'. *Theory and Society*, 33(3–4): 367–91.

KORBIN, S. J. (2001). 'Territoriality and the Governance of Cyberspace'. *Journal of International Business Studies*, 32(4): 687–704.

KRAUSE, L. and PETRO, P. (eds) (2003). *Global Cities: Cinema, Architecture, and Urbanism in a Digital Age*. New Brunswick, NJ and London: Rutgers University Press.

KUNTZE, M., ROTTMANN, S. and SYMONS, J. (2002). *Communications Strategies for World Bank and IMF-Watchers: New Tools for Networking and Collaboration*. London: Bretton Woods Project and Ethical Media, http://www.brettonwoodsproject.org/strategy/commosrpt.pdf, accessed 18 Mar. 2006.

LANNON, J. (2002). 'Technology and Ties that Bind: The Impact of the Internet on Non-Governmental Organizations Working to Combat Torture'. Unpub. MA thesis, University of Limerick.

LATHAM, R. and SASSEN, S. (2005). 'Introduction. Digital Formations: Constructing an Object of Study', in R. Latham and S. Sassen (eds), *Digital Formations: IT and New Architectures in the Global Realm*. Princeton NJ: Princeton University Press, 1–34.

LATOUR, B. (1996). *Aramis or the Love of Technology*. Cambridge, MA: Harvard University Press.

LEBERT, J. (2003). 'Writing Human Rights Activism: Amnesty International and the Challenges of Information and Communication Technologies', in M. McCaughey and M. Ayers (eds), *Cyberactivism: Online Activism in Theory and Practice*. London: Routledge; 209–32.

LIEVROUW, L. A. and LIVINGSTONE, S. (eds) (2002). *Handbook of New Media: Social Shaping and Consequences of ICTs*. London: Sage Publications.

LEIZEROV, S. (2000). 'Privacy Advocacy Groups versus Intel: A Case Study of How Social Movements Are Tactically Using the Internet to Fight Corporations'. *Social Science Computer Review*, 18(4): 461–83.

LESSIG, L. (1996). 'The Zones of Cyberspace'. *Stanford Law Review*, 48: 1403–12.

LOADER, B. D. (ed.) (1998). *Cyberspace Divide: Equality, Agency, and Policy in the Information Age*. London: Routledge.

—— (2007 forthcoming). *Beyond E-Government*. London and New York: Routledge.

LOVINK, G. (2002). *Dark Fiber: Tracking Critical Internet Culture*. Cambridge, MA: MIT Press.

—— (2003). *My First Recession: Critical Internet Culture in Transition*. Rotterdam: VP2/NAi Publishing.

LUSTIGER-THALER, H. and DUBET, F. (eds) (2004). 'Social Movements in a Global World.' SI of *Current Sociology*, 52(4): 555–725.

MACKENZIE, D. (2003). 'Long-Term Capital Management and the Sociology of Arbitrage'. *Economy and Society*, 32(3): 349–80.

—— with ELZEN, B. (1994). 'The Social Limits of Speed: The Development and Use of Supercomputers'. *IEEE Annals of the History of Computing*, 16(1): 46–61.

—— and WAJCMAN, J. (eds) (1999). *The Social Shaping of Technology: Second Edition*. Milton Keynes: Open University Press.

MacKenzie, D. and Millo, Y. (2003). 'Constructing a Market, Performing Theory: The Historical Sociology of a Financial Derivatives Exchange'. *American Journal of Sociology*, 109(1): 107–45.

McChesney, R. (2000). *Rich Media, Poor Democracy*. New York: New Press.

Mansell, R. and Silverstone, R. (1996). *Communication by Design: The Politics of Information and Communication Technologies*. Oxford: Oxford University Press.

—— and Steinmueller, W. E. (2002). *Mobilizing the Information Society: Strategies for Growth and Opportunity*. Oxford: Oxford University Press.

Mills, K. (2002). 'Cybernations: Identity, Self-Determination, Democracy, and the "Internet Effect" in the Emerging Information Order'. *Global Society*, 16(1): 69–87.

Monberg, J. (1998). 'Making the Public Count: A Comparative Case Study of Emergent Information Technology-Based Publics'. *Communication Theory*, 8(4): 426–54.

Morrill, R. (1999). 'Inequalities of Power, Costs and Benefits Across Geographic Scales: The Future Uses of the Hanford Reservation'. *Political Geography*, 18(1): 1–23.

Newman, J. (2001). 'Some Observations on the Semantics of Information'. *Information Systems Frontiers*, 3(2): 155–67.

Olesen, T. (2005). 'Transnational Publics: New Spaces of Social Movement Activism and the Problem of Long-Sightedness'. *Current Sociology*, 53(3): 419–40.

Pace, W. R. and Panganiban, R. (2002). 'The Power of Global Activist Networks: The Campaign for an International Criminal Court', in P. I. Hajnal (ed.), *Civil Society in the Information Age*. Aldershot: Ashgate: 109–26.

Panitch, L. (1996). 'Rethinking the Role of the State', in J. Mittleman (ed.), *Globalization: Critical Reflections*. Boulder, CO: Lynne Rienner Publishers, 83–111.

Pauly, L. (2002). 'Global Finance, Political Authority, and the Problem of Legitimation', in R. B. Hall and T. J. Biersteker (eds), *The Emergence of Private Authority and Global Governance*. Cambridge: Cambridge University Press, 76–90.

Pryke, M. and Allen, J. (2000). 'Monetized Time-Space: Derivatives—Money's "New Imaginary"?' *Economy and Society*, 29(2): 329–44.

Riemens, P. and Lovink, G. (2002). 'Local Networks: Digital City Amsterdam', in S. Sassen (ed.), *Global Network/Linked Cities*. New York: Routledge, 327–46.

Robinson, S. (2004). 'Towards a Neoapartheid System of Governance with IT Tools', SSRC IT & Governance Study Group. New York: SSRC, http://www.ssrc.org/programs/itic/publications/knowledge_report/memos/robinsonmemo4.pdf, accessed 18 Mar. 2006.

Rogers, R. (2004). *Information Politics on the Web*. Cambridge, MA: MIT Press.

Rosenau, J. N. and Singh, J. P. (eds) (2002). *Information Technologies and Global Politics: The Changing Scope of Power and Governance*. Albany, NY: State University of New York Press, 275–87.

Sack, W. (2005). 'Discourse Architecture, and Very Large-scale Conversation', in R. Latham and S. Sassen (eds), *Digital Formations: IT and New Architectures in the Global Realm*. Princeton, NJ: Princeton University Press, 242–82.

Sassen, S. (2006). *Territory, Authority, Rights: From Medieval to Global Assemblages*. Princeton, NJ: Princeton University Press.

—— (1999). 'Digital Networks and Power', in M. Featherstone and S. Lash (eds), *Spaces of Culture: City, Nation, World*. London: Sage, 49–63.

—— (1991/2001). *The Global City*. Princeton, NJ: University Press.

Schiller, H. I. (1995). *Information Inequality*. London: Routledge.

Schuler, D. (1996). *New Community Networks: Wired for Change*. Boston, MA: Addison-Wesley Publishing Co.

SEELY BROWN, J. and DUGUID, P. (2002). *The Social Life of Information*. Cambridge, MA: Harvard Business School Press.

SHARP, J. (1997). 'Communities of Practice: A Review of the Literature', 12 March, http://www.tfriend.com/cop-lit.htm, accessed 18 Mar. 2006.

SHAW, D. (2001). 'Playing the Links: Interactivity and Stickiness in .Com and "Not.Com" Web Sites'. *First Monday*, 6: http://www.firstmonday.dk/issues/issue6_3/shaw, accessed 18 Mar. 2006.

SMITH, P. J. (2001). 'The Impact of Globalization on Citizenship: Decline or Renaissance'. *Journal of Canadian Studies*, 36(1): 116–40.

SWYNGEDOUW, E. (1997). 'Neither Global nor Local: "Globalization" and the Politics of Scale', in K. R. Cox (ed.), *Spaces of Globalization: Reasserting the Power of the Local*. New York: Guilford, 137–66.

TAYLOR, P. J. (2003). *World City Network: A Global Urban Analysis*. London: Routledge.

TENNANT, E. W. (2007 forthcoming). 'Locating Transnational Activists: Solidarity with and Beyond Propinquity', in S. Sassen (ed.), *Deciphering the Global: Its Spaces, Scales and Subjects*. New York and London: Routledge.

THOMSONS FINANCIALS (1999). *1999 International Target Cities Report*. New York: Thomson Financial Investor Relations.

THRIFT, N. (2005). *Knowing Capitalism*. Thousand Oaks, CA: Sage.

TREND, D. (ed.) (2001). *Reading Digital Culture*. Oxford: Blackwell.

TSALIKI, L. (2002). 'Online Forums and the Enlargement of the Public Space: Research Findings from a European Project'. *The Public*, 9(2): 95–112.

VAN DE DONK, W., LOADER, B. D., MIXON, P. G. et al. (eds) (2005). Cyberprostest: New Media, Citizens, and Social Movements, London: Routledge.

WAESCHE, N. M. (2003). *Internet Entrepreneurship in Europe: Venture Failure and the Timing of Telecommunications Reform*. Cheltenham: Edward Elgar.

WARKENTIN, C. (2001). *Reshaping World Politics: NGOs, the Internet, and Global Civil Society*. Lanham, MD: Rowman & Littlefield.

WHITTEL, A. (2001). 'Toward a Network Sociality'. *Theory, Culture & Society*, 18(6): 51–76.

WILLIAMSON, T., ALPEROVITZ, G. and IMBROSCIO, D. L. (2002). *Making a Place for Community: Local Democracy in a Global Era*. London: Routledge.

WOOLGAR, S. (ed.) (2002). *Virtual Society? Technology, Cyberpole, Reality*. Oxford: Oxford University Press.

YANG, G. (2003). 'Weaving a Green Web: The Internet and Environmental Activism in China', *China Environment Series*, No. 6. Washington DC: Woodrow Wilson International Centers for Scholars.

ZALOOM, C. (2003). 'Ambiguous Numbers: Trading Technologies and Interpretation in Financial Markets'. *American Ethnologist*, 30(2): 258–72.

NOTES

1. For instance, the growth of electronic network alliances among financial exchanges located in different cities makes legible that electronic markets are partly embedded in the concentrations of material resources and human talents of financial centres, because

part of the purpose of these alliances is to capture the specific advantages of each of the financial centres (Sassen 2006: ch. 7). Thus, such alliances are not about transcending the exchanges involved or merging everything into one exchange.

2. I use the term imbrication to capture this simultaneous interdependence and specificity of both the digital and the nondigital. They work on each other, but they do not produce hybridity in this process. Each maintains its distinct irreducible character (Sassen 2006: ch. 7).

3. The model designed for Long Term Capital Management (LTCM) was considered a significant and brilliant innovation. Others adopted similar arbitrage strategies, despite the fact that LTCM did its best to conceal its strategies (MacKenzie 2003). MacKenzie and Millo (2003) posit that two factors ensured the success of option pricing theory (Black-Scholes) in the Chicago Board Options Exchange. First, the markets gradually changed (e.g. alterations of Regulation T, the increasing acceptability of stock borrowing, and better communications) so that the assumptions of the model became increasingly realistic. Secondly, the spread of what I would describe as a particular technical culture of interpretation in the context of globalized economic processes gradually reduced barriers to the model's widespread use. The performativity of this model was not automatic but 'a contested, historically contingent outcome, ended by a historical event, the crash of 1987' (MacKenzie 2003: 138). On the supervising of risk in financial markets see, e.g. Izquierdo (2001).

4. Elsewhere (Sassen 2006: chs 5 and 7) I have developed this thesis of finance today as being increasingly transaction-intensive and hence as raising the importance of financial centres because they contain the capabilities for managing this transactivity precisely at a time when the latter assumes whole new features given digitization.

5. Among the main sources of data for the figures cited in this section are the International Bank for Settlements (Basle); International Monetary Fund (IMF) national accounts data; specialized trade publications such as the *Wall Street Journal's WorldScope; Morgan Stanley Capital International; The Banker*; data listings in the *Financial Times* and in *The Economist*; and, especially for a focus on cities, the data produced by Technimetrics, Inc. (now part of Thomsons Financial, 1999).

6. This parallels cases where use of the Internet has allowed diasporas to be globally interconnected rather than confined to a one-to-one relationship with the country or region of origin (see, e.g. Glasius, Kaldor and Anheier 2002; Axel 2002; Bartlett forthcoming).

7. There are several organizations that work on adjusting to these constraints or providing adequate software and other facilities to disadvantaged NGOs. For instance, Bellanet (2002), a nonprofit organization set up in 1995, helps such NGOs gain access to online information and with information dissemination to the south. To that end it has set up web-to-email servers that can deliver web pages by email to users confined to low bandwidth. It has developed multiple service lines. Bellanet's Open Development service line seeks to enable collaboration among NGOs through the use of open source software, open content, and open standards; so it customized the Open Source PhP-Nuke software to set up an online collaborative space for the Medicinal Plants Network. Bellanet has adopted Open Content making all forms of content on its web site freely available to the public; it supports the development of an open standard for project information (International Development Markup Language—IDML). Such open standards enable information sharing.

8. A study of the web sites of international and national environmental NGOs in Finland, Britain, the Netherlands, Spain, and Greece, (Tsaliki 2002: 102) concludes that the Internet is mainly useful for intra- and interorganizational collaboration and networking, mostly complementing existing media techniques for issue-promotion and awareness-raising.

9. The possibility of exiting or avoiding scale hierarchies by actors lacking power does not keep powerful actors from using the existence of different jurisdictional scales to their advantage (Morrill 1999) nor does it keep states from constraining local resistance through jurisdictional, administrative, and regulatory orders (Judd 1998).

CHAPTER 15

E-DEMOCRACY: THE HISTORY AND FUTURE OF AN IDEA

STEPHEN COLEMAN

1 INTRODUCTION

THE post-Athenian democratic relationship, in which political representatives speak for the absent demos and media gatekeepers translate between the intimate sphere of individualized experience and the impersonal, public sphere in which strangers must live together as citizens, is blighted by inevitable problems of miscommunication. Political representatives are accused of being 'out of touch' and not listening to the public. The media are blamed for being simplistic, cynical, and sensationalist. The public are depicted as lacking the attentiveness, political literacy, and moral energy required of active citizens. There is a powerful desire for more effective communicative structures, techniques, and technologies that can facilitate the free spread of information and unrestricted communication between citizens. The purpose of this chapter is to explore ways in which, theoretically and empirically, new digital media technologies can support the norms and practices of democratic political communication.

2 MEDIA, DEMOCRACY, AND DETERMINISM

Rhetorical claims for the democratizing effects of new media have been a perennial feature of modernity, attributing to successive generations of communication technology the capacity to bring about what Peters (1992: 2) has referred to as 'a utopia where nothing is misunderstood, hearts are open, and expression is uninhibited'. For example, Lytton Butler was convinced that the rise of the popular press in the 1830s would mean that 'a new majority must be consulted, the sentiments and desires of poorer men than at present must be addressed; and thus a new influence of opinion would be brought to bear on our social relations and our legislative enactments' (Burke and Briggs 2001: 202). The invention of the telegraph in the 1850s led one member of the US Congress to predict that 'Space will be, to all practical purposes of information, annihilated between the States of the Union, as also between the individual citizens thereof'. Edward Bellamy's (1887/1996) popular nineteenth century utopia, *Looking Backward* (which William Morris dismissed as 'a cockney paradise') envisaged wireless as an instrument of cultural unification; in the 1930s H. G. Wells argued in favour of a 'World Brain': 'a unified, if not a centralized, world organ to "pull the mind of the world together"' (Wells 1937: 1) by collecting, indexing, summarizing, and disseminating all the knowledge in the world; and in 1945 Vannevar Bush envisaged the invention of a desk-sized computer called 'memex' which would provide access to an encyclopaedic array of facts, 'ready-made with a mesh of associative trails running through them' (Bush 1945: 108).

Deterministic claims that new media technologies are bound to lead to more democratic outcomes have been rightly criticized for neglecting the ways in which technologies are themselves socially shaped, and for conceiving political relationships in an excessively functional and mechanistic fashion that misses the cultural and ideological dynamics of social power. McLuhan's (1964: 23) famous distinction between 'hot media', which are 'low in participation', and 'cool media', which 'are high in participation or completion by the audience', exemplifies such determinism. Media technologies are neither inherently participatory nor exclusive, but depend upon cultural practices and policy contestations. The history of radio is a case in point. In the early twentieth century, amateur enthusiasts regarded radio technology as a tool for interpersonal (and inter-communal) communication, while governments conceived it as a means of centrally regulated broadcast transmission. Herbert Hoover as US Secretary of Commerce took the view that 'The use of the radio telephone for communication between single individuals...is a perfectly hopeless notion' (cited by Carty 1923: 3), whereas Brecht (1932: 53) argued that the 'broadcasting system would be the most wonderful communication apparatus...imaginable in public life, a fantastic channel system, that is, if it understood not only to transmit but also to receive, in other words, to make the listener not only hear but also speak, and not to isolate him [sic], but to involve him in a relationship'.

The hot or cool character of radio as a medium had less to do with its evolution as a centrally regulated system of broadcasting than did political concerns about the control of public information and (in the US rather than Britain) economic ambitions to commercialize the airwaves.

In the late 1960s, with the introduction of portable video and broadband cable television (TV), renewed hopes for a more participatory form of political communication were raised. According to Dutton (1992: 505), 'stimulated by the promises surrounding two-way interactive cable TV systems, proponents saw the convergence of computing and telecommunications as offering a technological fix to the many pragmatic constraints on more direct participation in governance'. In Canada, Henaut and Klein's pioneering work with the *Challenge for Change* project gave communities access to video technology, enabling them to record their social concerns, which were later shown at public meetings and to government officials. Experiments in community access to media technologies led to a revival of the Brechtian vision of interactive public communication. Shamberg, whose 1971 book, *Guerilla Television*, became a counter-cultural manifesto for the democratization of public communication, argued that 'The inherent potential of information technology can restore democracy in America if people will become skilled with information tools' (Shamberg and Raindance Corporation 1971: 28). The failure of Shamberg and his associates to recognize the more formidable politico-economic barriers to media democracy than simply providing citizens with video-production skills reflected a degree of naivete. As Enzensberger (1970: 34) observed, 'Anyone who expects to be emancipated by technological hardware . . . is the victim of an obscure belief in progress'.

The emergence of cable TV in the US, and the 1972 ruling by the Federal Communications Commission (FCC) that cable operators had an obligation to provide access channels for educational, local government and public use, was seen by enthusiasts as having 'the potential to rehumanize a dehumanized society, to eliminate the existing bureaucratic restrictions of government regulation common to the industrial world, and to empower the currently powerless public' (Streeter 1987: 181). This optimism was countered by harsh economic realities: the deregulatory atmosphere within which cable TV flourished was not ultimately conducive to civic imperatives and investment in viewer feedback declined, except for such services as teleshopping and evangelical pay-to-pray services.

Nonetheless, a number of interesting 'teledemocracy' experiments were pursued in the 1970s and 1980s, taking advantage of the growing convergence between computers, telecommunications and interactive cable TV (Hollander 1985; Arterton 1987; Grossman 1995). In 1972, Etzioni developed the MINERVA (Multiple Input Network for Evaluating Reactions, Votes and Attitudes) project, designed to enable 'masses of citizens to have discussions with each other, and which will enable them to reach group decisions without leaving their homes or crowding into a giant hall' (Etzioni 1972: 1). The system involved telephone conferencing, radio, two-way cable TV and satellites. In the 1980s Becker and Slaton were associated with a number of 'televote' experiments in Honolulu, Hawaii, and southern California, in which random groups of citizens were contacted by telephone, invited to study a brochure containing policy information and varied opinions and then asked to vote on a policy question. Few of these projects were sustained or integrated within the constitutional mechanisms of state governance, but they served to spur creative thinking among political theorists about the putative relationship between interactive communication technologies and more participatory forms of democratic governance.

It was the emergence in the 1990s of the Internet as a public communication network, however, which provided an impetus for some of the most grandiose narratives of technocratic determinism. This hyperbolic tendency had three main characteristics. First, cyber-visionaries depicted the Internet as a new frontier, a deterritorialized cyber-utopia beyond the comprehension or control of the political state. John Perry Barlow's *Declaration of the Independence of Cyberspace*, heralding a new world devoid of 'privilege or prejudice', in which 'legal concepts of property, expression, identity, movement, and context do not apply', exemplified what Barbrook and Cameron referred to as 'the Californian ideology' (Barlow 1996; Barbrook and Cameron 1997).

A second feature of this technocratic determinism was a belief that the feedback path of the Internet would enable mass democratic societies to transcend political representation and allow everyone to vote directly on every issue (Becker and Slaton 2000; Grossman 1995; Etzioni 1992). Dick Morris, who was at one time chief strategic adviser to President Bill Clinton, predicted the imminent arrival of plebiscitary, Jeffersonian democracy: 'Whether direct Internet democracy is good or bad is quite beside the point. It is inevitable. It is coming and we had better make our peace with it...Restricting the power of the people is no longer a viable option. The Internet made it obsolete' (Morris 2000: 5).

Thirdly, many of those who entertained sanguine hopes about the democratic potential of online politics failed to recognize the implicit codes of rationality built into the hardware and software through which most people access the Internet. As Street (1997) suggests, technical fixes are less about 'fixing' a problem than imposing a definition of that problem to which technology is often seen as a 'happy solution'. Such 'definitions' and 'solutions' reflect particular interests and perspectives, which are rarely transparent or accountable.

These elements of hyperbole and naiveté flourished in the heady atmosphere of the dotcom boom, supported by mantras such as 'the Internet changes everything' and 'information wants to be free'. After the dotcom bubble burst, a more sober, empirically-based research agenda emerged, exploring the effects of new information sources upon civic knowledge; the opportunities and risks associated with virtual communication; and the potential reconfiguration of political relationships within representative democracies—and beyond. Contributions to this new wave of e-democracy thinking include edited volumes on aspects of digital democracy by Tsagarousianou, Tambini, and Bryan (1998), Hague and Loader (1999), Coleman, Taylor, and van de Donk (1999), Horrocks, Hoff, and Tops (2000), Gibson and Ward (2000), Axford and Huggins (2001), and Hacker and van Dijk (2001). Each of these studies contributed to an examination of the ways in which the functions of leadership, government, and political parties are modified by new media. The remaining sections of this chapter explore the breadth and depth of these changes in the context of information, communication and power.

3 The Internet as a source of democratic information

Democracy depends upon common knowledge—information that possesses value because everyone knows it—such as news broadcasts, which provide common reference points for civic life, and leaflets explaining how to complain about poor services. But the mediation of common knowledge is complicated by three problems of information.

First, there is the question of who decides what is to be common knowledge. The means of disseminating information are costly and not equally shared. Governments and major media organizations have greater opportunities to set agendas than newspaper readers, phone-in callers or citizens who put up posters in their front windows. Knowledge production and selection are always political and susceptible to the effects of agenda-setting and censorship. 'The colonization of the public sphere by market forces' (Garnham 2000: 41) undermines the prospect of disseminating information on the basis of democratic need rather than private and unaccountable strategies.

Secondly, the costs of receiving information—especially from varied and balanced sources—are notoriously high and the fewer resources citizens have, in terms of time, education, and money, the harder it becomes to access civically valuable information. According to Tichenor, Donohue, and Olien's (1970) theory of knowledge gaps, people of higher socioeconomic status have better communication skills, can store information more easily, and are more selective in their exposure to and retention of information. The hopes of media theorists have been raised in the past by technologies that lower the cost of accesssible information. For example, reflecting in 1970 upon the democratic potential of TV, Blumler observed that as a mass medium it 'conveys impressions of the world of politics to individuals whose access to serious coverage of current affairs is otherwise quite limited' and could 'promote the development of more effective patterns of citizenship' (Blumler 1970: 100). The same optimism had previously been expressed in relation to the tabloid press and radio broadcasting.

Thirdly, there is the question of the status of information in democratic societies: the ways in which certain kinds of official knowledge are presented not only as epistemological truths, but as moral prompts to which 'informed citizens' are obliged to respond. For example, patients who are given medical information are deemed irresponsible if they fail to act upon it and citizens are increasingly urged to adopt prudential strategies designed to make them responsible for their own futures (Garland 1996; Bauman 1987). Barry notes that 'the very concept of information implies a reader who *should* be informed. It is a moral as well as a technical concept' (Barry 2001: 153). Whether information emancipates rather than controls citizens depends upon the extent to which there is scope to challenge, augment, or reject the authority of officially given knowledge.

The most obvious consequence of the Internet has been the creation of a condition of information abundance which has disrupted elite dominance in the sphere of knowledge production and dissemination (Bimber 2003). That this has amounted to disruption rather than rupture is evident in the key democratic contexts of election campaigning and news provision, where knowledge-shaping elites are still predominant, though increasingly challenged by new information mediators.

Some political scientists have suggested that the Internet has the capacity to democratize election campaigns by providing new opportunities for smaller parties and social movements to mobilize and receive a hearing (Foot and Schneider 2002; Benoit and Benoit 2000; Gibson and Ward 1998). Others have argued that the Internet reinforces traditional political and social inequalities (Margolis and Resnick 2000). Although it is premature to assess the long-term effect of online campaigning on electoral choice, the evidence so far is that parties are continuing to propagate their campaign messages online in much the same way as they had previously done offline: as one-to-many 'broadcasts' in which the interactive features of the Internet are not used. Gibson et al.'s (2003: 76) analysis of campaign websites in the US 2000 and UK 2001 elections concluded that the 'parties in the US and UK have used the technology relatively cautiously, to do things that they have always done, only more quickly and efficiently... Even where interactivity is available, it tends to be one way top-down, not two-way interactive.'

While online information abundance has not reconfigured electoral competition between traditional political parties, there is evidence to suggest that new media are having an impact on the capacity of non-party actors to influence election campaigns. For example, in recent elections bloggers, who previously lacked the resources to participate as media commentators, have played a significant role in broadening the style, if not the agenda, of the campaigns (Adamic and Glance 2005; Drezner and Farrell 2004). Coleman and Mesch (2006) have shown that more than one in ten Internet users during the UK general election of 2005 went online to voice opinions, influence friends and family, and pursue their own campaign agendas. Election campaigns are increasingly taking place at two levels: instrumentally-driven institutional actors, such as political parties, continue to conform to the propaganda model of message dissemination in both their online and offline activities; but civil-society organizations, citizen-bloggers, and network-activitated citizens are much more likely to participate in a secondary sphere of campaigning, characterized by online information-sharing and many-to-many interaction.

The same ambiguity applies to changes in the sources from which citizens learn about news. A 2005 US survey found that 31 per cent of 18–34 year-old males regarded the Internet as their main source of learning about news—compared with 22 per cent who cited local TV news and 6 per cent who cited national network news. (The response from females in the same age group was remarkably different: 18 per cent cited the Internet compared with 39 per cent who cited local TV news and 7 per cent who cited national network news (Carnegie 2005)). The trend away from TV and the press towards online news sources is undeniable, but does not necessarily imply that information sources are becoming more diverse or democratically accountable. In general, the most trusted sources of online news are provided by old-media organizations. Of the 12 most popular news sites in the US in June 2005, eight (CNN, Gannett Newspapers, *New York Times*, Knight Ridder, Tribune Newspapers, *USA Today*, *Washington Post*, and ABC News and Hearst Newspapers) had established reputations as broadcasters or newspaper publishers. The other four were run by Internet service providers (ISP) or search engines. The Internet has given rise to a vast array of news sources and political commentaries that could not have competed within any other medium, but the effect of this abundance of new information sources is not (yet) sufficient to undermine the resource and reputational advantages of the major news congolemerates.

For the Internet to redress the problem of information resource asymmetries, it would need to be just as easy to access online alternative accounts of reality (news, political messages, public information) as those promoted by powerful elites or well-resourced organizations. Most Internet users are only familiar with a small number of trusted web sites and only reach others via search engines. In a seminal analysis of the politics of search engines, Introna and Nissenbaum (2000: 185) observed 'the evident tendency of many of the leading search engines to give prominence to popular, wealthy and powerful sites at the expense of others'.

This is also an acute problem for users of multi-channel electronic programme guides (EPGs), which give page prominence to established and popular channels, while relegating educational and community channels to obscure positions in the guide. If the information costs of finding edifying or alternative information are raised as a result of the structure of search technologies, the effect is to reinforce the banal populism of the mass media paradigm. Information-seeking citizens are faced with a labyrinthine cornucopia of information abundance and choice without meaningful opportunities to select discriminately between different sources of knowledge.

This raises important questions about the extent to which citizens are free not only to receive, but to select, reject, and act upon civic information. The authority of broadcast and print media stems from its unidirectional message flow—the 'one-way conversation' (Postman 1986) to which viewers and readers cannot easily answer back. The interactivity of new media makes their content much more epistemologically vulnerable to challenge by the public. The way in which the modernist project of the encyclopaedia has been transformed through online collaboration exemplifies the shift from expert to lay authority in the production and dissemination of knowledge. The collaborative wikipedia project, which now has over a million entries in over 100 languages, comprises a form of social software that is dependent upon a degree of network co operation and trust. The emergence of social software, such as blogs, wikis, recommender systems and flickr, are characterized by a pluralistic ethos of shared and dynamic knowledge, in contradistinction to software that is designed to frame and constrain curiosity by replicating socio-politically dominant norms within its operational code. For example, the attention given by governments and IT companies to online voting, usually to the exclusion of a broader and potentially more empowering e-participation agenda, is indicative of the way in which technologies can be used to reinforce traditional practices, while diminishing the significance of new areas of empowerment (Coleman 2006a; Trechsel and Fernandez 2004). Another example is the way in which government-run portals organize information and discussion around bureaucratically devised categories that force public comment into artificially segmented policy silos (Rogers 2004).

It is a mistake, therefore, to characterize the relationship between new media and information structures as being either inherently replicative or transformative. Bellamy and Taylor's (1998: 165) assertion that 'ICTs and the information they convey are to be understood as active elements in the definition, reproduction and reshaping of institutional politics and power' can be applied to some uses of new media, particularly in the area of e-government. Zuboff's (1985) notion of informatization, which refers to the ways in which ICTs can give rise to organizational reflexivity, sometimes leading to unintended consequences, such as greater user empowerment, has explanatory force in other new media contexts. As with earlier media, relationships between message coders and user decoding are determined by wider factors than technological design.

4 THE INTERNET AS A SPHERE OF
DEMOCRATIC COMMUNICATION

A normative requirement of democracy is that citizens are not merely informed about the world, but are able to express freely their own considered views and listen to those of their fellow citizens. Contemporary democracies suffer from what might be called a deliberative deficit: an absence of spaces or occasions for the public to engage in open and critical discussion in which opinions can be exchanged and reviewed and policy decisions influenced. Several contemporary democratic theorists have adopted a critical stance towards the parsimonious, aggregatory model of democracy advanced by classical democratic theorists such as Schumpeter (1943/1976), in which voting for parties and leaders is the main role accorded to citizens. Deliberative democrats argue that the democratic relationship should comprise more than voting once every few years and that by exposing policy choices to inclusive public debate citizens' narrow preferences would become more flexible and political decisions more experientially connected.

Political talk 'transforms subconscious sentiments into conscious cognition and provides the basis for an active rather than a passive political involvement' (Mac-Kuen 1990: 60). Measuring levels and forms of political talk is problematic, because most of it takes place privately and self-reporting is not always reliable. Studies of political talk suggest that it is a highly differentiated activity, with a small minority of citizens in liberal democracies talking about politics a great deal, a similarly small minority never discussing politics, and most people engaging in political talk for less than an hour each week. Levels of political talk are unequally distributed, with poorer, less educated people engaging much less than those who are wealthier and formally educated (Bennett, Flickinger and Rhine 2000).

In early writing about the Internet, researchers speculated that it might provide a new space for virtual democratic interaction, with lowered costs of entry and an absence of cues that have traditionally inhibited political talk (Poster 1997; Herring 1993). To what extent has this happened?

A number of studies of online political talk have concluded that the Internet is at risk from flaming (Shirky 2004), identity deception (Donath 1999) and group herding (Sunstein 2001). Hill and Hughes (1998: 130) observe that 'chat rooms are a difficult format for thoughtful discussion. The short line space and the fast pace require people to make snap comments, not thoughtful ones.' Davis asserts that 'in Usenet political discussions, people talk past one another, when they are not verbally attacking each other. The emphasis is not problem solving, but discussion dominance. Such behavior does not resemble deliberation and it does not encourage participation, particularly by the less politically interested' (Davis 1999: 177; see also Davis 2005). Wilhelm concludes that 'the sorts of virtual political forums that were analysed do not provide viable sounding boards for signaling and thematizing issues to be processed by the political system' (Wilhelm 2000: 102). These studies all looked at informal, US-based chat fora, such as Usenet groups and chatrooms. Such fora were not intended to cultivate deliberative discourse, nor did they seek to arrive at any kind of conclusion. They were the online equivalent of people arguing in a bar. It would be a mistake to draw firm conclusions about the effects of all online political talk from these culturally-specific examples of informal chat. Even in this context, Kelly, Fisher, and Smith's (2005: 31) study of USENET newsgroups, utilizing the Netscan tool to map discursive patterns, found that 'even the most extremely opposed voices are talking to one another' and conclude that 'these environments are public commons that expose citizens to debate with diverse others. J. S. Mill would approve'.

Studies of more formally-structured modes of online talk, such as government-sponsored online consultations, policy networks or experimental deliberative exercises have reported positive findings about the potential for deliberative outcomes (Brants, Huizenga and van Meerten 1996; Walker and Akdeniz 1998; Sassi 2001). Coleman's (2004a,b) study of two online consultations run by the UK parliament concluded that online consultations provide a space for inclusive public deliberation; that such consultations generated and connected networks of interest or practice; and that a significant proportions of messages to both consultations referred to external information; frequent posters did not dominate the discussion to the exclusion of others; and there was a high level of interactivity between contributors. Luskin, Fishkin, and Iyengar's (2004: 18) study of the first ever online deliberative poll was particularly interesting, in that it compared the same process of experimental deliberation in online and offline contexts, concluding that the former showed 'significant potential for improving practices of public consultation'.

Central to the question of whether online political communication can foster heterogeneous, informed, and civilized discussion is the role of discursive structures and norms. Formal online talk is mediated through moderating structures. Edwards (2002: 3) argues that 'democratic regimes cannot function properly without intermediaries' and that the role of trusted moderators is crucial to the effectiveness of online discourse. According to Edwards, the role of a moderator is to contribute to the deliberative quality of an online discussion by promoting its openness and interactivity in a transparent and negotiable fashion. Coleman and Gotze (2001) have argued that 'mechanisms of moderation and mediation are crucial to the success of many-to-many asynchronous dialogue' and several other writers have argued that online civility requires regulation (Wilhelm 2000; Hron and Friedrich 2003; Wright 2006).

Arguments in favour of moderation run counter to the cyber-libertarian celebration of online disintermediation. At stake here is a theoretical debate about the regulatory basis of democracy. For cyber-libertarians, it is the absence of mediating rules and moderators that makes online interaction potentially democratic. Proponents of regulatory discursive structures argue that the only way to manage problems of scale, which have traditionally undermined norms of democratic inclusion, is by adopting and enforcing online protocols that encourage the widest possible participation in online discussions and promote listening as well as free expression. Dahlberg (2001: np) has suggested that rules of 'netiquette', as they have evolved in recent years, fall short of the deliberative standards required for truly democratic debate and that, for the purposes of enhancing the public sphere, rules of discourse could be adopted that 'structure online debate' and 'draw out rational-critical discourse from online interaction'.

Dahlberg's admonition begs the question of whether deliberative norms of 'rational-critical discourse' are the best measure of the democratic character of online talk. There are many other ways in which people communicate online—gossip, humour, emotionalism—which do not meet the lofty standards of deliberative democrats, but do constitute democratic expression. After recent terrorist bombings thousands of people contributed online tributes to the dead and injured. In web fora run by football clubs, reality TV shows, and soap operas many of the messages have a political dimension (van Zoonen 2004). During recent election campaigns online cartoons, jokes, and graffiti provided a popular outlet for public comment (Liffman, Coleman and Ward forthcoming). There has been too little research conducted on these tangentially political forms of online communication to draw robust conclusions, but it seems likely that many of the best examples of online democratic communication are not to be found within the dedicated political spaces of the Internet, but in discrete, peripheral, and ostensibly non-political online spaces.

Much online talk is informal and only tangentially political, but serves to sustain channels and networks through which interpersonal and civic relationships can be cultivated and enriched. A number of social theorists have argued that the health of democracy is linked intimately to everyday practices of talking, sharing, and imagining which are not ostensibly political, but which nurture participatory habits that lead to increased public engagement with political democracy. Putnam (1993: 167), for example, has argued that social capital inheres in networks 'that can improve the efficiency of society by facilitating coordinated actions' and that a key function of democratic political communication is to facilitate such informal associations. Several researchers have explored how new network relationships emerge online (Rheingold 1993; Jones 1995; Smith and Kollock 1996; Baym 1998; Agre 1998; Galston 1999).

Empirical evidence suggests that citizens can derive increased social capital from the experience of interacting online. Wellman et al. (2003) argue that online networks empower individuals rather than groups or communities (they refer to this phenomenon as 'networked individualism') by enabling them to personalize their associations: 'Each person is a switchboard, between ties and networks.

People remain connected, but as individuals, rather than being rooted in the home bases of work unit and household. Each person operates a separate personal community network, and switches rapidly among multiple sub-networks.'

Kavanaugh and Patterson (2001), on the basis of a three-year study of the Blacksburg Electronic Village, and Muller (1999), based on his study of chatroom and newsgroup participants, endorse Wellman et al.'s finding that being part of an online network enhances citizens' reciprocity, solidarity, and loyalty. All of these studies stress the fact that online networks are not self-contained communities in which people retreat from face-to-face physicality, but serve to support people in their existing social activities, contributing to 'the development of new communication formats which modify existing activities as well as help[ing] [to] shape new activities' (Altheide 1994: 666). Quan-Haase and Wellman (2004) have examined extensively the relationship between online networks and social capital and conclude that the former are an extension of, and supplement to, the world of offline interactions.

An interesting example of a democratic network that has emerged online is Netmums (http://www.netmums.com), which exists to support the quality of life for mothers with young children by helping them to find their local parent and toddler group, childcare facilities, playgroup; suggesting somewhere new to take the kids; recommending a good local GP; or helping them to make new friends in their local area. Sally Russell, a co-founder of Netmums, explains the value of being online in the following way:

The Internet is so dynamic: it allows a two-way conversation between members. It can be instantly updated by people who are providing classes and courses for parents or children, for example, and the members themselves can come and add on new information. So, it enables you to work as a cooperative rather than just providing information to parents one-way. (quoted in Coleman 2004a: 5)

The employment of online networks to support political mobilization, such as MoveOn.org during the 2004 US election campaign and the anti-globalization movement, has led Bennett (2003: 20) to conclude that:

When networks are not decisively controlled by particular organizational centers, they embody the Internet's potential as a relatively open public sphere in which the ideas and plans of protest can be exchanged with relative ease, speed, and global scope—all without having to depend on mass media channels for information or (at least, to some extent) for recognition. Moreover, the coordination of activities over networks with many nodes and numerous connecting points, or hubs, enables network organization to be maintained even if particular nodes and hubs die, change their mission, or move out of the network. Indeed, the potential of networked communication to facilitate leaderless and virtually anonymous social communication makes it challenging to censor or subvert broadly distributed communication even if it is closely monitored.

Bennett's analysis is useful and important for two reasons: it moves the debate about new media from a consideration of what technologies can do to what networks can do; and it connects new forms of democratic communication to new patterns and manifestations of political power. Indeed, Bennett's principal thesis in his writing about new media is that there is a dialectical relationship between emerging forms of networked communication and radical reconfigurations in the organization of global political power. In arguing that 'the underlying social and political dynamics of protest have changed significantly due to the ways in which economic globalization has refigured politics, social institutions, and identity formation within societies', Bennett (2003: 25) historicizes the relationship between new media and democracy, distancing his approach from deterministic assumptions (see also Bach and Stark 2004).

5 Conclusion: E-democracy and power

But still we are left, as is so commonly the case in studies of political communication, with the question of power. Even if information is more abundant, communication costs lower, and social networks easier to form, has power shifted in any discernible way from elites to the public? Have new media contributed to (in Giddens' (1990) terms) the 'democratization of democracy?' I want to conclude by setting out some claims that new media are implicated in an incipient reconfiguration of power relationships at three levels.

Representation

In post-Athenian constitutional democracies, the power of the public is mediated through representation. The task of political representation is to simulate the presence of the absent demos, speaking *for* the people as if they were speaking for themselves. This act of democratic ventriloquism is necessary because citizens are removed—physically, cognitively or otherwise—from the locus of public decision-making and their interests, preferences and values have to be expressed via an aggregating medium.

Historically, the problem of democratic mediation has been blighted by the problem of distance. The public is always somewhere else and the mechanisms of representation are inevitably indirect. This has resulted in a cultural chasm between formal mechanisms of democratic legitimacy and public confidence in the professional political elite's competence to empathize with, and reflect, the preferences and values of the sovereign demos. The ventriloquists stand accused of putting words in the mouth of the silently-represented electorate.

The feedback path inherent in digital media technologies makes possible a more direct communicative relationship between representatives and represented, allowing the former to consult the public regularly on matters of policy and the latter to feed their experience and expertise into the process of democratic governance. In its weakest form, this simply opens up representative institutions to greater transparency and public scrutiny (Coleman, Taylor and van de Donk 1999); in more radical ways this introduces opportunities for democratic co-governance (Ostrom 1990) and 'direct representation' (Coleman 2005b).

Whereas early conceptions of e-democracy envisaged a total transfer of power from elites to plebiscitary publics, current political interest in the concept stems from a growing unease among political elites about the unsustainability of indirect representative structures and processes and the need to mediate the relationship between representatives and represented in ways that can reconcile the democratic benefits of participation and the institutional complexities of governance. Innovative online experiments in more direct forms of representation have included consultations by parliamentary committees when considering legislation (UK, Canada, Scotland); e-rulemaking (US); consultation portals (Queensland, Estonia) and local issues forums (UK, US). The evaluation of these projects has been limited (Macintosh, White and Renton 2005; Coleman 2005c) and comparative indicators of success have yet to be introduced. It is too early to say how far these practices will become constitutionally embedded and integrated, but it would be very hard to imagine future governance without the presence of some of these levers of public communicative power, even if in time some of them emerge from outside government as external forces of public pressure.

The key question for research is not whether new media are capable of capturing, moderating and summarizing the voice of the public, but whether political institutions are able and willing to enter into a dialogical relationship with the public. The extent to which politicians, parties and bureaucrats can overcome institutional resistance to power sharing remains to be seen.

Space

Contemporary democracy suffers from a deficiency of 'institutional space where political will formation takes place, via the unfettered flow of relevant information and ideas' (Dahlgren 2001: 33). As Bauman (1987: 6) observed, 'the most powerful powers float or flow, and the most decisive decisions are taken in a space remote from the *agora* or even from the politically institutionalized public space; for the political institutions of the day, they are truly out of bounds and out of control'. The Habermasian notion of the public sphere in which all may participate in open, critical, and rational discussion has emerged as a normative aspiration for late-modern democracies.

In the past, public service broadcasting breathed life into the public sphere, and, in the case of the BBC, this has continued to happen in the new media arena, although it has been under strong pressure to become more competitive in its provision of online services (Graf 2004; Barwise 2004). But it is a mistake to confuse the public sphere, as a common ground for democratic mediation, with the mass media as institutions. In his more recent writings Habermas himself has come to realize that 'the public sphere cannot be conceived as an institution', but as 'a network for communicating information and points of view' which 'coalesce into bundles of topically specified public opinions' (Habermas 1996: 360). The development of a public sphere, therefore, entails 'finding ways to make the space transcending mass media supportive of public life' and 'developing social arrangements in which local discussions are both possible and able to feed into larger discussions mediated both by technology and by gatherings of representatives' (Calhoun 1989: 69). To this end, Blumler and Coleman have proposed the creation of a 'civic commons in cyberspace' as a protected space for public deliberation of local, national, and global issues. The commons would be run by an independent agency, funded by government, which would be charged with promoting inclusive public discussion and ensuring that relevant agencies within various sectors of government know about and are responsive to the public's views (Blumler and Coleman 2001). There is debate among proponents of e-democracy as to whether such a formal structure is needed or whether a civic commons is more likely to be an evolutionary outgrowth of grass-roots projects and experiments which effectively impose the voice of the online public upon reluctant political elites (Saco 2002).

At the global level, the Internet has opened up a space for communication between hitherto dispersed and less organized actors. The scope for global protest has been significantly increased. Moore (2003) has referred to the Internet as 'the second superpower', as institutions of global governance, such as the World Trade Organization, have come under unprecedented pressure from virtual publics to conduct their business accountably (Bennett and Fielding 1999). Resistance movements against dictatorial regimes have been strengthened by their use of the web, email, and mobile phones, and attempts to close them down fail to constrain the effects of diasporic solidarity (Ferdinand 2000).

But, as Lyon (2001) has noted, the other side of new media has been the extension of opportunities for panoptic surveillance by the state and other powerful actors. Computer records render citizens vulnerable to observation and control in the home and workplace; CCTV cameras watch us to an unprecedented degree in streets, shops, and playgrounds; network analyses of global networks categorize people and organizations in ways that cannot easily be challenged—or even recognized. As with all political spatiality, the search for democratic online space involves a power struggle between forces of liberty and control; Habermasian public space and the Foucauldian tyranny of conduct.

Everyday democracy

It would be a tragedy were 'digital democracy' merely to create virtual parallels of obsolescent political processes and structures. Conventional democratic forms have been radically challenged in recent times by what Bentley (2005) has called 'everyday democracy', and Bang and Sørensen (2000) refer to as the rise of 'the everyday maker'. These critiques of formal democracy argue for a more fluid and hybrid definition of the political, which is played out in an experiential public sphere 'that has to do with everybody and which is only realized in the heads of people, a dimension of their consciousness' (Negt and Kluge 1993: 3).

My own research on the political behaviour and attitudes of *Big Brother* viewers and voters (Coleman 2003/2006b) suggests that civic engagement can take many forms and that opportunities afforded by online and multimedia interaction can lead to reflections and negotiations about power that are not easily recognized by political scientists in search of conventional signs of 'civic participation'. The digitally-facilitated influence of supporters upon the corporate management of football teams, disabled people upon the governance of public transport, diasporas upon domestically-insulated dictatorships, and rock music fans upon government policies towards 'Third World' debt all suggest that the democratic affordances of new media are unlikely to be confined to the familiar world of constitutional politics. As new media become normalized and further integrated within routine circuits of power wielding, it is important for researchers to explore and acknowledge those currents of new mediation which nurture the non-politically political and sustain the democratizing practices of the disengaged.

REFERENCES

ADAMIC, L. and GLANCE, N. (2005). 'The Political Blogosphere and the 2004 U.S. Election: Divided They Blog'. Mimeo, http://www.blogpulse.com/papers/2005/Adamic-GlanceBlogWWW.pdf, accessed 18 Mar. 2006.

AGRE, P. (1998). 'Designing Genres for New Media: Social, Economic, and Political Contexts', in S. Jones (ed.), *CyberSociety 2.0: Revisiting CMC and Community*. Newbury Park, CA: Sage, 69–99.

ALTHEIDE, D. L. (1994). 'An Ecology of Communication'. *The Sociological Quarterly*, 35(4): 665–83.

ARTERTON, F. C. (1987). *Teledemocracy: Can Technology Protect Democracy?* Newbury Park, CA: Sage.

AXFORD, B. and HUGGINS, R. (2001). *New Media and Politics*. London: Sage.

BACH, J. and STARK, D. (2004). 'Link, Search, Interact: The Co-Evolution of NGOs and Interactive Technology'. *Theory Culture & Society*, 21(3): 101–17.

BANG, H. and SØRENSEN, E. (2000). 'The Everyday Maker: Building Political Rather than Social Capital', in P. Dekker and E. Uslaner (eds), *Social Capital and Participation in Every Day Life*. London: Routledge, 148–61.

BARBROOK, R. and CAMERON, A. (1997). 'The Californian Ideology'. *Science as Culture*, 26: 44–72.

BARLOW, J. P. (1996). *A Declaration of the Independence of Cyberspace*, http://homes.eff.org/~barlow/Declaration-Final.html, accessed 18 Mar. 2006.

BARRY, A. (2001). *Political Machines: Governing a Technological Society*. London: The Athlone Press.

BARWISE, P. (2004). *Independent Review of the BBC's Digital Television Services*. London: Department for Culture, Media and Sport.

BAUMAN, Z. (1987). *Legislators and Interpreters: On Post-modernity and Intellectuals*. Ithaca, NY: Cornell University Press.

BAYM, N. (1998). 'The Emergence of On-line Community', in S. Jones (ed.), *CyberSociety 2.0: Revisiting CMC and Community*. Thousand Oaks, CA: Sage, 35–68.

BECKER, T. and SLATON, C. (2000). *The Future of Teledemocracy*. Westport, CT: Praeger.

BELLAMY, C. and TAYLOR, J. (1998). *Governing in the Information Age*. Buckingham: Open University Press.

BELLAMY, E. (1887/1996). *Looking Backward: 2000–1887*. London: Penguin.

BENNETT, D. and FIELDING, P. (1999). *The Net Effect: How Cyberadvocacy is Changing the Political Landscape*. Washington DC: Capitol Advantage.

BENNETT, S., FLICKINGER, R. and RHINE, S. (2000). 'Political Talk Over Here, Over There, Over Time'. *British Journal of Political Science*, 30(1): 99–119.

BENNETT, W. L. (2003). 'New Media Power: The Internet and Global Activism', in N. Couldry and J. Curran (eds), *Contesting Media Power: Alternative Media in a Networked World*. Lanham, MD: Rowman and Littlefield, 17–38.

BENOIT, W. L. and BENOIT, P. J. (2000). 'The Virtual Campaign: Presidential Primary Websites in Campaign 2000'. *American Communication Journal*, 3(3): 1–22.

BENTLEY, T. (2005). *Everyday Democracy: Why We Get The Politicians We Deserve*. London: Demos.

BIMBER, B. (2003). *Information and American Democracy: Technology in the Evolution of Political Power*. Cambridge: Cambridge University Press.

BLUMLER, J. G. (1970). 'The Political Effects of Television', in J. Halloran (ed.), *The Effects of Television*. Manchester: Panther, 69–104.

—— and COLEMAN, S. (2001). *Realising Democracy Online: A Civic Commons in Cyberspace*. London: Institute for Public Policy Research.

BRANTS, K. HUIZENGA, M. and VAN MEERTEN, R. (1996). 'The New Canals of Amsterdam: An Exercise in Local Electronic Democracy'. *Media, Culture & Society*, 18(2): 233–47.

BRECHT, B. (1932). 'The Radio as an Apparatus of Communication', reprinted in J. G. Hanhardt (ed.) (1986), *Video Culture. A Critical Investigation*. Rochester, NY: Studies Workshop Press, 53–6.

BURKE, P. and BRIGGS, A. (2001). *A Social History of the Media: From Gutenberg to the Internet*. Cambridge: Polity Press.

BUSH, V. (1945). 'As We May Think'. *The Atlantic Monthly*, 176(1): 101–8.

CALHOUN, C. (1989). 'Tiananmen, Television and the Public Sphere'. *Public Culture*, 2(1): 54–71.

Carnegie Corporation of New York (2005). *Abandoning the News*. New York: Carnegie Corporation of New York.

CARTY, J. J. (1923). 'Electrical Communications', speech to the 11th Annual Meeting of the Chambers of Commerce of the United States, http://www.atlantic-cable.com/Article/ 1923Carty/, accessed 18 Mar. 2006.

COLEMAN, S. (2003). 'A Tale of Two Houses: The House of Commons, The *Big Brother* House and the People at Home'. *Parliamentary Affairs*, 56: 733–58.

—— (2004a). 'Connecting Parliament to the Public via the Internet: Two Case Studies of Online Consultations'. *Information, Communication and Society*, 7(1): 1–22.

—— (2004b). *The Network-Empowered Citizen*. London: Institute of Public Policy Research, http://www.ippr.org.uk/uploadedFiles/research/projects/Digital_Society/the_ networkempowered_citizen_coleman.pdf, accessed 18 Mar. 2006.

—— (2005a). 'The Lonely Citizen: Indirect Representation in an Age of Networks'. *Political Communication*, 22(2): 197–214.

—— (2005b). *Direct Representation: Towards a Conversational Democracy*. London: Institute for Public Policy Research.

—— (2005c). *From The Ground Up: An Evaluation of Community-focused Approaches to e-Democracy*. London: Office of the Deputy Prime Minister.

—— (2006a). 'Just How Risky is Online Voting?' *Information Polity*, 10(1–2): 95–104.

—— (2006b). *How the Other Half Votes: Big Brother Viewers and the 2005 General Election*. London: Channel 4 and Hansard Society.

—— and GOTZE, J. (2001). *Bowling Together: Online Public Engagement in Policy Deliberation*. London: Hansard Society.

—— and MESCH, G. (2006). 'British Internet Users and the 2005 Election Campaign'. Mimeo. University of Leeds.

—— , TAYLOR, J. and VAN DE DONK, W. (eds) (1999). *Parliament in the Age of the Internet*. Oxford: Oxford University Press.

DAHLBERG, L. (2001). 'Computer-Mediated Communication and The Public Sphere: A Critical Analysis'. *Journal of Computer Mediated Communication*, 7(1), http://jcmc. indiana.edu/vol7/issue1/dahlberg.html, accessed 18 Mar. 2006.

DAHLGREN, P. (2001). 'The Public Sphere and the Net: Structure, Space, and Communication', in W. L. Bennett and R. M. Entman (eds), *Mediated Politics: Communication in the Future of Democracy*. Cambridge: Cambridge University Press, 33–55.

DAVIS, R. (1999). *The Web of Politics: The Internet's Impact on the American Political System*. Oxford: Oxford University Press.

—— (2005). *Politics Online: Blogs, Chatrooms and Discussion in American Democracy*. London: Routledge.

DONATH, J. (1999). 'Identity and Deception in the Virtual Community', in M. Smith and P. Kollock (eds), *Communities in Cyberspace*. London: Routledge, 29–59.

DREZNER, D. and FARRELL, H. (2004). 'The Power and Politics of Blogs'. Paper presented at the American Political Science Association conference, August, http://www.danieldrezner. com/research/blogpaperfinal.pdf, accessed 24 Mar. 2006.

DUTTON, W. (1992). 'Political Science Research on Teledemocracy'. *Social Science Computer Review*, 10(4): 502–22.

EDWARDS, A. (2002). 'The Moderator as an Emerging Democratic Intermediary: The Role of the Moderator in Internet Discussions about Public Issues'. *Information Polity*, 7(1): 3–20.

ENZENSBERGER, H. M. (1970/1982). 'Constituents of a Theory of the Media', in H. M. Enzensberger (ed.), *Critical Essays*. New York: Continuum, 13–38.

ETZIONI, A. (1972). 'Minerva: An Electronic Town Hall'. *Policy Sciences*, 3(4): 457–74.

—— (1992). 'Teledemocracy'. *The Atlantic*, 270(4):34–9.

FERDINAND, P. (2000). *The Internet, Democracy and Democratization*. London: Frank Cass.

FOOT, K. and SCHNEIDER, S. (2002). 'Online Action in Campaign 2000: An Exploratory Analysis of the U.S. Political Web Sphere', *Journal of Broadcasting & Electronic Media*, 46(2): 222–44.

GALSTON, W. A. (1999). '(How) Does the Internet affect Community? Some Speculations in Search of Evidence' in E. Kamarck and J. S. Nye (eds), *Democracy.Com? Governance in a Networked World*. Hollis NH: Hollis Publishing Company, 40–58.

GARNHAM, N. (2000). *Emancipation, the Media, and Modernity: Arguments about the Media and Social Theory*. Oxford: Oxford University Press.

GARLAND, D. (1996). 'The Limits of the Sovereign State: Strategies of Crime Control in Contemporary Society'. *British Journal of Criminology*, 36(4): 445–71.

GIBSON, R. and WARD, S. (1998). 'UK Political Parties and the Internet: Politics as Usual in the New Media?' *Harvard International Journal of Press/Politics*, 3(3): 14–38.

GIBSON, R. and WARD, S. (2000). *Reinvigorating Democracy? UK Politics and the Internet*. Aldershot: Ashgate.

GIBSON, R., MARGOLIS, M., RESNICK, P. et al. (2003). 'Election Campaigning on the WWW in the US and UK: A Comparative Analysis'. *Party Politics*, 9(1): 47–76.

GIDDENS, A. (1990). *The Consequences of Modernity*. Stanford, CA: Stanford University Press.

GRAF, P. (2004). *Report of the Independent Review of BBC Online*. London: Department of Media, Culture, and Sport.

GROSSMAN, L. (1995). *The Electronic Republic: Reshaping Democracy in the Information Age*. New York: Viking.

HABERMAS, J. (1996). *Between Facts and Norms*. Cambridge: Polity Press.

HACKER, K. L. and VAN DIJK, J. (2001). *Digital Democracy: Issues of Theory and Practice*. London: Sage.

HAGUE, B. N. and LOADER, B. D. (eds) (1999). *Digital Democracy: Discourse and Decision Making in the Information Age*. London: Routledge.

HERRING, S. (1993). 'Gender and Democracy in Computer-mediated Communication'. *Electronic Journal of Communication*, 3(2): http://www.cios.org/www/ejc/v3n293.htm, accessed 18 Mar. 2006.

HILL, K. and HUGHES, J. (1998). *Cyberpolitics: Citizen Activism in the Age of the Internet*. Lanham, MD: Rowman & Littlefield.

HOLLANDER, R. S. (1985). *Video Democracy: The Vote-From-Home Revolution*. Mt Airy, MD: Lomond.

HORROCKS, I., HOFF, J., and TOPS, P. (2000). *Democratic Governance and New Technology: Technologically Mediated Innovations in Political Practice in Western Europe*. London: Routledge.

HRON, A. and FRIEDRICH, H. F. (2003). 'A Review of Web-based Collaborative Learning: Factors Beyond Technology'. *Journal of Computer Assisted Learning*, 19(1): 70–9.

INTRONA, L. D. and NISSENBAUM, H. (2000). 'Shaping the Web: Why the Politics of Search Engines Matters'. *The Information Society*, 16(3): 169–85.

JONES, S. G. (1995). 'Understanding Community in the Information Age', in S. G. Jones (ed.) *CyberSociety 2.0: Revisiting CMC and Community*. Newbury Park, CA: Sage, 10–35.

KAVANAUGH, A. and PATTERSON, S. (2001). 'The Impact of Community Computer Networks on Social Capital and Community Involvement'. *American Behavorial Scientist*, 45(3): 496–509.

KELLY, J., FISHER D. and SMITH, M. (2005). 'Debate, Division and Diversity: Political Discourse Networks in USENET Newsgroups'. Unpub. Working Paper presented at Stanford Online Deliberation Conference.

LIFFMAN, L., COLEMAN, S. and WARD. S. (forthcoming). 'Only Joking? Online Humour in the 2005 UK Election'. *Media, Culture & Society*.

LUSKIN, R. C., FISHKIN, J. S. and IYENGAR, S. (2004). 'Considered Opinions on US Foreign Policy: Face-to-Face versus Online Deliberative Polling'. Paper presented at the International Communication Association Conference, New Orleans, 27–31 May.

LYON, D. (2001). *Surveillance Society: Monitoring Everyday Life*. Buckingham: Open University Press.

McLUHAN, M. (1964). *Understanding Media: The Extensions of Man*. New York: McGraw-Hill.

MACINTOSH, A., WHITE, A. and RENTON, A. (2005). *From the Top Down: An Evaluation of e-Democracy Activities Initiated by Councils and Government*. London: Office of the Deputy Prime Minister.

MacKUEN, M. (1990). 'Speaking of Politics: Individual Conversational Choice, Public Opinion and the Prospects for Deliberative Democracy', in J. Ferejohn and J. Kuklinski (eds), *Information and Democratic Processes*. Champaign-Urbana, IL: University of Illinois Press, 59–99.

MARGOLIS, M. and RESNICK, P. (2000). *Politics As Usual: The Cyberspace 'Revolution'*. London: Sage.

MOORE, J. F. (2003). 'The Second Superpower Rears Its Beautiful Head', http://cyber.law.harvard.edu/people/jmoore/secondsuperpower.html, accessed 18 Mar. 2006.

MORRIS, D. (2000). *VOTE.COM: How Big Money Lobbyists and the Media are Losing their Influence, and the Internet is giving Power back to the People*. New York: Renaissance Books, http://extras.denverpost.com/books/chvote0227.htm.

MULLER, C. (1999). 'Networks of Personal Communities and Group Communities in Different Online Communication Services: First Results of an Empirical Study in Switzerland'. Paper presented at the Exploring Cyber Society Conference, University of Northumbria, July.

NEGT, O. and KLUGE, A. (1993). *Public Sphere and Experience*. Minneapolis, MN: University of Minnesota Press.

OSTROM, E. (1990). *Governing the Commons: The Evolution of Institutions for Collective Action*. Cambridge: Cambridge University Press.

PETERS, J. D. (1999). *Speaking Into the Air: A History of the Idea of Communication*. Chicago, IL: University of Chicago Press.

POSTER, M. (1997). 'Cyberdemocracy: Internet and the Public Sphere', in D. Porter (ed.), *Internet Culture*. London: Routledge, 201–18.

POSTMAN, N. (1986). *Amusing Ourselves to Death: Public Discourse in the Age of Show Business*. New York: Penguin Books.

PUTNAM, R. D. (1993). *Making Democracy Work: Civic Traditions in Modern Italy*. Princeton, NJ: Princeton University Press.

QUAN-HAASE, A. and WELLMAN, B. (2004). 'How Does the Internet Affect Social Capital?', in M. Huysmann and V. Wulf (eds), *Social Capital and Information Technology*. Cambridge, MA: MIT Press, 113–32.

RHEINGOLD, H. (1993). *The Virtual Community: Homesteading on the Electronic Frontier*. Reading, MA: Addison-Wesley.

ROGERS, R. (2004). *Information Politics on the Web*. Cambridge, MA: MIT Press.

SACO, D. (2002). *Cybering Democracy: Public Space and the Internet*. Minneapolis, MN: University of Minnesota Press.

SASSI, S. (2001). 'The Controversies of the Internet and the Revitalization of Local Political Life', in K. Hacker and J. van Dijk (eds), *Digital Democracy: Issues of Theory and Practice*. London: Sage, 90–104.

SCHUMPETER, J. A. (1943/1976). *Capitalism, Socialism, and Democracy* (5th edn). London: Allen and Unwin.

SHAMBERG, M. and Raindance Corporation (1971). *Guerrilla Television*. New York: Holt, Rinehart and Winston.

SHIRKY, C. (2004). *Voices from the Net*. Emeryville, CA: Ziff-Davis Press.

SMITH, M. and KOLLOCK, P. (1996). *Communities in Cyberspace*. London: Routledge.

STREET, J. (1997). 'Remote Control? Politics, Technology and "Electronic Democracy"'. *European Journal of Communication*, 12(1): 27–42.

STREETER, T. (1987). 'The Cable Fable Revisited: Discourse, Policy, and the Making of Cable Television'. *Critical Studies in Mass Communication*, 4 (June): 174–200.

SUNSTEIN, C. (2001). *Republic.com*. Princeton, NJ: Princeton University Press.

TICHENOR, P. J., DONOHUE, G. A. and OLIEN, C. N. (1970). 'Mass Media Flow and Differential Growth in Knowledge'. *Public Opinion Quarterly*, 34: 159–70.

TASAGAROUSIANOU, R., TAMBINI, D. and BRYAN, C. (1998). *Cyberdemocracy: Technology, Cities and Civic Networks*. London: Routledge.

TRECHSEL, A. and FERNANDEZ, F. (eds) (2004). *The European Union and e-Voting: Addressing the European Parliament's Internet Voting Challenge*. London: Routledge.

VAN ZOONEN, L. (2004). *Entertaining the Citizen: When Politics and Popular Culture Converge*. Lanham, MD: Rowman & Littlefield, 123–39.

WALKER, C. and AKDENIZ, Y. (1998). 'Virtual Democracy'. *Public Law*, Autumn: 489–506.

WELLMAN, B., QUAN-HAASE, A., BOASE, J., et al. (2003). 'The Social Affordances of the Internet for Networked Individualism'. *Journal of Computer-Mediated Communication*, 8(3), http://jcmc.indiana.edu/vol8/issue3/wellman.html, accessed 18 Mar. 2006.

WELLS, H. G. (1937). 'World Brain: The Idea of a Permanent World Encyclopaedia', Contribution to the new Encyclopédie Française, August, http://sherlock.berkeley.edu/wells/world_brain.html, accessed 18 Mar. 2006.

WILHELM, A. G. (2000). *Democracy in the Digital Age: Challenges to Political Life in Cyberspace*. London: Routledge.

WRIGHT, S. (2006). 'Government-run Online Discussion Fora: Moderation, Censorship and the Shadow of Control'. *British Journal of Politics & International Relations*, 8(4): 550–68.

ZUBOFF, S. (1985). 'Automate/Informate: The Two Faces of Intelligent Technology'. *Organizational Dynamics*, 14(2): 4–18.

CHAPTER 16

COMMUNICATIVE ENTITLEMENTS AND DEMOCRACY: THE FUTURE OF THE DIGITAL DIVIDE DEBATE

NICK COULDRY

there is a deep complementarity between individual agency and social arrangements. . . . To counter the problems we face, we have to see individual freedom as a social commitment.

(Sen 1999: xii)

[now] we can set out on the enormous task of redefining 'the right to the word' that is called for in the information age.

(Melucci 1996: 228)

1 INTRODUCTION*

IF individuals are to have a reasonable opportunity to participate regularly and effectively in the workings of democracy, they need some basic resources: a home, enough to eat and drink, basic personal security. But do they need more? In particular, do they need some share of a society's communicative resources and, if so, what form should this 'share' take? Not every account of democracy emphasizes effective citizen participation. Under elite models, only a minimally plausible degree of citizen monitoring is required; this chapter will not generally be concerned with such models. For other models, which connect democratic legitimacy to achieving a broad and effective degree of citizen *participation*, the distribution of communicative resources is a major issue,[1] unless (something few would argue) such resources are irrelevant to civic action. What we mean by 'communicative resources', of course, needs clarifying, as does the theoretical framework in which these questions are best formulated, whether in terms of specific civic 'rights' or in terms of an ethics based on an account of what individuals need if they are to have the chance to flourish as human beings (Sen 1992, 1999). I will adapt the term 'communicative entitlement' from Scannell (1989: see n. 1) to refer to the distributive outcome of both frameworks, but particularly the latter.

A remarkable result of the digital divide debate, for all its limitations, is to have pushed the distribution of communicative resources (and its consequences for democracy) to the centre of policy discussions, at least temporarily, in the late 1990s and early 2000s. Communications, of course, are often politically controversial, for example in disputes about public 'decency' or, while public service broadcasting models survive, in debates about how media should be funded. But the sight of policy makers debating the distribution of communicative resources among individuals is more striking, for here public and social imperatives conflict directly with deep-seated assumptions of consumer freedom. But, as Amartya Sen pointed out in the quotation at the start of this chapter, the separation of individual choice and social commitment is illusory. Never more so, we might add, than in relation to communication ('the way that people come to share things in common' (Dewey, quoted by Carey 1989: 22)). Indeed if, as one theorist of the network society claims, 'the position of people in media networks will largely determine their position in society' (van Dijk 1999: 78), then at some level the distribution of information and communication technology (ICT) resources must be central to social justice.

Digital divide debates suggested that, whether we look at democracy, social justice, or market functioning, ICT resources make enough of a difference to prompt governments, non-governmental organizations (NGOs) and corporations

* The author is grateful for the comments of an anonymous reader which greatly helped clarify this chapter's argument. Thanks also to Robin Mansell, whose Dixons lecture delivered at the London School of Economics on 23 October 2001 was an important inspiration for the thinking of this chapter.

consider intervention in their distribution. But how, and on the basis of what types of evidence? Here two uncertainties have complicated matters: first, an uncertainty about how governments could make a difference to the distribution of communicative resources and, through them, democracy and/or social life; secondly, an uncertainty about what exactly do we need to know about people's detailed uses of media and communications in order to answer the first question, or indeed to understand more generally how communications policy affects the social world (cf. Melody 1990: 32–3). Such questions matter less perhaps when discussing formal civic entitlements, but they matter a great deal if we want 'to safeguard the conditions and circumstances that ensure the range and reach of the democratic process'; this requires not abstract principles but 'effective practice' (Sen 1999: 158–9).

A single chapter can hardly claim to provide answers to such a challenge. Instead this chapter attempts to map the depth and importance of the problems at issue: first, in Section 2, through a review of digital divide debates at a time (2005) when in policy circles they are no longer in fashion; secondly in Sections 3 and 4, by linking this to recent debates in political sociology and media sociology about, respectively, the declining prospects for political engagement, and the public uses of people's media consumption; and finally in Section 5 by reviewing competing theoretical formulations of the communicative preconditions of democracy, and drawing particularly on Garnham's (1999) adaptation of Sen's human capabilities approach to the media field.

2 DIGITAL DIVIDE?

This is not the place to review exhaustively the history of the digital divide debate, or even to map all its recent critics. Instead, I will keep to the debate's main contours, outlining both its flaws and what of importance can and should be retained from it.

Brief history of the concept

There are at least two digital divides: the gap in communications resources between nations, and the analogous divides within nations. The first is concerned with absolute differences between countries' telecommunications infrastructures, information transmission capacity, aggregate numbers of computers, website hosts, telephone users, and the like; the second is concerned, within one nation, over the gap between those who have access to its communicative resources and those who do not. Both divides are important, but this chapter will concentrate on the second, since our focus on democratic efficacy requires, at least initially, a national scale; it is the complexities of analysing differences within already highly mediated societies that concern us here.

The limitations of the digital divide debate cannot, however, be understood outside of its international context. The term's currency in policy circles in the late 1990s was more closely related to economic, than to social or democratic, concerns. If the Global Information Highway was to enable 'a global information market-place, where consumers can buy and sell products' (Vice-President Al Gore, quoted in Schiller 1995: 17), then those across the world who could not afford a computer, modem, or even a local phone call represented a huge loss of market opportunity.

Telecommunications experts at the United Nations Development Programme (UNDP) and elsewhere had for a long time expressed concern about the impact on world economic development of a situation where 'more than half of the world's population lives more than two hours from a telephone' (d'Orville 1996: 2). The greater inequalities over who in the world had a modem raised even more serious obstacles to poor countries joining the global online consumer market, something that Microsoft and others hoped for (d'Orville 1996: ch. 5; cf. OECD 2001). Writing in 2001, Mark Malloch Brown—then administrator of the UNDP, and by 2005, assistant to the UN Secretary-General—maintained that economic emphasis, when he explained the role of the 'Digital Opportunity Task Force' (or 'DOTForce') thus: the point was 'encourag[ing] participation in global economic networks'; although he also wrote of 'build[ing] human capacity', a term to which we will return (Brown 2001: 4–5).

Meanwhile, within the US, there was increasing concern about home-grown inequality in computer access and its impacts on the US domestic market. The Clinton administration commissioned a series of studies by its Department of Commerce (DoC) (the 'Falling Through the Net' series 1995–2000) which by the late 1990s became crucial reference points in policy discussions about the so-called digital divide. Even if the term's inventor Lloyd Morrisett[2] had, and still has, a concern with issues of democracy (Morrisett 2003), the Clinton Administration's main emphasis was, once again, achieving 'participation in the digital economy' (US Department of Commerce 2000: 2).

At the international political level, the double-edged nature of the term digital divide provoked a rhetorical shift to 'digital opportunity' (World Economic Forum 2000: 10), although the underlying issue of the digital divide retained some momentum in debates leading to the World Summit on the Information Society (WSIS) in December 2003 and in 2005. (This is a huge topic, which we cannot broach here.) On the national scale, the divide in Internet take-up was more difficult to disguise rhetorically, at least at first. Taking as our reference point an authoritative definition of the digital divide as 'the differential access to and use of the Internet according to gender, income, race, and location' (Rice 2002: 106), a large body of

US government-sponsored and academic survey research confirmed a significant divide.[3] These results exercised governments in the US, the UK,[4] and elsewhere. By the early 2000s, however, such demographic gaps in the US had eased in certain respects, which enabled the incoming Bush administration to close down the debate altogether. In 2002, federal initiatives directed at the digital divide were shut down[5] against the backdrop of a new DoC report that claimed 'we are truly a nation online' (US Department of Commerce 2002: 2). The hollowness of this claim was clear, since, while on some indicators (race and gender, once adjusted to exclude other factors) the gap in digital access had narrowed, the report's own findings showed that income and education remained major determinants of whether people were online and whether, once online, they stayed online (US Department of Commerce 2002: 11, 18, 71, 75; cf. UCLA 2001: 13). Such 'below-the-line' subtleties were however ignored beneath the main message that markets would, in time, solve the problem (cf. Compaine 2001).

To understand why in evidential terms (leaving aside politics) such a closure might seem acceptable, we must notice the general silence in the 'Falling Through the Net' studies on the quality of people's Internet use. While in that series' final report (published in the last days of the Clinton administration) the Secretary of State for Commerce, Norman Mineta, proclaimed triumphantly that 'the data in this report show that, overall, our Nation is moving toward full digital inclusion' (US Department of Commerce 2000: 2), this same report admitted that quality of use was not even investigated (see Part II, under 'Location of Internet Use'). But quality of use could not go on being ignored, as became clear from academic research which showed that bare statistics of use disguised major differences between types of user. Heavy Internet users were more likely to spend their time online sending their own documents and information, rather than receiving public information (Pew 2002a; cf. Katz, Rice and Aspden 2001); whereas 'light' Internet users might do little more than access their web server, look at the headlines and a few links, and check a holiday option. Other major differences were found between online users with broadband and those without (Pew 2002c); length of online experience (the after-effect of the early digital divide) was also found to stratify users (Howard, Rainie and Jones 2002).

As the decade continued, differences in online use in the US remained shaped by gender, ethnicity, income, and education (Pew 2003); nor did the absolute figures for online access suggest that movement towards universal access was unstoppable. By 2004 around 75 per cent of US adults were online but 24.1 per cent remained non-users, with non-users likely to go online falling to the lowest level ever (Center for the Digital Future 2004). If US online use were to stabilize at around 75 per cent of the adult population (with 25 per cent excluded) that would be broadly consistent with the 2000 Pew Foundation report, which found that half of the then 50 per cent not online thought they would never go online (Pew 2000b). In addition, many researchers noted the phenomenon of Internet dropouts: people with online access who failed to maintain it, often because they no longer had a computer, but sometimes because they did not see the benefit (Katz and Rice 2002, chs. 4 and 5; Selwyn 2004; Center for the Digital Future 2004; Pew 2003; Wyatt, Thomas and Terranova 2002).

Explanations and implications

In spite, then, of earlier optimism, the digital divide remains significant and at some (as yet unknown) percentage may well become permanent. Why? First, computers are more complex communications goods than, say, televisions, and require more economic resources to maintain as goods (indeed they require regular replacement or updating (Golding 2000: 174)). They also require social resources if operating problems are to be effectively resolved (Kling 1999). As a result, mere 'technical access' to the online world is quite different from 'social access' (Kling 2000: 226). As Jan van Dijk argued in the most comprehensive rethinking so far of the digital divide concept, there are at least four hurdles to overcome before achieving effective Internet use: (i) a basic level of digital skills and confidence; (ii) material access to computer and modem; (iii) ease with usage style; and (iv) ongoing opportunities to practise use (van Dijk 1999: 148–55). Even if the early hurdles are overcome, later ones may remain, resulting not in a simple binary divide between digital 'haves' and 'have-nots', but a more complex usage gap between more skilled, broad users and less skilled, narrow users (van Dijk 1999: 153; cf. Mansell and Steinmueller 2000: ch. 2; and Livingstone in Ch. 21 of this handbook). The risk is that the social inequalities underlying that gap get rigidified in inequalities of use across a range of services (including political information)[6] offered online, resulting in a deepening of social inequality (van Dijk 1999: 235).[7]

Behind these complications lies a larger point: the use you or I make of the Internet may depend on our capacities to believe we can do something with the resources we find online. The online environment is 'decision-intensive' (Bucy and Newhagen 2004: x), but our capacity to take particular decisions is related to the range of actions more widely available to us. The Children's Partnership's (2000) study of online use by 'Underserved Americans' highlighted 'the Digital Divide's New Frontier...content': the gulf between what people need and what they actually find online.[8] People may need job and education information, yet not find it readily available, whether because such information assumes too high a literacy level, or is not in their first language, or is not 'culturally appropriate'. Hidden inequalities may be even more stark in the area of online information production, relating, ultimately, to what type of person you consider yourself to be. 'Low-income people think they're not *legitimate* information producers', said one community adviser interviewed (Children's Partnership 2000: 24 [emphasis added]).

Where does this take us? One practical policy direction is to insist on more appropriate online content for the full range of communities and social groups (Children's Partnership 2003). More pressing here is the uncertainty revealed about what is at stake in the digital divide debate. Clearly not just the provision of a computer and modem, but also the resources that allow effective Internet use. At which point, we have a choice. One path abandons the terrain of digital divide altogether and returns to considering Internet use (like any resource use) in relation to social exclusion (Warschauer 2003; cf. Norris 2001); the risk is that the issues of inequality just discussed fall permanently out of policy makers' view, as just another subtle consequence of social exclusion. The second path acknowledges that the digital divide is at best 'a simplifying metaphor' (Hacker and van Dijk 2001: 322), but holds onto its strategic importance in acknowledging real, permanent, and socially reinforced inequalities in digital resource use—how else to interrupt the rhetoric of inevitability surrounding terms such as 'Information Society'? It is this second path that I will pursue here.

Taking this second path however means addressing, if not resolving, some major definitional ambiguities. To start with the most basic point: *why* does it matter so much that citizens have a minimum level of communicative resources? Here I want to adapt from Scannell the notion of 'communicative entitlements'. Scannell (1989: 160) introduced this phrase to capture something over and above people's 'formal' communicative rights (freedom of speech, and so on): communicative entitlement means, for Scannell, citizens' rightful claim in a democracy to 'be listened to [and] be treated seriously'. Whereas Scannell pursues this in terms of representation in broadcasting (an important, but separate theme), I will pursue it in terms of individuals' claims on some minimum share of the resources to receive and produce communications; it is clear that how we conceive of such an entitlement changes, once we move outside the exclusive framework of broadcasting.

There are various ways we can ground the notion of communicative entitlement. We might first turn to broadly participatory democratic theory, where the notion of communicative entitlement would flow directly from some notion of mutuality: our requirement to recognize each other as agents capable of debating, and reaching shared decisions about, common issues (Benhabib 1995; Cohen 1995; Guttman and Thompson 1996; Young 2000). While questions of recognition (e.g. recognition of non-reducible differences between different cultural groups) have sometimes been seen as opposed to fair resource distribution, Nancy Fraser (2000) argued powerfully that recognition is closely interwoven with resource inequality. This is true above all, one might suggest, in relation to symbolic resources (the capacity to speak and be heard), especially in societies where the distribution of symbolic power is unequal. I want to leave until the final section the possibility of grounding the notion of communicative entitlement in a more general way, outside the framework of participatory democracy theory. The importance of doing so will emerge later.

The notion of communicative entitlement, then, has deep resonances. But to give it substance, we must clarify some of the specific purposes for which citizens need a fair share of communicative resources, and the specific means through which we imagine those resources operating. Here we confront a key uncertainty of current political sociology.

3 THE NEEDS OF DEMOCRACY?

What would be solved if the digital divide were ended? Where the term has an economic focus, the answer is, market functioning; more people online would increase the size, scale, and perhaps efficiency of markets. Where the term points purely towards pre-existing social inequalities (and here, as Warschauer (2003) argues, we could probably dispense with it), the answer is also clear—social 'functioning'—even if what counts as success is less easy to specify. But if we use digital divide to point to a political lack, then the answer is uncertain: a digitally more connected citizenry would result in what exactly for democracy?

To reply, 'a well-functioning democracy' begs the questions of what that means, and on what scale it can be achieved. Indeed one political sociologist, Alain Touraine (2000: 72), argues that 'desocialization' or 'the weakening of the social field' has reached such a point in late modernity that societies are no longer effective units of belonging (cf. Urry 2000). For Touraine, there is no coherent space of 'politics' remaining to which we should pay attention; this is not just because of a collapse of institutional legitimacy, but derives also from the contra-dictory scale of our personal lives:

Part of us is immersed in world culture, but, because there is no longer a public space where social norms could be formed and applied, another part of us . . . looks for a sense of belonging that is more immediate. . . . We are, on the one hand, world citizens who have neither responsibilities, rights nor duties, and, on the other, defenders of a private space that has been flooded by waves of world culture. (Touraine 2000: 5–6)

As a result, the very ideal of democracy must be rethought: no longer 'particip-ation in the general will' but 'institutions that safeguard the freedom of the Subject and permit communication between subjects' (Touraine 2000: 14). Clearly if Touraine is even half right, a major reassessment of what counts as citizen engagement is required, and it is interesting that communication forms part of Touraine's reformulation—but, strikingly, horizontal communication, not top-down communication.

Few political scientists or political sociologists in the US or the UK are as pessimistic as Touraine about the social underpinnings of democracy, although the fear that individualization will lead to an irreversible degeneration of the public sphere has found echoes in debates about the Internet's consequences for politics (Gitlin 1998; Sunstein 2001). But, whatever our pessimism or optimism, Touraine challenges easy assumptions that we know what sort of links between everyday experience and politics are either normal or desirable, or, therefore, what distribution of communicative resources is necessary if democracy is to flourish. Touraine's questioning of the contemporary social bond returns us, from a new direction, to recent digital divide research that asked how degrees of online connectedness affect the 'social fabric' (Matei and Ball-Rokeach 2003). While this work (drawing on the USC Annenberg 'Metamorphosis' project) suggests interesting contrasts between how different ethnic groups use the Internet for social connectedness, a problem is the project's functionalist assumption that the Internet *is* 'part of a general media system' contributing to social 'connectedness' (Matei and Ball-Rokeach 2003: 642, 647). But it is precisely this natural fit between individual/group uses of communication resources and wider social connectedness that Touraine challenges (cf. Bauman 2001).

If we turn to contemporary theorists of citizenship, the uncertainties multiply: 'what does it mean to belong to society?' asks Nick Stevenson (2002: 4); 'what counts as community and solidarity?' asks Anthony Elliott (2002: 55). Thomas Janoski and Brian Gras make the same point less rhetorically when they argue that 'theories of citizenship need to be developed to provide the informal aspects of citizenship *integrating* both the public and private sphere' (Janoski and Gras 2002: 42, emphasis added). What, in other words, *are* the practices that link private action to the public sphere, beyond the obvious act of walking down to the polling station to cast your vote?

Some in cultural studies would respond sceptically that there are no such practices, and the whole notion of the engaged citizen is a chimera (Miller 1999). Some sociologists would argue, with more regret, that those connecting practices between public and private spheres presupposed by citizenship are disappearing. Bryan Turner (2001) writes of 'the erosion of citizenship' by many factors including the changing organization of work and families; as a result, taken-for-granted contexts of civic action have been lost, although some new ones (television voting?) have been gained and arguably the whole nature of political engagement is changing (Bennett 1998). The question of attention is crucial here: the political sociologist Danilo Zolo (1992) argues that in complex societies the increasing demands made by mediated political messages on private citizens' finite attention spans reduce the likelihood of traditional civic engagement. Once again this returns us to a theme of the digital divide debate: the problem of 'attention scarcity' resulting from 'information abundance' online (DiMaggio et al. 2001: 313).

Network sociologists see no fundamental problem here and argue that the Internet accelerates a change already underway 'from all-encompassing, socially

controlling communities to individualized, fragmented personal communities'
(Haythornthwaite and Wellman 2002: 32), in which case Touraine is wrong to fear
for the future of society or indeed politics. Another strand of writing in sociology
and cultural studies relies on the notion of 'cultural citizenship' (Stevenson 1997;
Hermes 1998; Turner 2001) to fill the gap that Touraine perceives. But cultural
citizenship involves the rather traditional notion that a shared culture, generally a
shared national culture, is an essential lubricant of the wheels of politics. This idea
goes right back to the beginning of cultural analysis by Herder and others, and
remains important in T. H. Marshall's (1992: 8, 16, 44) famous post-World War II
analysis of citizenship: citizenship, for Marshall, includes 'the right to share to the full
in the social heritage' following 'the great expansion of the area of common culture
and common experience'. A recent discussion of cultural citizenship (Stevenson 1997:
42, 49) uses broadly similar language, so cultural citizenship comes to be defined
(Turner 2001: 12) as 'the capacity to participate effectively, creatively and successfully
within a national culture'.[9]

Whether we follow network sociology, or cultural citizenship debates, or neither,
it is too easy to assume that we have answers to some rather difficult empirical
questions: what does culture contribute to citizenship? What would a culture *of*
citizenship look like?[10] It is to the questions raised by empirical research into media
consumption and its possible links to civic culture that I now want to turn.

4 DIRECTIONS FOR EMPIRICAL RESEARCH?

Recently, writers have begun to move beyond general claims about 'cultural
citizenship' towards modelling in much greater detail what exactly *are* the preconditions for effective democratic practice. These models may help us think more
precisely about what we mean by 'communicative entitlement'.

When drawing on a well-known, but in many ways unsatisfactory, early literature
on civic culture (Almond and Verba 1963), Peter Dahlgren recently re-examined
this term:

civic culture points to those features of the socio-cultural world—dispositions, practices,
processes—that constitute pre-conditions for people's actual participation in the public
sphere, in civil and political society... civic culture is an analytic construct that seeks to
identify the possibilities of people acting in the role of citizens. (Dahlgren 2003: 154–5)

Dahlgren goes on to offer a multi-dimensional model of civic culture (in terms of a
'circuit' of six interlocking processes: values, affinity, knowledge, practices, identities, and discussion). A comparable approach is Ken Plummer's (2003: 81–2)

identification of five 'generic processes' through which new public spheres can appear: imagining/empathizing; vocalizing; investing identities through narrative; creating social worlds and communities of support; and creating a culture of public problems. Both models point to seeing the culture of citizenship as having at least three aspects: imaginative, cognitive and organizational/practical. Compare Michael Schudson's (2003: 59) point that citizenship (indeed the democratic 'lack' registered in digital divide debates) is about more than information possession, and Anthony Wilhelm's (2000: 98) point that online democracy requires more than political self-expression.

What do these (explicitly or implicitly) multi-dimensional models of civic culture engagement tell us about communicative entitlements, beyond the (obvious) point that formulating them is complex? First, they suggest that a basic level of information flow about common issues or problems is necessary: note that this need not be anything so coherent, or restrictive, as a shared culture, but simply an information space that enables prevailing life conditions to be seen, potentially, as objects of identification or dispute. Access to that information flow in a way that allows individuals to form their own opinions is basic. Secondly, access to opportunities to take part in collective discussion is also basic. So too, thirdly, is the opportunity to act as a citizen and, in so far as civic 'practices' (Dahlgren) go online, the effective opportunity to participate online.

So debates within political sociology can enrich our understanding of communicative entitlements, but the process is two-way since the digital divide literature can also enrich our understanding of the preconditions for an effective civic culture. Digital divide research, as we have seen, tells us that basic communicative entitlements of this sort will be ineffective without the technical capacity to use online resources, spaces and networks with confidence and fluency, and also the broader action-context(s) that make online opportunities for civic action meaningful. This last point is fundamental since, as Lloyd Morrisett (2003: 30) points out: 'Why should citizens enter into the hard work of education, discussion, deliberation and choice [online]? They must understand that when they go through that hard work, their choices and judgements will be used'.

But here we reach what we might call the hidden fallacy in discussing communicative entitlements: to forget that guaranteeing entitlements to communicative resources online even in the broadest sense (information, discussion spaces, sites for self-expression) will contribute little to democracy and civic engagement unless at the same time the mechanisms by which governments and other powerful institutions take account of people's uses of those resources are also rethought. Bill Melody made the same point more elegantly some years ago: 'To begin the process of defining the public interest in the information society, it is necessary to return to the essential functions of information and communication in modern participatory democracy, that is to provide opportunities for citizens to be informed and *to be heard*' (Melody 1990: 29, added emphasis). Apart from early visions of electronic democracy (often focused on the local scale), we have learned little about what it means for states in digital democracies to hear their citizens better.

The concept of communicative entitlement, then, implied by the digital divide debate and enriched by considerations of political sociology, depends on a wider context, which we are not yet able to fill in completely. Doing so would require further input from political theory (obviously beyond the scope of this chapter),[11] but it also requires input from empirical research on everyday media consumption that addresses Garnham's (1999: 118) fundamental question about 'the fields of action which are opened up or closed down' by people's use of the communicative resources available to them.[12] Acknowledging this incompleteness of the notion of communicative entitlements is not, however, to admit defeat; on the contrary, the value of the digital divide concept is to insert difficult and open-ended questions into debates about ICT provision that might otherwise be seen as 'merely' technical.

5 WHICH THEORETICAL FRAMEWORK?

So far in this chapter we have seen how posing the apparently simple question of what communicative resources people need in the age of digital media, takes us fairly quickly towards some fundamental issues (provided, that is, the debate is not arbitrarily closed down). These questions are:

- how in practice do people use communicative resources for purposes beyond the purely private?
- How might such use of communicative resources contribute to effective democratic practice?
- What do we mean by effective democratic practice?

It is this open-ended trajectory of questions about communications and democracy, carried by the term digital divide, that makes it still useful and provocative; the digital divide debate, in other words, has a future, and it would be absurd for this chapter to try now to reduce this complexity to a ready-made solution.

Instead, we can use the preceding discussion as a basis for broadening our understanding of the theoretical status of the term 'communicative entitlement', which, as we have seen, is implied by the debates on the digital divide. We saw earlier that it is relatively easy to ground the notion of communicative entitlement within theories of participatory democracy. From here we might build a notion of cultural 'rights',[13] including new rights for a digital age (resources to buy a modem, basic online training, and so on; cf. van Dijk (1999: 235)).

This would however unduly limit the scope of the notion of communicative entitlement, and thereby our understanding of the future of the digital divide debate. We must acknowledge here that lurking behind all discussions of democracy, social justice, and market functioning (the three areas where, at the outset, I suggested ICT resources have been acknowledged in digital divide debates to make a difference) are what Calabrese and Burgelman (1999: 8) call the 'fundamental and inextricable tensions between politics and economics'. It is easy, of course, to assume, as I have so far in this chapter, that political or social justice objectives can, in certain circumstances, have priority over economic objectives, notably when we are considering the institutional bases on which we should live together and resolve disputes over common resources. But it is better to acknowledge that others (e.g. Posner 2003) take a fundamentally different view (although, as such, that is not a question for debate here). Better, therefore, if we can, to formulate our notion of communicative entitlement in a way that is translatable into terms recognizable on both sides of the politics/economics divide.[14]

Here the work of Nobel-prize-winning economist and philosopher Amartya Sen on general human capabilities (and the ethical consequences of not allowing people the chance to fulfil their capabilities) is ultimately more helpful, I will argue, than work that starts out from rights to communicative resources, derived from a prescriptive model of active citizenship. The difference this makes now needs to be unpacked and explained.

Sen's capabilities approach

Sen's capabilities approach (1992, 1999) aimed to develop a globally applicable account of the principles on which development could be advocated; for this reason, he looked not for arguments that took democratic principles as automatic givens, but for arguments that could justify democratic principles in terms of some other broader human good (development), and ground development, in turn, in the concept of freedom. Sen was offering much more than an account of justice and fair distribution, based on the assumption of universal rights to certain goods. He was offering a regrounding of the principle of distributive rights, through a rethinking of the 'goods' that need to be fairly distributed (cf. Garnham 1999: 115). Sen's concern with human 'capabilities' links with the theme suppressed in digital divide debates about human 'capacity' (cf. Brown 2001). Clearly, if we can ground our notion of communicative entitlement in a theory of human goods and capacities for action, rather than the values of a specific normative position within political theory, we have broadened the concept's reach and potential applicability.

The goods of which we all deserve a fair share, as Sen sees it, are not the pleasures used by utilitarians as a reference point, nor the 'primary goods' used in Rawls'

Theory of Justice (Rawls 1972), but what Sen (1992: 6–8) calls 'functionings'. The problem, Sen argues, with those other ways of grounding a theory of just distribution is that they only measure the distribution of actual, achieved goods. But what if people vary greatly in the choices they exercise among a defined range of goods, and necessarily so, given 'the fundamental diversity of human beings' (Sen 1992: 8)? If this is so, then the best level at which to think about just distribution is not the level of goods, but the level of capabilities, more precisely 'a person's capability to achieve functionings that he or she has reason to value' (Sen 1992: 5). The concept of functionings provides stability amid the diversity of actual choice and the resulting diversity of human outcomes, since it points to underlying dimensions of human achievement that might generally be valued. These range from bodily health, to self-respect, to making choices about the development of one's life, to (crucially for the link to democracy) participation in the 'life of the community' (1992: 5). These functionings are 'constitutive elements of human well-being' (1992: 150). As a result, a person who lacks the capability to achieve these functionings (if they so choose), lacks something fundamental, something whose lack would not be clear from assessing simply what goods they possessed—what if they had chosen to give some of their goods away for some wider purpose?[15]

The link between Sen's theory of human capabilities/functionings and communicative entitlements was made by Garnham (1999). Garnham argued that informative media are 'enablers of a range of functionings' (1999: 121): this follows directly from Sen's inclusion of participation in the life of the community as one functioning (Sen 1992: 5); it follows indirectly from Sen's argument that an informed democracy is necessary to enable people to argue for fair treatment in the economic or other spheres (Sen 1999: 148–52). If this is so, access to informative media is a capability whose absence from an individual's 'capability set' (Sen 1992: 52) is a deficiency. Even more important, as Garnham (1999: 120–2) points out, this enables us to look at media's contribution not from the point of view of a consumption stream (which we 'take or leave'), but in terms of media's contribution to our range of capabilities, including our capability as citizens (cf. Gandy 2002). Mere availability of consumer choice in the media sphere is, in other words, insufficient; what matters is choice, *enabled by media*, which provides us with the opportunity of meeting our wider human needs on our own terms—and not just opportunity in the abstract, but 'the ability of people actually to make use of these options' (Garnham 1999: 121). This returns us to the questions of social stratification that emerged from the digital divide literature: for nominal access to a mediated stream of information essential, say, for awareness about one's political or economic rights does not amount to a real capability unless accompanied, for example, by the skills that would enable one to put that information to use. It is media's contribution to our capabilities in that enriched sense that we should assess.

Sen's capabilities approach has some additional advantages for thinking about communicative entitlements. First, it is grounded not in a particular model of democracy (for which there might not be consensus transnationally), but in an account of basic human needs and a related range of human functionings, on which more consensus might be possible. In its account of an objective set of human needs and functionings, Sen's approach is basically Aristotelian in spirit (Sen 1992: 39, cf. Garnham 1999: 119–20). Leaving aside difficult questions about the notion of human 'function' and more generally about the terms on which Aristotelian approaches can effectively be adapted to the contemporary world, there is the possibility here of developing a transculturally flexible frame for articulating questions of communications and democracy.[16] Relatedly, Sen's approach is applicable to all human beings equally, and therefore can ground a common approach to both types of digital divide, whether between or within nations. Third, Sen's emphasis on capabilities rather than actual goods helps us to distinguish between the *possibility* of access to particular communicative resources (which may be necessary), and actual *possession* of those resources. This might seem insignificant in a more traditional media environment where some media forms (television, newspapers) seem to constitute a basic minimum level of informational access, which must be achieved; but in a fluid digital media environment, where many choices over access options have to be exercised, it may be the capability of choosing, rather than the achievement of access to, a particular communicative resource that matters.

6 CONCLUSION

This chapter's argument has been that the digital divide exists and is likely to continue, so deepening existing social inequalities. But when we turn to the implications of the digital divide, particularly its implications for democracy, some clarifications become necessary. Here we used the term 'communicative entitlements', but found that the relation between communicative entitlements and effective democracy is not straightforward—not surprisingly since accounts of what constitutes democratic engagement, and how media might contribute to such engagement, remain in crucial respects undeveloped. Rather than complete the sociological account of what communicative entitlements might comprise in practice, and therefore what their fair distribution might achieve, we turned to a different question: how can the notion of communicative entitlements be best grounded philosophically (i.e in general terms, even if our understanding of their exact specifications remains incomplete)? Here we followed Sen's account of human needs and functioning, rather than relying on approaches built solely on the premises of participatory democratic theory, valuable though the latter theory remains for other purposes.

The aim, then, has been to review critically and reground debates about the digital divide and communicative entitlements. The plausibility of everything so far, nonetheless, relies on one fundamental point: the assumption that the digital divide, however contingent the factors that pushed it into the policy arena in the mid- to late-1990s, raises deep questions about the relations between communications and democracy—questions which long predate the digital era and affect all technologies of information and communication implemented on a large scale (cf. Garnham 1999; Peters 1999). These questions are, ultimately, ethical in nature (cf. Hacker and Mason 2003: 99–100; Stevenson 1999: 178). Once raised, they cannot be brushed aside on the basis that this or that measure of technical access distribution has been met. Nor do they fall away just because our understanding of how states can best facilitate a fair distribution of necessary communicative resources has shifted beyond an earlier, and rigid, model of state-directed funding of media production, and now includes, for example, models of 'subsidy' which give more scope for citizens to make their own media on their own terms (cf. Downing 2002); the breadth of, and multiple entry-points into, the digital media environment surely require greater flexibility in thinking about the policy implications of the (complex) divides of usage that persist. However they may be resolved, we can be sure that the questions—ethical, political, social—implicit in the digital divide debate will remain salient for a long time to come.

REFERENCES

ALMOND, G. and VERBA, S. (1963). *The Civic Culture*. Princeton, NJ: Princeton University Press.

BAUMAN, Z. (2001). *The Individualised Society*. Cambridge: Polity Press.

BENHABIB, S. (1995). 'Toward a Deliberative Model of Democratic Legitimacy', in S. Benhabib (ed.), *Democracy and Difference*. Princeton, NJ: Princeton University Press, 67–94.

BENNETT, L. (1998). 'The Uncivic Culture: Communication, Identity, and the Rise of Lifestyle Politics'. *Political Science and Politics*, 31(4): 740–61.

BROWN, M. M. (2001). 'Can ICTs Address the Needs of the Poor?', *Choices*, 10(2): 4–5.

BUCY, E. and NEWHAGEN, J. (2004). 'Preface: The New Thinking about Media Access', in E. Bucy and J. Newhagen (eds), *Media Access: Social and Psychological Dimensions of New Technology Use*. Mahwah, NJ: Lawrence Erlbaum, ix–xx.

CALABRESE, A. and BURGELMAN, J.-C. (1999). 'Introduction', in A. Calabrese and J.-C. Burgelman (eds), *Communication, Citizenship and Social Policy*. Lanham, MD: Rowman and Littlefield, 1–13.

CAREY, J. (1989). *Communication as Culture: Essays on Media and Society*. London: Routledge and Boston, MA: Unwin and Hyman.

Center for the Digital Future (2004). 'The Digital Future Report: Surveying the Digital Future: Year Four', http://www.digitalcenter.org/downloads/DigitalFuture Report–Year4–2004–pdt, accessed 18 Mar. 2006.

Children's Partnership, The (2000). 'Online Content for Low-income and Underserved Americans', http://whitepapers.zdnet.co.uk/0,39025945,60020807p-39000620q, 00htm, accessed 18 Mar. 2006.

—— (2003). 'The Search for High-Quality Online Content for Low-Income and Underserved Communities', http://www.childrenspartnership.org/AM/Template.cfm? Section=Home &CONTENTID=6646&TEMPLATE=/CM/HTMLDisplay.cfm, accessed 18 Mar. 2006.

COHEN, J. (1995). 'Procedure and Substance in Deliberative Democracy', in S. Benhabib (ed.) *Democracy and Difference*. Princeton, NJ: Princeton University Press, 95–119.

COMPAINE, B. (ed.) (2001). *The Digital Divide: Facing a Crisis or Creating a Myth?*. Cambridge, MA: MIT Press.

COULDRY, N. (2006). *Listening Beyond the Echoes: Media, Agency and Ethics in an Uncertain World*. Boulder, CO: Paradigm Books.

——, LIVINGSTONE, S. and MARKHAM, T. (2007 forthcoming). *Media Consumption and Public Engagement: Beyond the Presumption of Attention*. Basingstoke: Palgrave/Macmillan.

DAHLGREN, P. (2003). 'Reconfiguring Civic Culture in the New Media Milieu', in J. Corner and D. Pels (eds), *Media and the Restyling of Politics*. London: Sage, 151–70.

DIMAGGIO, P. J., HARGITTAI, E., NEUMAN, R. and ROBINSON, J. P. (2001). 'Social Implications of the Internet'. *Annual Review of Sociology*, 27: 307–36.

D'ORVILLE, H. (1996) 'UNDP and the Communications Revolution – Communications and Knowledge-Based Technologies For Sustainable Human Development', New York: UNDP, 30 April.

DOWNING, J. (2002). 'Radical Media Projects and the Crisis of Public Media', in R. Mansell, R., Samarajiva, and A. Mahan (eds), *Networking Knowledge for Information Societies*. Delft: Delft University Press, 300–7.

ELLIOTT, A. (2002). 'The Reinvention of Citizenship', in N. Stevenson (ed.), *Culture and Citizenship*. London: Sage, 47–61.

FRASER, N. (2000). 'Rethinking Recognition'. *New Left Review*, 3 (May–June): 107–20.

GANDY, O. (2002). 'The Real Digital Divide', in L. Lievrouw and S. Livingstone (eds), *The Handbook of New Media*. London: Sage, 448–60.

GARNHAM, N. (1999). 'Amartya Sen's "Capabilities" Approach to the Evaluation of Welfare and its Application to Communications', in A. Calabrese and J.-C. Burgelman (eds), *Communication, Citizenship and Social Policy*. Lanham, MD: Rowman and Littlefield, 113–24.

GITLIN, T. (1998). 'Public Sphere or Public Sphericules?', in T. Liebes and J. Curran (eds), *Media, Ritual and Identity*. London: Routledge, 38–52.

GOLDING, P. (2000). 'Forthcoming Features: Information and Communications Technologies and the Sociology of the Future'. *Sociology*, 34(1): 165–84.

GUTTMAN, A. and THOMPSON, D. (1996). *Democracy and Disagreement*. Cambridge, MA: Harvard University Press.

HACKER, K. L. and MASON, S. M. (2003). 'Ethical Gaps in Studies of the Digital Divide'. *Ethics and Information Technology*, 5(2): 99–115.

—— and VAN DIJK, J. (2001). *Digital Democracy: Issues of Theory and Practice*. Thousand Oaks, CA: Sage Publications.

HAYTHORNTHWAITE, C. and WELLMAN, B. (2002). 'The Internet in Everyday Life: An Introduction', in B. Wellman and C. Haythornthwaite (eds), *The Internet in Everyday Life*. Oxford: Blackwell, 3–41.

HERMES, J. (1998). 'Cultural Citizenship and Popular Fiction', in K. Brants, J. Hermes, and L. van Zoonen (eds), *The Media in Question*. London: Sage, 157–67.

JANOSKI, T. and GRAS, B. (2002). 'Political Citizenship: Foundations of Rights', in E. Isin and B. Turner (eds), *Handbook of Citizenship Studies*. London: Sage, 14–52.

HOWARD, P., RAINIE, L. and JONES, S. (2002). 'Days and Nights on the Internet: The Impact of a Diffusing Technology', in B. Wellman and C. Haythornthwaite (eds), *The Internet in Everyday Life*. Malden: Blackwell, 45–73.

KATZ, J. and RICE, R. (2002). *Social Consequences of Internet: Access, Involvement and Interaction*. Cambridge, MA: MIT Press.

——, —— and ASPDEN, P (2001). 'The Internet, 1995–2000: Access, Civic Involvement and Social Interaction'. *American Behavioral Scientist*, 45(3): 405–19.

KLING, R. (1999). 'Can the "Next Generation Internet" Effectively Support "Ordinary Citizens"?' *The Information Society*, 15(1): 57–63.

—— (2000) 'Learning about Information Technologies and Social Change: The Contribution of Social Informatics'. *The Information Society*, 16(3): 217–32.

LIVINGSTONE, S, BOBER, M. and HELSPER, E. (2004). 'Active Participation or Just More Information? Young People's Take Up of Opportunities to Act and Interact on the Internet'. London School of Economics, eprints.lse.ac.u.uk/archive/000003961, accessed 25 Oct. 2006.

MANSELL, R. and STEINMUELLER, W. E. (2000). *Mobilizing the Information Society: Strategies for Growth and Opportunity*. Oxford: Oxford University Press.

MARSHALL, T. (1992). 'Citizenship and Social Class', in T. Marshall and T. Bottomore, *Citizenship and Social Class*. London: Pluto, 31–51.

MATEI, S. and BALL ROKEACH, S. J. (2003). 'The Internet and the Communication Infrastructure of Urban Residential Communities: Macro- or Meso-Linkage?' *Journal of Communication*, 53(4): 642–57.

MAYHEW, L. (1997). *The New Public*. Cambridge: Cambridge University Press.

MELODY, W. (1990). 'Communication Policy in the Global Information Economy: Whither the Public Interest?', in M. Ferguson (ed.), *Public Communication: The New Imperatives: Future Directions for Media Resarch*. London: Sage, 16–39.

MELUCCI, A. (1996). *Challenging Codes*. Cambridge: Cambridge University Press.

MILLER, T. (1999) 'Television and Citizenship: A New International Division of Cultural Labor', in A. Calabrese and J.-C. Burgelman (eds), *Communication, Citizenship and Social Policy*. Lanham, MD: Rowman & Littlefield, 279–92.

MORRISETT, L. (2003). 'Technologies of Freedom?', in H. Jenkins and D. Thorburn (eds), *Democracy and New Media*. Cambridge, MA: MIT Press, 21–32.

MURDOCK, G. (1999). 'Rights and Representations: Public Discourse and Cultural Citizenship', in J. Gripsrud (ed.), *Television and Common Knowledge*. London: Routledge, 7–17.

—— and GOLDING, P. (1989). 'Information Poverty and Political Inequality: Citizenship in the Age of Privatised Communications'. *Journal of Communication*, 39(3): 180–95.

NORRIS, P. (2001). *Digital Divide: Civic Engagement, Information Poverty, and the Internet Worldwide*. Cambridge: Cambridge University Press.

OECD (2001). 'Understanding the Digital Divide', http://www.oecd.org/document/51/0,2340,en_2649_33757_1814131_1_1_1_1,00.html, accessed 18 Mar. 2006.

PETERS, J. D. (1999). *Speaking into the Air: A History of the Idea of Communication*. Chicago, IL: Chicago University Press.

Pew Internet & American Life Project (2000a). 'Who's Not Online', www.pewinternet.org, accessed 25 Mar. 2006.

—— (2000b) 'African-Americans and the Internet', www.pewinternet.org, accessed 25 Mar. 2006.

—— (2002a) 'Getting Serious Online', www.pewinternet.org, accessed 18 Mar. 2006.

—— (2002b) 'The Rise of the E-Citizen', www.pewinternet.org, accessed 18 Mar. 2006.

—— (2002c) 'The Broadband Difference', www.pewinternet.org, accessed 18 Mar. 2006.

—— (2003) 'American's Online Pursuits', www.pewinternet.org, accessed 18 Mar. 2006.

PLUMMER, K. (2003). *Intimate Citizenship: Private Decisions and Public Dialogues*. Seattle, WA: University of Washington Press.

POSNER, R. (2003). *Law, Pragmatism and Democracy*. Cambridge, MA: Harvard University Press.

RAWLS, J. (1972). *A Theory of Justice*. Oxford: Oxford University Press.

RICE, R. (2002). 'Primary Issues in Internet Use', in L. Lievrouw and S. Livingstone (eds), *The Handbook of New Media*. London: Sage, 105–129.

ROJAS, V., STRAUBHAAR, J., ROYCHOWDHURY, D., et al. (2004). 'Communities, Cultural Capital and the Digital Divide', in E. Bucy and J. Newhagen (eds), *Media Access: Social and Psychological Dimensions of New Technology Use*. Mahwah, NJ: Lawrence Erlbaum, 107–30.

SCANNELL, P. (1989). 'Public Service Broadcasting and Modern Public Life'. *Media Culture and Society*, 11: 135–66.

SCHILLER, H. (1995). 'The Global Information Highway: Project for an Ungovernable World', in J. Brook and I. Boal (eds) *Resisting the Virtual Life*. San Francisco, CA: City Lights Books.

SCHUDSON, M. (2003). 'Click Here for Democracy: A History and Critique of an Information-based Model of Citizenship', in H. Jenkins and D. Thorburn (eds), *Democracy and New Media*. Cambridge, MA: MIT Press, 49–59.

SELWYN, N. (2004). 'Reconsidering Political and Popular Understandings of the Digital Divide'. *New Media & Society*, 6(3): 341–62.

SEN, A. (1992). *Inequality Reexamined*. Oxford: Oxford University Press.

—— (1999). *Development as Freedom*. Oxford: Oxford University Press.

STEVENSON, N. (1997). 'Globalisation, National Cultures and Cultural Citizenship', *Sociological Quarterly*, 38(1): 41–66.

—— (1999). *The Transformation of Media: Globalisation, Morality and Ethics*. London: Longman.

—— (2002). 'Introduction', in M. Stevenson (ed.) *Culture and Citizenship*. London: Sage, 1–10.

—— (2003). 'Cultural Citizenship in the "Cultural" Society: A Cosmopolitan Approach'. *Citizenship Studies*, 7(3): 331–48.

SUNSTEIN, C. (2001). *Republic.com*, Princeton, NJ: Princeton University Press.

TOURAINE, A. (2000). *Can We Live Together?* Cambridge: Polity Press.

TURNER, B. (2001). 'The Erosion of Citizenship'. *British Journal of Sociology*, 52(2): 189–209.

UCLA (2000). 'The UCLA Internet Report 2000', http://www.worldinternetproject.net/default2.asp?page=published, accessed 18 Mar. 2006.

—— (2001). 'The UCLA Internet Report 2001: Surveying the Digital Future', http://www.worldinternetproject.net/default2.asp?page=published, accessed 18 Mar. 2006.

UK Cabinet Office (2000). 'Closing the Digital Divide: Information and Communication Technologies in Deprived Areas', www.socialexclusionunit.gov.uk/downloaddoc.asp?.id=137, accessed 20 Oct. 2006.

URRY, J. (2000). *Sociology Beyond Societies*. London: Sage.

US Department of Commerce (1998). 'Falling through the Net II: New Data on the Digital Divide', www.ntia.doc.gov/ntiahome/net2, accessed 18 Mar. 2006.

—— (1999). 'Falling through the Net: Defining the Digital Divide', www.ntia.doc.gov/ntiahome/fttn99/accessed 18 Mar. 2006.

—— (2000). 'Falling through the Net: Towards Digital Inclusion', www.ntia.doc.gov/pdf/fttnoo.pdf, accessed 18 Mar. 2006.

—— (2002). 'A Nation Online: How Americans are expanding their use of the Internet', www.ntia.doc.gov/ntiahome/dn/nationoline_20502.htm, accessed 18 Mar. 2006.

VAN DIJK, J. (1999). *The Network Society.* London: Sage.

WARSCHAUER, M. (2003). *Technology and Social Inclusion: Rethinking the Digital Divide.* Cambridge, MA: MIT Press.

WILHELM, A. G. (2000). *Democracy in the Digital Age.* New York: Routledge.

WILLIAMS, R. (1958). *Culture and Society.* Harmondsworth: Penguin.

WYATT, S., THOMAS, G. and TERRANOVA, T. (2002). 'They Came, They Surfed, They Went Back to the Beach: Conceptualizing Use and Non-use of the Internet', in S. Woolgar (ed.), *Virtual Society?* Oxford: Oxford University Press, 71–92.

World Economic Forum (2000). 'From the Global Digital Divide to the Global Digital Opportunity', http://www.ceip.org/files/projects/irwp/pdf/wef_gdd_statement.pdf, accessed 18 Mar. 2006.

YOUNG, I. M. (2000). *Democracy and Inclusion.* Oxford: Oxford University Press.

ZOLO, D. (1992). *Democracy and Complexity.* Cambridge: Polity Press.

NOTES

1. For a pioneering version of this argument, see Murdock and Golding (1989). Cf. also Stevenson (1999: 33) who calls for a 'politics of communication needs'.
2. For his credit for the invention, see Compaine (2001: xiv).
3. E.g. US Department of Commerce (1998, 1999); UCLA (2000); and specifically on ethnicity, see Pew (2000b). For a helpful overview, see Katz and Rice (2002: ch. 2).
4. See UK Cabinet Office (2000).
5. See Hacker and Mason (2003: 107), Bucy and Newhagen (2004: xi).
6. C.f. Pew (2002b) on the class differentials underlying the 'rise of the E-Citizen' in the US.
7. C.f. Livingstone, Bober, and Helsper (2004) on class stratification of UK young people's Internet use and Rojas et al. (2004) on class stratification of Hispanic and Afro-American Internet use in Texas.
8. For parallel UK research, see Selwyn (2004).
9. To be fair, Stevenson has recently modified his position slightly (Stevenson 2003: 333, 340), moving it towards cosmopolitanism.
10. It is a merit of Raymond Williams' well-known invocation of 'common culture' that it does not simplify such questions (1958: 259).
11. For interesting reflections on how mechanisms of representation might be rethought or enhanced in large-scale democracies with advanced communication infrastructures, see Mayhew (1997).

12. The author, together with Sonia Livingstone and Tim Markham, has recently completed an ESRC-funded project on 'public connection' that addresses aspects of this question: see www.publicconnection.org, and Couldry, Livingstone, and Markham (forthcoming 2007).

13. Cf. Murdock and Golding (1989: 183–84), Murdock (1999: 11–12).

14. That divide is being played out in interesting ways during the implementation of the UK Communications Act (2003) and the development of the UK's new super-regulator for the communications and telecommunications sector, the Office of Communciations (OFCOM).

15. Cf. Sen's discussion of fasting (1992: 51–2).

16. See Couldry (2006) for a similar argument in favour of a neo-Aristotelian approach to global media ethics.

CHAPTER 17

GOVERNANCE AND STATE ORGANIZATION IN THE DIGITAL ERA

PATRICK DUNLEAVY

1 INTRODUCTION

ATTITUDES to the impact of the Internet, the web, and modern information and communication technologies (ICTs) on government are highly polarized. At one end of the spectrum is a voluminous ICT-utopianist literature, constantly churned out in marketing-hype mode by software manufacturers, hardware suppliers, systems integrators, management consultancies, government departments, and agencies, and often politicians themselves. Here curves are always upwards sloping, phases are always progressive (never regressive), and the change process is always unilinear and 'transformational'. Corporate and agency leaflets and websites show smiling, empowered citizens revelling in the new transactional freedoms that this or that proprietary product has gifted them, while seriously-professional *uber*-bureaucrats in Armani suits look on complacently in the knowledge of a job well done. Even after the dot.bomb experience, much of this remains crude technological determinism—because the kit has changed, so must social arrangements. Of course, academic writers in the same boosterist vein (mainly from information technology (IT) departments and business schools) tread a more careful and sophisticated path. But many still anticipate sweeping changes, not just in state administrative processes, but also in the fabric of democratic political life itself.

At the other end of the spectrum is a voluminous public management and public administration literature, written in a conventional and often strongly backwards-looking vein. (In the US a failsafe hallmark of this literature is extended references to 'Jeffersonian democracy' or thinkers like Dwight Waldo; and in Europe, discussions of the Weberian ideal type of bureaucracy, as if it were an actually existing innovation.) Here, modern ICT developments are literally a footnote to history, about as important for the big issues of democratic governance and administration as the advent of the ballpoint pen in lieu of fountain pens. The role of ICTs in this literature is most commonly to be ignored or mentioned only in passing, usually for some obvious reason that links to this literature's established obsessions. For instance—using more ICT played a part in the 1980s, business-orientated, early 'new public management' (NPM); the large scale of government ICT projects adds to the 'complexity' of modern state administration; or the web can cut job advertising costs for public sector agencies. Apart from such almost random asides, however, the literature presents ICTs as of marginal significance for how government processes are organized or how deeper-seated public sector modernization is accomplished: 'Institutional theory has not accounted for information technology and its multi-faceted role in changing the contours of the landscape within which roles and structure influence perception and action' (Fountain 2001: 103).

It would be easy to dismiss these polarized positions as reconcilable in some blurred-over, middle way that presents a more 'realistic' picture by simply leaving out the hype on one side, and the neglect on the other. A small corpus of serious work already stresses the importance of institutional and political processes in shaping the adoption, dissemination, and use of new ICTs in governance. Behind an apparently boosterist title, Jane Fountain's *Building the Virtual State* in fact finds that:

The dot.coming of government is only just beginning. . . . The Internet is a revolutionary lever of institutional change. Yet inside the machinery of the state, amid a web of institutional structures that offer perverse incentives for innovation and efficiency gains, the action of this lever is complex, indirect and mediated significantly by institutional and organizational arrangements. (Fountain 2001: 201, 193)

Eugene Bardach sums up her themes conservatively as: 'Traffic in cyberspace, it turns out, still has to slow down and wait for institutions and human nature to do their thing'.[1] In the same vein, Darryl West's sweepingly titled but actually painstakingly empirical book *Digital Government* argues:

Revolutions do not have to be quick and abrupt for there to be widespread change. It may take a while for technological innovations to diffuse throughout a country. . . . While we have uncovered little evidence of transformational change in the e-government area, there is the possibility of more extensive change emanating from the Internet in the longer term. (West 2005: 7, 181)[2]

I want to argue here something rather different and more complex. In narrow and of course different ways, both the implied technological determinist views and the marginalizing public management views expressed above generate insights. Modern ICTs have an apparently inexhaustible capacity to demonstrate that 'everything must change so that everything can remain the same'.[3] The over-claiming, technological determinist hype, on the one hand, and the public management literature's time-warped stasis, on the other, are thesis and anti-thesis in a Hegelian dialectic. Despite their apparent orthogonality, each position captures something vital and important about modern governance, which I try to capture as synthesis in the concept of 'digital era governance'. Transcending the apparent contradictions of ICT-utopianism and ICT-rejectionism, allows the key insights of both views to illuminate a deeper process of change.

The chapter has three main parts. The first looks briefly at how successive waves of administrative and organizational theory have downplayed the role of admin-istrative technologies and technological change affecting government organiza-tions. Next I look at the key issues in post-1995 'e-government' debates and processes, briefly surveying the still little-researched changes of government ar-rangements brought in around web-based ICTs in advanced industrial countries. The third section sketches an emergent ideal type of 'digital era governance' focusing on the reintegration of government sector processes, a new effort at holism and a range of connected 'digitalization' changes in the organization of government information.[4]

2 WHY ICT CHANGES WERE MARGINALIZED IN THEORIES OF GOVERNMENT ORGANIZATION

Most people nowadays credit Max Weber with appreciating the importance of a simultaneous shift to relying on both written documentation and hierarchical organization at the end of the nineteenth century. In fact, this association had been noted many decades earlier (Albrow 1970: 28). The distinctiveness of Weber's analysis lay rather in his acute insistence that a bureau could *only* be constituted by bringing together well-trained, qualified, and impersonally-selected officials, in a corporate and systematized organizational configuration, together with the written papers and rules needed to conduct business. It was this simultaneity that created the inherent rationality advantages of bureaucracy compared with other forms of organization at the turn of the nineteenth century. In the language of a later era of industrial sociology, Weber correctly appreciated that offices are socio-technical systems where paperwork played a critical role in five main respects.

1 Official files and documents (covering rules, memos, letters, decisions, and case folders) provide a key underpinning for the impersonality and consistency of modern administration. They codify and express a common understanding that ensures that similarly trained officials will make identical decisions (Simon 1957: 158–60).

2 Well developed and systematically organized files provide what Montaigne called a 'paper memory', a collective capability many times larger and less fallible than any individual capacity. The critical facility here was the development of file registries with indexing and later cross-indexing systems, along with the capacity to store and re-find huge volumes of documents and papers. Essentially these paper-based systems endured from the late nineteenth century through to the 1980s and 1990s, when the first free text forms of searching began to be widely feasible. In this period newer indexing and document storage methods (such as punched card systems, most early mainframe computer indices, and automated storage and retrieval systems) changed only the size and capacity of government information systems, but not their fundamental operation (Margetts 1999). Registries became larger, more centralized, and their cross-indexing more automated and sophisticated. But their essential *modus operandi* did not change much. In most cases paper files still remained the most comprehensive and authoritative record, with big governments storing tens of millions of case files for long periods. (For instance, to this day the US Congress requires the storage of all citizenship documentation on paper for 75 years.) The development of relational databases with some structured query capabilities had some positive impacts later on how data were stored, especially how much text was computerized. But even here, most existing large administrative systems were surprisingly little affected up to the mid-1990s.

3 The joint development of file registries along with the impersonal occupation of offices and strengthening of bureaucratic training and socialization essentially gave bureaucratic organizations a capacity to operate continuously through time—Weber's permanence characteristic. In the government sector, turbulent competition between organizations is rarer and the selective culling of failing organizations weaker than in the private sector, so that serious analysts have wondered: 'Are government organizations immortal?'(Kaufman 1976).

4 The cumulative enhancement of bureaucratic modes of storing records and data had a widespread impact on the quality of 'information' itself. Government bureaucracies especially allied with newly expanded and powerful professions to advance the codification and certification of categories and classifications,

seen as enhancing the reliability and precision of the stored data. Some important results of this long-run change have been charted by the sociological literature on the spread of a 'governmentality' orientation. The combined political/official/professional/social science ambitions to monitor, categorize, control, or influence social behaviour have been greatly extended (see Rose 1999). The latest, turn of the twentieth century manifestation of this phenomenon has been an 'audit explosion' within the public sector itself, fuelled by a growth of internal regulators and the linking of KPIs (key performance indicators) to NPM reorganizations (Power 1994).

5 The large-scale storage of data and enhancement of data-handling and manipulation technologies also fuelled the development of calculations upon or modelling of data, which Weber also pointed out as distinctive to bureaucratic modernity a century ago. Increasingly official statistics and analyses have underpinned decisions made by all other actors in society, forming a key aspect of social capital.

Given this apparent centrality of data storing and accessing functions, why was it that paperwork systems and later government ICT operations played so little part in the development of public administration and public management theory? There are multiple strands in the answer, some immediate and rather obvious and others having a fairly indirect effect. In the immediate factors, both paperwork and later early waves of ICT and office automation concerned solely 'back office' functions, mostly carried out by relatively low status non-manual staffs doing work with a self-contained and technical character. This background work was hived off to generally quite separate divisions with servicing functions, and well-removed from the main lines of public policy and political decision-making. The post-war push for office automation and later the successive use of mainframe computers, networked systems, and eventually personal computer (PC) networks all came into government from outside businesses, with consultancies and experts as the main change agents. There were periods where governmental organizations pioneered important advances in data processing, as in Roosevelt's push for extended social security during the New Deal which relied in part on punched card technology; or the later 1950s and 1960s Cold War expansion of defence mainframe computing. But the more general post-war picture was of government agencies lagging behind large corporations, first in their adoption of new paperwork-handling systems and later with ICT systems. Add to these elements the fundamental endurance of paperwork models for handling data processing, and it is easy to see why government ICT generally seemed derivative of business practices, while intellectually, and in social status terms, a backwater.

Government organizations also reacted in an understandable, but perhaps slightly perverse way to the post-war advances in the routinization of paperwork, and later the advances in ICTs. In any organization where a function ceases to absorb human attention and operates in a stable and predictable way, that function will tend to move down the prioritization agenda for key decision makers, however fundamental or 'mission critical' it may be for organizational success. For instance, pricing goods and stock control in supermarkets has become much easier and less demanding of human time and capacity since the introduction of electronic tills that can hold and change product price details and automatically re-order products from central warehouses or suppliers as they are sold to customers. Hence, store managers have to think about this function less and assign fewer staff to monitor it, moving it down their list of concerns. This trend cannot easily be reversed. Perhaps only a power blackout or an ICT system collapse preventing the supermarket from selling any goods at all can actually bring home to the managers and staff involved how vital stock control still remains. In the same way within government organizations the primary impact of new systems of paperwork-handling, and later the development of simpler forms of well-functioning government ICT, was a tendency for it to drop off the top decision-makers' agenda in favour of continued, less routinized problems, chiefly human resource management, organizational culture issues, and managing crises.

A third factor for much of the twentieth century was that progress in automation and paperwork routinization was concentrated chiefly in the more old-fashioned, strongly hierarchical forms of government agency, which Mintzberg (1983) terms 'machine bureaucracies'. In these organizations the routine operations of government ICT were concentrated in services divisions, distinct from the 'middle line' of the organization, and 'on tap but non top' IT staff were organized in separate specialist staff hierarchies in the UK and many Commonwealth civil services, where generalist staff predominated in senior ranks. In countries like Japan and France with strong organizational cultures focused on departments, IT staff were few and were seen as peripheral to departmental culture. Only in some of the large US federal departments and agencies with scientific or technological briefs created in the Cold War were IT staff (or before them other technical staff) close to top-level decision makers.

More generally, however, Weber's prediction of the growing dominance of hierarchical bureaucracies seemed to be awry for much of the late twentieth century. The most rapidly growing forms of government organization were what Mintzberg (1983) terms 'professional bureaucracies'—such as hospitals, health service organizations, universities, schools, and social services departments. Professional groups grew fast under corporate and state patronage and their characteristic bureaucracies concentrated power in the professional staffs within the operating core, close to the clients being served. Until the 1990s, professional bureaucracies characteristically had simpler and more old-fashioned paperwork systems, which resisted computerization and automation for decades longer than large business corporations. Thus, the pattern of post-war welfare state growth favoured organizations with much less developed ICT systems and paper file registries, while the

Weberian machine bureaucracies with more developed information processing routines seemed less modern and more residual to contemporary public management tasks. The decentralization of professional bureaucracies to state or regional governments and to local authorities contributed a further twist to the weighting of late twentieth century government growth towards less ICT-intensive organizations. There has been a general and repeated pattern of a lower level of ICT development in smaller government units than in large national bureaucracies.

There were exceptions to this weighting, of course—notably the growth of very large 'divisionalized' bureaucracies in the US defence, intelligence, space, and nuclear energy sectors, with professional or machine bureaucracies as the component divisions. These agencies were strongly influenced by the parallel growth of an extensive 'para-state' of contractors. These agencies often handled issues with a high-technology or strongly scientific content, making far more intensive use of ICT. But they seemed like special cases compared with the rest of civilian government (Margetts 1999).

A final dimension of the neglect of ICT in public management theory was a strong theoretical blindspot about the importance of information in the delivery of government services. Pluralist and political science approaches concentrated on the nexus between politicians and the administration, tacitly assuming that an organizational capability to carry out political purposes was unproblematic. One or two isolated accounts, such as Deutsch's (1966) 'cybernetic' metaphor or Simon's (1957; 1973) focus on bounded rationality, did ascribe importance to information processing. But the even more influential theory of incrementalism suggested that crab-wise, exploratory movement was the most that could be expected of government organizations. The theory of organizations was also the source of many different interpretations, mainly derived from industrial firms whose experiences and processes read across poorly to government sector service organizations. Economic theories of bureaucracy began to be influential in the 1970s, but it was only in the 1980s that they started to be acknowledged by public administration or public management literatures, and only in the 1990s that they began to elucidate the importance of information demands and capabilities in structuring firms and government agencies' configurations.

Even today there are relatively few public management authors who recognize that government organizations exist in large part in order for their staff to process information, and then to take actions based on the results. Christopher Hood (1983) was one of the first to see theoretically that agencies need 'detector' tools for finding things out and then 'effector' tools for getting things done. Each of these broad types of tools he cross-groups into four categories, denoted by the 'NATO' mnemonic, using the first letters of each category. *Nodality* is the central position of government in society, such that other actors tell (a well-connected) government things for free and also assign special credibility and attention to messages or advice that government issues. *Authority* is the ability of government to requisition information or resources from other social actors and to mandate courses of action, using law and regulations. *Treasure* is the use of finance or other resources (like property or requisitioned assets, such as conscription labour) to purchase information, effort, or compliance, or to make resource transfers to particular social groups. Finally Hood's *organization* category includes the accumulation of an institutional capacity to process information and realize desired outcomes by employing staff, creating agencies, building up standard operating procedures, developing appropriate expertise, and so on.

The use of ICTs primarily relates to government's organization, of which these technologies are now a critical element, and to nodality, especially since many relevant networks are becoming digital. But governments also now rely integrally on ICTs to disperse treasure (especially for welfare state transfers) and for the contemporary exercise of authority functions. Yet these involvements and dependencies have been almost invisible in the public administration literature and not much more prominent in public management discussions and debates.

3 E-GOVERNMENT, WEB-BASED PROCESSES, AND GOVERNMENT ICT

The post-1994 development of e-government programmes differs radically from previous experience of ICTs in government in five key aspects:

- the presence of a long-run 'vision' of change;
- re-raising conventional dilemmas of governmental centralization and decentralization in new and specific forms;
- the developing incidence of technology advances across types of agencies;
- changes in ICT professionalism; and
- the extension and growing importance of the 'contract state' in ICTs.

The vision of change has proved critical in shaping government decision makers' perceptions for several reasons. First, it is apparent that the development of the Internet, the web, computer networks, and digital technologies has proceeded very rapidly and in hard-to-predict ways. The conventional governmental reaction to turbulent change conditions has often been to stay out of such areas in terms of major investments, until things have settled down and risks are reduced sufficiently to commit large amounts of public money. The major exceptions to this pattern have generally involved major political imperatives, as with the Cold War, the space race, and more recently, the 'war on terror'. However, the ICT industry and associated professionals successfully counteracted much of this government reluctance to engage by developing a 'phases model' of how long-run change in public sector ITs will progress. It is now hard to pin down exactly the genesis of this pervasive image, but its outlines are well known (see Figure 17.1).

The model arranges e-government changes into (usually) five successive phases of development, beginning with 'billboard' web sites, which simply make available existing information content in a web-accessible electronic form, while the underlying processes of the agencies involved remain essentially paper-based, with electronic file indices. The second phase is often described as 'e-publishing', with agencies going beyond special billboards to undertake more extensive dumping of information onto the web, but with little capacity for citizens to search interactively for information they need. The third phase involves the development of systematic interactive content, allowing citizens, enterprises, and other users to interrogate government information bases more, and to seek tailored electronic information closely suited to their needs. The fourth 'transactional' phase is where the ICT industry argues that all government should primarily aim to be, and within relatively short periods from the start of an e-government push, say five to ten years. Here citizens can undertake transactions directly with agencies, establishing their identities and filing forms electronically so as to complete whole sequences of operations and accomplish meaningful goals like paying the correct amounts of taxes, or establishing eligibility for, and commencing receipt of welfare payments.

Finally, the fifth and most vaguely specified 'transformational' phase is pictured as a nirvana period where government agencies are empowered by technology to work seamlessly together in purposeful, collaborative, and citizen-orientated ways, while

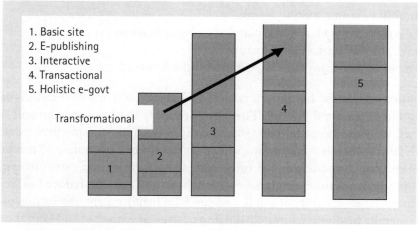

Fig. 17.1 The stages of e-government model
Source: Based on Fig. 2 in Dunleavy et al. (2002).

new forms of electronic community multiply in civil society and interact spontan-
eously in new e-democracy ways with government decision makers. Like all rhetorically effective long-run goals, the transformational period is acknowledged to be
as yet distant. But its ICT-utopianist characteristics often work strongly to allay
concerns by politicians and officials that perhaps extensive ICT spending may not
work, in a triumph of hope over experience. Aiming forward to 'transformational
government' also provides the basis for a multiplicity of press releases guaranteed to
identify the politicians involved as far-sighted strategists on the issue.

Despite its pervasiveness the theoretical or evidential basis for the five-phase
image is extremely slender. That there will likely be a long-run pattern of improvement and change in e-government is not in doubt, but that it will fit closely to the
phases identified or proceed in some form of linear sequence is. The phase diagram
has been used to justify diverting large amounts of public money into 'transactional' projects, even if the task involved is something as straightforward and minor
as applying for, and paying for, a fishing licence on-line—effectively just giving a
name, address, and credit card details to a government agency. Completing projects
of this kind allows governments to portray themselves as already entering
the 'transactional' phase, even if their information-provision arrangements more
generally are elementary or un coordinated. In research interviews for a recent
book on government ICT in seven countries (Dunleavy et al. 2006b) we commonly
encountered officials running very large e-government investment projects
(designed to reap transactional goals) who reacted with a kind of disdain to
questions about why their existing web sites were of elementary design or how
they can accurately understand citizens' or enterprises' needs without first building
up a detailed picture of users' electronic behaviours. Their standard response was
that their project 'is far more than just a web site', when what they often seemed to
mean is that it 'is not even a web site'.

The tragic history of public sector information-giving investments also captures
in an acute form what is wrong with the five-phase model. In the period from
around 1994 to 2003, governments and politicians were often keen to skip over the
merely 'interactive' phase of providing information content in a fashion that was
readily electronically searchable. When this kind of intermediate and unfashionable
objective got any priority at all, changes were largely accomplished by spawning
new special purpose websites with discrete domain names (often not recognizable
as government names). In most countries the government domain showed a strong
proliferation of web pages and URLs, layered one on top of another, creating a
confusing jungle of sites for civil society actors (and even for officials in other
agencies) to navigate. Commonly there was little effort to develop coherent
government web site strategies and search facilities were lamentable.

The rise and market launch of Google in 2004 (and the growth in other search
engines and portals), produced some reappraisal, recognizing the centrality of

informational tools within government. But it is as yet hard to point to any country where this has extended to a reconsideration of the five-phase model and a recognition instead that achieving genuine and connected-up interactivity is likely to be the major challenge for at least the next two decades of e-government. Few officials can yet see that this challenge will be only partially addressed after the 'low hanging fruit' of web-enabling easy transactional targets has long gone. For instance, as yet no e-government system anywhere in the world has moved beyond text-based access to its services, despite the well-known problems of at least one in six citizens even in advanced industrialized countries having very low levels of functional literacy and numeracy, especially with unfamiliar and difficult materials. In the commercial sector, on line gaming has been successful in developing highly sophisticated and accessible graphical interfaces with wide market appeal and a capacity to handle simultaneously thousands of fast-interacting players. Yet at the time of writing (2006) any form of graphical interface for government remains in a distant future.

Centralization/decentralization dilemmas have been a staple theme in public management and they have recurred in e-government in two ways. First, the provision of electronic information and services can be organized in either a central, whole-of-government way, or in a decentralized, agency-by-agency way. Since modern government systems assign the vast bulk of administrative tasks and associated funding to the departments and agencies with implementation responsibilities, the early development of web sites in the late 1990s was unsurprisingly undertaken by them. The result was to 'let a thousand nettles bloom', with US citizens, enterprises, and other officials confronted by literally thousands of websites—over 4,000 sites for the Pentagon alone by 2000.

In many countries indexing this labyrinth was a distinctly second order priority, with no organization clearly capable of co ordinating developments. For instance, in the US four different attempts to co ordinate a whole-of-government index site failed before the experimental www.first.gov portal was finally established (at an initial cost of just $4 million, in a government system spending at that time more than $1.5 trillion a year). In the NPM countries the stress on disaggregating previous large, hierarchical departments into agencies, quasi-governments, or independent bodies, and on competition, meant that co ordination of web site provision was especially difficult. For instance, the NPM pioneer country New Zealand ended up with 40 ministries and over 300 central agencies (for a population of under 4 million people) and did not even attempt an e-government programme until late 2001.

In the UK a relatively strong e-government programme with centralized targets was established in 1998 and some substantial investments made in joint facilities like identity authentication and a government portal. But the direct results of successive rounds of centralized investments were disappointing—even in areas like the establishment of inter operability or metadata standards across government. In Japan strongly entrenched departmentalism, and the lack of expertise as a result of outsourcing of all government ICT to corporations, meant that a coherent e-government programme was launched only in 2002. By contrast the Canadian federal government successfully organized a cross-departmental effort, coordinated by central departments, but bringing together the major spending agencies, which kept the country top of most e-government rankings in the early 2000s.

The second dimension of centralization–decentralization dilemmas involves coordination across tiers of government—an especially critical set of issues in federal countries where national and state or regional governments parcel out key functions affecting citizens and enterprises between them. Since the 1970s, most large, advanced industrial countries that were previously unitary have switched towards at least quasi-federal arrangements, thanks to a pluralization of elected tiers of government in previously Bonapartist countries (France, Spain, and Italy), and the late advent of devolution in the UK. The conspicuous exception remains Japan. But even there, and within England, the rise of e-government raises new issues about the balance of e-government efforts for citizens and enterprises between local authorities and central governments. E-government centralization makes most sense for large or medium-size enterprises where the staff interacting with government may be chiefly specialists single-mindedly carrying out repeat operations (such as exporting goods, checking property deeds, paying corporate taxes or VAT, or filing company accounts).

Generally, most citizens' relationships with central governments are relatively restricted to taxation, social security, and a few regulatory issues. In other aspects their relations with many central agencies are relatively episodic—as with renewing a passport only once every ten years. By contrast, citizens may have most chance of interacting regularly with government at the state or local level, where multiple services are often provided in specific and accessible ways. Hence, if citizens are ever to learn how government web sites operate, or are to come across new and useful information while browsing a government portal, the greatest potential may lie at the regional or local levels. (It is hard to be sure here because the available evidence on patterns of use of government e-services remains very elementary.) But if so, efforts (such as that in the UK) to build a dominant, centrally-funded public sector portal may run against the grain of how most citizens interact with government.

At the least, these reflections suggest that an integrated e-government effort to involve citizens will need a high level of integration between three tiers: centrally-provided, cross-government facilities; national or federal departments' information provision; and state and local governments. The prospects here are not conspicuously good, however, with most research showing that state or regional governments lag far behind national governments in their expenditures and development of e-services. Local authorities are generally even further behind, with the smallest and most rural municipalities least likely to have the funding or expertise to provide facilities—even though these are often also areas where spatial access to services is also poor. However, there have been a few efforts, notably in the UK and Scandinavia, to 'pump-prime' local e-government with central funds in such a way that e-services become mainstreamed. Spending to counteract digital divide problems in local communities is a little more widespread.

Technology advances across machine and professional bureaucracies have added their own variations to e-government patterns. I have already pointed out that government ICT efforts in the period up to the 1990s concentrated on more traditional and large-scale 'machine bureaucracy' agencies, running functions like taxation, social security, and immigration. The diffusion of PC networks and related 'general purpose' software across most government agencies in the 1980s and early 1990s changed this pattern a bit, converting previously computer-free professional bureaucracies towards more standard patterns of business organization with smallish amounts of ICT and more computerized processes.

The early part of the Internet and web-influenced period saw the emphasis on achieving 'transactional' changes and focused attention again on machine bureaucracies. E-taxation processes were spectacularly developed in the Scandinavian countries and some other small states such as Singapore. And Australia and the US both achieved early gains with e-filing of income taxes by cooperating with software firms or tax accountants to make e-filing systems readily available and encouraging tax accountants to submit on their clients' behalf electronically. Even in lagging countries such as the UK, where these elementary steps were not taken, by 2005 around a quarter of self-assessed tax forms were submitted electronically. By contrast, electronic social security processes have lagged much further behind, chiefly because government restrictions require more paper documentation and signatures and because social security forms are often complex and loaded with restrictions on citizens' eligibility and requirements for personal identification and signatures. However, there has been a considerable shift towards phone-based processes, and their effective operations actually rely chiefly on web-enabled call centres accessing joined-up back-office ICT systems. In most large countries, the underlying integration of taxation and social security ICT systems remains deeply problematic. The departments running such systems often have any number of different mainframes, or other computers running networks and registers, interconnecting in rather fragile ways and dependent upon millions of lines of legacy code that is extremely expensive to maintain.

In one other machine bureaucracy area, immigration, the political investment in homeland security after the 9/11 attack in the US in 2001 has wrought something of a technological transformation. Systems that were once run in at best lightly automated ways, with extensive reliance on inspecting paper documentation, have been transformed by moves to adopt biometric identification (at considerable cost since initial documentation must be issued in person). The US, the UK, and other countries plan to use biometrics pervasively in monitoring inward and outward flows, not just of home-country citizens, but of foreigners required to have biometric passports. Some countries have ambitious schemes for electronic automation, as with the UK's programme of identity cards, 'e-borders' (stopping undesirable entrants before they board planes to reach the UK), and I-visas (electronic monitoring of foreigners within the UK).

Since 2000, the development of web-based ICT systems has had a renewed, if delayed, impact on a large swathe of public sector professional bureaucracies which have previously lagged in their ICT development, especially hospitals, social welfare agencies, universities, and legal bureaucracies. For these areas, significant new possibilities have been opened up by the ability to quickly and cheaply digitize an enormous range of information and to network it so that it becomes easily available to multiple actors involved in case-managing individual clients and co-ordinating treatments. In general, the past ICT investments in these areas have been relatively small scale, but this pattern is changing. For instance, after 15 years of minimal ICT spending the UK's National Health Service hospitals were engaged in the mid-2000s in a centralized programme for developing standardized patient record systems (at a cost of some £13 billion)—a change essential to deliver a political promise to expand patient choice within a previously rationing-based system.

The inrush of modern ICT into such laggard areas has gone along with the transition of some machine bureaucracies towards much more sophisticated technological solutions, as already discussed, and the traditional strength of ICT development in scientific, intelligence, and defence areas, so as to create a considerably enlarged high-tech government ICT sector that may radically change the character of government operations. Ambitious plans exist to create further hi-tech machine bureaucracies to undertake existing functions in different ways. For example, defence sector automation in the US may offer possibilities for centrally directing armed forces with far fewer military personnel on the ground, using fully automated equipment such as sensors, response systems, and drone aircraft, all co ordinated by satellite positioning systems. Somewhat similarly the UK government at one time planned to introduce road-charging technology on a national scale based on the European Union's Gallileo satellite system, tracking all car and truck movements, either countrywide or in extensive congested areas. Whether the high-tech armed forces ever arrive in significant numbers, or whether the direct taxation of car use can ever displace the current much simpler means to collect UK car taxes (car registrations and petrol taxes included in the pump price), remains unclear. But even to articulate such large and complex plans implies a potentially different scale of government dependence on ICT systems, and on the professional and corporate expertise needed to design and maintain them.

Developing IT professionalism has been crucial to the evolution of e-government systems in several ways. There are multiple major occupations in the ICT area, all somewhat fragmented from each other in terms of their education, socialization, and training. Although the traditionalists' idea of the ultimate core ICT occupational groups is computer science and computer engineering, Denning (2001) lists 19 occupations as 'IT-specific disciplines', 16 'IT-intensive disciplines' (of which nine are primarily IT-focused), and an additional nine 'IT-supportive occupations' (such as computer technicians, help desk technicians, or web designers). As a result, a cohesive or effective 'ICT profession' does not exist in any advanced industrial country.

There are additional lags and complexities in the public sector, where we might otherwise have expected that there was scope for ICT professionalism to find a niche. Many government systems work by assigning the management of different agencies or sectors to dominant professional groups or communities (such as doctors, lawyers, government scientists). In return for accepting political direction and socializing their members extensively into respect for the public interest, these occupational groups receive large amounts of public funding to deliver services and often develop partly autonomous spheres of delegation, as well as largely professionally-run agencies or networks.

However, fragmented ICT professionals have instead been split up in small packets across public agencies, and rarely run their own organizations. Apart from a few small specialized technology advice and assessment agencies, whose role has often been limited, or even abolished, under NPM arrangements, ICT professionals have almost never achieved a secure institutional base of their own. Because of their internal fragmentation between numerous occupations they have rarely developed the powerful cross-cutting mechanisms that have helped other dispersed occupational groups (such as government economists, statisticians, or scientists) to establish a clear identity anyway. In the US, Congressional insistence led to the appointment of Chief Information Offices (CIOs) in all federal departments and major agencies. At the federal-wide level, the Council of CIOs became an important force on some issues, especially for instance the year 2000, or Y2K, preparations. Elsewhere, in the Netherlands government, the importance of 'informatization' changes has been intellectually recognized. A somewhat different balance of political and professional power has been achieved, so that Dutch politicians generally have to do far more to demonstrate that the new ICT systems, necessary for new laws, exist before they can be implemented. But these are rare examples of ICT professionalism within government systems. In every country ICT professionals as an occupational group still fall a long way short of the influence of comparable occupational groups, such as government accountants, financial experts, or lawyers.

A strong factor maintaining and accentuating this relative lack of influence has been the inability of most agencies within government to retain key ICT professionals within the sector. In the 1960s and even into the 1970s some of the largest and most technically challenging computer projects were introduced by government, and the public sector could often attract key talent to work on their projects (Margetts 1999). However, with outsourcing beginning to take a strong hold in the 1980s, and pushed furthest in NPM countries (the UK, Australia, and New Zealand) governments have generally lost much of their former ability to retain key expertise compared with large ICT companies. The big systems integrator companies in particular can offer ICT professionals far more interesting flows of work tasks and much longer and better-paid career paths than all but the very largest and most specialized or high-tech government agencies. So the influence of ICT professionals within government has been hugely constrained by the impacts of outsourcing in attracting away into private corporations and ICT consultancies many of the most talented and critical staff.

Contracting for information technology is the final dimension of e-government change, with government ICT work dominated by very large companies in some countries. In Japan, the wholesale outsourcing of government ICT to companies has prevailed since the 1960s, with powerful departments maintaining over decades long-term contracting relationships exclusively with major Japanese hardware manufacturers (but including eventually IBM Japan). In the NPM countries (again the UK, Australia, and New Zealand) private sector dominance of government ICT systems development work has been more recent. By 2000, it was common to find that the top five companies in these countries accounted for 90 to 95 per cent of the government ICT market by value. In the UK a single company (EDS) at one time controlled three-fifths of the market, before government took forceful action in 2003 to re-create more diversity of supply. Contract scales and time periods also increased sharply in the bigger and richer NPM countries (except New Zealand). In the UK typical contract lengths went to ten years, with contract scales often reaching several billion pounds. And new forms of private sector involvement (such as private finance initiative (PFI) 'build, own, and operate' contracts) were used to purchase ICT systems for a time—until some inherent problems in respect of risk transfer for ICT systems emerged, leading to PFI deals for ICT projects being banned by the UK Treasury in 2004.

The implications of wholesale outsourcing for governments' abilities to even retain an 'intelligent customer' capability in ICTs were also adverse. In the UK in the late 1990s, government departments with major ICT dependencies and projects costing hundreds of millions often retained very few technical staff. In some cases, such as the Inland Revenue department, the most senior ICT personnel were three or four tiers below the level of departments' management boards. In the US the huge scale of the civilian government ICT market, combined with a vigorous federal stance of maintaining strong competition, produced much lower industrial concentration, with the top five corporations accounting for around a quarter of the total market. But across most countries the importance of attracting and managing big ICT corporations' involvement to the successful delivery of government projects has increased sharply, especially in sectors outside physical science, high-tech, or defence agencies (where contractual dominance of ICT development was already very high).

However, some countries (such as Canada) have followed countervailing practices designed to maintain a strong capacity to develop ICT systems in-house and to create a competitive tension between government provision and outsourcing to contractors. Other countries, such as the Netherlands, achieved a similar effect by cutting up their ICT projects into small parts and then tendering them in a proactive way so as to maintain a strong diversity of suppliers. Typically there are around eight to ten contractors per Netherlands central department and most contract sizes are kept below a few million euros.

4 DIGITAL ERA GOVERNANCE

There are strong grounds for believing that over the next 20 years (to 2025) a connected set of institutional, organizational, conceptual, and technological changes will continue to extensively transform public management and government systems.

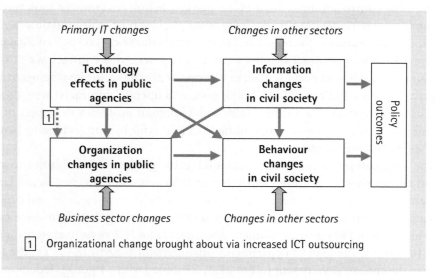

Fig. 17.2 The centrality of ICT changes in contemporary public management change

Source: Based on Dunleavy et al. (2006b)

I term this new constellation of factors 'digital era governance'. As Figure 17.2 shows, it has several roots and processes, in all of which a technological colouration or component is important, but in which there is no simple technological determination of changes. In itself, the feeding through of technological changes within government has no direct effects upon policy outcomes in the figure. Instead ICT changes work through indirectly, in several different ways.

First, organizational changes, and organizational culture changes take place inside the government sector. Digital era changes are already triggering numerous significant shifts in how government conducts business—a large-scale switchover to email in internal and external communications; the rising salience of web sites and intranets in organizational information networks; the development of electronic services for different client groups; the growth of electronic procurement systems; a fundamental transition from paper-based to electronic record-keeping, and so on. A tipping point in many organizations' development towards digital agency status is when they move over from files and documentation recognizably the same as in Weber's day, where the authoritative version of policy is recorded on paper, to holding the authoritative version electronically (usually on an intranet) and simply printing off paper copies as needed. This transition reflects the ineradicability of serious 'version control' problems in any mixed paper/electronic systems. Full digital agency status is potentially achievable by many government agencies in advanced states, especially at the central or federal government tier and in regulatory areas, but of course less so for delivery agencies that physically fulfil service needs themselves. In former NPM countries there is an influential additional pathway for organizational change, the impact of large-scale contractor involvement in delivering ICT-related administration processes on the organizational arrangements and cultures of the agencies they supply, denoted as Flow 1 in Figure 17.2.

Contemporary ICT changes also operate via shifts in societal information-handling norms and patterns, as modes of informing consumers, and involving them with corporations change across leading-edge business sectors. Particularly influential for government have been the disintermediation changes affecting the most cognate or similar private sector services industries, such as banking, insurance, comparator specialists, travel firms, and even electronic merchandisers. Similarly, the business-to-business interactions in fields like procurement spill over directly into what civil society actors expect of government. As consumers' and corporations' behaviours in the private sector change, so there are direct demands for government information and transaction practices to shift in parallel ways. The lags involved here are considerable, of the order of half a decade, but there are strong similarities in the patterns of diffusion of innovations across public and private sectors. Figure 17.2 shows that changes in information systems and alterations in citizen behaviours, partly shaped by government ICT and organizational changes, are the key pathways along which alterations in policy outcomes are accomplished.

At every point in Figure 17.2 the impact of digital era governance influences is also externally conditioned. The key influences on primary ICT changes are commercial, the demands from the business sector for new capabilities and then the oligopolistic (or in software near-monopolistic) supply-side responses. The major external influences on state organizational changes remain business managerialism, although a different vintage from the now dated NPM influences, with many current effects also shaped strongly by digital era influences. Societal information systems are integrally linked and civil society behavioural changes reflect much more general contextual shifts. In more specific terms the impact of digital era governance practices can be considered under three main themes: reintegration, needs-based holism, and digitalization.

Reintegration components reflect the key opportunities for exploiting digital era technology changes by simplifying the institutional structure of government, making it more transparent and purposeful both for officials involved in it and for citizens or enterprises trying to use it or influence the state. In countries like the UK and Australia the potential benefits are enhanced by the savings possible from reversing some of the disaggregation changes built up in these strong NPM systems. Reintegration approaches are not simple reruns of the old centralization phases of centralization/decentralization cycles. Instead they cover a range of different strategies:

- some re-governmentalization of privatized services (as with airport security in the US or Railtrack in the UK);
- joining up government, both organizationally and electronically or virtually;
- cutting out complexities and duplications in order to radically squeeze down back-office costs in favour of either front-line services or slimmer government;
- the re-centralization of some services; and
- the development of business process outsourcing towards shared services— especially in a mixed economy mode where in-house and private corporate suppliers compete to deliver key back-office services to client agencies in areas such as ICTs, call centres, human resources, financial management, citizen redress functions, legal services, and many other functions.

Needs-based holism goes beyond the internally-focused reforms included in the reintegration theme, and seeks additionally to simplify and change the wider relationship between agencies and their clients. One foundation for such changes is the development of sophisticated interactive information-giving for citizens or enterprises. Another pillar is creating larger and more encompassing administrative blocs focused around client needs, linked with 'end-to-end' re-engineering of processes, stripping out unnecessary steps, compliance costs, checks, and forms and putting in their place 'ask-once' administrative processes and different forms of 'one-stop' shops, some electronic and others organizational. Holistic government also stresses developing a more 'agile' state apparatus that can respond speedily and flexibly in real time to a wide range of changes in the social environment or to external threats.

Digitization changes seek to realize contemporary productivity gains from ICT in radical ways, especially by achieving a transition to fully digital operations. One possibility is a form of radical disintermediation analogous to that in commercial sectors, a process of cutting out the 'middle man' (in this case the mass of the government bureaucracy) and allowing citizens to interact more directly with policy systems. For example, 'zero touch technology' systems can allow citizens to interact with government without any human staff intervention being needed, as with the London congestion charge or some significant smart card systems already in use. Active 'channel streaming' and customer segmentation could mean that instead of electronic channels being seen as supplementary to conventional administrative and business processes (at additional cost), they instead become genuinely core processes, with only 'exceptions handling' running through paper-based or front-office processes. In most liberal democracies closing down non-electronic routes (using either pricing mechanisms or regulatory compulsion) can follow only if large-scale switches to electronic channels have already been achieved. Not all possible digitization changes are positive. In particular, if constitutional and legal controls on data misuse are not strong, there are severely adverse potentials in the creation of huge, pooled, government data warehouses, making available sophisticated data-mining and matching techniques to state personnel. For instance, under the banner of acting against terrorist or criminal threats these changes might all too easily be extended in highly regressive ways undermining key democratic freedoms of speech and movement. But in liberal democracies with secure constitutional safeguards for privacy and data protection the most optimistic potential impacts of digitization changes would see the creation of 'isocratic' (that is, do-it-yourself) government, in which citizens and enterprises increasingly manage their own compliance, leaving slimmed down state agencies with more focused roles of 'holding the ring' against defectors and non-compliance.

5 CONCLUSION

The radical thinker Ivan Illich brilliantly attacked the pervasive tendency to reify information, insisting instead that we recognize the essentially temporary, ephemeral, and 'in use' character of human knowledge:

The world does not contain any information. It is as it is. Information about it is created in the organism [a human being] through its interaction with the world. To speak about the storage of information is to fall into a semantic trap. Books or computers are parts of the world. They can yield information when they are looked upon. We move the problem of learning and cognition nicely into the blind spot of our intellectual vision if we confuse vehicles for potential information with information itself. (Illich 1973: 101)

Most practitioner accounts of the role of ICTs in government fail at this first hurdle, committing errors of perception so deep-rooted that their exponents literally cannot see that any given technology exists only in use. But equally it is important to recognize that the prevalent non-technological (even anti-technological) emphasis of public administration and public management studies commits similarly serious errors, almost blanking out critical aspects of contemporary government organizations' fundamental operations. The anthropologist Mary Douglas has stressed the importance of 'how institutions think', not by having 'minds of their own' but instead by being founded on analogies, conferring identities on people, 'doing the classifying' and remembering and forgetting: 'Institutions create shadowed places in which nothing can be seen and no questions asked. They make other areas show finely discriminating detail, which is closely scrutinized and ordered' (Douglas 1988: 69). These kinds of processes, both in government organizations themselves and in the academic institutions studying them, explain why it is that the role of ICTs has been marginalized so extensively and for so long.

The approach advocated here recognizes two partly divergent propositions as equally important. On the one hand, as Illich reminds us, government organizations are socio-technical systems in which technology changes never exert an autonomous influence, but are always endlessly being constructed and reconstructed in use. On the other hand, the ICT elements of contemporary bureaucracy are increasingly fundamental, and their management involves some of the most critical aspects of state administration. At a limit, government organizations could 'become their web site' (as one Australian official put it), moving beyond 'adhocracy' to an organizational form that exists as a system primarily in cyberspace. The optimistic take of the 'digital era governance' concept is that in the next few decades, in the most privileged of 'advanced countries', this development can co-exist with and even positively foster the development of 'isocratic government' in which citizens solve their own problems (as they always have and must), yet with proactive ICT facilitation by government of the largest and most inherently collective endeavours (such as 'holding the ring' on cooperative behaviours and maintaining a public realm).

There are also numerous ways in which this vision can be deformed and limited. Governing elites may reify systems or technologies—for example, using modern ICTs to construct a pervasive 'surveillance state', a possible outcome of some countries' contemporary pushes for 'homeland security'. At the same time, elites may simply ignore or mis-appreciate the specific ICTs characteristics of contemporary governance, producing the large-scale crises and failures in ICT investments characteristic of the UK government from the 1980s to around 2000. These all too likely recurring possibilities emphasize the importance of correctly assessing the role of ICTs in government and of assigning to it academic attention and resources commensurate with its increasing importance in terms of contemporary government operations and the key collective endeavours of modern societies.

References

ALBROW, M. (1970). *Bureaucracy.* London: Palgrave Macmillan.

DENNING, P. J. (2001). 'The Profession of IT'. *Communications of the ACM*, 44(2): 15–19.

DEUTSCH, K. (1966). *The Nerves of Government.* New York: Free Press.

DOUGLAS, M. (1988). *How Institutions Think.* London: Routledge & Kegan Paul.

DUNLEAVY, P., MARGETTS, H., BASTOW, S. et al. (2002). *Government on the Web II*, National Audit Office 'value for money' study number HC 764, Session 2001–2. London: The Stationery Office.

——, ——, —— et al. (2006a). 'New Public Management is Dead—Long Live Digital Era Governance'. *Journal of Public Administration Research and Theory*, 16(3): 467–94.

——, ——, —— et al. (2006b). *Digital Era Governance: IT Corporations, the State and e-Government.* Oxford: Oxford University Press.

FOUNTAIN, J. (2001). *Building the Virtual State: Informational Technology and Institutional Change.* Washington DC: Brookings Institution.

HOOD, C. (1983). *The Tools of Government.* Basingstoke: Macmillan.

ILLICH, I. (1973). *Tools for Conviviality.* London: Caldar and Boyars.

KAUFMAN, H. (1976). *Are Government Organizations Immortal?* Washington DC: Brookings Institution.

MARGETTS, H. (1999). *Information Technology in Government: Britain and America.* London: Routledge.

MINTZBERG, H. (1983). *Structure in Fives.* Prentice Hills, NJ: Wiley.

POWER, M. (1994). *The Audit Explosion.* London: Demos.

ROSE, N. (1999). *Powers of Freedom: Reframing Political Thought.* Cambridge: Cambridge University Press.

SIMON, H. (1957). *Administrative Behavior: A Study of Decision-Making Processes in Organizations* (2nd edn). New York: Free Press.

—— (1973). 'Applying Information Technology to Organizational Design'. *Public Administration Review*, 485–503.

WEST, D. (2005). *Digital Government: Technology and Public Sector Performance.* Princeton, NJ: Princeton University Press.

NOTES

1. Quoted, backcover of Fountain's *Building the Virtual State*.
2. In fact it is hard to see from West's findings why he is optimistic. Immediately after the passage quoted, he muses in a curiously vague way: 'There are several factors that presage an optimistic future for e-government: the engagement of young people in Internet technology, societal trends that encourage the adoption of new technology, and the generally favourable views that most Americans hold towards Internet technology' (West 2005: 181).
3. In Lampedusa's oft-quoted phrase from his novel, *The Leopard*.
4. Throughout this chapter I draw heavily on joint work with Helen Margetts, Simon Bastow and Jane Tinkler, whose contributions I gratefully acknowledge (see Dunleavy et al. 2006a, b).

CHAPTER 18

PRIVACY PROTECTION AND ICT: ISSUES, INSTRUMENTS, AND CONCEPTS

CHARLES D. RAAB

1 INTRODUCTION

THE protection or invasion of privacy is usefully seen in terms of different dimensions. Privacy of the body, the self, personal space, correspondence, and personal information are among the main categories that feature in an academic literature that is, by now, enormous and diffuse. The overlapping or discreteness of the dimensions, whether they are sub-types of some overarching concept of 'privacy', and whether the concepts can travel across cultures and eras, are among the themes of a good deal of sociology, anthropology, social and individual psychology, philosophy, history, law, political science, and the literary and performing arts. Whether privacy is possible in a globalized, consumerist world that is heavily dependent upon the use of information and communication technologies (ICTs) to process large quantities of personal data,[1] and in an increasingly edgy socio-political world of terrorism, counter-terrorism and surveillance, is also a large question that is approached from a variety of perspectives, from the fatalist to the Panglossian, with many way-stations in between.

Far from being an obscure 'nerd's charter', rendered even more impenetrable when called 'data protection', the study of information privacy is enlivened by its engagement with practical issues and controversies. The interest in this subject has rocketed over the last 30 years or so as major social, economic, and governance patterns and processes have become restructured and globalized around the importance of information about identifiable individuals. Among these underlying processes is surveillance—or 'dataveillance' in Clarke's (1988) coinage[2]—construed broadly to include the monitoring, tracking, sorting and profiling of persons for a variety of purposes, and involving an array of sophisticated technologies including closed-circuit television (CCTV) and mobile and tracking technologies such as radio-frequency identification (RFID) devices.

This chapter focuses on the privacy of personal information. Following a short, indicative literature survey, it frames the discussion in terms of a very few illustrative themes that open up a larger number of avenues for further research; the cited literature, albeit not comprehensive, enables deeper understanding.[3] Three prominent areas of information privacy are selected for review and comment, with a view to identifying some critical questions and issues that are to the fore in policy and governance debates as well as in research. The first area is the ways in which governments and other organizations have attempted to regulate the increasingly intensive, extensive, and global processing of personal data. The second concerns the prevalent practice of sharing data across organizational boundaries, giving scope to further invasions of privacy alongside benefits realized by organizations as well as individuals, and involving uncertainties about control and related matters. The third is especially, but not exclusively, associated with the contemporary preoccupation with terrorist and criminal threats to society, law, and order, and reflects on the effect of the safety and security agenda upon the protection of privacy. The first two involve the erosion, to one extent or another, of different kinds of boundary. All of these areas generate questions and policy issues for debate as well as items for an agenda of future research. The chapter concludes by drawing the latter together to point a way forward.

2 BRIEF OVERVIEW

A vast body of social scientific, legal, and technological scholarship, as well as more popular writing on information privacy, has borne upon the possibility and means of providing safeguards for privacy—however construed—in the dynamic, complex and diverse activities in which a growing volume of information about living individuals is processed. These activities take place in public places, workplaces, and in a host of other social and spatial settings, and increasingly over the Internet and in ambient intelligence or ubiquitous computing. While they are often celebrated as the hallmarks of a modernized government and of a technologically powered, consumer-oriented economy, they have also fuelled concern about the extent and lack of transparency of these information processing phenomena. The practical attention of lawmakers, regulatory officials, and industrial and commercial decision makers in the extensive domains of the state and the market, as well as of groups and individuals in civil society, has also been engaged. With differing interests, these participants interact in the broadly political processes of exploiting the benefits of the 'information age', or in limiting the adverse effects of surveillance and dataveillance. Many works (e.g. Ball and Webster 2003; Davies 1996; Garfinkel 2000; Lyon 2003a; Marx 1999, 2003; Norris and Armstrong 1999; Whitaker 1999) tackle the impact of these practices on privacy, civil liberty, and other important societal values. In one sense, such sources have served to re-focus an older dystopian literature as the information age or information (super)highway entered new territory.

Persuasive literature (e.g. Bowker and Star 1999; Flaherty 1989; Gandy 1993; Lyon 1994; 2001, 2003a) suggests that privacy, while an important human value at stake in the use of ICTs, may be a less significant focus of attention than other values, such as dignity, selfhood, equality, and sociality, with which privacy is closely associated, but which may be seriously and directly affected by information practices even where privacy invasion is less at issue. Much depends on the way privacy is understood as a value and as a right (Neill 2001); but this chapter will not grapple with this conceptual issue, except in one of its facets, as will be seen later.[4]

Privacy protection is sometimes seen as an obstacle to commercial and governmental purposes, but it is also—and in many respects—construed as a facilitator of the conditions required for the use of ICTs when personal data are involved. Technical security solutions are to the fore (e.g. Denning and Denning 1998), increasingly seen as the promoters of the confidence and trust that are considered to be essential elements, especially in online transactions (e.g. Camp 2001; Mansell and Collins 2005; 6 1998; Raab 1998). Scholarly writing has paid some attention to security and privacy issues in commerce or public administration (e.g. Bekkers, Koops and Nouwt 1996; Bellamy and Taylor 1998; van de Donk, Snellen and Tops 1995), and in the context of electronic democracy (Coleman, Taylor and van de Donk 1999; Hague and Loader 1999), but has also grappled with more primal issues of crime and policing (e.g. Ericson and Haggerty 1997; Thomas and Loader 2000), national and personal security (Lyon 2003b), and genetics (Laurie 2002); these are likely to remain at the forefront of investigation for a considerable time. Legal literature on privacy has been especially profuse, much of it dealing with major policy and regulatory issues, and some of it exploring or surmounting the limits of statutory or common law in providing protection for online transactions and transborder flows of personal data.[5]

3 THE FORMATION OF PRIVACY REGIMES

The question of regulation has occupied a central position in policy debates and research on information privacy over a long period of time, and each new generation of ICTs has added more issues to the agenda even while some early ones fade in importance. This chapter, therefore, gives this question pride of place, for it also allows reference to be made to many ICT-related issues and developments. This section reviews and comments upon the main lines of the history of attempts to protect privacy, structured in terms of the tools or instruments that have been fashioned. The response to technological, economic, and governmental developments implicating personal data has been largely national, within an international framework that has played an important, although sometimes secondary, role. The relationship between these levels has become highly important in recent years, and will be revisited in the conclusion to this chapter.

Policy responses to the extensive and intensive use of personal information go back a long way in industrialized countries, where the advent of the computer and subsequent ICT instruments, and the increased pressure to exploit personal data in a host of economic and governmental applications, led to concerns that privacy and other individual and social values might be under threat (e.g. Rule 1974; Sieghart 1976; Westin 1967). Privacy protection was identified as an important regulatory issue in the early 1980s' environment of telephony and cable television for interactive services (Flaherty 1985), and in more general contexts (Simitis 1987).

The formation of country-based regimes for protecting privacy has been the main tendency arising from those perceptions, and it continues still in many parts of the world. Yet information processes and systems stretch beyond the national containers in which both they, and attempts to regulate them, may have originated. One of the most dramatic recent developments in practice has been the solidification of inter- and supra-national trajectories of change—referred to by some as globalization—as the volume and pace of the flow of personal data across jurisdictions have increased, largely owing to the advent of the Internet. The growth of the Internet, the ubiquity of increasingly sophisticated ICTs from, roughly, the early 1990s, and new governmental and business purposes have combined to elevate both privacy threats and privacy solutions to a new level. This erosion of boundaries has challenged the enforcement of privacy and related rights, hastening the obsolescence of practical measures taken to regulate change, and of many of their underlying nation-state-based, offline, assumptions. In many fields, they have generated a very large academic industry, one that also incorporates or revisits analyses relevant to non-Internet activity. Analytical and prescriptive writing on the regulatory problems of cyberspace has burgeoned (e.g. Kahin and Nesson 1997), but so rapid and so recent has been the acceleration of change and of the ferment in the regulatory world that scholarship, too, is rapidly becoming outdated.

Over nearly 40 years, and in many countries and regions, a variety of strategies have been developed by governments and other organizations for protecting privacy in personal information (Bennett 1992; Bennett and Raab 2006; Flaherty 1989). They include a mixture of types of instruments and involve a range of institutional and individual actors, including business firms, regulatory agencies, governments, international bodies, technologists, lawyers, citizens or consumers, and others. Activity to protect privacy takes place at many jurisdictional and geographical levels, from the micro to the macro, in the private and public sector, and at many places along the flow of personal data. New tools have been debated or developed as privacy protection has evolved to cope with new conditions, and as shortcomings have been found in the established repertoire of instruments. Not all of this activity can be taken as especially heartening news for privacy advocates, for the results are frequently weak, patchy in coverage, and intermittent, if not entirely absent. Nevertheless, regulatory regimes for privacy protection have become institutionalized and centralized on well-known principles and assumptions.

The search for protective instruments first turned to legislation to regulate information processing, and to the delineation of guidelines and principles. These principles[6] came to be authoritatively articulated in documents devised in international arenas (Council of Europe 1981; OECD 1981; Commission of the European Communities 1995), and guided the legislation of the 1980s and beyond, although these documents are showing their age in the twenty-first century. To date, information privacy or data protection laws have been passed in a large number of countries, with the most recent examples coming mainly from the Asia-Pacific region, South America, and countries in East and Central Europe. Laws have also been created at sub-national levels, such as the separate states of the US, the Canadian provinces, Germany's *Länder*, and states in Australia. Many countries—especially EU member states prior to the recent expansion—have moved into further stages of amended or renewed legislation; others are recent first-timers; and still others, including China, have yet to enact general laws. Some laws achieve the gold standard of general, comprehensive coverage with important supervisory and sanctioning powers exercised by regulatory bodies often termed commissions. But there are many instances where the information processing activities of only one sector or another are regulated by law, in piecemeal fashion and without special oversight machinery, reacting to brush-fires of public concern: the US legislation for children's online privacy and for video rental data are famous make cases in point.

Most countries have legislated to protect personal data in both the public and private sectors. Some, however—the US, Canada, and Australia furnish prominent examples—have shown great reluctance to regulate the activities of private business firms, although the public/private distinction has itself become somewhat tenuous: another case of boundaries being eroded, as business and government undergo transformation in their processes and relationships. In many countries, such blurring has promoted policy efforts to ensure that all sectors be regulated appropriately, because modern public administration increasingly contracts with the private and voluntary sectors to provide services to the public, using identifiable and often highly sensitive personal data in, for example, health and social care, and the criminal justice system.

Yet, while the laws embrace internationally agreed principles, there have been significant differences among the laws over the years, in terms of their coverage of manual as well as automatically processed data, their sectoral applicability, their means of enforcement, their provisions for oversight and redress, and their relation to other instruments of regulation. Variations reflect differences in legal and administrative traditions, political emphases, and cultural factors (Bennett 1992). This unevenness was seen as a major problem for fair economic competition within Europe at the beginning of the 1990s, prompting a solution in terms of member states' conformity to a new, ostensibly make higher level, and more prescriptive set of institutional and legal requirements. As was anticipated, this piece of supranational legislation, the EU Data Protection Directive (Commission of the European Communities 1995), has come to have global repercussions. It has therefore been at the centre of attention and debate for the way it attempts to protect the personal information of citizens of the EU wherever in the world it flows.

The 'Safe Harbor', negotiated at considerable length and with much controversy between the US and the European Commission, is a direct result of the Directive's potential bite upon transatlantic westward flows of personal data to a country which, in the eyes of Brussels, lacks 'adequate' data protection (Charlesworth 2000; Shaffer 2000; Swire and Litan 1998; Bennett and Raab 1997; Farrell 2002). It enables US firms formally to register their declared adherence to a set of rules within a scheme monitored by the Federal Trade Commission (FTC). At the global level, the World Trade Organization (WTO) is a potentially significant player in disputes between countries concerning the effect of privacy protection upon international trade, although not directly involved in shaping the laws of states and regions. The attempt at supranational regulation also includes the effort of creating standards through bodies such as the International Organization for Standardization (ISO) and the Comité Européen de Normalisation/Information Society Standardization System (CEN/ISSS), although the future of global regulatory activity, especially through legislative and standardization pathways, cannot easily be foretold (Bennett and Raab 2006; Raab 2006).

The rapid development of the electronic communication of personal data and, in particular, the spread of the Internet as a vehicle for commercial transactions, has led to increasing exploration of the possibilities of technological solutions to privacy issues. This accompanied a growing disillusionment with the efficacy of laws, by themselves, to afford sufficient protection to consumers and citizens as the flow of personal data across national boundaries accelerated. Building privacy safeguards into ICTs, as well as allowing individuals to select their desired levels of safeguard, have become some of the main foci of attention in the world of information privacy policy and practice.

Cognizance of technological means for privacy protection was not, however, greatly evident among regulatory officials until their attention had been brought to applications of encryption (Diffie and Landau 1998) and other privacy-enhancing technologies (PETs) enabling anonymity in systems of electronic cash payments (Chaum 1992) and in other commercial processes. A joint project between the Ontario and Dutch data protection regulatory authorities (Ontario 1995) boosted the credibility of the PET approach amongst the community of officials and agencies that had been brought into existence with the formation of data protection laws in a large number of countries and lesser jurisdictions. Scholarly works in the borderland between law and technology pointed to the rule-making property of ICTs as an important way forward (Lessig 1999a; Reidenberg 1998). The interest shown in designing privacy into the technology, rather than relying solely on organizational, cultural, or legal solutions, arguably reflects Winner's (1989) perception that the structure of artefacts manifests social or political tendencies. If that is so, then ICTs can be fashioned to protect privacy rather than to threaten it. The realization of this possibility has become a main thrust in developments in recent years, incidentally allowing connections to be forged among technologists, lawyers, and ethicists who debate and often promote the PET route as the key solution to privacy problems. With some justification, critics have disparaged such solutions as a technological fix if they are proffered as the only or best way of protecting privacy.

Going back to at least the 1990s, the increasing policy interest in electronic commerce exhibited by international organizations has registered a concern with consumer trust and the trustworthiness of electronic transactions, both business-to-business and business-to-consumer. Data security has been at issue, but so also have been wider conceptions of privacy protection for the personal information necessary for ordering, shipping, payment, and customer-relations management; as Burkert (1997) argues, PETs should be distinguished from security devices. Somewhat ironically, a supposed attrition of deference to technological expertise manifested in late twentieth-century public opinion, and the technophobia of many early privacy activists, appear to have been stemmed in the incorporation of technological innovations for trustworthiness and privacy protection within information infrastructures. An EU ministerial conference on Global Information

Networks in 1997 highlighted these trust issues, pointing out the relevance of encryption and digital signatures alongside legal mechanisms. But the public availability of cryptography was a highly controversial issue in the 1990s, pitting government law-enforcement interests against both business and privacy groups (Koops 1999). Technological provisions for making secure payments online, and for allowing consumers to choose the level of privacy protection they may seek for their personal details—the Platform for Privacy Protection (P3P)—have been important PET innovations, although P3P's claims aroused scepticism in the privacy community.

Laws and PETs do not exhaust the inventory of instruments for the protection of information privacy. A wide range of invasive practices, involving the excessive or surreptitious collection of personal information online and the amassing and commodification of enormous amounts of data on identifiable individuals, has grown up over the years. These practices pose a threat to personal privacy, but in business circles it is also realized that the worry of significant proportions of the public about what happens to their information poses a threat to commerce itself; such public concern is amply documented by public opinion surveys in many countries (Bennett and Raab 2006). Although it comes in several different models (Priest 1997–8) and involves various instruments (Bennett and Raab 2006), self-regulation has secured an important place in regulatory systems, in which data controllers, in the jargon of the data-protection world, develop and subscribe to codes of practice and other pledges and commitments to their customers (data subjects). In some countries where legislation is desired to be avoided, self-regula-tion has been put forward as a better option or at least as an alternative worth entertaining seriously, if not necessarily as a panacea (e.g. Swire 1997; Mulligan and Goldman 1997), and an entire philosophy and rhetoric of free consumer choice and responsible private enterprise have often been deployed to strengthen the claims of self-regulation as superior to bureaucratic state regulation.[7]

Self-regulation occurs at the level of the individual firm or of an entire industry, such as direct marketing or the provision of financial services. In a climate of increasing identity fraud, and especially with regard to electronic commerce, there has been a proliferation of tools developed to give online consumers a way of judging the trustworthiness of the invisible merchants with whom they transact business. Privacy seal programmes offered by WebTrust, TrustE, BBBOnline, and others have attracted favourable attention and have been heavily promoted, although here, too, scepticism about the efficacy, reliability, and extent of adoption of these devices has accompanied their development, generating lively debate (Froomkin 2000).

The distinction between legally based state regulation and self-regulation has even been taken, quite crudely, to represent the US *versus* the European approach to data protection. Where laws do exist, or where they do not, but are seen as a necessary albeit insufficient regulatory tool, self-regulatory codes of practice have been acknowledged, in official regulatory policy and in law, as playing an integral part in the regulatory armoury. In Australia, for example, 'co-regulation' has been the legitimizing ideology for this, while Dutch, Irish, British, New Zealand, and Canadian legislation encourages or gives legal recognition to codes; so too does the EU Directive.

This brief overview of the main types of policy mechanism[8] shows that the attempt to regulate the processing of personal data occurs over an extremely wide range of actors and institutions, from the individual to the global. For some countries, there have been successive phases in the development of systems and regimes for privacy protection. However, such periodization is difficult to illustrate universally, for the most recent national members of the data protection 'club' have often had to embrace prefabricated and inherited packages of instruments representing international best practice. If the EU Directive's concern about its citizens' privacy—that it must not be compromised when their personal information is transmitted to 'third countries'—is implemented rigorously, such historical telescoping and leapfrogging may be observed in many countries as they seek to conform to the strictures about adequacy by developing sound protective regimes.

4 PRIVACY AND THE SHARING OF INFORMATION

A second, but perhaps less remarked-upon and less researched, practical development in the processing of personal data also involves the erosion of boundaries: in this case, not jurisdictional ones, but organizational boundaries, as personal data become increasingly shared and matched even within the borders of one country or of one government or business organization.[9] These information disclosures have become particularly prevalent in the public sector—at least, in policy initiatives if not fully or smoothly in practice—as co-working takes root in health and social care, in the criminal justice system, and in combating welfare-state fraud.

The UK provides only one among many national examples of how privacy protection, including technological safeguards, has become an important theme in the development of systems for electronic public service delivery and for the intensified sharing of personal data within agencies and across the public sector (6, Raab and Bellamy 2005; Performance and Innovation Unit 2002; Prime Minister and Minster of State for the Cabinet Office 1999; Raab 2001). In many countries and lesser jurisdictions, the push towards information age government, involving electronic transactions and one-stop shops for public services (Bellamy and Taylor 1998; Hagen and Kubicek 2000; Prins 2001) is well established. However, achievements are more mixed as governments struggle with ICT system failures, legacies of technological incompatibilities, fluctuating policy inputs, cost escalation, inadequate organization and training, and other impediments.

Nevertheless, under the aegis of joined-up government, personal information and the databases in which they are held are seen as crucial resources for the better, more efficient and effective operation of public services on an integrated basis. Integrating sources of personal data for these ends, and processing them using the latest ICTs, throw up issues for privacy and the maintenance of confidentiality, especially regarding what are considered to be particularly sensitive data: physical and mental health records, criminal records, social service case notes, benefit payments data, and the like. Here too, the efficacy of the instruments that comprise existing regulatory regimes is challenged.

Discussion of this second dimension is useful, for it casts light on further aspects of privacy and its protection in practice that the first dimension does not so easily reveal. Here, assumptions and work practices about the control and disclosure of personal information among professionals and administrators, dating from an era of administrative and service 'silos', have been shaken in the age of integrated, multi-agency public service provision, although older practices are tenacious and fragmentation has remained the rule (6, Raab and Bellamy 2005; Bellamy, 6 and Raab 2005). The impetus to share or to pool personal data about persons, especially where they are deemed to be at risk—for example, young children, the mentally ill, the elderly, and persons with disabilities—often confronts other important, human rights-based, policy imperatives to protect privacy, as well as professional codes concerning confidentiality. This situation frequently presents a conundrum for policy makers and, particularly, for service professionals at the front line who are charged with making often fateful decisions about those entrusted to their care.

It was not until the mid-1990s that privacy considerations were prominently discussed in regard to the 'informatization' of public administration and service to the citizen (Performance and Innovation Unit 2002; Raab 1998; Snellen and van de Donk 1998). The prospect of wholesale integration of personal data threatened to undermine citizens' trust in public authorities if these innovations were not effectively regulated. At one level, responses to this prospect centred on the improvement of security through systems design and the tightening up of the rules governing professionals' or administrators' access to stored data; the promulgation of 'role-based access control' in the UK's National Health Service (NHS) National Programme for IT is an interesting example. The NHS has also innovated with the creation of a special supervisory and decision-making role within health service units—the 'Caldicott Guardian' (Department of Health 1997)—that has been extended to the world of social care. Where disclosure or the pooling of information between agencies is concerned, protocols for the sharing of data have been developed within programmes such as the Scottish Executive's eCare

Programme (Raab et al. 2004) or under the guidance given by central bodies (Department for Constitutional Affairs 2003).

It is important to note that, while the attention paid to better security and to explicit agreements about disclosure addresses some of the important principles that are found in legal and self-regulatory instruments, there are other important information–privacy principles in the sharing of personal data that need similar attention. The accuracy, currency, length of retention, and parsimony of collections of personal data are also crucial parts of privacy protection. They are placed under strain, especially when the policy impetus is towards the maximum exploitation of personal data in part to avert blame for having neglected to use and to share data when, for example, tragic cases of child abuse erupt into the limelight. The application of these principles may not be so straightforward: the difficulty of determining appropriate retention periods has been highlighted in recent cases of child murder (Bichard 2004). Yet shortcomings in the application of these data quality criteria give grounds for concern, especially where the construction of comprehensive, and in the view of some, disproportionately large, databases is contemplated in public policy. The UK's *Identity Cards Act* 2006 and the database envisaged under *The Children Act* 2004 are highly prominent cases where critics have emphasized the threats to privacy.

It is with such new departures in the use of ICTs in government that the relevance of a new, fairly experimental, regulatory instrument can be seen. Privacy Impact Assessment (PIA) is 'an assessment of any actual or potential effects that an activity or proposal may have on individual privacy and the ways in which any adverse effects may be mitigated' (Stewart 1996: 61). This technique is mandated in the US and Canada for new federal-level public-sector projects where personal data are to be processed, and a wealth of models and templates, albeit diverse, can be found for implementing PIAs (Raab 2005a). PIAs are based on the assessment of risks to privacy: this itself may be a daunting task, both conceptually and empirically. They take into account not only the proposed system's compliance with privacy laws and principles, but with ways in which the organization(s) concerned aim to ensure that the risks can be avoided or managed through the application of a variety of means that are available to them or that can be developed, such as intensive staff training. Although PIAs have not yet solved many problems, perhaps their unique value—if they are not applied as a perfunctory exercise merely to satisfy auditing rituals—is in the opening up of privacy issues to in-depth scrutiny, debate, and remedy within the organization, or within a multi-agency partnership in which boundaries are blurred, rather than in any specific verdict that may result. They also may stimulate an appreciation of where decisions need to be made between the competing interests of the organizations and their clients or customers; or at least point up the difficulty of making them and the need for wider debate about decision criteria. If PIAs are made public documents, gains in transparency and in the elevation of privacy as a public issue may be realized.

Making difficult judgements where privacy is at stake has a wider importance than within the context of the PIA process. Up to a point, the rules for information sharing in multi-agency working can be specified. However, there are many instances—for example, where vulnerable children or adults are at risk of harm—in which the rules necessarily fall short of determining the judgements that front-line workers, including the police, must make. These are decisions concerning, for example, whether to inform other agencies about an apparently abused child, about a potential child molester where the accuracy of the information is contestable, or about a possibly dangerous mental patient. ICT innovations for sharing data cannot automate the interpretation of information and the subsequent decisions that are required for action, whether it is better to be safe than sorry, or to act only when the likelihood of harm is 'beyond a reasonable doubt'. Privacy invasions in some of these cases may be unavoidable; regulators would hold that an invasion must be proportionate to the likely harm, but judging this may be extremely difficult and disputable.

5 PRIVACY IN DANGEROUS CIRCUMSTANCES

Shifting the example to the collection, collation, analysis, and communication of information for counter-terrorist purposes, the privacy of individuals or of categories of persons may be under threat from another quarter, and by means of other ICTs. In a rights-based society, counter-terrorist privacy invasion is justifiable and publicly acceptable only in terms of preventing even greater harm to the general public. The genesis of policy initiatives and technological developments for intensified surveillance (Ball and Webster 2003, Lyon 2003b) antedated the recent terrorist incidents of 9/11 in the US and 7/7 in the UK. But the tracking of human mobility, the interception of communications, the preoccupation with verifying identities and profiling individuals, and the matching, merging, and newly legitimized disclosure of hitherto protected data to other agencies or countries highlight privacy concerns, however cogent the rationales for the use of these tools in extremely dangerous circumstances.

More generally than in counter-terrorism, the advent of the 'safety state' (Raab 2005b) and the 'surveillance society' (Lyon 2001) renders the protection of privacy that much more difficult, no matter what regulatory instruments and precepts may be available. Where public policy and public opinion elevate physical safety as the most important value to be furthered and protected, debates about privacy may be marginalized, and the policy emphasis upon increasing the ICT and other resources available to make society safer is likely to be difficult to counter. On the other hand, recent world events have at least served to increase the prominence of debates about privacy issues, including the role of ICTs and systems, as well as the strengths and weaknesses of the gamut of regulatory rules and roles. Apocalyptic warnings of a unified, centralized, and malign 'Big Brother' at the national level, and even beyond those borders, may be at least premature, if not based on fallacious premises.

In some respects, it is misleading to weigh up safety and privacy on counter-poised balancing pans, construing a trade-off in terms of society versus the individual. Three reasons for scepticism about such a construction cast useful light on the meaning of privacy and its relation to other values. First, balancing may be more a slogan than a coherent concept and a practical course of action, because it implies that these values can be easily measured and compared, and because the notion of equilibrium may be misapplied to the detriment of the right to privacy (Raab 1999). Even if this reason were not considered cogent, a second reason is that, although the politics, law, and rhetoric of information privacy issues often sets individual rights against the public interest, the way in which the values and interests involved may be understood does not make these antagonisms inevitable. This is because the public interest is also served by the preservation of individual rights such as privacy: the public sphere of a democratic society and polity cannot itself function without the protection of the privacy of the individuals whose participation in its affairs is central. Therefore, the main antagonism may be between competing conceptions of the public interest; that is a more complex matter.

This line of thought critically confronts Etzioni's (1999) communitarian theory-based critique of privacy, while taking a step away from considering privacy in conventional terms solely as an individual, defensive right and a personal value. It moves, rather, towards a conceptualization that reflects the insights of Regan (1995) and of Schoeman (1992) in validating privacy's collective, common, and public value as well. This view enables it to be argued that the protection of privacy should be understood more robustly as part of public and social policy, and not merely as a personal preference whose protection or loss is of no consequence for the fabric of society beyond the individual. This view, incidentally, can be used in support of criticism of those PETs that enable some, but not all, persons to increase their own privacy protection, and in favour of the equitable provision of ICT privacy solutions as systemic, built-in, common goods available to all.

The third reason is that privacy itself can be thought of instrumentally as valuable for safety, and is often so promoted. It can be a protective, defensive, and risk-averse value, guarding against the harm caused by encroachments whether informational, spatial, or other senses. Opponents of telephone calling-line identification, for example, point out the risks of physical harm to which vulnerable women and children might be subject if their whereabouts could be traced through knowledge of their telephone number. More generally, anonymity—which, along with pseudonymity, is a main goal in the development of PETs—is often desired for reasons that do not necessarily distinguish between safety and privacy. Privacy advocates themselves invoke the precautionary principle concerning risk exposure in criticizing state security policies and the heavy reliance on surveillance technologies; their stance on the potential adverse effects of identity-card databases, congestion-charge technologies, and mobile tracking telematics also gives evidence of this. The use of encryption and other PETs in electronic commerce and in online public service provision can be seen as safeguards for individuals against identity theft and the loss of property. Individual privacy and the security of society or of the state can therefore be seen as two 'takes' on safety, with privacy invasions considered to be a safety risk for persons, and conventional public interest rationales seen, in some circumstances, as transferring risk to the individual. This prompts the thought that privacy and its social distribution can usefully be explored as an issue in social policy, and not only as one of individual rights (Bennett and Raab 2006).

6 CONCLUSION

Only some ten years after the Internet became widely available, information privacy is an issue and a subject of study that has come of age, perhaps just at a time when it is most difficult to assert its claims and to ensure that technologies and organizational systems or networks take these into account. There is much scope for fresh thinking about information privacy, its relation to other dimensions of privacy, and the ways in which it can or cannot be regulated. There are many further issues and analytical problems, frequently ignored, that point to a long list of items for future research alongside what has been mentioned in passing, as well as for policy making at many levels. A few of these issues and items have been canvassed here, and others may be constructed from the wealth of documentary and academic literature that is now available, and—perhaps especially—from the lessons learnt from events that will continue to unfold at grand as well as mundane levels. While this chapter has only highlighted some of the topics that are frequently discussed within the scholarly and practical communities that focus upon privacy and its relation to the development and use of ICTs, they prompt some fruitful lines of investigation that may engage future research.

As we have seen, privacy protection involves ensuring that the processing of personal data is subjected to controls, including those exercised by the individual. The first two sections of the chapter showed how jurisdictional and organizational boundaries have come under pressure as information practices migrate to global and holistic contexts, thereby casting doubt on the efficacy of privacy protection at a time when new solutions have not yet been well developed for these contexts. Privacy-invading ICTs are involved in the attack on boundaries, but are not themselves best understood as the cause: they are more properly thought of as the vehicles for the purposes and policies of states and organizations that seek to process personal data. Recent concerns about privacy, and efforts to safeguard it, respond in part to the challenge of the decline of national and other jurisdictional boundaries to information processes by seeking to create supranational mechanisms to cope with the effects of the worldwide flow of personal information.

This raises the prospect of comprehending, and shaping, a multi-level governance (Bache and Flinders 2004) regime for privacy protection, in which controls are exerted in complex and variable patterns, across several jurisdictional levels, that relate to different kinds and purposes of information processing, different sectors or industries, and the like. They may also be exerted through combinations of tools or instruments, including the main ones described earlier, as well as the newer ones— binding corporate rules and model contractual clauses, for example—that have been fashioned explicitly for flows of personal data across national boundaries. But in terms of understanding the way regimes work, it is insufficient to view the various instruments as stand-alone tools, each suited to a special purpose that it is best capable of fulfilling on its own. Although policy discourse talks of a toolkit, Bennett and Raab (2006) question whether this is an appropriate term to describe a situation in which a perception of the often complex and dynamic interactions among the instruments, including their symbiosis, may lead to more accurate description within an analytical framework that concerns governance seen in a more comprehensive light. For this, research is needed on how these combinations evolve and perform.

This is not merely an analytical and perhaps Durkheimian fine point of preferring the organic solidarity of complementarity to a view that tools are equivalent and interchangable, for an interactive or holistic conception of privacy protection may have practical value in helping to design these regimes, rather than only in describing them; Lessig (1999b) has taken an interesting step towards this goal. To pursue this, one would also have to take into account the variety of actors—and their motives and interests—whose activities shape regimes and outcomes, and to understand the political processes through which they conflict or negotiate agreements. With rare exceptions (e.g. Bennett 1992; Raab and Bennett 1994; Regan 1995) however, the literature on privacy and data protection has not focused on processes of policy making and implementation so much as it has on substantive matters of law, technology, and outcomes. Future research—whether basic or applied—into multi-level, multi-instrument patterns would have to be process-focused to a considerable degree; this, in turn, implies the further development of broader social-science empirical methodologies beyond legal and computer-science scholarship.

With regard to the second issue described in this chapter, privacy concerns respond to the possible erosion of privacy-safeguarding organizational or 'silo' boundaries, by seeking to negotiate and codify the terms under which personal data are disclosed across these boundaries, and by pressing for closer supervision of compliance with these rules. Within and across organizational lines, there is also an emergent precautionary control through the assessment of the impact upon privacy of new ICT systems and processes. A research agenda can be contemplated that aims to understand, and perhaps to address in practical terms, the reasons why organizations and their staff share, or fail to share, the personal data of their clients within new frameworks of inter-agency working (6, Raab and Bellamy 2005; Bellamy, 6 and Raab 2005). This involves teasing out the cultural, structural, and behavioural variables that shape the activity of sharing or not sharing, and understanding the effect of new ICT infrastructures on the volume and patterning of the information flows. Inherent in this is also a comprehension of the effect of legal and professional privacy or confidentiality rules as they engage daily practice in new contexts of joint working across traditional dividing lines. A further research prospect involves the development of PIA techniques, but also the evaluation of their efficacy where they have been applied, and a more effective tailoring of such assessments to the circumstances prevailing in inter- or multi-organizational situations.

The research agenda for this dimension also pertains to the third, concerning privacy and social, national, or global safety. Both dimensions are especially bound up with the evaluation of risk, although the approach to risk analysis in the field of information privacy has not yet received attention commensurate with what might be its growing importance. This is perhaps among the most intractable areas of investigation, inherently so in the case of counter-terrorism and its effect on privacy, but also fraught with difficulty in less dramatic contexts to which, of course, the questions of risk and safety also pertain. Much conceptual work as well as close understanding of technologies, social processes, and public attitudes are required, but the research focus might well be less on the question of information and systems security, and more on the many other requirements that are placed on information processing by law and best practice.

Whether reliable knowledge can be gained from researching the issue of privacy risk and safety, such that public policy can be informed, is by no means certain. But, as was outlined in the previous section, theoretical work towards reconceptualizing the public interest, and safety, may help to clarify the meaning of privacy and, in turn, the extent and ways in which it may be protected.

References

6, P. (1998). *The Future of Privacy, Volume 1: Private Life and Public Policy.* London: Demos.
——, RAAB, C., and BELLAMY, C. (2005). 'Joined-up Government and Privacy in the United Kingdom: Managing Tensions between Data Protection and Social Policy. Part I'. *Public Administration,* 83(1): 111–33.

BACHE, I. and FLINDERS, M. (eds) (2004). *Multi-level Governance*. Oxford: Oxford University Press.

BALL, K. and WEBSTER, F. (eds) (2003). *The Intensification of Surveillance: Crime, Terrorism and Warfare in the Information Age*. London: Pluto Press.

BEKKERS, V., KOOPS, B.-J. and NOUWT, S. (eds) (1996). *Emerging Electronic Highways: New Challenges for Politics and Law*. The Hague: Kluwer Law International.

BELLAMY, C. and TAYLOR, J. (1998). *Governing in the Information Age*. Buckingham: Open University Press.

——, 6, P. and RAAB, C. (2005). 'Joined-up Government and Privacy in the United Kingdom: Managing Tensions between Data Protection and Social Policy. Part II'. *Public Administration*, 83(2): 393–415.

BENNETT, C. (1992). *Regulating Privacy: Data Protection and Public Policy in Europe and the United States*. Ithaca, NY: Cornell University Press.

—— and RAAB, C. (1997). 'The Adequacy of Privacy: The European Union Data Privacy Directive and the North American Response'. *The Information Society*, 13(3): 245–63.

—— and —— (2006). *The Governance of Privacy: Policy Instruments in Global Perspective*, (2nd edn). Cambridge, MA: MIT Press.

BICHARD, SIR M. (2004). *The Bichard Inquiry Report*, HC 653. London: The Stationery Office.

BING, J. (1999). 'Data Protection, Jurisdiction and the Choice of Law'. Paper presented at the 21st Annual Conference on Privacy and Personal Data Protection, Office of the Privacy Commissioner for Personal Data, Hong Kong.

BLUME, P. (2002). *Protection of Informational Privacy*. Copenhagen: DJOF Publishing.

BOWKER, G. C. and STAR, S. L. (1999). *Sorting Things Out: Classification and its Consequences*. Cambridge, MA: MIT Press.

BURKERT, H. (1996). 'Data-protection Legislation and the Modernization of Public Administration'. *International Review of Administrative Sciences*, 62(4): 557–67.

—— (1997). 'Privacy Enhancing Technologies: Typology, Critique, Vision', in P. Agre and M. Rotenberg (eds), *Technology and Privacy: The New Landscape*. Cambridge, MA: MIT Press, 125–43.

BYGRAVE, L. (2002). *Data Protection Law: Approaching its Rationale, Logic and Limits*. The Hague: Kluwer Law International.

CAMP, L. (2001). *Trust and Risk in Internet Commerce*. Cambridge, MA: MIT Press

CHARLESWORTH, A. (2000). 'Clash of the Data Titans? US and EU Data Privacy Regulation'. *European Public Law*, 6(2): 253–74.

CHAUM, D. (1992). 'Achieving Electronic Privacy'. *Scientific American*, 267(2): 96–101.

CLARKE, R. (1988). 'Information Technology and Dataveillance'. *ACM*, 31(5): 498–512.

COLEMAN, S., TAYLOR, J. and VAN DE DONK, W. (eds) (1999). *Parliament in the Age of the Internet*. Oxford: Oxford University Press.

Commission of the European Communities (1995). 'Directive 95/46/EC of the European Parliament and of the Council on the Protection of Individuals with Regard to the Processing of Personal Data and on the Free Movement of such Data'. Brussels: OJ No. L281, 24 Oct.

Council of Europe (1981). 'Convention for the Protection of Individuals with Regard to Automatic Processing of Personal Data (Convention 108)'. Strasbourg: Council of Europe.

DAVIES, S. (1996). *Big Brother: Britain's Web of Surveillance and the New Technological Border*. London: Pan Books.

DENNING, D. and DENNING, P. (eds) (1998). *Internet Besieged: Countering Cyberspace Scofflaws*. New York: ACM Press.

DEPARTMENT FOR CONSTITUTIONAL AFFAIRS (2003). *A Toolkit for Data Sharing*. London: Department for Constitutional Affairs.

DEPARTMENT OF HEALTH (1997). *Report on the Review of Patient Identifiable Information* (Report of the Caldicott Committee). London: Department of Health.

DIFFIE, W. and LANDAU, S. (1998). *Privacy on the Line: The Politics of Wiretapping and Encryption*. Cambridge, MA: MIT Press.

ERICSON, R. and HAGGERTY, K. (1997). *Policing the Risk Society*. Oxford and Toronto: Clarendon Press and Toronto University Press.

ETZIONI, A. (1999). *The Limits of Privacy*. New York: Basic Books.

FARRELL, H. (2002). 'Negotiating Privacy Across Arenas: The EU-US "Safe Harbor" discussions', in A. Héritier (ed.), *Common Goods: Reinventing European and International Governance*. Lanham, MD: Rowman & Littlefield, 101–23.

FLAHERTY, D. (1985). *Protecting Privacy in Two-way Electronic Services*. London: Mansell Publishing Limited.

—— (1989). *Protecting Privacy in Surveillance Societies: The Federal Republic of Germany, Sweden, France, Canada, and the United States*. Chapel Hill, NC: University of North Carolina Press.

FROOMKIN, M. (1997). 'The Internet as a Source of Regulatory Arbitrage', in B. Kahin and C. Nesson (eds) *Borders in Cyberspace: Information Policy and the Global Information Infrastructure*. Cambridge, MA: MIT Press, 129–63.

—— (2000). 'The Death of Privacy?' *Stanford Law Review*, 52(5): 1461–543.

GANDY, O. Jr (1993). *The Panoptic Sort: A Political Economy of Personal Information*. Boulder, CO: Westview Press.

GARFINKEL, S. (2000). *Database Nation: The Death of Privacy in the Twenty-first Century*. Sebastopol, CA: O'Reilly.

GELLMAN, R. (1993). 'Fragmented, Incomplete and Discontinuous: The Failure of Federal Privacy Regulatory Proposals and Institutions'. *Software Law Journal*, 6(2): 199–238.

—— (1996). 'Can Privacy be Regulated Effectively on a National Level? Thoughts on the Possible Need for International Privacy Rules'. *Villanova Law Review*, 41(1): 129–72.

—— (1997). 'Conflict and Overlap in Privacy Regulation: National, International, and Private', in B. Kahin and C. Nesson (eds), *Borders in Cyberspace: Information Policy and the Global Information Infrastructure*. Cambridge, MA: MIT Press, 255–82.

GREENLEAF, G. (1998). 'An Endnote on Regulating Cyberspace: Architecture vs Law?' *University of New South Wales Law Journal*, 21(2): 593–622.

GUTWIRTH, S. (2002). *Privacy and the Information Age*. Lanham, MD: Rowman & Littlefield.

HAGEN, M. and KUBICEK, H. (eds.) (2000). *One-stop Government in Europe: Results from 11 National Surveys*. Bremen: University of Bremen.

HAGUE, B. N. and LOADER, B. D. (eds) (1999). *Digital Democracy: Discourse and Decision Making in the Information Age*. London: Routledge.

KAHIN, B. and NESSON, C. (eds) (1997). *Borders in Cyberspace: Information Policy and the Global Information Infrastructure*. Cambridge, MA: MIT Press.

KOOPS, B.-J. (1999). *The Crypto Controversy: A Key Conflict in the Information Society*. The Hague: Kluwer Law International.

LAUDON, K. (1996). 'Markets and Privacy'. *Communications of the Association for Computing Machinery*, 39(9): 92–104.

LAURIE, G. (2002). *Genetic Privacy: A Challenge to Medico-Legal Norms.* Cambridge: Cambridge University Press.

LESSIG, L. (1999a). *Code and Other Laws of Cyberspace.* New York: Basic Books.

—— (1999b). 'The Law of the Horse: What Cyberlaw Might Teach'. *Harvard Law Review*, 113: 501–46.

LYON, D. (1994). *The Electronic Eye: The Rise of Surveillance Society.* Minneapolis, MN: University of Minnesota Press.

—— (2001). *Surveillance Society: Monitoring Everyday Life.* Buckingham: Open University Press.

—— (ed.) (2003a). *Surveillance as Social Sorting: Privacy, Risk, and Digital Discrimination.* London and New York: Routledge.

—— (2003b). *Surveillance after September 11.* Cambridge: Polity Press.

MANSELL, R. and COLLINS, B. (eds), (2005). *Trust and Crime in Information Societies.* Cheltenham: Edward Elgar.

MARX, G. T. (1999). 'Ethics for the New Surveillance', in C. Bennett and R. Grant (eds), *Visions of Privacy: Policy Choices for the Digital Age.* Toronto: University of Toronto Press, 38–67.

—— (2003). 'A Tack in the Shoe: Neutralizing and Resisting the New Surveillance'. *Journal of Social Issues*, 59(2): 369–90.

MILL, J. S. (1859). *Three Essays.* Oxford: Oxford University Press.

MULLIGAN, D. and GOLDMAN, J. (1997). 'The Limits and the Necessity of Self-regulation: The Case for Both', in US Department of Commerce, National Telecommunications and Information Administration (ed.), *Privacy and Self-regulation in the Information Age.* Washington DC: US Department of Commerce, 65–73.

NEILL, E. (2001). *Rites of Privacy and the Privacy Trade; On the Limits of Protection for the Self.* Montreal and Kingston, McGill-Queen's University Press.

NOAM, E. (1997). 'Privacy and Self-regulation: Markets for Electronic Privacy', in US Department of Commerce, National Telecommunications and Information Administration (ed.), *Privacy and Self-regulation in the Information Age.* Washington DC: US Department of Commerce, 21–33.

NORRIS, C. and ARMSTRONG, G. (1999). *The Maximum Surveillance Society: The Rise of CCTV.* Oxford: Berg.

Ontario (Office of the Information and Privacy Commissioner and Netherlands Registratiekamer) (1995). *Privacy-enhancing Technologies: The Path to Anonymity.* Toronto: Office of the Information and Privacy Commissioner and Netherlands Registratiekamer.

OECD (1981). *Guidelines on the Protection of Privacy and Transborder Flows of Personal Data.* Paris: OECD.

PENNOCK, J. and CHAPMAN, J. (1971). *Privacy: Nomos XIII.* New York, NY: Atherton Press.

Perfomance and Innovation Unit (2002). *Privacy and Data-sharing: The Way Forward for Public Services.* London: Cabinet Office, Performance and Innovation Unit.

POULLET, Y. (2002). 'How to Regulate Internet: New Paradigms for Internet Governance— Self-regulation: Value and Limits', in Cahiers du centre de recherches informatique et droit (CRID) (ed.), *Variations sur le droit de la société de l'information*, Cahiers du CRID No. 20. Brussels: Bruylant, 79–114.

PRIEST, M. (1997–98). 'The Privatization of Regulation: Five Models of Self-regulation'. *Ottawa Law Review*, 29: 233–302.

PRIME MINISTER AND MINISTER OF STATE FOR THE CABINET OFFICE (1999). *Modernising Government*, Cm 4310. London: The Stationery Office.

PRINS, J. (ed.) (2001). *Designing e-Government: On the Crossroads of Technological Innovation and Institutional Change*. The Hague: Kluwer Law International.

RAAB, C. (1998). 'Electronic Confidence: Trust, Information and Public Administration', in I. Snellen and W. van de Donk (eds), *Public Administration in an Information Age: A Handbook*. Amsterdam: IOS Press, 113–33.

—— (1999). 'From Balancing to Steering: New Directions for Data Protection', in C. Bennett and R. Grant (eds), *Visions of Privacy: Policy Choices for the Digital Age*. Toronto: University of Toronto Press, 68–93.

—— (2001). 'Electronic Service Delivery in the UK: Proaction and Privacy Protection', in J. Prins (ed.), *Designing e-Government: On the Crossroads of Technological Innovation and Institutional Change*. The Hague: Kluwer Law International, 41–62.

—— (2005a). 'The Future of Privacy Protection', in R. Mansell and B. Collins (eds), *Trust and Crime in Information Societies*. Cheltenham: Edward Elgar, 282–318.

—— (2005b). 'Governing the Safety State', Inaugural Lecture, University of Edinburgh, 7 June.

—— (2006). 'The Governance of Global Issues: Protecting Privacy in Personal Information', in M. Koenig-Archibugi and M. Zürn (eds), *New Modes of Governance in the Global System: Exploring Publicness, Delegation and Inclusiveness*. London: Palgrave Macmillan.

—— and BENNETT, C. (1994). 'Protecting Privacy Across Borders: European Policies and Prospects'. *Public Administration*, 72(1): 95–112.

——, 6, P., BIRCH, A. and COPPING, M. (2004). *Information Sharing for Children at Risk: Impacts on Privacy*. Edinburgh: Scottish Executive.

REGAN, P. (1995). *Legislating Privacy: Technology, Social Values and Public Policy*. Chapel Hill, NC: University of North Carolina Press.

REIDENBERG, J. (1992). 'Privacy in the Information Economy: A Fortress or Frontier for Individual Rights?' *Federal Communications Law Journal*, 44(2): 195–243.

—— (1993). 'Rules of the Road for Global Electronic Highways: Merging the Trade and Technical Paradigms'. *Harvard Journal of Law & Technology*, 6 (Spring): 287–305.

—— (1996). 'Governing Networks and Rule-making in Cyberspace'. *Emory Law Journal*, 45(3): 912–30.

—— (1998). 'Lex Informatica: The Formulation of Information Policy Rules through Technology'. *Texas Law Review*, 76(3): 553–93.

—— (1999). 'Restoring Americans' Privacy in Electronic Commerce'. *Berkeley Technology Law Journal*, 14(2): 771–92.

—— (2000). 'Resolving Conflicting International Data Privacy Rules in Cyberspace'. *Stanford Law Review*, 52(5): 1315–71.

RULE, J. (1974). *Private Lives and Public Surveillance: Social Control in the Computer Age*. New York: Schocken Books.

—— and HUNTER, L. (1999). 'Towards Property Rights in Personal Data', in C. Bennett and R. Grant (eds), *Visions of Privacy: Policy Choices for the Digital Age*. Toronto: University of Toronto Press, 168–81.

SCHOEMAN, F. (ed.) (1984). *Philosophical Dimensions of Privacy: An Anthology*. Cambridge: Cambridge University Press.

—— (1992). *Privacy and Social Freedom*. Cambridge: Cambridge University Press.

SCHWARTZ, P. (2000a). 'Beyond Lessig's *Code* for Internet Privacy: Cyberspace Filters, Privacy Control and Fair Information Practices'. *Wisconsin Law Review*, 2000(4): 743–88.

—— (2000b). 'Internet Privacy and the State'. *Connecticut Law Review*, 32(3): 815–59.

—— (2004). 'Property, Privacy, and Personal Data'. *Harvard Law Review*, 117(7): 2055–128.

—— and REIDENBERG, J. (1996). *Data Privacy Law: A Study of United States Data Protection*. Charlottesville, VA: Michie.

SHAFFER, G. (2000). 'Globalization and Social Protection: The Impact of EU and International Rules in the Ratcheting up of U.S. Data Privacy Standards'. *Yale Journal of International Law*, 25(1): 1–88.

SIEGHART, P. (1976). *Privacy and Computers*. London: Latimer.

SIMITIS, S. (1987). 'Reviewing Privacy in an Information Society'. *University of Pennsylvania Law Review*, 135: 707–46.

—— (1995). 'From the Market to the Polis: The EU Directive on the Protection of Personal Data'. *Iowa Law Review*, 80(3): 445–69.

SNELLEN, I. and VAN DE DONK, W. (eds) (1998). *Public Administration in an Information Age: A Handbook*. Amsterdam: IOS Press.

SOLOVE, D. (2002). 'Conceptualizing Privacy'. *California Law Review*, 90: 1087–155.

STEWART, B. (1996). 'Privacy Impact Assessments'. *Privacy Law and Policy Reporter*, 3(4): 61–4, http://www.austlii.edu.au/au/journals/PLPR/1996/39.html, accessed 18 Mar. 2006.

SWIRE, P. (1997). 'Markets, Self-regulation, and Government Enforcement in the Protection of Personal Information', in US Department of Commerce (ed.), *Privacy and Self-regulation in the Information Age*. Washington DC: US Department of Commerce, National Telecommunications and Information Administration, 3–19.

—— and LITAN, R. (1998). *None of Your Business: World Data Flows, Electronic Commerce, and the European Privacy Directive*. Washington DC: Brookings Institution Press.

THOMAS, D. and LOADER, B. D. (eds) (2000). *Cybercrime: Law Enforcement, Security and Surveillance in the Information Age*. London: Routledge.

VAN DE DONK, W., SNELLEN, I. and TOPS, P. (eds) (1995). *Orwell in Athens: A Perspective on Informatization and Democracy*. Amsterdam: IOS Press.

WACKS, R. (1989). *Personal Information: Privacy and the Law*. Oxford: Clarendon Press.

—— (1995). *Privacy and Press Freedom*. London: Blackstone Press.

WARREN, S. and BRANDEIS, L. (1890). 'The Right to Privacy'. *Harvard Law Review*, 4(5): 193–220.

WESTIN, A. (1967). *Privacy and Freedom*. New York: Atheneum.

WHITAKER, R. (1999). *The End of Privacy: How Total Surveillance is Becoming a Reality*. New York: New Press.

WINNER, L. (1989). *The Whale and the Reactor: A Search for Limits in the Age of High Technology*. Chicago, IL: University of Chicago Press.

YOUNG, J. (ed.) (1978). *Privacy*. New York: Wiley.

NOTES

1. For the purposes of this chapter, 'processing' of personal data is paraphrased from the UK Data Protection Act 1998, §1.1 to mean obtaining, recording, or holding the information or data, or carrying out any operations on them, including: organization, adaptation, or alteration; retrieval, consultation, or use; disclosure; alignment, combination, blocking,

erasure, or destruction. This is a wide definition and its meaning is subject to interpretation and, ultimately, to judicial ruling.

2. Roger Clarke's website, at http://www.anu.edu.au/people/Roger.Clarke/DV/, provides a wealth of technical and policy resources, including bibliographies, for the study of many privacy topics.

3. Owing to limited space, the points illustrated in this chapter are drawn mainly from the UK. For fuller descriptions and discussion, see Bennett and Raab (2006) and Raab (2005a).

4. Philosophical treatments of privacy can be found in the anthologies of Schoeman (1984), Young (1978), and Pennock and Chapman (1971). Other seminal, controversial, or informative sources bearing upon the concept of privacy go back to Mill (1859) and include Westin (1967), Warren and Brandeis (1890), Etzioni (1999), Neill (2001), Solove (2002), and Gutwirth (2002). A critique of the received 'privacy paradigm', mentioning other sources, is found in Bennett and Raab (2006).

5. Among many others, see Bing (1999), Blume (2002), Burkert (1996, 1997), Bygrave (2002), Charlesworth (2000), Froomkin (2000, 1997), Gellman (1993, 1996, 1997), Greenleaf (1998), Lessig (1999a,b), Poullet (2002), Reidenberg, (1992, 1993, 1996, 1998, 2000), Schwartz (2000a, 2000b, 2004), Schwartz and Reidenberg (1996), Simitis (1987, 1995), Solove (2002), Swire and Litan (1998), and Wacks (1989, 1995).

6. To paraphrase these principles as embodied in the UK's Data Protection Act 1998, data that relate to living individuals must: (1) be obtained and processed fairly and lawfully, and subject to general conditions, either under consent or under necessity for a limited number of general purposes; (2) be used only for the purpose(s); (3) be adequate, relevant, and not excessive for the purpose(s); (4) be accurate and, where necessary, kept up to date; (5) be retained no longer than necessary for the purpose(s); (6) be processed in ways that respect the data subject's rights, include the right of subject access (the right of the individual to see information held about him or her); (7) be subject to appropriate technical and organizational measures to prevent unauthorized and unlawful processing, accidental loss of, destruction of, or damage to the information; and (8) not be transferred outside the European Economic Area, except to countries where levels of data protection are deemed adequate.

7. Reidenberg (1999: 776), however, argues that 'the American experience during the last two decades shows that the theory of self-regulation is pure sophistry'.

8. See also Froomkin (2000). There are, of course, other mechanisms, including contracts between data controllers, binding corporate rules, and consumer or citizen education. Some writers propose, or critically evaluate, market solutions in which personal information is treated as the person's property that can be sold, thus leaving privacy up to the individual to preserve or relinquish (Laudon 1996; Noam 1997; Rule and Hunter 1999; Schwartz 2004).

9. This discussion is informed by research undertaken in 2003–5 by the author, Christine Bellamy, and Perri 6 in a project funded by the UK Economic and Social Research Council, entitled 'Joined-up Public Services: Data-sharing and Privacy in Multi-Agency Working', RES/000/23/0158.

CHAPTER 19

SURVEILLANCE, POWER, AND EVERYDAY LIFE

DAVID LYON

1 INTRODUCTION

SURVEILLANCE grows constantly, especially in the countries of the global north. Although as a set of practices it is as old as history itself, systematic surveillance became a routine and inescapable part of everyday life in modern times and is now, more often than not, dependent on information and communication technologies (ICTs). Indeed, it now makes some sense to talk of 'surveillance societies', so pervasive is organizational monitoring of many kinds. Fast developing technologies combined with new governmental and commercial strategies mean that new modes of surveillance proliferate, making surveillance expansion hard to follow, let alone analyse or regulate.

Since the mid-1970s traffic in personal data has expanded explosively, touching numerous points of everyday life and leading some to proclaim the 'end of privacy'. But while questions of privacy are both interesting and important (see Raab, Ch. 18 of this handbook), others that relate to the ways in which data are used for 'social sorting', discriminating between groups that are classified differently, also need urgently to be examined. Who has the power to make such discriminatory judgements, and how this becomes embedded in automated systems, is a matter of not merely academic interest. Such questions are likely to be with us for some time, both because of what might be called the 'rise of the safety state', which requires more and more surveillance, and also because the politics of personal information is becoming increasingly prominent.

Literally, surveillance means to 'watch over' and as such it is an everyday practice in which human beings engage routinely, often unthinkingly. Parents watch over children, employers watch over workers, police watch over neighbourhoods, guards watch over prisoners, and so on. In most instances, however, surveillance has a more specific usage, referring to some focused and purposive attention to objects, data, or persons. Agricultural experts may do aerial surveillance of crops, public health officials may conduct medical surveillance of populations, or intelligence officers may put suspects under observation.

Such activities have several things in common, among which are that in the world of the twenty-first century some kind of technical augmentation or assistance of surveillance processes is often assumed. ICTs are utilized to increase the power, reach, and capacity of surveillance systems. The specific kind of surveillance discussed here is perhaps the fastest growing and almost certainly the most controversial, namely the processing of personal data for the purposes of care or control, to influence or manage persons and populations. In this and every other respect, power relations are intrinsic to surveillance processes.

This being so, it immediately becomes apparent that actual 'watching over' is not really the main issue, or at least not literally. While CCTV (Closed Circuit Television) surveillance certainly does have a watching element, other kinds of ICT-enabled surveillance include the processing of all kinds of data, images, and information. Some, of which we are most aware, include the multiple checks that we go through at an airport, from the initial ticketing information and passport check, through to baggage screening and the ID and ticket check at the gate. In this example, both public (governmental; customs and immigration) and private (commercial; airlines and frequent flyer clubs) data are sought. Others, of which we may be less consciously aware, include 'loyalty cards' at supermarkets and other stores that offer customers discounts and member privileges, but which are simultaneously the means of garnering consumer data from shoppers.

All these count as surveillance of one kind or another, in which we are (usually) individuated—distinguished from others, identified—according to the criteria of the organization in question, and then some sort of analysis of our transaction, communication, behaviour, or activity is set in train. Thus, some kinds of surveillance knowledge are produced that are then used to mark the individual, to locate him or her in a particular niche or category of risk proneness, and to assign social places or opportunities to the person according to the ruling criteria of the organization. It is not merely that some kinds of surveillance seem invasive or intrusive, but rather that social relations and social power are organized in part through surveillance strategies.

It should be noted that surveillance involving direct watching or monitoring continues to be an important part of social life, but the kind of surveillance discussed here is supported, enabled, or assisted by ICTs. In the latter part of the twentieth century the idea became popular that 'information societies' were in the making wherever computer and telecommunication technologies formed essential infrastructures for administrative and organizational life. Although a certain technological determinism drove some of these ideas—after all, paper file-based bureaucracies created 'information societies' long before vacuum tubes, transistors, or silicon chips had been invented—the notion that significant changes occur with the use of digital infrastructures should not simply be discounted. One of the key changes is that routine, mundane, everyday surveillance is enabled by those infrastructures. Indeed, one can argue that the 'surveillance societies' of today are a byproduct of the so-called 'information society'.

2 SURVEILLANCE SOCIETY

From time-to-time social scientists propose labels and phrases that highlight crucial aspects of contemporary change and 'surveillance society' is one of these. First used by sociologist Gary T. Marx in the mid-1980s (Marx 1985, see also Gandy 1989), the phrase is now in common use, frequently by those who wish to make the same kinds of points as Marx did then. His concern was that new technologies were helping to create situations in which 'one of the final barriers to total social control is now crumbling'. Soon afterwards, historian David Flaherty commented that Western countries in general were becoming surveillance societies, 'as one component of becoming information societies' (Flaherty 1989: 1). Two decades later, in 2004, the British Information Commissioner, Richard Thomas, warned that with the proposed introduction of a national identification card the UK was in danger of sleepwalking into a surveillance society (*The Times* [London], 28 August 2004).

What kinds of processes would have to be in place to warrant the use of a phrase like 'surveillance society'? For Richard Thomas, the issue was that the UK government would be enabled through the 'Citizens' Information Project' of the Office of the Census to collect far more personal data than are necessary for the purposes of the ID card. At the same time, he questioned what exactly is the main purpose of the proposed card—to regulate immigration, to combat terrorism, or to provide access to services and benefits? For Thomas, the surveillance society clearly relates to state activities, similar to those in *Nineteen Eighty-four* perhaps, but which are augmented by the use of new technologies—the Citizens' Information Project is a national database. He also refers to other twentieth century examples of state rule by surveillance, such as in the older Eastern European societies and in Franco's Spain.

A similar kind of analysis, though more rigorously sociological, was made by James Rule in the early 1970s, when he suggested that an 'ideal type'—a 'total surveillance society'—could be imagined, by which to judge increases in surveillance. Surveillance capacities were rapidly being expanded, he showed, through the use of computerization that permitted increasing file size, greater centralization, higher speeds of data flow between points in the system, and a larger number of contact points between the system and the subject (Rule 1973: 37–40). While Rule's studies related in part to government administration, in the form of drivers' licences, national insurance, and policing in the UK, he also studied consumer credit reporting and credit cards systems in the US. Already, then, hints of a surveillance *society* rather than just a surveillance *state* were becoming visible. And with it came new forms of power, of subtle shifts in governance.

This is the point of considering the surveillance society. That which was once thought to refer primarily to affairs of state now has become societally pervasive. Surveillance, assisted by new technologies, appears in everyday commercial life, as people pay with credit cards and as their shopping habits are monitored through credit reporting. Today, however, this process is vastly magnified, such that all manner of everyday activities are recorded, checked, traced, and monitored for a variety of purposes. Consumers are profiled by corporations as never before, and several new technical developments such as the Internet and cell phones, unknown to Rule and others in the 1970s and 1980s, make available new thick layers of surveillance data.

One advantage of thinking in terms of a surveillance society is that this term deflects attention from other totalitarian or disciplinary models of how surveillance works. The main such models are the Orwellian apparatus of a totalitarian state, depicted in the novel *Nineteen Eighty-four* and Jeremy Bentham's penitentiary plan for a 'Panopticon' or 'all-seeing place'. The former provided the starting point for several sociological studies (such as James Rule's), whereas the latter became the centrepiece of Michel Foucault's study of discipline in the modern world. The point is not to dismiss these models but to place them in a larger context.

The idea that state power could be augmented by surveillance systems in ways that are at least reminiscent of totalitarianism is quite plausible. This can be seen in some South-East Asian countries, such as Singapore, and also in Western societies, such as the US following the attacks of 9/11 (Lyon 2003, Ball and Webster 2003). The analysis of self-discipline, induced by the uncertainty and fear associated with unseen observers, not only within a closed environment such as a prison, but also in more public venues, does give the panopticon considerable credibility. There is evidence that people do alter their behaviours when, for instance, they are aware that they are under video surveillance (Norris and Armstrong 1999, McCahill 2002, Cole 2001). These forms of analysis have not simply been superseded. Rather they are inadequate on their own.

There is much more to contemporary surveillance than totalitarianism or panopticism, significant though these concepts are. Several writers have pointed to other features of surveillance that are difficult to squeeze into either of those frames. Gilles Deleuze, for example, suggested in a brief statement on 'societies of control' that we all now live in situations where 'audio-visual protocols'—such as cameras, personal identification numbers (PINs), barcodes, radio frequency identification (RFID)—help to determine which opportunities are open, and which closed to us in daily life (Deleuze 1992). His (and Felix Guattari's) idea of the 'assemblage' of surveillance activities has also been taken up by a number of sociological authors (such as Ericson and Haggerty 2000).

The notion of assemblage in this context points to the increasing convergence of once discrete systems of surveillance (administration, employment, health, insurance, credit, and so on) such that (in this case) digital data derived from human bodies flows within networks. At particular points the state, or totalizing institutions such as prisons, may focus or fix the flows to enable control or direction of the actions of persons or groups. But in this view surveillance becomes more socially levelled out, non-hierarchical, and inclusive of others who might once have felt themselves impervious to the gaze. At the same time, it is suggested, surveillance itself will not be slowed merely by resisting a particular technology or institution.

Others, sometimes indirectly, have also proposed fresh ways of examining surveillance beyond those classic foci on the 'state' or total institutions as its perpetrators. Nikolas Rose, for instance, argues that surveillance should be seen as part of contemporary governmentality, the way that governance actually happens, rather than thinking of it as an aspect of institutional state activities. Modern systems of rule, says Rose, depend on a complex set of relationships between state and non-state authorities, infrastructural powers, authorities that have no 'established' power and networks of power (Rose 1996: 15). Surveillance that pays close attention to personal details, especially those that are digitally retrievable, contributes to such governmentality. Indeed, it may, paradoxically, use 'freedom' (conventionally considered in opposition to state power) to further its ends. Consumer 'freedom' and surveillance is a case in point.

Perspectives such as Rose's offer much to critical thought. The powers of which he writes, expressed in part through surveillance, now spill over the territories once associated with the nation state. In their work on 'empire', Richard Hardt and Antonio Negri argue that surveillance is effectively globalized and indeed is vital to new regimes of imperial power (Hardt and Negri 2000). Moreover the ways in which contemporary surveillance works lead to new forms of exclusion (rather than control through inclusion that was characteristic of Foucault's understanding of the Benthamite panopticon). This is clear from empirical studies (such as Norris 2003 on public CCTV), Bauman (2000) on super-max prisons, and also from the theoretical work of Giorgio Agamben (1998) (which criticizes Foucault for never demonstrating *how* 'sovereign power produces biopolitical bodies').

Such exclusionary power has come more clearly into focus since 9/11, not only in the attempts to identify 'terrorists' and to prevent them from violent action, but also in the more general sorting of foreign workers, immigrants, and asylum seekers into 'desirable' and 'undesirable' categories. As Bigo and Guild (2005: 3) say, while

Foucault thought of surveillance as something that affects citizens equally, in fact 'the social practices of surveillance and control sort out, filter and serialize who needs to be controlled and who is free of that control'. Such sorting is becoming increasingly evident not only in Europe, but in North America and elsewhere. And it is facilitated by new surveillance measures such as biometric passports and electronic ID cards, currently being established in the UK and the USA (Lyon 2004).

The notion of a surveillance society is also given credence by the fact that in ordinary everyday life not only are people constantly being watched, they are also willing, it seems, to use technical devices to watch others. Plenty of domestic technologies are on the market, for providing video camera 'protection' to homes; CCTV is commonplace in schools and on school buses, and many schools are adopting automated identification systems; spouses may use surreptitious means to check on each other; and there is a burgeoning trade in gadgets that allow parents to 'watch' their children. Day Care cams permit parents to see what their toddlers are up to, Nanny cams monitor for suspected abuse, and cell phones are often given to children so that their parents may 'know where they are'. Those technologies, which originated in military and police use and later migrated to large organizations and government departments, may now be used for mundane, civilian, local, and familial purposes.

At the same time, the broader frames for understanding surveillance, such as governmentality, that acknowledge its ambiguity as well as its ubiquity, permit consideration of how new technologies may also empower the watched. While global imperial power is undoubtedly stretched by surveillance, and social exclusion is automated by the same means, Internet blogs, cell phone cameras, and other recent innovations may be used for democratic and even counter-surveillance ends. While such activities have none of the routine and systematic character let alone the infrastructural resources of most institutional surveillance, they may nevertheless contribute to alternative perspectives and to the organizational capacities of counter-hegemonic social movements.

Surveillance technologies

The very term 'surveillance technologies' is somewhat misleading. If one visits the 'spy stores' that seem to spring up in every city, the term seems clear enough. You can purchase disguised video cameras, audio surveillance and telephone tapping equipment, GPS (Global Positioning Satellite) enabled tracking devices, and of course counter-surveillance tools as well. But each of these is intended for very small-scale use—usually one surveillor, one person under surveillance, and they are often people already known to each other—and is decidedly covert. In policing and other investigative activities, such specifically targeted and individually triggered surveillance may be called for, but the kinds of surveillance discussed here are different in almost every respect. In terms of power relations, individual surveillance is one thing; institutional surveillance is quite another.

Surveillance that has developed as an aspect of bureaucratic administration in the modern world (see Dandeker 1990) is large-scale, systematic, and now is increasingly automated and dependent on networked computer power. It depends above all on searchable databases (Lessig 1999) to retrieve and process the relevant data. Although some systems depend on images or film (such as CCTV), even these possess far greater surveillance power when yoked to searchable databases. In most cases surveillance is not covert. It is often known about, at least in a general way, by those whose data are extracted, stored, manipulated, concatenated, traded, and processed in many other ways. Those buying houses are aware that checks will be made on them, patients know that health care agencies keep detailed records, video surveillance cameras are visible on the street, Internet surfers know their activities are traced, and so on. I return to this point later.

Surveillance technologies enable surveillance to occur routinely, automatically, but only in some cases is the surveillance aspect primary. Clearly, the point of public CCTV is to 'keep an eye' on the street or train station (although even here the larger goal may be public order or maximizing consumption). In the UK, there are more than 4 million cameras in public places (Norris and McCahill 2004). Police and intelligence services also use technologies such as fingerprinting devices, wiretaps, CCTV, and so on for surveillance purposes and all these depend (or are coming to depend) on searchable databases. For this reason, among others, they contribute to qualitatively different situations, sometimes amounting to a challenge to traditional conceptions of criminal justice (Marx 1988, 1998). In many cases, however, surveillance is the byproduct, accompaniment, or even unintended consequence of other processes and practices. It is sometimes not until some system is installed for another purpose that its surveillance potential becomes apparent.

Marketers claim that they 'want to know and serve their customers better' and this entails finding out as much as possible about tastes, preferences, and past purchases, which has now developed into a multi-billion dollar industry using Customer Relationship Marketing (CRM; see 6: 2005). Retailers may install ceiling mounted cameras in stores to combat shoplifting only to discover that this is also a really good way of monitoring employees as well. In the 'privacy' field this latter process is often referred to, using Langdon Winner's phrase, as 'function creep' (Winner 1977). Winner, like David Thomas almost 30 years later, warned that once a digitized national ID number has been assigned—say, to combat terrorism—its use is likely to be expanded to cover many cognate areas.

Whatever the specific characteristics of surveillance technologies, they also have to be located culturally in certain discourses of technology. Especially in the Western world and above all in the US, technology holds a special place in popular imagination and in public policy. Technical 'solutions' to an array of perceived social, economic, and political questions are all-too-quickly advanced and adopted, particularly in the aftermath of some crisis or catastrophe. This is not the start of an anti-technology argument—I have already claimed that surveillance is in part a necessary aspect of the technology-enhanced administrative and organizational regimes that have ordered social life for more than a century in the West— but rather an observation that technical responses have become commonplace, taken for granted.

In the mid-twentieth century, Jacques Ellul famously insisted that in the 'technological society', *la technique*, or the 'one best way of doing things' had become a kind of holy grail, especially in the US. In a world where from the late-nineteenth century 'progress' associated with undeniable technological advancement (at least in some domains) had been proclaimed, to fall back on technical solutions was both understandable, straightforwardly manageable, and, of course, lucrative for the companies concerned. By the end of the twentieth century Robert Wuthnow (1998), a sociologist of religion, could argue that technology remains one of the few beliefs that unites Americans. And if it was not clear before the twenty-first century, the challenge of terrorism certainly made it clear that technical responses were highly profitable. Share prices in security and surveillance companies surged after the attacks of 9/11 and also after the Madrid (2003) and London (2005) bombings (see, e.g. siliconvalley.com July 7 2005). The political economy of surveillance should not be overlooked; technology companies constantly press for procurements.

The steady and often subtle adoption of new technologies—including surveillance devices and systems—into everyday life is highly significant from a sociological point of view. If it was ever appropriate to think of social situations in a technological vacuum those days are definitely over. Because, for example, machines such as cell phones and computers have become essential for so many everyday communications, analyses of networks of social relations cannot but include reference to them. This is the 'technoculture'. Frequently, however, the focus is on how fresh forms of relationship are *enabled* by the new technologies rather than on how power may also be involved in ways that *limit or channel* social activities and processes. In a post-9/11 environment, the main things that come to mind in this connection may be the threats to civil liberties from the hasty deployment of supposedly risk-reducing technologies in the name of national security. But equally, the mundane activities of shopping using credit and loyalty cards may also contribute to profoundly significant processes of automated social sorting into newer spatially-based, social class categories that modify older formations of class and status. Sociology itself is obliged to readjust to such shifts (see Burrows and Gane 2006).

The explosion of personal data

It is difficult to exaggerate the massive surge in traffic in personal data from the 1970s to today. The quantitative changes have qualitative consequences. It is not merely that more and more data circulate in numerous administrative and commercial systems, but that ways of organizing daily life are changing as people interact with surveillance systems. One of the biggest reasons for this is hinted at in the word that I just used to describe it—'traffic'. There is constant growth in the volume of personal data that flow locally, nationally, and internationally through electronic networks. But one cause of this is 'traffic' in another, economic, sense, in which personal data are sought, stored, and traded as valuable commodities.

Long before notions of the 'surveillant assemblage' came to the fore, Australian computer scientist Roger Clarke had proposed another term to capture the idea of 'surveillance-by-data': 'dataveillance' (Clarke 1988, but cf. Genosko and Thompson 2006). A surge in surveillance could be traced, he argued, to the convergence of new technologies—computers and telecommunications—that rendered Orwell's ubiquitous two-way television unnecessary. The novel combinations made possible by ICTs permitted quite unprecedented flows of data, illustrated by Clarke in the case of EFT or 'Electronic Funds Transfer'.

It is hard for those who now assume the constant 'networks of flows' (this term is Manuel Castells') to recall how revolutionary EFT seemed at the time. It enabled supermarket shoppers, for instance, to have their accounts conveniently debited at the point of sale, thus bypassing several stages of financial transaction that would previously have had to occur. Such transfers are not only now commonplace, they also occur across a range of agencies and institutions that once had only indirect and complex connections. Clarke's point about *Nineteenth Eighty-four* was a critical one, pointing to the potentially negative surveillance capacities of dataveillance. Without minimizing that point, however, it is crucial to note that the major difference between the two is that EFT and its descendants are not centralized. Indeed, to the contrary, they are diffuse, shifting, ebbing and flowing—and yet as we shall see, not without discernible patterns of their own.

Even when Clarke was writing about dataveillance, a further innovation had yet to become a household word. What is often referred to as the 'Internet' (meaning a range of items, usually including email systems and the World Wide Web) was only coming into being as a publicly accessible tool in the early 1990s. The debate over its threatened commercialization was hot; until then it was the preserve of the military, academics, and computer enthusiasts, many of whom saw it as an intrinsically open medium. Its eventual role as a global purveyor of information, ideas, images, and data, under the sign of consumerism, signals a major augmentation of surveillance.

Not only were computers and communications systems enabling new data-flows of many kinds, now consumers could participate directly in the process. Online purchasing of goods and services, from groceries, to airline tickets, to banking, meant that personal data were moving on a massive scale. Who had access to these data, and how they could be secured and protected became a central question as quite new categories of crime appeared, such as 'identity theft', and as corporations fell over themselves to gain access to increasingly valuable personal data. Knowing people's preferences and purchasing habits was to revolutionize marketing industries—right down to targeting children (Steeves 2005).

A third phase of dataveillance began to take off only at the turn of the twenty-first century. It involves a device that had been in the analytical shadow of the Internet during much of the 1990s, but which, some argue, may be at least as, if not more, profound in its social implications. The cell phone (or mobile phone) is the single most important item in what might be termed 'mobiveillance'. If dataveillance started in the world of places such as supermarkets, police stations, and offices, then the use of networked technologies such as the Internet virtualized it, producing what might be called 'cyberveillance'. Surfing data became significant within the virtual travels of the Internet user. The advent of mobile or 'm-commerce', in which the actual location of consumers becomes an important value-added aspect of personal data—using RFID, automated road tolling, or other technologies as well as cell phones—brings the activity that characterized 'surfing' back into the world of place, only now it can be any place in which signals are accessible (Andrejevic 2004, Lyon 2006).

The result is that personal data now circulate constantly, not only within, but also between organizations and even countries. Personal data flow internationally for many reasons, in relation, for example, to police data-sharing arrangements (such as the Schengen Agreement in Europe), especially with the rise of perceived threats of terrorism, or to 'outsourcing', the set of processes whereby banks, credit card companies, and other corporations use call centres in distant countries for dealing with customer transaction data. While for much of the time publics in countries affected by such increased data flows seem to assume that their data are secure and that they are used only for the purposes for which they were released, notorious cases of fraud and sheer error do seem to proliferate with the result that some consumers and citizens are more cautious about how they permit their data to travel. The language used to mobilize such concerns is, more often than not, 'privacy'. Even if it is a notion of 'information privacy' rather than, say, a right to be 'left alone' that is in question, privacy dominates the discourse.

3 THE END OF PRIVACY?

From the late twentieth century, a common response to the massive growth of surveillance systems in the global north has been to ask whether we are witnessing the 'end of privacy'. What is meant by this? On the one hand, as many socially critical authors assert, there are fewer and fewer 'places to hide' (see, e.g. O'Harrow

2005) in the sense that some surveillance systems record, monitor, or trace so many of our daily activities and behaviours that, it seems, nothing we do is exempt from observation. On the other, a different set of authors see the 'end of privacy' as something to celebrate, or at least not to lament. In the face of growing e-commerce and the consequent mass of personal data circulating, Scott McNealy, of Sun Microsystems, most famously declared, 'Privacy is dead. Get over it!'

It is important to note that privacy is a highly mutable concept, both historically and culturally relative. If privacy is dead, then it is a form of privacy—legal, relating to personal property, and particularly to the person as property—that is a relatively recent historical invention in the Western world. At the same time, this Western notion of privacy is simply not encountered in some South-Eastern Asian and Eastern countries. The Chinese have little sense of personal space as Westerners understand it, and the Japanese have no word for privacy in their language (the one they use is imported from the West).

The best-known writer on privacy in a computer era is Alan Westin, whose classic book, *Privacy and Freedom* (Westin 1967) has inspired and informed numerous analysts and policy makers around the world. For him, privacy means that 'individuals, groups or institutions have the right to control, edit, manage and delete information about themselves and to decide when, how and to what extent that information is communicated to others'. However, although this definition seems to refer to more than the 'individual', the onus of responsibility to 'do something' about the inappropriate use of personal (and other) data is on data subjects. That is, rather than focusing on the responsibilities of those who collect data in the first place, it is those who may have grievances who have rights to have those addressed.

This emphasis has been questioned, for example by Priscilla Regan (1995) who argues that privacy has intrinsic common, public, and social value, and therefore that not only may individuals have a right to seek protection from the effects of misused personal data, but also organizations that use such data have to give account. The huge increase in surveillance technologies, for instance in the workplace and in policing, underscores this point. Today, data are not only collected and retrieved, but analysed, searched, mined, recombined, and traded, within and between organizations, in ways that make simple notions of privacy plain inadequate. Valerie Steeves maintains that while Westin started out (in the 1960s) with a broader definition of privacy, the overwhelmingly individualistic context of American business and government interests, in conjunction with pressure to adopt new technology 'solutions' has served to pare down privacy to its present narrow conception (Steeves 2005).

Surveillance as social sorting

To argue that privacy may not have the power to confront contemporary surveillance in all its manifestations is one thing. To propose an alternative approach is another. For, as in the case of the Orwellian and the panoptic imagery for capturing what surveillance is about, the language of privacy has popular cachet. It is difficult to explain why 'privacy' is not the (only) problem that surveillance poses (Stalder 2002) when this is so widely assumed by lawyers, politicians, mass media, and Western publics. The best way of deflecting attention from a singular focus on privacy, in my view, is to consider surveillance as 'social sorting'.

It could be said that 'to classify is human' but in modern times classification became a major industry. From medicine to the military, classification is crucial. As Geoffery Bowker and Susan Star show, the quest for meaningful content produces a desire for classification, or 'sorting things out' (Bowker and Star 1999). Human judgements attend all classifications and, from our perspective, these are critical. Classification allows one to segregate undesirable elements (such as those susceptible to certain kinds of disease), but it is easy for this to spill over into negatively discriminatory behaviours. South Africa under apartheid had a strong population classification system, but it served to exclude, on 'racial' criteria, black people from any meaningful access to opportunity structures. Classification may be innocent and humanly beneficial, but it can also be the basis of injustice and inequity. The modern urge to classify found its ideal instrument in the computer.

One way of thinking about surveillance as social sorting is to recall that today's surveillance relies heavily on ICTs. Both security measures and marketing techniques exploit the interactivity of ICTs to identify and isolate groups and individuals of interest to the organizations concerned. By gathering data about people and their activities and movements and analysing secondary data (by 'mining' other databases) obtained through networked technologies, marketers can plan and target their advertising and soliciting campaigns with increasingly great accuracy. Equally, security personnel use similar strategies to surveil 'suspects' who have been previously identified or who fit a particular profile, in the hope of building a fuller picture of such persons, keeping tabs on their movements, and forestalling acts of violence or terror.

These actuarial plans for opportunity maximization (marketing strategies for widening the range of target groups for products and services) and for risk management (such as security strategies for widening the net of suspect populations) represent a new development in surveillance. Though they have a long history, they contrast with more conventional reactive methods of marketing or security delivery. They are future rather than past oriented, and are based on simulating and modelling situations that have yet to occur. They cannot operate without networked, searchable databases and their newness may be seen in the fact that unsuspecting persons who fit, say, an age profile, may be sent email messages promoting devices guaranteeing enhanced sexual performance, and others—much less amusingly—who simply fit an ethnic or religious profile, may be watched and detained without explanation, or worse detained by security forces.

The 'surveillant assemblage' works by social sorting. Abstract data of all kinds—video images, text files, biometric measures, genetic information, and so on—are manipulated to produce profiles and risk categories within a fluid network. Planning, prediction, pre-emption, permitting, all these and more goals are in mind as the assemblage is accessed and drawn upon. Social sorting is in a sense an ancient and perhaps inevitable human activity, but today it has become routine, systematic, and above all technically assisted or automated (and in some sense driven). The more new technologies are implicated, however, the more the criteria of sorting becomes opaque to the public. Who knows by what standards a credit was unexpectedly turned down or an innocent terrorist suspect was apprehended? Of course, the sorting may be innocent and above question—surveillance, after all, is always ambiguous—but it is also the case that social sorting has a direct effect, for good or ill, on life-chances (see Lace 2005: 28–32 for consumer examples).

The main fears associated with automated social sorting, then, are that through relatively unaccountable means, large organizations make judgements that directly affect the lives of those whose data are processed by them. In the commercial sphere, such decisions are made in an actuarial fashion, based on calculations of risk, of which insurance assessments provide the best examples. Thus people may find themselves classified according to residential and socio-demographic criteria, and paying premiums that bear little relation to other salient factors. Equally, customers are increasingly sorted into categories of worth to the corporation, according to which they can obtain benefits or are effectively excluded from participation in the marketplace. In law enforcement contexts, the actuarial approach is replicated; indeed, Feely and Simon warned in the mid-1990s that forms of 'actuarial justice' were becoming evident. The 'new penology', they argue, 'is concerned with techniques for identifying, managing and classifying groups sorted by levels of dangerousness' (Feely and Simon 1994: 180). Rather than using evidence of criminal behaviour, newer approaches intervene on the basis of risk assessment, a trend that has become even more marked after 9/11.

Surveillance society and safety state

The growth of the surveillance dimension of modern states warrants special attention and one way of indicating this is to refer to current conditions of social life as living in a 'surveillance society'. This is no more meant to be sinister than it is to refer to everyday practices of extracting personal data in the supermarket, for example, as 'surveillance'. It simply draws attention to a key feature of contemporary life which is both so routine and taken-for-granted that it seems unremarkable and yet simultaneously has such far-reaching consequences that it demands social scientific scrutiny.

At the same time, life in a surveillance society reflects in part some expanding dimensions of the nation state. Whereas in the mid- and later-twentieth century it may have been true to say that several more liberal countries considered themselves to be 'welfare states' in the early twentieth century the designation 'safety state' began to be more plausible as an overall descriptor (Raab 2005). More and more, the criteria by which policies of many kinds are judged is not the positive benefit for all so much as the minimization of risk. New technologies designed to reduce risk are central to the emerging quest for the 'safety state', and they all entail surveillance of one kind or another.

In their work on policing, Ericson and Haggerty (1997: 431) show how new communication technologies make possible faster transmission and contribute to a shift from local spatial emphases to 'microcentres of inscription' such as computer terminals in police cars. Organizational hierarchies are challenged by the same trends, and at the same time more 'remote control' becomes possible. In combination, the new technologies enable faster surveillance of the population for risk management purposes (as well as making the police themselves more vulnerable to scrutiny). What they say about policing has a familiar ring in other sectors as well. Surveillance is vital to risk communication because it 'provides knowledge for the selection of thresholds that define acceptable risks and justify inclusion and exclusion'. Thus, they go on, 'coercive control gives way to contingent categorization' and everyone is 'assumed to be "guilty" until the risk communication system reveals otherwise' (Ericson and Haggerty 1997: 449).

Such trends have become more widespread and controversial in the West since 9/11. Airport and border management systems are on heightened alert according to just the same kind of criteria. The same kinds of surveillance systems, now further bolstered by the adoption of 'new' biometrics technologies (distinguished from the 'old' not because they have transcended their often racist and colonial 'anthropometric' origins, but rather by their extensive use of ICTs) are used for making 'biographical' profiles of human populations to determine whether or not they may travel, exchange large sums of money, or be employed within given companies. Hence the scandals, from a civil liberties perspective, of 'no-fly lists' based on ethnicity, religion, or country of origin, that can also easily include 'mistaken identities'. Hence too, the ironic exacerbation of risk (to travellers and citizens) from the increasing reliance on other agencies (such as airports) to whom tasks have been outsourced, especially in countries such as the US.

It is also, at least in part, the role played by ICTs that makes it important to consider both 'surveillance society' and 'safety state' together. For the kinds of risk communication (that may also be read as 'opportunity calculation') carried out by firms in relation to customers, and providing of detailed profiles, are also of interest to the nation state. Not only are the methods of assembling profiles based on similar algorithms, the actual data gathered and analysed by those firms are also of interest to law enforcement agencies, especially in the so-called 'war on terrorism'. Thus in

2006, for instance, Google refused to hand over its search records to the US Department of Justice (DoJ), citing the privacy of its users and the protection of its trade secrets. In this particular case, the DoJ claimed they wished to test the effectiveness of web-filtering software, but many civil libertarians and privacy advocates saw it as the thin end of the wedge. Government could also use search records to obtain highly personal records, in the name of 'national security'.

Thus, while it is worth examining both the development of the surveillance society for its routine dependence on the garnering and processing of personal data, and the safety state for its use of surveillance for risk communication, it is also important to see that the two work in an increasingly symbiotic relation. If present trends continue, this particular social-economic-political nexus will become more and more significant in coming decades.

Politics of personal data

Surveillance studies, as this sub-field is increasingly known (see Lyon, forthcoming), has often focused on the large-scale systems, institutions, and technologies that promote and produce surveillance. This can result in some rather negative and dystopian perspectives however, that give the impression that ordinary people whose everyday activities are surveilled are simply pawns, ciphers in an increasingly global surveillance machine. Without suggesting that such views have no merit, or that the balance of power is not tipped overwhelmingly in favour of those large institutions, it is nevertheless important to note that surveillance is an interactive process. What sociologists of technology call 'co-construction' well describes the world of surveillance (Lyon, 2004).

In order to work, surveillance systems frequently depend on their subjects (indeed, as Foucault (1979) observed a long time ago, subjects become 'the bearers of their own surveillance'). Although there is a sense in which the subjects of surveillance become 'objectified' as their data double become more real to the surveillance system than the bodies and daily lives from which the data have been drawn, their involvements with surveillance systems often remain active, conscious, and intentional. People comply (but not as dupes), negotiate, and at times resist the surveillance systems in which their lives are enmeshed.

It is very important to consider the ways in which so-called 'data subjects' of contemporary surveillance engage with and respond to having their data collected and used by organizations. Much depends on the purposes for which those data are collected. Righteous indignation at being shut out of a flight may be the response of a passenger with a 'suspicious' name, even though that same passenger may be delighted with the 'rewards' from his frequent flyer programme with which he 'bought' the ticket. In each case, extensive personal data are used to determine the outcome, whether the privileged category of an 'elite' passenger or the excluded category of a name on the no-fly list. Consumers appear most willing to provide their personal data, in the belief that some benefit awaits them; employees and citizens are much more likely to exercise caution or express complaint at the over-zealous quest of organizations for their details.

Other variables in the analysis of the interactions between the 'watchers and the watched' include the extent of the knowledge of 'data subjects' of their being watched. In the classic case of panoptic surveillance, prison inmates were supposed to subject themselves to self-discipline based on the assumption that the unseen inspector might just be watching. The uncertainty is essential to the success of the system. But what of situations where cameras are hidden, or when customer details are simply extracted without the knowledge of the person concerned? Life-chances and choices are still affected, for better or for worse, but the opportunity to engage with the surveillance system is severely restricted. As ICTs help to reduce the visibility of surveillance through miniaturization or automation, this will become an increasingly significant area for social and political analysis.

The evidence suggests that the politics of information is becoming more im-portant, even though some leading theorists of information may miss it. Manuel Castells, for instance, reassures his readers that for most of the time contemporary surveillance is a rather benign set of processes, and Scott Lash (2002: 112) argues that with the 'predominance of communication the logic of classification disap-pears'. Yet as I have tried to show here, the use of ICTs within new regimes of risk management in the surveillance society and the safety state is contributing to new modes of classification that have profound social, economic, and political ramifi-cations. This is where the struggle over information will take place.

4 CONCLUSION

Questions of surveillance and privacy have become more important as so-called information societies—dependent upon electronic technologies—have developed since the 1970s. Thus ICTs are centrally implicated in these developments because their establishment may be prompted by them or they may be harnessed to add power to surveillance systems. At the same time, surveillance grows because of certain economic and political priorities and because of the emergence of cultural contexts in which self-disclosure is not merely acceptable, but sometimes positively valued and sought. Surveillance has also been expanding since the start of the twenty-first century in an international response to global terrorism, and it is now much more internationally networked itself, which again indicates how its dom-inant forms are structurally dependent on ICTs.

Calls for greater privacy, once the standard response to increased surveillance, continue to be made, with varying results. Yet regulative bodies, especially ones based on legislative regimes, have a very hard time keeping up with the changes occurring. At the same time, the onus of law has tended to be on the individual, who feels (assuming she even knows) that she has been violated or invaded, and not necessarily on the organizations that process the data in the first place. Data protection regimes have more to offer here, dependent as they are on registering their activities, and more recent laws—for instance PIPEDA (Personal Information Protection and Electronic Documents Act 2001) in Canada—do require organizations, in this case including commercially-based ones, to attend to the stipulations of the law.

However, large and urgent questions about social sorting remain, even after privacy and data protection policies and laws have done their work. It is quite possible for negative discrimination to be carried out, automatically and systematically, against ethnic (such as categories relating to the likelihood of terrorist involvement), or social-economic (such as those living in low-income districts of cities) minorities, despite having such policies and laws in place. The codes by which persons and groups are categorized are seldom under public scrutiny (and if they relate to 'national security' they may well be veiled in official secrecy), and yet they have huge potential and actual consequences for the life chances and the choices of ordinary citizens.

Thus, in terms of both accurate analysis and informed political action, much remains to be done in the emerging realm of database-enabled surveillance. It seems unlikely that the issues will be tackled in ways appropriate to the present challenge while the mass media encourage complacency about self-disclosure, high technology companies persuade governments and corporations that they have surveillance 'solutions' to their problems, actuarial practices deriving from insurance and risk management dominate the discourse that supports surveillance, and legal regimes are couched in the language of supposed rights to individual privacy.

One upshot of this kind of argument is that analysts and practitioners in the ICT field have special responsibilities to understand and to intervene in an informed way in current developments. There is also as I have argued, an urgent need to go beyond tired notions of 'privacy'—that tend to place the onus of care over personal data back on the individual—to assessing the need for greater accountability in organizations processing personal data, as well as for greater awareness among publics, politicians, and policy makers. While common prudence may be expected, to assume that ordinary people have the time, expertise, or motivation to be constantly vigilant about surveillance is to sidestep questions of justice and informational fairness. The politics of information in the twenty-first century will increasingly be about how to increase the accountability of those who have responsibility for processing personal data.

REFERENCES

6, P. (2005). 'The Personal Information Economy: Trends and Prospects for Consumers', in S. Lace (ed.), *The Glass Consumer: Living in a Surveillance Society*. Bristol: Policy Press, 17–43.

ANDREJEVIC, M. (2004). *Reality TV: The Work of Being Watched*. Lanham, MD: Rowman & Littlefield.

AGAMBEN, G. (1998). *Homo Sacer: Sovereign Power and Bare Life*. Stanford, CA: Stanford University Press.

BAUMAN, Z. (2000). 'Social Issues of Law and Order'. *British Journal of Criminology*, 40: 205–21.

BALL, K. and WEBSTER, F. (eds) (2003). *The Intensification of Surveillance: Crime, Terrorism and Warfare in the Information Age*. London: Pluto Press.

BIGO, D. and GUILD, E. (eds) (2005). *Controlling Frontiers: Free Movement Into and Within Europe*. Aldershot: Ashgate.

BOWKER, G. C. and STAR, S. L. (1999). *Sorting Things Out: Classification and its Consequences*. Cambridge, MA: MIT Press.

BURROWS, R. and GANE, N. (2006). 'Geodemographics, Software and Class'. *Sociology*, 40(5): 793–812.

CLARKE, R. (1988), 'Information Technology and Dataveillance'. *Communications of the ACM*, 31(5): 498–512.

COLE, S. (2001). *Suspect Identities: A History of Fingerprinting and Criminal Identification*. Cambridge, MA: Harvard University Press.

DANDEKER, C. (1990). *Surveillance Power and Modernity*. Cambridge: Polity Press.

DELEUZE, G. (1992). 'Postscript on the Societies of Control'. *October*, 59: 3–7.

ERICSON, R. and HAGGERTY, K. (1997). *Policing the Risk Society*. Oxford and Toronto: Clarendon Press and Toronto University Press.

FEELY M. and SIMON, J. (1994). 'Actuarial Justice: The Emerging New Criminal Law', in D. Nelken (ed.), *The Futures of Criminology*. London: Sage, 173–201.

FLAHERTY, D. (1989). *Protecting Privacy in Surveillance Societies: The Federal Republic of Germany, Sweden, France, Canada, and the United States*. Chapel Hill, NC: University of North Carolina Press.

FOUCAULT, M. (1979). *Discipline and Punish*. New York: Vintage.

GANDY, O. Jr (1989). 'The Surveillance Society: Information Technology and Bureaucratic Social Control'. *Journal of Communication*, 39(3): 61–76.

GENOSKO, G. and THOMPSON, S. (2006). 'Tense Theory: The Temporalities of Surveillance', in D. Lyon (ed.), *Theorizing Surveillance: The Panopticon and Beyond*. Cullompton: Willan Publishing, Ch. 9.

HAGGERTY, K. and ERICSON, R. (2002). 'The Surveillant Assemblage'. *British Journal of Sociology*, 51(4): 605–62.

HARDT, R. and NEGRI, A. (2000). *Empire*. Cambridge, MA: Harvard University Press.

LACE, S. (2005). *The Glass Consumer: Living in a Surveillance Society*. Bristol: The Policy Press.

LASH, S. (2002). *Critique of Information*. London: Sage.

LESSIG, L. (1999). *Code and Other Laws of Cyberspace*. New York: Basic Books.

LYON, D. (2003). *Surveillance after September 11*. Cambridge: Polity Press.

—— (2004). *ID Cards: Social Sorting by Database*. Oxford: Oxford Internet Institute Issue Brief, www.oii.ox.ac.uk/resources/publications/IB3all.pdf, accessed 18 Mar. 2006.

—— (2004). 'Surveillance Technologies and Surveillance Societies', in T. Misa, P. Brey, and A. Feenberg (eds), *Modernity and Technology*. Cambridge, MA: MIT Press, 161–84.

—— (2006). 'Why Where You are Matters: Mundane Mobilities, Transparent Technologies and Digital Discrimination', in T. Monahan (ed.) *Surveillance and Security: Technological Politics and Power in Everyday Life*. New York and London: Routledge, Ch. 13.

—— (2007). *Surveillance Studies* An Overview. Cambridge: Polity Press.

MARX, G. T. (1985). 'The Surveillance Society: The Threat of 1984-style Techniques'. *The Futurist*, 19: 21–6.

—— (1988). *Undercover: Police Surveillance in America*. Berkeley, CA: University of California Press.

—— (1998). 'An Ethics for the New Surveillance'. *The Information Society*, 14(3): 171–85.

McCAHILL, M. (2002). *The Surveillance Web: The Rise of Visual Surveillance in an English City*. Cullompton: Willan.

NORRIS, C. (2003). 'From Personal to Digital: CCTV, the Panopticon and the Technological Mediation of Suspicion and Social Control', in D. Lyon (ed.), *Surveillance as Social Sorting: Privacy, Risk, and Digital Discrimination*. London and New York: Routledge, 249–81.

—— and ARMSTRONG, G. (1999). *The Maximum Surveillance Society: The Rise of CCTV*. Oxford: Berg.

—— and McCAHILL, M. (2004). *CCTV in London*. Berlin: Urban Eye, www.urbaneye.net/results/ue_wp6.pdf, accessed 18 Mar. 2006.

O'HARROW, R. (2005). *No Place to Hide*. New York: Free Press.

RAAB, C. D. (2005). 'Governing the Safety State'. Inaugural Lecture at the University of Edinburgh, 7 June.

REGAN, P. (1995). *Legislating Privacy: Technology, Social Values and Public Policy*. Chapel Hill, NC: University of North Carolina Press.

ROSE, N. (1996). *Powers of Freedom*. Cambridge: Cambridge University Press.

RULE, J. (1973). *Private Lives, Public Surveillance*. London: Allen Lane.

STALDER, F. (2002). 'Privacy is not the Antidote to Surveillance'. *Surveillance and Society* 1(1): 120–4.

STEEVES, V. (2005). 'It's Not Child's Play: The Online Invasion of Children's Privacy'. *University of Ottawa Law and Technology Journal*, 2(2), http://www.uoltj.ca/articles.php, accessed 18 Mar. 2006.

WESTIN, A. (1967). *Privacy and Freedom*. New York: Atheneum.

WINNER, L. (1977). *Autonomous Technology: Technics Out of Control as a Theme in Human Thought*. Cambridge, MA: MIT Press.

WUTHNOW, R. (1998). *The Restructuring of American Religion*. Princeton, NJ: Princeton University Press.

PART IV

··

CULTURE, COMMUNITY, AND NEW MEDIA LITERACIES

··

THEME EDITOR: ROGER SILVERSTONE

Introduction

THIS part addresses the social aspects of ICTs from the perspective of their significance for experience and practice. They are seen principally as resources for social, political, and personal action, and as having consequences for the ways in which cultures form and change. Each chapter in its own way offers a version of the dialectic at the heart of technological and social change, recognizing that understanding its complexity is also a matter of understanding its variety and its instability.

Graham and Goodrum in Chapter 20 take a long term overview, both historical and predictive, of how literacies emerge and change with the emergence of new media. In their account, which draws on critical discourse analysis as well as on the political economy of ICTs, literacy is a matter of the capacity to participate in public discourse, and to command it. In this sense literacy is both a political project and a pedagogic one, but it ultimately resides in the capacity of individuals to be able to mobilize the resources for effective participation in the changing cultures of an increasingly technology-dependent world.

Livingstone picks up these themes in Chapter 21 by focusing much more directly on the capacity of young people to use the Internet in a creative way. The skills required bring the young greater access to a world of information and communication, but they also bring greater risks. This would always have been the case, of course. However, Livingstone focuses on youthful experience of the Internet to argue for the significance of a continuing divide between those with and those without the relevant skills, but also, more significantly, between those who can and will engage with the resources available online in creative and participative ways, and those who, for one reason or another, cannot.

Questions of literacy raise questions of the nature of the relationship between what goes on on line and what off line. Orgad reviews the wide range of areas where this agenda has been identified, but in each case where it still needs further discussion: in e-commerce, in journalism, in civil society, but above all in the fine grain of action in everyday life. In Chapter 22 she argues that it is still the case that thinking is dominated by a kind of 'two-realm' approach, which will consistently fail to understand the intensity of their interrelationship. What is required is a political economy which stresses the materiality of power inscribed across both domains, and a broadly ethnographic perspective, where, likewise, there is every intention of exploring the mutual contextualization of life which is simultaneously both on line and off.

This is a theme that underpins both of the chapters that follow, the first on the significance of ICTs for political movements, and the second on the formation and sustaining of community. Downing and Brooten address the first in Chapter 23.

They review the key theoretical issues relevant to an understanding of the changing nature of ICTs and contrary politics: the public sphere, counter-hegemony, and civil society. And they then discuss a number of significant case studies of alternative political mobilization, spanning a range of media from community radio to mobile telephony and the web, and of specific cases where these technologies have been utilized in situations of direct mobilization as well as sustained engagement in alternative politics at local, community, and global levels.

So it is not just the relationship between online and offline action and discourse which is at issue. There is also an inevitable tension between global and local levels of communication and action which ICTs dramatically bring to the fore. Jung, Ball-Rokeach, Kim, and Matei discuss these in Chapter 24 in the context of community, where once again the tendency in the literature is to offer a polarized dystopian or utopian account of the significance of ICTs. In an age of rapid social change and increasing social and geographical mobility, the capacity to use the Internet creatively is in great degree determined not by the technology, but by the social, economic, and political resources available to communities and networks on the ground.

The final chapter addresses the complex and subtle agenda of identity, and of the relationship between identity and inequality. Wajcman's focus on gender, and in particular on the significance of ICTs for the role, status, and empowerment of women, also reviews the polarized debates that have defined much of the discourse thus far. In the realms of education and work, above all, it is clear that there has been a sustained regime of inequality across the sexes in both access and participation. On the other hand, arguments have emerged that have suggested that ICTs have the capacity to liberate women from their dependent status in technological environments. Wajcman argues against such essentialism and determinism to explore a more synthetic and sympathetic techno-feminism, one that requires the rejection of the polarities of many of the arguments around gender and technology in favour of a more sociologically and historically sophisticated account of their mutual determination.

CHAPTER 20

NEW MEDIA LITERACIES: AT THE INTERSECTION OF TECHNICAL, CULTURAL, AND DISCURSIVE KNOWLEDGES

PHIL GRAHAM
ABBY ANN GOODRUM

1 INTRODUCTION

THE global spread of ICTs surprisingly has not coincided with an intellectual burst of energy focused on literacies of all kinds: technological, financial, reflective, rhetorical, critical, scientific, visual—the list of new and seemingly essential literacies is endless. In this chapter we focus on the cultural and discursive aspects of literacies, noting that the term 'literacy' has moved to encompass much more than the mere comprehension and manipulation of letters and words. In fact none of the terms we are dealing with are singular or uncontested and so some definition is in order. By literacy we mean the ability to understand and make meanings of the universe of symbolic resources to which we have access, including access to the technical means to do this (see Lankshear and Knobel 2003: ch. 1). By culture we mean the universe of symbolic resources drawn upon and deployed by specific groups of people joined in historical association, whether on religious, ethnic, nationalistic, geographic, or some other corporate basis (see Bernstein 1996/2000). By discourse and discursive we refer to the patterns of representation and evaluation that typify, identify, and differentiate cultural groups (see Lemke 1995). We therefore necessarily see culture and discourse as being historically intertwined: culture is the pool of symbolic resources through which specific groups of people typically express themselves, while discourse refers to the patterns of representation and evaluation through which a culture maintains, extends, and transforms itself in time, and which are simultaneously discursive resources and cultural markers. The significance of new media in the transformation of cultural and discursive trends further entails an historical view because new mediations necessarily include incursions of one culture upon another resulting in what can be called cultural hybridity, an innately historical process (see Lemke 1995; Fairclough 2000).

As a field of study, media literacy emerges with the study of radio propaganda in the 1930s. More recently it has been a field of research that has responded to the television saturated consumer cultures of the late-1960s onwards. Unlike literacies of pre-electronic media environments, those that have been studied within electronic environments have been almost solely concerned with analytical ways of reading multimedia texts. In contrast, literacies in the written word have typically involved the production of written texts as integral to curricula. The new media environment provides opportunities and challenges for research in new media literacies, not the least of which is understanding what it means for people to have a widespread potential to write themselves into global, multimediated conversations. This not only involves technical, cultural, discursive, and aesthetic knowledges, it also involves the need to be politically and economically literate in the implications of a dispersed, participatively produced, multimedia environment as distinct from the 'broadcast' literacies of past media environments. In this chapter, we situate new media literacies in an historical framework, emphasizing the close connections among technology, culture, discourse, and related changes in political economic structures.

2 MEDIA LITERACIES IN HISTORY

The technological impacts of new digital media on cultural and discursive literacies cannot be fully understood outside media history more generally. Rather than simply seeing an historically unique rupture in the media environment that has spurred a sudden interest in new kinds of literacies for the production of culture and discourse, a longer historical view reveals that not only do literacy drives emerge historically with new communication technologies, but that the current environment appears to be reverting to more participatory, localized, cultural, formations of pre-industrial eras (see Lessig 2004; Mumford 1934/1963). Such a view invites charges of determinism and reductionism. But Walter Ong (1988: 701) argues that to see such movements in terms of technological change 'is not reductionist but relationist'. He uses the historical move from primarily oral cultures to ones in which the printed word becomes dominant to exemplify the point:

By no means do all changes in culture identifiable after the introduction of writing reduce to the shift from orality to literacy. But an astonishing number of them relate massively to this shift (and later to the shifts to printing and electronic processing of the word). Although we can isolate certain general traits that differentiate literate cultures from oral, these general traits never occur without admixtures of specific differences. (Ong 1988: 701)

The 'specific differences' that Ong mentions are cultural differences, and they make any definitive set of 'media effects' almost impossible to identify, at least as homogeneous functions of any particular communication technology.

However, the most emphasized aspect in studies of media history is the advent of the printing press, developed in the Western world by Gutenberg more than 400 years after its invention in the Orient. The new medium of moveable type had impacts upon Western societies that did not occur elsewhere, even in societies where the same medium appeared much earlier. Mumford (1964/1970: 139–40) argues that this is because 'the initial step in mechanization, the creation of perfectly standardized hand-lettering, had long been achieved in the monastery, where a deliberately mechanized habit of life laid the groundwork for wider mechanizations'. Ong (1984) also notes the significance of the mediaeval move from oral- and manuscript-based communication media to an industrialized print system, emphasizing the move from sound-based recognition of 'sameness' between two literary works to a mode of recognition based on visual sameness: 'If a person could not read, he or she could never tell if two manuscript books were the same work or not' unless someone was reading them and converting them into sound (Ong 1984: 2). The sharp distinction that has emerged in recent years between literate and non-literate persons is directly related to the massification of language and culture and can be summarized as follows.

The relationship of language to writing begins when someone devises a way of putting the words of a language into a script. But the fact that a writing system has been devised for a particular language does not necessarily make any difference at all to a language or its speakers.... Many languages, now as in the past, have never had enough speakers to make writing worthwhile. If only five hundred speakers know a language, what sort of effort could they put into teaching how to write it, and what would they use writing for on any continuous basis? (Ong 1984: 5)

However, as soon as writing 'has been devised for a language, various stages of limited literacy can develop': these include 'semiliteracy or craft literacy, the literacy of a scribal culture', and, 'if writing becomes more widespread, the culture itself, as a whole or in significant parts, can become fully literate' (Ong 1984: 5). At such a point, 'writing provides new resources for thought' which can 'alter the mental processes of a culture in significant ways', producing 'a body of discursive texts' that need 'no independent oral existence. To be fully at home in such a culture, one needs to be able to read' (Ong 1984: 5–6). At this point:

[o]rality and textuality now interplay vigorously in the language. Consciously or unconsciously, speakers model their oral utterance on forms of thought and expression which have come into existence only because of the resources provided by writing, while written language continually accommodates itself to oral variations. A language at this stage is a literary language. (Ong 1984: 6)

In fully literate, massified, industrialized cultures tied together and amplified by nationalized, standardized education systems, the widespread 'experience of physically matching books, together with our late typographic habit of silent reading... altered our sense of the text by dissociating it notably, though never of course entirely, from the oral world' (Ong 1984: 5). And, while many such as Ong (1984) and McLuhan (1964) argue that electronic media herald a reversion to oral and aural (or preliterate) modes of communication, many others argue that the visual bias of print has so exerted itself in the appearance everywhere of screen-based interfaces, that a move towards understanding 'multimodal', and especially visual literacies, has become imperative for contemporary curricula (e.g. Kress and van Leeuwen 1996).

Educating readers

Contemporary 'literacy drives' can be traced back to the establishment of universities in Western Europe under Charlemagne. After the collapse of Roman influence in Western Europe, literacy went into severe decline (Thurow 1996: 281–8). In response, Charlemagne issued his *admonitio generali*, a significant aim of which was to establish 'schools near the cathedrals or in the monasteries' (Ganshof 1949: 522). One main purpose of issuing this edict—the other equally significant part being concerned with setting up a system of law—was to carefully transcribe and correct 'biblical and liturgical texts', and to ensure at least minimal literacy stand-ards among the clergy (Ganshof 1949: 522). Charlemagne's admonition was to be the basis for Western university systems and began the slow but steady movement to textual literacies.

Adams and Hamon (2001: 33) note that until very recently 'literacy was squeezed into an established framework of reading and writing', but that with new tech-nologies, the 'meaning' of literacy 'has changed as new circumstances and new approaches to teaching have opened up a much wider range of possibilities'. Also Kress and Van Leeuwen point out that while new ICTs are clearly language-based technologies—with the bulk of exchanges they facilitate being comprised of written and spoken words (e.g. through email, mobile phones, and web pages) and their functional reliance is on quasi-linguistic code—in some views the most obvious changes facilitated by digital information and communication technologies (ICTs) are related to what linguists call 'multimodality' (Kress 2001; 2003; Kress and Van Leeuwen 1996). Multimodal technologies are those that give us the combined ability to manipulate words, images, music, and sounds in order to communicate. Modes can be roughly conceived of in this context as meaning-making resources that appeal to different aspects of the human perceptive apparatus, a clear example being those that appeal to the eye rather than the ear, and vice versa (Innis 1951; McLuhan 1964; Ong 1984).[1]

The development and diffusion of digital, multimodal ICTs (hereafter new media) are closely tied to a new emphasis on literacy teaching in contemporary education research (see Lankshear and Knobel 2003; Cazden et al. 1996; Kalantzis and Cope 2001). Beyond the state-based cultural media of education systems, new media proliferation has had significant impacts on all cultural heritage institutions: 'mere' textual literacy is not enough for the traditional keepers of cultural and discursive literacies, such as libraries and museums (Goodrum 2006). For example, libraries and schools now find themselves under pressure to be major community bridges across 'the digital divide', with about 95 per cent of all public libraries in the US providing computer and Internet access to the public (ALA 2001). Similarly to education systems, libraries have come under increasing pressure to provide training in 'information literacy' as well as traditional literacy skills. Information literacy means the ability to use 'digital technology, communications tools, and/or networks to access, manage, integrate, evaluate, and create information in order to function in a knowledge society' (IICT Literacy Panel 2002: 16). The International Information and Communication Technologies (IICT) Literacy Panel outlines five skills that comprise information literacy: the ability to access information in the digital environment; knowledge of how to manage information effectively; the ability to interpret and integrate the results of research; the ability to evaluate the quality of these results; and, the ability to create new information by adapting, applying, designing, inventing, or authoring information (IICT Literacy Panel 2002: 14–16).

As an applied intellectual force, the 'New London Group' (hereafter NLG)(Cazden et al. 1996) has had the most significant global impacts upon curriculum policies for new media literacies and is comprised of leading scholars in critical literacy studies. In an effort to draw together global perspectives for literacy teaching and learning, this (fairly disparate) group developed a theory of 'multiliteracies', a term that captures the issues for pedagogy emerging from changes in the 'cultural, institutional, and global order: the multiplicity of communications channels and media, and the increasing salience of cultural and linguistic diversity' (Cazden et al. 1996: 63). Rather than 'mere literacy', which 'remains centred on language only':

a pedagogy of multiliteracies, by contrast, focuses on modes of representation much broader than language alone. These differ according to culture and context, and have specific cognitive, cultural, and social effects. In some contexts—in an Aboriginal community or in a multimedia environment, for instance—the visual mode of representation may be much more powerful and closely related to language than 'mere literacy' would ever be able to allow. Multiliteracies also creates [sic] a different kind of pedagogy, one in which language and other modes of meaning are dynamic representational resources, constantly being remade by their users as they work to achieve their various cultural purposes. (Cazden et al. 1996: 64)

Here we see a consciousness of the close interactions among new technologies, culture, and discourse, and of the complex interplay of the human sensorium upon these relationships. The main aim of the NLG's efforts is to encourage literacy educators and students to 'see themselves as active participants in social change, as learners and students who can be active designers—makers—of social futures', with the 'key concept' being 'that of Design, in which we are both inheritors of patterns and conventions of meaning and at the same time active designers of meaning' (Cazden et al. 1996: 64–5). The strength of the group's approach to multiliteracies is its grounding in history, context, discourse, and culture. It consequently recognizes the significant impacts of new media on modes of expression and the interrelatedness of these with work practices, social practices, citizenship, the conduct of war and business, and imperatives for literacy education. As an historical statement, the NLG is significant for its recognition of the nation-building role that language-focused literacies have played, and of the complex and contradictory functions of new media that push in opposite directions: the 'balkanization' of cultures, the demise of the great state-building exercises of New Deal politics, and the strong tensions developing between local, global, public, and private aspects of human association (Cazden et al. 1996: 64–9).

Designing futures through literacy

For NLG, 'design' has three elements: 'available designs', or 'existing resources' in all modes of meaning; 'designing', or the process of shaping emergent meanings; and 'the redesigned', or the 'new meaning... through which meaning-makers remake themselves' (Cazden et al. 1996: 73–6). The group provides a tentative 'grammar', described as 'elements of design', which is functional, analytical, and linguistically based (Cazden et al. 1996: 78–85). In the 'metalanguage' the group develops for understanding multiliteracies, one might argue that some unhelpful divisions are made: for example, sound and spoken language are treated as separate rather than closely related categories; image, architecture, writing, and personal appearance are also separated; the inseparable relationships between spatial, visual, and audio design also fall to distinctions based in linguistic (i.e. primarily oral and aural) traditions (Cazden et al. 1996: 83). For example, there is little recognition by the group that the written word is entirely comprised of images. Like the unspecified Aboriginal culture used by the group as an example to describe how images can be more powerful than words in certain cultural contexts, in the industrialized world written words—word images—are a far more powerful and official form of language than oral forms, to which anybody who has dealt with a bureaucracy, legal system, or auditor can attest: the 'paper trail' is everything: the frozen word-image is the most sacred, powerful, and official form of meaning in industrialized societies. After the historical experience of text-based literate cultures, multimodal literacies now appear to be essential, especially given rapid technological change. But it is also important to realize that new media have been introduced into a fundamentally textual culture.

The last comparable period to that of the contemporary milieu in terms of intense changes in the media environment was between 1916 and 1945. The very best propagandists of the early twentieth century well understood that mastery of cultural literacies and multimedia production was essential to designing or 'engineering' social futures by shaping public discourse. Evidence of the power of the propagandists' media literacy can be found in George Creel's description of one of the most successful public education campaigns in history. It turned an isolationist, fragmented, and pacifist US public into a militarized mass prepared to enter World War I. The year is 1920:

There was no part of the great war machinery that we did not touch, no medium of appeal that we did not employ. The printed word, the spoken word, the motion picture, the telegraph, the cable, the wireless, the poster, the sign-board—all these were used in our campaign to make our own people and all other peoples understand the causes that compelled America to take arms. All that was fine and ardent in the civilian population came at our call until more than one hundred and fifty thousand men and women were devoting highly specialized abilities to the work of the Committee, as faithful and devoted in their service as though they wore the khaki.

[...] What we had to have was no mere surface unity, but a passionate belief in the justice of America's cause that should weld the people of the US into one white-hot mass instinct with fraternity, devotion, courage, and deathless determination. The war-will, the will-to-win, of a democracy depends upon the degree to which each one of all the people of that democracy can concentrate and consecrate body and soul and spirit in the supreme effort of service and sacrifice. What had to be driven home was that all business was the nation's business and every task a common task for a single purpose. (Creel 1920: 5)

This is a clear example of the power of multimodal literacies combined with the means to deploy them *en masse*. The effects of the Creel Committee remain quite overt today. Creel was almost instantly successful, even though his campaign was conducted without the aid of today's instantaneous mass media. The same emphasis that Creel places on 'multimodality'—the necessity of deploying every form of media available—can also be found in Lasswell, Bernays, and Lippman, all members of Creel's Committee for Public Information; all pioneers of modern public relations, propaganda, and advertising methods (Graham and Luke 2003, 2005). The same sensitivities can be seen in the early literacy drives *against* the design techniques developed by Creel et al., such as The Institute for Propaganda Analysis formed in 1937 to educate the US public about the workings of propaganda, and to introduce these findings into literacy education.

The Institute was 'founded by nationally prominent educators, historians, psychologists, and social scientists' concerned with the effects of new media techniques on culture (Hayakawa 1939: 197). The Institute's efforts quickly became part of literacy curricula throughout the US. By as early as 1938, the first 'critical literacy' drive of the modern era was being implemented in classrooms with the national release in the US of a curriculum package designed by the Institute for Propaganda Analysis (Davis 1939: 26). Davis enthuses that it is 'exciting days in the English classroom for the teacher who is not tied to a textbook. Indeed they are challenging days in which to be alive and to teach changing pupils in a changing world' (Davis, 1939: 26). Davis again emphasizes the role of language, considering English to be 'the most far-reaching and functional subject in the modern high school curriculum', and that 'the publications and study guides of the recently organised Institute for Propaganda Analysis' are essential to the teaching 'of fourth-term English' (Davis 1939: 26). Here, almost 70 years ago, new communication technologies, 'multimodality', and media production literacies become key concerns for literacy education:

Through the first of its publications, *Propaganda and How To Recognize It*, we were given methods for studying the meaning and scope, power, confusions, and dangers in all kinds of propaganda. Journalism, movies, radio—all channels of communication of social and political idea—are presented. . . . The need to vitalize the teaching of composition, especially exposition; the need to stimulate our students to read decent magazines and newspapers; the responsibility of the teacher of English to bring his [*sic*] students closer to the life and problems of our difficult and confusing 1938 world—these demands upon my knowledge and courage were satisfyingly met with peculiar efficacy by the institute studies. (Davis 1938: 26)

It can be said unequivocally that multimodal literacies are neither new nor dependent on new media; they have been essential means of persuasion and expression throughout history. Aristotle's *Poetics* tells us 'genre', 'medium', and 'mode' are the basic categories for understanding how to make meaning (Aristotle (trans. M. Heath) 1996: 1). But various of these aspects clearly become more apparent during times of change in the media environment. Throughout the twentieth century, industrial and governmental propagandists honed the new multiliteracies developed by Creel and his cohort in 1916 (Graham and Luke 2003). There is no doubt that Creel, Lasswell, Bernays, and the many thousands that have followed them into the public opinion professions were in the business of 'designing social futures' through mass mediated education (Graham and Luke 2003, 2005). The NLG, along with many excellent contemporary 'anti-propagandist' literacy researchers, has made its greatest contributions in emphasizing that new media literacies can provide opportunities for people to design their own social futures, ones that promote greater cultural and social equality; that new media in the transformative view bring previously disparate contexts and cultures into contact with each other, which means unpredictable interactions and potentials; and that literacies are always culturally 'situated practices', which are therefore always discursive in nature and are best understood as such (Cazden et al. 1996: 83–5; see also Gee 2000; Lankshear and Knobel 2003; Kalantzis and Cope 2001: 19–21; Kress 2001, 2003; Kapitzke 1995, 2003, 2005; Luke 1997; Luke and Freebody 1997; Luke et al. 2005). Common to these closely related, but often disparate approaches is a sensitivity to culture, and it is to this aspect we now turn.

3 Culture, context, and communication

The changed political economic context of literacies: From monopoly to monopsony

As has been established by scholars of media history and literacy education, cultural, technological, and political economic change are closely intertwined. Such approaches entail an understanding of political economic contexts: relations of production, distribution, exchange, and the power that derives from these. From the Creel Committee's assault on the American public in 1916 to the turn of the twenty-first century, the means of producing and distributing multimodal texts on a mass scale have been concentrated in the hands of relatively few people, largely because of entry costs. During this period, what many have called a 'media monopoly' emerged as a global force for industrial and nationalistic formations of culture, discourse, and the regulation of consumption (Bagdikian 1997; Innis 1944, 1951; McChesney 2000; Smythe 1981). Today's new media, though, are facilitating a radical assault on the media monopoly's economic structure, giving the media monopoly view a strange twist as well as an analytical opportunity. Apart from the loudly stated pirating concerns of major publishing companies felt in almost every sphere of life, vastly increased access to cheap and good means of production for video, audio, and still imagery has removed the foundation of what Horkheimer and Adorno (1947/1998) called *The Culture Industry*, in which cultural and discursive literacies for national and international populations were shaped during the twentieth century in a centralized and very conscious way.

Multimedia production suites that would have cost many thousands of dollars only ten years ago are today given away with operating systems or made available for free on the Internet (Graham 2006a). Broadcast quality materials that would previously have cost many thousand of dollars to use legally are available today for public use at no cost. More important—because production costs have been falling fairly steadily for 20 years or so—is the direct threat posed by new media to the last stronghold of what is typically called the media monopoly: the means of distribution. These changes in new media give us a new view of twentieth century media monopolies or culture industries: what once appeared as monopoly now appears as monopsony. A monopoly view is by definition 'consumption-sided' because it focuses on 'selling': one seller, many buyers: *monopoly*. Focus on the effects that industry structures and practices have upon cultural 'consumption' cannot recognize that the existence of a small group of organizations as the largest *buyers* of cultural materials in a global media system has serious implications for the character of culture and discourse. This perspective, in which monopolies are seen from the view of producers, is called *monopsony*: one buyer, many sellers. It provides a far reaching and very different view of cultural and discursive literacies than can be derived from monopoly-based perspectives.

One implication of a monopsony view is that mass mediated, or 'monopoly' culture tends to lower the financial value of cultural materials to zero. That is to say: unless specific people's words, dances, songs, music, photographs, movies, or scripts are bought, promoted, and distributed through the key institutions of mass mediated culture, they are generally considered to be of no significant financial or cultural worth. Since it is in the interests of commercially-driven mass media industries to buy cultural products for the lowest possible price, and because these industries have been the only *buyers* of mass culture, and because the number of producers increases daily, the overall trend is the devaluation of culture to zero (Graham 2006a).

New media patterns of cultural production and distribution highlight this fairly mundane fact of mass culture, but only because they threaten established cultural production order so radically. In response, the organs of cultural monopsony react by centralizing even more, further limiting the number of sellers it buys from. Here is an example of how this dynamic plays out in a most powerful aspect of culture—news:

There are two main news footage agencies—Reuters and APTN [Associated Press Television News]—AP having bought the third, WTN [Worldwide Television News] some years ago.

You might think that this would double the amount of available material but this is not the case. Since neither agency wants to miss pictures which the other one can offer its subscribers exclusively, they follow each other around! This is exacerbated by the Eurovision system in Europe whereby public service broadcasters exchange material. This allows the agencies to send their pictures back to London (where they are both based) for free—they do not have to pay for their own satellite time. If the agencies both have the same pictures then they get what is known as a 'common' which means that either APTN feeds its pictures and Reuters has access to them or vice versa. Another incentive for both agencies to get the same shots rather than seek an alternative view (Bill Hayton, Europe Editor, Newsroom, BBC World Service, email correspondence, 26 August 2004).

This is one example of how a monopsony devalues cultural and discursive production; how it reduces cultural and discursive production to the lowest possible price; and the resultant lack of creativity, novelty, and difference that occurs as a consequence. While it would be anachronistic to wish for a return to the 'village pump' model of news telling, it is worth drawing the analogy to emphasize the participative way in which new information—news—has been historically introduced into cultures, and to foreground the cultural function of 'news' more generally.

News and how it is chosen and distributed is a key component of any culture. It is a unique and influential form of 'ritual' drama for members of a culture; 'a portrayal of the contending forces in the world' that positions people within the 'dramatic action' portrayed by news; 'a presentation of reality that gives life an overall form, order, and tone' (Carey 1989: 20–1). In other words, news is an important 'form of culture' and an essential component of public and private discourse (Carey 1989: 21). What we call 'news' is probably the earliest precursor of mass mediated culture and its historical progress towards an ironic lack of novelty, diversity, and creativity exemplifies the progress of mass culture more generally. The deterioration of news gathering and reporting for mass consumption cannot be explained by any single factor: its changing nature is a combined function of technological, institutional, cultural, political, economic, and discursive changes.

Competing cultural and discursive literacies: nationalism, globalism, localism

To comprehend the phenomena that pertain to mass production of culturally specific discourses, we rely on the following assumptions. Cultures extend only as far in time and space as the systems of technologies and practices that mediate them permit because they rely for their existence on those systems (Innis 1944, 1951). New patterns of mediation produce new cultural interactions and new ways of extending, reinforcing, and otherwise transforming the character of any culture that is touched by the new patterns that the new interactions entail (Silverstone 1999). Cultures are primarily axiological—values based—which is to say that any culture is initially identifiable as such because of the unique patterns of evaluation that characterize it (Graham 2006b). Evaluations are a definitive aspect of any discursive formation, none more so than the delineation of a cultural entity (Lemke 1998). Cultures are distinguishable only by the way their members express themselves, in words, images, colours, foods, dress, dance, prayer, and song. New media systems, especially those that span larger and larger geographical spaces, therefore tend to promote intense axiological interactions, conflicts, and syntheses, moving beyond nationalistic concerns to cultural aggregations that are at once globally dispersed yet in the process of reforming on a supra-nationalistic basis.

During the moments in history when they collide, cultures change quickly and at numerous levels, as exemplified by the strong globalizing movements of the 1990s and the subsequent rapid cultural fragmentation that characterizes the early twenty-first century (Graham and Luke 2003). To understand and to be able to participate in the ways in which new media environments might affect cultures and discourses, an axiological or values-based approach to discursive and cultural literacies is therefore implicated (Graham 2002; Lemke 1998). At the technological intersection of culture and discourse in the new global economic context—that is, *how* new political economic contexts come into formation (White 1940: 15)—is an interdisciplinary potpourri of symbolic endeavours and struggles between computer programmers, system administrators, librarians, museum curators, journalists, historians, engineers, sociologists, artists in all media, mathematicians, linguists, lawyers, business people, communication researchers, educators—people from throughout almost the entire spectrum of human cultural endeavours are involved in 'designing' the global universe of culture and discourse: they (we) are engaged daily in the design of global 'futures'. No longer are libraries, museums, archives, and education systems the elite arbiters of cultural memory. Organizations of all kinds now have enormous digital collections: corporations, schools, universities, religious organizations, political movements, military organizations, and local communities: in new mediated cultures, everyone has become part of massive cultural and discursive production and distribution networks. This heralds a 'reversion' of sorts (though certainly not an identical manifestation) to a literate global network of people who daily produce, distribute, exchange, and hoard objects of cultural significance.

Reversion, reversioning, and revisioning: The troublesome resurgence of participatory culture

Long before the radio was successfully deployed as the first instantaneous mass medium, the participatory character of culture had been diminishing for centuries, due largely to the influence of industrialization and its technologies. Diminishing participation in the quotidian performance of music is a case in point noted by Lewis Mumford:

The workshop song, the street cries of the tinker, the dustman, the pedlar, the flower vendor, the chanties of the sailor hauling the ropes, the traditional songs of the field, the wine-press, the taproom were slowly dying out during this period. Labor was orchestrated by the number of revolutions per minute, rather than by the rhythm of song or chant or tattoo.... No one any longer thought of asking the servants to come to the living room to take part in a madrigal or ballad. What happened to poetry had happened likewise to pure music. (Mumford 1934/1963: 201)

Once industrialized, music became, like every other industrial 'occupation', a specialized occupation dedicated to producing commodities. But sustainable cultural vibrancy requires widespread participation, experience, and education in the Arts: in short, cultural and discursive literacies are required for the renewal of culture:

Art... cannot become a language, and hence an experience, unless it is practiced. To the man [sic] who plays, a mechanical reproduction of music may mean much, since he already has the experience to assimilate. But where reproduction becomes the norm, the few music makers will grow more isolate and sterile, and the ability to experience music will disappear. The same is true with cinema, dance, and even sport. (Mumford 1934/1962: 343, citing Waldo Frank)

Under the influence of industrialization, culture, like nature, appears as an alien force to be conquered, codified, objectified, commodified, and deployed in the pursuit of profit. For industrial societies, literacy became both a nationalistic and commercial concern. In order to 'unify' the industrial system, 'the characteristic limitations' of the factory 'were introduced as far as possible into the school: silence, absence of motion, complete passivity, response only upon the application of an outer stimulus, rote learning, verbal parroting, piece-work acquisition of knowledge—these gave the school the happy attributes of jail and factory combined' (Mumford 1934/1963: 176).

Similarly today, the waning of Arts faculties in universities, and the corollary appearance of 'Creative Industries' faculties in their place, indicate the broad impact of cultural monopsonies: whether made by mind, mouth, or gesture, objects of culture must enter the official processes of the monopsony before realizing pecuniary worth. This is confirmed in the frenzy of intellectual and policy activity focused on the concept of 'creative industries' and their increasing economic value to society (DEST 2002; NOIE 2002). Such activities are most overtly concerned with developing policies and curricula designed to service monopsonies, and with how universities and other organs of education can best tailor their skills training to the industrial structures and practices of waning mass cultural industries.

The simultaneous marketization and devaluation of the Arts in universities, and of universities more generally, is in large part an effect of a functioning global cultural monopsony given surprising impetus by the productive and distributive affordances of new media (Graham 2005). The practices of the academic cultural 'industry' exemplify the practices of cultural producers more generally: academics write research papers and manuscripts and submit them to publishers in the hope they will be accepted, even though acceptance usually brings little or no direct financial reward (although promotion and tenure may follow a successful publishing record). Prior to being accepted through official processes of peer review and so on, academic discourses are considered to have little or no 'official' status as knowledge. The same is true for producers of music, film, dance, poetry, and theatre: unless their productions are vetted, shaped, and purchased by the cultural monopsony, then passed through their institutional mediation processes, they are typically relegated to obscurity, their status as art attributed with the derogatory epithet 'amateur', and they do not form a part of mass culture.

But in the new media environments, even the academic publishing industry, tightly controlled for centuries, is giving way to new forms of production and distribution through such projects as, for example, the University of British Columbia's Public Knowledge Project (Willinsky 2005), MIT's D-Space (Smith 2005), and the many library-led 'e-prints' and digital theses initiatives designed to enhance literacies across places, times, and cultures (RCUK 2005). Similarly, and despite (or perhaps because of) the intellectual property wars being waged by the corporate monopsony for control of public discourse and official culture, powerful new media initiatives are underway that facilitate the production and distribution of multimodal forms, examples of which include The Internet Archive, Open Sound, Creative Commons, and Australian Creative Resources Online.[2] Such initiatives, especially The Internet Archive, which daily indexes and archives large portions of the Internet, are at the same time extensions and transformations of traditional cultural heritage institutions and applied exercises in the promotion of participatory culture.

Information literacy

Information literacy as a field of research and pedagogy emerged in the early 1980s as a response to the increasing availability of computerized databases and library catalogues on the one hand, and a growing body of research in the area of human information seeking behaviour, on the other. Information literacy, is generally defined as the ability to identify one's personal need for information, to be able to identify gaps in one's understanding, and to be able to identify, locate, evaluate, and effectively use information for the issue or problem at hand. Among the earliest proponents of information literacy were libraries and library researchers who began building information literacy education into existing bibliographic instruction programmes. The focus shifted from teaching users to find books and articles in the library, to helping users to assess their own knowledge gaps and anomalous states of knowledge (Belkin, Oddy and Brooks 1982), and then to match their needs to the myriad resources available. Librarians, teachers, and other cultural heritage workers, began to position themselves within a rich information environment as guides rather than gatekeepers. They became, as Nardi and O'Day (1999) describe, 'keystone species' in the 'information ecology'.

Cultural heritage institutions—largely conservative bastions of cultural and discursive literacies for close on two centuries, and the historical precursor of contemporary cultural monopsonies—were radically transformed by the demands entailed by new media. A globally connected, widely accessible system for the production, storage, and distribution of culture and discourse presents historically unique challenges to these institutions. As Mackenzie Smith notes:

It took two centuries to fill the U.S. Library of Congress in Washington, D.C., with more than 29 million books and periodicals, 2.7 million recordings, 12 million photographs, 4.8 million maps, and 57 million manuscripts. Today it takes about 15 minutes for the world to churn out an equivalent amount of new digital information. It does so about 100 times every day, for a grand total of five exabytes annually. That's an amount equal to all the words ever spoken by humans, according to Roy Williams, who heads the Center for Advanced Computing Research at the California Institute of Technology, in Pasadena. (Smith 2005)

Apart from the overwhelming volume of globally mediated culture and discourse—a further case for literacy in respect of sorting the informational wheat from the chaff—there are the attendant problems of preservation, typically the domain of 'high-culture' heritage preservation institutions (Smith 2005). Because the software and hardware of new media continue to change at a rapid pace, the problems of preservation, retrieval, and access are accentuated, especially for such institutions. Smith frames the problem as follows:

In an era when the ability to read a document, watch a video, or run a simulation could depend on having a particular version of a program installed on a specific computer platform, the usable life span of a piece of digital content can be less than 10 years. That's a recipe for disaster when you consider how much we rely on stored information to maintain our scholarly, legal, and cultural record and to help us with, and profit from, our digital labor. Indeed, the ephemeral nature of both data formats and storage media threatens our very ability to maintain scientific, legal, and cultural continuity, not on the scale of centuries, but considering the unrelenting pace of technological change, from one decade to the next. (Smith 2005)

Cultural heritage institutions are where the technical dynamics of new media overtly intersect with 'official' culture and discourse, and where problematic issues of cultural and discursive literacies have clearly begun to compound exponentially.

It is well recognized that libraries, museums, and schools in particular have been fundamental to the projects of nationalism (Valencia 2002). The fast-moving, dynamic tensions between various national, global, local, religious, and ethnic discourses are exemplified in the pressures being brought to bear on these institutions. Regardless of whether one considers them as organs of repression, as conservative bastions of the status quo, or as intrinsic cultural and social goods, the importance of cultural heritage institutions cannot be understated:

Our cultural heritage finds its expression in the common, everyday activities, which are the sum and substance of our character as a people and as a nation. We must not lose this heritage, and we must understand it. Knowledge of the antecedents of this heritage is the keystone of any conscious effort to achieve meaningful goals for ourselves as individuals and as a people. (Valencia 2002: 3, citing Burr 1952)

But as Hunter and Choudhury (2004: 270) point out, 'there is no single best solution to digital preservation. The most appropriate strategy depends on the particular requirements of the custodial organization, the producers and consumers of its collection and the nature of the objects in the collection.' Decisions on such strategies must therefore take into account the varying cultural, discursive, and technical needs of entire preservation sectors, their associated institutions, and their sponsors.

Prior to the emergence of new media, cultural heritage institutions such as museums, libraries, and schools, typically provided both access to cultural history and to the tools and training in the various skills required to critically assess, and create personal meaning from the artefacts contained in their collections (Goodrum 2006). However, on top of the pressure for these institutions to provide new media literacies, as well as digital access to cultural heritage, the provision of traditional literacy training remains a priority for public libraries and national education systems worldwide, largely because 'mere literacy' is still lacking even in first-world countries. For example, in 1992, the American Library Association (ALA) reported that approximately 44 million adults in the US could not read well enough to 'fill out an application, read a food label, or read a story to a child. These individuals lack the literacy skills needed to find and keep decent jobs, support their children's education, and participate actively in civic life' (ALA 2001).

In other words, to be 'literate' in the new media age means having mastery of skills and knowledge that were formerly the domain of, *inter alia*, academic researchers, librarians, curators, artists, writers, politicians, and multimedia producers. Add to this the infrastructure that allows people to distribute their multimediated discursive products worldwide, and the potential structural ruptures in culture and discourse production across national, global, and local contexts become immense. The level of cultural and discursive literacies now expected of individuals impinges upon all the institutions traditionally ordained as the arbiters of official cultural memory and, therefore, public discourse. The IICT Literacy Panel's description of information literacy reflects the scope and scale of transformation of what it means to be literate in the current new media age: literacy is 'a continuum of knowledge, skills, and strategies that individuals acquire over the course of their lives in various contexts and through interactions with their peers and with the larger communities in which they participate' (IICT 2002: 14). In this view, 'literacy' amounts to the lifetime of experience and spans the entirety of interactions, knowledges, and skills acquired by a person—a catch-all term for an individualized totality of cultural and discursive experience.

4 CONCLUSION

Scanning the definitions, issues, and political economic forces bearing upon new technological, cultural, and discursive literacies, we consistently find imperatives for participatory approaches. New media literacies must be 'conceived as a political, social, and cultural practice' within a framework of critical pedagogy (Scholle and Denski 1995: 17). The 'primary objective' of such literacies 'is critical autonomy in relationship to all media ... including informed citizenship, aesthetic appreciation and expression, social advocacy, self-esteem, and consumer competence' (Aufterheide 1993). People will ideally become 'active, free participants' in media processes 'rather than static, passive and subservient to the images and values communicated in a one-way flow from media sources' (Brown 1998: 47). But such ideals have yet to be realized in any way that has substantive effects on the democratic ends at which they are ostensibly aimed, except perhaps in a negative sense.

The apparent results of greatly increased access to the means of cultural and discursive production and distribution, while making the ideal objectives of cultural and discursive literacy advocates seemingly achievable, include a resurgence in violent, culture-based conflicts; an increased sense of remoteness in processes of governance; and a withering of public discourse, especially in broadcast media environments. At a legal and institutional level, conflicts have emerged between mass media monopsonies and their greatest consumers: youth and the institutions of education. It is notable in this respect that the first major institutional targets of the latest copyright wars were schools and universities (Latonero 2000). Where accessibility is a matter of concern, disciplinary conflicts have broken out between advocates of standards-based approaches to metadata developed by librarians and computer scientists in relatively strict taxonomies and more sociological, participatory approaches to developing information 'folksonomies' involving users and user communities (see Apps 2005; Mathes 2004). Global and international coalitions of corporate, political, community, religious, and issues-based groups have declared open warfare on each other, with information being a central focus for these groups.

None of this is surprising when the history of communication technologies is considered. Control over the structures of power, wealth, culture and meaning, and intellectual supremacy is always at stake in the seemingly banal term 'new media literacies'. Innis's theses on the historical significance of knowledge monopolies have never seemed so relevant as they are in the context of this new movement. In the current environment an inversion of sorts is apropos: a culturally oriented, monopsony perspective reveals entirely different potentials, including the potential for new, participatory, globally dispersed cultural forms. Yet it is too early to tell whether the implementation of new cultural and discursive literacies, as envisaged by critical educators such as the NLG, will bear the political and material fruit to which they aspire. Potentials for better understandings and conversations between antithetical cultures certainly exist thanks to the new media environment. But throughout history, the privileged and powerful have never easily given up control of what is at stake in this environment: knowledge, meaning, experience, social order, and the value of various aspects of culture. All of these are at stake in the development of new technological, cultural, and discursive literacies.

REFERENCES

ADAMS, D. and HAMON, M. (2001). *Literacy in a Multimedia Age*. Norwood, MA: Christopher-Gordon.

AMERICAN LIBRARY ASSOCIATION. (2001). '21st Century Literacy', *ALA Action, 1*, http://www.ala.org/ala/proftools/21centurylit/21stcenturyliteracy.htm, accessed 18 Mar. 2006.

APPS, A. (2005). *Guidelines for Encoding Bibliographic Citation Information in Dublin Core Metadata*. Dublin Core Metadata Initiative Citation Working Group: Dublin Core Metadata Initiative, http://dublincore.org/documents/dc-citation-guidelines/, accessed 23 Aug. 2006.

ARISTOTLE, A. (1996). *Poetics* (trans. M. Heath). London: Penguin.

AUFDERHEIDE, P. (ed.) (1993). *Media Literacy: A Report of the National Leadership Conference on Media Literacy*. Aspen, CO: Aspen Institute.

BAGDIKIAN, B. H. (1997). *The Media Monopoly (5th Edn)*. Boston, MA: Beacon Press.

BELKIN, N. J., ODDY, R. N. and BROOKS, H. M. (1982). 'ASK for Information Retrieval: Part I. Background and Theory'. *Journal of Documentation*, 38(2): 61–71.

BERNSTEIN, B. (1996/2000). *Pedagogy, Symbolic Control, and Identity: Theory, Research, Critique*. Oxford: Rowman & Littlefield.

BROWN, J. A. (1998). 'Media Literacy Perspectives'. *Journal of Communication*, 48(1): 44–57.

CAREY, J. (1989). *Communication as Culture: Essays on Media and Society*. London: Routledge and Boston, MA: Unwin and Hyman.

CAZDEN, C., COPE, B., FAIRCLOUGH, N., et al. (The New London Group) (1996). 'A Pedagogy of Multiliteracies: Designing Social Futures'. *Harvard Educational Review*, 66(1): 60–92.

CREEL, G. (1920). *How We Advertised America*. New York: Harper and Brothers, 3–9, http://www.historytools.org/sources/creel.html, accessed 18 Mar. 2006.

DAVIS, H. I. (1939). 'Propaganda Enters the English Classroom'. *The English Journal*, 28(1): 26–31.

DEST (2002). *Frontier Technologies for Building and Transforming Australian Industries: Stimulating the Growth of World-class Australian Industries using Innovative Technologies Developed from Cutting-edge Research*. Canberra: Commonwealth of Australia.

FAIRCLOUGH, N. (2000). 'Discourse, Social Theory, and Social Research: The Discourse of Welfare Reform'. *Journal of Sociolinguistics*, 4(2): 163–95.

GEE, J. P. (2000). 'New People in New Worlds: Networks, the New Capitalism and Schools', in B. Cope and M. Kalantzis (eds), *Multiliteracies: Literacy Learning and the Design of Social Futures*. London: Routledge, 43–68.

GANSHOF, F. L. (1949). 'Charlemagne'. *Speculum*, 24(4): 520–8.

GOODRUM, A. (2006). 'Surrogation, Mediation and Collaboration: Access to Digital Images in Cultural Heritage Institutions', in C. Kapitzke and A. Luke (eds), *Libr@ries and the Arobase: Changing Information Space and Practice*. Mahwah, NJ: Lawrence Erlbaum Associates, 73–90.

GRAHAM, P. (2002). 'Predication and Propagation: A Method for Analysing Evaluative Meanings in Technology Policy'. *TEXT*, 22(2): 227–68.

—— (2005). 'Issues in Political Economy', in A. O. Albarran, S. M. Chan-Olmsted and M. B. Wirth (eds), *Handbook of Media Management and Economics*. Mahwah, NJ: Lawrence Erlbaum, 493–519.

—— (2006a). 'Monopoly, Monopsony, and the Value of Culture in a Knowledge Economy: An Axiology of Two Multimedia Resource Repositories', in C. Kapitzke and A. Luke (eds). *Libr@ries and the Arobase: Changing Information Space and Practice*. Mahwah, NJ: Lawrence Erlbaum Associates, 253–70.

—— (2006b). *Hypercapitalism: Language, New Media, and Social Perceptions of Value*. New York: Peter Lang.

—— and LUKE, A. (2003). 'Militarising the Body Politic: New Media as Weapons of Mass Instruction'. *Body and Society*, 9(4): 149–68.

—— and —— (2005). 'The Language of Neofeudal Corporatism and the War on Iraq'. *Journal of Language and Politics*, 4(1): 11–40.

HAYAKAWA, S. I. (1939). 'General Semantics and Propaganda'. *Public Opinion Quarterly*, 3(2): 197–208.

HORKHEIMER, M. and ADORNO, T. W. (1947/1998). *The Dialectic of Enlightenment* (trans. J. Cumming). New York: Continuum.

HUNTER, J. and CHOUDHURY, S. (2004). 'A Semi-Automated Digital Preservation System based on Semantic Web Services'. *Proceedings of the Fourth ACM/IEEE Joint Conference on Digital Libraries*, JCDL 2004: Tucson, Arizona 7–11 June, 269–78, http://metadata.net/panic/Papers/JCDL2004_paper.pdf, accessed 18 Mar. 2006.

IICT Literacy Panel (2002). *Digital Transformation: A Framework for ICT Literacy*. Princeton, NJ: Educational Testing Services.

INNIS, H. A. (1944). 'On the Economic Significance of Culture'. *Journal of Economic History*, 4, [Issue supplement: The Tasks of Economic History]: 80–97.

—— (1951). *The Bias of Communication*. Toronto: University of Toronto Press.

KALANTZIS, M. and COPE, B. (2001). 'Multiliteracies as a Framework for Action', in M. Kalantzis and B. Cope (eds), *Transformations in Language and Learning: Perspectives on Multiliteracies*. Australia: Common Ground, 19–32.

KAPITZKE, C. (1995). *Literacy and Religion: The Textual Politics and Practice of Seventh-day Adventism*. Amsterdam: John Benjamins.

KAPITZKE, C. (2003). 'Information Literacy: The Changing Library', in B. C. Bruce (ed.), *Literacy in the Information Age: Inquiries into Meaning Making with New Technologies*. Neward, DE: International Reading Association, 59–69.

—— (2005). 'Whose Community? Which Knowledge? A Critical (Hyperliteracies) Take on Information Literate School Communities', in J. Henri and M. Asselin (eds), *The Information Literate School Community 2: Issues of Leadership*. Westport, CT: Libraries Unlimited, 27–38.

KRESS, G. (2001). 'Issues for a Working Agenda in Literacy', in M. Kalantzis and B. Cope (eds), *Transformations in Language and Learning: Perspectives on Multiliteracies*. Australia: Common Ground, 33–52.

—— (2003). *Literacy in the New Media Age*. London: Routledge.

—— and VAN LEEUWEN, T. (1996). *Reading Images: The Grammar of Visual Design*. London: Routledge.

LANKSHEAR, C. and KNOBEL, M. (2003). *New Literacies: Changing Knowledge and Classroom Learning*. Buckingham: Open University Press.

LATONERO, M. (2000). *Survey of MP3 Usage: Report on a University Consumption Community*. The Norman Lear Center, Annenberg School for Communication. University of Southern California, http://www.learcenter.org/pdf/mp3.pdf, accessed 18 Mar. 2006.

LEMKE, J. L. (1995). *Textual Politics*. London: Taylor and Francis.

—— (1998). 'Resources for Attitudinal Meaning: Evaluative Orientations in Text Semantics'. *Functions of Language*, 5(1): 33–56.

LESSIG, L. (2004). *Free Culture: How Big Media Uses Technology and the Law to Lock Down Culture and Control Creativity*. New York: Penguin.

LUKE, C. (1997). 'Media Literacy and Cultural Studies', in P. Muspratt, A. Luke and P. Freebody (eds), *Constructing Critical Literacies: Teaching and Learning Textual Practice*. Australia: Allen and Unwin, 18–49.

—— and FREEBODY, P. (1997). 'Critical Literacy and the Question of Normativity', in P. Muspratt, A. Luke and P. Freebody (eds), *Constructing Critical Literacies: Teaching and Learning Textual Practice*. Cresskill, NJ: Hampton Press, 1–18.

——, LAU, S. and GOPINATHAN, S. (2005). 'Towards Research-based Innovation and Reform: Singapore Schooling in Transition'. *Asia Pacific Journal of Education*, 25(10): 5–28.

MATHES, A. (2004). *Folksonomies: Cooperative Communication through Shared Metadata*, http://www.adammathes.com/academic/computer-mediated-communication/folksonomies.html, accessed 18 Mar. 2006.

McCHESNEY, R. W. (2000). 'The Political Economy of Communication and the Future of the Field'. *Media, Culture & Society*, 22(1): 109–16.

McLUHAN, M. (1964). *Understanding Media: The Extensions of Man*. New York: McGraw Hill.

MUMFORD, L. (1934/1963). *Technics and Civilization*. New York: Harcourt Brace and Co.

—— (1964/1970). *The Myth of the Machine: The Pentagon of Power*. New York: Harcourt Brace, Jovanovich.

NARDI, B. A. and O'DAY, V. L. (1999). *Information Ecologies: Using Technology with Heart*. Cambridge, MA: MIT Press.

NOIE (2002). *Creative Industries Cluster Study: Stage One Report*. Canberra: NOIE, DCITA, Commonwealth of Australia.

ONG, W. J. (1984). 'Orality, Literacy, and Medieval Textualization'. *New Literary History*, 16(1): 1–12.

—— (1988). 'A Comment on "Arguing about literacy" '. *College English*, 50(6): 700–1.

RCUK (2005). *Supporting Open Access: E-prints*, http://www.eprints.org/, accessed 18 Mar. 2006.

SHOLLE, D. and DENSKI, S. (1995). 'Critical Media Literacy: Reading, Remapping, Rewriting', in P. McLaran, R. Hammer, D. Sholle, et al. (eds), *Rethinking, Media Literacy: A Critical Pedagogy of Representation*. New York: Peter Lang, 7–31.

SILVERSTONE, R. (1999). *Why Study the Media?* London: Sage.

SMITH, M. (2005). 'Eternal Bits: How Can We Preserve Digital Files and Save our Collective Memory? *IEEE Spectrum Online*, 5 July, http://www.spectrum.ieee.org/jul05/1568, accessed 18 Mar. 2006.

SMYTHE, D. (1981). *Dependency Road: Communications, Capitalism, Consciousness, and Canada*. Norwood, NJ: Ablex.

THUROW, L. C. (1996). *The Future of Capitalism: How Today's Economic Forces Shape Tomorrow's World*. New York: William Morrow & Company.

VALENCIA, M. (2002). 'Libraries, Nationalism, and Armed Conflict in the Twentieth Century'. *Libri*, 52: 1–15.

WHITE, L. Jr (1940). 'Technology and Invention in the Middle Ages'. *Speculum*, 15(2): 141–59.

WILLINSKY, J. (2005). 'The Unacknowledged Convergence of Open Source, Open Access, and Open Science'. *First Monday*, 10(8), http://firstmonday.org/issues/issue10_8/willinsky/index.html, accessed 18 Mar. 2006.

NOTES

1. Of course there are tactile and otherwise sensual aspects of new media that impact upon their communicative potentials, such as the prestige value of owning, using, and displaying new technologies, but these are beyond the scope of this chapter except in so far as particular ICTs accrue symbolic value for their owners in particular cultural settings. For example, in corporate contexts all-in-one mobile devices such as the Blackberry[tm] carry with them a certain prestige value. Similarly, the absence of ICTs in an executive's office can denote a level of prestige.

2. The Internet Archive can be found at www.archive.org, Open Sound can be found at www.opsound.org, Creative Commons can be found at www.creativecommons.org, and Australian Creative Resources Online initiatives can be found at www.acro.edu.au.

CHAPTER 21

YOUTHFUL EXPERTS? A CRITICAL APPRAISAL OF CHILDREN'S EMERGING INTERNET LITERACY

SONIA LIVINGSTONE

Through confident use of communications technologies people will gain a better understanding of the world around them and be better able to engage with it.

(Ofcom 2004: para 3).

Despite the growth in the numbers of Internet users, a rather small minority of these users has the capability to use the Internet in ways that are creative and that augment their ability to participate effectively in today's knowledge societies.

(Mansell 2004: 179).

1 INTRODUCTION

THE growing importance of the Internet in our lives raises many questions for social scientists, policy makers, and the public regarding the implications for work, education, community, politics, family life, and social relationships. Yet the research literature provides only moderate evidence that the Internet is bringing about any great changes; rather, the emerging picture stresses the (unequal) social conditions that influence how we fit the Internet into our lives. The contrast between the above quotations illustrates, the gap between the hopes held out for the Internet and the realities of people's experiences. As research, especially in industrialized countries, begins to shift its focus from questions of access and diffusion to questions about the nature and quality of Internet use, attention is being directed towards the skills and competence that 'using' the Internet implies. These are far from straightforward, and many people are struggling to come to terms with this complex and changing bundle of technologies, which, supposedly, can deliver new opportunities for information, communication, entertainment, or even, more grandly, 'empower' them in relation to identity, community, participation, creativity, and democracy.

The speculation surrounding children, media, and social change requires an especially critical stance from the academy, since all three terms seem to be catalysts for public anxiety. Children and young people are widely perceived on the one hand, as the youthful experts or pioneers leading the way in using the Internet and yet, on the other hand, as peculiarly vulnerable to the risks consequent on failing to use it wisely. This chapter draws on the 'UK Children Go Online' (UKCGO) project for empirical evidence regarding how young people are striking a balance between maximizing opportunities and minimizing risks as they explore the Internet. By unpacking the nature of 'use', this chapter reveals some of the ways in which the Internet poses significant challenges for its users, requiring the rapid development and continual updating of a range of skills, competences, and knowledge, from the already-familiar to the very-new, and from the most basic to the highly sophisticated. As we shall see, despite considerable enthusiasm for going online and becoming 'youthful experts', children and young people (like many adults) are finding that access and motivation are necessary but insufficient for using the Internet in a complex and ambitious manner.

The skills and knowledge that underpin Internet use are increasingly conceptualized in terms of 'literacy' (Marcum 2002; Potter 2004; Snyder 1998; Tyner 1998). Livingstone, Van Couvering, and Thumim (forthcoming) compare and contrast the analysis of media literacy from audiovisual studies, media education, and cultural studies with the analysis of information literacy from information science, library studies, and technology studies, arguing that these traditions are converging along with the technologies. The former, we suggest, has strengths in researching audiences' understanding, comprehension, and, particularly, their critical and creative literacies, including a politicized account of their social positioning in relation to powerful media institutions and texts. The latter, meanwhile, has strengths in the analysis of access and use, particularly focusing on standards for and the evaluation of skills and abilities, resulting in a policy-oriented account of the barriers/enablers to access and use.

This is not just an academic discussion, but also a growing area of policy making. As the content available across media platforms expands, policy makers are asking whether people, including parents on behalf of their children, are competent to manage their personal media environment (Livingstone and Bober 2006). In the UK, The Communications Act (2003) requires Ofcom, the communications in-dustry regulator, to 'promote media literacy' among the population of the UK. Media literacy is also being addressed at the European level, with the Council of Europe (2005) seeking 'to give special encouragement to training for children in media literacy, enabling them to benefit from the positive aspects of the new communication services and avoid exposure to harmful content' (Resolution 3, para 17) and so to 'support steps to promote, at all stages of education and as part of ongoing learning, media literacy which involves active and critical use of all the media, including electronic media' (Draft action plan, para 20).

Before asking whether the Internet does, in practice, facilitate significant oppor-tunities for children and young people, we must look a little more closely at this generation of supposed 'youthful experts'.

The Internet generation

My younger cousins, they're all under the age of eleven—and they're now coming into an age where the Internet is all they've ever known. Where we, really, when we were young, we were still doing all the [outdoor] activities, and the Internet wasn't really around. So we've got balance. But maybe in five or ten years time that will change. (Lorie, 17, from Essex)

The first generation to grow up with the Internet from early childhood, today's children proudly proclaim themselves to be the experts online, especially compared with the struggles of their parents and teachers to keep up with, let alone to inform and guide, their Internet use. Amir (15) from London states confidently, 'I don't find it hard to use a computer because I got into it quickly. You learn quick because it's a very fun thing to do.' Nina (17, from Manchester) adds scathingly, 'my Dad hasn't even got a clue. Can't even work the mouse . . . So I have to go on the Internet for him.' Yet of the growing number of research projects exploring the social contexts and consequences of Internet use surprisingly few include children and young people, even though those under 18 constitute a sizeable proportion of the total population and, in households with children, access is more common than in those without children, making young people the 'pioneers' of new media cultures (Drotner 2000).

Responding to this gap in the literature, the UKCGO research project conducted a thorough investigation of 9 to 19-year-olds' use of the Internet between 2003 and 2005. Through all phases of the research we worked with children from diverse backgrounds in terms of socio-economic status, ethnicity, family status, geographic region, and so forth. The project combined parent–child paired interviews, in-home observations, group discussions, and a major national in-home face-to-face survey of 1,511 9 to 19-year-olds and 906 of their parents. The research followed a child-centred approach in regarding children as active, motivated, and imaginative, though not necessarily knowledgeable or sophisticated agents, who contribute to shaping the meanings and consequences of the 'new' through the lens of their established social practices (James, Jenks and Prout 1998). For, whether information and communication technologies (ICTs) are incorporated into the ongoing stream of social life, or whether they reorient or open up alternative trajectories, the perspective of their users plays a key role in mediating just how this occurs, notwithstanding the many and influential constraints that frame the choices and possibilities in children's lives (Bakardjieva 2005).

The findings confirm that Internet access and use is widespread among UK children and young people (Livingstone and Bober 2004). Among 9 to 19-year-olds, home access is growing: 75 per cent have accessed the Internet from home, and school access is near universal (92 per cent); two-thirds have also used the Internet elsewhere. Homes with children indeed are in the lead in gaining Internet access, since, by February 2004, only 58 per cent of UK adults had used the Internet (Office for National Statistics 2004), compared with 98 per cent of 9 to 19-year-olds. This represents a dramatic increase in just a few years: in 1997, 53 per cent of 6 to 17-year-olds in the UK had a personal computer at home, only 7 per cent had Internet access, and only 19 per cent had used the Internet anywhere (Livingstone 2002). Today, 'access' is a complicated phenomenon, and continuing changes in the nature and quality of access indicate fast-rising expectations as well as placing considerable demands on households to 'keep up' (Facer et al. 2003). The pace of change sets a challenge not only for the general public, but also for researchers, in keeping track of technological, market and policy developments.

Although 'some people can't afford it, which is just a sad truth', as Steve (17, from Manchester) put it, few children and young people are wholly excluded. But variation in the breadth and richness of access and use requires a reframing of the 'digital divide' as a continuum of digital inclusion and exclusion (Livingstone and Helsper forthcoming, Selwyn 2004; Warschauer 2003). Access platforms are diversifying, with growing numbers accessing the Internet not only through a computer, but also via digital television, games consoles, and mobile phones. Families with children are also acquiring multiple computers, plus broadband access to the Internet. One-fifth of 9 to 19-year-olds has Internet access in their bedrooms, furthering a media-rich 'bedroom culture', and making Internet use a highly privatized activity (Livingstone 2002). Across Europe (EU-25), on average three quarters of 16 to 25-year-olds had used the Internet in 2004 (Eurostat 2005), as had 49 per cent of children under 18 years old (Eurobarometer 2004), confirming that households with children 'lead' in gaining Internet access. In the US, 85 per cent of 12 to 19-year-olds had access at home, though only 63 per cent had it at school in 2003 (USC 2004), contrasting with the UK's greater access at school (92 per cent of 9 to 19-year-olds) than at home (75 per cent).

Significant inequalities persist, especially in home access, with more middle-class than working-class children accessing the Internet at home (UKCGO figures show a difference of 88 per cent versus 61 per cent). Since technological innovation is a moving target, requiring recurrent rather than one-off investment, social stratification is likely to continue (Golding 2000). These complexities of access mean that understanding 'Internet use' is no easy matter for the quality of access affects, though by no means determines, the quality of use. We found that those from middle-class homes not only have better quality of access, but they also spend longer online and have greater online expertise (Livingstone, Bober and Helsper 2005a). For low users and non-users, access and expertise remain significant barriers, and for children, parents' experience of the Internet also matters, with more frequent users having more expert parents with more positive attitudes to the Internet.

2 NEW TECHNOLOGIES, NEW ACTIVITIES?

If we didn't have the Internet, we'd get everything we have on the Internet somewhere else. And I don't think the Internet is the solution to anything. And especially not education because there are too many distractions . . . I just think the Internet can be an easy way of doing things. (Marie, 16, from Essex)

Children and young people are using the Internet in many ways. Yet, Marie has a point: the Internet makes a range of activities easier, altering the pattern of young people's social and leisure activities, but radical change is little in evidence. When this 'Internet generation' was asked which medium they would most miss if it disappeared tomorrow, only 10 per cent named the Internet.

As of 2004, in the UK, half of all 9 to 19-year-olds had been online for over four years and most use the Internet frequently though for moderate amounts of time; most are either daily (41 per cent) or weekly (43 per cent) users; few use it less often (13 per cent), and just 3 per cent count as non-users (compared with 22 per cent of their parents) (Livingstone and Bober 2004). Most are online for less than an hour, meaning that more time is spent watching television and with the family, though amount of time online is similar to that spent doing homework or playing computer games and greater than time spent on the phone or reading. They go online for a wide range of purposes. The Internet is fast becoming central to the learning experience: 90 per cent of 9 to 19-year-old weekly users go online for school work, and 60 per cent of pupils regard the Internet as the most useful tool for getting information for homework.

In addition, nearly all (94 per cent) use the Internet to get information for other things, most use it for email (72 per cent) or games (70 per cent); half send instant messages (55 per cent) and download music (45 per cent). As Nina, 17, from Manchester, told us: 'You don't, like, buy CDs from HMV any more. You just get them off the Internet or off one of your mates who copies CDs'. Further, many look for information on careers and further education (44 per cent) or for products online (40 per cent), while a quarter read the news (26 per cent) and use chat rooms (21 per cent). Some use it for less-approved activities: among 12 to 19-year-olds who go online daily or weekly, 21 per cent admit to having copied something from the Internet for a school project and handed it in as their own, and a few claim to have hacked into someone else's website or email, to have visited an online dating site or sent a message to make someone feel uncomfortable or threatened, and 2 per cent admitted to having gambled online.

These figures chime with parallel surveys conducted elsewhere. In a European comparison (Larsson 2003), 66 per cent of 9 to 16-year-old boys used the Internet to play games and 49 per cent to download music, while the most popular activities for girls were email (58 per cent) and using the Internet for homework (43 per cent). In Norway, Sweden, and Ireland, 60 per cent found downloading music acceptable, but only 4 per cent thought the same about hacking. In the US in 2003, 84 per cent of 12 to 19-year-old Internet users went online to send/receive emails, 69 per cent for instant messaging, and 51 per cent for games (USC 2004).

Clearly, research must continue to track the diversifying uses of the Internet, both because learning how to use the Internet is a cognitive and cultural process (Bakardjieva 2005; Haddon 2004) and because the opportunities afforded by the Internet are themselves changing. But it is crucial also to make sense of this range of uses, and to identify the institutional and social influences on children's Internet use. When Linda, 13, from Derbyshire, says, 'I use it for, like, homework, emailing my cousin in Australia and keeping in touch with my friend in Cornwall', one wonders whether this is what was meant by empowering young people or democratizing participation? Do such uses reflect a growing breadth and sophistication of use? Do they justify the investment made by governments, teachers, and parents? What do we hope Linda will use the Internet for next? And, will it be worth running the attendant risks for?

Before getting too ambitious, we should recognize that even these uses have not come easily to many households. Ethnographic research, following a 'domestication of new technology' approach (Miller 1987; Silverstone and Hirsch 1992), focuses on how families are appropriating the Internet within domestic practices of space, time, and social relations (Van Rompaey, Roe and Struys 2002) and integrating it within the already complex media environment (Drotner 2000; Livingstone and Bovill 2001). This research finds that the Internet remains a fragile and opaque medium for many families, being experienced as unfamiliar, confusing, easier to get wrong than right, and far from taken for granted (e.g. Facer et al. 2003).

Thus Amir (15, from London) describes a fairly typical family when he says: 'Well, my mum doesn't use the computer, she doesn't even log on. But my dad—he doesn't know how to use the computer as well—but he always asks me "how do you do . . . ?" It doesn't take a day to learn how to use a computer, it's very difficult to use it. But when you get used to it, you're able to use it.' Indeed, although children usually consider themselves more expert than their parents, gaining in social status within the family as a result, neither children nor parents claim great expertise: in the UKCGO survey, 28 per cent of parents and 7 per cent of children who use the Internet described themselves as beginners; 12 per cent of parents and 32 per cent of children considered themselves advanced users. Such findings lead some, therefore, to challenge the 'myth' of the young computer or Internet expert (Facer et al. 2003), though within the home, the perceived 'reverse generation gap' in skills allows children to tease, or guide, or undermine, parental authority over children's Internet use (Holloway and Valentine 2003).

Such struggles are of growing importance not least because the home is changing, becoming the site of content production as well as reception, of education and work as well as entertainment and leisure. In other words, it is not only the technologies that are converging: the ways in which people use technologies are also converging, as people integrate information and communication services in their everyday lives. This raises new questions about the links between children's different activities, as learning becomes fun, as play may (or may not) be educational, as online chat serves (perhaps) to sustain networks, and so on. It also raises new questions regarding the links between the institutions (parents, teachers, government) that regulate children's lives (Livingstone and Bober 2006) as Internet literacy increasingly mediates not just leisure, but many aspects of cultural, economic and political participation.

3 INTERNET LITERACY

Literacy is not, nor ever has been, a personal attribute or ideologically inert 'skill' simply to be 'acquired' by individual persons. . . . It is ideologically and politically charged—it can be used as a means of social control or regulation, but also as a progressive weapon in the struggle for emancipation. (Hartley 2002: 136)

I have suggested that the evident gap between the grand hopes held out for the Internet and the more mundane realities of its day-to-day use (Lievrouw 2004) can be framed in terms of Internet literacy. This may be defined as the ability to access, understand and create information and communication online (Livingstone, Bober and Helsper 2005a), abilities that are, as Warschauer (2003: 9) puts it, 'critical to social inclusion in today's era'. In what follows, I shall also show how Internet literacy arises from the social knowledge that shapes people's lives and, further, from the design and implementation of online contents and services.

In other words, literacy should not be understood purely in terms of the acquisition of individual skills. Rather, it emerges from the interactions among a motivated and skilled individual, a well-resourced socio-cultural context and a well-designed interface. In everyday life, the context is commonly stratified, serving to differentiate among people and thus, often, to perpetuate and reproduce inequalities. The interface, similarly, can be understood in social, textual, technical and institutional terms, and in each of these respects may hinder or facilitate the activities of those using the Internet. Thus we need a broad ranging conception of literacy, one that mediates all aspects of access and use, not merely a tracking of specific skills or expertise. To sustain this conception, Internet literacy must be theorized in relation to the long history of intellectual debate and policy initiatives regarding literacy—mainly print literacy though recently also (audiovisual) media literacy, and, most recently, information literacy.

Internet literacy is of little value in and of itself; rather, its value lies in the opportunities that it opens up. Indeed, debates over literacy can be read as debates about the manner and purposes of public participation in society (Kellner 2002; Livingstone 2004; Luke 1989). Critical commentators on literacy from diverse perspectives assert three broad purposes to which media and information literacies are expected to make a contribution (Livingstone, Van Couvering and Thumim, forthcoming):

Democracy, participation and active citizenship: in a democratic society, a media and information-literate individual is more able to gain an informed opinion on matters of the day, and to be able to express their opinion individually and collectively in public, civic, and political domains, while a media and information-literate society supports a critical and inclusive public sphere.

Knowledge economy, competitiveness and choice: in a market economy increasingly based on information, often in a complex and mediated form, a media and information-literate individual is likely to have more to offer and so achieve at a higher level in the workplace, and a media and information-literate society is innovative and competitive, sustaining a rich array of choices for the consumer.

Lifelong learning, cultural expression and personal fulfilment: since our highly reflexive, heavily mediated symbolic environment informs and frames the choices, values and knowledge that give significance to everyday life, media and information literacy contributes to the critical and expressive skills that support a full and meaningful life, and to an informed, creative, and ethical society.

In the remainder of this chapter, I shall examine some of the online opportunities open to children and young people—focusing on communicating, interacting, and participating—to illustrate their steps towards, perhaps, these grand ambitions. My purpose is to assess the gap between hopes and realities as this is mediated by Internet literacy, in order to determine the challenges ahead.

4 Communication

Children and young people's main interest in going online is the new opportunities to communicate with peers. 'Communication' here must be read broadly, for as Clark (2005: 206) observes, despite the apparently mundane nature of much online conversation, it is through online (and other) communication, that teens engage in a protracted, sometimes experimental, sometimes cautious negotiation with their peers over 'everything from appropriate attire to appropriate academic and career aspirations' (see also Turkle 1995, on identity play online). This is to extend life offline to the online domain, albeit with, arguably, more freedom to experiment away from the adult gaze, to exercise control, and also to save face.

Consensus is emerging that the popular opposition between online and offline, or virtual and real communication was misguided. Young people integrate on- and offline communication to sustain their social networks, moving freely between different communication forms (Drotner 2000; Pew 2001; Slater 2002). Most contacts are local rather than distant (or 'virtual'): 'even if you've just seen them at school like, it'll be like you're texting them or talking to them on the phone or on MSN' (Kim, 15, from Essex). Since the perceived benefit is being in constant contact with one's friends (Clark 2005), there is rather little interest in communicating with strangers, although 'friends of friends' whom one has not met (and whom parents may consider 'strangers') are popular. Despite the early findings of the HomeNet project (Kraut et al. 1998), it seems that for all but the already isolated, the Internet fosters rather than undermines existing social contacts (Mesch 2001), permitting a continuation of, rather than an escape from, face-to-face communication in daily life. In the US, 45 per cent of 12 to 19-year-olds said their online use has increased communication with their family, and 54 per cent thought it had increased the number of people they stay in touch with, though others considered that the time spent with family and friends is unchanged (USC 2004). Pew (2001) found two-thirds of US teens thought the Internet keeps them from spending time with their family while half said they use it to improve relationships with friends, suggesting a shift away from familial to peer relations for this generation.

Whether the quality of relationship remains the same is contested (Kraut et al. 2006). Significantly, rather than seeing face-to-face communication as automatically superior, as many adults do, young people evaluate the different forms of communication available to them according to distinct communicative needs, often making careful choices among these forms depending on their characteristics—cost, control, temporal and spatial constraints and conventions, and so forth. (Livingstone 2006). Talking online is seen as less satisfying than face-to-face conversation, and can raise problems of trust: 'if you're talking to someone on the Internet who's a friend, you actually talk to them saying stuff, but feelings and everything are real . . . but if you're talking to someone you haven't met, how do you know if what they're telling you is the truth?', asks Mark (17, from Essex). It has its advantages, however: half of email, instant message and chat room users think that talking to people on the Internet can be as much or more satisfying as talking to them in real life, and a quarter identify significant advantages with online communication in terms of privacy, confidence, and intimacy (Livingstone and Bober 2004). As Cameron (13, from Derbyshire), confessed, 'I once dumped my old girlfriend by email . . . Well, it was cowardly really. I couldn't say it face-to-face.' Pew (2001) found that 37 per cent of US teenagers had used instant messaging to say something they would not have said in person, and 18 per cent had looked for sensitive information and advice online. In the UKCGO project, we also found a growth in teenagers seeking advice online. A quarter of 12 to 19-year-olds who use the Internet at least weekly say they go online to get advice, this being more common among older teens and, interestingly, boys; again, though, some worry about the reliability and privacy of online advice-seeking.

Online communication is not always a positive experience for children and young people, and the benefits must be balanced against the risks. One-third of children and young people report having received unwanted sexual or nasty comments via email, chat, instant messages or text messages. For example, Laura (13, from Essex) told us that 'my friend's family kind of used to send me horrible messages. I gave my email address to my friend, and then she used it, and somehow her friend got it, and half of her mates did . . .'. Since far fewer parents think their child has received sexual or hostile comments online, they may underestimate children's potential need for guidance. Further, contacts made online may not be safe, a risk that many have become aware of from media information campaigns. As Rosie (13, from Derbyshire) says, 'I've got about five buddies on my thing, but you can't really say, oh, this is a young girl, she's got brown hair, blue eyes,' 'cause she could be an old – she could be a he, and it's an old man, but I suppose it's quite nice to just say, oh, I've met someone on the Internet.' Yet her pleasure in making such friends suggests that fun may override good sense on occasion.

Indeed, one-in-three have made an online acquaintance, and 8 per cent say they have met face-to-face with someone they first met on the Internet. Similar figures are reported across Europe (Larsson 2003). In the US, 24 per cent of 12 to 17-year-old teens have pretended to be someone else in chatrooms, 60 per cent have received and 50 per cent have exchanged messages with a stranger (see also Mitchell, Finkelhor and Wolak 2003; Pew 2001). The Chatwise, Streetwise Report (Internet Crime Forum 2000) charted mounting evidence of actual crimes against children, suggesting that incidents of adult sex offenders meeting children online and gaining their trust are increasing in both the UK and US (see also Arnaldo 2001). Beyond the use of opinion polls, however, little research has explored the nature or consequences of unwanted sexual contact.

In consequence, many parents seek to manage their children's Internet use through restriction, although one-in-ten parents say they do not know what their child does on the Internet, and a fifth say they do not know how to help their child use the Internet safely, suggesting a clear need to improve and extend the reach of awareness and Internet literacy initiatives. Specifically, in the UK, many parents ban such interactive uses as chat rooms, downloading, instant messaging, and email. Understandable though such strategies are, these rules, and the anxieties behind them, also restrict children's freedoms to explore online communication in creative and satisfying ways (Livingstone, Bober and Helsper 2005a).

5 INTERACTIVITY

The interactive character of the Internet (McMillan 2006) supposedly encourages its users to 'sit forward', click on the options, find the opportunities exciting, begin to contribute content, come to feel part of a community, and so, perhaps by gradual steps, to shift from acting as a consumer to acting as a citizen. Indeed, the UKCGO survey found that over half report at least one form of interactive engagement with a website (out of sending an email/SMS to a site, voting for something online, contributing to a message board, offering advice to others, filling in a form or signing a petition online), suggesting a high level of interest and motivation among children and young people to be active online. Yet, on average, notwithstanding the many invitations to interact or 'to have your say', each individual has interacted in just one or two of these eight possible ways. Those who engage the most interactively with websites are also most likely to have made their own webpage, this being 34 per cent of Internet users aged 9–19. Yet of these, one-third never managed to get their webpage online and a further third have not maintained the site.

Interactivity and website creation are more common among boys and among middle-class youngsters. Since they are also the most privileged in terms of domestic access and use of the Internet, they have developed their online skills, discovering the advantages of the Internet not only for communication, games, and music, but also for advice, news, and content creation. In short, these young people are more likely than some others to spread their interests in using the Internet widely, being ready to take up new opportunities as offered.

Online skills mediate online opportunities and risks: children and young people's levels of online skills have a direct influence on the breadth of online opportunities and risks, over and above the effects of demographics, access, and use (Livingstone, Bober and Helsper 2005a). Perhaps surprisingly, more skilled young people do not avoid the risks; quite the contrary. It often assumed that, as children become more skilled and experienced Internet users, they simultaneously embrace more opportunities and manage to avoid the risks, so that 'expert' children can be more or less left to their own devices while attention is devoted to more naive users. The UKCGO findings contradict this assumption, finding that opportunities and risks go hand-in-hand—the more children and young people experience the one, the more they also experience the other, pointing up a dilemma for parents and regulators since reducing risks also reduces opportunities.

As already noted, parents are particularly likely to restrict the interactive uses of the Internet, notwithstanding that interactive engagement is essential for peer-to-peer connection, participation, identity play, and creative experimentation. Hazel (17, from Essex) recounts one among many such instances when she reports that 'my dad . . . doesn't let me go on the Internet very often because we had an incident one day where my sister . . . she was on MSN, and someone sent her something through. And it was actually like – it was like porn. So my dad saw it, and he was like very angry, so he doesn't let us use MSN now.' Toby (13, from Derbyshire) similarly tells us: 'We have different names to log on to the computer, it's not just one. You can set up your own thing. So my dad's got hardly any [restrictions] on it. I've got, you know, quite a bit. But my brothers, they've blocked out most of the stuff, so they can only go on very limited sites.'

Hence, parental concerns serve both to protect children and also to limit them, and UK parents seem more restrictive than others in Europe (Eurobarometer 2003), being closer to American parents (Pew 2001). For example, 86 per cent of parents whose child has home access to the Internet do not allow their children to give out personal information online, although 46 per cent of children and young people say that they have given out personal information. Significantly, the existence of a parental rule bears little or no relation to whether or not the child has given out such information (Livingstone, Bober and Helsper 2005a). Still, parental concerns have some justification. For example, coming into contact with pornography is, the UKCGO survey shows, a commonplace, but often unwelcome experience for children and young people. Among 9 to 19-year-olds who go online at least once a week, 57 per cent have come into contact with online pornography. Most exposure is accidental and much is unwelcome, at times disturbing or upsetting, particularly when encountered unexpectedly. As Tanya (15, from London) explains, 'yeah, these boys, they just go onto the Internet, they download it [porn], they put it on as screensaver. . . . It's just disgusting.' Similarly, Stuart (17, from Manchester) complains: 'What annoys me is when you get into something like "Open this website, it's a good website". . . You open it, it's something highly illegal.'

Parents and children are clear that pornography and other forms of undesirable content are more available online than via other media. However, unwanted or undesirable content varies considerably, from the mildly distasteful to hard core or illegal material, and too little attention has been paid to the definition of pornography. While acknowledging the ethical issues involved in researching this with children, it remains the case that the consequences of exposure to unwanted or inappropriate content is a key research gap: little is known of how children and young people respond to exposure to different kinds or levels of content or, especially, whether or when this has adverse consequences for their sexual or personal development (Feilitzen and Carlsson 2003; Thornburgh and Lin 2002).

6 PARTICIPATION

The possible role of the Internet in facilitating the step from communication and interactivity to civic participation has attracted considerable attention, especially given the apparent crisis in youth participation (Coleman 2003; Dahlgren 2003; Livingstone, forthcoming). The Center for Media Education in the US has argued strongly for the creation of an economically viable 'youth civic media' that asserts children's rights to self-expression, creativity, and participation, in effect to cultural citizenship online as well as offline (Montgomery, Gottlieb-Robles and Larson 2004).

The UKCGO research identified several ways in which the Internet encourages civic participation: 54 per cent of 12 to 19-year-olds who use the Internet at least weekly have sought out sites concerned with political or civic issues, although two-fifths are not interested. However, only one in three of those who have visited such sites responded to or contributed to them in any way, the other two-thirds claiming merely to 'check out' the site. Also evident, however, were ways in which traditional factors—age, gender and social background—play a part in supporting some and hindering others, with girls, and older and middle-class teens visiting a broader range of civic and political sites (Livingstone, Bober and Helsper 2005b). Although one middle-class 15-year-old girl declares, with some despair—'I really don't understand how people could have said that they aren't interested in politics! What about the "Don't attack Iraq" rallies and marches? There was a massive under-18 turn out!'—politics is boring'. And as Lorie (17, from Essex) adds wisely, 'At the end of the day, you're going to look at what you're interested in. And if you haven't got an interest in politics, you're not going to get one from having the Internet.'

Online participation, it seems, tends to be short-lived. Young people are enthusiastic about interacting with the Internet, but they often do not follow through, taking up only a few opportunities to visit civic sites, tending just to check out the sites rather than contributing to them, rarely discussing civic or political topics with their peers (Livingstone, Bober and Helsper 2005b). This is partly because young people are cynical about the invitation to have their say, as they feel their contributions are not taken seriously, and they are not listened to. Anne (15, from Essex), complains: 'young people's opinions are not at all valued, especially not by politicians.' Since many have 'tested the water', but taken few steps beyond this, there is a challenge for policy makers in developing a more genuinely interactive environment in which young people's contributions are directly responded to in such a way that their efforts at participation can be sustained and experienced as rewarding. For the shift from providing opportunities to 'have your say' to also providing opportunities for two-way engagement depends less on young people than on the adults who seek to engage them. As Hazel (17, from Essex) asks, 'you can email your MP, but is he going to listen?' Thus the online opportunity structure available to young people may be no better than that established offline. And in everyday life, as the sociology of childhood makes clear, the trends are more towards the sequestration of children away from adult society, the commodification of childhood being perhaps a key exception (James, Jenks and Prout 1998; Livingstone 2002).

Nonetheless, young people are more likely to participate online than to take part in more traditional forms of politics (Gibson, Lusoli and Ward 2002): while only 10 per cent of 15–24-year-olds in the UK took part in any form of political activity offline, three times as many did something political on the Internet. In the US too, 38 per cent of 12–17-year-olds said they go online to express their opinion (Pew 2001), and 26 per cent of the UKGCO teenagers go online to read the news. The lower commitment required for online participation, compared with attending meetings or other offline activities, may yet encourage young people. As Poppy (16, from London), reported, 'there's a Greenpeace website which had a petition about like global warming and stuff and we should do something about it. And I signed that just because it's easy and you might as well put your name down.'

Countering optimistic visions of public participation online are the critical accounts of the privatization or commercialization of online content targeted towards young people (Buckingham 2005; Kinder 1999). The Center for Media Education identifies several new forms of online marketing practices targeted at children, including 'branded communities', 'viral marketing', and so on, expressing particular concern over the economic pressure towards alliances between civic sites and commercial ventures (Montgomery 2001; Turow 2001). Little research, however, has yet examined the user's perspective to discover how teens respond to such sites and whether they can recognize and/or distance themselves from commercial approaches. The UKCGO survey found that young people who rate themselves as beginners in using the Internet lack critical skills and so are more distrustful towards Internet content than those who call themselves experts (see similar findings from the OxIS survey of adults, Dutton and Shepherd 2004).

Yet still little is known of how children and young people's critical literacy skills develop as they become experienced in a greater range of types of online content, whether they can identify the new forms of promotion, sponsorship, paid-for-content, and merchandizing on the Internet, and whether they extend distinctions—of reliability, trustworthiness, credibility—learned in relation to broadcast or print media, or whether they are developing a new approach to content evaluation. Seiter (2005) is sceptical about this, not because children cannot gain such skills, but because, without decisive intervention, it seems that in practice they do not. Arguing provocatively that computers and the Internet are, in key ways, 'fundamentally unsuited to children's needs', drawing them into an invidiously commercialized and branded environment for which their critical literacy skills are (even designed to be) insufficient, she joins many who call for greater critical literacy interventions.

7 CONCLUSION

For most children and young people, the Internet is not yet used to its full potential. As an information medium, the Internet has rapidly become central in children's lives, and as a communication medium, it represents a significant addition to the existing means of communication available to them. In a plethora of ways, children and young people are taking steps towards deepening and diversifying their Internet use, many of them gaining in sophistication, motivation, and skills as they do so. But many are not yet taking up the potential of the Internet.

These young people worry about the risks, visit only a few sites, fail to upload and maintain personal websites, and treat sites more as ready-made sources of entertainment or information than as opportunities for critical engagement, user-generated content production, or active participation.

As noted in the definition of Internet literacy offered at the outset, and as developed especially by work on information literacy and the digital divide, literacy first and foremost includes the ability to access media and information technologies. Construing access as a dimension of literacy means focusing not only on the economic, educational and social resources to know which domestic goods and services to acquire and how to appropriate them at home, but also on the skills and competences required to maintain and upgrade domestic ICTs, together with knowing how to ensure they provide access to desired contents (from installing software to knowing how to access, search, and navigate complex databases effectively and efficiently), and also how to avoid undesired contents (that is, regulating for content and contact risks, whether through technical or social practices). No longer are children and young people only, or even mainly, divided by access, though 'access' is a moving target in terms of its speed, location, quality, and support, and inequalities in access do persist. Increasingly, children and young people are divided into those for whom the Internet is an increasingly rich, diverse, engaging, and stimulating resource of growing importance in their lives, and those for whom it remains a narrow, unengaging, if occasionally useful, resource of rather less significance.

Hence, a new divide is opening up, mapping out a continuum in the quality of use in which middle-class children, children with Internet access at home, children with broadband access, and children whose parents use the Internet more often are more likely to be daily users and to gain more Internet skills. Consequently, they experience the Internet as a richer, if riskier, medium than do less privileged children. This is because literacy also includes the ability to understand media and information technologies. This includes knowledge of the range of technologies, contents, and services available so as to make meaningful choices, an awareness of the institutional, economic, and political contexts of production in order that the choices available can be critically appraised, the know-how to ensure that the available facilities match one's own interests and needs, and the critical literacy to evaluate and, if necessary reject, problematic, biased, or otherwise flawed information and communication. Now that almost anyone can produce and disseminate Internet contents, with fewer and different kinds of filters, critical literacy requires skills of searching across a wide range of heterogeneous sources, evaluating them, and identifying what is authoritative, trustworthy, and relevant.

In addition to access and understanding, the third dimension of literacy is the ability to produce or create media and information contents, crucial since the changing media environment potentially serves to democratize content creation and dissemination in hitherto unprecedented ways. This stresses the knowledge and competence required to participate as a creator as well as a receiver of information and communication contents and services, ICTs representing a key route to participation in a modern democratic society. Just as writing as well as reading has long been required of a print-literate person (and society), so too is the know-how required to undertake successfully a wide range of activities concerned with content creation and dissemination deemed central to an Internet- or ICT-literate individual (and society). Here too, children and young people face challenges, though not primarily because their skills are limited. Rather, more critical attention is needed to the social contexts that sustain skills and competence, and to examining how interfaces are designed to invite and illuminate or obscure and impede (Isaacs and Walendowski 2002). Literacy depends on an effective interaction between people and the Internet, and this process may be both enabled and undermined by individual or societal factors as well as by the institutional, textual and technological factors that shape the interface with the user or audience.

REFERENCES

ARNALDO, C. A. (2001). *Child Abuse on the Internet: Ending the Silence.* Paris: Berghahn Books and UNESCO Publishing.

BAKARDJIEVA, M. (2005). *Internet Society: The Internet in Everyday Life.* London: Sage.

BUCKINGHAM, D. (2005). 'The Electronic Generation? Children and New Media', in L. Lievrouw and S. Livingstone (eds), *The Handbook of New Media: Updated Student Edition.* London: Sage, 75–91.

CLARK, L. S. (2005). 'The Constant Contact Generation: Exploring Teen Friendship Networks Online', in S. Mazzarella (ed.), *Girl Wide Web.* New York: Peter Lang, 203–22.

COLEMAN, S. (2003). 'A Tale of Two Houses: The House of Commons, the Big Brother House and the People at Home'. *Parliamentary Affairs*, 56: 733–58.

COUNCIL OF EUROPE (2005). *Integration and Diversity: The New Frontiers of European Media and Communications Policy,* http://www.coe.int/T/E/Com/Files/Ministerial-Conferences/2005-kiev/texte_adopte.asp, accessed 25 Apr. 2005.

DAHLGREN, P. (2003). 'Reconfiguring Civic Culture in the New Media Milieu', in J. Corner and D. Pels (eds), *Media and the Restyling of Politics.* London: Sage, 151–70.

DROTNER, K. (2000). 'Difference and Diversity: Trends in Young Danes' Media Use'. *Media, Culture & Society*, 22(2): 149–66.

DUTTON, W. H. and SHEPHERD, A. (2004). *Confidence and Risk on the Internet.* Oxford: Oxford Internet Institute.

EUROBAROMETER (2003, 2004). *Eurobarometer 59.2.* Brussels: European Commission, Directorate-General for Information, Communication, Culture and Audiovisual Media.

—— (2004). *Illegal and Harmful Content on the Internet.* Brussels: European Commission, Directorate-General for Information, Communication, Culture and Audiovisual Media.

EUROSTAT (2005). *The Digital Divide in Europe.* Statistics in Focus, Industry, Trade and Services, http://europea.eu.int/comm/eurostat/, accessed 23 Jan 2005.

FACER, K., FURLONG, J., FURLONG, R. et al. (2003). *ScreenPlay: Children and Computing in the Home*. London: Routledge.

GIBSON, R., LUSOLI, W. and WARD, S. (2002). *UK Political Participation Online: The Public Response. A Survey of Citizens' Political Activity via the Internet*. Salford: ESRI, www. ipop.org.uk.

GOLDING, P. (2000). 'Forthcoming Features: Information and Communications Technologies and the Sociology of the Future'. *Sociology*, 34(1): 165–84.

HADDON, L. (2004). *Information and Communication Technologies in Everyday Life: A Concise Introduction and Research Guide*. Oxford: Berg.

HARTLEY, J. (2002). *Communication, Cultural and Media Studies: The Key Concepts*. London: Routledge.

HOLLOWAY, S. L. and VALENTINE, G. (2003). *Cyberkids: Children in the Information Age*. London: Routledge.

INTERNET CRIME FORUM (2000). *Chat Wise, Street Wise: Children and Internet Chat Services*. UK: The Internet Crime Forum IRC Sub-group.

ISAACS, E. and WALENDOWSKI, A. (2002). *Designing from Both Sides of the Screen: How Designers and Engineers Can Collaborate to Build Cooperative Technology*. Indianapolis, IN: New Riders.

JAMES, A., JENKS, C. and PROUT, A. (1998). *Theorizing Childhood*. Cambridge: Cambridge University Press.

KELLNER, D. (2002). 'New Media and New Literacies: Reconstructing Education for the New Millenium', in L. Lievrouw and S. Livingstone (eds), *The Handbook of New Media*. London: Sage, 90–104.

KINDER, M. (ed.) (1999). *Kids' Media Culture*. Durham, NC: Duke University Press.

KRAUT, R., KIESLER, S., BONEVA, B., et al. (2006). 'Examining the Impact of Internet Use: on Television Viewing in R. Kraut, M. Brynin and S. Kiesler (eds), *Computers, Phones, and the Internet: Domesticating Information Technology*. Oxford: Oxford University Press, 70–83.

—— LUNDMARK, V., PATTERSON, M., et al. (1998). 'Internet Paradox: A Social Technology That Reduces Social Involvement and Psychological Well-being?' *American Psychologist*, 53(9): 1017–32.

LARSSON, K. (2003). 'Children's On-line Life – And What Parents Believe: A Survey in Five Countries', in C. von Feilitzen and U. Carlsson (eds), *Promote or Protect? Perspectives on Media Literacy and Media Regulations*. Goteborg: NORDICOM, 113–20.

LIEVROUW, L. (2004). 'What's Changed About New Media? Introduction to the Fifth Anniversary Issue of New Media and Society'. *New Media & Society*, 6(1): 9–15.

LIVINGSTONE, S. (2002). *Young People and New Media: Childhood and the Changing Media Environment*. London: Sage.

—— (2004). 'Media Literacy and the Challenge of New Information and Communication Technologies'. *Communication Review*, 7: 3–14.

—— (2006). 'Children's Privacy Online', in R. Kraut, M. Brynin and S. Kiesler (eds), *Computers, Phones, and the Internet: Domesticating Information Technology*. Oxford: Oxford University Press, 128–44.

—— (2007). 'Interactivity and Participation on the Internet: A Critical Appraisal of the Online Invitation to Young People', in P. Dahlgren (ed.), *Young Citizens and New Media: Strategies for Learning Democratic Engagement*. London: Routledge.

LIVINGSTONE, S. and BOBER, M. (2004). *UK Children Go Online: Surveying the Experiences of Young People and their Parents.* London: London School of Economics and Political Science.

—— and —— (2006). 'Regulating the Internet at Home: Contrasting the Perspectives of Children and Parents', in D. Buckingham and R. Willett (eds), *Digital Generations.* Mahwah NJ: Lawrence Erlbaum Associates, 93–113.

——, —— and HELSPER, E. J. (2005a). *Internet Literacy among Children and Young People.* London: LSE Report, February, www.children-go-online.net.

——, —— and —— (2005b). 'Active Participation or just more Information? Young People's Take Up of Opportunities to Act and Interact on the Internet'. *Information, Communication and Society,* 8(3): 287–314.

—— and HELSPER, E. J. (forthcoming) 'Gradations in Digital Inclusion: Children, Young People and the Digital Divide. New Media & Society.

—— and BOVILL, M. (eds). (2001). *Children and their Changing Media Environment: A European Comparative Study.* Mahwah, NJ: Lawrence Erlbaum Associates.

——, VAN COUVERING, E. and THUMIM, N. (forthcoming). 'Converging Traditions of Research on Media and Information Literacies: Disciplinary and Methodological Issues', in D. J. Leu, J. Coiro, M. Knobel, et al. (eds), *Handbook of Research on New Literacies.* Mahwah, NJ: Lawrence Erlbaum Associates.

LUKE, C. (1989). *Pedagogy, Printing and Protestantism: The Discourse of Childhood.* Albany, NY: State University of New York Press.

MANSELL, R. (2004). 'The Internet, Capitalism, and Policy', in M. Consalvo, N. Baym, J. Hunsinger, et al. (eds), *Internet Research Annual* (vol. 1). New York: Peter Lang, 175–84.

MARCUM, J. W. (2002). 'Rethinking Information Literacy'. *Library Quarterly,* 72(1): 1–26.

MCMILLAN, S. (2006). 'Interactivity: Users, Documents, and Systems', in L. Lievrouw and S. Livingstone (eds), *The Handbook of New Media: Updated Student Edition.* London: Sage Publications, 205–29.

MESCH, G. (2001). 'Social Relationships and Internet Use among Adolescents in Israel'. *Social Science Quarterly,* 82(2): 329–39.

MILLER, D. (1987). *Material Culture and Mass Consumption.* Oxford: Blackwell.

MITCHELL, K. J., FINKELHOR, D. and WOLAK, J. (2003). 'The Exposure of Youth to Unwanted Sexual Material on the Internet: A National Survey of Risk, Impact, and Prevention'. *Youth and Society,* 34(3), 330–58.

MONTGOMERY, K. (2001). 'The New On-line Children's Consumer Culture', in D. Singer and J. Singer (eds), *Handbook of Children and the Media.* London: Sage, 635–50.

——, GOTTLIEB-ROBLES, B. and LARSON, G. O. (2004). *Youth as E-Citizens: Engaging the Digital Generation.* Washington DC: Center for Social Media, American University, http://www.centerforsocialmedia.org/ecitizens/youthreport.pdf, accessed 8 Jan. 2006.

OFCOM (2004). *Ofcom's Strategy and Priorities for the Promotion of Media Literacy: A Statement.* London: Ofcom.

OFFICE FOR NATIONAL STATISTICS (2004). *Internet Access: 12.1 Million Households Now Online,* http://www.statistics.gov.uk/, accessed 8 Jan. 2006.

PEW (2001). *Teenage Life Online: The Rise of the Instant-Message Generation and the Internet's Impact on Friendships and Family Relationships.* Washington DC: Pew Internet and American Life Project, http://www.pewinternet.org/, accessed 11 Jan 2006.

POTTER, W. J. (2004). *Theory of Media Literacy: A Cognitive Approach.* Thousand Oaks, CA: Sage.

SEITER, E. (2005). *The Internet Playground: Children's Access, Entertainment, and Mis-education*. New York: Peter Lang.

SELWYN, N. (2004). 'Reconsidering Political and Popular Understandings of the Digital Divide'. *New Media & Society*, 6(3): 341–62.

SILVERSTONE, R. and HIRSCH, E. (eds). (1992). *Consuming Technologies: Media and Information in Domestic Spaces*. London: Routledge.

SLATER, D. (2002). 'Social Relationships and Identity Online and Offline', in L. Lievrouw and S. Livingstone (eds), *The Handbook of New Media*. London: Sage, 534–47.

SNYDER, I. (ed.). (1998). *Page to Screen: Taking Literacy into the Electronic Era*. London: Routledge.

THORNBURGH, D. and LIN, H. S. (2002). *Youth, Pornography, and the Internet*. Washington DC: National Academy Press.

TURKLE, S. (1995). *Life on the Screen: Identity in the Age of the Internet*. New York: Simon and Schuster.

TUROW, J. (2001). 'Family Boundaries, Commercialism, and the Internet: A Framework for Research'. *Journal of Applied Developmental Psychology*, 22(1): 73–86.

TYNER, K. (1998). *Literacy in a Digital World: Teaching and Learning in the Age of Information*. Mahwah, NJ: Lawrence Erlbaum Associates.

USC (2004). *The Digital Future Report: Surveying the Digital Future Year Four – Ten Years, Ten Trends*: USC Annenberg School, Centre for the Digital Future, www.digitalcenter.org.

VAN ROMPAEY, V., ROE, K. and STRUYS, K. (2002). 'Children's Influence on Internet Access at Home: Adoption and Use in the Family Context'. *Information, Communication and Society*, 5(2): 189–206.

VAN FEILITZEN, C., and CARLSSON, U. (eds) (2003). *Promote or Protect? Perspectives on Media Literacy and Media Regulations*. Goteborg: NORDICOM.

WARSCHAUER, M. (2003). *Technology and Social Inclusion: Rethinking the Digital Divide*. Cambridge, MA: MIT Press.

CHAPTER 22

THE INTERRELATIONS BETWEEN ONLINE AND OFFLINE: QUESTIONS, ISSUES, AND IMPLICATIONS

SHANI ORGAD

1 INTRODUCTION

THE distinction between the online and offline has been essential to the understanding of the Internet from its earliest days. Some of the early research on Internet and computer mediated communication (CMC), and popular discourse on the Internet even today, have depicted the online space as an autonomous, self-contained realm, separate from the offline world. For example, Turkle's (1996) infamous *Life on the Screen* shows how participants in cyberspace—particularly simulated MUDs (multi-user dungeons) and MOOs (multi-user object oriented environments), invest in constructing identities and lives online as a way of liberating themselves from the confines of their real-life identities.

Although Turkle's analysis actually demonstrates how individuals' experimentation with their online identities is closely connected to their offline selves, for example by developing a certain role, or escaping from it, it was commonly seen as representing a separation and opposition between online and offline identities. Other studies reinforced the idea that the online and the offline are two distinct, and often oppositional, communicative realms. Schofield (1998: 182), for example, described chatrooms for teenagers as a space outside of everyday life, for the development of a 'pure' relationship 'that is fulfilling and liberating, ultimately and primarily, to the self'. This notion that Internet spaces are independent of and separate from offline relations and practices, endorsed a view of cyberspace as a plausible research field site (Hine 2000: 9), advancing the development of 'virtual methodologies', such as 'virtual ethnography', implemented exclusively by and through the Internet (e.g. Hine 2000; Kendall 2002; Markham 1998; Schaap 2002).

However, the separation between online and offline has been increasingly challenged on a conceptual, analytical, and methodological level. Researchers have recognized that online spaces and relations do not evolve in isolation from existing social and cultural processes and institutions. Rather, cyberspace is fundamentally embedded within specific social, cultural, and material contexts (e.g. Baym 2000; Halavais 2000; Khiabany 2003; Mansell 2004; Mesch 2006; Miller and Slater 2000; Sassen 2004). There is a growing body of research on the interrelations between various online phenomena and offline structures, practices, discourses, and factors, which shows that the assumption 'that only things that happen on the Internet were relevant to understanding the Internet' can no longer be sustained (Haythornthwaite and Wellman 2002: 5).

The broader agenda underlying the interest in the online and offline concerns how and with what effect the Internet alters and becomes integrated into daily life. Any exploration of this is interested also in the reverse relationship, that is, how everyday offline structures, practices, texts, and behaviours shape Internet and CMC environments.

This interest in the interrelations between online and offline shifts the focus from the technology (the Internet) to the communication processes it facilitates, and the movement of meanings between the two realms. It urges a view of communication as a process where meanings move across different technologies, channels, realms, spaces, and structures. For example, in my research on participation in Internet spaces of women with breast cancer and their engagement in telling their personal stories online (Orgad 2005a), rather than asking about the impact of the Internet on participants' lives, I focused on the communicative activities and social processes that emerged from women's participation in online spaces, and how they became interwoven in the management of their illness. Enquiring about the Internet's impact, and how online participation interweaves with participants' lives, may seem just a different way of asking the same question. However, I suggest that framing the question as an attempt to enquire into online–offline interrelations, rather than an attempt to study the Internet's impact on the offline realm, is more productive for several reasons.

Focusing on online–offline interrelations avoids both technological determinism (claims such as, 'the Internet radically changes the way patients relate to each other and their doctors'), and extreme constructivism, which ignores the technology's material characteristics and the structural contexts within which it is embedded (claims such as, 'patients' online sites constitute alternative spaces that fundamentally challenge conventional medicine'). Rather it invites a qualified and balanced analysis, which takes account of the movement of meanings between the two communicative realms, their varying directions, and their multiple and unpredictable consequences.[1]

This chapter investigates the interrelations between the online and offline. Drawing on earlier research (Orgad 2005a) into breast cancer patients' online communication, I explore some of the questions and issues surrounding the current debate on the relations between online and offline, and particularly: (1) the transition from offline to online and its consequences (e.g. the migration of journalism and news to online space); (2) the transition from online to offline and its consequences (e.g. evolution from online to offline interpersonal relationships); and (3) the interweaving of the online and offline realms (e.g. how a particular online discourse is embedded within broader offline public discourses and cultures, and how offline public discourses are shaped by discursive online elements). The objective is to enhance understanding about the conceptual, analytical, and methodological aspects of studying the relations between the online and the offline.

2 FROM OFFLINE TO ONLINE

Research on the move from offline to online has focused on texts or discourses (e.g. news), institutions (e.g. business firms), networks (e.g. civil society organizations), practices (e.g. shopping, brand management, journalistic professional conventions), and interactions (e.g. between customers and sellers), and how the nature of the object that originated offline has been altered by the move to online. In this chapter, I examine three areas: commercial business and branding, news and journalism (in particular), and civil society networking. These areas demonstrate the transformation of different types of objects from offline to online (organizational structures and communication strategies, texts and professional practices, and interactions) in different areas of life (economy, media, and politics/social action).[2] In reviewing key claims and findings, I draw broader conclusions to improve our understanding of the online in the context of offline behaviours, practices, and structures.

The move to e-commerce

The possibilities offered by e-commerce have tempted many businesses to integrate online practice into their activities, to become what are known as 'click and mortar' or 'clicks and bricks' firms. This move has necessitated the translation of their brand into a significant and profitable online presence.

Research has shown that online brands or businesses are not a mere transfer of traditional offline counterparts to the online space. For instance, the reduced physical, verbal, and visual cues, and the increased impersonality of online communication, introduces uncertainty and raises questions about trust in electronic interactions; thus brand awareness and trust may be more important online than offline (Ben-Ner and Putterman 2002; Strebinger and Treiblmaier 2004: 159; Wallace 2001). On the other hand, there is growing evidence that in some cases e-commerce, and branding in particular, tend to mirror the offline commercial arena (Strebinger and Treiblmaier 2004), or that the most popular areas of web content of online media firms converge with those of the traditional offline commercial media (McChesney 2000).

Whether emphasizing the significant differences between online and offline branding and marketing, or highlighting their similarities, one important conclusion from these studies is that the move from offline to online must satisfy the requirements of the offline firm, for instance its organizational structure and corporate culture and strategy, while responding to the needs and exploiting the opportunities of the online environment (Strebinger and Treiblmaier 2004: 155). For example, firms that are well resourced financially can invest more in hardware, software, and technical training, and therefore are likely to become more extensively involved in e-commerce. More generally, the values, beliefs, and needs of an organization are significant determinants of the scope of its e-commerce adoption (Gibbs and Kraemer 2004).

In this context, Steinfeld (2004) calls for a 'situated' view, which regards e-commerce as connected to the firm's physical infrastructure. The situatedness of e-commerce also has a significant cultural aspect, as shown by studies highlighting the national and organizational cultures within which e-commerce (production and use) is embedded (Thanasankit 2003). These studies show how aspects such as values, religion, symbols, and even meanings of colours influence the design, adoption, implementation, and use of e-commerce. A key theme in these studies is how attitudes towards e-business, both within the organization and among consumers, are influenced by culture. For instance, cultural conflicts between the Japanese and Singaporeans resulted in an e-commerce project being abandoned (Pan and Flynn 2003). These studies also point to the crucial role of governments in providing clear policy and incentives for the adoption of e-commerce. Lack of a supportive regulatory environment has significant negative effects on e-commerce use (Gibbs and Kraemer 2004).

Thus, e-commerce studies have increased awareness that the online is shaped by wider offline factors, and that the two realms are interdependent, and must be understood to be so if a company is to successfully extend its activities from the offline to the online. Furthermore, understanding the role of contextual elements such as culture, in the adoption, implementation, and use of e-commerce may help organizations formulate appropriate business strategies, and conduct more effective and efficient business online (Thanasankit 2003).

Although studies on the move to e-commerce focus on the move of an offline object to the online world, they also show that there is a transformation in the other direction. That is, the move from offline to online may alter the 'original' offline brand or business landscape. For instance, e-commerce may alter the cost–benefit ratio of brands in the offline world (Strebinger and Treiblmaier 2004), the patterns of price discovery enabled by e-commerce can change how buyers and sellers set prices (Bakos 2001), and automated information exchanges in e-commerce transactions may lower wholesalers' perceived bargaining power (Nakayama 2000). Thus, the relationship between the online and the offline in the commercial context is bilateral, entailing mutual effects that cannot be simply assumed nor easily predicted.

The migration of news and journalism to online space

Research on online news has focused on the consequences of the migration of news discourse and journalistic practice to online space. The debate has been largely fuelled by the promise of the online environment to create a new generation of journalistic conventions that could affect old media (Boczkowski 2004; Matheson 2004: 444). There has been particularly lively discussion in academia and beyond about the potential for blogging to alter the nature of journalism by nudging print media towards richer, deeper, and more balanced sourcing outside the traditional local sources of government and corporations (Matheson 2004; Nieman Reports 2003).

However, despite enthusiasm about the promise of online journalism, and journalistic blogging in particular, to rearticulate journalistic practices in the new forms available online and take advantage of the possibilities afforded by networked computing, newspapers have been slow to realize the potential (Boczkowski 2004; Matheson 2004). In his analysis of the *Guardian* weblog, for instance, Matheson (2004) shows that it is not in any way revolutionary, nor does it challenge the 'old media' in any meaningful way. He and Zhu (2002) confirm this finding in their study of online newspapers in China, showing that generally online newspapers mirror their print versions in terms of objectives, basic tone, and content.

One lesson that can be drawn from these studies is that the consequences of transformation of an object—be it an organization, a brand, a text, discourse, or practices—from offline to online, cannot be simply assumed or easily predicted. Its development must be empirically investigated and critically evaluated to allow development of concepts and theories to explain transformations in other areas.

One important aspect of empirical investigations of the online–offline relationship is participants' perceptions and experiences. This requires questions such as: how do journalists perceive the impact of the move from offline to online? How do they differentiate between the two realms? And, do they see any connections between the two? At the same time, analysis of the online–offline relationship needs to be qualified by participants' realities and actual experiences. For instance, journalists may be very enthusiastic about the potential to rearticulate journalistic practices in the new forms available online, and thus will endorse the view of a strong and meaningful connection between offline and online, while in reality there is little evidence of this. The reverse may also occur: in my study of breast cancer patients' online activities, participants often conveyed a very weak (if any) connection between their online and offline experiences, depicting their engagement in online spaces as insignificant in coping with their illness. However, the actual evidence of their active participation in breast cancer Internet spaces suggested a close and meaningful connection between their online experiences and the handling of their illness.[3]

These analyses are significant from a design point of view for parties interested in implementing offline to online moves, and accommodating the changes they entail. For example, a medical organization designing an online space for patients to communicate, would need to attend to users' views, expectations, and experiences, but would also need to draw on other sources of information to fully understand patients' online practices and the meanings they derive from them.

Civil society networks go online

Cammaerts and Carpentier's (2005) study of civil society actors' participation in the World Summit on the Information Society (WSIS) makes a similar argument about the limited extent to which the promise of the move from offline to online is realized. In addition to offline consultation meetings, an online platform was developed specifically directed at involving civil society actors in the WSIS preparation process. The authors show that despite this, actual decision-making in relation to the WSIS occurred exclusively in offline meetings.[4] They argue that the Internet played a limited role in facilitating participation in global governance processes.

While this account of participation in the WSIS shows that the move from offline to online had limited (if any) consequences, many studies on the role of the Internet and CMC in political struggle, collective action, and social movements present contradictory findings. Various works on the role of the Internet in the organization of the anti-globalization protests (e.g. Bennett 2003; Van Aelst and Walgrave 2002), the resistance to corporate culture (e.g. Carty 2002; Meikle 2002), and political struggle such as the Zapatistas' in Mexico (Russell 2001) have shown that the introduction of the online component into activists' struggles—either in offering new tools and practices or in enhancing and helping maintain old (offline) ones—enhanced their political action and assisted the mobilization of their goals in meaningful ways.

What is important is that these contradictory findings about the impact of the introduction of online components into existing offline contexts emerge from a similar principle: online intervention does not work independently of the offline world. In the WSIS case it was the unequal access to the infrastructure and skills that prevented members from utilizing the Internet (Cammaerts and Carpentier 2005), while the online activism studies show that the development, organization, and success of online networks are fundamentally shaped by offline realities. For example, the development and survival of the Belgrade radio station B92 online, which campaigned against the censorship imposed by Milosevic, was largely facilitated by the strong offline network of solidarity combined with the support of international service providers, and it was Milosevic's very extreme censorship that eventually rendered it toothless (Meikle 2002).

The other lesson from these studies is that the success and implications of the introduction of online components into offline contexts depend not only on offline realities, but also on online realities. For instance, Cammaerts and Carpentier (2005) explain the relatively low use of online protests by civil society organizations as being the result of the rise of spam and filtering software. In my study, I found that the reluctance of many interviewees to participate in chats to discuss their illness was nourished by mediated representations of chatrooms as dangerous places, for example, discussion about sexual harassment and paedophilia on online chats. Thus, broader aspects that extend the specific online phenomenon, such as popular representations of cyberspace or certain trends and practices that become popular in online spaces, coupled with offline elements, shape specific online environments and users' participation in them in significant ways.

3 FROM ONLINE TO OFFLINE

The move between the two communicative realms also occurs from online to offline. Research on issues such as romantic relationships, diasporic communities, and health-related communication has explored how an object that originated online moved into the offline context, what the consequences were, and how the online and offline objects differed.

One area where this transition has been examined is that of interpersonal relationships, where the focus is the differences and similarities between individuals' online and offline development of relationships and interactions. For example, Baker (1998) and Sveningsson (2002) explored how participants established romantic relationships in online spaces such as chatrooms, and later evolved to face-to-face meetings with these partners. Sveningsson (2002) describes the phases involved in offline relationships as occurring in reverse order to how they occur online: in the initial stages of offline relationships, the emphasis is on physical 'extrinsic' qualities, whereas in online relationship it is 'intrinsic' qualities that are more important. At the same time, Sveningsson (2002) stresses that there are also important similarities between the online and offline, and that even if there are differences, it is not certain that they will have the kind of consequences often predicted.

Discussion of the move of interpersonal relationships from online to offline also explores whether and how participants re-engage online after they have met their partners offline. Sveningsson (2002: 68) describes the return to CMC after face-to-face meetings as 'retrogression in the progressive phases of relationship development' and likens it to a withdrawal; participants who meet partners online often lose interest in, and stop visiting chatrooms after they take their relationship offline. For many, the online became frustrating for communication, and lost its relevance.

Eichhorn (2001), Gajjala (2002), and Orgad (2005b) reflect on the move from online to offline, and back, in another context: how the move from online to offline with research informants altered their understanding of the online phenomenon and the practices they studied. In her study of a girls' textual online community ('zines'), Eichhorn (2001) notes how, as a consequence of a face-to-face encounter with one of her study participants, an issue that had initially been peripheral (the way people 'recycle' old technologies as tools of resistance) became a central concern, and that meeting the participant face-to-face forced her to recognize the significance of her research participants' bodies in understanding the online community.

Similarly, the move from online relationships, which emerged and were maintained primarily via e-mail, to face-to-face meetings with breast cancer patients, challenged my understanding of their experience in fundamental ways. Hearing women's stories face-to-face revealed much more complex relationships between their online experiences and their illness experience than had emerged from their initial email accounts. For example, while in their emails respondents often described 'the Internet' in utopian terms such as 'empowering' or 'dazzling', in their face-to-face accounts they described complex and sometimes contradictory experiences of Internet use: positive and negative, informative and unhelpful, sometimes misleading, engaging, and alienating. The face-to-face meetings forced me to reconsider concepts such as empowerment and even 'the Internet' to describe participants' online experience, and seek alternative frameworks to account more adequately for its complexities and subtleties (see Orgad 2004). Thus, explorations of the move from online to offline show that the meanings of online and offline are neither fixed nor singular.

The move from online to offline has another implication. Consideration of the move from offline to online has often centred on what is lost in this transition, and how it is compensated for. Moving the relationship in the opposite direction, as in the case of couples who met online and then moved offline, or researchers who recruited their informants online and then met them face to face, reverses this thinking. As argued in Orgad (2005b: 63), we could equally 'decry the many things we have lost in the move from online to offline, and think of face-to-face inter-action as a form of communication which is rather limited'.

In my research, one of the things that in some cases was lost in the move from online to offline was the interviewees' level of openness and self-disclosure. While the anonymous and disembodied medium encouraged detailed disclosure of intimate experiences of using the Internet in the context of the illness, talking face-to-face made some participants more reticent. Also, the degree of control over the interaction was far more limited for both parties: neither I nor my informants had as much control over the offline interaction as we had had over the email interactions.[5]

The move from online to offline reverses common thinking about the online–offline relationship in yet another way. Common analysis treats the offline as chronologically preceding the online; the offline is perceived as the broader setting that existed before, and can thus explain and contextualize the online phenomenon being studied. For instance, much of the discussion on the performance of gender online usefully analyses online environments and interactions as being fundamen-tally shaped by the broader realities of gender inequities in participants' offline lives and in society at large.[6]

However, when the online is the setting where the relationship between partici-pants initially emerges, and the offline follows chronologically, the online can serve as the broader setting for making sense of the offline. For instance, I first learned about participants' interactions with the Internet through email exchanges and my observation of their forums. The information I obtained online enabled me to explain and contextualize much of the information gleaned later about their illness experience from face-to-face interviews. In particular, I learned that one of the main online activities of participants was looking for similar illness cases. This reflected a more general aspect of coping with illness: the need for reassurance that others have similar problems, and the need to locate oneself in relation to these others.

From online to offline in the study of the Internet and everyday life

Beyond the focus on the migration of specific objects or relations to online space, the concern with the transition from online to offline is at the heart of the enquiry into the role of the Internet in people's everyday lives more generally. It is concerned with how individuals' or groups' online activities affect their offline contexts, identities, and experiences.

Wellman's (1999, 2004; see also Hampton and Wellman 2003) work is a good case in point. It explores the relationship between individuals' connection to the Internet and their online activities, and their levels of loneliness and connectivity in their offline local communities. Rather than isolating users in a virtual world, argues Wellman, the Internet extends communities in the real world; people use it to connect within individualized and flexible social networks. Similarly, Baym (2000: 208) demonstrates how soap opera fans' engagement in an online community influences their involvement in offline communities, fostering an interest, for example, in women's shelters and support for them. She also describes how she herself met people in her local community through the online community she was studying, and formed relationships that allowed her to break through professional and institutional boundaries.

Some of the surveys of the Pew Internet & American Life Project also attempt to show how users' online activities affect their offline lives. For example, seeking health information online affected how individuals managed their health and, more particularly, their offline interactions with doctors and health professionals (Pew Internet & American Life Project 2002, 2005). My study of breast cancer patients' participation in online spaces showed how their online activities, and particularly configuring their experience into a story online (storytelling) — helped them cope with their illness.

However, the effect of online participation on people's offline lives can also be negative or harmful. Kraut et al.'s (1998) study is a highly cited (and criticized) example of Internet use exacerbating depression and loneliness.[7] Viégas (2005) found that a substantial percentage of bloggers have run into legal or professional problems over entries in their blogs. The recent reports on the arrests of bloggers who tried to encourage others to join the riots in France (Jarvis 2005) are one example. Probably the most extreme demonstration of the harmful effects of online participation are the cases of people forming suicide pacts through online chatrooms. Though this may be a quantitatively marginal phenomenon (Rajagopal 2004), it suggests that online participation could have huge consequences for people's identities, experiences, and actions.

4 LIMITATIONS TO STUDIES OF THE TRANSITION BETWEEN THE REALMS

Notwithstanding the merits of discussions about the move from offline to online, and online to offline, and the more refined analyses of the Internet's role in everyday life, they suffer from one major limitation.

Discussion of the move from offline to online or online to offline, to an extent maintains the dualism between the Internet and the everyday, and the separation between online and offline. Even in studies such as Wellman's, which stress the need to consider the Internet as embedded in everyday life, questions about the impact of the Internet on the everyday start from the implicit assumption that the two realms are separate. Wellman analyses the two communicative domains separately, and then establishes the connections between them, for example, the link between being wired or not, and people's informal contacts with neighbours (Hampton and Wellman 2003).

This conceptual and analytical issue is closely related to the influence of Castells approach on Wellman's work. On the one hand, Castells (2001) stresses that the Internet and its use are closely tied to everyday life. On the other hand, his emphasis on the network society as producing disembodied relationships that introduce 'the culture of real virtuality' (Castells 1998: 349), and his opposition between 'the Net' and 'the Self', reinforce a view of the Internet as an autonomous, monolithic, and reified structure, whose impact on society is then investigated (Miller and Slater 2000: 8; van Dijk 1999). This view fails to recognize that social and media networks, including the Internet, are contextually embedded, that is, that they are always connected to their material, organic, social, physical, and biological contexts (Thacker 2004; van Dijk 1999: 134).

However, there are several studies that offer a more complex approach, which acknowledges the interrelations between the online and offline realms, and examines how they are mutually interwoven (or not), and how they may reinforce and/or challenge each other. This subject is discussed in the following section.

5 INTERWEAVING AND EMBEDDEDNESS

Scholars are increasingly recognizing that 'much of what happens in electronic space is deeply inflected by the cultures, the material practices, and the imaginaries that take place outside electronic space' (Sassen 2004: 298). In this context, four approaches are reviewed, which have contributed to this recognition of the embeddedness and intermeshing of the online and the offline, namely: (1) social informatics; (2) the analysis of culture and discourse online; (3) the ethnographic approach to the Internet; and (4) the political economy of new media. This is a selective account of approaches, each focusing on different aspects of the online and offline, illuminating the different ways in which they may interact. These approaches are not mutually exclusive; there are possible overlaps between them, and they should be seen as complementing one another.

Social informatics

Social informatics (SI) has greatly contributed to the study of the embedded nature of information and communication technologies (ICTs). Informed by research and theories on the social shaping of technology, SI examines the role of the social and cultural context of ICT development and use, and the consequences of this context for work, organizations, and social life more broadly (Kling 2000; Kling, Rosenbaum, and Sawyer 2005). SI research does not focus only on the Internet; nor does it explicitly study the interrelations between online and offline. Rather, it looks at the ways in which the technology in use and the social world co-constitute each other. Its contribution to our discussion is in offering an analytical model, which enables researchers to ask contextual questions that locate their inquiry of online-related phenomena in specific times and places, and in relation to specific actors and particular goals. For example, in examining the use of the Internet to seek health information, the SI approach is to ask about the times when people use the Internet for this purpose; the conditions that prompt this activity; the kind of information they seek in varying circumstances; the role the information derived plays in their lives; the life circumstances that lead some people and not others to search for health information online.[8] These kinds of questions help to operationalize and specify the interrelations between online and offline.

However, the SI approach has two limitations for the study of online and offline relations. First, it focuses on technology implementation in design and use, but is not concerned with (and therefore has limited tools to investigate) communicative and discursive practices. My study, for instance, which explored participants' engagement in storytelling online, could generally benefit from the emphasis of SI on contextual inquiry and contingency questions about information technologies and social life. However, SI cannot explain the ways participants' discursive practices, such as storytelling, are embedded within broader social and cultural contexts, for example, public discourses of health and illness. Secondly, SI analyses are heavily oriented to the way technologies relate to their settings. These are often organizational settings where the primary participants are located within a few identifiable institutions (Kling et al. 2000: 15). However, in many studies of CMC environments, the setting in which the communicative space and practices are embedded is not tangible, and is often difficult to locate. In fact, CMC environments are usually not bounded within a specific organization that constitutes their 'social context'. Rather, the researcher must explore and theorize these 'social contexts'. The analysis of discourse, ethnography, and political economy discussed in the sections below, are attempts to identify and theorize 'social contexts' and how they shape, and are shaped by, the online.

The embeddedness of discourse

Analyses of online discourses attempt to explain interactions that occur at a representational level (text) as embedded in broader social and material realities. For example, studies have looked at the Internet as a communicative space embedded within wider public gender discourses that tend to reproduce traditional representations and gendered stereotypes, for instance of women as consumers (Rodino 2003; van Zoonen 2001: 69), and of girls and young women as technologically inept and socially frail (Silver and Garland 2004). Similarly, Orgad (2005a) shows how the colloquy of empowerment, survival, triumphalism, and the exclusion of expressions of despair that govern breast cancer online spaces, are significantly shaped by wider public discourses of the disease in the media, and in the rhetoric of national and international health systems.

The study of the embeddedness of online discourse within broader offline contexts emphasizes the connections and continuities between online and offline. At the same time, online discourses and behaviour can challenge offline discourses. For example, Silver and Garland (2004: 168) discuss how offline discourses are being resisted by actual patterns of online communication and Internet use: 'Although advertisements portray American female teen cyberculture as an activity firmly focused on consumption, their actual use is quite diverse and favors communication, entertainment, and information seeking over commerce'. This contradiction between offline representations and online patterns of communication does not mean, however, that the online and offline are two separate realms, and that teen online cultures are detached from public discourses and teenagers' popular constructions. Rather, what Silver and Garland (2004) describe as resistance to offline (advertising) representations can be seen as the other side of embeddedness. That is, the cultures and spaces that girls and young women create online respond to offline cultures and discourses through resistance. Thus, rather than being a self-contained space where 'teen cyberculture' is formed, female teen online cultures should be understood in terms of their (resistant) relation to wider (offline) cultures and discourses.

Ethnography

Methodologically, the commitment to explore the interface between online and offline has led some researchers, such as Wilson and Atkinson (2005), to conduct ethnographies. The premise of an ethnographic approach, as Miller and Slater (2000) posit, is not only that the online and the offline shed light on one another, but that one cannot be understood without the other; the online is seen as embedded in specific offline places, which it in turn transforms.

Wilson and Atkinson's (2005) analysis of the Internet youth cultures of 'Rave' and 'Straighthedge' in Canada highlights that as much as the online is embedded within the offline, so too are aspects of offline subcultural communities influenced by online participation. Similarly, studies of global activism and political action online (e.g. Bennett 2003; Carty 2002) show how the construction of offline relationships among activists as a globally oriented community are largely facilitated and influenced by their online activities.

Exploring the mutual influence of online and offline cultures implies a more complex and holistic approach than that suggested by studies of the move from one realm to another. Rather than focusing on either their online or offline manifestations, or the effect of online on offline, this approach examines the ways in which online and offline elements intermesh and intersect in a particular context, such as members' practice of their subcultural lifestyles (Wilson and Atkinson 2005).

Sanders' (2005) study of the sex workers' community in Britain demonstrates the usefulness of a holistic ethnographic approach to the study of the relationship between online and offline realms. Sanders does not simply ask how sex workers use or appropriate the Internet (online) in their work (offline). Rather, she treats the sex worker community holistically, as a culture whose members manage their actions and interactions, through various media, including the Internet. The Internet plays an important role in transforming their work culture, facilitating, for instance, interaction between sex workers who work in secrecy and are isolated from colleagues (Sanders 2005: 69).

An ethnographic holistic approach invites a multi-layered research design, which includes both online and offline components. Sanders (2005) started her ethnography offline, later turned to the Internet to collect online data, and then realized that in order to fully understand the role of the Internet in sustaining the identities of sex workers, she needed to move back offline to recruit participants who use the Internet for face-to-face interviews. Miller and Slater (2000) also conducted an ethnographic study of the Internet in Trinidad, in offline settings such as Internet cafés, and online spaces such as the chatroom 'de Rumshop Lime' and the Miss Universe website, through which Trinidadians construct and represent their 'Trininess'.

Political economy

Like SI the political economy of communication is interested in the varying situated contexts in which ICTs are being developed and experienced. Both fields examine the choices made by social actors about the design of, and engagement with, new technologies (Mansell 2005). One important contribution of the political economy approach is the articulation of power and its embeddedness in socio-technical systems such as ICTs.[9] The political economy of new media rejects any detachment of what the Internet means and the actors for whom it has meaning, from the structures and processes of power (Mansell 2004), and emphasizes the need to understand the choices of social actors as being highly situated in specific offline contexts and embedded in values and perceptions of power (Mansell 2004; 2005).

The critical contribution to the study of the Internet, and specifically the relationship between the online and offline, is political economy's insistence on the online space not as simply textual or representational, but as material. For example, in *Protocol: How Control Exists after Decentralization* (Galloway 2004), by looking closely at the technical specifications of Transmission Control Protocol/ Internet Protocol (TCP/IP) and Domain Name System (DNS), and regarding networks as a set of technical procedures for defining, managing, modulating, and distributing information throughout a delivery infrastructure, the author demonstrates how power and control are shaping the experience of online partici- pation and the nature of these participatory spaces: how participation is subjected to surveillance and managed by codes, standards, and regulatory bodies. Similarly, studies of linking on the web (Walker 2002), and search engines (Introna and Nissenbaum 2000; Van Couvering 2005), challenge the view of online space as neutral, equally accessible, and decentralized, highlighting the structures of power that shape Internet sites, practices, and developments.

In short, understanding online as a fundamentally material realm, underscores from the outset the inseparability of online from offline. The point of departure for a political economy analysis is not that there is online and we need to add the offline to make sense of the former, but rather that the online is already inscribed into material realities. In a sense, from a political economy perspective the distinc- tion between the online and offline does not exist.

The other contribution of critical political economy is the importance it gives to historical processes, particularly late capitalism, that set the stage for the online context being studied (Golding and Murdock 1991; Webster 1995: 75). For instance, how the changing role of state and government intervention—from ARPA to DARPA to dot.coms (Thacker 2004: xv)—has shaped online space as we know it today.[10] A political economy approach would ask: what are the specific historical circumstances under which new media and communications products and services are produced under capitalism, and what is the influence of these circumstances over their consumption? (see Mansell 2004). The implication is that the relation- ship between the online and offline has to be understood historically, and needs to be located in a specific time. In my study, accounting for the historical absence of a communicative infrastructure for breast cancer patients to talk to each other, was crucial for acknowledging the meaning and value of contemporary online spaces as therapeutic public spaces for patients' communication.

6 METHODOLOGICAL IMPLICATIONS

To acknowledge the complex relationship between online and offline is to invite researchers to problematize their methods and rethink the boundaries of the fields and the objects that they study. Even if the object of study is located online, researchers need to ground their investigations in, and take stock of the material context and the broader structures within which it is situated. The boundaries of the field cannot be sustained exclusively online; the methods and the analysis need to allow room for consideration of the intersections between online and offline. This will be achieved only if claims about the Internet and its meanings are anchored in rigorous empirical work, and if we bear in mind, as Miller and Slater (2000: 1) contend, that 'the Internet as a meaningful phenomenon only exists in particular places'. Equally, studying offline contexts without reference to or consideration of an online component is problematic and limited. In this context, Beaulieu (2004) exhorts anthropologists to follow their subjects online.

In my research into the online communication of women suffering from breast cancer (Orgad 2005a), employing both online and offline methods, and obtaining both online and offline data regarding participants' lives and experiences, were crucial for making sense of the Internet phenomenon that I was studying. In order to understand patients' online contexts, it was necessary to know about their offline contexts, that is, of the everyday aspects of coping with breast cancer. This information was obtained mainly through face-to-face interviews. Similarly, to make sense of patients' experience of breast cancer (offline), it was necessary to understand their online engagement, which played a significant part in their experience of managing their illness. This was achieved through textual analysis of related websites, and e-mail interviews.

The recognition that online life cannot be investigated as an integral and coherent culture in its own right has encouraged researchers to extend the boundaries of 'virtual ethnography', and investigate the connections and intersections between online and offline (e.g. Boczkowski 2004; Miller and Slater 2000; Wilson and Atkinson 2005).[11] Indeed, challenging the online–offline distinction requires us also to think about innovative and creative methods that move beyond bounded sites, and trace connections and movements between online and offline contexts. Leander and McKim (2003) stress the need to develop a methodology that follows participants' practices of moving between online and offline, and involves a wider and more hybrid mediascape. In their analysis of adolescents' Internet practices, the authors develop the concept of 'siting' to trace participants' experiences across online and offline spaces. More efforts in this direction are needed.

Another methodological implication of the disruption of the online–offline distinction is related to authenticity. The online was often seen as less authentic (or inauthentic) than the offline, a depiction fuelled by the focus on identity play and deception that occurs online. As a consequence, the data obtained by virtual methods, for example participant observation in Internet spaces, has been often considered less truthful and valid than data obtained offline. Breaking down the online–offline dualism abolishes the notion that an analysis based on online data is less authentic or valid. In gathering offline data the aim should be not to introduce some external criteria for judging whether it is safe to believe what informants say (Hine 2000: 49), but to add context, to enhance information, and to yield insights into aspects that would otherwise remain invisible, but which are consequential to the research (Orgad, forthcoming). Researchers should be guided by the particular research contexts and the demands of their research goals, and not some general presuppositions about the nature of the online and offline environments.

7 Conclusion: Emerging challenges and opportunities for future research

Against the mid-1990s celebration of the disappearance of life's materiality 'into the weightlessness of cyberspacetime' (Nguyen and Alexander 1996: 102), the effort to disrupt the online–offline distinction highlights the importance of recognizing the material in even the most dematerialized and digitized activities (Sassen 2004: 299). Online spaces, products, services, and interactions are fundamentally integrated into social everyday life, and thus must be understood within this context.

The online–offline distinction is a conceptual, analytical, and methodological device, which is part of what Robins (1996: 26) calls 'the mythology of cyberspace': a view of online space and virtual reality as separated from social reality and from physical and localized existences. The way to disrupt the online–offline distinctions and achieve a critical understanding of Internet practices is to abandon the mythology of cyberspace and advance the sociology of the Internet (Robins 1996). A sociological enquiry of the Internet converges with a significantly different set of agendas to those characterizing the (mythological) online–offline distinction.

First, while the online–offline distinction was underpinned by an ethos of freedom and lack of governance that supposedly characterizes cyberspace (Slater 2002), the sociology of the Internet brings to the fore issues of power, highlighting the limits and constraints that cannot be simply escaped online. Studying the Internet sociologically and critically means recognizing that the online space is structured and fundamentally embedded within 'sited materialities' (Sassen 2004) and is not fluid, free, and ungoverned. Secondly, and closely related to the first point, a sociology of the Internet emphasizes the ongoing significance of the material world and its economic relations and flows (Sassen 2004), even in the case of the most dematerialized economic relations and flows: i.e. how, despite enthusiasm for the novelty of online news and its potential to radically challenge the realities of offline newspapers, the distribution of online newspapers often follows the pattern of uneven development of geographical regions (He and Zhu 2002). Thirdly, if early writing on the Internet has been characterized by a fascination with identity play and the deconstruction of authentic identities, a sociology of the Internet emphasizes the realness and the embeddedness of this space and the identities performed in it. Participants' most deconstructed 'unreal' online identities can still be strongly connected to their offline selves.

Recognizing the embeddedness of online within offline, and their intermeshing also demands a 'historicization' of the analysis of new media. The virtual is never ahistorical; it develops under specific historical circumstances and is embedded within a particular historical context that shapes its structure and nature.

In fact, it might prove fruitful to abandon the online–offline terminology, and talk instead of spaces and processes of mediation. An account of mediation looks at what happens *between* the online and the offline, and more generally between technology and society (Miller and Slater 2000: 8, based on Latour 1991). It urges a move away from the qualities of virtual versus body-to-body communication, a concern raised earlier in relation to older media such as the telephone (Marvin 1988) and the radio (Peters 1999). Alternatively, drawing on Silverstone (2005), thinking about Internet and CMC in terms of mediation requires us to understand how processes of CMC shape society and culture, and the relationships that participants, both individual and institutional, have with their environment and with each other. At the same time such an analysis requires consideration of how the Internet and the meanings that are delivered by it are appropriated through reception and consumption.

Analysis of mediation is likely to marginalize the Internet as an object of study. Instead, it demands a broader focus on a communicative space. In this space, the Internet may have a role, but certainly not an exclusive or even necessarily a primary one. Furthermore, as the space of media and communication becomes more hybrid and multi-layered, and with the increasing trend towards the convergence of technology, the lines between online and offline communication are blurring (Herring 2004; Slater 2002).

The Internet, like electric communication in the late nineteenth century, has been seen as embracing 'distinct and self-contained codes or spheres of interpretive activity' (Marvin 1988: 7). However, as scholars have increasingly acknowledged, and I have argued in this chapter, this view cannot be sustained. Instead, it may be useful to adapt Marvin's lesson on old media to the study of new media, and to think about the Internet and online communication as 'constructed complexes of habits, beliefs and procedures embedded in elaborate cultural codes of communication'

(Marvin 1988: 8). It is in the intersections, overlaps, and contradictions between media, technologies, and society that the significance lies.

REFERENCES

BAKER, A. (1998). 'Cyberspace Couples Finding Love Online then Meeting for the First Time in Real Life', http://oak.cats.ohiou.edu/~bakera/ArticleC.htm, accessed 20 Oct. 2006.

BAKOS, Y. (2001). 'The Emerging Landscape for Retail E-Commerce'. *Journal of Economic Perspectives*, 15(1): 69–80.

BAUSINGER, H. (1984). 'Media, Technology and Everyday Life'. *Media, Culture & Society*, 6(4): 343–52.

BAYM, N. K. (2000). *Tune in, Log on: Soap, Fandom, and Online Community*. London: Sage.

BEAULIEU, A. (2004). 'Mediating Ethnography: Objectivity and the Making of Ethnographies of the Internet'. *Social Epistemology*, 18(2–3): 139–63.

BEN-NER, A. and PUTTERMAN, L. (2002). 'Trust in the New Economy', *HRRI Working Paper 11-02*, University of Minnesota, Industrial Relations Centre, ideas.repec.org/p/hrr/papers/1102.htm, accessed 20 Oct. 2006.

BENNETT, W. L. (2003). 'Communicating Global Activism: Strengths and Vulnerabilities of Networked Politics'. *Information, Communication & Society*, 6(2): 143–68.

BOCZKOWSKI, P. J. (2004). *Digitizing the News: Innovation in Online Newspapers*. Cambridge, MA: MIT Press.

CAMMAERTS, B. and CARPENTIER, N. (2005). 'The Unbearable Lightness of Full Participation in a Global Context: WSIS and Civil Society Participation', Media@LSE Electronic Working Paper 8.

CARTY, V. (2002). 'Technology and Counter-Hegemonic Movements: The Case of Nike Corporations'. *Social Movement Studies*, 1(2): 129–46.

CASTELLS, M. (1998). *The Information Age: Economy, Society and Culture, Vol. III: End of Millennium*. Oxford: Blackwell.

—— (2001). *The Internet Galaxy: Reflections on the Internet, Business and Society*. Oxford: Oxford University Press.

CAWSON, A., HADDON, L. and MILES, I. (1995). *The Shape of Things to Consume: Delivering Information Technology Into the Home*. Aldershot: Avebury.

EICHHORN, K. (2001). 'Sites Unseen: Ethnographic Research in a Textual Community'. *Qualitative Studies in Education*, 14(4): 565–78.

GAJJALA, R. (2002). 'An Interrupted Postcolonial/Feminist Cyberethnography: Complicity and Resistance in the "Cyberfield"'. *Feminist Media Studies*, 2(2): 177–93.

GALLOWAY, A. R. (2004). *Protocol: How Control Exists after Decentralization*. Cambridge, MA: MIT Press.

GIBBS, J. L. and KRAEMER, K. L. (2004). 'A Cross-Country Investigation of the Determinants of Scope of E-commerce Use: An Institutional Approach'. *Electronic Markets*, 14(2): 124–37.

GOLDING, P. and MURDOCK, G. (1991). 'Culture, Communication and Political Economy', in J. Curran and M. Gurevitch (eds), *Mass Media and Society*. London: Edward Arnold, 15–32.

HALAVAIS, A. (2000). 'National Borders on the World Wide Web'. *New Media & Society*, 1(3): 7–28.

HAMPTON, K. and WELLMAN, B. (2003). 'Neighboring in Netville: How the Internet Supports Community and Social Capital in a Wired Suburb'. *City and Community*, 2(4): 277–311.

HAYTHORNTHWAITE, C. and WELLMAN, B. (2002). 'The Internet in Everyday Life: An Introduction', in B. Wellman and C. Haythornwaite (eds), *The Internet in Everyday Life*. Oxford: Blackwell, 3–41.

HE, Z. and ZHU, J. (2002). 'The Ecology of Online Newspapers: The Case of China'. *Media, Culture and Society*, 24(1): 121–37.

HERRING, S. C. (2004). 'Slouching Toward the Ordinary: Current Trends in Computer-Mediated Communication'. *New Media & Society*, 6(1): 26–36.

HINE, C. (2000). *Virtual Ethnography*. London: Sage.

INTRONA, L. D. and NISSENBAUM, H. (2000). 'Shaping the Web: Why the Politics of Search Engines Matters'. *The Information Society*, 16(3): 169–85.

JARVIS, J. (2005). 'Chaos Spreads from the Web to the Streets'. The *Guardian*, 14 Nov. Media Section, 3.

KENDALL, L. (2002). *Hanging Out in the Virtual Pub: Masculinities and Relationships Online*. Berkeley, CA: University of California Press.

KHIABANY, G. (2003). 'Globalization and the Internet: Myths and Realities'. *Trends in Communication*, 11(2): 137–53.

KLING, R. (2000). 'Learning About Information Technologies and Social Change: The Contribution of Social Informatics'. *The Information Society*, 16(3): 217–32.

——, CRAWFORD, H., ROSENBAUM, H. et al. (2000). 'Learning from Social Informatics: Information and Communication Technologies in Human Contexts', *The Center for Social Informatics*, http://rkcsi.indiana.edu/media/SI_report.pdf, accessed 20 Oct. 2006.

——, ROSENBAUM, H. and SAWYER, S. (2005). *Understanding and Communication Social Informatics: A Framework for Studying and Teaching the Human Contexts of Information and Communication Technologies*. New York: Information Today Inc.

KRAUT, R. E., KEISLER, S., BONEVA, B., et al. (2002). 'Internet Paradox Revisited'. *Journal of Social Issues*, 58(1): 49–74.

——, PATTERSON, M., LUNDMARK, V., et al. (1998). 'Internet Paradox: A Social Technology that Reduces Social Involvement and Psychological Well-Being?' *American Psychologist*, 53(9): 1017–32.

LATOUR, B. (1991). 'Technology is Society Made Durable', in J. Law (ed.), *A Sociology of Monsters: Essays on Power, Technology and Domination*. London: Routledge, 103–31.

LEANDER, K. M. and McKIM, K. K. (2003). 'Tracing the Everyday "Sitings" of Adolescents on the Internet: A Strategic Adaptation of Ethnography Across Online and Offline Spaces'. *Education, Communication & Information*, 3(2): 211–40.

McCHESNEY, R. (2000). 'So Much for the Magic of Technology and the Free Market: The World Wide Web and the Corporate Media System', in A. Herman and T. Swiss (eds), *The World Wide Web and Contemporary Cultural Theory*. London: Routledge, 5–35.

MANSELL, R. (2004). 'Political Economy, Power and New Media'. *New Media & Society*, 6(1): 96–105.

—— (2005). 'Social Informatics and the Political Economy of Communications', *Information Technology and People*, 18(1): 21–5.

MARKHAM, A. N. (1998). *Life Online: Researching Real Experience in Virtual Space*. Walnut Creek, CA: Altamira Press.

MARVIN, C. (1988). *When Old Technologies Were New: Thinking About Electric Communication in the Late Nineteenth Century.* Oxford: Oxford University Press.

MATHESON, D. (2004). 'Weblogs and the Epistemology of the News: Some Trends in Online Journalism'. *New Media & Society*, 6(4): 443–68.

MEIKLE, G. (2002). *Future Active: Media Activism and the Internet.* London: Routledge and Sydney: Pluto Press.

MESCH, G. (ed.) (2006). 'E-Relationships: The Blurring and Reconfiguration of Offline and Online Social Boundaries', SI of *Information, Communication and Society*, 9(6).

MILLER, D. and SLATER, D. (2000). *The Internet: An Ethnographic Approach.* Oxford: Berg.

NAKAYAMA, M. (2000). 'E-commerce and Firm Bargaining Power Shift in Grocery Marketing Channels: A Case of Wholesalers' Structured Document Exchanges'. *Journal of Information Technology*, 15(3): 195–210.

NGUYEN D. T. and ALEXANDER, J. (1996). 'The Coming of Cyberspace Time and the End of the Polity', in R. Shields (ed.), *Cultures of Internet: Virtual Spaces, Real Histories, Living Bodies.* Thousand Oaks, CA: Sage, 99–124.

NIEMAN REPORTS (2003). 'Weblogs and Journalism', http://www.nieman.harvard.edu/reports/03-3NRfall/V57N3.pdf, accessed 12 Dec. 2005.

ORGAD, S. (2004). 'The Use of the Internet in the Lives of Women with Breast Cancer: Narrating and Storytelling Online and Offline'. Unpub. Ph.D. thesis, London School of Economics.

—— (2005a). *Storytelling Online: Talking Breast Cancer on the Internet.* New York: Peter Lang.

—— (2005b). 'From Online to Offline and Back: Moving from Online to Offline Relationships with Research Informants', in C. Hine (ed.), *Virtual Methods: Issues in Social Research on the Internet.* Oxford: Berg, 51–65.

—— (forthcoming). 'How Does a Researcher Grapple With the Issues of Online versus Offline Data in the Qualitative Internet Research Project?', in A. Markham and N. K. Baym (eds), *Qualitative Internet Inquiry: A Dialogue Among Researchers.* Thousand Oaks, CA: Sage.

PAN, G. S. C. and FLYNN, D. (2003). 'Gaining Knowledge from Post-Mortem Analyses to Eliminate Electronic Commerce Project Abandonment', in T. Thanasankit (ed.), *E-commerce and Cultural Values.* Hershey, PA: Idea Group, 108–25.

PETERS, J. D. (1999). *Speaking Into the Air: A History of the Idea of Communication.* Chicago, IL: Chicago University Press.

PEW INTERNET & AMERICAN LIFE PROJECT (2002). 'Vital Decisions', Washington, http://www.pewinternet.org/, accessed 25 Mar. 2006.

—— (2005). 'Health Information Online', Washington, http://www.pewinternet.org/, accessed 25 Mar. 2006.

RAJAGOPAL, S. (2004). 'Suicide Pacts and the Internet'. *British Medical Journal*, 329(7478): 1298–9.

ROBINS, K. (1996). 'Cyberspace and the World We Live In', in J. Dovey (ed.) *Fractal Dreams: New Media in Social Context.* London: Lawrence and Wishard, 1–30.

RUSSELL, A. (2001). 'The Zapatistas Online: Shifting the Discourse of Globalization'. *Gazette*, 63(5): 399–413.

RODINO, M. (2003). 'Mobilizing Mother'. *Feminist Media Studies*, 3(3): 375–77.

SANDERS, T. (2005). 'Researching the Online Sex Work Community', in C. Hine (ed.), *Virtual Methods: Issues in Social Research on the Internet.* Oxford: Berg, 67–79.

SASSEN, S. (2004). 'Sited Materialities with Global Span', in P. N. Howard and S. Jones (eds), *Society Online: The Internet in Context.* London: Sage, 295–306.

SCHAAP, F. (2002). *The Words that Took Us There: Ethnography in a Virtual Reality*. Somerset, NJ: Transaction Publishers.

SCHOFIELD, C. L. (1998). 'Dating on the Net: Teens and the Rise of "Pure" Relationships', in S. Jones (ed.) *Cybersociety 2.0: Revisiting Computer-Mediated Communication and Community*. Thousand Oaks, CA: Sage, 159–83.

SILVER, D. and GARLAND, P. (2004). 'sHoP onLiNE!', in P. N. Howard and S. Jones (eds), *Society Online: The Internet in Context*. London: Sage, 157–71.

SILVERSTONE, R. (1994). *Television and Everyday Life*. London: Routledge.

—— (2005). 'Mediation and Communication', in C. Calhoun, C. Rojek and B. S. Turner (eds.), *The International Handbook of Sociology*. London: Sage, 188–207.

SLATER, D. (2002). 'Social Relationships and Identity Online and Offline', in L. Lievrouw and S. Livingstone (eds), *The Handbook of New Media*. London: Sage, 534–47.

STEINFELD, C. (2004). 'Situated Electronic Commerce: Toward a View as Complement Rather than Substitute for Offline Commerce'. *Urban Geography*, 25(4): 353–71.

STREBINGER, A. and TREIBLMAIER, H. (2004). 'E-Adequate Branding: Building Offline and Online Brand Structure within a Polygon of Interdependent Forces'. *Electronic Markets*, 14(2): 153–64.

SVENINGSSON, M. (2002). 'Cyberlove: Creating Romantic Relationships on the Net', in J. Fornäs, K. Klein, M. Ladendorf, et al. (eds), *Digital Borderlands: Cultural Studies of Identity and Interactivity on the Internet*. New York: Peter Lang, 48–78.

THACKER, E. (2004). 'Protocol Is as Protocol Does', in A. R. Galloway, *Protocol: How Control Exists after Decentralization*. Cambridge, MA: MIT Press, xi–xxii.

THANASANKIT, T. (2003). *E-commerce and Cultural Values*. Hershey, PA: Idea Group.

TURKLE, S. (1996). *Life on the Screen: Identity in the Age of the Internet*. London: Weidenfeld & Nicolson.

VAN AELST, P. and WALGRAVE, S. (2002). 'New Media, New Movements? The Role of the Internet in Shaping the "Anti-Globalization" Movement'. *Information, Communication and Society*, 5 (4): 465–93.

VAN COUVERING, E. (2004). 'New Media? The Political Economy of Internet Search Engines'. Presented at the Annual Conference of the International Association of Media & Communications Researchers, Porto Alegre, Brazil, 25–30 July.

VAN DIJK, A. G. M. (1999). 'The One-Dimensional Network Society of Manuel Castells'. *New Media & Society*, 1(1): 127–38.

VAN ZOONEN, L. (2001). 'Feminist Internet Studies'. *Feminist Media Studies*, 1(1): 67–72.

VIÉGAS, F. (2005). 'Blog Survey: Expectations of Privacy and Accountability: An Initial Survey'. *Journal of Computer-Mediated Communication*, 10(3): art. 12.

WALKER, J. (2002). 'Links and Power: The Political Economy of Linking on the Web', proceedings of ACM Hypertext conference, Baltimore, http://huminf.uib.no/~jill/txt/linksandpower.html, accessed 20 Oct. 2006.

WALLACE, P. (2001). *The Psychology of the Internet*. Cambridge: Cambridge University Press.

WEBSTER, F. (1995). *Theories of the Information Society*. London: Routledge.

WELLMAN, B. (1999). 'The Network Community', in B. Wellman (ed.), *Networks in the Global Village*. Boulder, CO: Westview, 1–48.

—— (2004). 'Connecting Communities: On and Offline'. *Contexts*, 3(4): 22–8.

WILSON, B. and ATKINSON, M. (2005). 'Rave and Straightedge, The Virtual and the Real: Exploring Online and Offline Experiences in Canadian Youth Subcultures'. *Youth and Society*, 36(3): 276–311.

NOTES

1. In this sense, the discussion of the online–offline interrelation follows the rich work on media (mainly television) and everyday life (e.g. Bausinger 1984; Cawson, Haddon and Miles 1995; Silverstone 1994), which has contributed to understanding and the critical evaluation of the social significance of media and communication technologies.
2. There are, of course, many more areas where the move from offline to online has occurred, including political activities, education and learning.
3. See (Orgad 2005b) for possible explanations for this contradiction.
4. The authors also acknowledge the benefits of this platform, but this discussion is beyond the scope of this chapter.
5. Arguably, if we had communicated in online synchronous settings, for instance Internet Relay Chats, we would have had less control over our online interactions.
6. On this issue see also Slater (2002: 544).
7. Kraut and colleagues revisited their work in a later study (Kraut et al. 2002), which produced contrasting findings.
8. Based on Kling's (2000: 218–19) discussion of the example of Internet courses.
9. This is not to suggest that SI analyses do not account for questions of power, but rather that these are not usually their explicit concern.
10. ARPA (Advanced Research Projects Agency); DARPA (Defense Research Projects Agency), both US.
11. This is not to suggest that we necessarily need offline methods, and information obtained offline to be able to adequately account for participants' online experiences. It depends on the questions being asked and the specific context being studied. While it might be more sensible and context-sensitive to seek access to online and offline data, this is not always essential (see Orgad forthcoming).

CHAPTER 23

ICTs AND POLITICAL MOVEMENTS

JOHN D. H. DOWNING

LISA BROOTEN

1 INTRODUCTION[*]

WE live in a world of extremely rapid social change, but one in which the structures
that perpetuate profound and widespread social injustice seem impervious. Nonetheless, other worlds and directions, as the *altermondialiste*/global social justice
movement insists, are not beyond human wit and wisdom. The vital question is
how to get within hailing distance of them, since travelling the largely uncharted
territory in their direction is also at one and the same time the only practical way to
begin to visualize them, discuss them, and test them out through prefigurative
projects embedded in political movements. Political movements (Right or Left)
cannot however exist without communication processes, internal and external.
Communication technologies, despite their huge corporate, military, and surveillance applications, also afford opportunities within political movements to debate,

* Our thanks go to Clemencia Rodríguez, Cao Yong, Robin Mansell, the late Roger Silverstone, and
an anonymous reviewer for their help in preparing this chapter.

mobilize, reflect, imagine, fantasize, critique, archive, and inform, and will be pivotal to developing a future for humans rather than for capital.

In this chapter we focus on some possibilities offered by three such technologies, radio, the Internet and the mobile phone, to political movements. We provide a variety of illustrations of their uses and applications in social struggles, large and small. First, however, we dwell briefly on some of the issues and concepts in the air at the time of writing, which we think may help to frame and thus interpret the specifics.

2 Issues and concepts

Much recent writing on the democratic or community-building potential of information and communication technologies (ICTs) has fetishized the Internet, some of it as wildly optimistic as were earlier forecasts concerning a whole series of now familiar communication technologies. We will not pause to dismantle that discourse here, as its moment has largely passed. Furthermore, by including radio along with newer WiFi and Internet technologies, we evidently set ourselves at odds with the fetishism of the latest machine (which is at the same time an implicit dismissal of the needs of the global poor). For despite the growing accessibility of mobile phones and the Internet, for much of the world's population, radio continues to be the crucial communication tool, quite closely followed by street theatre (Gumucio Dagron 2001).

Nonetheless, as already affirmed, ICTs present us with democratic opportunities. We do not have in mind the sphere of liberal democracy's formal procedures, but rather the turbulent, unpredictable world of social movements and their forms of mobilization, which may engage with particular nodes within formal democratic structures, but are in no way subsumed by them. Let us then summarize our definitions of social movements and political mobilization, and also of three other concepts: *Öffentlichkeit* (public sphere),[1] counter-hegemony, and civil society, which have figured largely in debates about ICTs and the expansion of democracy.

The research literature on social movements and political mobilization has exploded since the early 1990s (for summaries see McDonald 2002 and Tarrow 2005), and has certainly left far behind older, elite-originated notions of 'the mob' and 'the crowd'. It has largely bifurcated into studies of resource mobilization and political opportunity structures, in which movements are perceived no longer as mobs but rather as 'rational actors' drawing upon the resources at their disposal (strikes, occupations, the state's openness to social protest, etc.), and studies of collective identity, where supposedly the defining characteristic of a contemporary social movement is its generation of a valued collective self (feminists, peace activists, environmentalists), rather than specific objectives to be wrestled from the power structure, such as the eight-hour day. This latter position is generally termed the New Social Movements (NSM) approach. However, it suffers from the academic tunnel-vision syndrome, seeing only what its chosen lens permits. Feminists want good and affordable childcare facilities, not just a state of mind. It also suffers from Occidentocentrism. The South African anti-apartheid movement and the Brazilian Landless Farmworkers' Movement are but two major recent social movements that did not fit the NSM frame.[2]

As many critics have also observed, the adjective new implies an evolutionary shift, not unlike the term 'postmodernity'. For example, McDonald's (2002) analysis of contemporary direct action protest in Australia and the US, while perceptive in many ways, falls into an implicit evolutionary trap. He identifies 'network society', à la Castells (1996), as current reality rather than concept, and then proceeds to specify a culture of 'immediacy'/'simultaneity'/'fluidarity' [sic] (McDonald 2002: 11) now supposedly characterizing the present epoch: 'a new grammar of action is emerging...a shared struggle for personal experience' (McDonald 2002: 124, 125). His interviewees' cited comments echo this view, but somehow the shared reason for their participation in protests against structured global injustice vanishes along the way and the exercise almost becomes one of finding themselves. Some participants may indeed think and feel precisely thus, but in his relief at current activists' dismissal of old leftist utopias McDonald appears to glide past the semi-structured utopia of *altermondialisme*, that other worlds are possible even though as yet unrealizable and only vaguely definable, more easily specified by what will *not* characterize them than by what *will*. Like NSM analysts, and despite his commitment to avoiding rigid categories, his argument ends up by fastening its teeth into his own perception of the new and then extrapolating from it.

In short, the protean qualities of social movements mean especially that they repeatedly erupt beyond the confines of our categories. This does not mean we should give up on categorizing, only that the task is particularly complex and demands considerable caution and comparative research. Nonetheless, movements' uses of ICTs are particularly important, even though mainstream social movement research literature, paradoxically, to date spends rather little time on them.

We should also note that social movements are not necessarily positive, nor a post-socialist *deus ex machina* substituting for the Leninist working class and its organized revolutionary party. Fascism was a political movement, the Klu Klux Klan in its multiple heydays was a political movement, rightist Christian fundamentalism in the US and Latin America is a political movement. 'Protean', as a characterization of social movements, does not exaggerate.

Lastly, there has been a focus in recent research on the issue of mobilization, with ongoing debates especially in the journals *Mobilization* and *Social Movement Studies*. One of the paradoxes of this literature is relatively how little of it includes attention to communication media or issues in popular culture.[3] The following summary by Tarrow of what he sees as the multi-disciplinarity of social movement research illustrates the problem:

> Political economists and economic sociologists offered the broadest vision, emphasizing global capitalism, countermovements, and the shifting arenas of conflict from the local to the global level. New-institutional sociologists provided a broad picture of trends in global culture, focusing on the growth of international organizations and the diffusion of Western 'rationalizing' values. At the other extreme of generality, anthropologists and students of global public opinion were beginning to track the impact of global trends on local actors, while scholars of international politics provided precious information on transnational advocacy networks and on how nonstate actors interacted with powerful international financial institutions like the World Bank, the IMF, and the WTO. Finally, advocates of global civil society offered stimulating proposals... with one or another version of 'globalization from below'. (Tarrow 2005: 65–6)

As one of us has written elsewhere (Downing 1996: 1, 18–27), approaches of these conventional social science kinds, despite all they have to offer, are always liable to portray social movement actors as astute, but mute pieces on a chessboard. The texture of social movement actors' ongoing engagement with each other, the ways in which they research, share, and archive information relevant to their goals, the impact of mainstream media coverage on their tactics and strategies, their deployment of their own media and other cultural forms, such as street theatre, hacktivism, or culture-jamming, the communication problems and achievements of organizing international protest strategies, all more or less disappear from view. Mische (2004) is one of the few recent voices from those quarters to have proposed intensive attention to what she terms the 'culture-network link'.

We may now proceed much more briefly to establish our own working definitions of *Öffentlichkeit*, counter-hegemony, and civil society. By *Öffentlichkeit*, originally coined by Jürgen Habermas, we mean the process of public debate. This also includes the realities both that this process operates in multiple spheres (Bastien and Neveu 1999), and that it is a process ever more colonized by huge communication corporations, advertisers, and government public relations operations. These corporations include, by now perhaps self-evidently, Microsoft, Google, Lexis Nexis, and other Internet giants.

Counter-hegemony is a term that was never used by Gramsci, but is one that derives from hegemony in its Gramscian sense, though without his evolutionist vision. We use the master-term to mean the cumulative emergence over decades and centuries of multi-faceted national cultures of mass political consent—cultures that are not rigid carapaces, or mutually interchangeable, but which shift and develop over time and whose weave may be rent apart and even disintegrate at times of social crisis. This is why they constantly interact with the disciplinary force of state coercion. Socially, these cultures of consent are generated, sustained, repaired, reformulated, and communicate themselves through an array of religious, educational, mediatic, military, sporting, and other organisms, exhibiting myriad, shifting, often contradictory, processes.

Counter-hegemony, then, covers attempts to dislodge and disrupt the sway of the status quo, although its actual use is often no more than a synonym for 'oppositional' or 'resistive' to a particular government or policy (Carty 2002), and does not engage with the deeper questions of ideological saturation addressed by Gramsci's *egemonia*. Given the historical sedimentation and multi-faceted character of the hegemonic process, such small, local upsurges might be thought to be tilting at windmills, trivial pinpricks at best. And indeed, so some are. Yet in riposte however, the very acceleration of change characteristic of capitalism and now evident on a truly global scale, continually generates newly dissonant energies and opens up fresh scenarios for political contestation.

Over the years, *Öffentlichkeit*, too, has been extended to address contestatory debate, or *Gegenöffentlichkeit* (counter public sphere). The proletarian public sphere (Negt and Kluge 1972/1993), alternative public spheres (Downing 1988), counter public spheres (Fraser 1993), are a variety of the ways in which this has been done. The small media of diasporic groups are another quasi-contestatory or at least dissonant zone, which has attracted researchers' attention (Riggins 1992; Naficy 1993, 2001; Cunningham and Sinclair 2002; Karim 2003). The notions of counter-hegemonic and/or alternative public sphere activity, in turn leach into the final concept to be addressed here, namely 'civil society'.

Civil society had quite different meanings in the works of earlier European philosophers (Locke, Kant, Hegel, Marx), ranging, for example, from the attempt to contrast disciplined social organization among humans with what was seen as brutish animal life, to the distinction between economic and political life. As one might still use the now-discredited term 'Third World' solely for convenience, here we use civil society to signify a collection of highly disparate entities, activities, projects, and ongoing protests, which have in common only that to a greater or lesser extent they overlap partially with, or feed off, social movements, and are not state or corporate entities. Today this grab-bag term is global in scope. It does not, however, in our usage equate with global non-governmental organizations (NGOs), despite the error made by far too many researchers of mistaking the part (NGOs) for the whole (the global justice movement). That equation would in reality tilt the category much more strongly in the direction of state and corporate influence. The lines are often blurry, but as a matter of emphasis, we insist that global civil society is not the same as global NGOs. Smith (2005) attempts to address this problem by separating out Transnational Social Movement Organizations (TSMOs) from NGOs as a whole, focusing in her study on women's rights, human rights, environmental, and economic justice activist organizations. However, her conclusion, that political opportunity structures determine TSMOs' functions, inexorably pulls us right back into the blurry definitional zone of interaction among states, NGOs, and contestatory movements.

These terms—social movements, political mobilization, *Öffentlichkeit*, counter-hegemony, civil society—now broadly defined as we propose to deploy them, all endeavour to capture various dimensions of social movements and their communication formations within which ICTs are applied. The communication research literature on this theme, despite its tendential absence from the political science and sociology social movement research literature, is developing rapidly, with a rich series of empirical and conceptual contributions, frequently relating to the Internet (Rodríguez 2001; Granjon 2001; Meikle 2002; Rheingold 2002; Lovink 2002, 2003; Granjon and Cardon 2003; Couldry and Curran 2003; Opel and Pompper 2003; Jordan and Taylor 2004; Krohling Peruzzo 2004; van de Donk et al. 2004; Atton 2001, 2005; de Jong, Shaw and Stammers 2005; Langlois and Dubois 2005). From these we will select a small sample of contributions we judge particularly relevant to the Internet dimension of ICTs.

3 FORAYS INTO INTERNET USES WITHIN POLITICAL MOVEMENTS

Granjon (2001) carried out one of the relatively few systematic surveys of political movements' Internet use. He interviewed 250 French activists in 1999, and the results challenged some conventional expectations. He found, for example, that the most common use of the Internet was for summons to action, with debate online, the *Öffentlichkeit* or *Gegenöffentlichkeit* function, relatively rare, reserved for special protest co-ordinations or assemblies. Just 8 per cent of his respondents had debated online, with one respondent speaking for many in expressing irritation with the verbal prolixity and irrelevance often encountered in online fora (Granjon 2001: 107–8, 137–8). Only a third said they felt themselves to be part of an online community, and 80 per cent of those who said this had already met in various activist settings, especially demonstrations (Granjon 2001: 111–12), indicating thereby both that face-to-face interaction was a key component of these forms of Internet use, and also that the Internet was not being used as a recruitment tool.

An activity Granjon found especially prominent among his respondents (60 per cent) was the role of forwarder of information (Granjon 2001: 122ff.), including people who printed out and distributed material to activists not on the listserv. As between Internet activists and others, there was sometimes an attitude divide (Granjon 2001: 151–3, 161–2): activists operating in more conventional modes were prone to see the internauts as armchair *intellos*, while the latter, over 70 per cent by their own accounts spending 30 minutes to over 2 hours a day in Internet activist work, often because their jobs were only lightly supervised, found the conventional activists lacking in perception of how the technology could be used to strengthen social movements.

In a later four-nation study of Internet use by ATTAC,[4] the global social justice organization originating in France, Granjon and Cardon (2003) found that in each country ATTAC had a team of four to eight individuals who functioned as editors (dovetailing documents), co-producers, translators, proofreaders, and technicians. Interestingly, the information activists usually did not read what they themselves produced, very much fulfilling the forwarder function noted in Granjon's earlier study. Moreover, in a fascinating echo of the commercial origins of non-partisan reporting in the late nineteenth century press, they avoided offering analytical frameworks for their content in order not to risk alienating their broad movement public with its many constituencies. In a different study of ATTAC's online culture, le Grignou and Patou (2004) argue that it facilitated an exchange of opinions rather than of reasoned arguments, but also that it often re-inscribed a division between experts and lay-activists.

Lovink (2003: 86–129) offers an important account of the rise and demise of Syndicate, a pan-European listserv network launched in the early 1990s in the heady aftermath of the collapse of East-Central and Balkan Europe's sovietized regimes. It is important because it illustrates the problematic character of the Internet as *Öffentlichkeit*. Syndicate's purpose was summarized by one of its early activists as 'a digging, excavating, tunneling process toward greater understanding . . . which fully recognizes different starting points and possible directions: a collaborative process with a shared desire for making connection' (Lovink 2003: 93). However, the connections were not based on digital communication as such. As with Granjon's study, Syndicate's facilitators noted that 'the meetings and personal contacts off-list were an essential part of the Syndicate network: they grounded the Syndicate' (Lovink 2003: 94).

The objective was positive, even if overly marked by a definition of Eastern Europe from the Cold War years, rather than as a new field of forces. Nonetheless, the listserv fell apart as a result of two factors. The first was the tensions generated by NATO's bombing of Serbian targets, supposedly to prevent massacres of Kosovar Albanians and to force Serbia's Milosevic regime to the negotiating table. The bombings generated a furious and bitter exchange between advocates of the bombing, their opponents, and those espousing the 'plague upon both your houses' position. The other was the aggressive attack-postings, sustained at the rate of some ten a day, by a single arrogant spoiler, in the absence of a listserv policy on excluding such activity. Together these mark 'the end of the romantic concept of open, unmoderated exchange' (Lovink 2003: 129), and similarly warn against defining the Internet as smoothly facilitating *Öffentlichkeit*.

Salazar (2003) presents an analysis of some 25 websites operated by Mapuche people of Chilean citizenship around the world, not only in Chile, but in Belgium, Britain, France, Germany, the Netherlands, Spain, and Sweden. The Mapuche are some 10 per cent of Chile's population (and a smaller percentage of Argentina's), and suffer from the usual history of massive land-dispossession and abuse that characterizes indigenous peoples throughout the Americas. Salazar summarizes a number of issues these sites amplify, seeking to vault over the alternating silence and hostility with which mainstream Chilean media have typically represented Mapuche life: the negative consequences of urban migration; loss of cultural identity; state land, health, and development policies; assimilation and racism; lack of voice; dam and highway construction that disrupts their terrain; deforestation. The websites connect up Mapuche communities and individuals, and also seek to engage transnational attention to their often dire situations as a way of bringing pressure for change to bear on Chile's typically uninterested governments.

Atton (2005) reviews a variety of alternative Internet uses, from extreme Rightist movements to fanzines, and counter-hegemonic applications from hacktivism to copyleft and e-commons approaches to intellectual property issues, the last a theme also addressed by Meikle (2002: 88–112). Van de Donk et al. (2004) provide case studies of new media use by global justice activists, solidarity activism with East Timor, women's groups in the Netherlands, Hong Kong, and Australia, and disablement activists in Portugal. Jordan and Taylor (2004) offer an informative exploration of digitally organized protest actions, including centralized, distributed, and client-side Denial of Service 'drownings' of a targeted website, along with reviews of the notion of electronic civil disobedience, actions by the Electronic Disturbance Theatre, and the publications of the Critical Art Ensemble group.[5] They argue that actions by a mass of computer activists to shut down a site or replace or *détourne*[6] its flash page are equivalent to a virtual sit-in, and politically an entirely different statement from purely technical 'bombing' operations by a lone 'cracker' (the term preferred by hacktivists for such destructive individuals, rather than 'hacker'). They also argue that hackers tend to be masculinist, as the trope of the Wild West so popular in their circles suggests, and to be more obsessed with efficient systems than social, cultural, and economic questions (Jordan and Taylor 2004: 117–19, 132–4).

4 ICTs AND SOCIAL MOVEMENTS IN PRACTICE

The particular examples which we propose to discuss are: (1) the rather early uses of the Internet by Burmese opposition, solidarity, and human rights groups; (2) cellphone uses in anti-government protests in Thailand and the Philippines; (3) community radio in Latin America in the 1990s and 2000s; and (4) the Indymedia network and its challenges to conventional journalism. All these instances have formed an integral dimension of political movements, some of them directly involved in counter-hegemonic political mobilization (the South-East Asian examples), others such as Latin American community radio stations mostly offering scope for very local debate and analysis (*Gegenöffentlichkeit*), some presenting examples of ongoing civil society organizations (the Indymedia network, the Burma solidarity group), others seemingly more spontaneous (notably the Thai and Philippines cases, although it is likely that the history of prior networking and habits of mobilization contributed significantly to galvanizing those movements).

The campaign for Burma (Myanmar)[7]

An early example of global Internet activism was the international grassroots movement in support of democracy in Burma (Brooten 2003). Because of the restrictive nature of Internet use under the country's military dictatorship, this campaign was initiated and has been maintained from outside the country, spearheaded early on by the coordinating group, the Free Burma Coalition (FBC), and now by the US Campaign for Burma.[8] This Internet campaign has challenged the authoritarian actions of the Burmese regime and provided a platform for the opposition to communicate widely, without great expense, in the attempt to enact change in Burma.

The FBC claimed its high-profile Internet campaign as the largest cyber-campaign devoted to human rights in a single country, and the campaign was often cited as an example of a new international cyber-activism that was fundamentally changing global activist strategies (Doherty 1997; Holloway 1996; Matthews 1996; O'Neill 1997; Tyson 1995; Urschel 1996). During the mid-1990s, the FBC claimed member groups in over 100 universities and high schools in the US and overseas, as well as affiliations with a large number of environmentalists, labour organizers, and human rights campaigners worldwide. The coalition successfully pressured corporations to rethink their Burma connections by effectively linking their business decisions to human rights abuses in Burma, especially the regime's use of forced labour. The campaign created a powerful sense of camaraderie among hundreds of people corresponding over vast distances about a country that many of them had never visited, especially the North American and European students and activists who were involved. Activists often began their online postings with 'Dear fellow spiders', in reference to the campaign's motto, 'When spiders unite they can tie down a lion'.

The FBC campaign made use of its international reach to create a bottom-up strategy that drew a cause as dramatic as that found in any legendary tale to bring activists into battle against the Burmese regime. The regime rendered itself easy for activists to vilify: a repressive military dictatorship in power since 1962; a massive general strike in 1988 in which troops killed unknown thousands of unarmed demonstrators; a 1990 election won in a landslide by the opposition National League for Democracy (NLD), but never honoured by the regime; and repression of the photogenic Aung San Suu Kyi, the Nobel Peace Prize-winning opposition leader standing strong against constant surveillance and years of house arrest. One example of many harsh decrees the regime issued is the 1996 Computer Science and Development Law, which authorizes an automatic 7–15 year jail sentence for anyone found with an unauthorized modem or fax machine. The FBC's use of the Internet capitalized on the power of Burma's story and the global nature of the web, cultivating an identity among democracy-loving activist spiders around the world.

The BurmaNet listserv, which was founded in 1993, quickly became the primary source of daily information for most Burma watchers. The impact of BurmaNet took the regime by surprise, and it soon recognized that effective control of communication required new strategies. Shortly after the founding of BurmaNet, and despite protests from some listserv subscribers, in 1994 BurmaNet's editors decided in the interests of free speech and full debate to allow the Burmese military and its representatives to subscribe and post their messages. The regime and members of the opposition-in-exile attacked, cajoled, and poked fun at each other, at times even managing a debate. The listserv arguably became the most significant forum for discussion between the regime and the opposition. Thus BurmaNet made a significant step toward a more polycentric, non-hierarchical system of communication among the Burmese despite the limited access to the Internet for many inside and even outside Burma.

The use of ICTs has enabled the development of more complex networks of information between activists and civilians inside and outside Burma, and between activists and the regime. Burma's border areas are home to a variety of opposition media whose messages are either referenced or directly placed on the Internet, so that online connectivity has influenced all media. The Burmese regime regularly posts information online, and Burmese opposition groups in exile in Thailand obtain information from their contacts inside Burma, then feed their statements, news, and opinion pieces to BurmaNet and Burma-related websites. These listservs and websites are regularly read and often reported on by the wire services and other news services, including major international broadcasters such as the Burmese services of the Voice of America (VOA), British Broadcasting Corporation (BBC), Radio Free Asia (RFA), and the opposition Democratic Voice of Burma (DVB) radio, which then broadcast much of the information back into Burma. With improvements in computer skills and the use of desktop publishing software, opposition groups also smuggle their publications inside the country on CD-ROM or computer diskettes, which are generally easier to hide than hard copies of a publication, and lessen the risks for those smuggling the information.

The Internet also makes possible media that otherwise would be unviable, such as the DVB radio station, based in Oslo, Norway, which bases much of its own reporting on the information it collects from wire services and major publications throughout Asia using the Internet. The Internet is also important because it enables field reporters to send reports as email attachments, saving the editors back in Oslo the trouble of retyping them during the editing process (Khin Maung Win, personal communication, 23 August 2000). Thus, the Internet is a source of information for the multiplicity of media published and distributed along Burma's borders and elsewhere outside the country, and then smuggled or excerpted for broadcast back into Burma. In this way, even those without access to the newest communication technologies are affected by the increased number of sources these technologies make available for the more traditional media.

The Burma opposition case-study illustrates many features of ICTs and political movements: their global scope; their usefulness as a platform to demonstrate how the global actions of transnationals have consequences in local areas; their potential accessibility in significant indirect ways, despite the barriers the Burmese economy and state put in their path; their interaction with other media, such as radio; and not least in this case, the emergence for a while of a mutually antagonistic and unanticipated *Öffentlichkeit* involving state and opposition representatives, something impossible in physical space inside Burma itself.

Mobile telephones in Thailand and the Philippines

Mobile telephones, video cameras, and fax machines played a crucial role in motivating students and workers to turn back an attempted coup in Thailand in 1992, during which three days of violence left dozens dead, hundreds wounded, and thousands in prison. Massive street protests were fuelled by rising resentment of military dominance in politics and business, and protesters demanded the resignation of the unelected Prime Minister, General Suchinda Kraprayoon, who had imposed a state of emergency in Bangkok and surrounding provinces. According to the US State Department, excessive use of force by the military led to at least 52 deaths, and nearly 200 protesters remained 'disappeared' at the year's end. In addition, during the three days of protest, military and police forces took into custody and detained over 3,500 people, including onlookers and some 500 children, who were reportedly treated very harshly (US Department of State 1993). The tension eased and General Suchinda resigned only after King Bhumibol Adulyadej stepped in and called for reconciliation.

During the violence, new censorship rules created confusion about the demonstrations. The government-controlled radio and TV stations featured announcers insisting that everything was normal. When the stations did report on the events, they showed only the rioters and no army manoeuvres. The public severely

548 HANDBOOK OF ICTs

criticized Thailand's five television channels for kowtowing to the government, and some claimed that the media worsened the situation, in that its one-sided coverage caused many people to go to see for themselves what was happening (US Department of State 1993).

All newspapers were prohibited from printing documents threatening national security or disturbing public law and order. One of two English-language dailies, the *Bangkok Post*, was published with large blank spaces in place of articles and editorials that according to its editors could be defined as violating the order. Police also used a felt-tip pen to censor the front page of the *International Herald Tribune* before it was distributed, blacking out information critical of the military's involvement in the Thai economy, although two other items reporting directly on the demonstrations remained untouched (US Department of State 1993). Because the other English language paper, *The Nation*, and two Thai-language dailies virtually ignored the order, the director of police closed them, only to rescind his order a few hours later.

Unlike past anti-government protests, however, which had been organized mainly by students, this round of demonstrations was joined by an older generation of Thailand's middle class, which had grown dramatically during the previous decade. This time protestors included business men with cell phones and beepers on their belts, who used these new technologies to relay information from one pro-democracy protest to another (Shennon 1992; Watson and Moreau 1992). Thus although the Thai government imposed a virtual television blackout of the demonstrations, the affluent middle class in Bangkok moved quickly to make use of their widespread telephone network. For this reason, the demonstrators have been described as 'the handy telephone mob' (Connolly 1992), or 'yuppie revolutionaries', who used their mobile telephones to call their friends and relatives to join the demonstrations and to castigate the hosts of radio call-in shows for providing one-sided information (Ungphakron 1992). Many believe that if protestors had not had access to cell phones, they could not have rallied their own numbers to show massive public resistance and force the military to surrender. In addition, Thai protesters certainly capitalized on the advent of 24/7 television news as they hoisted signs in English and other languages to communicate with the foreign journalists covering the events. In the aftermath of the 1992 protests, the Internet also played an important role in providing a source of information about the events.

In 2001 in the Philippines, a not dissimilar upsurge unseated a president, once again enabled by intensive mobile phone use, though this time mercifully unaccompanied by bloodshed (Coronel 2001; Rafael 2003). The brazenly corrupt Filipino president, Joseph Estrada, was under impeachment proceedings, and the Senate hearing was being televised. Huge numbers were watching, and inside an hour after a crucial vote, some hundreds were on the streets of Manila honking their car horns, banging on pans, and demanding Estrada's resignation. Within two hours, by midnight the very same day, thousands had gathered on the Edsa Highway, the historic location of the 'people power' demonstrations that peacefully toppled US-backed dictator Marcos 15 years earlier.

This lightning mobilization was coordinated by Filipinos texting on their cell phones, and gathered strength and determination over the next four days until Estrada finally conceded and resigned. Coronel (2001) notes that, unlike in the Thai case, Filipino media—after initial hesitation due to Estrada's record of intimidating news media—aggressively covered the situation, but could not match the speed and safety of texting, since it was difficult to trace the source of text messages. In addition to up-to-the-minute news, stories circulated about Estrada's scandalous lifestyle along with jokes at his and his Senate cronies' expense. Imagination and humour are not always evoked by 'information society' discourses, but they represent a vital zone in both hegemonic and counter-hegemonic communication (Downing 2001: 105–80). In addition, some 200 anti-Estrada websites were set up and about 100 listservs.

Rafael (2003: 409) makes some interesting further observations about Generation TxT (as the young texters called themselves), and notes specifically one respondent who, not wishing to spread unfounded rumours, had waited to text until the church-owned radio station offered to broadcast the same information. Once sent, not only did his message return to him, but it returned threefold. Rafael notes that the power of texting in this case 'requires, at least in the eyes of this writer and those he sends messages to, another power to legitimate the text's meaning; and second, that such a power is felt precisely in the multiple transmissions of the same text' (Rafael 2003: 409).

This observation rather clearly distinguishes the use of cell phones in this Filipino protest from the *Öffentlichkeit* concept, emphasizing instead their mobilizing dimension. The extent to which their usage was counter-hegemonic is also problematic, in that as Rafael (2003: 410) emphasizes, the demands of People Power II addressed neither the nature of the state nor the class divisions of the Philippines, only the corruption of the President and his cronies. A final observation is in order about the Philippines case: it was the unofficial alternative media whose performance effectively pressured the mainstream media to abandon their craven stance and fulfil their supposed role as watchdogs. This chimes with our observations on the challenge to mainstream journalism posed by the Indymedia network and its analogues later in this chapter.

Community radio stations

As already emphasized, radio continues to be the most widely used ICT across the planet.[9] The term 'community radio' loosely designates small, generally poorly funded, non-government stations, often broadcasting on a fairly to very weak signal (typically 10–20 watts).[10] Despite their minuscule size, governments have frequently closed them down, citing one or other pretext—the US Federal Communications Commission (FCC) at one stage, singing to the tune of corporate broadcasters such as NBC and CBS, solemnly asserted they were a danger to air traffic safety. These low-power FM stations have been at the centre of battles between the broadcasting industry, working through the FCC, and local community radio activists (Sakolsky and Dunifer 1998; Soley 1998; Opel 2004). Some of them in Latin America and Africa, as we shall see, have also begun to utilize the Internet as part of their operation.

In a number of countries in the 2000s, there has been a wave of repression of community radio stations. Between 1998 and 2004 according to police figures, Brazil's Federal government closed down nearly 13,000 such stations and over 10,000 trials were instituted against radio activists (Milan 2004). This pattern is visible in other Latin American nations, notably Argentina, Guatemala, and even Peru, where after a long period of government tolerance, these stations were suddenly banned from even the minimal advertising they carried, normally their only source of income. In Chile the government only permitted community stations to broadcast at a single watt.

At the time of writing (2006), the governments of South Korea and Uruguay were bucking this repressive trend, and some other Latin American governments were taking cautious steps to permit a very select few radio stations to operate, for example a single Argentinean station in the Mapuche indigenous region in the Andes foothills (other stations have existed in Argentina, such as the movement station La Tribu since 1989,[11] but illegally and under constant threat of closure). In Indonesia, where radio stations other than the government station were banned from broadcasting news once the long-running US-backed military dictatorship collapsed in 1998, community stations jumped in number from 60 in the 68H Radio Network in August 1999, to 200 by the end of 2000 (Hala and Santoso 2003).

It is important not to move instantly to romanticize all such stations simply because they are often under attack, for they constitute a vast spectrum of effectiveness and democratic organization. The remarkable miners' radio stations of Bolivia represented a high point in the community radio movement in Latin America and while their experiences are well known there, they deserve much more study outside the continent (Huesca 1995; O'Connor 2004). Gumucio Dagron (2001) provides short accounts of the contributions of a scatter of such stations across the global South as development and social change agents. Geerts, van Oeyen and Villamayor (2004) also provide fairly brief, but equally evocative accounts of some 32 Latin American radio stations, along with a lengthier analysis of the continental situation during the first part of the 2000s.

While these stations do not all represent social movements in a dramatic mode, in their different ways they all represent the attempts of groups to claw out, through communicating, some 'spaces of hope' where they actually are, not necessarily where they would like to be. Such projects are often discussed under the misleading heading of 'development communication', a label that all too often signifies in the speaker's mind pathetic forms of communication practised by the world's unfortunate in order to improve the equally pathetic state of their agriculture. Nor are these examples simply of 'identity politics'. Our is a sharply different, and robust, interpretation of these projects. Questions of social class, of imperial power, of racism, are only some of their dimensions. The examples that follow articulate the communication politics of migrant labour, of children's rights, and of indigenous Aymara and Afro-Brazilian identities.

Radio Callos y Guatita[12] communicated weekly between members of the 400,000-strong Ecuadorean migrant community in Spain, predominantly undocumented workers, and their families, mostly from southern Ecuador (Dávila and López 2004). The station ran programmes on immigrant rights, had call-in programmes so that migrants could speak with their families, did pieces on opportunities for small-scale savings investment back in southern Ecuador, giving advice on how to send remittances and exposing rip-off firms, and in general sought to combat the misinformation current in each nation about the other country. In Ecuador the call-in programmes were in a studio, while in Spain, due to the legal vulnerability of many migrants, the station staff went to a local park frequented by Ecuadoreans.

Radio Cumiches had a particular focus on school children and young people (Gutiérrez 2004). Nicaragua is one of the very poorest nations in the hemisphere, and Estelí at the time of the research was plagued by juvenile gangs. The station's focus was an attempt to harness young people's energies to reconstruct the community. It had developed a network of some 60 school-based activists, and 30 city neighbourhood correspondents focusing on children's rights. It strove to balance girls and boys among its young activists. It ran programmes on sexual and reproductive health, and served as a training centre for similar youth communicators nationally.

Radio Ondas del Titicaca (Lake Titicaca Waves Radio) especially served Aymara indigenous communities in Bolivia (Mamani Jiménez 2004). In 2000 and 2001, during violent confrontations with government troops across the nation, it was protected by community support even when invaded by the police (their shouts and orders went out over the air and mobilized the community). In 2001, its transmitter mast was blown up by an army unit, but community contributions quickly built a new and more powerful one. Radio Favela (Tough Neighbourhood Radio)[13] began as an unlicensed station in 1980, and had frequently been threatened with closure (Barbosa 2004). One of its favourite station identifiers was 'This station is a piece of shit!' Its active community support, which included surrounding it at times when the police were set to raid, kept it alive. On one occasion no less than 700 police and two helicopters arrived to arrest the director. It featured Afro-Brazilian music of all kinds, including local hip-hop and rap, and its voices almost exclusively conversed in *favela* argot. The station also ran call-in programmes with local prisons (in Brazil, as in the US and Europe, filled with people of colour). Its campaigns against drug barons, and its critical solidarity with the petty pushers striving to survive as best they could, won it UN anti-drug campaign prizes over two consecutive years.

In Colombia, indigenous peoples, comprising some 2 per cent of the population inhabiting 30 per cent of national territory, adopted a spectrum of policies regarding radio—from the Kogi people who saw it as an instrument of their cultural destruction and wanted nothing to do with the technology on any terms, to the Nasa and Guambiano peoples who embraced it for several reasons, including as a means to preserve their languages, to the Wayuu people whose stations were led by women and whose operations were conceptualized within the matrix of traditional culture (Rodríguez and El Gazi 2005). The authors of this absorbing study emphasize how differently the dynamics of technology and indigenous collective self-assertion pan out in Colombia, as elsewhere.

The emerging relation between community radio and the Internet is explored by a number of writers in AMARC director Bruce Girard's collection *The One To Watch* (2003). Examples are drawn from Senegal, Mali, Sri Lanka, Indonesia, and Latin America. The studies indicate the persistence of language and literacy as key obstacles to Internet use, and also the technological issue of downloading audio files over phone lines (it would often take an hour to download a 15-minute file in Mali, several hours to download a 30-minute audio file in Indonesia). The Simbani Project, which sought to make audio programmes available to a variety of stations in sub-Saharan Africa, quickly ran into this technical problem. Text files, which could be voiced locally, presented far fewer problems, though electricity breakdowns commonly interfered with that process as well. In Indonesia, a partial solution was found by gaining access to a satellite audio channel, though the cost of up-linking back through the satellite meant the traffic was one-way.

Yet the challenge was to make non-local information accessible through these radio stations, whose pre-eminent strength lay precisely in being bound to their locales, but which, in a global era, also needed to be able to open up a wider world and make information sources available to listeners. One solution adopted in a number of places was to run a regular radio web-browsing programme, where a speaker would report on a series of sites, often in English or a non-local language, and read key portions of them in translation to listeners. While doing this, it was possible also to offer guidance to listeners on how to browse the Internet themselves if they had access to a telecentre computer. By these means, a trickle of Internet access and use became possible.

The Indymedia network [14]

The Indymedia network was founded at the time of the extraordinary mobilization against the World Trade Organization (WTO) in Seattle toward the close of 1999. Extraordinary as much for the wide spectrum of those involved as for its numbers and global impact, this network quite quickly established itself as a major presence (Brooten 2004a, b; Kidd 2003; Downing 2002; 2003a, b, c). The primary regions of activity over its first five years were in the US, Canada, and Western Europe, but it fairly quickly came to include chapters in a number of 'Third World' nations too. At the time of writing, its sites numbered some 170 worldwide, but since the Brazil and Italy sites were quasi-federal in the sense that they embraced a considerable number of localities within those two nations, the true number was probably nearer 200.

Indymedia sites consisted in essence of a connected server and a group of activists prepared to sign on to the network's general principles. In the main, the network had an open postings policy, though a number of sites were adopting more restrictive editorial policies in response to a slew of hate-filled, racist and sexist postings. The splash-page format was initially identical on all sites, which may have given a false impression of central direction from the Seattle site, but in reality was chosen because it made hyper-linking far easier technically. Behind this apparent homogeneity, however, there were considerable differences not only in the levels of energy in the different sites, but also in emphasis. The typical political commitment at many sites appeared to be anarchist (though that term too telescopes multiple and significantly different positions), but some sites from time to time seemed to become, at least temporarily, colonized by a single organization's viewpoint, such as 'Earth First!', the Popular Front for the Liberation of Palestine, and others.

The formation of many of these sites coincided with a major local mobilization against a national or global pro-corporate gathering, such as the WTO, the International Monetary Fund (IMF), the World Bank, the G8, or the Free Trade Association of the Americas. Thus both the local and the global were permanently locked together into energetic activism in the formation of the Indymedia network.

With each site hyper-linked to all the others, detailed and up-to-the-minute global news on social movement activity and resistance to corporate globalization was available cost-free to users. During the turbulent years of protest in Argentina against both the governmental elite and the IMF from 2001 to 2003, the Indymedia Argentina site for example was running some 20–30 news updates a day. The network primarily operated in English, but also—depending on the site—in Dutch, French, German, Greek, Italian, Portuguese, Russian, and Spanish, among other languages. It made particularly good use of photojournalism. For example, on 17 June 2005, it showed half a dozen stills of US Representative John Conyers at the White House gates handing in a petition to halt the Iraq war, signed by over half a million Americans.

Let us now turn to ways in which conventional journalism as practised by corporate news media has been continually challenged by the Indymedia network (see Atton 2005: 25–60). This has taken shape through development of a collective process of research and critique in which the discussion becomes an integral part of the finished text (Brooten 2004b). Indymedia is more a facilitation mechanism than a news service, and as such is not usefully examined through the lens used to judge traditional journalism. Yet the network is challenging the nature of news, how we get it, and how we make it.

Indymedia challenges people's passive acceptance of the authority naturalized through corporate media news, by encouraging them to take control of the story-telling, to place current events in their historical, social, and geographic contexts, and to attend to and challenge the process through which reporting dehumanizes victims and trivializes outrage. As web users have become comfortable with getting and ranking news from a variety of sources, they have begun to share the role of searching for information once held by journalists (Jones 2000). Meikle (2003: 4) maintains that in addition to a form of direct citizen-to-politician communication, and with the shifting nature of news consumption in the online world, 'there is also a corresponding ongoing shift in the boundaries of what constitutes newsmakers'. Indymedia presents an interesting example of this ongoing shift.

Many Indymedia activists openly challenge the concept of 'objectivity' in jour-nalism, arguing that it is better to be honest about one's biases, in contrast to corporate media. The network has introduced several alternative ideas about what makes for a good and credible writer. Writers gain legitimacy or credibility in two primary ways: (i) when they present ample evidence to back up the claims they make, in the form of links and citations, and (ii) when they have had direct experience with an issue, often as an eyewitness. A consistent theme is that no single information source should be relied upon exclusively, and that readers must be aware of who owns the source and their ideological assumptions.

Indymedia has in essence taken on the watchdog function traditionally associ-ated with mainstream media, arguing that because they have become lapdogs for corporate interests, these media now need their own watchdog. Indymedia's achievements support the claim that web use can encourage a collective process of critique in which, as Jones (2000: 178) suggests, 'the sum of connections makes a content greater than the sum of its parts'. The network also takes Burnett and Marshall's (2003) claim that web users are increasingly taking the researcher's role a step further, in that the research being conducted is not carried out exclusively on the web, but also in the streets or people's homes, stretching the boundaries of what constitutes a newsmaker.

In offering a tool for media activism characterized by decentralized networks and hyperlinks between multiple information sources, Indymedia opens the kind of 'deliberative spaces' required to maintain an active democratic citizenry (Dahl-berg 2001). This process not only challenges mainstream media messages outright, but also reframes normative concepts of 'expert' status and 'objectivity', calling into question a profit-driven media that many argue leaves out as much as it reports. With the call for eyewitness accounts, links, and citations to establish legitimacy, the Independent Media Center (IMC) at times demands a level of accountability corporate media would find hard to meet.

5 Conclusion

Krohling Peruzzo (2004: 302) concludes from her study of Brazilian alternative media and social movements that participatory communication supports the activity of building a democratic culture and educational process; helps to know, reclaim, and valorize the roots of the general public's culture; transforms various dimensions of everyday behaviour; makes technical expertise accessible; demystifies communication technologies; encourages group creativity; makes available information directly relevant to local communities; gives voice to the supposedly voiceless; and is steadily expanding, as witness the increase in the number of grassroots radio and video projects. She does not address the Internet or cellphones, but the evidence we have summarized here is very suggestive of ways in which their potential mobilizing uses fit her summary.

In terms of the case studies noted in this chapter, cell phones clearly operated most effectively in short-term mobilizing situations, whereas community radio stations and IMCs functioned both over the long term and the short. At the same time, with the rapid spread of WiFi and the increasing capacity of cell phones, we may anticipate that as users access the Internet through them their uses will stretch into the long term too.

To understand contemporary political movements, just as much as for movements in the past, their communicative aspects and communicative competence are clearly central. Both long-term and short-term mobilization can be provided with new facility through ICTs, though at present radio is much more central for people at large across the planet than more recent technologies. Understanding their potential and practice through the lenses of *Öffentlichkeit*, counter-hegemony, and global civil society helps to anchor them as vital functions of activist movements, though not all ICT uses within political movements come close to fitting all three terms. Whatever the future of global social justice movements, it is impossible to imagine their functioning without a range of ICTs, even while other movement forms, such as street theatre and graffiti, continue to have tremendous resonance.

References

Atton, C. (2001). *Alternative Media*. London: Sage.
—— (2005). *An Alternative Internet: Radical Media, Politics and Creativity*. Edinburgh: Edinburgh University Press.
Barbosa, L. (2004). 'Radio Favela, Belo Horizonte, Brasil: Una Forma "Favela" de Hacer Radio', in A. Geerts, V. van Oeyen and C. Villamayor (eds), *La Práctica Inspira: La Radio*

Popular y Comunitaria Frente al Nuevo Siglo. Quito: Associación Latinoamericana de Educación Radiofónica, 179–87.

BASTIEN, F. and NEVEU, E. (eds) (1999). *Espaces Publiques Mosaïques: Acteurs, Arènes et Rhétoriques des Débats Publics Contemporains*. Rennes: Presses Universitaires de Rennes.

BROOTEN, L. (2003). 'Global Communications, Local Conceptions: Human Rights and the Politics of Communication among the Burmese Opposition-in-exile'. Unpublished Ph.D. dissertation, College of Communication, Ohio University, Athens, OH.

—— (2004a). 'Digital Deconstruction: The Independent Media Center as a Process of Collective Critique', in R. Berenger (ed.), *Global Media Go to War*. Spokane, WA: Marquette Books, 265–79.

—— (2004b). 'The Power of Public Reporting: The Independent Media Center's Challenge to the "Corporate Media Machine"', in L. Artz and Y. R. Kamalipour (eds), *Bring 'Em On! Media and Power in the Iraq War*. Lanham, MD: Rowman & Littlefield, 239–54.

BURNETT, R. and MARSHALL, P. D. (2003). *Web Theory: An Introduction*. New York: Routledge.

CARTY, V. (2002). 'Technology and Counter-Hegemonic Movements: The Case of Nike Corporation'. *Social Movement Studies*, 1(2): 129–46.

—— (2004). 'Transnational Labor Mobilizing in Two Mexican Maquiladoras: The Struggle for Democratic Globalization'. *Mobilization: An International Journal*, 9(3): 295–310.

CASTELLS, M. (1996). *The Information Age: Economy, Soceity and Culture Volume I: The Rise of the Network Society*. Oxford: Blackwell Publishers.

COLECTIVO LA TRIBU (2004a). 'La Radio es su Consecuencias', in N. Vitelli and C. Rodríguez Esperón (eds), *Contrainformación: Medios Alternativos para la Acción Política*. Buenos Aires: Ediciones Continente, 167–77.

—— (2004b). 'FM La Tribu, Buenos Aires, Argentina', in A. Geerts, V. van Oeyen and C. Villamayor (eds), *La Práctica Inspira: La Radio Popular y Comunitaria Frente al Nuevo Siglo*. Quito: Asociación Latinoamericana de Educación Radiofónica, 303–11.

CONNOLLY, A. (1992). 'Phones Keep Thai Protesters Honed'. *Herald Sun*, 26 June.

CORONEL, S. (2001). 'The Media, the Market and Democracy: The Case of the Philippines'. *Javnost/The Public*, VIII(2): 109–24.

COULDRY, N. and CURRAN, J. (eds) (2003). *Contesting Media Power: Alternative Media in a Networked World*. Lanham, MD: Rowman & Littlefield.

CRITICAL ART ENSEMBLE (2001). *Digital Resistance: Explorations in Tactical Media*. New York: Autonomedia.

CUNNINGHAM, S. and SINCLAIR, J. (eds) (2002). *Floating Lives: The Media and Asian Diasporas*. Lanham, MD: Rowman & Littlefield.

DAHLBERG, L. (2001). 'The Internet and Democratic Discourse'. *Information, Communication and Society*, 4(4): 615–33.

DÁVILA, L. and LÓPEZ, J. M. (2004). 'Callos y Guatita: Una receta radial sobre la emigración, el desarrollo y la comunicación', in A. Geerts, V. van Oeyen and C. Villamayor (eds), *La práctica inspira: La radio popular y comunitaria frente al nuevo siglo*. Quito: Associación Latinoamericana de Educación Radiofónica, 68–78.

DAVIS, D. E. and ROSAN, C. A. (2004). 'Social Movements in the Mexico City Airport Controversy: Globalization, Democracy, and the Power of Distance'. *Mobilization: An International Journal*, 9(3): 279–93.

DE JONG, W., SHAW, M. and STAMMERS, N. (eds) (2005). *Global Activism, Global Media*. London: Pluto Press.

DOHERTY, C. J. (1997). 'Free Burma Drive has Global Impact: Grassroots Pressure Forces US Firms Out'. *The Arizona Republic*, A16, 18 Sept.

DOWNING, J. (1988). 'The Alternative Public Realm: The Organization of the 1980s Anti-nuclear Press in West Germany and Britain'. *Media, Culture & Society*, 10: 163–81.

—— (1996). *Internationalizing Media Theory*. London: Sage.

—— (2001). *Radical Media: Rebellious Communication and Social Movements*. Thousand Oaks, CA: Sage.

—— (2002). 'Independent Media Centers: A Multi-local, Multi-media Challenge to Global Neo-liberalism', in M. Raboy (ed.), *Global Media Policy in the New Millennium*. Luton: Luton University Press, 215–32.

—— (2003a). 'The IMC Movement beyond "The West"', in A. Opel and D. Pompper (eds), *Representing Resistance: Media, Civil Disobedience, and the Global Justice Movement*. Westport, CT: Praeger, 241–58.

—— (2003b). 'The Indymedia Phenomenon: Space-Place-Democracy and the New Independent Media Centers', in J.-G. Lacroix and G. Tremblay (eds), *2001 Bogues: globalisme et pluralisme* (vol. 2). Montréal: Les Presses de l'Université Laval, 57–67.

—— (2003c). 'The Independent Media Center Movement and the Anarchist Socialist Tradition', in N. Couldry and J. Curran (eds), *Contesting Media Power*. Lanham, MD: Rowman & Littlefield, 243–57.

FRASER, N. (1993). 'Rethinking the Public Sphere: A Contribution to the Critique of Actually Existing Democracy', in C. Calhoun (ed.), *Habermas and the Public Sphere*. Cambridge, MA: MIT Press, 109–42.

GEERTS, A., VAN OEYEN, V. and VILLAMAYOR, C. (eds) (2004). *La práctica inspira: la radio popular y comunitaria frente al nuevo siglo*. Quito: Associación Latinoamericana de Educación Radiofónica.

GIRARD, B. (1992). *A Passion for Radio: Radio Waves and Community*. Montreal: Black Rose Books.

—— (2003). *The One To Watch: Radio, New ICTs and Interactivity/Secreto a Voces: Radio, Nuevas Tecnologías de Información y Comunicación (NTICs) e interactividad*. Rome, FAO and Geneva: Friedrich Ebert Stiftung.

GRANJON, F. (2001). *L'Internet Militant: Mouvement Social et Usage des Réseaux Télématiques*. Paris: Éditions Apogée.

GRANJON, F. and CARDON, D. (2003). 'Mouvement altermondialiste et militantisme informationnel. Le cas d'attac hors du FSM 2003', www.attac.info/txt/fabin=poa2003-fr.pdf, accessed 20 Oct. 2006.

GUMUCIO DAGRON, A. (2001). *Making Waves*. New York: Rockefeller Foundation.

GUTIÉRREZ, H. (2004). 'Radio Cumiches, Estelí, Nicaragua', in A. Geerts, V. van Oeyen and C. Villamayor (eds), *La práctica inspira: La radio popular y comunitaria frente al nuevo siglo*. Quito: Associación Latinoamericana de Educación Radiofónica, 109–18.

HALA, M. and SANTOSO (2003). 'Awaking from the Big Sleep: Kantor Berita 68H', in B. Girard (ed.) *The One To Watch: Radio, New ICTs and Interactivity*. Rome, FAO and Geneva: Friedrich Ebert Stiftung, 136–44.

HOLLOWAY, N. (1996). 'Caught in the Net: US Sanctions Debate Moves to Cyberspace'. *Far Eastern Economic Review*, 159(Nov.): 28, 30.

HUESCA, R. (1995). 'A Procedural View of Participatory Communication: Lessons from Bolivian Tin Miners' Radio'. *Media, Culture and Society*, 17: 101–19.

JONES, S. (2000). 'The Bias of the Web', in A. Herman and T. Swiss (eds), *The World Wide Web and Contemporary Cultural Theory*. New York: Routledge, 171–82.

JORDAN, T. and TAYLOR, P. A. (2004). *Hacktivism and Cyberwars: Rebels with a Cause?* London: Routledge.

KARIM, K. H. (ed.) (2003). *The Media of Diaspora*. London and New York: Routledge.

KIDD, D. (2003). 'Become the Media: The Global IMC Network', in A. Opel and D. Pompper (eds), *Representing Resistance: Media, Civil Disobedience, and the Global Justice Movement*. Westport, CT: Praeger, 224–40.

KROHLING PERUZZO, C. M. (2004). *Comunicação nos movimentos populares: A participação na construção da cidadania*. Petrópolis: Editora Vozes (3rd edn).

LANGLOIS, A. and DUBOIS, F. (eds) (2005). *Autonomous Media: Activating Resistance and Dissent*. Montreal: Cumulus Press.

LE GRIGNOU, B. and PATOU, C. (2004). 'ATTAC(k)ing Expertise: Does the Internet Really Democratize Knowledge?', in W. Van de Donk, B. D. Loader, P. G. Nixon and D. Rucht (eds), *Cyberprotest: New Media, Citizens and Social Movements*. London: Routledge, 164–79.

LOVINK, G. (2002). *Dark Fiber: Tracking Critical Internet Culture*. Cambridge, MA: MIT Press.

—— (2003). *My First Recession: Critical Internet Culture in Transition*. Rotterdam: V2_/NAi Publishers.

MAMANI JIMÉNEZ, C. (2004). 'Radio Ondas del Titicaca, Huarina, La Paz, Bolivia: En defensa de la comunidad y la cultura Aymara', in A. Geerts, V. van Oeyen and C. Villamayor (eds), *La práctica inspira: La radio popular y comunitaria frente al nuevo siglo*. Quito: Associación Latinoamericana de Educación Radiofónica, 216–22.

MARTIN, G. (2002). 'Conceptualizing Cultural Politics in Subcultural and Social Movement Studies'. *Social Movement Studies*, 1(1): 73–88.

MATTHEWS, P. (1996). 'Changing the World with a PC and a Modem'. *The Times*, 7 Aug.

McDONALD, K. (2002). 'From Solidarity to Fluidarity: Social Movements beyond "Collective Identity" – The Case of Globalization Conflicts'. *Social Movement Studies*, 1(2): 109–28.

MEIKLE, G. (2002). *Future Active: Media Activism and the Internet*. London: Routledge and Sydney: Pluto Press.

—— (2003). 'Indymedia and the New Net News'. *Media Development* XLX(4): 3–6.

MILAN, S. (2004). 'Brazil: Community Media Muzzled'. *InterPress Service*, 8 Aug.

MISCHE, A. (2004). 'Cross-Talk in Movements: Reconceiving the Culture-network Link', in M. Diani and D. McAdam (eds), *Social Movements and Networks: Relational Approaches to Collective Action*. New York: Oxford University Press, 258–80.

NAFICY, H. (1993). *The Making of Exile Cultures: Iranian Television in Los Angeles*. Minneapolis, MN: University of Minnesota Press.

—— (2001). *An Accented Cinema: Exilic and Diasporic Film-making*. Princeton, NJ: Princeton University Press.

NEGT, O. and KLUGE, A. (1972/1993). *Öffentlichkeit und Erfahrung*. Frankfurt am Main: Suhrkamp Verlag/ *Public Sphere and Experience*. Minneapolis, MN: University of Minnesota Press.

O'CONNOR, A. (ed.) (2004). *Community Radio in Bolivia: The Miners' Radio Stations*. Lewiston, NY: The Edwin Mellen Press.

O'NEILL, J. (1997). 'Laptop-toting Sleuth brings Burma to the World'. *The Ottawa Citizen,* A9, 21 Dec.

OPEL, A. (2004). *Micro Radio and the FCC: Media Activism and the Struggle over Broadcast Policy.* Westport, CT: Praeger.

—— and POMPPER, D. (eds) (2003). *Representing Resistance: Media, Civil Disobedience, and the Global Justice Movement.* Westport, CT: Praeger.

OPENNET INITIATIVE. (2005). *Internet Filtering in Burma in 2005: A Country Study,* http://www.opennetinitiative.net/studies/burma/, accessed 20 Oct. 2006.

RAFAEL, V. L. (2003). 'The Cell-Phone and the Crowd: Messianic Politics in the Contemporary Philippines'. *Public Culture,* 15(3): 399–425.

RHEINGOLD, H. (2002). *Smart Mobs: The Next Social Revolution.* New York: Basic Books.

RIGGINS, S. (ed.) (1992). *Ethnic Minority Media: An International Perspective.* Thousand Oaks, CA: Sage.

RODRÍGUEZ, C. (2001). *Fissures in the Mediascape: An International Study of Citizens' Media.* Cresskill, NJ: Hampton Press.

—— and EL GAZI, J. (2005). 'La Poética de la Radio Indígena en Colombia', *Códigos* (Puebla, Mexico) 1(2): 17–34.

RUCHT, D. (2005). 'Appeal, Threat, and Press Resonance: Comparing Mayday Protests in London and Berlin'. *Mobilization: An International Journal,* 10(1): 163–81.

SAKOLSKY, R. and DUNIFER, S. (eds) (1998). *Seizing The Airwaves: A Free Radio Handbook.* Edinburgh and San Francisco: AK Press.

SALAZAR, J. F. (2003). 'Articulating an Activist Imaginary: Internet as Counter Public Sphere in the Mapuche Movement, 1997/2002'. *Media International Australia,* 107: 19–30.

SHEFNER, J. (2004). 'Current Trends in Latin American Social Movements'. *Mobilization: An International Journal,* 9(3): 219–22.

SHENNON, P. (1992). 'Deaths Mount as Troops Fire on Thais'. *New York Times,* A1, 19 May.

SMITH, J. (2005). 'Building Bridges or Building Walls? Explaining Regionalization among Transnational Social Movement Organizations'. *Mobilization: An International Journal,* 10(2): 251–69.

SOLEY, L. (1998). *Free Radio: Electronic Civil Disobedience.* Boulder, CO: Westview Press.

STEINBERG, M. W. (2004). 'When Politics Goes Pop: On the Intersections of Popular and Political Culture and the Case of Serbian Student Protests'. *Social Movement Studies,* 3(1): 3–29.

TARROW, S. (2005). 'The Dualities of Transnational Contention: "Two Activist Solitudes" or a New World Altogether?' *Mobilization: An International Journal,* 10(1): 53–72.

TYSON, A. S. (1995). 'Political Activism on Campus Takes on a Cyberspace Twist'. *Christian Science Monitor,* 3, 31 Oct.

UNGPHAKRON, P. (1992). 'Bangkok Shows its Anger at the Generals' Grip on P: Why the People of Thailand have Taken to Mass Protest'. *Financial Times* (London), 12 May, 5.

URSCHEL, J. (1996). 'College Cry: "Free Burma" Activists make Inroads with US Companies'. *USA Today,* A1, 29 April.

US Department of State (1993). *Thailand Human Rights Practices, 1992.* Department of State Dispatch, vol. 3. Washington DC: US State Department.

VAN DE DONK, W., LOADER, B. D., NIXON, P. G. and RUCHT, D. (eds) (2004). *Cyberprotest: New Media, Citizens and Social Movements.* London: Routledge.

WATSON, R. and MOREAU, R. (1992). 'Blood and Beepers'. *Newsweek,* 1 June, 50.

NOTES

1. The English translations 'public sphere' or 'public realm' restate the German term, itself fairly fuzzy, within an implicitly spatial and consequently static metaphor, whereas the original conveys social interactivity, in a much more kinetic sense (Downing 1988).
2. See Shefner (2004) for a critique of the NSM approach within a Latin American context.
3. For some exceptions, see Martin (2002); Rucht (2005); Steinberg (2004). For more typical examples, which touch on media issues in passing, see Carty (2004: 306–7), or Davis and Rosan (2004: 288–90).
4. Association pour la Taxation des Transactions Financières pour l'Aide aux Citoyens.
5. See also Critical Art Ensemble (2001).
6. *Détournement* was a favourite term of the French Situationists, and could loosely be translated as 'hijacking,' as in the case of the Canadian Adbusters website's 're-purposing' of ads (also referred to as culture-jamming), www.adbusters.org.
7. The country's name has taken on intensely political connotations since 1989, when the military government changed it to the Union of Myanmar. While the government claimed the new name was ethnically neutral and would provide a greater sense of national unity, the opposition movement rejected the name change, since it was made without a referendum. While the UN has accepted the name change, the US government has not, and the terms have become an indicator of one's political position. Since this work focuses on the opposition to the regime, we use the name 'Burma' here. The term 'Burman' is used to refer to the ethnic majority of the country, while 'Burmese' is used as an adjective to refer to both the language and Burma's various peoples.
8. Burma's military regime has used the open source filtering software DansGuardian to implement its censorship of websites (especially those of a political nature), and observers believe the regime is now moving toward use of a firewall product produced by the US company Fortinet to more efficiently control the Internet (OpenNet Initiative 2005). Nonetheless, those with tech savvy and perseverance can find ways around this, and recent discussions with Burmese activists outside the country indicated a growing use of the Internet by activists inside Burma.
9. See Girard (1992) for a substantial collection of essays on radio stations of this kind. Other sources are the AMARC organization, based in Montréal, which provides updates through its subscription news service (InteRadio), and the InterPress Service (IPS), based in Rome, through its subscription news service, archived under the heading 'Community Radio.' Krohling Peruzzo (2004: chs 4, 5) provides a further account of a variety of Latin American examples.
10. The term 'community' is used for convenience here, but suffers from extreme vagueness (Downing 2001: 39–40).
11. For more information on this station, a key player in the Argentinean tumults of the early 2000s and a classic instance of social movement *Gegenöffentlichkeit* (see Colectivo La Tribu (2004a, b)).
12. Spain's and Ecuador's terms, respectively, for a popular tripe dish.
13. *Favela* has come to mean something especially Brazilian, part of its racially defined exotic mystique almost. This translation is partial, but an attempt to emphasize the commonalities of *favelas* with similar neighbourhoods across the planet, including in 'First World' cities.
14. Some elements of this section are drawn from Brooten (2004b).

CHAPTER 24

ICTs AND COMMUNITIES IN THE TWENTY-FIRST CENTURY: CHALLENGES AND PERSPECTIVES

JOO-YOUNG JUNG

SANDRA J. BALL-ROKEACH

YONG-CHAN KIM

SORIN ADAM MATEI

1 INTRODUCTION

As we begin our review of the literature on information and communication technologies (ICTs) and community networks, we cannot help but wonder why it has been such a difficult project to establish a concrete and widely accepted conceptualization of the relationship between ICTs and community. By way of reflecting on this issue, this chapter is organized around four of the major challenges that seem necessary to address in the effort to tease out this complex relationship. After introducing the challenges, we examine how past studies have tackled them. We conclude with an assessment of how well these challenges have been addressed and where we should go, in theory and research, to move beyond the present understandings.

One of the first challenges (Section 2) is to go beyond utopian and dystopian visions of the new ICTs. New communication technologies that reach a critical mass of adoption generate a litany of hopes and fears—utopian and dystopian visions of how the technology will afford solutions to previously intractable problems, or will create intractable problems. In the case of ICTs in the late twentieth and early twenty-first centuries, the perceived decline in the viability and vitality of communities of place was one of the main problems addressed by ICT visionaries. Some imagined a world in which place would no longer matter; community formations would spawn and thrive in the cyberspaces of the Internet. Others imagined that community would give way to a libertarian form of individualism. While we have passed the early period of the ICT visionaries, it is worth problematizing the dominant ideology of that era as it situates early studies of ICT and community issues.

The challenge examined in Section 3, is to resist the tendency towards technological determinism fostered by myopic approaches to studying ICTs and community. Technological determinism is seductive, even when disavowed. This problem is exacerbated when theoretical perspectives *and* methodological orientations are decontextualized. As a result, neither the ICT nor the individual is set in context of its grounded environments—the host environments, or ecology of established communication technologies, where people in communities (and other social networks) construct and reconstruct their communication ecologies as new ICTs emerge.

A related challenge (Section 4) is to critically examine ICTs in the contexts of existing place and non-place communities where people lead their everyday lives. In the process of asking if real or 'virtual' communities can exist in cyberspaces, an emphasis upon identifying the characteristics of virtual communities that are similar or different from the 'real' community often fails to consider the integration of ICTs into established residential and other community formations.

Finally, we argue in Section 5 that it is a challenge to articulate ICT-community relations at a time of rapid socio-demographic and cultural change. Many contemporary residential spaces are more fluid than they once were with respect to in and out flows of culturally diverse populations. ICTs emerged in an era of increased migration—diasporic movement or ethnoscapes (Appadurai 1996). Thus, over and above the issue of community form (e.g. *gemeinschaft*, networked formations), we have cultural variations along lines of ethnicity/race and class that hold open the likelihood that different 'communities' will engage ICTs at different rates and in different ways. The challenge becomes how to be sensitive to the cultural variations that modulate the manner in which people engage ICTs. It may require new theoretical and methodological orientations to capture such variations which we address in the conclusion.

2 MOVING BEYOND UTOPIAN AND DYSTOPIAN VISIONS OF ICTs

Historically, the advent of communication technologies has been greeted as a breakthrough in the quest for solutions to long unresolved problems of communities (Czitrom 1982; Fischer 1992; Marvin 1988). Each time a new communication technology emerges, it is accompanied by dreams of reviving a civic society, interpersonal ties, or organizational cohesion; concerns about the decline of community replaced with hopeful expectations. On the other hand, communication technologies have been seen as causing a decline in community life and sense of belonging. Telephones were held responsible for pulling people out of their local communities (Fischer 1992; Marvin 1988), and television was accused of loosening social ties in American communities (Putnam 2000). Rothenbuhler (2001) argued that both utopian and dystopian positions share a fundamental idea, that is, that community is based on a commonality where communication is an essential element. While dystopians believe that mass communication and new communication technologies, as opposed to interpersonal communications, are likely to give rise to 'false' community, optimists believe that mass media are important supplements to interpersonal communication and local social organization (Rothenbuhler 2001: 162).

During the early growth period of ICTs (1980s to early 1990s), discussions about the social impact of communication technology were quite positive, even utopian (e.g. Rheingold 1987, 1990, 1991). Many in this camp believed in the emergence of a new type of social aggregation, the 'virtual' or 'online community'. These terms, mainly articulated by activist-analyst proponents (Barlow 1994, 1996; Hauben and Hauben 1997; Hiltz and Turoff 1978; Horn 1998; Rheingold 1993; Rushkof 1994; Schuler 1996; Watson 1997), describe a new form of human association—facilitated by networks of communication powered by computers—in which distant and local face-to-face interactions are stimulated or enhanced beyond space or time constraints.

The early supporters of the idea of virtual community believed not only in the virtues of virtual communities, but also in their potential to offer superior and progressive forms of social aggregation (Horn 1998; Rheingold 1993; Rushkof 1994; Smith 1992; Watson 1997). The virtual community envisioned was egalitarian and allowed authenticity of feeling and involvement because, purportedly, communication through computer networks allowed freedom of expression and wide access to other people, communities, institutions, or information. These ideas made the virtual community project very appealing, especially as it displayed strong 'elective affinities' with the cultural, social, and political projects of the sixties, which informed the public sensibilities of the early adopters of new communication technologies in North America, Europe, Japan, or in the Anglo-Saxon nations outside Europe (Roszak 1986, 1994).

The drawing power of the virtual community dream appears to derive from its promise that establishing a new social covenant or inventing new types of social personality are possible (Hiltz and Turoff 1978; Kiesler, Siegel and McGuire 1984; Matei 2005; Sproull and Kiesler 1991; Turkle 1984; Valee 1982). In a more practical vein, the virtual community dream has fuelled a libertarian–individualist project, which at least in the US spans the gamut of political ideologies, from the radical, anarchist left to the libertarian right (Barlow 1994; Dyson 1997; Etzioni 1993; Gingrich 1995; Katz 1997; Kelly 1995, 1998; Meeks 1997; Mitchell 1995; Rheingold 1993; Rushkof 1994; Schuler 1996; Toffler and Toffler 1995).

However, these views did not go without challenge. A number of academic and non-academic critics vigorously questioned them. Overall, these critics were more likely to see ICTs as agents of social control and massification than as agents of social and individual liberation (Boal 1995; Downey and McGuigan 1999; Robins 1999). The whole progressive ideal of reformulating the social covenant through computer technologies was found to be at fault by those who rejected the premise that the Internet, or any similar system, is owned or ruled by no one. Scholars and practitioners pointed to the fact that ICTs are lodged in specific government, corporate and individual settings, each with the capacity to impose agendas that are shaped by specific interests (Robins 1999).

To claims of ease of access came counterclaims of a 'gapping' digital divide (Barbrook and Cameron 1997). In this context, the degree to which ICTs or the communities they may support 'want to be freed' is put in great doubt (Boal 1995; Downey and McGuigan 1999; Robins 1999; US Department of Commerce 1999). Other critics pointed to the fact that identity switching can weaken social responsibility (Slouka 1995; Sunstein 2001). They also pointed to the fact that while communication technologies might create communities, these might fall short of the ideal since their directing principle is that of common interest, often quite narrowly defined (e.g. hobbies, consumption, or instrumental needs). The communication ideology, which equates presence of online connections or infrastructure access with social connectedness, was indicted as a type of heterotopic discourse, whose goal was to shift attention from real problems to imaginary solutions (Lievrouw 1998).

Coming from a different perspective, rooted in the social psychological research paradigm, a number of scholars have indicted the Internet for its deleterious effects on human well-being. Nie and Erbring (2000) concluded that the Internet leads to social atomization. They announced that the Internet replicates the social isolation effects of television and of the automobile (Markoff 2000; Nie and Erbring 2000; Putnam 1995). In an early and much publicized study (Kraut et al. 1998), Kraut and his co-authors argued that those that spent more time online became lonelier and more depressed. After a temporary reversal (Kraut et al. 2002), the authors reconfirmed their initial findings (Shklovski and Kraut 2004).

For many scholars, the utopian–dystopian debate seemed to pose a false dilemma. Although not rejecting the proposition that online communication environments can and do foster social groups that display community characteristics, such as group-sanctioned identities or jargons, norms, or strong personal relationships (Baym 1998; McLaughlin, Osborne and Ellison 1997; Parks and Floyd 1996), they shifted the focus to what happens to people's pre-existing community-oriented social and spiritual resources when they migrate online (Baym 1998; Calhoun 1998; Doheny-Farina 1996; Hampton and Wellman 1999, 2000; Matei 2004; Matei and Ball-Rokeach 2002, 2003; Putnam 2000; Rainie and Kohut 2000; Wellman and Gulia 1999). The thrust of this literature is the idea that online groups grow out of pre-existing social formations (Calhoun 1986, 1998; Jones 1997; Matei 2003; Wellman 1997; Wellman and Gulia 1999), or as Calhoun aptly put it 'the Internet mainly makes it easier for us to do some things we were already doing and allows those with the resources to do some things that they already wanted to do' (Calhoun 1998: 382).

In a series of innovative research projects, Wellman, Haythornthwaite, Hampton, and other scholars advanced new and productive concepts, such as that of 'networked individualism', where online and offline ties intersect and support people in an increasingly unstable social universe (Quan-Haase et al. 2002; Wellman 2001; Wellman et al. 2001; Wellman and Haythornthwaite 2002). The Metamorphosis Project, conducted in Los Angeles, uncovered the subtle ways in which online and offline ties are linked, with sociability online leading, and being reinforced by, sociability offline (Matei and Ball-Rokeach 2002). It also showed that the Internet has been increasingly woven through the communication infrastructure of local residential communities, contributing in certain situations to consolidating social ties (Matei and Ball-Rokeach 2003). These findings are consistent with those produced by other projects. For example, a number of empirically oriented social research projects, such as Syntopia (Katz, Rice, and Aspden 2001) or the Pew Internet rolling polls (Howard, Rainie and Jones 2002), emphasize the fact that online and offline lives are inextricably united. That is, people's online communications are examined in the context of their offline social and communication lives.

3   RESISTING THE TENDENCY TOWARDS TECHNOLOGICAL DETERMINISM

One of the driving forces that often lead to the duality of either utopian or dystopian visions is implicit or explicit technological determinism. The dynamic interplay between technology and people articulated in the social construction of technology approaches is absent, such that the capacities of people to participate in the construction of the technology and its everyday meanings are ignored and go unobserved (MacKenzie 1999). Technological determinism, whether by default or by intention, is usually most evident in early studies of emerging communication technologies (see Czitrom 1982; Dutton 1996; Fischer 1992; Marvin 1988).

However, both ICTs and communities are changing while being studied. At the same time as ICTs increase their capacities for communication, there are increased flows of people across national borders that make many communities of place more demographically and culturally diverse. In order to avoid leaning towards a techno-logical deterministic perspective, it is necessary to examine ICTs in the context of existing social and communication ecologies, and to analyse the relationship between the two. As Rothenbuhler (2001: 165–73) suggests, the relationship between commu-nication and community should be studied with three things in mind; first, commu-nity and communication are both based on differences rather than commonalities; second, conflicts and 'bad things', as well as a 'good life' exist in communities; and third, community is not external to the individuals that constitute it.

Dutton (1999) pointed out that social factors are likely to shape the design and use of ICTs. These social factors include economic resources and constraints, ICT paradigms and practices, conceptions and responses of users, geography of space and place, and institutional arrangements and public policy. Similarly, several researchers overcame the tendency towards technological determinism by consid-ering factors that condition or mediate the relationship between ICTs and individ-uals in community contexts. These factors range from individual-level (e.g. Internet experience, personality, age), interpersonal-level (e.g. social capital) to community-level (e.g. communication action context), as will be explained next.

Length of Internet experience seems to condition the social and civic engage-ment outcomes of Internet communications. Generally speaking, time connected operates in favour of engagement; that is, as people go beyond the novelty of a new technology to develop a history of Internet connection, they are somewhat more likely to be involved in their place-based communities. In their studies of Blacks-burg Electronic Village, for example, Kavanaugh and Patterson (2002: 336) found 'the longer people are users of the Internet the more likely they are to use the Internet for a variety of social capital building activities, such as communicating with local friends, church members, and formal and informal social groups'.

Age or generation may be another conditional factor. Shah, McLeod, and Yoon (2001) found that after controlling for other factors, Internet use was more strongly related to trust in people and civic participation among young adults than older people. Kraut et al.'s (2002) HomeNet study also found that age was an important conditional factor. Teens were more likely than adults to experience enhanced social support as a function of their Internet use. On the other hand, adults were more likely than teens to increase their face-to-face interaction with family and friends through their Internet use.

Personality/motivational factors also can influence how individuals use the Internet and, therefore, its engagement consequences. For example, Kraut et al.'s (1998) study reported an interaction between extroversion and Internet use for community involvement. They found that Internet use was positively related to community involvement among extroverts, while it was negatively related to community involvement among introverts. Also, the motivations driving Internet use may condition the relationship between Internet use and community engagement. For example, several studies have found that individuals who use the Internet to get news or information, or to communicate with others, are more likely to get involved in community activities than those whose primary reason for using the Internet is having fun or entertainment (Bimber 2000; Norris 1998; Shah, McLeod and Yoon 2001).

Pre-existing connections to social resources also condition the effects of Internet communications. For example, Kavanaugh and Patterson (2002) found that individuals with high levels of community involvement (e.g. keeping up with local news, having ideas for improving local areas, getting together with other people, and working to bring change to the local area) were more likely to use the Internet for acquiring additional social capital, such as communicating with local friends, family, church members, and formal or informal social groups.

Finally, community-level contextual characteristics that affect communication can condition the way the Internet is deployed with regard to community engagement. From the communication infrastructure perspective (Ball-Rokeach, Kim and Matei 2001; Kim and Ball-Rokeach 2004), Matei and Ball-Rokeach (2002) found that the role of the Internet in shaping 'belonging' to residential communities is complex, and mediated by ethnicity. Internet connections had a positive effect on belonging in Anglo residential communities in Los Angeles. This effect, however, was indirect, being mediated by participation in community organizations. In the Asian and Latino communities, being an Internet connector had neither a positive nor a negative effect on local neighbourhood belonging. Borgida and colleagues (Borgida et al. 2002) compared two small Minnesota cities with similar demographics, and found that the existing culture of the communities and their approach to the new technology influenced how an electronic network developed. In one community where the goal of reducing inequality was seen as an important issue, the electronic network diffused throughout income groups. In the other community where the network was considered more of a private good, income disparities were reflected in people's access to the electronic network.

4 GROUNDING THE ANALYSIS IN THE EVERYDAY LIVES OF COMMUNITIES OF PLACE

Researchers often isolate a new ICT from existing ways of communicating and from communities of place where people lead their everyday lives. One crucial, but difficult, way to avoid such myopic inquiry is to study the process through which people integrate ICTs into their everyday lives in the communities in which they live. Berry Wellman and his colleagues pioneered this effort. They studied ICTs in Netville (Hampton and Wellman 2000), a suburban neighbourhood of 109 detached, closely spaced, single-family homes outside Toronto, Canada, and an early adopter of high-speed Internet access—still unusual in 1997. Of the 109 homes in Netville, 64 were Internet connected. The authors found that wired compared to non-wired residents remembered the names of three times as many neighbours, talked with about twice as many, and had been invited or had invited one and a half times as many neighbours to their homes. They also observed that wired Netville residents used their email lists to organize social activities (e.g. bands, sports teams, or bowling leagues), to talk about events and what was happening in their community (such as a burglary, vandalism or unsafe traffic conditions), and to mobilize actions against the housing developers (e.g. in-person strategy meetings) (Hampton and Wellman 2000: 303).

Kavanaugh and Patterson (2002) found that spending more time on the Internet was associated with using the Internet to communicate with local friends, church members, and with formal/informal social groups as well as communicating more frequently with non-local families and friends. Using Pew Internet and American Life Project data from October 2001, Howard, Rainie, and Jones (2002) found that Internet users were more likely to visit friends or relatives, had more people they could turn to for support, and made calls to friends or relatives just to talk. Based on US national telephone survey data gathered in 1995, and again in 2000, Katz, Rice and Aspden (2001) found that Internet users were more likely to belong to community organizations than non-users, and they were more likely to have, and meet with, local friends. From a study of people's reactions to the 9/11 attack, Kim, Jung, Cohen, and Ball-Rokeach (2004) reported that individuals with broader and more intense Internet connectedness relationships were more likely to participate in civic behaviours following the attack than those who used the Internet in a more limited way.

ICTs and local community building

In a more practical vein, several studies have examined how ICTs are being incorporated into local communities to enhance community networks. For example, a group of scholars proposed the term, 'community informatics' to actively examine the ways in which ICTs are serving as tools to improve information networks in different communities (Gurstein 2003, 2000; Keeble and Loader 2001). Shearman (2003: 14–15) identified the missions of community networks as a number of (re)connecting goals: to create 'connecting communities' by reconnecting people with others; reconnecting people with themselves in the sense of building up self-confidence and self-esteem; reconnecting people with economic opportunities; reconnecting people with educational opportunity, providing pathways to future employment for those who are outside the formal education system; and reconnecting people with their locality and culture, helping people to develop and access relevant information to give voice to their identity. Researchers and practitioners have developed a variety of ICT-based community networks to increase community capacity. We briefly identify these efforts in terms of the community-level benefit they are designed to achieve.

Improving residents' participation in the democratic process

There have been many attempts to use ICTs to build civic networks. These include Amsterdam's Digital City, Bologna's IperBolE, Philadelphia's Neighborhoods Online, the Blacksburg Electronic Village, the Public Electronic Network (PEN) in Santa Monica, California, and the Milan Community Network. Neighbourhood councils in the city of Los Angeles use email as a main communication channel to communicate with each other and with city officials and agencies (Weare et al. 2003). In these city-level or neighbourhood-level computer network projects, ICTs were designed as civic community forums where local residents exchange community news and information, discuss important community issues, and mobilize community activities.

Providing access to practical information

ICTs can also be used to provide access to basic social and civic information such as local events, education, health, or emergency services. The Public Electronic Network (PEN) in Santa Monica, and the Seattle Community Network (SCN) provide a government information channel. Another example is the CIRCE project, a British Library-funded project designed for community members to access information brought together from distributed databases in a user-friendly way (Leech 1999).

Providing access to health information has been a major focus of a number of ICT-based efforts. Indeed, Tom Grunder's Cleveland Free-Net, an electronic bulletin board with the mission of delivering health information to the general public, is regarded as the first community network project, following which a number of health information community networks (HICNs) have been developed. They afford local residents and groups the capacities to come together to share information, prioritize issues, resolve conflicts, estimate the impact of policy initiatives, and plan, organize, manage, and evaluate programmes and projects dealing with such community health issues as teenage pregnancy, violence, suicide, unemployment, poverty, and housing (Duhl 2000).

Supporting local economic development

ICTs also have been developed to contribute to regional or neighbourhood economic revitalization by creating new jobs, increasing efficiencies of local business, and improving local buyer–seller relationships. Community networks in Ipswich City, Australia, the Blacksburg Electronic Village in Virginia, Liberty Net in Philadelphia, Pennsylvania, and the Appalachian Center for Economic Networks (ACE-net) in Southern Ohio were set up especially to deal with unemployment problems and regional economic development.

CTCs—Providing opportunities for the disadvantaged

Communication Technology Centers (CTCs) in the US are one of the ways in which ICTs become concretely incorporated into multiple aspects of existing community networks. According to Servon and Nelson (2001), almost two-thirds (64.2 per cent) of CTCs are located in, and serve, urban areas, and more than three-quarters of CTCs target low-income populations (Servon and Nelson 2001: 283). These researchers identify three types of CTCs based on the services they provide: CTCs that focus on providing access to ICTs, CTCs designed to develop information technology (IT) skills in order to address economic and job-related issues, and CTCs that connect residents to resources, create materials residents can use, and teach residents how to create relevant content. Ideally, CTCs would provide all of these services to maximize their impact on underserved populations. The real world funding and the staffing conditions under which most CTCs operate usually work against this goal. Therefore, Servon (2002) calls for collaboration between CTCs and community-based organizations (CBOs) that have complementary programmatic mandates. Similarly, the Computers in Our Future Project (Fowells and Lazarus 2001) envisioned the role of CTCs in a larger community context:

[CTCs] could accomplish more than providing valuable direct services to participants. They could serve as a technology resource to public and private entities in the community, meeting a pressing need that otherwise would not have been met....[CTCs could] spread benefits beyond the individual center to the community. (p. ii)

Shaw and Shaw (1999) view many of the issues concerning the empowerment of lower class people as a matter of enhancing their local information infrastructure.

From their study of community networks in low-income communities in Boston and New Jersey, they found that community networks helped members of these communities rebuild a fractured social setting.

In their study of CTCs in the Los Angeles area, Hayden and Ball-Rokeach (2005) conceptualized the role of CTCs as 'a unique element in a communication infra-structure—*a digital hub*—that facilitates connectivity and communicative capacity for the essential community components of a local urban environment' (p. 4, emphasis in original). The authors join the call for the incorporation of CTCs into the existing network of community organizations, residents, and geo-ethnic media (media targeted to particular geographic and ethnic communities) (Kim, Jung, and Ball-Rokeach, in press).

5 Which community? Observing cultural variations in ICT–community relations

Once established communities are taken into consideration in studying ICTs, the challenge becomes the observation of 'difference' among communities. Janowitz (1952: 11) stated in 1952 that 'the community press acts as a mechanism which seeks to maintain local consensus through the emphasis on *common values* rather than on the solution of conflicting values'. In contemporary communities, media serve cultur-ally diverse populations. As Wilson and Gutiérrez (1985: 234) state, 'racial minorities will be more fully served by an expanding communication media system than were racial minorities in the past ... the socialization function of media in developing and transmitting the common culture of the society will be less important'.

Although new ICTs may enhance the frequency and quality of communication among ethnic groups spread across the globe, this does not mean the deterioration of local communities. Castells (1997: 65) argued that 'ethnicity, while being a funda-mental feature of our societies ... may not induce communes on its own. Rather, it is likely to be processed by religion, nation, and locality, whose specificity it tends to reinforce.' Local communities are where people live and interact on a daily basis, a process that goes hand in hand with local and distant Internet communications.

Ball-Rokeach and her colleagues at the University of Southern California (Gibbs et al. 2004) argue that participation in Internet communications does not magically translate into a 'global village' where people of different backgrounds come together to connect with one another. From their survey and focus group studies of seven new and old immigrant groups in the Los Angeles area, they found that: (a) a significant divide existed among different socioeconomic and ethnic groups regarding computer ownership and Internet access; and (b) people's Internet communications were ethnically bound—connecting mostly with friends and family and visiting websites of their countries of origin (in the case of new immigrants), rather than making 'new friends' or visiting websites of other cultures (Gibbs et al. 2004).

Indeed, many people who, for a variety of reasons, are away from their home countries use media to connect both to their local community and to their home countries and cultures (Grossberg 1996; Silverstone 2001). As Silverstone states, 'the populations that are involved are both local and global at the same time: they are local insofar as they are minority cultures living in particular places, but they are global in their range and reach' (Silverstone 2001: 21).

So-called global communications are often transformed into local/regional communications (Karim 2003; Parham 2004). Parham (2004) studied a diasporic network called Haiti Global Village. One of the main observations in her study was that this diasporic network was not placeless. After a few years of involvement in the Haiti Global Village, people in the US formed another group called CHAH (Coalition of Haitians for the Advancement of Haiti), which had its base in Tampa, Florida. The formation of CHAH illustrates the evolution of an online diasporic network into a mix of online and offline organization. Mandaville (2003), who studied Muslims living in the diaspora, concludes that 'the new interpretations of Islam that emerge in diasporic Islamic contexts are often rather "local" in nature insofar as they seek to make Islam relevant to the circumstances of particular communities living in the West' (Mandaville 2003: 146).

Access to ICTs does not in itself mean that people will engage in diasporic communications via new communication technologies. After an in-depth study of a Ghanaian diasporic group, Ackah and Newman (2003: 206) argued that for most people, ICTs were not particularly beneficial, and they did not hold much interest because ICTs were not compatible with the goals and desires of the Ghanaian people. Ackah and Newman's study cautions against assuming that everyone will move to new media when they become available, and make use of them in the same way.

A study conducted by the University of Southern California's Metamorphosis Project examined the effects of 'geo-ethnicity', a concept developed to examine ethnicity in context of an ecological and dynamic communication infrastructure. Defining geo-ethnicity as ethnically-articulated attitudes and behaviours grounded in a specific temporal and spatial situation (Kim, Jung, and Ball-Rokeach, forthcoming), the Metamorphosis researchers offer an ecological framework to understand ethnicity as a multilevel phenomenon embedded in a specific geographical, temporal, and cultural context (Eriksen 1991; Featherston and Lash 1999; Flora 1999). Based on data from ethnically diverse communities in Los Angeles, they have demonstrated geo-ethnic effects on the breadth, intensity, and depth of Internet connectedness (Kim et al. 2002) and the level of neighbourhood engagement (Kim et al. forthcoming). These geo-ethnic effects on individuals' connections to both ICTs and local communities are based on the combination of two sets of factors: who they are (e.g. immigration history, level of acculturation/assimilation, ethnic identification, cultural attitudes towards technology and community involvement, etc.) and where they are (e.g. level of access to basic political, economic, technological, or health resources, area-level poverty, quality of communication infrastructure, population characteristics such as ethnic diversity or residential stability, etc.).

6 Conclusion

In this chapter, we identified major challenges to the study of ICTs and communities, and critically reviewed research literatures in relation to each challenge. The challenges considered are: (1) getting beyond utopian and dystopian visions; (2) resisting the tendency toward technological determinism; (3) grounding the analysis in the everyday lives of communities of place; and (4) observing cultural variations in ICT-community relations. To conclude our discussion, we assess how well past studies have met each challenge, and make recommendations for future research.

Utopian and dystopian challenge

The possibility of a completely new form of 'Internet' community has been widely discussed in academic and public settings. However, as the new technology has matured, fantasies about virtual communities and fears about the breakdown of established ways of living have toned down. Scholars have turned their attention away from discovering revolutionary effects to investigating the ways in which ICTs relate to other aspects of people's everyday lives. As new ICTs continue to emerge, we should incline our gaze away from a search for the revolutionary to the more likely evolutionary, at the same time recognizing that the objective 'potential' of a new technology should not be the main rationale for predicting its outcomes. For example, with all the technical features of the Internet, it did not enable a global village, or even a national village, where people can be free from their offline socioeconomic and demographic associations and live a life online via virtual connections, nor did it destroy our pre-existing social networks and organizations.

Resisting implicit or explicit technological determinism

Since the early studies of ICTs (e.g. Dutton 1996; Fulk, Schmitz and Steinfield 1990), which proposed 'social influence' models of communication technologies, continuous efforts have been made to resist inclinations towards technological determinism. Many of the arguments against technological determinism have been conceptual or theoretical. The challenge that remains is to overcome the often-unintended technological determinism embedded in research methodologies. It is challenging to design research that not only systematically examines an ICT–community relation, but also takes into account pre-existing media-community relations. Yet our position is that this challenge must be met, and that this can be achieved by researchers developing ecological, recursive, transactional, and multi-level models and the methods to evaluate them. The new models should be ecological, in describing how new ICTs enter a pre-existing social and media ecology; recursive, in empirically testing how ICTs and communities influence each other; transactional, in offering analytical tools to articulate a process (e.g. structuration), in which both ICTs and communities are being restructured while influencing one another; and multilevel, in incorporating contextual factors that influence the ways in which ICTs and communities are related.

Grounding ICTs in local community

The studies that we reviewed in this chapter examined the role of ICTs in local communities, and how ICTs can be deployed to address issues of inequality and to improve community networks. Few studies, however, have examined 'where ICTs fit in' in the larger communication system of a community. That is, an ecological framework to examine ICTs within community contexts was missing. A programme utilizing ICTs to improve community networks, for example, should understand what has been lacking in established community networks, examine the roles that ICTs are playing in relation to other actors in those networks (Matei and Ball-Rokeach 2003), and then think through how ICTs (probably in combination with other ways of communicating) might establish relations that improve the capacity of community networks to operate in the service of community constituencies. Put more briefly, research should begin with a network diagnostic and an assessment of how community groups are/are not connected to ICTs and, only then, design an informatic or programme to strengthen network relations. Methodologically, a multi-level research design that incorporates theory-driven selections of micro-, meso-, and macro-level variables is required.

ICTs in diverse communities

In this age of globalization with in and out flows of diverse populations and technological developments, communities—and especially urban communities—are more culturally diverse. When ICTs are studied in relation to who is connecting to them, and where, and why, the analysis should include the full array of extant cultural and ethnic groups. Many studies do take ethnicity into consideration; however, ethnicity is usually treated as an individual characteristic without contextualization of where certain ethnic groups live and what kind of social and communication environments surround them. In order to examine the ways in which various ethnic groups construct ICT communications in the context of their communities, ethnicity and geographic/community-level factors should be studied in relation to one another.

We suggest three things to consider when conducting research with diverse ethnic groups. First, when collecting data through surveys, focus groups, interviews, ethnographies or other methods, researchers should go out of their way to be accessible and friendly, by using, for example, the native language of participants and paying attention to culturally-sensitive linguistic and cultural practices. Secondly, when studying the communication patterns of various cultural and ethnic groups, the media as a whole (traditional and new media, mainstream and ethnic media), rather than just a new communication technology, should be taken into consideration in order to be able to observe ethnic/cultural variations in media relations (Ackah and Newman 2003; Ball-Rokeach, Kim and Matei 2001; Gibbs et al. 2004; Silverstone 2001). Thirdly, comparative studies, whether intra- or international, afford an examination of how different social, cultural and communication factors interact with people's everyday communication practices.

REFERENCES

ACKAH, W. and NEWMAN, J. (2003). 'Ghanaian Seventh Day Adventists On and Offline: Problematizing the Virtual Communities Discourse', in K. H. Karim (ed.), *The Media of Diaspora*. London and New York: Routledge, 203–14.

APPADURAI, A. (1996). *Modernity at Large: Cultural Dimensions of Globalization*. Minneapolis, MN: University of Minnesota Press.

BALL-ROKEACH, S. J., KIM, Y.-C. and MATEI, S. (2001). 'Storytelling Neighborhood: Paths to Belonging in Diverse Urban Environments'. *Communication Research*, 28(4): 392–428.

BARBROOK, R. and CAMERON, A. (1997). 'The Californian Ideology'. *Science as Culture*, 16: 44–72.

BARLOW, J. P. (1994). 'Jack In, Young Pioneer'. *Keynote Essay for the 1994 Computerworld College Edition*, http://www.eff.org/Misc/Publications/John_Perry_Barlow/HTML/jack_-in_young_pioneer.html, accessed 20 Oct. 2006.

—— (1996). 'A Declaration of the Independence of Cyberspace', http://homes.eff.org/~barlow/Declaration-Final.html, accessed 18 Mar. 2006.

BAYM, N. (1998). 'The Emergence of on-Line Community', in S. Jones (ed.), *Cybersociety 2.0: Revisiting CMC and Community*. Thousand Oaks, CA: Sage, 35–68.

BIMBER, B. (2000). 'The Study of Information Technology and Civic Engagement'. *Political Communication*, 17(4): 329–33.

BOAL, I. (1995). 'A Flow of Monsters: Luddism and Virtual Technologies', in J. Brook and I. Boal (eds), *Resisting the Virtual Life: The Culture and Politics of Information*. San Francisco, CA: City Lights, 3–16.

BORGIDA, E., SULLIVAN, J. L., OXENDINE, A., et al. (2002). 'Civic Culture Meets the Digital Divide: The Role of Community Electronic Networks'. *Journal of Social Issues*, 58(1): 125–141.

CALHOUN, C. (1986). 'Computer Technology, Large-Scale Social Integration, and the Local Community'. *Urban Affairs Quarterly*, 22(2): 329–49.

—— (1998). 'Community without Propinquity Revisited: Communications Technology and the Transformation of the Urban Public Sphere'. *Sociological Inquiry*, 68(3): 373–97.

CASTELLS, M. (1997). *The Power of Identity*. Malden, MA: Blackwell.

CZITROM, D. L. (1982). *Media and the American Mind: From Morse to McLuhan*. Chapel Hill, NC: University of North Carolina Press.

DOHENY-FARINA, S. (1996). *The Wired Neighborhood*. New Haven, CT: Yale University Press.

DOWNEY, J. and McGUIGAN, J. (eds) (1999). *Technocities: The Culture and Political Economy of the Digital Revolution*. London: Sage.

DUHL, L. J. (2000). 'Health Information Community Networks'. *Public Health Reports*, 115(2/3): 271.

DUTTON, W. H. (1999). *Society on the Line: Information Politics in the Digital Age*. Oxford and New York: Oxford University Press.

—— (ed.), (1996). *Information and Communication Technologies – Visions and Realities*. Oxford: Oxford University Press.

DYSON, E. (1997). *Release 2.0: A Design for Living in the Digital Age* (1st edn). New York: Broadway Books.

ERIKSEN, T. H. (1991). 'The Cultural Contexts of Ethnic Differences'. *Man*, 26(1): 127–44.

ETZIONI, A. (1993). *The Spirit of Community: Rights, Responsibilities and the Communitarian Agenda*. New York: Crown Publishers, Inc.

FEATHERSTONE, M. and LASH, S. (1999). *Spaces of Culture: City-Nation-World*. London: Sage.

FISCHER, C. S. (1992). *America Calling: A Social History of the Telephone to 1940*. Berkeley, CA: University of California Press.

FLORA, P. (1999). *State Formation, Nation-Building and Mass Politics in Europe: The Theory of Stein Rokkan*. Oxford: Oxford University Press.

FOWELLS, L. and LAZARUS, W. (2001). *What Works in Closing the Technology Gap? Lessons from a Four Year Demonstration in 11 Low Income California Communities*. Los Angeles, CA: Computers In Our Future.

FULK, J., SCHMITZ, J. and STEINFIELD, C. W. (1990). 'A Social Influence Model of Technology Use', in J. Fulk and C. W. Steinfield (eds), *Organizations and Communication Technology*. Newbury Park, CA: Sage Publications, 71–94.

GIBBS, J., BALL-ROKEACH, S. J., JUNG, J.-Y., KIM, Y.-C., et al. (2004). 'The Globalization of Everyday Life: Visions and Reality', in M. Sturken, D. Thomas and S. J. Ball-Rokeach (eds), *Technological Visions: The Hopes and Fears that Shape New Technologies*. Philadelphia, PA: Temple University Press, 339–58.

GINGRICH, N. (1995). 'Foreword', in A. Toffler and H. Toffler (eds), *Creating a New Civilization*. Atlanta, GA: Turner Publishing, Inc., 13–18.

GROSSBERG, L. (1996). 'Identity and Cultural Studies: Is That All There Is?' in S. Hall and P. D. Gay (eds), *Questions of Cultural Identity*. London: Sage, 87–107.

GURSTEIN, M. (2003). 'Perspectives on Urban and Rural Community Informatics: Theory and Performance, Community Informatics and Strategies for Flexible Networking', in S. Marshall, W. Taylor, and Y. Xu (eds), *Closing the Digital Divide: Transforming Regional Economies and Communities with Information Technology*. Westport, CT: Greenwood Publishing Group, 1–11.

—— (ed.). (2000). *Community Informatics: Enabling Communities with Information and Communication Technologies*. Hershey, PA: Idea Group Publishing.

HAMPTON, K. N. and WELLMAN, B. (1999). 'Netville On-Line and Off-Line. Observing and Surveying a Wired Suburb'. *American Behavioral Scientist*, 43(3): 475–92.

—— (2000). 'Examining Community in the Digital Neighborhood. Early Results from Canada's Wired Suburb', in T. Ishida and K. Isbister (eds), *Digital Cities: Technologies, Experiences, and Future Perspectives*. New York/Berlin: Springer-Verlag, 194–208.

HAUBEN, M. and HAUBEN, R. (1997). *Netizens. On the History and the Impact of Usenet and the Internet*. Hoboken, NJ: Wiley/IEEE Computer Society Press.

HAYDEN, C. and BALL-ROKEACH, S. J. (2005). 'Maintaining the Digital Hub: Locating the Community Technology Center in a Communication Infrastructure'. Unpub. mss., Los Angeles, CA.

HILTZ, S. R. and TUROFF, M. (1978). *The Network Nation: Human Communication Via Computer*. Reading, MA: Addison-Wesley.

HORN, S. (1998). *Cyberville: Clicks, Culture, and the Creation of an on-Line Town*. New York: Warner Books.

HOWARD, P., RAINIE, L. and JONES, S. (2002). 'Days and Nights on the Internet: The Impact of a Diffusing Technology', in B. Wellman and C. Haythornthwaite (eds), *The Internet in Everyday Life*. Malden, MA: Blackwell, 45–73.

JANOWITZ, M. (1952/1967). *The Community Press in an Urban Setting: The Social Elements of Urbanism*. Chicago, IL: The University of Chicago Press.

JONES, S. (1997). 'The Internet and Its Social Landscape', in S. Jones (ed.), *Virtual Culture: Identity and Communication in Cybersociety*. Thousand Oaks, CA: Sage, 7–35.

KARIM, K. H. (2003). *The Media of Diaspora*. London and New York: Routledge.

KATZ, J. (1997). 'Birth of a Digital Nation'. *Wired* 5(4), http://www.wired.com/wired/5.04/netizen.html, accessed 25 Mar. 2006.

——, RICE, R. E. and ASPDEN, P. (2001). 'The Internet, 1995–2000: Access, Civic Involvement, and Social Interaction'. *American Behavioral Scientist*, 45(3): 405–20.

——, —— and —— (2001). 'The Internet, 1995–2000: Access, Civic Involvement and Social Interaction'. *American Behavioral Scientist*, 45(3): 404–19.

KAVANAUGH, A. L. and PATTERSON, S. J. (2001). 'The Impact of Community Computer Networks on Social Capital and Community Involvement'. *American Behavioral Scientist*, 45(3): 469–509.

—— and —— (2002). 'The Impact of Community Computer Networks on Social Capital and Community Involvement in Blacksburg', in B. Wellman and C. Haythornthwaite (eds), *The Internet in Everyday Life*. Malden, MA: Blackwell, 325–44.

KEEBLE, L. and LOADER, B. (eds) (2001). *Community Informatics: Shaping Computer-Mediated Social Relations*. London: Routledge.

KELLY, K. (1995). *Out of Control: The New Biology of Machines, Social Systems and the Economic World*. Reading, MA: Addison-Wesley.

—— (1998). *New Rules for the New Economy: 10 Radical Strategies for a Connected World*. New York: Viking.

KIESLER, S., SIEGEL, J. and McGUIRE, T. (1984). 'Social Psychological Aspects of Computer Mediated Communication'. *American Psychologist*, 39(10): 1123–34.

KIM, Y.-C. and BALL-ROKEACH, S. J. (2004). 'Civic Engagement from a Communication Infrastructure Perspective'. Paper presented at the Voice and Citizenship Conference, Seattle, WA.

——, JUNG, J.-Y. and BALL-ROKEACH, S. J. (forthcoming). ' "Geo-Ethnicity" and Neighborhood Engagement: A Communication Infrastructure Perspective'. *Political Communication*.

——, ——, —— et al. (2002). 'Ethnicity, Place and Communication Technology: Geo-Ethnic Effect on Multi-Dimensional Internet Connectedness in Urban Communities'. Paper presented at the International Communication Association Convention, Seoul, Korea, 15–19 July.

——, ——, COHEN et al. (2004). 'Internet Connectedness Before and After September 11th 2001'. *New Media & Society*, 6(5): 611–631.

KRAUT, R., KIESLER, S., BONEVA, B., et al. (2002). 'Internet Paradox Revisited'. *Journal of Social Issues*, 58(1): 49–74.

——, PATTERSON, M., LUNDMARK, V. et al. (1998). 'Internet Paradox: A Social Technology That Reduces Social Involvement and Psychological Well-Being?' *American Psychologist*, 53(9): 1017–32.

LEECH, H. (1999). CIRCE: *Better Communities through Better Information* (Library and Information Commission Research Report 1). London: Library and Information Commission.

LIEVROUW, L. (1998). 'Our Own Devices: Heterotopic Communication, Discourse and Culture in Information Society'. *The Information Society*, 14(2): 83–96.

MacKENZIE, D. (1999). 'Technological Determinism', in W. Dutton (ed.), *Society on the Line: Information Politics in the Digital Age*. Oxford: Oxford University Press, 39–41.

MANDAVILLE, P. (2003). 'Communication and Diasporic Islam: A Virtual Ummah?', in K. H. Karim (ed.), *The Media of Diaspora*. London: Routledge, 135–47.

MARKOFF, J. (2000). 'Portrait of a Newer, Lonelier Crowd is Captured in an Internet Survey'. *New York Times*, 16 Feb., 1.

MARVIN, C. (1988). *When Old Technologies Were New: Thinking About Communications in the Late Nineteenth Century*. Oxford: Oxford University Press.

MATEI, S. (2003). 'The Internet as Magnifying Glass: Marital Status and On-Line Social Ties'. *The Public*, 10(1): 101–12.

—— (2004). 'The Impact of State-Level Social Capital on Emergence of Virtual Communities'. *Journal of Broadcasting and Electronic Media*, 48(1): 23–40.

—— (2005). 'From Counterculture to Cyberculture: Virtual Community Discourse and the Dilemma of Modernity'. *Journal of Computer Mediated Communication*, 10(3): art. 14, http://jcmc.indiana.edu/vol10/issue3/matei.html.

—— and BALL-ROKEACH, S. J. (2002). 'Belonging in Geographic, Ethnic and Internet Spaces', in B. Wellman and C. A. Haythornthwaite (eds), *The Internet in Everyday Life*. Malden, MA: Blackwell, 404–30.

—— and —— (2003). 'The Internet in the Communication Infrastructure of Ethnically-Marked Neighborhoods: Meso or Macro-Linkage?' *Journal of Communication*, 53(4): 642–57.

McLAUGHLIN, M., OSBORNE, K. K. and ELLISON, N. (1997). 'Virtual Community in a Telepresence Environment', in S. Jones (ed.) *Virtual Culture: Identity and Communication in Cybersociety*. Thousand Oaks, CA: Sage, 146–68.

Meeks, B. (1997). 'Better Democracy through Technology. The Next 50 Years: Our Hopes, Our Visions, Our Plans'. *Communications of the ACM*, 40(2): 75–8.

Mitchell, W. J. (1995). *City of Bits: Space, Place, and the Infobahn*. Cambridge, MA: MIT Press.

Nie, N. H. and Erbring, L. (2000). *Internet and Society: A Preliminary Report*. Palo Alto, CA: Stanford Institute for the Quantitative Study of Society, Stanford University.

Norris, P. (1998). 'Virtual Democracy'. *Harvard International Journal of Press Politics*, 3: 1–4.

Parham, A. A. (2004). 'Diaspora, Community and Communication: Internet Use in Transnational Haiti'. *Global Networks*, 4(2): 199.

Parks, M. R. and Floyd, K. (1996). 'Making Friends in Cyberspace'. *Journal of Communication*, 46(1): 80–97.

Putnam, R. (1995). 'Bowling Alone: America's Declining Social Capital'. *Journal of Democracy*, 6(1): 65–78.

—— (2000). *Bowling Alone: The Collapse and Revival of American Community*. New York: Simon and Schuster.

Quan-Haase, A., Wellman, B., Witte, J. et al. (2002). 'Capitalizing on the Net: Social Contact, Civic Engagement, and Sense of Community', in B. Wellman and C. Haythornthwaite (eds), *The Internet in Everyday Life*. Oxford: Blackwell, 291–324.

Rainie, L. and Kohut, A. (2000). *Tracking Online Life: How Women Use the Internet to Cultivate Relationships with Family and Friends* (Internet Life Report No. 1). Washington DC: Pew Internet and American Life.

Rheingold, H. (1987). 'Virtual Communities'. *Whole Earth Review*, Winter: 78–81.

—— (1990). 'Travels in Virtual Reality'. *Whole Earth Review*, Summer: 80–8.

—— (1991). 'Electronic Democracy; the Great Equalizer'. *Whole Earth Review*, Summer: 4–8.

—— (1993). *The Virtual Community: Homesteading on the Electronic Frontier*. Reading, MA: Addison Wesley.

Robins, K. (1999). 'Foreclosing on the City? The Bad Idea of Virtual Urbanism', in J. Downey and J. McGuigan (eds), *Technocities*. London: Sage, 34–59.

Roszak, T. (1986). *From Satori to Silicon Valley: San Francisco and the American Counterculture*, San Francisco, CA: Don't Call It Frisco Press.

—— (1994). *The Cult of Information: A Neo-Luddite Treatise on High-Tech, Artificial Intelligence, and the True Art of Thinking* (2nd edn). Berkley, CA: University of California Press.

Rothenbuhler, E. W. (2001). 'Revising Communication Research for Working on Community', in G. J. Shepherd and E. W. Rothenbuhler (eds), *Communication and Community*. Mahwah, NJ: Lawrence Erlbaum Associates Publishers, 159–79.

Rushkof, D. (1994). *Cyberia*. San Francisco, CA: Harper.

Schuler, D. (1996). *New Community Networks: Wired for Change*. Reading, MA: Addison-Wesley.

Servon, L. (2002). *Bridging the Digital Divide: Technology, Community, and Public Policy*. Oxford: Blackwell.

—— and Nelson, M. K. (2001). 'Community Technology Centers: Narrowing the Digital Divide in Low-Income Urban Communities'. *Journal of Urban Affairs*, 23(3–4): 279–90.

Shah, D. V., McLeod, J. M. and Yoon, S. H. (2001). 'Communication, Context, and Community: An Exploration of Print, Broadcast and Internet Influences'. *Communication Research*, 28(4): 464–506.

Shaw, A. and Shaw, M. (1999). 'Social Empowerment through Community Networks', in D. Schon, B. Sanyal and W. Mitchell (eds), *High Technology and Low-Income Communities*. Cambridge, MA: MIT Press, 315–35.

SHEARMAN, C. (2003). 'Strategies for Reconnecting Communities: Creative Use of ICTs for Social and Economic Transformation', in S. Marshall, W. Taylor and X. Yu (eds), *Closing the Digital Divide: Transforming Regional Economies and Communities with Information Technology*. Westport, CT: Praeger, 13–26.

SHKLOVSKI, I. and KRAUT, R. (2004). 'The Internet and Social Participation: Contrasting Cross-Sectional and Logitudinal Analyses'. *The Journal of Computer-Mediated Communication*, 10(1), art. 1, http://jcmc.indiana.edu/vol10/issue11/shklovski_kraut.html

SILVERSTONE, R. (2001). 'Finding a Voice: Minorities, Media and the Global Commons'. *Emergences*, 11(1): 13–27.

SLOUKA, M. (1995). *War of the Worlds: Cyberspace and the High-Tech Assault on Reality*. New York: Basic Books.

SMITH, M. (1992). *Voices from the Well: The Logic of Virtual Commons*. Unpub. Masters thesis, University of California at Los Angeles, Los Angeles.

SPROULL, L. and KIESLER, S. B. (1991). *Connections: New Ways of Working in the Networked Organization*. Cambridge, MA: MIT Press.

SUNSTEIN, C. R. (2001). *Republic.Com*. Princeton, NJ: Princeton University Press.

TOFFLER, A. and TOFFLER, H. (1995). *Creating a New Civilization: The Politics of the Third Wave*. Atlanta, GA: Turner Publishing, Inc.

TURKLE, S. (1984). *The Second Self: Computers and the Human Spirit*. New York: Simon and Schuster.

US DEPARTMENT OF COMMERCE (1999). 'Falling through the Net: Defining the Digital Divide', Washington DC: US Department of Commerce, www.ntia.doc.gov/reportsarch-ives.html, accessed 18 Mar. 2006.

VALEE, J. (1982). *The Network Revolution: Confessions of a Computer Scientist*. Berkeley, CA: And/Or Press.

WATSON, N. (1997). 'Why We Argue About Virtual Community: A Case Study of the Phish.Net Fan Community', in S. G. Jones (ed.), *Virtual Culture*. London, Thousand Oaks, CA, New Delhi: Sage, 102–32.

WEARE, C., OZTAS, N., LOGES, W. E. and MUSSO, J. A. (2003). 'Neighborhood Governance and Networks of Community Power'. Paper presented at the Democratic Network Governance, Roskilde University, Helsingor, Denmark.

WELLMAN, B. (1997). 'An Electronic Group Is Virtually a Social Network', in S. Kiesler (ed.), *Culture of the Internet*. Mahwah, NJ: Lawrence Erlbaum Associates. 179–205.

—— (2001). 'Physical Place and Cyber Place: The Rise of Personalized Networks'. *International Journal of Urban and Regional Research*, 25(2): 227–52.

——, and GULIA, M. (1999). 'Net Surfers Don't Ride Alone: Virtual Communities as Communities', in B. Wellman (ed.), *Networks in the Global Village*. Boulder, CO: Westview Press, 331–67.

——, QUAN-HAASE, A. WITTE, J. and HAMPTON, K. (2001). 'Does the Internet Increase, Decrease, or Supplement Social Capital? Social Networks, Participation, and Community Commitment'. *American Behavioral Scientist*, 45(3): 436–55.

—— and HAYTHORNTHWAITE, C. A. (eds) (2002). *The Internet in Everyday Life*. Oxford and Malden, MA: Blackwell.

WILSON II, C. C. and GUTIÉRREZ, F. (1985). *Minorities and Media: Diversity and the End of Mass Communication*. Beverly Hills, CA: Sage.

CHAPTER 25

ICTs AND INEQUALITY: NET GAINS FOR WOMEN?

JUDY WAJCMAN

1 INTRODUCTION

Do information and communication technologies (ICTs) have a sex? Until recently, popular stereotypes have associated technology strongly with masculinity. However, in the new digital age, many contemporary feminists surmise that the link between technology and male privilege is finally being severed. While ICTs have had a reputation in feminist theory for being biased towards the interests and styles of men, post-modern theories, such as cyberfeminism, see the virtuality of cyberspace and the Internet as spelling the end of the embodied basis for sex difference. In these accounts, digital technologies are seen as gender free and as potentially opening up fresh possibilities for a new gender order for women.

In this chapter I consider the gender relations of ICTs, canvassing both pessimistic and optimistic perspectives. Drawing on the social studies of technology, I argue that ideas about and practices of gender inform the design, production, and use of ICTs, and that, in turn, technical artefacts and culture are integral to the formation of gender identity. Technologies embody and advance political interests and agendas and they are the product of social structure, culture, values, and politics as much as the result of objective scientific discovery. While new ICTs can be constitutive of new gender dynamics, they can also be derivative of and reflect older patterns of gender inequality. My argument is that social science needs to continually engage with the process of technological change, as it is a key aspect of gender power relations.

The chapter is organized in five sections. Section 2 examines how technology and technical expertise came to be so closely identified with masculinity. The marginalization of women from technically-oriented work has traditionally led to much pessimism in feminist analyses of technology. ICTs however have evoked much more optimism. Section 3 then, considers work in the new media, widely regarded as prefiguring the sexism-free future of work. Section 4 evaluates contemporary cyberfeminist theory, particularly the claim that digital technologies are inherently liberating. A critical weakness of this literature is its leaning towards technological determinism, addressed in Section 5. Finally, in Section 6, I present technofeminism as the alternative, that is, the mutual shaping of ICTs and gender with feminist politics situated firmly at its centre.

2 TECHNOLOGY, WORK, AND MASCULINITY

What role does technology play in embedding gender power relations? Let us begin with the traditional conception of what technology is taken to be. We tend to think about technology in terms of industrial machinery and cars for example, overlooking other technologies that affect most aspects of everyday life. The very definition of technology, in other words, has a male bias. This emphasis on technologies dominated by men conspires in turn to diminish the significance of women's technologies, such as horticulture, cooking and childcare, and so reproduces the stereotype of women as technologically ignorant and incapable (Stanley 1995). The enduring force of the identification between technology and manliness, therefore, is not inherent in biological sex difference. It is rather the result of the historical and cultural construction of gender.

Indeed, it was only with the formation of engineering as a white, male middle-class profession that 'male machines rather than female fabrics' became the modern markers of technology (Oldenziel 1999). During the late nineteenth century, mechanical and civil engineering increasingly came to define what technology is, diminishing the significance of both the artefacts and forms of knowledge associated with women. The rise of engineering as an elite, with exclusive rights to technical expertise, involved the creation of a male professional identity based on educational qualifications and the promise of managerial positions, sharply distinguished from shop-floor engineering and blue-collar workers. It also involved an ideal of manliness, characterized by the cultivation of bodily prowess and individual achievement. The discourse about manliness was mobilized to ensure that class, race, and gender boundaries were drawn around the engineering bastion.

It was during and through this process that the term technology took on its modern meaning. Whereas the earlier concept of useful arts had included needlework and metalwork as well as spinning and mining, by the 1930s this had been supplanted with the idea of technology as applied science. At the same time, femininity was being reinterpreted as incompatible with technological pursuits. The legacy of this relatively recent history is our taken-for-granted association of technology with men.

Technology thus needs to be understood as a culture that expresses and consolidates relations among men. Feminist writing has long identified the ways in which gender-technology relations are manifest not only in institutions, but also in cultural symbols, language and identities. Technical competence is central to the dominant ideal of masculinity, and its absence a key feature of stereotyped femininity. Men's affinity with technology is thus integral to the constitution of subjectivity for both sexes. A classic example is the archetypal masculine culture of engineering, where mastery over technology is a source of both pleasure and power for the predominantly male profession (Faulkner and Lohan 2004; Mellstrom 2003). Engineering is represented as the very epitome of cool reason, as a detached, abstract activity, the antithesis of 'feminine' feeling. This resonates with the dominant image of computing work in the nineties, the young, white, male 'nerds' or 'hackers' who enjoyed (and still do) working 16-hour days (Grundy 1996; Panteli et al. 2001; Star 1995). Indeed, during the dot.com boom of the 1990s it was rare to see a female face among the millionaires. The 'cyber-brat pack' for the new millennium—those wealthy and entrepreneurial young guns of the Internet—consists almost entirely of men. Castells (2001), and other writers, eulogize the counterculture hacker origins of the Internet, but fail to notice that the culture of computing was predominantly the culture of the white American male.

This is not to imply that there is a single form of masculinity. Gender theory has challenged the singular and unitary conception of gender identity, arguing that there is a multiplicity of masculinities and femininities (e.g. Jackson and Scott 2002). Sexual ideologies are remarkably diverse and fluid, and for some men technical expertise may be as much about their lack of power as the realization of it. It is indubitably the case however, that in contemporary Western society, the hegemonic form of masculinity is still strongly associated with technical prowess and power (Connell 1995). Feminine identity, on the other hand, has been seen as being ill suited to technological pursuits. Different childhood exposure to technology, the prevalence of different role models and forms of schooling, and the extreme gender segregation on the job market all lead to what Cockburn (1983: 203) described as 'the construction of men as strong, manually able and technologically endowed, and women as physically and technically incompetent'. Entering technical domains has therefore required women to sacrifice major aspects of their gender identity.

A report by Millar and Jagger (2001) comparing six countries, including the UK, found that women are generally under-represented among graduates in the information technology (IT), electronics and communications-related subjects, despite the fact that they form the majority of university graduates overall (see also the Greenfield Report 2002). Indeed, over the last 20 years, the number of women entering computer science at tertiary level has fallen.[1] In the US, too, women are particularly under-represented among graduates in computer and information science (34 per cent) and engineering (21 per cent) (National Science Foundation 2004). At the doctoral level, in computer and information science women are but 19 per cent, and only 17 per cent in engineering. The exception is the biological sciences, where women continue to be well represented.

This bias in women's and girls' education choices has major repercussions because employment in the IT, electronics and communications sector is graduate intensive. In the US, for example, women's participation in these occupations declined from 37 per cent in 1993 to 28 per cent at the start of the twenty-first century (Millar and Jagger 2001). Where women are relatively well represented is in the lower status occupations, such as telephone operators, data processing equipment installers and repairers, and communications equipment operators. By contrast, male graduates are heavily concentrated among computer systems analysts and scientists, computer science teachers, computer programmers, operations and systems researchers and analysts, and broadcast equipment operators. These sexual divisions in the labour market mean that women are largely excluded from the processes of technical design that shape the world we live in.

In sum, then, much feminist research on gender, technology and work has focused on the processes and practices that have systematically marginalized women from jobs and professions that are defined as scientific, technical or technological (Cockburn 1983; Hacker 1989; Wajcman 1991). The central theme running through all this literature is that in defining what technology is, how it should be used, what technical skills are, or in other words what 'counts' as valuable knowledge and skills, gender functions as a cultural category in sorting out high-tech from low-tech or no-tech (Lie 2003: 20). But is such a pessimistic reading of the woman–machine relationship still warranted given the dramatic changes that are occurring both in the economy and in gender relations? The following section considers work in the new media as a test case.

3 GENDER AND NEW MEDIA WORK

Much has been written about the transformative effects of the ICT industries and the emergence of the new knowledge economy. The millennial reflections of both social theorists and popular commentators, whether it be theories of globalization, risk, or the network society, all stress that ICTs are dramatically changing the character of capitalism and the nature of work. For example, Manuel Castells (1996: 477) argues that labour and capital, the central variables of the industrial society, are replaced by information and knowledge. In the resulting 'network society', information is the key ingredient of social organization, and flows of messages and images between networks constitute the basic thread of social structure. Or, in the words of Nicholas Negroponte, 'being digital is different . . . in the digital world, previously impossible solutions become viable' (Negroponte 1995: 231). The literature on the knowledge economy and the changes generated is discussed in Chapter 1 of this handbook. Here I will consider the gender implications of these changes, a subject conspicuously absent from the usual accounts.

There is no doubt that the digital age has spawned brand new fields of work, just since the 1990s. This has generated a whole new range of practitioners: web designers, digital animators, multimedia producers, electronic artists, webcasters, computer game designers, and so on. Taken together, these new media workers are said to be at the forefront of the new economy or the knowledge economy. Indeed, they have acquired an iconic status in terms of representing the future of work. And many commentators and politicians pin high hopes on the opportunities for women in the ICT sector. It is therefore worth considering the emerging empirical evidence on the gender aspects of this new economic sector.

In her study of freelance new media workers in six European countries, Rosalind Gill (2002) assesses the extent to which the image of this work as cool, creative, autonomous, and egalitarian matches the experience of these workers. She found that most of the workers were young (between 25 and 35 years), white, and highly educated, and they were unanimous about the attractions of working in their field. Its youth, dynamism, and creativity were mentioned repeatedly, as were the pleasures of working autonomously with no managerial control, flexible working hours, and the intrinsically challenging and fulfilling nature of the work. Similarly, Diane Perron's (2003) study of new media companies in the south-east of England reports that the vast majority of owners, managers and employees surveyed derive enormous satisfaction from their work. They identify with the media image of the work as intellectually challenging and providing independence and freedom as to when and where the work is done. Rather than women being alienated from technology, new media work, based on brain rather than brawn, on networks rather than hierarchy, might herald a new relationship between women and machines.

Both studies, however, report clear divergences between the experiences of women and men in new media work. Not only is the new media sector 'characterized by a number of entrenched and all too old-fashioned patterns of gender inequality relating to education, access to work and pay', but also 'a number of *new* forms of gender inequality are emerging, connected—paradoxically—to many of the features of the work that are valued: informality, autonomy, flexibility and so on' (Gill 2002: 71). The studies found that women own and manage fewer and smaller companies, women freelancers obtain significantly fewer work contracts than men (often in the public or voluntary sector), earn less than men, and are much more likely to work from home, despite having a strong preference for working from a rented workspace. The informality of work practices and relationships, regarded as a major attraction of the work by both sexes, posed particular problems for women. Finding and securing contracts was heavily based on informal networks and interpersonal connections, resulting in a form of gender exclusion based on an 'old boys' network'. Moreover, informal hiring practices also raised grave concerns about equal opportunities. While traditional bureaucratic organizations and careers may have had a gendered character, new organizational forms and portfolio careers are not necessarily more conducive to gender equality (Edwards and Wajcman 2005; Hebson and Grugulis 2005).

The issue of flexibility, raised here in relation to new media work, is also seen more broadly as central to current discussions of gender equality. Much has been made of the way that personal computers (PCs), the Internet and mobile phones have made the boundaries that once separated the public world of work and the private home more permeable.[2] The historical separation of these spheres has been seen as key to women's oppression, so increasing permeability should help to erode strict sex-role demarcation. By transcending the link between time and space, ICTs offer greater control over the location and scheduling of tasks. Those who belong to the flexible workforce, especially managers and professionals, increasingly work from and at home, and when they are on the move. The notion of flexible hours suggests that the individual is able to exercise some control over when, where, and how long she works. Working from home is seen as offering the freedom of self-regulated work, and making the organization of both paid and unpaid work time more manageable. Media images of a woman working while the baby happily crawls across a computer are ubiquitous.

New media workers are generally very positive about the way their work and life are merging. They regularly take work home, work in the evenings, and work long hours in order to fulfil the demands of project work with extremely tight deadlines, regarding 'work excitement and work pressure as opposite sides of the same coin' (Perrons 2003: 81). The pattern is one of irregular work, with very intense periods followed by several weeks with no work at all, a pattern that has been described as the 'bulimic career' (Pratt 2000; see also Terranova 2000). Such working patterns, however, are not conducive to combining work with family life. Perrons concludes that while new media work does provide flexibility and time sovereignty that could facilitate a better work–life balance, the current situation where women are mainly responsible for childcare and domestic life remains resilient to change. While mothers are particularly seen as the beneficiaries of this development, the flexibility in new media work turns out to be most cherished by young people without children or other caring responsibilities. In any event, it would appear that ICTs are almost always used to facilitate the transfer of work into the home, rather than the transfer of home concerns into the workplace.

In sum, a mixed picture of developing gender patterns in the new industries is apparent. While there is less gender segregation of jobs, and signs that women are readily taking up opportunities to acquire technical expertise, some familiar patterns of gendered work organization persist. Perhaps frustrated with the tenacity of the masculine culture of technology in the workplace, feminist scholars have turned their attention to other aspects of everyday life and women's interaction with ICTs.

4 SUSPENDING GENDER IN CYBERSPACE

Contemporary feminist commentary has been much more positive about the possibilities of ICTs to empower women and transform gender relations. Indeed, early concerns about women being left out of the communications revolution, victims of the digital divide, now seem misplaced. The proliferation of mobile phones, the Internet, and cyber cafes are providing new opportunities and outlets for women. Around the world, although women still account for a lower proportion of Internet users than men, their share is rapidly rising. While the early adopters of the Internet were overwhelmingly men, US studies have been finding that gender and racial differences in Internet use disappear after other socio-economic variables (such as income and education) are taken into account (Rice and Katz 2003). China, a country where Internet take-up is relatively recent, shows how rapidly change can occur. Over a five-year period from 1997, the proportion of Internet users who were female rose from 12 per cent to 39 per cent (CNNIC 2002). Similarly, while men initially dominated mobile phone use, already there seems to be no gender gap whatsoever, neither in relation to ownership, nor access to the mobile phone. Especially among younger people, this artefact is not culturally coded as either masculine of feminine. There is no equivalent of the hacker stereotype that has had so much traction in relation to computing.

As a result of these dramatic changes in the ownership and use of ICTs, many feminists surmise that the link between technology and male privilege is finally being severed. The emergence of cyberfeminism has given voice to some new strands of gender theory that embrace the idea that web-based technology generates a culture of unlimited freedom. The writings of Sadie Plant (1998), acclaimed by some as the most radical 'techno theorist' of the day, have been particularly influential. Cyberfeminist discourse appeals to a new young generation that grew up with computers and pop culture in the 1990s and their themes of 'grrrl power' and 'wired worlds'. At this point it is worth looking at Sadie Plant's work in more detail, as representative of this trend within feminism.

In part, cyberfeminism needs to be understood as a reaction to the pessimism of the earlier feminist vision that stressed the inherently masculine nature of technoscience. In contrast, cyberfeminism emphasizes women's subjectivity and agency, and the pleasures immanent in new digital technologies. They accept that industrial technology did indeed have a patriarchal character, but ICTs are much more diffuse and open. The Internet in particular is seen as providing the technological basis for a new form of society and a multiplicity of innovative subjectivities. As such, cyberfeminism marks a new relationship between gender and technology.

For Plant, technological innovations have been pivotal in the fundamental shift in power from men to women that occurred in Western cultures in the 1990s—the genderquake. Old expectations, stereotypes, senses of identity and securities have been challenged as women gained unprecedented economic opportunities, technical skills, and cultural powers. Automation has reduced the importance of muscular strength and hormonal energies and replaced them with demands for speed, intelligence, and transferable, interpersonal, and communication skills (Plant 1998: 37–8). This has been accompanied by the feminization of the workforce, which favours independence, flexibility, and adaptability. While men are ill prepared for a postmodern future, women are ideally suited to the new technoculture.

The digital revolution heralds the decline of the traditional hegemonic structures and power bases of male domination because it represents a new kind of technical system. For Plant, it is technology without *logos*. The standard way of thinking about technology is in terms of the application of reason in the domination and mastery of natural and social environments. Social hierarchies are put to work on nature in an orderly way to produce highly organized systems of social and technological power. For Plant, as for other feminist writers, this is fundamental to technology as a patriarchal system and it is bound up with masculine identities. This includes sexual identities. The 'ones' of Plant's title *Zeros and Ones* describe a singular male identity against which female identity is measured and found to be a nothing, a 'zero'. She cleverly uses the digital language of computers—sequences of zeros and ones—to evoke a new gendering of technology. There is a decided shift in the woman–machine relationship, because there is a shift in the nature of machines. 'Zeros' now have a place and they displace the phallic order of 'ones'.

The Net, cyberspace, virtual reality, the matrix epitomize the shape of a new 'distributed nonlinear world'. They do not develop in predictable and orderly ways and cannot be subject to control. Innovations occur at different points in the web and create effects that outrun their immediate origins. The web is therefore the ideal feminine medium where women should feel at home. This is because women excel within fluid systems and processes: their distinctive mode of being fits perfectly with the changes associated with ICT. The metaphors for this new technology are drawn from women's worlds and, looking back at the emergence of the new technology, Plant finds women have been central to it. She traces a history of female superiority as programmers—or 'weavers of information'—from women's skills in weaving to their contributions to modern computing. Far from being a technology of male dominance, computing is technology that is freeing up women for a post-patriarchal future.

The idea that the Internet can transform conventional gender roles, altering the relationship between the body and the self via a machine, is a popular theme in postmodern feminism. The message is that young women in particular are colonizing cyberspace where, like gravity, gender inequality is suspended. In cyberspace, all physical, bodily cues are removed from communication. As a result, our interactions are fundamentally different because they are not subject to judgements based on sex, age, race, voice, accent, or appearance, but are based only on textual exchanges. In *Life on the Screen*, Sherry Turkle (1995: 12) enthuses about the potential for people 'to express multiple and often unexplored aspects of the self, to play with their identity and to try out new ones ... the obese can be slender, the beautiful plain, the "nerdy" sophisticated'. It is the increasingly interactive and creative nature of computing technology that now enables millions of people to live a significant segment of their lives in virtual reality. Moreover, it is in this computer-mediated world that people experience a new sense of self that is decentred, multiple, and fluid. In this respect, Turkle argues, the Internet is the material expression of the philosophy of postmodernism.

Like many other authors, Turkle (1995: 314) argues that gender-swapping, or virtual cross-dressing, encourages people to reflect on the social construction of gender, to acquire 'a new sense of gender as a continuum'. In a similar vein, Stone (1995) celebrates the myriad ways that the interactive world of cyberspace is challenging traditional notions of gender identity. Complex virtual identities rupture the cultural belief that there is a single self in a single body. Stone's discussion of phone and virtual sex, for example, describes how female sex workers disguise crucial aspects of identity and can play at reinventing themselves. She takes seriously the notion that virtual people or selves can exist in cyberspace, with no necessary link to a physical body. Our relationship to technology and technical culture, then, is pivotal to the discourse of gender dualisms and gender difference. ICTs provide a new site of transgender politics, enabling women and men to escape from bodily gender definitions and to construct new gender identities, or even genderless identities. This could be a Net gain for women.

5 Cyberfeminism and technological determinism

Postmodern feminist cultural theories, then, see the digital revolution as offering a whole new realm of human experience. Mirroring cyber-gurus, from Nicholas Negroponte (1995) to Manuel Castells (1996, 2001), they proclaim that the Internet and cyberspace are bringing about a technological and social revolution. Electronic networks are said to create new forms of sociability that will result in enhanced communities and greater world harmony. An optimistic—almost utopian—vision of the electronic community as foreshadowing the 'good society' is also characteristic of cyberfeminism. Although the mainstream literature is silent on gender issues, it shares with some new strands of feminism the idea that web-based technology generates a zone of unlimited freedom.

While this blend of technology, networks, and freedom is intoxicating, it risks fetishizing the new. Such a discourse of radical discontinuity, whether it be by cyber-gurus or cyberfeminists, has echoes of technological determinism. Technology itself is seen as empowering women, as though these new technologies were an autonomous, gender-neutral force reconfiguring social relations. Digital technologies, like older technologies, are malleable and contain contradictory possibilities, but they also reveal continuities of power and exclusion, albeit in new forms. Let me elaborate.

Plant claims that women's affinity with digitalization means that it is inherently freeing. For Plant, there is a direct causal relationship between communication technologies and the particular cultural forms they come to be associated with. Her homage to the Internet closely echoes Marshall McLuhan's (1962) famous aphorism, 'the medium is the message', and she acknowledges his legacy. But as did McLuhan, she fails to distinguish between technical inventions (the digitilization of data), socially instituted technology (the Internet), and its attendant cultural forms (email, websites, interactive multimedia, etc). As a result, the crucial influence of media corporations and communications institutions within which technologies develop, and which circumscribe their use, is ignored (Jones 1998). Indeed, the three properties of digital networks—decentralized access, simultaneity, and interconnectivity—have produced strikingly different outcomes in the private, firewalled sites of global finance from the distributed power of the public-access cyberspaces (Sassen 2002; see also Chapter 14 in this handbook). There are trends towards increasing privatization of the Internet, with multiple classes of service and access to information depending upon the ability of users to pay (Mansell 2002; Thomas and Wyatt 2000). Network power is not inherently distributive, as cyberfeminists among others would have us believe. In the hands of multinational corporations and capital markets, it can concentrate power.

Plant's abstract theory of the Internet thus reproduces McLuhan's technological determinism, and can be criticized in precisely the terms that Raymond Williams applied to McLuhan in *Television: Technology and Cultural Form*:

It is an apparently sophisticated technological determinism which has the significant effect of indicating a social and cultural determinism: a determinism, that is to say, which ratifies the society and culture we now have, and especially its most powerful internal directions. For if the medium—whether print or television—is the cause, all other causes, all that men [*sic*] ordinarily see as history, are at once reduced to effects. Similarly, what are elsewhere seen as effects, and as such subject to social, cultural, psychological and moral questioning, are excluded as irrelevant by comparison with the direct physiological and therefore 'psychic' effects of the media as such. (Williams 1974: 127)

As Williams so forcefully points out in relation to McLuhan, the political consequence of this avant-gardist celebration of the 'new media' is paradoxically to legitimate the existing social order. Plant is similarly exposed as politically conservative. If digital technology is inherently feminine whoever controls or uses it, then no political action is necessary. Cyberfeminism may appear to be anarchist and anti-establishment but, in effect, it requires for its performances all the latest free market American capitalist gizmos.

Moreover, Plant's utopian version of the relationship between gender and technology is perversely post-feminist. Rather than wanting to erase gender difference, Plant positively affirms women's radical sexual difference, their feminine qualities. It is a version of radical or cultural feminism dressed up as cyberfeminism and is similarly essentialist. The belief in some inner essence of womanhood as an a-historical category lies at the very heart of traditional and conservative conceptions of womanhood. What is curious is that Plant holds on to this fixed, unitary version of what it is to be female while, at the same time, arguing that the self is decentred and dispersed. Her melange of postmodern/French feminist/psychoanalytic theories of the fractured identities of woman, with sets of embodiments, might have led her to emphasize the differences between, as well as within, individuals. However, she does not connect these theories on multiple identities and bodies with the multiple lived experiences that give rise to them. Rather, throughout Plant's analysis there is dissonance between her appeal to universal feminine attributes and her conceptualization of women's fragmented identities.

As with much of the literature on cyberculture, Plant does not consider in any depth the more prosaic findings about women's actual experience of computer facilities. For example, the Internet Café is often seen as exemplary of a gender-neutral public space. Yet emerging fieldwork on cybercafés confounds this picture (Liff and Laegran 2003; Wakeford 1998). While new gender alliances are being forged through interactions between computers, staff and customers at cafés, old stereotypes of gender and technology are also in evidence. Most obviously, women's bodies are used to encapsulate the cybervibe of the café, as in the recurring sculpture of glossy red lips clamped around a computer disc. Observers of Internet use conclude that specific local cultures of place and space, including the 'offline landscapes' of cybercafés, are decisive in interpreting the feminist potential of the Net.

6 TECHNOFEMINISM

How then do we get beyond seeing ICTs as either inherently patriarchal or essentially a woman's medium? What would be an alternative approach to understanding the relationship between gender and ICTs?

Over the last decade or so, feminist writing within the field of science and technology studies (STS) has theorized the relationship between gender and technology as one of mutual shaping. Social scientists increasingly recognize that technological innovation is itself shaped by the social circumstances within which it takes place. Crucially, the notion that technology is simply the product of rational technical imperatives has been dislodged. Within STS, objects and artefacts are no longer seen as separate from society, but as part of the social fabric that holds society together; they are never merely technical or social. Rather, the broad social shaping or constructivist approach treats technology as a sociotechnical product—a seamless web or network combining artefacts, people, organizations, cultural meanings and knowledge.[3] It follows that technological change is a contingent and heterogeneous process in which technology and society are mutually constituted.

In terms of gender and ICTs, feminist STS scholarship has explored the effects of gender power relations on design and innovation, as well as the impact of technological change on the sexes. This technofeminist approach conceives of technology as both a source and consequence of gender relations (Berg 1996; Lie 2003; Wajcman 1991, 2004). In other words, gender relations can be thought of as materialized in technology, and gendered identities and discourses as produced simultaneously with technologies. Several empirical studies have demonstrated that the marginalization of women from the technological community has a profound influence on the design, technical content, and use of artefacts (Cockburn and Ormrod 1993; Cowan 1983; Lerman et al. 2003; Oudshoorn 1994, 2003). Importantly, this gendering of technology takes place during the entire life trajectory or biography of an artefact, from design, development, production and marketing to distribution, sales, use, and cultural consumption. For this reason, technofeminism stresses that gendering involves several dimensions, involving material, discursive and social elements. It is precisely this intricate interweaving of artefacts, culture, and gendered identities in technoscientific practice that helps to explain why this link has proved so durable.

Feminist critics have pointed out that gender blindness persists in mainstream STS studies that overlook how technological systems implicitly place men's experiences and men's investments at the centre.[4] The corollary is the simultaneous denial of other realities such as those of women. In their concern to identify and study the social groups or networks that actively seek to influence technological design, STS studies have generally neglected the effects of structural exclusion on technological development. As a result, agents in these studies are most commonly male heroes, big projects, and important organizations. Moreover, the narrow lens of actor-network theory, for example, upon observable conflict in the processes of innovation, eclipses those absent from the network. A parallel point can be made in relation to Lawrence Lessig's (2001) argument about the importance of maintaining the Internet as an 'innovation commons'. Nowhere does he acknowledge the gendered character of the free communities of entrepreneurs he so celebrates. By contrast, a feminist analysis widens the focus to show how preferences for different technologies are shaped by a set of social arrangements and institutions that reflect men's power and resources in the wider society.

Let us take the example of the wired house to illustrate the gender politics of design. One of the great paradoxes of domestic technologies is that, despite being universally promoted as time and labour saving, these technologies have been singularly unsuccessful in lessening women's domestic load (Cowan 1983; Bittman et al. 2004). We might have hoped that the electronic home would achieve the wholesale elimination of household labour. The smart houses occupied by the very affluent display what high-technology dwellings might offer the family of the future. Magazines like *Wired* and futuristic films, present home networking as the backbone infrastructure of the twenty-first century lifestyle. But it seems that the designers and producers of the technological home, such as the MIT (Massachusetts Institute of Technology) 'House of the Future', have little interest in housework.[5] Home informatics is mainly concerned with the centralized control of heating, lighting, security, information, entertainment and energy consumption in a local network or 'house-brain'. Prototypes of the intelligent house tend to ignore the whole range of functions that come under the umbrella of housework. The target consumer is implicitly the technically-interested and entertainment-oriented male, someone in the designer's own image. The smart house is a deeply masculine vision of a house, rather than a home, somewhat like Corbusier's 'machine for living'. The routine neglect of women's knowledge, experience and skills as a resource for technical innovation in the home is symptomatic of the gendered character of the process. So too is the slant in research effort towards technologies that absorb time (home entertainment goods such as television and CD players) rather than save time (such as dishwashers and washing machines) (Hamill 2003). The space-age design is directed to a technological fix rather than envisioning social changes that would see a less gendered allocation of housework and a better balance between working time and family time. The wired home may have much to offer, but democracy in the kitchen is not part of the package.

Electronic games are another domain in which ICTs reflect cultural expressions of gender. In fact video games began at one of the places where computer culture itself got started. The first video game was Space War, built at MIT in the early 1960s (Turkle 1984). Computer games partly originated as training and simulation technologies for US fighter pilots. Many of the most popular games today are simply programmed versions of traditional non-computer games, involving shooting, blowing up, speeding, or zapping in some way or another. They often have militaristic titles such as 'Destroy All Subs' and 'Brute Force' highlighting their themes of adventure and violence, and the most ubiquitous electronic toy is called 'Gameboy'. Given that it is predominantly young men (often computer hackers) who design games software, it is hardly surprising that their inventions typically appeal to male fantasies, and reinforce a particular brand of masculinity. While much has been made of the postmodern possibilities of parody, and subversive readings of figures such as Lara Croft of Tomb Raiders, the bodily images and the identities available for womanhood in games are still very limited and appeal to the male fantasies of their predominantly male designers. Indeed, sex has played a defining role in the development and advance of ICTs. Cybersex entrepreneurs were the driving force behind key technical innovations, such as interactive CD-ROM software and improved on-screen image definition. Online pornography remains a major use of the Internet worldwide. According to some estimates, over half of all spending on the Internet is related to sexual activity (Griffiths 2003).

Up to this point, I have been stressing the impact of gender power relations on the design and meanings of ICTs. Nonetheless, it is striking that the web and the media more generally are host to an enormous diversity of contemporary representations of masculinity and femininity (Gill 2006). ICTs, gender relations and feminist ideas are themselves changing and in flux. The social meanings of technological artefacts are contingent and contestable, and open up space for feminine appropriations as well. Rather than conceiving of users as passive consumers, STS scholars have increasingly focused on how users interact with artefacts to become agents of technological change (Oudshoorn and Pinch 2003). This is also a key theme in recent technofeminist studies.

The diffusion of the fixed-line telephone is a classic case of how women can actively subvert the original inscription of a technology. The early phone, like the mobile, was designed for business and professional purposes. However, there was a generation-long mismatch between how the consumers used the telephone and how the industry thought it should be used (Fischer 1992; Martin 1991). The people who developed, built, and marketed telephone systems were predominantly telegraph men who assumed that the telephone's main use would be to replicate that of the parent technology, the telegraph. Although sociability (phoning relatives and friends) was and still is the main use of the residential telephone, the telephone industry resisted such uses until the 1920s, condemning this use of the technology for 'trivial gossip'. Until that time the telephone was sold as a practical business and household tool. When the promoters of the telephone finally began to advertise its use for sociability, this was at least partly in response to subscribers' insistence on, and rural women's innovative uses of, the technology for personal conversation. Similarly, the heavy use of mobiles by adolescents exchanging SMS (short message service) text as well as audio messages was unanticipated. In both cases, it was users rather than designers who established what was to become the typical pattern of use.

The relationship between gender and ICTs, then, is not immutably fixed. While the design process is decisive, technologies also yield unintended consequences and unanticipated possibilities. ICTs are sociotechnical or sociomaterial configurations that exhibit different degrees of determination and contingency at different moments in their relationship. The capacity of women users to produce new, advantageous readings of artefacts is dependent on their broader economic and social circumstances. The same technological device can mean very different things to different groups of women. For example, a young woman in the West experiences her silver cell phone as a liberating extension of her body. For her mother, it may primarily be a tool to keep track of her daughter. For women working as traders in Bangladesh, the mobile phone provides the means to run businesses selling communication services to other women. For women in rural and low-income areas of Africa, such as Botswana, Uganda, Ghana, it is a way to communicate with friends and family about significant events (e.g. funerals and festivals), and financial matters, as well as for keeping in touch generally (Scott et al. 2004). There is enormous variability in gendering by place, nationality, class, race, ethnicity, sexuality, and generation and thus women's experience of ICTs will be diverse.

At the same time, ICTs are themselves changing at an extremely rapid pace. At present the use of the Internet takes place mainly through the PC at home. While the computer's image has to some extent been reconfigured from a masculinized technology to a postfeminist tool for working wives and mothers, it enters an already gendered-space of the family home (Cassidy 2001). It is not surprising then that a detailed study of Internet use among young, childless, Dutch couples found that it is the particularly masculine codes of the PC that resound in the household's routine practices of usage (van Zoonen 2002). However, as the author notes, the Internet may soon be an ordinary extension of each and every domestic technology from televisions and mobile phones to microwaves and dishwashers. Each of these appliances has its own gendered uses and codes that may result in new and different articulations of gender and the Internet. These novel techno-practices in turn have the potential to reshape the sexual micropolitics of the home.

7 CONCLUSION

The electronic revolution has coincided with massive social transformations associated with the increasing emancipation of women worldwide, economically, culturally, politically. The old discourse of sex difference has been made increasingly untenable by the dramatic changes in ICTs, by the challenge of feminism, and by awareness of the mutating character of the natural world. Feminism has long been conflicted about the impact of technology on women, torn between utopian and dystopian visions of what the future may hold. The same technological innovations have been categorically rejected as oppressive to women, and uncritically embraced as inherently liberating. But for all the diversity of feminist voices, there is a shared concern with the hierarchical divisions between men and women that order the world we inhabit. The process of technical change is integral to the renegotiation of gender power relations and, therefore, an important site of feminist scholarship and political practice.

Empirical research on the gender relations of ICTs is still in its infancy. Moreover, 'post-industrial' technologies, like ICTs, genomics, and nanotechnology, are much more complex and flexible than the technologies that preoccupied earlier generations of feminist scholars. A technofeminist approach foregrounds the need to investigate the ways in which women's identities, needs, and priorities are being reconfigured together with digital technologies. This opens up fresh possibilities for studies that are more attuned to how different groups of women users creatively respond to and assimilate numerous ICTs in diverse real-world locations.

Such an approach also suggests the limitations of attempts to specify in advance the desirable design characteristics of artefacts and information systems. Rather, research should be aimed at ensuring that women are involved throughout the processes and practices of shaping technological innovation. With the increasing recognition that the development of effective ICTs requires detailed knowledge of the sites and practices in and through which the new technologies will literally be made to work, this may indeed become imperative. A foundational premise of feminist theory is that the traditional boundaries between production and consumption, work and home, public and private, do not correspond with women's experience. Research projects that challenge these familiar dualisms will be better able to capture the increasingly complex interconnections between gender and ICTs.

REFERENCES

Berg, A. J. (1996). *Digital Feminism.* Report No. 28 Dragvoll, Norway: Senter for Tenologi og Samfunn, Norwegian University of Science and Technology.

BIJKER, W., HUGHES, T. and PINCH, T. (eds) (1987). *The Social Construction of Technological Systems: New Directions in the Sociology and History of Technology*. Cambridge, MA: MIT Press.

BITTMAN, M., RICE, J. and WAJCMAN, J. (2004). 'Appliances and their Impact: The Ownership of Domestic Technology and Time Spent on Household Work'. *The British Journal of Sociology*, 55(3): 401–23.

CASSIDY, M. (2001). 'Cyberspace Meets Domestic Space: Personal Computers, Women's Work, and the Gendered Territories of the Family Home'. *Critical Studies in Media Communications*, 18(1): 44–65.

CASTELLS, M. (1996). *The Information Age: Economy, Society and Culture, Volume 1, The Rise of the Network Society*. Oxford: Blackwell.

—— (2001). *The Internet Galaxy: Reflections on the Internet, Business, and Society*. Oxford: Oxford University Press.

CNNIC (2002). 11th Survey Report, www.cnnic.net.cn, accessed 18 Mar. 2006.

COCKBURN, C. (1983). *Brothers: Male Dominance and Technological Change*. London: Pluto Press.

—— and ORMROD, S. (1993). *Gender and Technology in the Making*. London: Sage.

CONNELL, R. W. (1995). *Masculinities*. Cambridge: Polity Press.

COWAN, R. S. (1983). *More Work for Mother: The Ironies of Household Technology from the Open Hearth to the Microwave*. New York: Basic Books.

EDWARDS, P. and WAJCMAN, J. (2005). *The Politics of Working Life*. Oxford: Oxford University Press.

FAULKNER, W. (2001). 'The Technology Question in Feminism: A View from Feminist Technology Studies'. *Women's Studies International Forum*, 24(1): 79–95.

—— and LOHAN, M. (2004). 'Masculinities and Technologies'. *Men and Masculinities*, 6(4): 319–29.

FISCHER, C. S. (1992). *America Calling: A Social History of the Telephone to 1940*. Berkeley, CA: University of California Press.

GILL, R. (2002). 'Cool, Creative and Egalitarian? Exploring Gender in Project-Based New Media Work in Europe. *Information, Communication and Society*, 5(1): 70–89.

—— (2006). *Gender and the Media*. Cambridge: Polity Press.

GREENFIELD, S. (2002). *SET Fair: A Report on Women in Science, Engineering and Technology*. London: Department of Trade and Industry.

GRIFFITHS, M. (2003). 'Sex on the Internet', in J. Turow and A. Kavanaugh (eds), *The Wired Homestead*. Cambridge, MA: MIT Press, 261–82.

GRUNDY, F. (1996). *Women and Computers*. Exeter: Intellectual Books.

HACKER, S. (1989). *Pleasure, Power and Technology*. Boston, MA: Unwin Hyman.

HACKETT, E., AMSTERDAMSKA, O., LYNCH, M. et al. (forthcoming). *New Handbook of Science and Technology Studies*, Cambridge, MA: MIT Press.

HAMILL, L. (2003) 'Time as a Rare Commodity in Home Life', in R. Harper (ed.), *Inside the Smart House*. London: Springer, 63–78.

HEBSON, G. and GRUGULIS, I. (2005). 'Gender and New Organizational Forms', in M. Marchington, D. Grimshaw, J. Rubery and H. Willmott (eds), *Fragmenting Work*. Oxford: Oxford University Press, 217–38.

HENWOOD, F., PLUMERIDGE, S. and STEPULEVAGE, L. (2000). 'A Tale of Two Cultures?: Gender and Inequality in Computer Education', in S. Wyatt, F. Henwood, N. Miller, and

P. Senker (eds), *Technology and In/equality: Questioning the Information Society*. London: Routledge, 111–28.

HUWS, U. (2003). *The Making of a Cybertariat: Virtual Work in a Real World*. London: Merlin Press.

JACKSON, S. and SCOTT, S. (eds) (2002). *Gender: A Sociological Reader*. London: Routledge.

JONES, P. (1998). 'The Technology Is Not the Cultural Form? Raymond Williams's Sociological Critique of Marshall McLuhan'. *Canadian Journal of Communication*, 23(4): 423–54.

LAW, J. and HASSARD, J. (eds) (1999). *Actor-Network Theory and After*. Oxford: Blackwell.

LERMAN, N. E., OLDENZIEL, R. and MOHUN, A. P. (eds) (2003). *Gender and Technology: A Reader*. Baltimore, MD: Johns Hopkins University Press.

LESSIG, L. (2001). *The Future of Ideas: The Fate of the Commons in a Connected World*. New York: Vintage.

LIE, M. (ed.) (2003). *He, She and IT Revisited: New Perspectives on Gender in the Information Society*. Oslo: Gyldendal.

LIFF, S. and LAEGRAN, A. (eds) (2003). *New Media & Society*, 5(3), SI on cybercafés.

MACKENZIE, D. and WAJCMAN, J. (eds) (1999). *The Social Shaping of Technology: Second Edition*. Milton Keynes: Open University Press.

MANSELL, R. (2002). 'From Digital Divides to Digital Entitlements in Knowledge Societies'. *Current Sociology*, 50(3): 407–26.

MARTIN, M. (1991). *'Hello Central?': Gender, Technology, and the Culture in the Formation of Telephone Systems*. Montreal and Kingston: McGill-Queen's University Press.

MARTIN, U., LIFF, S., DUTTON, W. et al. (2004). *Rocket Science or Social Science? Involving Women in the Creation of Computing*. Oxford Internet Institute, Forum Discussion Paper No. 3.

MCLUHAN, M. (1962). *The Gutenberg Galaxy*. London: Routledge & Kegan Paul.

MELLSTROM, U. (2003). *Masculinity, Power and Technology: A Malaysian Ethnography*. Aldershot: Ashgate.

MILLAR, J. and JAGGER, N. (2001). *Women in ITEC Courses and Careers*. London: Women and Equality Unit, DTI.

NATIONAL SCIENCE FOUNDATION (2004). *Women, Minorities, and Persons with Disabilities in Science and Engineering*. NSF04-317. Arlington, VA: Division of Science Resources Statistics.

NEGROPONTE, N. (1995). *Being Digital*. New York: Vintage Books.

OLDENZIEL, R. (1999). *Making Technology Masculine: Men, Women and Modern Machines in America*. Amsterdam: Amsterdam University Press.

OUDSHOORN, N. (2003). *The Male Pill: A Biography of a Technology in the Making*. Durham, NC: Duke University Press.

—— (1994). *Beyond the Natural Body: An Archaeology of Sex Hormones*. London: Routledge.

—— and PINCH, T. (eds) (2003). *How Users Matter: The Co-construction of Users and Technology*. Cambridge, MA: MIT Press.

PANTELI, N., STACK, J. and RAMSAY, H. (2001). 'Gendered Patterns in Computing Work in the Late 1990s'. *New Technology, Work and Employment*, 16(1): 3–17.

PERRONS, D. (2003). 'The New Economy and the Work-Life Balance: Conceptual Explorations and a Case Study of New Media'. *Gender, Work & Organization*, 10(1): 65–93.

PLANT, S. (1998). *Zeroes and Ones: Digital Women and The New Technoculture*. London: Fourth Estate.

PRATT, A. (2000). 'New Media, the New Economy and New Spaces'. *Geoforum*, 31(4): 425–36.

RICE, R. and KATZ, J. (2003). 'Comparing Internet and Mobile Phone Usage: Digital Divides of Usage, Adoption, and Dropouts'. *Telecommunications Policy*, 27(8–9): 597–623.

SASSEN, S. (2002). 'Towards a Sociology of Information Technology'. *Current Sociology*, 50(3): 365–88.

SCOTT, N., McKEMEY, K. and BATCHELOR, S. (2004). 'The Use of Telephones Amongst the Poor in Africa: Some Gender Implications'. *Gender, Technology and Development*, 8(2): 185–207.

SISMONDO, S. (2004). *An Introduction to Science and Technology Studies*. Malden, MA: Blackwell.

STANLEY, A. (1995). *Mothers and Daughters of Invention*. New Brunswick, NJ: Rutgers University Press.

STAR, S. L. (ed.) (1995). *The Cultures of Computing*. Oxford: Blackwell.

STONE, A. R. (1995). *The War of Desire and Technology at the Close of the Mechanical Age*. Cambridge, MA: MIT Press.

TERRANOVA, T. (2000). 'Free Labor: Producing Culture for the Digital Economy'. *Social Text*, 18(2): 33–58.

THOMAS, G. and WYATT, S. (2000). 'Access is Not the Only Problem: Using and Controlling the Internet' in S. Wyatt, F. Henwood, N. Miller, and P. Senker (eds), *Technology and In/equality: Questioning the Information Society*. London: Routledge, 21–45.

TURKLE, S. (1984). *The Second Self: Computers and the Human Spirit*. London: Granada.

VAN ZOONEN, L. (2002). 'Gendering the Internet'. *European Journal of Communication*, 17(1): 5–23.

—— (1995). *Life on the Screen: Identity in the Age of the Internet*. New York: Simon and Schuster.

WAJCMAN, J. (1991). *Feminism Confronts Technology*. Cambridge: Polity Press.

—— (2004). *TechnoFeminism*. Cambridge: Polity Press.

WAKEFORD, N. (1998). 'Gender and the Landscapes of Computing in an Internet Café', in M. Crang, P. Crang and J. May (eds), *Virtual Geographies: Bodies, Spaces and Relations*. London: Routledge, 178–201.

WILLIAMS, R. (1974). *Television: Technology and Cultural Form*. London: Fontana.

NOTES

1. For a discussion of gender inequality in computing education, see Henwood, Plumeridge, and Stepulevage (2000), and in the computing professions, see Martin et al. (2004).
2. Indeed, telework was the focus of several weighty policy documents in the mid-1980s, when similar issues were raised about flexible work (see Huws 2003, ch. 7).
3. For an introduction to STS see, e.g. Bijker, Hughes, and Pinch (1987), Hackett et al. (forthcoming), Law and Hassard (1999), MacKenzie and Wajcman (1999), and Sismondo (2004).
4. See, e.g. Faulkner (2001) and Wajcman (2004).
5. http://architecture.mit.edu/house_n, accessed 18 Mar. 2006.

INDEX